Get the eBooks FREE!

(PDF, ePub, Kindle, and liveBook all included)¯

We believe that once you buy a book from us, you should be able to read it in any format we have available. To get electronic versions of this book at no additional cost to you, purchase and then register this book at the Manning website.

Go to https://www.manning.com/freebook and follow the instructions to complete your pBook registration.

That's it!
Thanks from Manning!

Time Series Forecasting in Python

Time Series Forecasting in Python

MARCO PEIXEIRO

MANNING
SHELTER ISLAND

For online information and ordering of this and other Manning books, please visit
www.manning.com. The publisher offers discounts on this book when ordered in quantity.
For more information, please contact

    Special Sales Department
    Manning Publications Co.
    20 Baldwin Road
    PO Box 761
    Shelter Island, NY 11964
    Email: orders@manning.com

Manning Publications Co.
20 Baldwin Road
PO Box 761
Shelter Island, NY 11964

Development editor:	Bobbie Jennings
Technical development editor:	Al Krinker
Review editor:	Adriana Sabo
Production editor:	Andy Marinkovich
Copy editor:	Andy Carroll
Proofreader:	Katie Tennant
Technical proofreader:	Karsten Strøbaek
Typesetter:	Dennis Dalinnik
Cover designer:	Marija Tudor

ISBN: 9781617299889
Printed in the United States of America

To my wife, my parents, and my sister,
even though you will probably never read it.

brief contents

contents

preface

Working at a bank, I quickly realized how time is an important factor. Interest rates vary over time, people's spending varies over time, asset prices vary over time. Yet I found most people, including me, were uncomfortable with time series. So I decided to learn time series forecasting.

It turned out to be harder than expected because every resource I found was in R. I am comfortable with Python, and Python is undoubtedly the most popular language for data science in the industry. While R constrains you to statistical computing, Python allows you to code websites, perform machine learning, deploy models, build servers, and more. Therefore, I had to translate a lot of R code into Python to learn time series forecasting. That's when I recognized the gap, and I was lucky enough to be given the opportunity to write a book about it.

With this book, I hope to create a one-stop reference for time series forecasting with Python. It covers both statistical and machine learning models, and it also discusses automated forecasting libraries, as they are widely used in the industry and often act as baseline models. This book greatly emphasizes a hands-on, practical approach, with various real-life scenarios. In real life, data is messy, dirty, and sometimes missing, and I wanted to give readers a safe space to experiment with those difficulties, learn from them, and easily transpose those skills into their own projects.

This book focuses on time series forecasting. Of course, with time series data, we can also perform classification or anomaly detection, but this book addresses only forecasting to keep the scope manageable.

In each chapter, you will find exercises you can use to practice and hone your skills. Each exercise comes with a full solution on GitHub. I strongly suggest that you take the time to complete them, as you will gain important practical skills. They offer a great way to test your knowledge, see what you need to revisit in a given chapter, and apply modeling techniques in new scenarios.

After reading the chapters and completing the exercises, you will have all the necessary tools to tackle any forecasting project with confidence and great results. Hopefully, you will also gain the curiosity and motivation to go beyond this book and become a time series expert.

acknowledgments

First, I would like to thank my wife, Lina. Thank you for listening when I struggled, for your feedback on large parts of the book, and for correcting my grammar. You supported me from the very beginning and ultimately made this possible.

Next, I want to acknowledge my editor, Bobbie Jennings. You made the entire process of writing my first book so easy, it makes me want to write a second one! You taught me a lot about writing and keeping my audience in mind, and you weren't scared to challenge parts of the book, which greatly improved it.

To all the reviewers—Amaresh Rajasekharan, Ariel Andres, Biswanath Chowdhury, Claudiu Schiller, Dan Sheikh, David Paccoud, David R King, Dinesh Ghanta, Dirk Gomez, Gary Bake, Gustavo Patino, Helder C. R. Oliveira, Howard Bandy, Igor Vieira, Kathrin Björkelund, Lokesh Kumar, Mary Anne Thygesen, Mikael Dautrey, Naftali Cohen, Oliver Korten, Paul Silisteanu, Raymond Cheung, Richard Meinsen, Richard Vaughan, Rohit Goswami, Sadhana Ganapathiraju, Shabie Iqbal, Shankar Swamy, Shreesha Jagadeesh, Simone Sguazza, Sriram Macharla, Thomas Joseph Heiman, Vincent Vandenborne, and Walter Alexander Mata López—thank you. You all helped make this a better book.

Finally, a special thank you goes to Brian Sawyer. I guess you saw something in me. You gave me this incredible opportunity to write a book, and you trusted me the entire time. Writing a book is a dream come true for me, and it's happened because you started this entire process. I am very grateful for that.

about this book

This book was written to help data scientists master time series forecasting and help professionals transition from R to Python for time series analysis. It starts off by defining time series data and highlighting the uniqueness of working with that type of data (for example, you cannot shuffle the data). It then walks through developing baseline models and explores when forecasting does not make sense.

Subsequent chapters dive deep into forecasting techniques and gradually increase the complexity of the models, from statistical models to deep learning models. Finally, the book covers automated forecasting libraries, which can greatly speed up the forecasting process. This will give you a sense of what is being done in the industry.

Who should read this book?

This book is for data scientists who know how to perform traditional regression and classification tasks but find themselves stuck when it comes to time series. If you have been dropping the date column up until now, this book is definitely for you!

The book is also for professionals proficient in R looking to transition to Python. R is a great language for time series forecasting, and many methods have been implemented in R. However, Python is the most popular language for data science, and it has the advantage of being applied to deep learning models, which is something R can't do.

How this book is organized: A roadmap

The book has 4 parts and 21 chapters.

Part 1 is an introduction to time series forecasting. We'll formalize the concept of time series data, develop baseline models, and see when forecasting is not a reasonable avenue:

- Chapter 1 defines time series data and explores the lifecycle of a forecasting project.
- In chapter 2 we'll develop baseline models, as a model can only be evaluated in relation to another model. It is therefore important to first have a simple forecasting model before moving on to more complex techniques.
- In chapter 3 we'll study the random walk model, which is a special scenario where forecasting cannot reasonably be performed with advanced models, and we must resort to simple baseline models.

Part 2 focuses on forecasting with statistical models:

- In chapter 4 we'll develop the moving average model, $MA(q)$, one of the building blocks of more complex forecasting techniques.
- In chapter 5 we'll develop the autoregressive model, $AR(p)$, the other foundational model for more complicated scenarios.
- In chapter 6 we'll combine the $AR(p)$ and $MA(q)$ models to form the $ARMA(p,q)$ model and design a new forecasting procedure.
- In chapter 7 we'll build on the previous chapter to model non-stationary time series with the $ARIMA(p,d,q)$ model.
- In chapter 8 we'll add yet another layer of complexity and model seasonal time series with the $SARIMA(p,d,q)(P,D,Q)_m$ model.
- In chapter 9 we'll add the last layer of complexity and reach the SARIMAX model, allowing us to use external variables to forecast our data.
- In chapter 10 we'll explore vector autoregression, $VAR(p)$, models, which allow us to forecast many time series simultaneously.
- Chapter 11 concludes part 2 with a capstone project, giving us the chance to apply what we learned since chapter 4.

Part 3 covers forecasting with deep learning. When your dataset becomes very large, with nonlinear relationships and high dimensionality, deep learning is the most appropriate tool for forecasting:

- Chapter 12 introduces deep learning and the types of models we can build.
- Chapter 13 explores the data windowing step, which is crucial to ensuring the success of forecasting using deep learning models.
- In chapter 14 we'll develop our first simple deep learning models.
- In chapter 15 we'll use the LSTM architecture for forecasting. This architecture is specifically built to process sequential data, just like time series.

- In chapter 16 we'll explore the CNN architecture, which can effectively filter the noise in a time series with the convolution operation. We'll also combine the CNN with the LSTM architecture.
- In chapter 17 we'll develop an autoregressive deep learning model, which is an architecture that is proven to generate state-of-the-art results, as the model's output is fed back in as an input to produce the next forecast.
- In chapter 18 we'll conclude part 3 with a capstone project.

Part 4 explores the use of automated forecasting libraries, especially Prophet, as it is one of the most widely used libraries in the industry:

- Chapter 19 explores the ecosystem of automated forecasting libraries, and we'll work through a project using Prophet. We'll also use a SARIMAX model to compare the performance of both methods.
- Chapter 20 is a capstone project where you are invited to use Prophet and a SARIMAX model and see which performs best in that situation.
- Chapter 21 concludes the book and aims to inspire you to go above and beyond and explore what else can be done with time series data.

About the code

This book contains many examples of source code both in numbered listings and in line with normal text. In both cases, source code is formatted in a `fixed-width font` `like this` to separate it from ordinary text.

In many cases, the original source code has been reformatted; we've added line breaks and reworked indentation to accommodate the available page space in the book. In some cases, even this was not enough, and listings include line-continuation markers (➥). Additionally, comments in the source code have often been removed from the listings when the code is described in the text. Code annotations accompany many of the listings, highlighting important concepts.

You can get executable snippets of code from the liveBook (online) version of this book at https://livebook.manning.com/book/time-series-forecasting-in-python-book/. The entire source code for this book is available on GitHub at https://github.com/marcopeix/TimeSeriesForecastingInPython. You can also find the solutions to all the exercises there, and the code for the figures is also included. Creating visualizations is sometimes an overlooked skill, but I believe it is an important one.

All the code was run on Windows using Jupyter Notebooks in Anaconda. I used Python 3.7, but any later release should work as well.

liveBook discussion forum

Purchase of *Time Series Forecasting in Python* includes free access to liveBook, Manning's online reading platform. Using liveBook's exclusive discussion features, you can attach comments to the book globally or to specific sections or paragraphs. It's a snap to make notes for yourself, ask and answer technical questions, and receive help from the author and other users. To access the forum, go to https://livebook.manning.com/book/time-series-forecasting-in-python-book/discussion. You can also learn more about Manning's forums and the rules of conduct at https://livebook.manning.com/discussion.

Manning's commitment to our readers is to provide a venue where a meaningful dialogue between individual readers and between readers and the author can take place. It is not a commitment to any specific amount of participation on the part of the author, whose contribution to the forum remains voluntary (and unpaid). We suggest you try asking the author some challenging questions lest his interest stray! The forum and the archives of previous discussions will be accessible from the publisher's website as long as the book is in print.

Author online

You can follow me on Medium for more articles on data science (https://medium.com/@marcopeixeiro). My approach to blogging is similar to how I approached this book: theory first and a hands-on project second. You can also reach out to me on LinkedIn (https://www.linkedin.com/in/marco-peixeiro/).

about the author

MARCO PEIXEIRO is a senior data scientist at one of Canada's largest banks. Being self-taught, he is especially aware of what one needs to know to land a job and work in the industry. Marco is a big proponent of hands-on approaches to learning, which is the approach taken in his Medium blog, his freeCode-Camp crash course on data science, and in his Udemy course.

about the cover illustration

The figure on the cover of *Time Series Forecasting in Python* is captioned "Homme de Kamtschatka," or "Kamchatka man," taken from a collection by Jacques Grasset de Saint-Sauveur, published in 1797. Each illustration is finely drawn and colored by hand.

In those days, it was easy to identify where people lived and what their trade or station in life was just by their dress. Manning celebrates the inventiveness and initiative of the computer business with book covers based on the rich diversity of regional culture centuries ago, brought back to life by pictures from collections such as this one.

Part 1

Time waits for no one

Very few phenomena are unaffected by time, which in itself is enough to justify the importance of understanding what time series are. In this first part of the book, we'll define time series and explore the particularities of working with them. We'll also develop our very first forecasting models using naive methods. These will serve as baseline models, and we'll reuse these techniques throughout the book. Finally, we'll study a situation where forecasting is not possible, so that we identify and avoid falling into that trap.

Understanding time series forecasting

This chapter covers

- Introducing time series
- Understanding the three main components of a time series
- The steps necessary for a successful forecasting project
- How forecasting time series is different from other regression tasks

Time series exist in a variety of fields from meteorology to finance, econometrics, and marketing. By recording data and analyzing it, we can study time series to analyze industrial processes or track business metrics, such as sales or engagement. Also, with large amounts of data available, data scientists can apply their expertise to techniques for time series forecasting.

You might have come across other courses, books, or articles on time series that implement their solutions in R, a programming language specifically made for statistical computing. Many forecasting techniques make use of statistical models, as you will learn in chapter 3 and onwards. Thus, a lot of work was done to develop packages to make time series analysis and forecasting seamless using R. However, most data scientists are required to be proficient with Python, as it is the most widespread language in the field of machine learning. In recent years, the community and large companies have developed powerful libraries that leverage Python to perform statistical computing and machine learning tasks, develop websites, and much more. While Python is far from being a perfect programming language, its versatility is a strong benefit to its users, as we can develop models, perform statistical tests, and possibly serve our models through an API or develop a web interface, all while using the same programming language. This book will show you how to implement both statistical learning techniques and machine learning techniques for time series forecasting using only Python.

This book will focus entirely on time series forecasting. You will first learn how to make simple forecasts that will serve as benchmarks for more complex models. Then we will use two statistical learning techniques, the moving average model and the autoregressive model, to make forecasts. These will serve as the foundation for the more complex modeling techniques we will cover that will allow us to account for non-stationarity, seasonality effects, and the impact of exogenous variables. Afterwards, we'll switch from statistical learning techniques to deep learning methods, in order to forecast very large time series with a high dimensionality, a scenario in which statistical learning often does not perform as well as its deep learning counterpart.

For now, this chapter will examine the basic concepts of time series forecasting. I'll start by defining time series so that you can recognize one. Then, we will move on and discuss the purpose of time series forecasting. Finally, you will learn why forecasting a time series is different from other regression problems, and thus why the subject deserves its own book.

1.1   Introducing time series

The first step in understanding and performing time series forecasting is learning what a time series is. In short, a *time series* is simply a set of data points ordered in time. Furthermore, the data is often equally spaced in time, meaning that equal intervals separate each data point. In simpler terms, the data can be recorded at every hour or every minute, or it could be averaged over every month or year. Some typical examples of time series include the closing value of a particular stock, a household's electricity consumption, or the temperature outside.

Time series

A time series is a set of data points ordered in time.

The data is equally spaced in time, meaning that it was recorded at every hour, minute, month, or quarter. Typical examples of time series include the closing value of a stock, a household's electricity consumption, or the temperature outside.

Let's consider a dataset representing the quarterly earnings per share in US dollars of Johnson & Johnson stock from 1960 to 1980, shown in figure 1.1. We will use this dataset often throughout this book, as it has many interesting properties that will help you learn advanced techniques for more complex forecasting problems.

As you can see, figure 1.1 clearly represents a time series. The data is indexed by time, as marked on the horizontal axis. Also, the data is equally spaced in time, since it was recorded at the end of every quarter of each year. We can see that the data has a trend, since the values are increasing over time. We also see the earnings going up and down over the course of each year, and the pattern repeats every year.

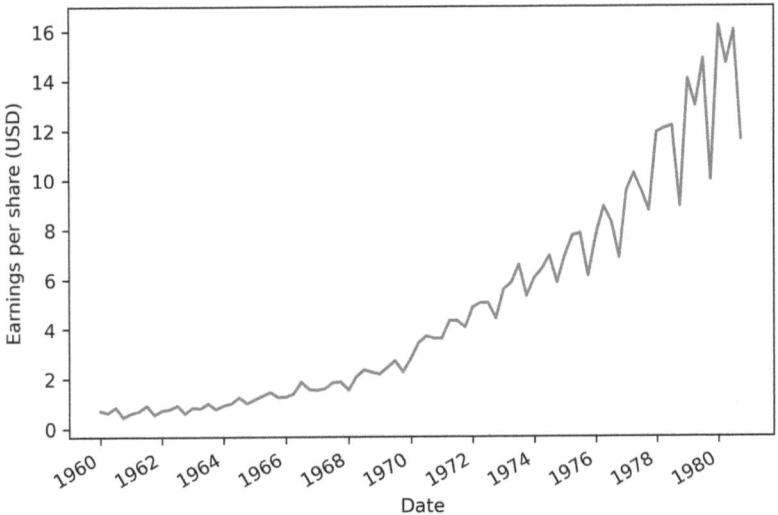

Figure 1.1   Quarterly earnings of Johnson & Johnson in USD from 1960 to 1980 showing a positive trend and a cyclical behavior

1.1.1   Components of a time series

We can further our understanding of time series by looking at their three components: a trend, a seasonal component, and residuals. In fact, all time series can be decomposed into these three elements.

Visualizing the components of a time series is known as decomposition. *Decomposition* is defined as a statistical task that separates a time series into its different components. We can visualize each individual component, which will help us identify the trend and seasonal pattern in the data, which is not always straightforward just by looking at a dataset.

Let's take a closer look at the decomposition of Johnson & Johnson quarterly earnings per share, shown in figure 1.2. You can see how the Observed data was split into Trend, Seasonal, and Residuals. Let's study each piece of the graph in more detail.

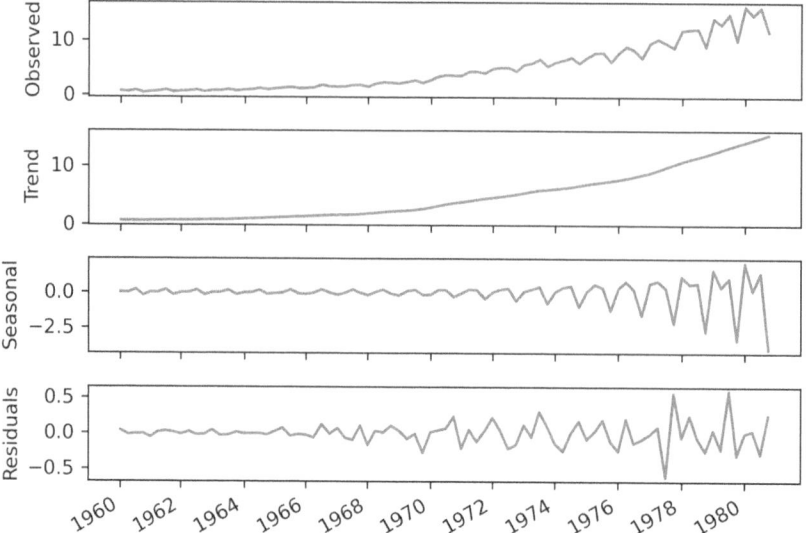

Figure 1.2   Decomposition of quarterly earnings of Johnson & Johnson from 1960 to 1980

First, the top graph, labeled as Observed, simply shows the time series as it was recorded (figure 1.3). The *y*-axis displays the value of the quarterly earnings per share for Johnson & Johnson in US dollars, while the *x*-axis represents time. It is basically a recreation of figure 1.1, and it shows the result of combining the Trend, Seasonal, and Residuals graphs from figure 1.2.

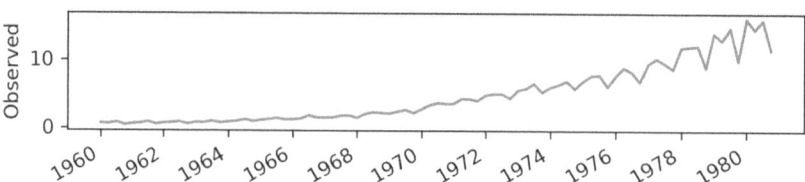

Figure 1.3   Focusing on the Observed plot

Then we have the trend component, as shown in figure 1.4. Again, keep in mind that the *y*-axis represents the value, while the *x*-axis still refers to time. The trend is defined as the slow-moving changes in a time series. We can see that it starts out flat and then steeply goes up, meaning that we have an increasing, or positive, trend in our data. The trend component is sometimes referred to as the *level*. We can think of the trend

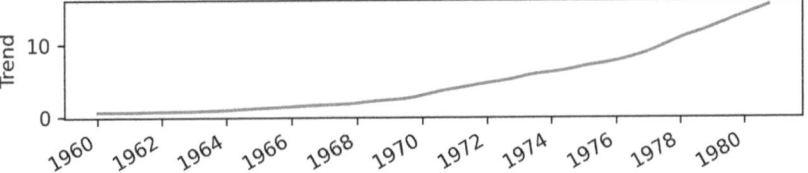

Figure 1.4 **Focusing on the trend component. We have a trend in our series, since the component is not flat. It indicates that we have increasing values over time.**

component as trying to draw a line through most of the data points to show the general direction of a time series.

Next we see the seasonal component in figure 1.5. The seasonal component captures the seasonal variation, which is a cycle that occurs over a fixed period of time. We can see that over the course of a year, or four quarters, the earnings per share start low, increase, and decrease again at the end of the year.

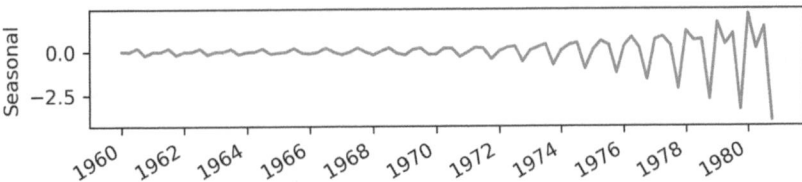

Figure 1.5 **Focusing on the seasonal component. Here we have periodic fluctuations in our time series, which indicates that earnings go up and down every year.**

Notice how the *y*-axis shows negative values. Does this mean that the earnings per share are negative? Clearly, that cannot be, since our dataset strictly has positive values. Therefore, we can say that the seasonal component shows how we deviate from the trend. Sometimes we have a positive deviation, and we get a peak in the Observed graph. Other times, we have a negative deviation, and we see a trough in Observed.

Finally, the last graph in figure 1.2 shows the residuals, which is what cannot be explained by either the trend or the seasonal components. We can think of the residuals as adding the Trend and Seasonal graphs together and comparing the value at each point in time to the Observed graph. For certain points, we might get the exact same value as in Observed, in which case the residual will be zero. In other cases, the value is different from the one in Observed, so the Residuals graph shows what value must be added to Trend and Seasonal in order to adjust the result and get the same value as in Observed. Residuals usually correspond to random errors, also termed *white noise*, as we will discuss in chapter 3. They represent information that we cannot model or predict, since it is completely random, as shown in figure 1.6.

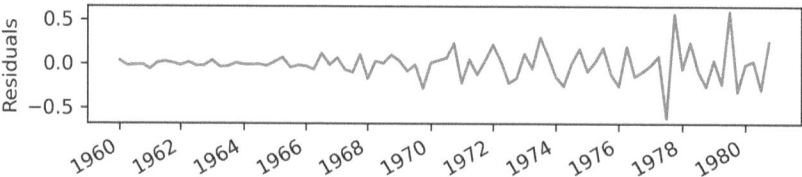

Figure 1.6   Focusing on the residuals. The residuals are what cannot be explained by the trend and seasonal components.

> ## Time series decomposition
>
> Time series decomposition is a process by which we separate a time series into its components: trend, seasonality, and residuals.
>
> The trend represents the slow-moving changes in a time series. It is responsible for making the series gradually increase or decrease over time.
>
> The seasonality component represents the seasonal pattern in the series. The cycles occur repeatedly over a fixed period of time.
>
> The residuals represent the behavior that cannot be explained by the trend and seasonality components. They correspond to random errors, also termed white noise.

Already we can intuitively see how each component affects our work when forecasting. If a time series exposes a certain trend, then we'll expect it to continue in the future. Similarly, if we observe a strong seasonality effect, this is likely going to continue, and our forecasts must reflect that. Later in the book, you'll see how to account for these components and include them in your models to forecast more complex time series.

1.2   *Bird's-eye view of time series forecasting*

Forecasting is predicting the future using historical data and knowledge of future events that might affect our forecasts. This definition is full of promises and, as data scientists, we are often very eager to start forecasting by using our scientific knowledge to showcase an incredible model with a near-perfect forecast accuracy. However, there are important steps that must be covered before reaching the point of forecasting.

Figure 1.7 is a simplified diagram of what a complete forecasting project might look like in a professional setting. Note that these steps are not universal, and they may or may not be followed, depending on the organization and its maturity. These steps are nonetheless essential to ensure good cohesion between the data team and the business team, hence providing business value and avoiding friction and frustration between the teams.

Let's dive into a scenario that covers each step of a forecasting project roadmap in detail. Imagine you are planning a one-week camping trip one month from now, and

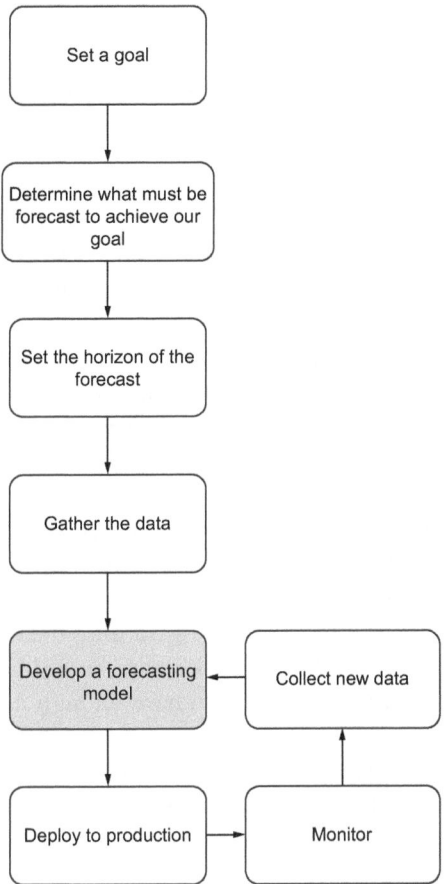

Figure 1.7 **Forecasting project roadmap. The first step is naturally to set a goal that justifies the need for forecasting. Then you must determine what needs to be forecast in order to achieve that goal. Then you set the horizon of the forecast. Once that's done, you can gather the data and develop a forecasting model. Then the model is deployed to production, its performance is monitored, and new data is collected in order to retrain the forecasting model and make sure it is still relevant.**

you want to know which sleeping bag to bring with you so you can sleep comfortably at night.

1.2.1 Setting a goal

The very first step in any project roadmap is to set a goal. Here it is explicit in the scenario: you want to know which sleeping bag to bring to sleep comfortably at night. If the nights will be cold, a warm sleeping bag is the best choice. Of course, if nights are expected to be warm, then a light sleeping bag would be the better option.

1.2.2 Determining what must be forecast to achieve your goal

Then you move to determining what must be forecast in order for you to decide which sleeping bag to bring. In this case, you need to predict the temperature at night. To simplify things, let's consider that predicting the minimum temperature is sufficient to make a decision, and that the minimum temperature occurs at night.

1.2.3   Setting the horizon of the forecast

Now you can set the horizon of your forecast. In this case, your camping trip is one month from now, and it will last for one week. Therefore, you have a horizon of one week, since you are only interested in predicting the minimum temperature during the camping trip.

1.2.4   Gathering the data

You can now start gathering your data. For example, you could collect historical daily minimum temperature data. You could also gather data on possible factors that can influence temperature, such as humidity and wind speed.

This is when the question of how much data is enough data arises. Ideally, you would collect more than 1 year of data. That way, you could determine if there is a yearly seasonal pattern or a trend. In the case of temperature, you can of course expect some seasonal pattern over the year, since different seasons bring different minimum temperatures.

However, 1 year of data is not the ultimate answer to how much data is sufficient. It highly depends on the frequency of the forecasts. In this case, you will be creating daily forecasts, so 1 year of data should be enough.

If you wanted to create hourly forecasts, a few months of training data would be enough, as it would contain a lot of data points. If you were creating monthly or yearly forecasts, you would need a much larger historical period to have enough data points to train with.

In the end, there is no clear answer regarding the quantity of data required to train a model. Determining this is part of the experimentation process of building a model, assessing its performance, and testing whether more data improves the model's performance.

1.2.5   Developing a forecasting model

With your historical data in hand, you are ready to develop a forecasting model. This part of the project roadmap is the focus of this entire book. This is when you get to study the data and determine whether there is a trend or a seasonal pattern.

If you observe seasonality, then a SARIMA model would be relevant, because this model uses seasonal effects to produce forecasts. If you have information on wind speed and humidity, you could take that into account using the SARIMAX model, because you can feed it with information from exogenous variables, such as wind speed and humidity. We will explore these models in detail in chapters 8 and 9.

If you managed to collect a large amount of data, such as the daily minimum temperature of the last 20 years, you could use neural networks to leverage this very large amount of training data. Unlike statistical learning methods, deep learning tends to produce better models, as more data is used for training.

Whichever model you develop, you will use part of the training data as a test set to evaluate your model's performance. The test set will always be the most recent data points, and it must be representative of the forecasting horizon.

In this case, since your horizon is one week, you can remove the last seven data points from your training set to place them in a test set. Then, when each model is trained, you can produce one-week forecasts and compare the results to the test set. The model's performance can be assessed by computing an error metric, such as the mean squared error (MSE). This is a way to evaluate how far your predictions are from the real values. The model with the lowest MSE will be your best-performing model, and it is the one that will move on to the next step.

1.2.6 Deploying to production

Once you have your champion model, you must deploy it to production. This means that your model can take in data and return a prediction for the minimum daily temperature for the next 7 days. There are many ways to deploy a model to production, and this could be the subject of an entire book. Your model could be served as an API or integrated in a web application, or you could define your own Excel function to run your model. Ultimately, your model is considered deployed when you can feed in data and have forecasts returned without any manual manipulation of the data. At this point, your model can be monitored.

1.2.7 Monitoring

Since the camping trip is 1 month from now, you can see how well your model performs. Every day, you can compare your model's forecast to the actual minimum temperature recorded for the day. This allows you to determine the quality of the model's forecasts.

You can also look for unexpected events. For example, a heat wave can arise, degrading the quality of your model's forecasts. Closely monitoring your model and current events allows you to determine if the unexpected event results from a temporary situation, or if it will last for the next 2 months, in which case it could impact your decision for the camping trip.

1.2.8 Collecting new data

By monitoring your model, you necessarily collect new data as you compare the model's forecasts to the observed minimum temperature for the day. This new, more recent, data can then be used in retraining your model. That way, you have up-to-date data you can use to forecast the minimum temperature for the next 7 days.

This cycle is repeated over the next month until you reach the day of the camping trip, as shown in figure 1.8. By that point, you will have made many forecasts, assessed their quality against newly observed data, and retrained your model with new daily minimum temperatures as you recorded them. That way, you make sure that your model is still performant and uses relevant data to forecast the temperature for your camping trip.

Finally, based on your model's predictions, you can decide which sleeping bag to bring with you.

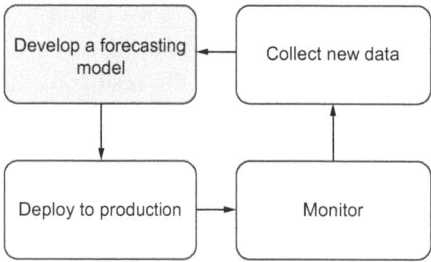

Figure 1.8   Visualizing the production loop. Once the model is in production, you enter a cycle where you monitor it, collect new data, and use that data to adjust the forecasting model before deploying it again.

1.3   How time series forecasting is different from other regression tasks

You probably have encountered regression tasks where you must predict some continuous target given a certain set of features. At first glance, time series forecasting seems like a typical regression problem: we have some historical data, and we wish to build a mathematical expression that will express future values as a function of past values. However, there are some key differences between time series forecasting and regression for time-independent scenarios that deserve to be addressed before we look at our very first forecasting technique.

1.3.1   Time series have an order

The first concept to keep in mind is that time series have an order, and we cannot change that order when modeling. In time series forecasting, we express future values as a function of past values. Therefore, we must keep the data in order, so as to not violate this relationship.

Also, it makes sense to keep the data in order because your model can only use information from the past up until the present—it will not know what will be observed in the future. Recall your camping trip. If you want to predict the temperature for Tuesday, you cannot possibly use the information from Wednesday, since it is in the future from the model's point of view. You would only be able to use the data from Monday and before. That is why the order of the data must remain the same throughout the modeling process.

Other regression tasks in machine learning often do not have an order. For example, if you are tasked to predict revenue based on ad spend, it does not matter when a certain amount was spent on ads. Instead, you simply want to relate the amount of ad spend to the revenue. In fact, you might even randomly shuffle the data to make your model more robust. Here the regression task is to simply derive a function such that given an amount on ad spend, an estimate of revenue is returned.

On the other hand, time series are indexed by time, and that order must be kept. Otherwise, you would be training your model with future information that it would not have at prediction time. This is called *look-ahead bias* in more formal terms. The resulting model would therefore not be reliable and would most probably perform poorly when you make future forecasts.

1.3.2 *Time series sometimes do not have features*

It is possible to forecast time series without the use of features other than the time series itself.

As data scientists, we are used to having datasets with many columns, each representing a potential predictor for our target. For example, consider the task of predicting revenue based on ad spend, where the revenue is the target variable. As features, we could have the amount spent on Google ads, Facebook ads, and television ads. Using these three features, we would build a regression model to estimate revenue.

However, with time series, it is quite common to be given a simple dataset with a time column and a value at that point in time. Without any other features, we must learn ways of using past values of the time series to forecast future values. This is when the moving average model (chapter 4) or autoregressive model (chapter 5) come into play, as they are ways to express future values as a function of past values. These models are foundational to the more complex models that then allow you to consider seasonal patterns and trends in time series. Starting in chapter 6, we will gradually build on those basic models to forecast more complex time series.

1.4 *Next steps*

This book will cover different forecasting techniques in detail. We'll start with some very basic methods, such as the moving average model and autoregressive model, and we will gradually account for more factors in order to forecast time series with trends and seasonal patterns using the ARIMA, SARIMA, and SARIMAX models. We will also work with time series with high dimensionality, which will require us to use deep learning techniques for sequential data. Therefore, we will have to build neural networks using CNN (convolutional neural network) and LSTM (long short-term memory). Finally, you will learn how to automate the work of forecasting time series. As mentioned, all implementations throughout the book will be done in Python.

Now that you have learned what a time series is and how forecasting will be different than any traditional regression tasks you might have seen before, we are ready to move on and start forecasting. However, our first attempt at forecasting will focus on naive methods that will serve as baseline models.

Summary

- A time series is a set of data points ordered in time.
- Examples of time series are the closing price of a stock or the temperature outside.
- Time series can be decomposed into three components: a trend, a seasonal component, and residuals.
- It is important to have a goal when forecasting and to monitor the model once it's deployed. This will ensure the success and longevity of the project.
- Never change the order of a time series when modeling. Shuffling the data is not allowed.

A naive prediction
of the future

This chapter covers

- Defining a baseline model
- Setting a baseline using the mean
- Building a baseline using the mean of the previous window of time
- Creating a baseline using the previous timestep
- Implementing the naive seasonal forecast

In chapter 1 we covered what time series are and how forecasting a time series is different from a traditional regression task. You also learned the necessary steps in building a successful forecasting project, from defining a goal to building a model, deploying it, and updating it as new data is collected. Now you are ready to start forecasting a time series.

You will first learn how to make a naive prediction of the future, which will serve as a baseline. The baseline model is a trivial solution that uses heuristics, or simple statistics, to compute a forecast. Developing a baseline model is not always an exact science. It will often require some intuition that we'll gain by visualizing the data and detecting patterns that can be used to make predictions. In any modeling project, it is important to have a baseline, as you can use it to compare the performance

14

of the more complex models you'll build down the road. The only way to know that a model is good, or performant, is to compare it to a baseline.

In this chapter, let's imagine that we wish to predict the quarterly earnings per share (EPS) of Johnson & Johnson. We can look at the dataset in figure 2.1, which is identical to what you saw in chapter 1. Specifically, we will use the data from 1960 to the end of 1979 in order to predict the EPS for the four quarters of 1980. The forecasting period is illustrated by the gray zone in figure 2.1.

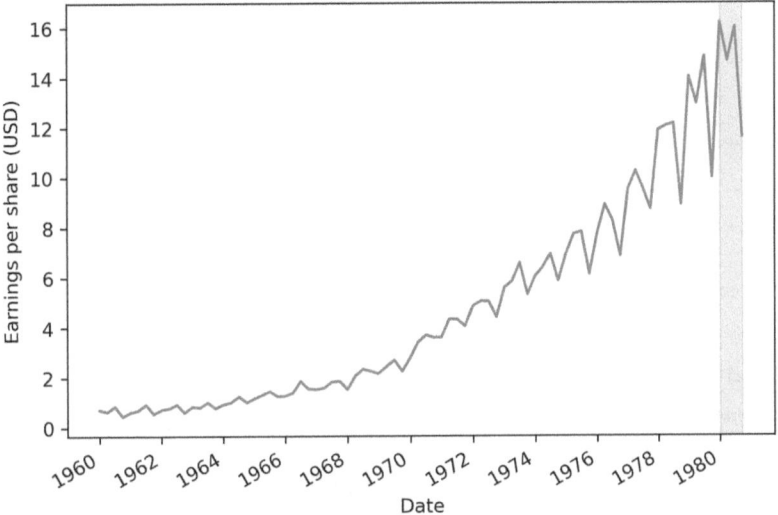

Figure 2.1 Quarterly earnings per share of Johnson & Johnson in US dollars (USD) between 1960 and 1980. We will use the data from 1960 to the last quarter of 1979 to build a baseline model that will forecast the earnings per share for the quarters of 1980 (as illustrated by the gray area).

You can see in figure 2.1 that our data has a trend, since it is increasing over time. Also, we have a seasonal pattern, since over the course of a year, or four quarters, we can observe peaks and troughs repeatedly. This means that we have seasonality.

Recall that we identified each of these components when we decomposed our time series in chapter 1. The components are shown in figure 2.2. We will study some of these components in detail later in the chapter, as they will help us gain some intuition about the behavior of the data, which in turn will help us develop a good baseline model.

We will first define what a baseline model is, and then we will develop four different baselines to forecast the quarterly EPS of Johnson & Johnson. This is the time when we'll finally get our hands dirty with Python and time series forecasting.

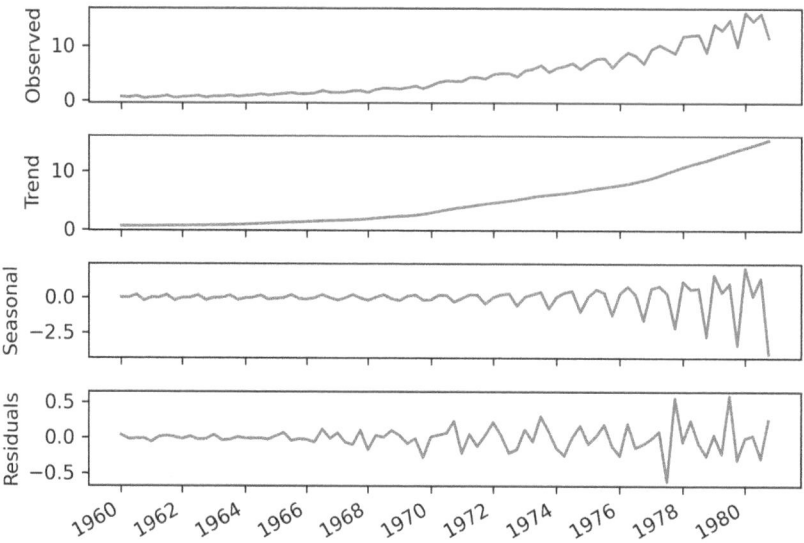

Figure 2.2   Decomposition of quarterly earnings of Johnson & Johnson from 1960 to 1980

2.1   *Defining a baseline model*

A *baseline model* is a trivial solution to our problem. It often uses heuristics, or simple statistics, to generate predictions. The baseline model is the simplest solution you can think of—it should not require any training, and the cost of implementation should be very low.

> **Can you think of a baseline for our project?**
> Knowing that we want to forecast the EPS for Johnson & Johnson, what is the most basic, most naive, forecast you can make?

In the context of time series, one simple statistic we can use to build a baseline is the arithmetic mean. We can simply compute the mean of the values over a certain period and assume that future values will be equal to that mean. In the context of predicting the EPS for Johnson & Johnson, this is like saying

The average EPS between 1960 and 1979 was $4.31. Therefore, I expect the EPS over the next four quarters of 1980 to be equal to $4.31 per quarter.

Another possible baseline is to naively forecast the last recorded data point. In our context, this would be like saying

If the EPS is $0.71 for this quarter, then the EPS will also be $0.71 for next quarter.

Or, if we see a cyclical pattern in our data, we can simply repeat that pattern into the future. Staying in the context of Johnson & Johnson, this is like saying

> *If the EPS is $14.04 for the first quarter of 1979, then the EPS for the first quarter of 1980 will also be $14.04.*

You can see these three possible baselines rely on simple statistics, heuristics, and patterns observed in our dataset.

Baseline model

A baseline model is a trivial solution to your forecasting problem. It relies on heuristics or simple statistics and is usually the simplest solution. It does not require model fitting, and it is easy to implement.

You might wonder if those baseline models are any good. How well can those simple methods forecast the future? We can answer this question by forecasting for the year of 1980 and testing our forecasts against the observed data in 1980. This is called *out-of-sample* forecasting because we are making predictions for a period that was not taken into account when the model was developed. That way we can measure the performance of our models and see how they would perform when we forecast beyond the data we have, which in this case is 1981 and later.

In the next sections, you will learn how to develop the different baselines mentioned here to predict the quarterly EPS of Johnson & Johnson.

2.2   Forecasting the historical mean

As mentioned at the beginning of the chapter, we are going to work with the quarterly EPS in US dollars (USD) of Johnson & Johnson from 1960 to 1980. Our goal is to use the data from 1960 to the end of 1979 to predict the four quarters of 1980. The first baseline we'll discuss uses the historical mean, which is the arithmetic mean of past values. Its implementation is straightforward: calculate the mean of the training set, and it will be our prediction for the four quarters of 1980. First, though, we need to do some preliminary work that we'll use in all of our baseline implementations.

2.2.1   Setup for baseline implementations

Our first step is to load the dataset. To do so, we will use the `pandas` library and load the dataset into a `DataFrame` using the `read_csv` method. You can either download the file on your local machine and pass the file's path to the `read_csv` method, or simply type in the URL where the CSV file is hosted on GitHub. In this case, we will work with the file:

```
import pandas as pd

df = pd.read_csv('../data/jj.csv')
```

NOTE   The entire code for this chapter is available on GitHub: https://github
.com/marcopeix/TimeSeriesForecastingInPython/tree/master/CH02.

A `DataFrame` is the most-used data structure in `pandas`. It is a 2-dimensional labeled
data structure with columns that can hold different types of data, such as strings, integers, floats, or dates.

Our second step is to split the data into a train set for training and a test set for
testing. Given that our horizon is 1 year, our train set will start in 1960 and go all the
way to the end of 1979. We will save the data collected in 1980 for our test set. You can
think of a `DataFrame` as a table or a spreadsheet with column names and row indices.

With our dataset in a `DataFrame`, we can display the first five entries by running

```
df.head()
```

This will give us the output shown in figure 2.3.

	date	data
0	1960-01-01	0.71
1	1960-04-01	0.63
2	1960-07-02	0.85
3	1960-10-01	0.44
4	1961-01-01	0.61

**Figure 2.3   The first five entries of quarterly
earnings per share for the Johnson & Johnson
dataset. Notice how our `DataFrame` has two
columns: date and data. It also has row indices
starting at 0.**

Figure 2.3 will help you better understand what type of data our `DataFrame` is holding.
We have the date column, which specifies the end of each quarter, when the EPS is
calculated. The data column holds the value of the EPS in US dollars (USD).

We can optionally display the last five entries of our dataset and obtain the output
in figure 2.4:

```
df.tail()
```

	date	data
79	1979-10-01	9.99
80	1980-01-01	16.20
81	1980-04-01	14.67
82	1980-07-02	16.02
83	1980-10-01	11.61

**Figure 2.4   The last five entries of our dataset. Here
we can see the four quarters of 1980 that we will try
to predict using different baseline models. We will
compare our forecasts to the observed data in 1980
to evaluate the performance of each baseline.**

In figure 2.4 we see the four quarters of 1980, which is what we will be trying to forecast using our baseline models. We will evaluate the performance of our baselines by

comparing our forecasts to the values in the data column for the four quarters of 1980. The closer our forecasts are to the observed values, the better.

The final step before developing our baseline models is to split the dataset into the train and test sets. As mentioned earlier, the train set will consist of the data from 1960 to the end of 1979, and the test set will consist of the four quarters of 1980. The train set will be the only information we use to develop our models. Once a model is built, we will forecast the next four timesteps, which will correspond to the four quarters of 1980 in our test set. That way, we can compare our forecasts to the observed data and evaluate the performance of our baselines.

To make the split, we'll specify that our train set will contain all the data held in `df` except the last four entries. The test set will be composed of only the last four entries. This is what the next code block does:

```
train = df[:-4]
test = df[-4:]
```

2.2.2 Implementing the historical mean baseline

Now we are ready to implement our baseline. We will first use the arithmetic mean of the entire train set. To compute the mean, we'll use the numpy library, as it is a very fast package for scientific computing in Python that plays really well with `DataFrames`:

```
import numpy as np

historical_mean = np.mean(train['data'])        ◁──┤ Compute the arithmetic
                                                    │ mean of the data column
print(historical_mean)                              │ in the train set.
```

In the preceding code block, we first import the numpy library and then compute the average of the EPS over the entire train set and print it out on the screen. This gives a value of 4.31 USD. This means that from 1960 to the end of 1979, the quarterly EPS of Johnson & Johnson is on average 4.31 USD.

Now we will naively forecast this value for each quarter of 1980. To do so, we'll simply create a new column, pred_mean, that holds the historical mean of the training set as a forecast:

```
test.loc[:, 'pred_mean'] = historical_mean       ◁──┤ Set the historical
                                                     │ mean as a forecast.
```

Next, we need to define and calculate an error metric in order to evaluate the performance of our forecasts on the test set. In this case, we will use the *mean absolute percentage error* (MAPE). It is a measure of prediction accuracy for forecasting methods that is easy to interpret and independent of the scale of our data. This means that whether we are working with two-digit values or six-digit values, the MAPE will always be expressed as a percentage. Thus, the MAPE returns the percentage of how much the forecast values deviate from the observed or actual values on average, whether the prediction was higher or lower than the observed values. The MAPE is defined in equation 2.1.

$$\text{MAPE} = \frac{1}{n} \sum_{i=1}^{n} \left| \frac{A_i - F_i}{A_i} \right| \times 100$$

Equation 2.1

In equation 2.1, A_i is the actual value at point i in time, and F_i is the forecast value at point i in time; n is simply the number of forecasts. In our case, because we are forecasting the four quarters of 1980, $n = 4$. Inside the summation, the forecast value is subtracted from the actual value, and that result is divided by the actual value, which gives us the percentage error. Then we take the absolute value of the percentage error. This operation is repeated for each of the n points in time, and the results are added together. Finally, we divide the sum by n, the number of points in time, which effectively gives us the mean absolute percentage error.

Let's implement this function in Python. We'll define a mape function that takes in two vectors: y_true for the actual values observed in the test set and y_pred for the forecast values. In this case, because numpy allows us to work with arrays, we will not need a loop to sum all the values. We can simply subtract the y_pred array from the y_true array and divide by y_true to get the percentage error. Then we can take the absolute value. After that, we take the mean of the result, which will take care of summing up each value in the vector and dividing by the number of predictions. Finally, we'll multiply the result by 100 so the output is expressed as a percentage instead of a decimal number:

```
def mape(y_true, y_pred):
    return np.mean(np.abs((y_true - y_pred) / y_true)) * 100
```

Now we can calculate the MAPE of our baseline. Our actual values are in the data column of test, so it will be the first parameter passed to the mape function. Our forecasts are in the pred_mean column of test, so it will be our second parameter for the function:

```
mape_hist_mean = mape(test['data'], test['pred_mean'])
print(mape_hist_mean)
```

Running the function gives a MAPE of 70.00%. This means that our baseline deviates by 70% on average from the observed quarterly EPS of Johnson & Johnson in 1980.

Let's visualize our forecasts to better understand our MAPE of 70%.

Listing 2.1   Visualizing our forecasts

```
import matplotlib.pyplot as plt

fig, ax = plt.subplots()

ax.plot(train['date'], train['data'], 'g-.', label='Train')
ax.plot(test['date'], test['data'], 'b-', label='Test')
```

```
ax.plot(test['date'], test['pred_mean'], 'r--', label='Predicted')
ax.set_xlabel('Date')
ax.set_ylabel('Earnings per share (USD)')
ax.axvspan(80, 83, color='#808080', alpha=0.2)
ax.legend(loc=2)

plt.xticks(np.arange(0, 85, 8), [1960, 1962, 1964, 1966, 1968, 1970, 1972,
    1974, 1976, 1978, 1980])

fig.autofmt_xdate()
plt.tight_layout()
```

In listing 2.1, we use the `matplotlib` library, which is the most popular library for generating visualizations in Python, to generate a graph showing the training data, the forecast horizon, the observed values of the test set, and the predictions for each quarter of 1980.

First, we initialize a `figure` and an `ax` object. A figure can contain many `ax` objects, which allows us to create a figure with two, three, or more plots. In this case, we are creating a figure with a single plot, so we only need one `ax`.

Second, we plot our data on the `ax` object. We plot the train data using a green dashed and dotted line and give this curve a label of "Train." The label will later be useful for generating a legend for the graph. We then plot the test data and use a blue continuous line with a label of "Test." Finally, we plot our predictions using a red dashed line with a label of "Predicted."

Third, we label our *x*-axis and *y*-axis and draw a rectangular area to illustrate the forecast horizon. Since our forecast horizon is the four quarters of 1980, the area should start at index 80 and end at index 83, spanning the entire year of 1980. Remember that we obtained the indices of the last quarter of 1980 by running `df.tail()`, which resulted in figure 2.5.

	date	data
79	1979-10-01	9.99
80	1980-01-01	16.20
81	1980-04-01	14.67
82	1980-07-02	16.02
83	1980-10-01	11.61

Figure 2.5 The last five entries of our dataset

We give this area a gray color and specify the opacity using the `alpha` parameter. When `alpha` is 1, the shape is completely opaque; when `alpha` is 0, it is completely transparent. In our case, we'll use an opacity of 20%, or 0.2.

Then we specify the labels for the ticks on the *x*-axis. By default, the labels would show the data for each quarter of the dataset, which would create a crowded *x*-axis with unreadable labels. Instead, we'll display the year every 2 years. To do so, we'll gen-

erate an array specifying the index at which the label must appear. That's what
`np.arange(0, 81, 8)` does: it generates an array starting at 0, finishing at 80, because
the end index (81) is not included, with steps of 8, because there are 8 quarters in 2
years. This will effectively generate the following array: [0,8,16,...72,80]. Then we
specify an array containing the labels at each index, so it must start with 1960 and end
with 1980, just like our dataset.

Finally, we use `fig.automft_xdate()` to automatically format the tick labels on the
x-axis. It will slightly rotate them and make sure that they are legible. The final touch-up
is using `plt.tight_layout()` to remove any excess white space around the figure.

The end result is figure 2.6. Clearly, this baseline did not yield accurate predictions, since the Predicted line is very far from the Test line. Now we know that our
forecasts are, on average, 70% below the actual EPS for each quarter in 1980. Whereas
the EPS in 1980 was consistently above $10, we predicted only $4.31 for each quarter.

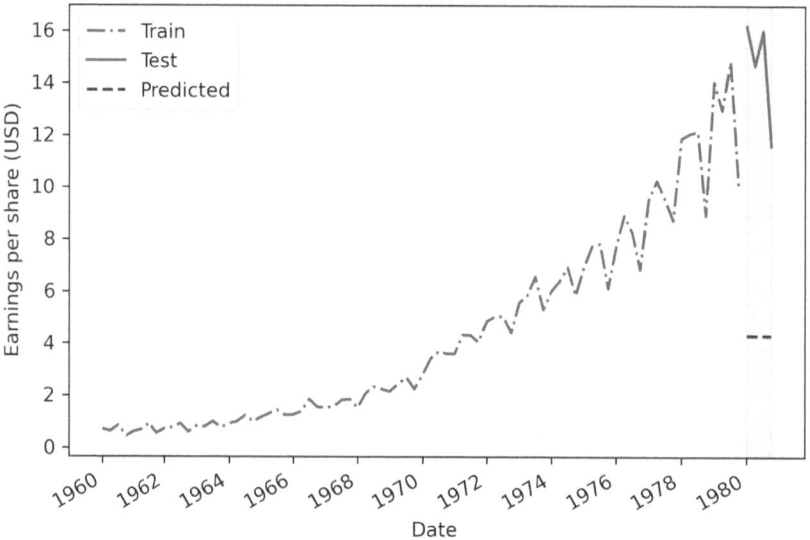

**Figure 2.6   Predicting the historical mean as a baseline. You can see that the prediction
is far from the actual values in the test set. This baseline gives a MAPE of 70%.**

Still, what can we learn from it? Looking at our training set, we can see a positive
trend, as the EPS is increasing over time. This is further supported by the trend component coming from the decomposition of our dataset, shown in figure 2.7.

As you we can see, not only do we have a trend, but the trend is not constant
between 1960 and 1980—it is getting steeper. Therefore, it might be that the EPS
observed in 1960 is not predictive of the EPS in 1980, because we have a positive
trend, and EPS values are increasing with time and are doing so at a faster rate.

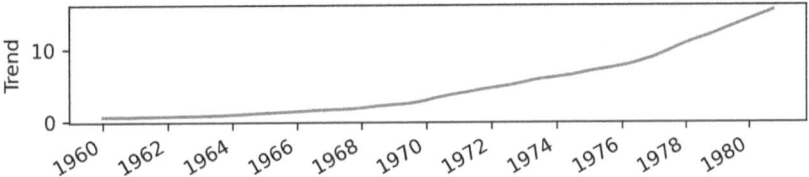

Figure 2.7   Trend component of our time series. You can see that we have a positive trend in our data, as it increases over time.

Can you improve our baseline?

Before moving on to the next section, can you think of a way to improve our baseline while still using the mean? Do you think that taking the mean of a shorter and more recent period of time would help (from 1970 to 1979, for example)?

2.3   *Forecasting last year's mean*

The lesson learned from the previous baseline is that earlier values do not seem to be predictive of future values in the long term because of the positive trend component in our dataset. Earlier values seem to be too small to be representative of the new level the EPS reaches toward the end of 1979 and onwards into 1980.

What if we use the mean of the last year in our training set to forecast the following year? This means that we would compute the average EPS in 1979 and forecast it for each quarter of 1980—the more recent values that have increased over time should potentially be closer to what will be observed in 1980. For now, this is simply a hypothesis, so let's implement this baseline and test it to see how it performs.

Our data is already split into test and train sets (done in section 2.2.1), so we can go ahead and calculate the mean of the last year in the train set, which corresponds to the last four data points in 1979:

```
last_year_mean = np.mean(train.data[-4:])    ◁─────  Compute the average EPS for the four
                                                     quarters of 1979, which are the last
print(last_year_mean)                                four data points of the train set.
```

This gives us an average EPS of $12.96. Therefore, we will predict that Johnson & Johnson will have an EPS of $12.96 for the four quarters of 1980. Using the same procedure that we used for the previous baseline, we'll create a new pred_last_yr_mean column to hold the mean of last year as our predictions:

```
test.loc[:, 'pred__last_yr_mean'] = last_year_mean
```

Then, using the mape function that we defined earlier, we can evaluate the performance of our new baseline. Remember that the first parameter is the observed values, which are held in the test set. Then we pass in the predicted values, which are in the pred_last_yr_mean column:

```
mape_last_year_mean = mape(test['data'], test['pred__last_yr_mean'])
print(mape_last_year_mean)
```

This gives us a MAPE of 15.60%. We can visualize our forecasts in figure 2.8.

Can you recreate figure 2.8?
As an exercise, try to recreate figure 2.8 to visualize the forecasts using the mean of the quarters of 1979. The code should be identical to listing 2.1, only this time the predictions are in a different column.

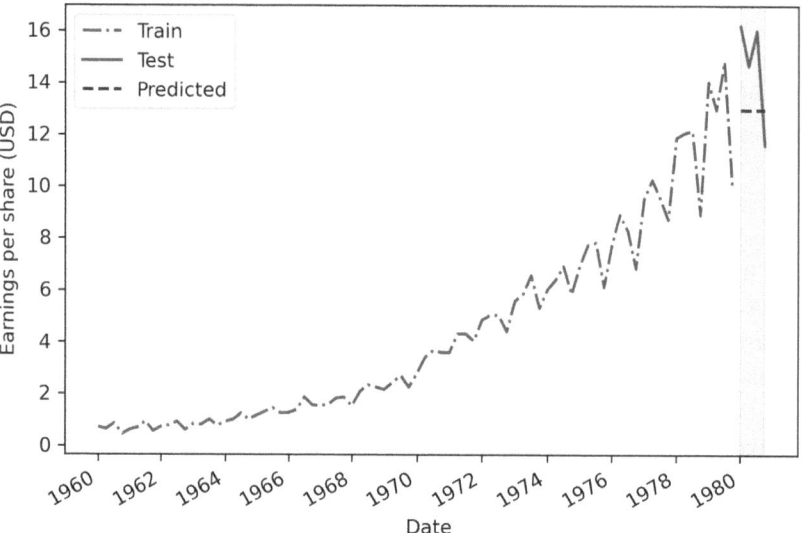

Figure 2.8 Predicting the mean of the last year in the training set (1979) as a baseline model. You can see that the prediction is closer to the actual values of the test set when compared to the previous baseline that we built in figure 2.6.

This new baseline is a clear improvement over the previous one, even though its implementation is just as simple, as we decreased the MAPE from 70% to 15.6%. This means that our forecasts deviate from the observed values by 15.6% on average. Using the last year's mean is a good step in the right direction. We want to get a MAPE as close to 0% as possible, since that would translate into predictions that are closer to the actual values in our forecast horizon.

We can learn from this baseline that future values likely depend on past values that are not too far back in history. This is a sign of *autocorrelation*, and we will dive deep into this subject in chapter 5. For now, let's look at another baseline that we could develop for this situation.

2.4 *Predicting using the last known value*

Previously we used the mean over different periods to develop a baseline model. So far, the best baseline has been the mean of the last recorded year in our training set, since it yielded the lowest MAPE. We learned from that baseline that future values depend on past values, but not those too far back in time. Indeed, predicting the mean EPS from 1960 to 1979 yielded worse forecasts than predicting the mean EPS over 1979.

Therefore, we could suppose that using the last known value of the training set as a baseline model will give us even better forecasts, which would translate to a MAPE closer to 0%. Let's test that hypothesis.

The first step is to extract the last known value of our train set, which corresponds to the EPS recorded for the last quarter of 1979:

```
last = train.data.iloc[-1]

print(last)
```

When we retrieve the EPS recorded for the last quarter of 1979, we get a value of $9.99. We will thus predict that Johnson & Johnson will have an EPS of $9.99 for the four quarters of 1980.

Again, we'll append a new column called pred_last to hold the predictions.

```
test.loc[:, 'pred_last'] = last
```

Then, using the same MAPE function that we defined earlier, we can evaluate the performance of this new baseline model. Again, we pass to the function the actual values from the test set and our prediction from the pred_last column of test:

```
mape_last = mape(test['data'], test['pred_last'])

print(mape_last)
```

This gives us a MAPE of 30.45%. We can visualize the forecasts in figure 2.9.

> **Can you recreate figure 2.9?**
> Try to produce figure 2.9 on your own! As data scientists, it is important for us to convey our results in a way that is accessible to people who do not work in our domain. Thus, producing plots showing our forecasts is an important skill to develop.

It seems that our new hypothesis did not improve upon the last baseline that we built, since we have a MAPE of 30.45%, whereas we achieved a MAPE of 15.60% using the

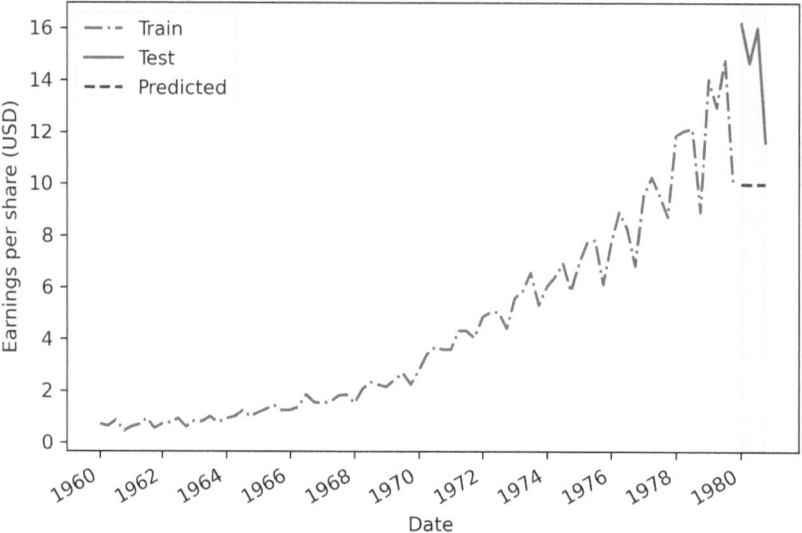

Figure 2.9   Predicting the last known value of the train set as a baseline model. We can see that this baseline, with a MAPE of 30.45%, is better than our first baseline, but less performant than our second one.

mean EPS over 1979. Therefore, these new forecasts are farther from the observed values in 1980.

This can be explained by the fact that the EPS displays a cyclical behavior, where it is high during the first three quarters and then falls at the last quarter. Using the last known value does not take the seasonality into account, so we need to use another naive forecasting technique to see if we can produce a better baseline.

2.5   *Implementing the naive seasonal forecast*

We considered the trend component for the first two baselines in this chapter, but we have not studied another important component from our dataset, which is the seasonal component shown in figure 2.10. There are clear cyclical patterns in our data, and that is a piece of information that we could use to construct one last baseline: the naive seasonal forecast.

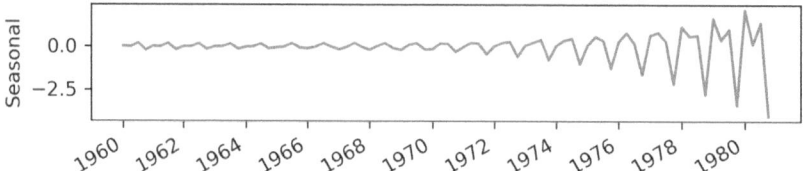

Figure 2.10   Seasonal component of our time series. We can see periodic fluctuations here, which indicate the presence of seasonality.

The naive seasonal forecast takes the last observed cycle and repeats it into the future. In our case, a full cycle occurs in four quarters, so we will take the EPS from the first quarter of 1979 and predict that value for the first quarter of 1980. Then we'll take the EPS from the second quarter of 1979 and predict that value for the second quarter of 1980. This process will be repeated for the third and fourth quarters.

In Python, we can implement this baseline by simply taking the last four values of the train set, which correspond to the four quarters of 1979, and assigning them to the corresponding quarters in 1980. The following code appends the pred_last_season column to hold our predictions from the naive seasonal forecast method:

```
test.loc[:, 'pred_last_season'] = train['data'][-4:].values
```

Our predictions are the last four values of our train set, which correspond to the quarters of 1979.

Then we calculate the MAPE the same way we did in the previous sections:

```
mape_naive_seasonal = mape(test['data'], test['pred_last_season'])

print(mape_naive_seasonal)
```

This gives us a MAPE of 11.56%, which is the lowest MAPE from all the baselines in this chapter. Figure 2.11 illustrates our forecast compared to the observed data in the test set. As an exercise, I strongly suggest that you try to recreate it on your own.

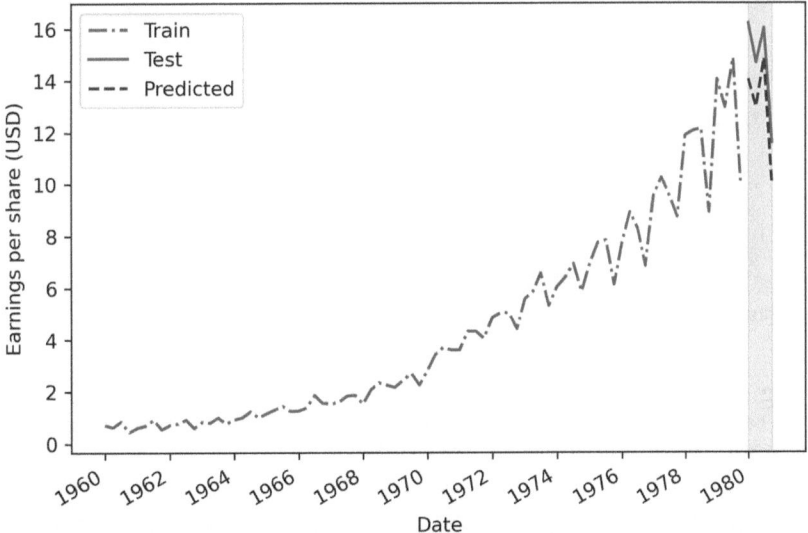

Figure 2.11   Result of the naive seasonal forecast on the test set. This forecast is more similar to the data observed in the test set, and it resulted in the lowest MAPE. Clearly, the seasonality of this dataset has an impact on future values, and it must be considered when forecasting.

As you can see, our naive seasonal forecast resulted in the lowest MAPE of all the baselines we built in this chapter. This means that seasonality has a significant impact on future values, since repeating the last season into the future yields fairly accurate forecasts. Intuitively, this makes sense, because we can clearly observe a cyclical pattern being repeated every year in figure 2.11. Seasonal effects will have to be considered when we develop a more complex forecasting model for this problem. I will explain in detail how to account for them in chapter 8.

2.6   *Next steps*

In this chapter, we developed four different baselines for our forecasting project. We used the arithmetic mean of the entire training set, the mean of the last year in the train set, the last known value of the train set, and a naive seasonal forecast. Each baseline was then evaluated on a test set using the MAPE metric. Figure 2.12 summarizes the MAPE of each baseline we developed in this chapter. As you can see, the baseline using the naive seasonal forecast has the lowest MAPE, and therefore the best performance.

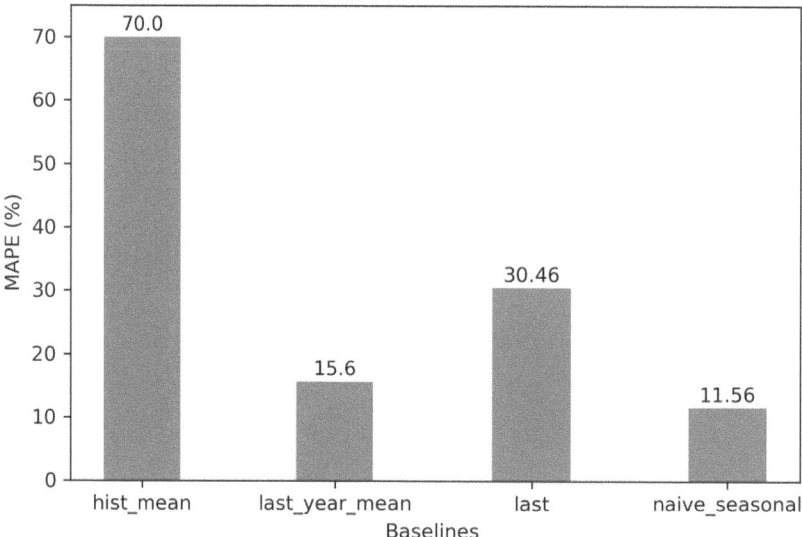

Figure 2.12   The MAPE of the four baselines developed in this chapter. The lower the MAPE, the better the baseline; therefore, we'll choose the naive seasonal baseline as our benchmark and compare it to our more complex models.

Keep in mind that a baseline model serves as a basis for comparison. We will develop more complex models by applying statistical learning or deep learning techniques, and when we evaluate our more complex solutions against the test set and record our error metrics, we can compare them to those of the baseline. In our case, we'll compare the MAPE from a complex model against the MAPE of our naive seasonal forecast. If the MAPE of a complex model is lower than 11.56%, then we'll know that we have a better-performing model.

There will be special situations in which a time series can only be forecast using naive methods. These are special cases where the process moves at random and cannot be predicted using statistical learning methods. This means that we are in the presence of a random walk—we'll examine this in the next chapter.

Summary

- Time series forecasting starts with a baseline model that serves as a benchmark for comparison with more complex models.
- A baseline model is a trivial solution to our forecasting problem because it only uses heuristics, or simple statistics, such as the mean.
- MAPE stands for *mean absolute percentage error,* and it is an intuitive measure of how much a predicted value deviates from the actual value.
- There are many ways to develop a baseline. In this chapter, you saw how to use the mean, the last known value, or the last season.

Going on a random walk

In the previous chapter, we compared different naive forecasting methods and learned that they often serve as benchmarks for more sophisticated models. However, there are instances where the simplest methods will yield the best forecasts. This is the case when we face a random walk process.

In this chapter, you will learn what a random walk process is, how to recognize it, and how to make forecasts using random walk models. Along the way, we will look at the concepts of differencing, stationarity, and white noise, which will come back in later chapters as we develop more advanced statistical learning models.

For this chapter's examples, suppose that you want to buy shares of Alphabet Inc. (GOOGL). Ideally, you would want to buy if the closing price of the stock is expected to go up in the future; otherwise, your investment will not be profitable. Hence, you decide to collect data on the daily closing price of GOOGL over 1 year and use time series forecasting to determine the future closing price of the stock. The closing price of GOOGL from April 27, 2020, to April 27, 2021, is shown in figure 3.1. At the time of writing, data beyond April 27, 2021, was not available yet.

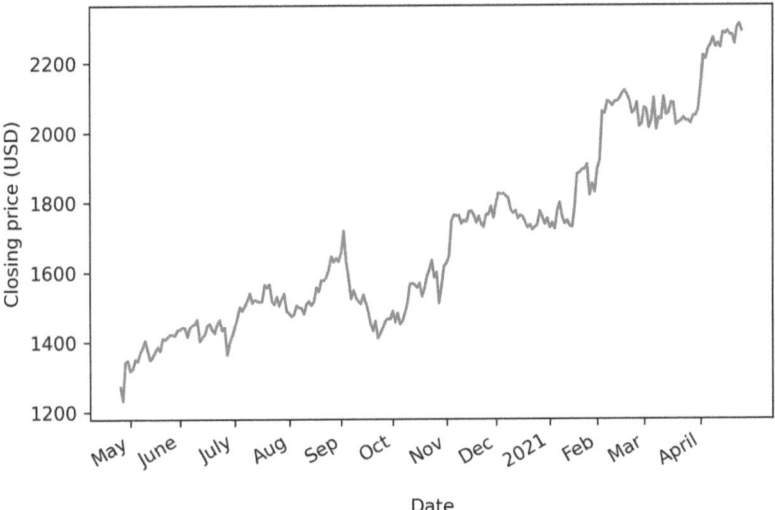

Figure 3.1   Daily closing price of GOOGL from April 27, 2020, to April 27, 2021

In figure 3.1 you can clearly see a long-term trend, since the closing price increased between April 27, 2020, and April 27, 2021. However, there are also abrupt changes in the trend, with periods where it sharply decreases before suddenly increasing again.

It turns out that the daily closing price of GOOGL can be modeled using the random walk model. To do so, we will first determine whether our process is *stationary* or not. If it is a non-stationary process, we will have to apply transformations, such as *differencing*, in order to make it stationary. Then we will be able to use the *autocorrelation function* plot to conclude that the daily closing price of GOOGL can be approximated by the random walk model. Both differencing and the autocorrelation plot will be covered in this chapter. Finally, we'll wrap up the chapter with forecasting methods that attempt to predict the future closing price of GOOGL.

By the end of this chapter, you will have mastered the concepts of stationarity, differencing, and autocorrelation, which will return in later chapters as we further develop our forecasting skills. For now, let's focus on defining the random walk process.

3.1   The random walk process

A *random walk* is a process in which there is an equal chance of going up or down by a random number. This is usually observed in financial and economic data, like the daily closing price of GOOGL. Random walks often expose long periods where a positive or negative trend can be observed. They are also often accompanied by sudden changes in direction.

In a random walk process, we say that the present value y_t is a function of the value at the previous timestep y_{t-1}, a constant C, and a random number ϵ_t, also termed *white noise*. Here, ϵ_t is the realization of the standard normal distribution, which has a variance of 1 and a mean of 0.

Therefore, we can mathematically express a random walk with the following equation, where y_t is the value at the present time t, C is a constant, y_{t-1} is the value at the previous timestep $t-1$, and ϵ_t is a random number.

$$y_t = C + y_{t-1} + \epsilon_t \qquad \textbf{Equation 3.1}$$

Note that if the constant C is nonzero, we designate this process as a random walk with drift.

3.1.1 *Simulating a random walk process*

To help you understand the random walk process, let's simulate one with Python—that way you can understand how a random walk behaves, and we can study its properties in a purely theoretical scenario. Then we'll transpose our knowledge onto our real-life example, where we'll model and forecast the closing price of GOOGL.

From equation 3.1, we know that a random walk depends on its previous value y_{t-1} plus white noise ϵ_t and some constant C. To simplify our simulation, let's assume that the constant C is 0. That way, our simulated random walk can be expressed as

$$y_t = y_{t-1} + \epsilon_t \qquad \textbf{Equation 3.2}$$

Now we must choose the first value of our simulated sequence. Again, for simplification, we will initialize our sequence at 0. This will be the value of y_0.

We can now start building our sequence using equation 3.2. We'll start off with our initial value of 0 at time $t = 0$. Then, from equation 3.2, the value at $t = 1$, represented by y_1 will be equal to the previous value y_0 plus white noise.

$$y_0 = 0$$

$$y_1 = y_0 + \epsilon_1 = 0 + \epsilon_1 = \epsilon_1 \qquad \textbf{Equation 3.3}$$

The value at $t = 2$, denoted as y_2, will be equal to the value at the previous step, which is y_1, plus some white noise.

$$y_1 = \epsilon_1$$

$$y_2 = y_1 + \epsilon_2 = \epsilon_1 + \epsilon_2 \qquad \textbf{Equation 3.4}$$

Then the value at $t = 3$, denoted as y_2, will be equal to the value at the previous step, which is y_2, plus some white noise.

$$y_2 = \epsilon_1 + \epsilon_2$$

$$y_3 = y_2 + \epsilon_3 = \epsilon_1 + \epsilon_2 + \epsilon_3 \qquad \textbf{Equation 3.5}$$

Looking at equation 3.5, you should start seeing a pattern. By initializing our random walk process at 0 and setting the constant C to 0, we determine that the value at time t is simply the sum of white noise from $t = 1$ to time t. Thus, our simulated random walk will respect the equation 3.6, where y_t is the value of the random walk process at time t, and ϵ_t is a random number at time t.

$$y_t = \sum_{t=1}^{T} \epsilon_t \qquad \textbf{Equation 3.6}$$

Equation 3.6 establishes that at any point in time t, the value of our simulated time series will be the cumulative sum of a series of random numbers. We can visualize how our simulated random walk takes shape in figure 3.2.

Simulated random walk

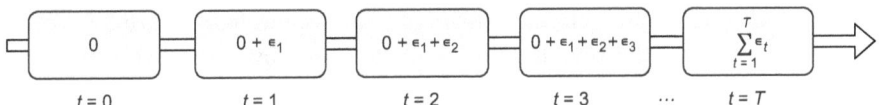

Figure 3.2   Visualizing the construction of our simulated random walk. As you can see, our initial value is 0. Then, since the constant was also set to 0, the value of our random walk at any point in time is simply the cumulative sum of random numbers, or white noise.

We are now ready to simulate our random process using Python. In order for this exercise to be reproducible, we will need to set a *seed*, which is an integer that we pass to the random.seed method. That way, no matter how many times we run the code, the same random numbers will be generated. This ensures that you will obtain the same results and plot as outlined in this chapter.

> **NOTE**   At any time, you can refer to the source code for this chapter here: https://github.com/marcopeix/TimeSeriesForecastingInPython/tree/master/CH03.

Then we must decide on the length of our simulated process. For this exercise, we will generate 1,000 samples. The numpy library allows us to generate numbers from a normal distribution by using the standard_normal method. This ensures that the numbers come from a distribution with mean of 0, as per the definition of white noise; I've also given it a variance of 1 (a normal distribution). Then we can set the very first value of our series to 0. Finally, the cumsum method will calculate the cumulative sum of white noise for each timestep in our series, and we will have simulated our random walk:

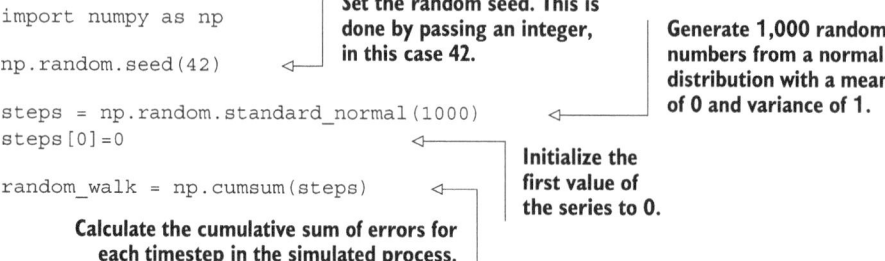

```
import numpy as np

np.random.seed(42)

steps = np.random.standard_normal(1000)
steps[0]=0

random_walk = np.cumsum(steps)
```

Set the random seed. This is done by passing an integer, in this case 42.

Generate 1,000 random numbers from a normal distribution with a mean of 0 and variance of 1.

Initialize the first value of the series to 0.

Calculate the cumulative sum of errors for each timestep in the simulated process.

We can plot our simulated random walk and see what it looks like. Since our *x*-axis and *y*-axis do not have a real-life meaning, we will simply label them as "timesteps" and "value," respectively. The following code block generates figure 3.3:

```
fig, ax = plt.subplots()

ax.plot(random_walk)
ax.set_xlabel('Timesteps')
ax.set_ylabel('Value')

plt.tight_layout()
```

You can see the defining characteristics of a random walk in figure 3.3. You'll notice a positive trend over the first 400 timesteps, followed by a negative trend, and a sharp

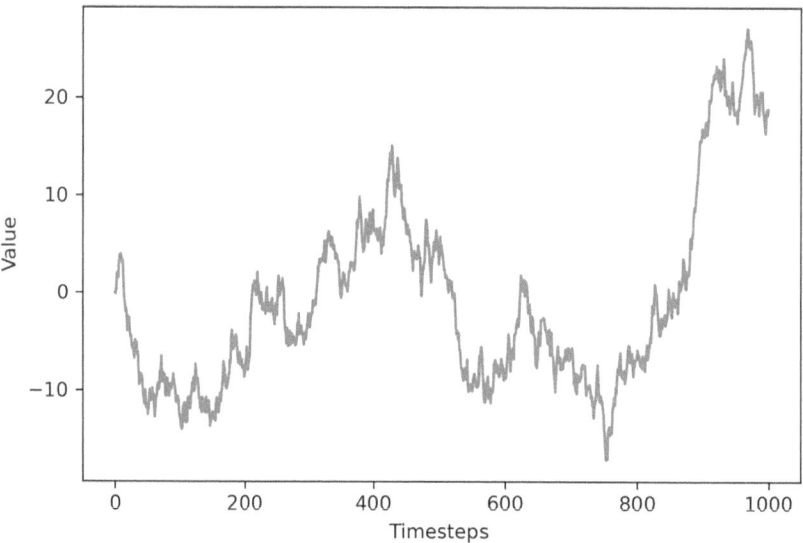

Figure 3.3 A simulated random walk. Notice how we have a positive trend during the first 400 timesteps, followed by a negative trend, and a sharp increase toward the end. These are good hints that we have a random walk process.

increase toward the end. Therefore, we have both sudden changes and long periods where a trend is observed.

We know this is a random walk because we simulated it. However, when dealing with real-life data, we need to find a way to identify whether our time series is a random walk or not. Let's see how we can achieve this.

3.2   *Identifying a random walk*

To determine if our time series can be approximated as a random walk or not, we must first define a random walk. In the context of time series, a *random walk* is defined as a series whose first difference is stationary and uncorrelated.

> **Random walk**
>
> A random walk is a series whose first difference is stationary and uncorrelated.
>
> This means that the process moves completely at random.

I've just introduced a lot of new concepts in a single sentence, so let's break down the steps to identify a random walk into a process. The steps are outlined in figure 3.4.

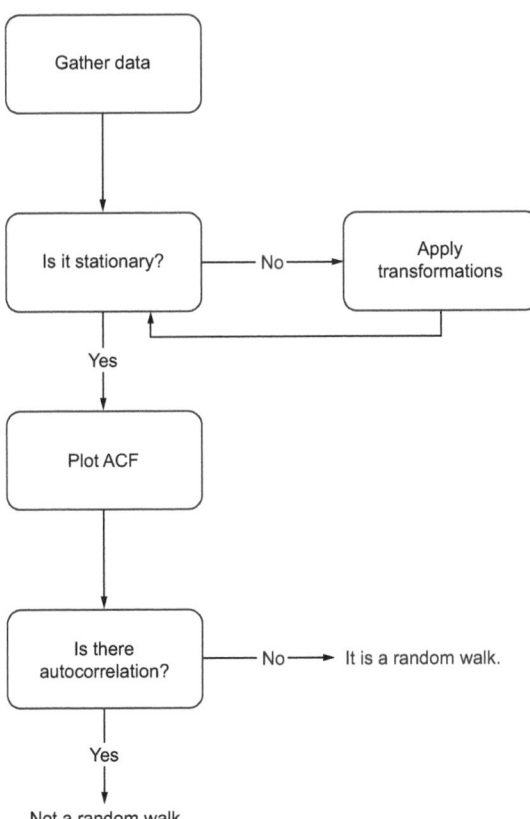

Figure 3.4   **Steps to follow to identify whether time series data can be approximated as a random walk or not. The first step is naturally to gather the data. Then we test for stationarity. If it is not stationary, we apply transformations until stationarity is achieved. Then we can plot the autocorrelation function (ACF). If there is no autocorrelation, we have a random walk.**

In the following subsections, we will cover the concepts of stationarity and autocorrelation in detail.

3.2.1   *Stationarity*

A *stationary time series* is one whose statistical properties do not change over time. In other words, it has a constant mean, variance, and autocorrelation, and these properties are independent of time.

Many forecasting models assume stationarity. The moving average model (chapter 4), autoregressive model (chapter 5), and autoregressive moving average model (chapter 6) all assume stationarity. These models can only be used if we verify that the data is indeed stationary. Otherwise, the models will not be valid, and the forecasts will not be reliable. Intuitively, this makes sense, because if the data is non-stationary, its properties are going to change over time, which would mean that our model parameters must also change through time. This means that we cannot possibly derive a function of future values as a function of past values, since the coefficients change at each point in time, making forecasting unreliable.

We can view stationarity as an assumption that can make our lives easier when forecasting. Of course, we will rarely see a stationary time series in its original state because we are often interested in forecasting processes with a trend or with seasonal cycles. This is when models like ARIMA (chapter 7) and SARIMA (chapter 8) come into play.

> **Stationarity**
>
> A stationary process is one whose statistical properties do not change over time.
>
> A times series is said to be stationary if its mean, variance, and autocorrelation do not change over time.

For now, since we are still in the early stages of time series forecasting, we'll focus on stationary time series, which means that we will need to find ways to *transform* our time series to make them stationary. A transformation is simply a mathematical manipulation of the data that stabilizes its mean and variance, thus making it stationary.

The simplest transformation one can apply is differencing. This transformation helps stabilize the mean, which in turn removes or reduces the trend and seasonality effects. Differencing involves calculating the series of changes from one timestep to another. To accomplish that, we simply subtract the value of the previous timestep y_{t-1} from the value in the present y_t to obtain the differenced value y'_t.

$$y'_t = y_t - y_{t-1} \qquad \textbf{Equation 3.7}$$

Transformation in time series forecasting

A transformation is a mathematical operation applied to a time series in order to make it stationary.

Differencing is a transformation that calculates the change from one timestep to another. This transformation is useful for stabilizing the mean.

Applying a log function to the series can stabilize its variance.

Figure 3.5 illustrates the process of differencing. Notice that taking the difference makes us lose one data point, because at the initial point in time, we cannot take the difference with its previous step, since $t = -1$ does not exist.

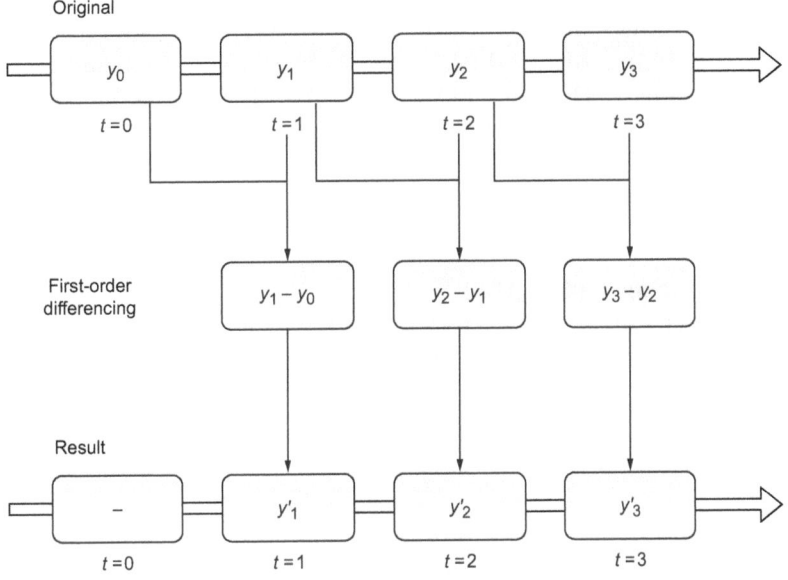

Figure 3.5 Visualizing the differencing transformation. Here, a first-order differencing is applied. Notice how we lose one data point after this transformation because the initial point in time cannot be differenced with previous values since they do not exist.

It is possible to difference a time series many times. Taking the difference once is applying a *first-order* differencing. Taking it a second time would be a *second-order* differencing. It is often not necessary to difference more than twice to obtain a stationary series.

While differencing is used to obtain a constant mean through time, we must also make sure we have a constant variance in order for our process to be stationary. Logarithms are used to help stabilize the variance.

Keep in mind that when we model a time series that has been transformed, we must *untransform* it to return the results of the model to the original units of measurement. The formal term for undoing a transformation is *inverse transform*. Therefore, if you apply a log transformation to your data, make sure you raise your forecast values to the power of 10 in order to bring the values back to their original magnitude. That way, your predictions will make sense in their original context.

Now that we know what type of transformations we need to apply on a time series to make it stationary, we need to find a way to test whether a series is stationary or not.

3.2.2 *Testing for stationarity*

Once a transformation is applied to a time series, we need to test for stationarity to determine if we need to apply another transformation to make the time series stationary, or if we need to transform it at all. A common test is the augmented Dickey-Fuller (ADF) test.

The ADF test verifies the following null hypothesis: there is a unit root present in a time series. The alternative hypothesis is that there is no unit root, and therefore the time series is stationary. The result of this test is the ADF statistic, which is a negative number. The more negative it is, the stronger the rejection of the null hypothesis. In its implementation in Python, the p-value is also returned. If its value is less than 0.05, we can also reject the null hypothesis and say the series is stationary.

> **Augmented Dickey-Fuller (ADF) test**
>
> The augmented Dickey-Fuller (ADF) test helps us determine if a time series is stationary by testing for the presence of a unit root. If a unit root is present, the time series is not stationary.
>
> The null hypothesis states that a unit root is present, meaning that our time series is not stationary.

Let's consider a very simple time series where the present value y_t only depends on its past value y_{t-1} subject to a coefficient α_1, a constant C, and white noise ϵ_t. We can write the following general expression:

$$y_t = C + \alpha_1 y_{t-1} + \epsilon_t \qquad \text{Equation 3.8}$$

In equation 3.8, ϵ_t represents some error that we cannot predict, and C is a constant. Here, α_1 is the root of the time series. This time series will be stationary only if the root lies within the unit circle. Therefore, its value must be between −1 and 1. Otherwise the series is non-stationary.

Let's verify this by simulating two different series. One will be stationary and the other will have a unit root, meaning that it will not be stationary. The stationary process follows equation 3.9, and the non-stationary process follows equation 3.10.

$$y_t = 0.5y_{t-1} + \epsilon_t \qquad\qquad\qquad \textbf{Equation 3.9}$$

$$y_t = y_{t-1} + \epsilon_t \qquad\qquad\qquad \textbf{Equation 3.10}$$

In equation 3.9, the root of the series is 0.5. Since it is between −1 and 1, this series is stationary. On the other hand, in equation 3.10, the root of the series is 1, meaning that it is a unit root. Therefore, we expect this series to be non-stationary.

By looking at both series in figure 3.6, we can gain some intuition about how stationary and non-stationary series evolve through time. We can see that the non-stationary process has long periods of positive and negative trends. However, the stationary process does not seem to increase or decrease over the long term. This high-level qualitative analysis can help us intuitively determine if a series is stationary or not.

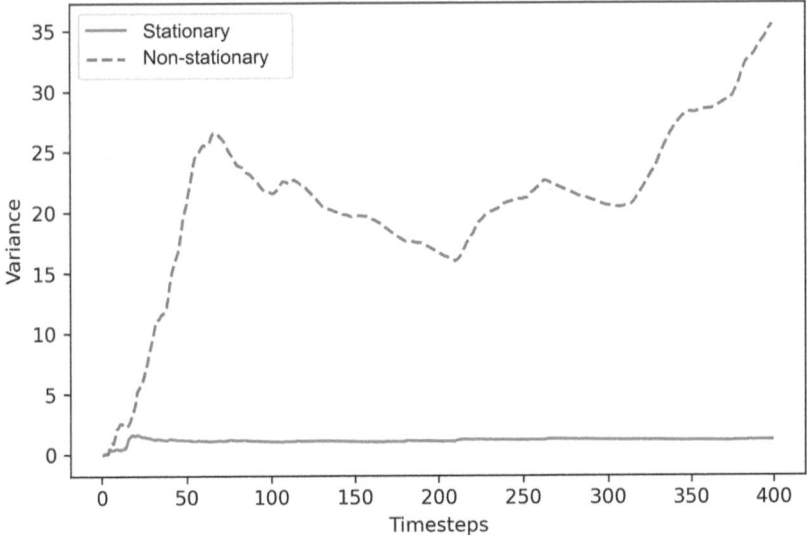

Figure 3.6 Simulated stationary and non-stationary time series over 400 timesteps. You can see that the stationary series does not increase or decrease over the long term. However, the non-stationary process has long periods of positive and negative trends.

A stationary series has constant properties over time, meaning that the mean and variance are not a function of time, so let's plot the mean of each series over time. The mean of a stationary process should be flat over time, whereas the mean of a non-stationary process should vary.

As you can see in figure 3.7, the mean of the stationary process becomes constant after the first few timesteps. This is the expected behavior of a stationary process. The fact that the mean does not change as a function of time means that it is independent of time, as per the definition of a stationary process. However, the mean of the non-stationary process is clearly a function of time, as we can see it decreasing and increasing

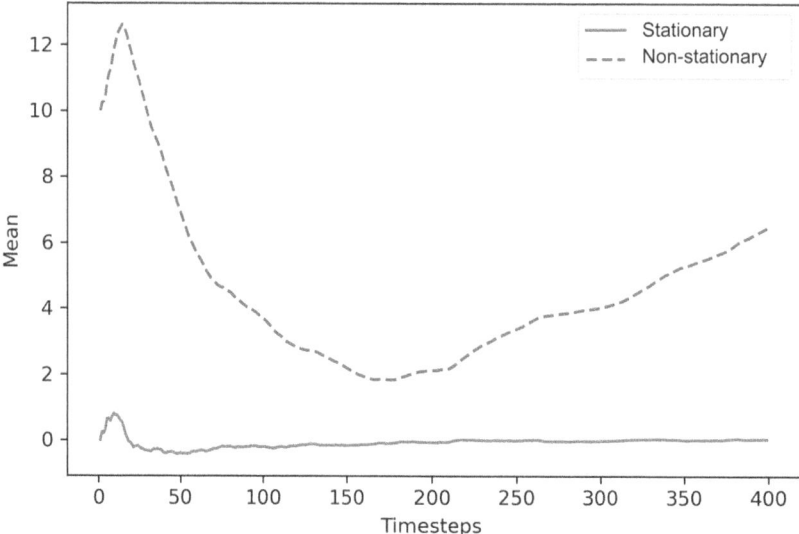

Figure 3.7 Mean of stationary and non-stationary processes over time. You can see how the mean of the stationary process becomes constant after the first few timesteps. On the other hand, the mean of the non-stationary process is a clear function of time, as it is constantly changing.

again over time. Thus, the presence of a unit root makes the mean of the series dependent on time, so the series is not stationary.

Let's further prove to ourselves that a unit root is a sign of non-stationarity by plotting the variance of each series over time. Again, a stationary series will have a constant variance over time, meaning that it is time independent. On the other hand, the non-stationary process will have a variance that changes over time.

In figure 3.8 we can see that after the first few timesteps the variance of the stationary process is constant over time, which follows equation 3.9. Again, this corresponds to the definition of a stationary process, since variance does not depend on time. On the other hand, the process with a unit root has a variance that depends on time, since it greatly varies over the 400 timesteps. Therefore, this series is not stationary.

By now, you should be convinced that a series with a unit root is not a stationary series. In both figures 3.7 and 3.8, the mean and variance were dependent on time, as their values kept changing. Meanwhile, the series with a root of 0.5 displayed a constant mean and variance over time, demonstrating that this series is indeed stationary.

All these steps were performed to justify the use of the augmented Dickey-Fuller (ADF) test. We know that the ADF test verifies the presence of a unit root in the series. The null hypothesis, stating that a unit root is present, means that the series is not stationary. If the test returns a p-value less than a certain significance level, typically 0.05 or 0.01, then we can reject the null hypothesis, meaning that there are no unit roots, and so the series is stationary.

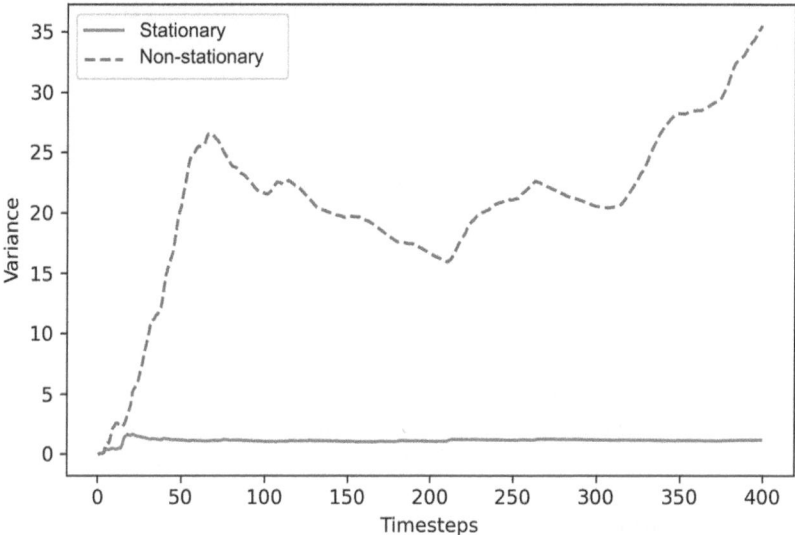

Figure 3.8 **Variance of the simulated stationary and non-stationary series over time. The variance of the stationary process is independent of time, as it is constant after the first few timesteps. For the non-stationary process, the variance changes over time, meaning that it is not independent.**

Once we have a stationary series, we must determine whether there is autocorrelation or not. Remember that a random walk is a series whose first difference is stationary and uncorrelated. The ADF test takes care of the stationarity portion, but we'll need to use the autocorrelation function to determine if the series is correlated or not.

3.2.3 The autocorrelation function

Once a process is stationary, plotting the autocorrelation function (ACF) is a great way to understand what type of process you are analyzing. In this case, we will use it to determine if we are studying a random walk or not.

We know that correlation measures the extent of a linear relationship between two variables. Autocorrelation therefore measures the linear relationship between lagged values of a time series. Thus, the ACF reveals how the correlation between any two values changes as the lag increases. Here, the lag is simply the number of timesteps separating two values.

Autocorrelation function

The autocorrelation function (ACF) measures the linear relationship between lagged values of a time series.

In other words, it measures the correlation of the time series with itself.

For example, we can calculate the autocorrelation coefficient between y_t and y_{t-1}. In this case, the lag is equal to 1, and the coefficient would be denoted as r_1. Similarly, we can calculate the autocorrelation between y_t and y_{t-2}. Then the lag would be 2, and the coefficient would be denoted as r_2. When we plot the ACF function, the coefficient is the dependent variable, while the lag is the independent variable. Note that the autocorrelation coefficient at lag 0 will always be equal to 1. This makes sense intuitively, because the linear relationship between a variable and itself at the same time-step should be perfect, and therefore equal to 1.

In the presence of a trend, a plot of the ACF will show that the coefficients are high for short lags, and they will decrease linearly as the lag increases. If the data is seasonal, the ACF plot will also display cyclical patterns. Therefore, plotting the ACF function of a non-stationary process will not give us more information than is available by looking at the evolution of our process through time. However, plotting the ACF for a stationary process can help us identify the presence of a random walk.

3.2.4 *Putting it all together*

Now that you understand what stationarity is, how to transform a time series to make it stationary, what statistical test can be used to assess stationarity, and how plotting the ACF function can help you identify the presence of a random walk, we can put all these concepts together and apply them in Python. In this section, we will work with our simulated data (from section 3.1.1) and cover the necessary steps to identify a random walk.

The first step is to determine whether our random walk is stationary or not. We know that since there are visible trends in our sequence, it is not stationary. Nevertheless, let's apply the ADF test to make sure. We will use the `statsmodels` library, which is a Python library that implements many statistical models and tests. To run the ADF test, we simply pass it our array of simulated data. The result is a list of different values, but we are mainly interested in the first two: the ADF statistic and the p-value.

```
from statsmodels.tsa.stattools import adfuller

ADF_result = adfuller(random_walk)        ←─── Pass the simulated random
                                               walk to the adfuller function.

print(f'ADF Statistic: {ADF_result[0]}')  ←─── Retrieve the ADF statistic, which is
print(f'p-value: {ADF_result[1]}')         ←──  the first value in the list of results.
                                               Retrieve the p-value, which is the
                                               second value in the list of results.
```

This prints an ADF statistic of –0.97 and a p-value of 0.77. The ADF statistic is not a large negative number, and with a p-value greater than 0.05, we cannot reject the null hypothesis stating that our time series is not stationary. We can further support our conclusion by plotting the ACF function.

The `statsmodels` library conveniently has a function to quickly plot the ACF. Again, we can simply pass it our array of data. We can optionally specify the number of lags, which will determine the range on the *x*-axis. In this case, we will plot the first 20 lags, but feel free to plot as many lags as you wish.

```
from statsmodels.graphics.tsaplots import plot_acf

plot_acf(random_walk, lags=20);
```

The output is shown in figure 3.9.

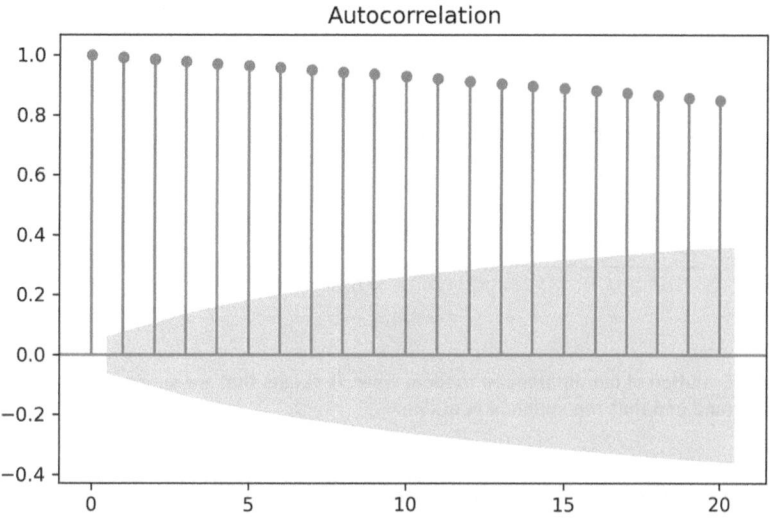

Figure 3.9   Plot of the ACF of our simulated random walk. Notice how the autocorrelation coefficients slowly decrease. Even at lag 20, the value is still autocorrelated, which means that our random walk is not stationary at the moment.

In figure 3.9 you'll notice how the autocorrelation coefficients slowly decrease as the lag increases, which is a clear indicator that our random walk is not a stationary process. Note that the shaded area represents a confidence interval. If a point is within the shaded area, then it is not significantly different from 0. Otherwise, the autocorrelation coefficient is significant.

Because our random walk is not stationary, we need to apply a transformation to make it stationary in order to retrieve useful information from the ACF plot. Since our sequence mostly displays changes in the trend without seasonal patterns, we will apply a first-order differencing. Remember that we'll lose the first data point every time we difference.

To difference, we will use the `numpy` method `diff`. This will difference a given array of data. The n parameter controls how many times the array must be differenced. To apply a first-order differencing, the n parameter must be set to 1:

```
diff_random_walk = np.diff(random_walk, n=1)
```

We can visualize the differenced simulated random walk in figure 3.10.

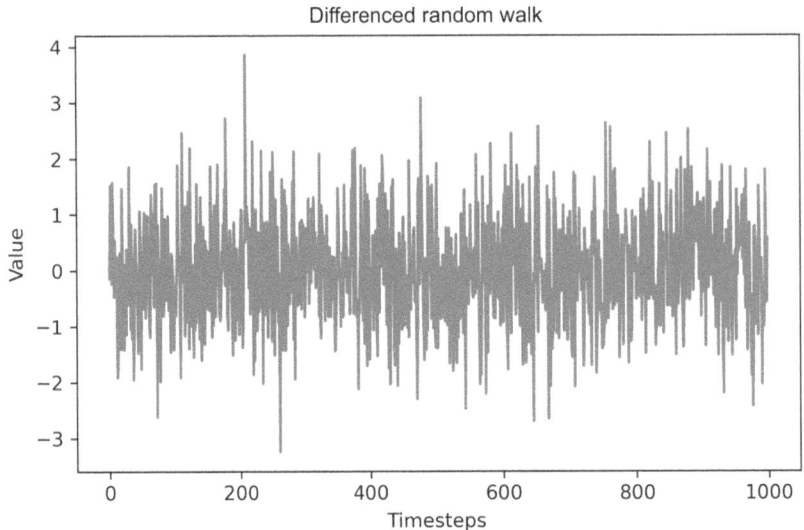

Figure 3.10   Evolution of our differenced random walk. It seems that we successfully removed the trend and that the variance is stable.

As you can see in figure 3.10, we have removed the trend from our series. Furthermore, the variance looks quite stable. Let's test for stationarity again, using the ADF test:

```
ADF_result = adfuller(diff_random_walk)          ⟵┐   Here we pass in
                                                  │   our differenced
print(f'ADF Statistic: {ADF_result[0]}')         │   random walk.
print(f'p-value: {ADF_result[1]}')
```

This prints out an ADF statistic of –31.79 with a p-value of 0. This time the ADF statistic is a large negative number, and the p-value is less than 0.05. Therefore, we reject the null hypothesis, and we can say that this process has no unit root and is thus stationary.

We can now plot the ACF function of our newly stationary series:

```
plot_acf(diff_random_walk, lags=20);
```

Looking at figure 3.11, you'll notice that there are no significant autocorrelation coefficients after lag 0. This means that the stationary process is completely random and can therefore be described as *white noise*. Each value is simply a random step away from the previous one, with no relation between them.

We have demonstrated that our simulated data is indeed a random walk: the series is stationary and uncorrelated after a first-order differencing, which corresponds to the definition of a random walk.

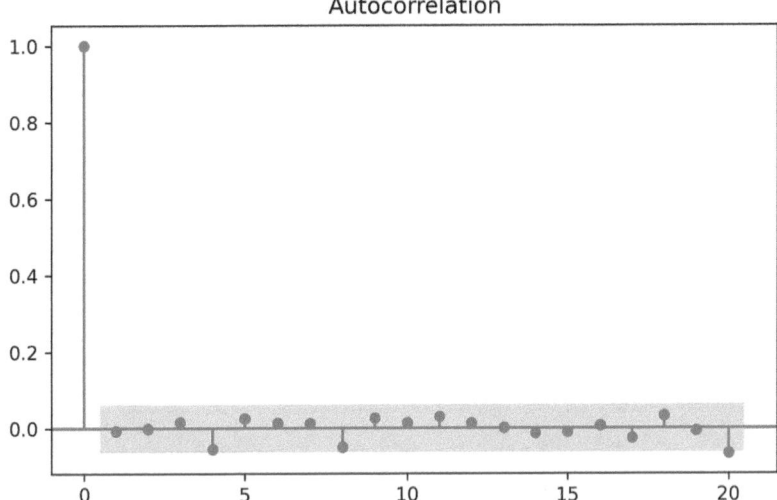

Figure 3.11 An ACF plot of our differenced random walk. Notice how there are no significant coefficients after lag 0. This is a clear indicator that we are dealing with a random walk.

3.2.5 *Is GOOGL a random walk?*

We've applied the necessary steps to identify a random walk on our simulated data, so this is a great time to test our knowledge and new skills on a real-life dataset. Taking the closing price of GOOGL from April 27, 2020, to April 27, 2021, from finance.yahoo.com, let's determine whether the process can be approximated as a random walk or not.

You can load the data in a DataFrame using the read_csv method from pandas:

```
df = pd.read_csv('data/GOOGL.csv')
```

Hopefully, your conclusion is that the closing price of GOOGL is indeed a random walk process. Let's see how we arrive at this conclusion. For visualization purposes, let's quickly plot our data, which results in figure 3.12:

```
fig, ax = plt.subplots()

ax.plot(df['Date'], df['Close'])
ax.set_xlabel('Date')
ax.set_ylabel('Closing price (USD)')

plt.xticks(
    [4, 24, 46, 68, 89, 110, 132, 152, 174, 193, 212, 235],
    ['May', 'June', 'July', 'Aug', 'Sep', 'Oct', 'Nov', 'Dec', 2021, 'Feb',
➥   'Mar', 'April']              ◁─────┐  Nicely label the
                                        │  ticks on the x-axis.
fig.autofmt_xdate()
plt.tight_layout()
```

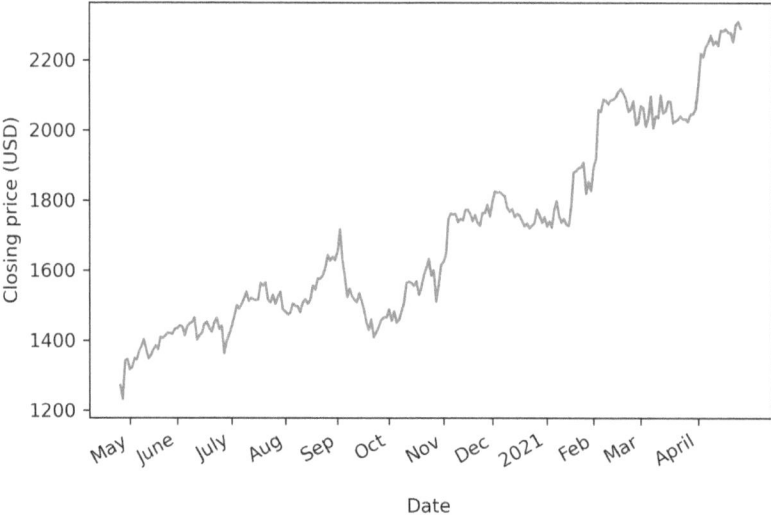

Figure 3.12   Closing price of GOOGL from April 27, 2020, to April 27, 2021

Looking at figure 3.12, we can see a trend in the data as the closing price is increasing over time; therefore, we do not have a stationary process. This is further supported by the ADF test:

```
GOOGL_ADF_result = adfuller(df['Close'])

print(f'ADF Statistic: {GOOGL_ADF_result[0]}')
print(f'p-value: {GOOGL_ADF_result[1]}')
```

This returns an ADF statistic of 0.16 and a p-value greater than 0.05, so we know that our data is not stationary. Hence, we will difference our data to see if that makes it stationary:

```
diff_close = np.diff(df['Close'], n=1)
```

Next, we can run the ADF test on the differenced data:

```
GOOGL_diff_ADF_result = adfuller(diff_close)

print(f'ADF Statistic: {GOOGL_diff_ADF_result[0]}')
print(f'p-value: {GOOGL_diff_ADF_result[1]}')
```

This gives an ADF statistic of –5.3 and a p-value smaller than 0.05, meaning that we have a stationary process.

Now we can plot the ACF function and see if there is autocorrelation:

```
plot_acf(diff_close, lags=20);
```

Figure 3.13 might make you scratch your head and wonder if there is autocorrelation or not. We do not see any significant coefficients, except at lags 5 and 18. This situation can arise sometimes, and it is due to chance only. In such a situation, we can safely assume that the coefficients at lags 5 and 18 are not significant, because we do not have consecutive significant coefficients. It just happened by chance that the differenced values are slightly correlated with the ones at lags 5 and 18.

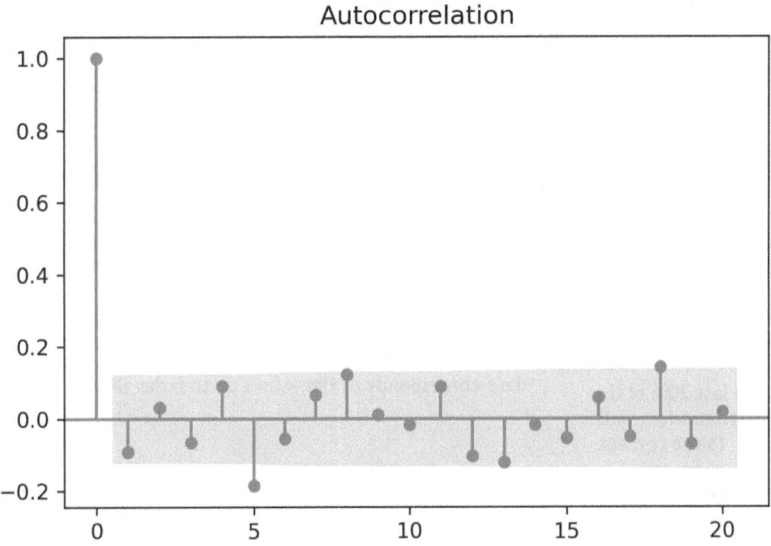

Figure 3.13   We can see that there are no significant coefficients in the ACF plot. You might notice that at lags 5 and 18 the coefficients are significant, while the others are not. This happens by chance with some data, and these points can be assumed to be non-significant, because we do not have consecutive significant coefficients between lags 0 and 5 or lags 0 and 18.

Therefore, we can conclude that the closing price of GOOGL can be approximated by a random walk process. Taking the first difference makes the series stationary, and its ACF plot shows no autocorrelation, meaning that it is purely random.

3.3   *Forecasting a random walk*

Now that we know what a random walk is and how to identify one, we can start forecasting. This might sound surprising, since we established that a random walk takes random steps as time progresses.

Predicting a random change is impossible, unless we predict a random value ourselves, which is not ideal. In this case, we can only use naive forecasting methods, or baselines, which we covered in chapter 2. Since the values change randomly, no statistical learning model can be applied. Instead, we can only reasonably predict the historical mean, or the last value.

Depending on the use case, your forecasting horizon will vary. Ideally, when dealing with a random walk, you will only forecast the next timestep. However, you may be required to forecast many timesteps into the future. Let's look at how to tackle each of these situations.

3.3.1 *Forecasting on a long horizon*

In this section, we'll forecast a random walk on a long horizon. This is not an ideal case—a random walk can unexpectedly increase or decrease because past observations are not predictive of changes in the future. Here we'll continue working with our simulated random walk from section 3.1.1.

To make things easier, we will assign the random walk to a `DataFrame` and split the dataset into train and test sets. The train set will contain the first 800 timesteps, which corresponds to 80% of the simulated data. The test set will thus contain the last 200 values:

```
import pandas as pd

df = pd.DataFrame({'value': random_walk})     ◁─┐   Assign the simulated random walk
                                                │   to a DataFrame. It will contain a
                                                │   single column called value.
train = df[:800]     ◁─┐
test = df[800:]      ◁─┤   The first 80% of the data is assigned to the train set.
                       │   Since we have 1,000 timesteps, 80% of our simulated
   Assign the last 20% of the   data corresponds to the values up to index 800.
   simulated random walk
   to the test set.
```

Figure 3.14 illustrates our split. Using the train set, we must now predict the next 200 timesteps in the test set.

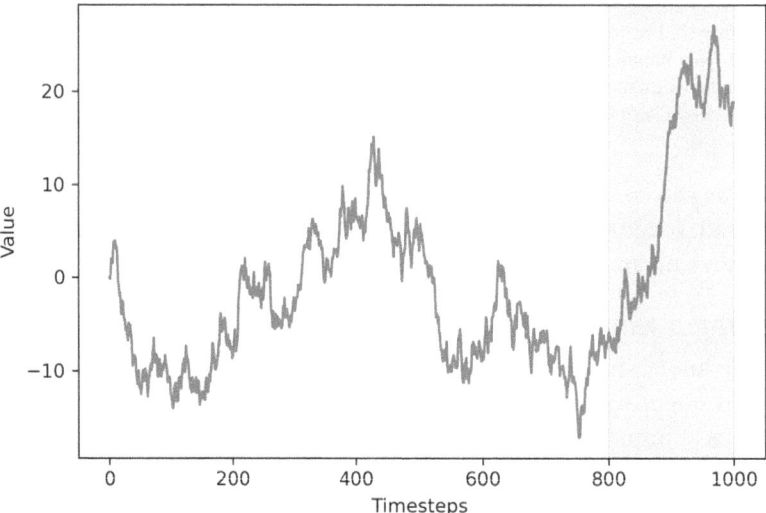

Figure 3.14   The train/test split of our generated random walk. The first 800 timesteps are part of the train set, and the remaining values are part of the test set. Our goal is to forecast the values in the shaded area.

As mentioned, we can only use naive forecasting methods for this situation, since we are dealing with a random walk. In this case, we will use the historical mean, the last known value, and the drift method.

Forecasting the mean is fairly straightforward. We'll simply calculate the mean of the train set and say that the next 200 timesteps will be equal to that value. Here, we'll create a new column pred_mean that will hold the historical mean as a prediction:

```
mean = np.mean(train.value)          ◄──┤ Calculate the mean
                                          of the train set.

test.loc[:, 'pred_mean'] = mean      ◄──┐ Predict the historical
                                          mean for the next 200
test.head()    ◄──┤ Show the first five   timesteps.
                    rows of test.
```

You will get a historical mean of –3.68. This means that we'll forecast that the next 200 timesteps of our simulated random walk will have a value of –3.68.

Another possible baseline is to predict the last known value of the train set. Here, we'll simply extract the last value of the train set and assign its value as our prediction for the next 200 timesteps:

```
                                       ┤ Retrieve the last
                                         value of the train set.
last_value = train.iloc[-1].value   ◄─┘
test.loc[:, 'pred_last'] = last_value   ◄──┐ Assign the last value as a prediction
                                             for the next 200 timesteps under
test.head()                                  the pred_last column.
```

This method yields forecasts with a constant value of –6.81.

Finally, we'll apply the drift method, which we have not covered yet. The *drift* method is a modification of predicting the last known value. In this case, we allow the values to increase or decrease over time. The rate at which values will change in the future is equal to that seen in the train set. Therefore, it is equivalent to calculating the slope between the first and last value of the train set and simply extrapolating this straight line into the future.

Remember that we can calculate the slope of a straight line by dividing the change in the *y*-axis by the change in the *x*-axis. In our case, the change in the *y*-axis is the difference between the last value of our random walk y_f and its initial value y_i. Then, the change in the *x*-axis is equivalent to the number of timesteps minus 1, as shown in equation 3.11.

$$\text{slope} = \frac{\Delta y}{\Delta x} = \frac{y_f - y_i}{\# \text{ timesteps} - 1} \qquad \textbf{Equation 3.11}$$

We calculated the last value of the train set when we implemented the last known value baseline, and we know that the initial value of our simulated random walk is 0; therefore, we can plug the numbers into equation 3.11 and calculate the drift in equation 3.12.

$$\text{drift} = \frac{-6.81 - 0}{800 - 1} = -0.0085 \qquad \textbf{Equation 3.12}$$

Let's implement this in Python now. We will calculate the change in the *x*-axis and the *y*-axis, and simply divide them to obtain the drift:

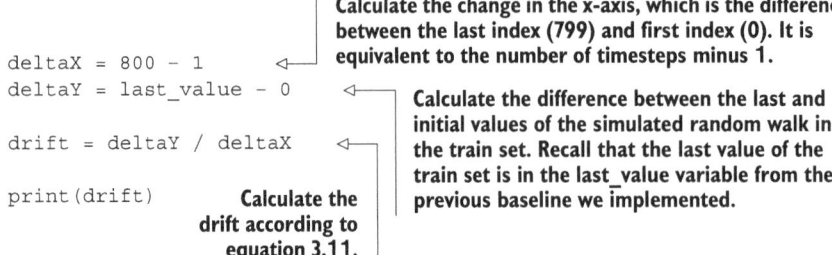

```
deltaX = 800 - 1
deltaY = last_value - 0

drift = deltaY / deltaX

print(drift)
```

As expected, this gives us a drift of –0.0085, which means that the values of our forecasts will slowly decrease over time. The drift method simply states that the value of our forecast is linearly dependent on the timestep, the value of the drift, and the initial value of our random walk, as expressed in equation 3.13. Keep in mind that our random walk starts at 0, so we can remove that from equation 3.13.

$$\text{forecast} = \text{drift} \times \text{timestep} + y_i$$

$$\text{forecast} = \text{drift} \times \text{timestep} \qquad \text{Equation 3.13}$$

Since we want to forecast the next 200 timesteps following the train set, we'll first create an array containing the range of timesteps starting at 800 and ending at 1000 with a step of 1. Then we simply multiply each timestep by the drift to get our forecast values. Finally, we assign them to the pred_drift column of test:

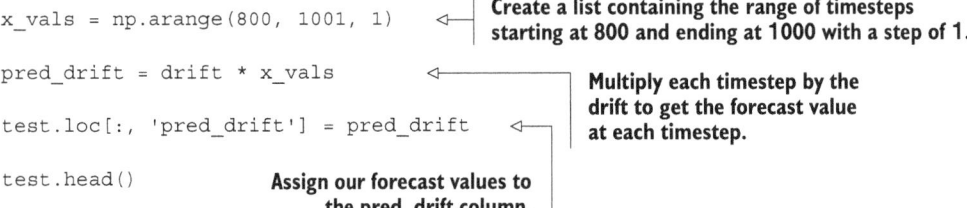

```
x_vals = np.arange(800, 1001, 1)

pred_drift = drift * x_vals

test.loc[:, 'pred_drift'] = pred_drift

test.head()
```

With all three methods, we can now visualize what our forecasts look like against the actual values of the test set:

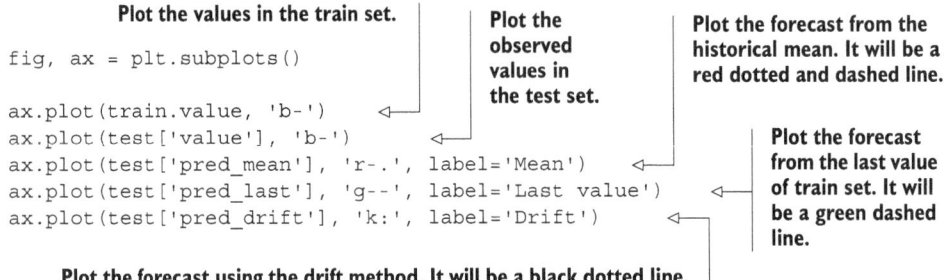

```
fig, ax = plt.subplots()

ax.plot(train.value, 'b-')
ax.plot(test['value'], 'b-')
ax.plot(test['pred_mean'], 'r-.', label='Mean')
ax.plot(test['pred_last'], 'g--', label='Last value')
ax.plot(test['pred_drift'], 'k:', label='Drift')
```

```
ax.axvspan(800, 1000, color='#808080', alpha=0.2)          ◁─────┐  Shade the
ax.legend(loc=2)                      ◁───────┐                   │  forecast
                                              │  Place the legend │  horizon.
ax.set_xlabel('Timesteps')                    │  in the upper-left
ax.set_ylabel('Value')                        │  corner.

plt.tight_layout()
```

As you can see in figure 3.15, our forecasts are faulty. They all fail to predict the sudden increase observed in the test set, which makes sense, because the future change in a random walk is completely random, and therefore unpredictable.

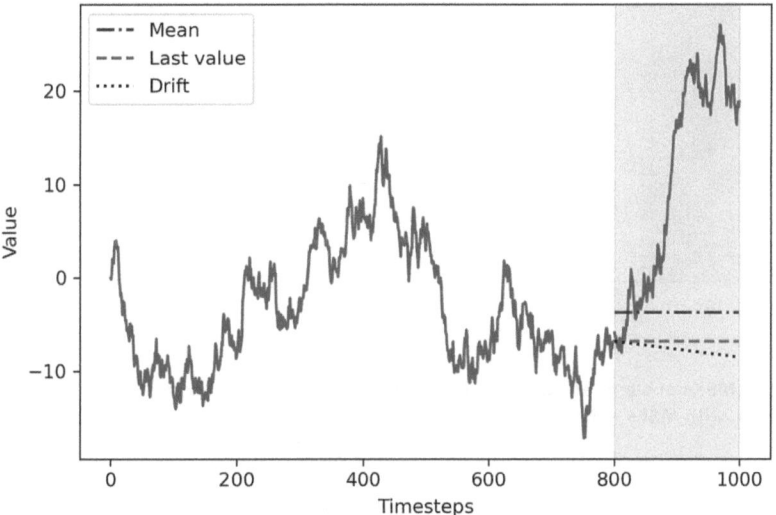

Figure 3.15 Forecasting our random walk using the mean, last known value, and drift methods. As you can see, all predictions are fairly poor and fail to predict the sudden increase observed in the test set.

We can further demonstrate that by calculating the mean squared error (MSE) of our forecasts. We cannot use the MAPE, as in chapter 2, because our random walk can take the value 0—it is impossible to calculate the percentage difference from an observed value of 0 because that implies a division by 0, which is not allowed in mathematics.

Therefore, we opt for the MSE, as it can measure the quality of the fit of a model, even if the observed value is 0. The `sklearn` library has a `mean_squared_error` function that simply needs the observed and predicted values. It will then return the MSE.

```
from sklearn.metrics import mean_squared_error

mse_mean = mean_squared_error(test['value'], test['pred_mean'])
mse_last = mean_squared_error(test['value'], test['pred_last'])
mse_drift = mean_squared_error(test['value'], test['pred_drift'])

print(mse_mean, mse_last, mse_drift)
```

You will obtain an MSE of 327, 425, and 466 for the historical mean, last value, and drift methods, respectively. We can compare the MSEs for these three baselines in figure 3.16.

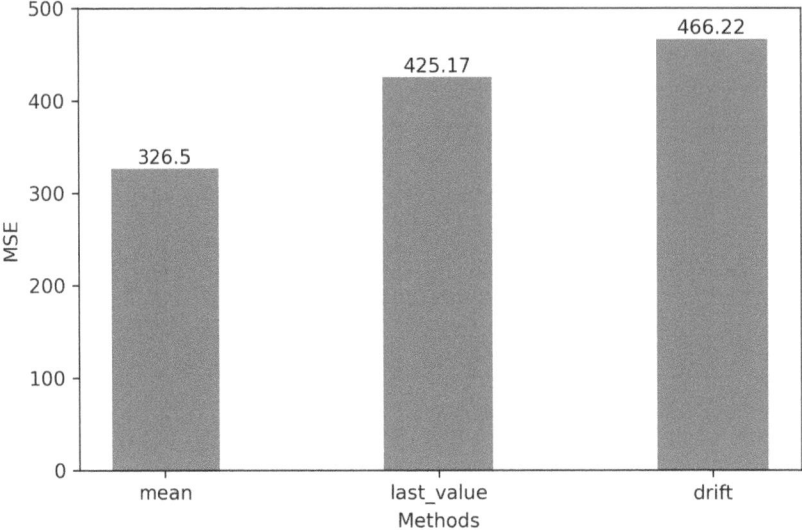

Figure 3.16 MSEs of our forecasts. Clearly, the future of a random walk is unpredictable, with MSEs exceeding 300.

As you can see in figure 3.16, the best forecast was obtained by predicting the historical mean, and yet the MSE exceeds 300. This is an extremely high value considering that our simulated random walk does not exceed the value of 30.

By now, you should be convinced that forecasting a random walk on a long horizon does not make sense. Since the future value is dependent on the past value plus a random number, the randomness portion is magnified in a long horizon where many random numbers are added over the course of many timesteps.

3.3.2 *Forecasting the next timestep*

Forecasting the next timestep of a random walk is the only reasonable situation we can tackle, although we will still use naive forecasting methods. Specifically, we will predict the last known value. However, we will make this forecast only for the next timestep. That way, our forecast should only be off by a random number, since the future value of a random walk is always the past value plus white noise.

Implementing this method is straightforward: we take our initial observed value and use it to predict the next timestep. Once we record a new value, it will be used as a forecast for the following timestep. This process is then repeated into the future.

Figure 3.17 illustrates this process. Here, the observed value at 8:00 a.m. is used to forecast the value for 9:00 a.m., the actual value observed at 9:00 a.m. is used to forecast the value at 10:00 a.m., and so on.

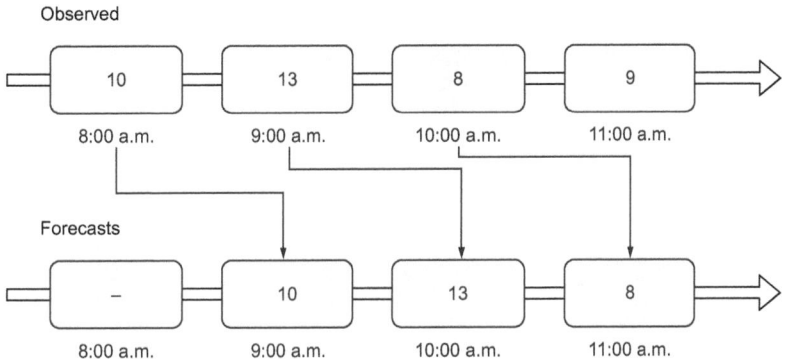

Figure 3.17 Forecasting the following timestep of a random walk. Here, the observed value at a point in time will be used as a forecast for the next point in time.

Let's apply this method to our random walk process. For the sake of illustrating this method, we will apply it over the entire random walk. This naive forecast can look deceptively amazing, when we are actually only predicting the last known value at each timestep.

A good way to simulate this process is by shifting our data, and the pandas library has a shift method that does exactly what we want. We simply pass in the number of periods, which in our case is 1, since we are forecasting the next timestep:

```
df_shift = df.shift(periods=1)

df_shift.head()
```

df_shift is now our forecast over the entire random walk, and it corresponds to the last known value at each timestep.

You will notice that at step 1, the value is 0, which corresponds to the observed value at step 0 in the simulated random walk. Therefore, we are effectively using the present observed value as a forecast for the next timestep. Plotting our forecast yields figure 3.18.

```
fig, ax = plt.subplots()

ax.plot(df, 'b-', label='actual')
ax.plot(df_shift, 'r-.', label='forecast')

ax.legend(loc=2)

ax.set_xlabel('Timesteps')
ax.set_ylabel('Value')

plt.tight_layout()
```

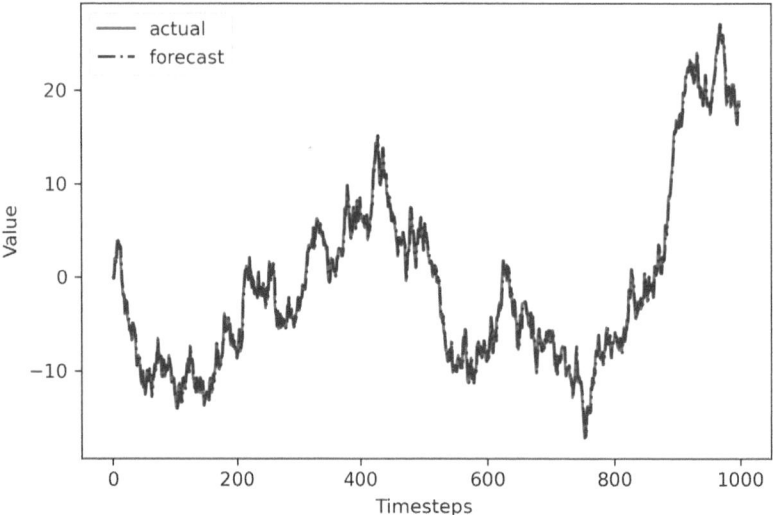

Figure 3.18   A naive forecast of the next timestep of a random walk. This plot gives the illusion of a very good model, when we are in fact only predicting the value observed at the previous timestep.

Looking at figure 3.18, you might think that we have developed an amazing model that is almost a perfect fit to our data. It seems that we do not have two separate lines in the graph, since both of them almost perfectly overlap, which is a sign of a perfect fit. Now, we can calculate the MSE:

```
mse_one_step = mean_squared_error(test['value'], df_shift[800:])

print(mse_one_step)                              Calculate the MSE on the test set.
```

This yields a value of 0.93, which again might lead us to think that we have a very performant model, since the MSE is very close to 0. However, we know that we are simply forecasting the value observed at the previous timestep. This becomes more apparent if we zoom in on our graph, as shown in figure 3.19.

Therefore, if a random walk process must be forecast, it is better to make many short-term forecasts. That way, we do not allow for many random numbers to accumulate over time, which will degrade the quality of our forecasts in the long term.

Because a random process takes random steps into the future, we cannot use statistical or deep learning techniques to fit such a process: there is nothing to learn from randomness and it cannot be predicted. Instead, we must rely on naive forecasting methods.

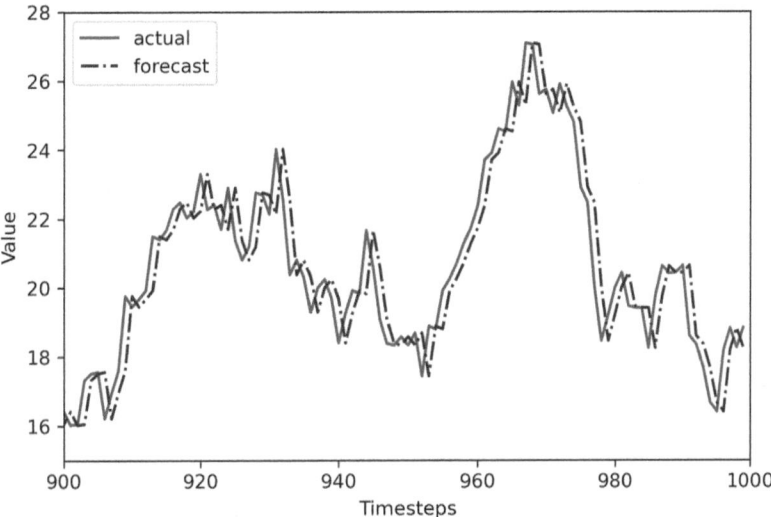

Figure 3.19 Close-up on the last 100 timesteps of our random walk. Here we can see how our forecasts are a simple shift of the original time series.

3.4 Next steps

So far you've learned how to develop baseline models, and you've discovered that in the presence of a random walk you can only reasonably apply baseline models to make forecasts. You cannot fit a statistical model or use deep learning techniques on data that takes random steps in the future. Ultimately, you cannot predict random movements.

You learned that a random walk is a sequence where the first difference is not autocorrelated and is a stationary process, meaning that its mean, variance, and autocorrelation are constant over time. The steps required to identify a random walk are shown in figure 3.20.

But what happens if your process is stationary and autocorrelated, meaning that you see consecutive significant coefficients on the ACF plot? For now, figure 3.20 simply states that it is not a random walk, so you have to find another model to approximate the process and forecast it. In such a situation, you are facing a process that can be approximated by the moving average (MA) model, an autoregressive (AR) model, or the combination of both processes, leading to an autoregressive moving average (ARMA) model.

In the next chapter, we will focus solely on the moving average model. You'll learn how to identify such processes and how to use the moving average model to make forecasts.

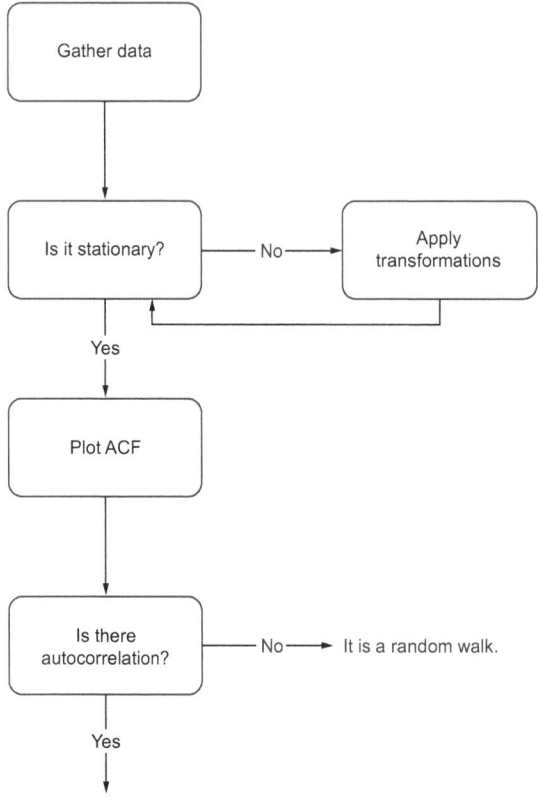

Figure 3.20   Steps to identify a random walk

3.5   *Exercises*

Now is a great time to apply the different skills you learned in this chapter. The following three exercises will test your knowledge and understanding of random walks and forecasting a random walk. The exercises are in order of difficulty and the time required to complete them. The solutions to exercises 3.5.1 and 3.5.2 are on GitHub: https://github.com/marcopeix/TimeSeriesForecastingInPython/tree/master/CH03.

3.5.1   *Simulate and forecast a random walk*

Simulate a different random walk than the one we have worked with in this chapter. You can simply change the seed and get new values:

1 Generate a random walk of 500 timesteps. Feel free to choose an initial value different from 0. Also, make sure you change the seed by passing a different integer to `np.random.seed()`.
2 Plot your simulated random walk.
3 Test for stationarity.
4 Apply a first-order difference.

5 Test for stationarity.

6 Split your simulated random walk into a train set containing the first 400 time-steps. The remaining 100 timesteps will be your test set.

7 Apply different naive forecasting methods and measure the MSE. Which method yields the lowest MSE?

8 Plot your forecasts.

9 Forecast the next timestep over the test set and measure the MSE. Did it decrease?

10 Plot your forecasts.

3.5.2 *Forecast the daily closing price of GOOGL*

Using the GOOGL dataset that we worked with in this chapter, apply the forecasting techniques we've discussed and measure their performance:

1 Keep the last 5 days of data as a test set. The rest will be the train set.

2 Forecast the last 5 days of the closing price using naive forecasting methods and measure the MSE. Which method is the best?

3 Plot your forecasts.

4 Forecast the next timestep over the test set and measure the MSE. Did it decrease?

5 Plot your forecasts.

3.5.3 *Forecast the daily closing price of a stock of your choice*

The historical daily closing price of many stocks is available for free on finance.yahoo .com. Select a stock ticker of your choice, and download its historical daily closing price for 1 year:

1 Plot the daily closing price of your chosen stock.

2 Determine if it is a random walk or not.

3 If it is not a random walk, explain why.

4 Keep the last 5 days of data as a test set. The rest will be the train set.

5 Forecast the last 5 days using naive forecasting methods, and measure the MSE. Which method is the best?

6 Plot your forecasts.

7 Forecast the next timestep over the test set, and measure the MSE. Did it decrease?

8 Plot your forecasts.

Summary

- A random walk is a process where the first difference is stationary and not auto-correlated.
- We cannot use statistical or deep learning techniques on a random walk, since it moves at random in the future. Therefore, we must use naive forecasts.

- A stationary time series is one whose statistical properties (mean, variance, auto-correlation) do not change over time.
- The augmented Dickey-Fuller (ADF) test is used to assess stationarity by testing for unit roots.
- The null hypothesis of the ADF test is that there is a unit root in the series. If the ADF statistic is a large negative value and the p-value is less than 0.05, the null hypothesis is rejected, and the series is stationary.
- Transformations are used to make a series stationary. Differencing can stabilize the trend and seasonality, while logarithms stabilize the variance.
- Autocorrelation measures the correlation between a variable and itself at a previous timestep (lag). The autocorrelation function (ACF) shows how the auto-correlation changes as a function of the lag.
- Ideally, we will forecast a random walk in the short term or the next timestep. That way, we do not allow for random numbers to accumulate, which will degrade the quality of our forecasts in the long term.

Part 2

Forecasting with statistical models

In this part of the book, we'll explore statistical models for time series forecasting. When performing statistical modeling, we need to perform hypothesis testing, study our data carefully to extract its properties, and find the best model for our data.

By the end of this part, you will have a robust framework for modeling any type of time series using statistical models. You will develop $MA(q)$ models, $AR(p)$ models, $ARMA(p,q)$ models, $ARIMA(p,d,q)$ models for non-stationary time series, $SARIMA(p,d,q)(P,D,Q)_m$ for seasonal time series, and SARIMAX models to include external variables in your forecast. We'll also cover the $VAR(p)$ model for predicting many time series at once. We'll conclude this part of the book with a capstone project, so that you'll get to apply what you've learned on your own.

There are, of course, many other statistical models for time series forecasting. For example, exponential smoothing basically takes a weighted average of past values to predict future values. The general idea behind exponential smoothing is that past values are less important than more recent values when predicting the future, so they are assigned a smaller weight. This model can then be extended to include trend and seasonal components. There are also statistical approaches to modeling time series with different seasonal periods, such as the BATS and TBATS models.

To keep this section manageable, we won't address those models, but they are implemented in the `statsmodels` library, which we will use extensively.

Modeling a moving average process 4

This chapter covers

- Defining a moving average process
- Using the ACF to identify the order of a moving average process
- Forecasting a time series using the moving average model

In the previous chapter, you learned how to identify and forecast a random walk process. We defined a random walk process as a series whose first difference is stationary with no autocorrelation. This means that plotting its ACF will show no significant coefficients after lag 0. However, it is possible that a stationary process may still exhibit autocorrelation. In this case, we have a time series that can be approximated by a moving average model MA(q), an autoregressive model AR(p), or an autoregressive moving average model ARMA(p,q). In this chapter, we will focus on identifying and modeling using the moving average model.

Suppose that you want to forecast the volume of widget sales from the XYZ Widget Company. By predicting futures sales, the company will be able to better manage its production of widgets and avoid producing too many or too few. If not enough widgets are produced, the company will not be able to meet their clients' demands, leaving customers unhappy. On the other hand, producing too many widgets will increase inventory. The widgets might become obsolete or lose their value, which will increase the business's liabilities, ultimately making shareholders unhappy.

In this example, we will study the sales of widgets over 500 days starting in 2019. The recorded sales over time are shown in figure 4.1. Note that the volume of sales is expressed in thousands of US dollars.

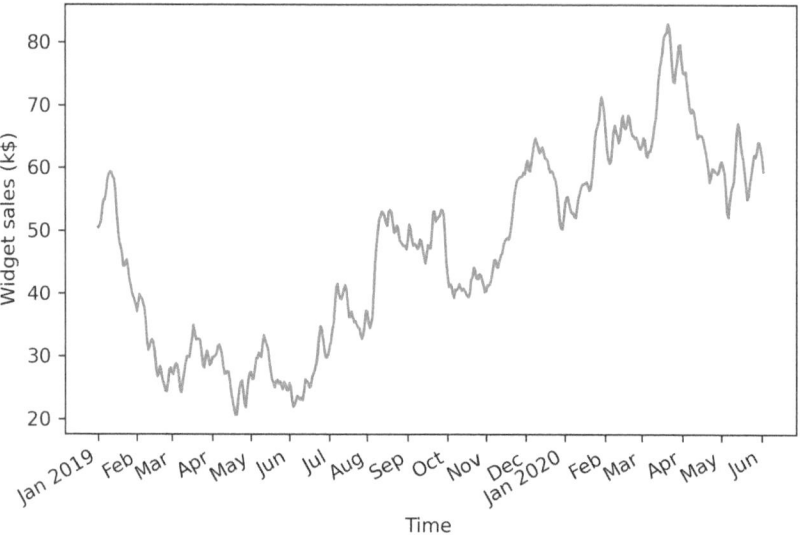

Figure 4.1   Volume of widget sales for the XYZ Widget Company over 500 days, starting on January 1, 2019. This is fictional data, but it will be useful for learning how to identify and model a moving average process.

Figure 4.1 shows a long-term trend with peaks and troughs along the way. We can intuitively say that this time series is not a stationary process, since we can observe a trend over time. Furthermore, there is no apparent cyclical pattern in the data, so we can rule out any seasonal effects for now.

In order to forecast the volume of widget sales, we need to identify the underlying process. To do so, we will apply the same steps that we covered in chapter 3 when working with a random walk process, shown again in figure 4.2.

Once the data is gathered, we will test for stationarity. If it is not stationary, we will apply a transformation to make it stationary. Then, once the series is a stationary process, we will plot the autocorrelation function (ACF). In our example of forecasting widget sales, our process will show significant coefficients in the ACF plot, meaning that it cannot be approximated by the random walk model.

In this chapter, we will discover that the volume of widget sales from the XYZ Widget Company can be approximated as a moving average process, and we will look at

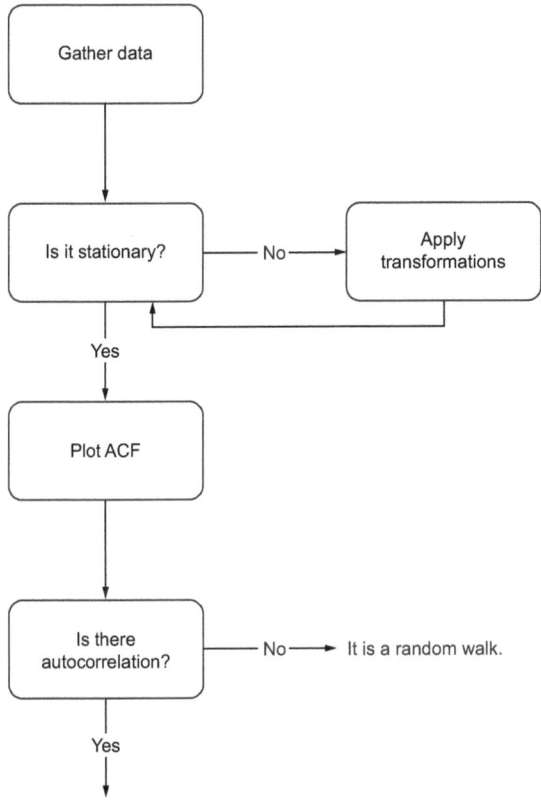

Figure 4.2 Steps for identifying a random walk

the definition of the moving average model. Then you'll learn how to identify the order of the moving average process using the ACF plot. The order of this process determines the number of parameters for the model. Finally, we will apply the moving average model to forecast the next 50 days of widget sales.

4.1 Defining a moving average process

A *moving average process*, or the moving average (MA) model, states that the current value is linearly dependent on the current and past error terms. The error terms are assumed to be mutually independent and normally distributed, just like white noise.

A moving average model is denoted as MA(q), where q is the order. The model expresses the present value as a linear combination of the mean of the series μ, the present error term ϵ_t, and past error terms ϵ_{t-q}. The magnitude of the impact of past errors on the present value is quantified using a coefficient denoted as θ_q. Mathematically, we express a general moving average process of order q as in equation 4.1.

$$y_t = \mu + \epsilon_t + \theta_1\epsilon_{t-1} + \theta_2\epsilon_{t-2} + \cdots + \theta_q\epsilon_{t-q}$$

Equation 4.1

Moving average process

In a moving average (MA) process, the current value depends linearly on the mean of the series, the current error term, and past error terms.

The moving average model is denoted as MA(q), where q is the order. The general expression of an MA(q) model is

$$y_t = \mu + \epsilon_t + \theta_1\epsilon_{t-1} + \theta_2\epsilon_{t-2} + \cdots + \theta_q\epsilon_{t-q}$$

The order q of the moving average model determines the number of past error terms that affect the present value. For example, if it is of order 1, meaning that we have an MA(1) process, the model is expressed as in equation 4.2. Here we can see that the present value y_t is dependent on the mean μ, the present error term ϵ_t, and the error term at the previous timestep $\theta_1\epsilon_{t-1}$.

$$y_t = \mu + \epsilon_t + \theta_1\epsilon_{t-1} \qquad \textbf{Equation 4.2}$$

If we have a moving average process of order 2, or MA(2), then y_t is dependent on the mean of the series μ, the present error term ϵ_t, the error term at the previous timestep $\theta_1\epsilon_{t-1}$, and the error term two timesteps prior $\theta_2\epsilon_{t-2}$, resulting in equation 4.3.

$$y_t = \mu + \epsilon_t + \theta_1\epsilon_{t-1} + \theta_2\epsilon_{t-2} \qquad \textbf{Equation 4.3}$$

Hence, we can see how the order q of the MA(q) process affects the number of past error terms that must be included in the model. The larger q is, the more past error terms affect the present value. Therefore, it is important to determine the order of the moving average process in order to fit the appropriate model—if we have a second-order moving average process, then a second-order moving average model will be used for forecasting.

4.1.1 *Identifying the order of a moving average process*

To identify the order of a moving average process, we can extend the steps needed to identify a random walk, as shown in figure 4.3.

As usual, the first step is to gather the data. Then we test for stationarity. If our series is not stationary, we apply transformations, such as differencing, until the series is stationary. Then we plot the ACF and look for significant autocorrelation coefficients. In the case of a random walk, we will not see significant coefficients after lag 0. On the other hand, if we see significant coefficients, we must check whether they become abruptly non-significant after some lag q. If that is the case, then we know that we have a moving average process of order q. Otherwise, we must follow a different set of steps to discover the underlying process of our time series.

Let's put this in action using our data for the volume of widget sales for the XYZ Widget Company. The dataset contains 500 days of sales volume data starting on January 1,

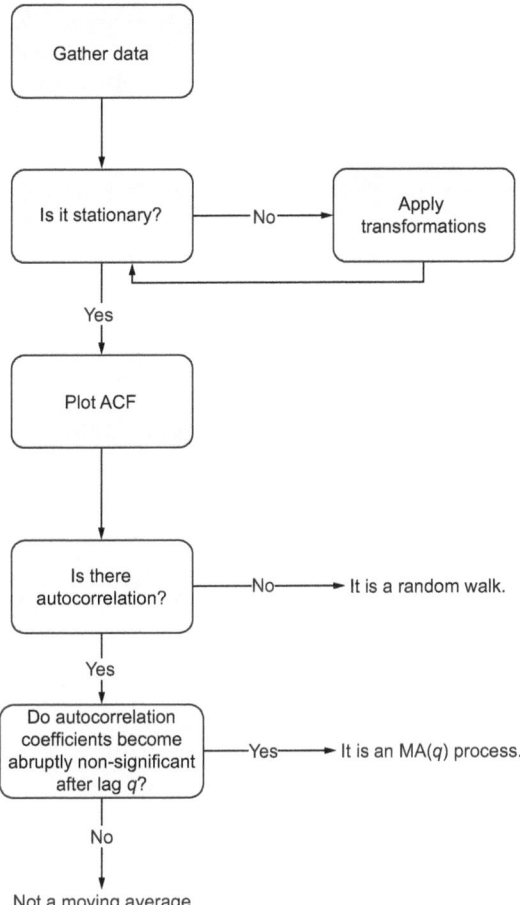

Figure 4.3   Steps to identify the order of a moving average process

2019. We will follow the steps outlined in figure 4.3 and determine the order of the underlying moving average process.

The first step is to gather the data. This step has already been done for you, so this is a great time to load the data into a DataFrame using pandas and display the first five rows of data. At any point, you can refer to the source code for this chapter on GitHub: https://github.com/marcopeix/TimeSeriesForecastingInPython/tree/master/CH04.

```
import pandas as pd

df = pd.read_csv('../data/widget_sales.csv')     ⟵  Read the CSV file
df.head()      ⟵  Display the first                   into a DataFrame.
                  five rows of data.
```

You'll see that the volume of sales is in the widget_sales column. Note that the volume of sales is in units of thousands of US dollars.

We can plot our data using `matplotlib`. Our values of interest are in the widget_ sales columns, so that is what we pass into `ax.plot()`. Then we give the *x*-axis the label of "Time" and *y*-axis the label of "Widget sales (k$)." Next, we specify that the labels for the ticks on the *x*-axis should display the month of the year. Finally, we tilt the *x*-axis tick labels and remove extra whitespace around the figure using `plt.tight_layout()`. The result is figure 4.4.

```
import matplotlib.pyplot as plt

fig, ax = plt.subplots()

ax.plot(df['widget_sales'])                    Plot the volume
                                               of widget sales.
ax.set_xlabel('Time')                          Label the x-axis.
ax.set_ylabel('Widget sales (k$)')             Label the y-axis.

plt.xticks(
    [0, 30, 57, 87, 116, 145, 175, 204, 234, 264, 293, 323, 352, 382, 409,
    439, 468, 498],
    ['Jan', 'Feb', 'Mar', 'Apr', 'May', 'Jun', 'Jul', 'Aug', 'Sep', 'Oct',
    'Nov', 'Dec', '2020', 'Feb', 'Mar', 'Apr', 'May', 'Jun'])        Label the
                                                                     ticks on
                                                                     the x-axis.
fig.autofmt_xdate()          Tilt the labels on the x-axis ticks
plt.tight_layout()           so that they display nicely.

                             Remove extra whitespace
                             around the figure.
```

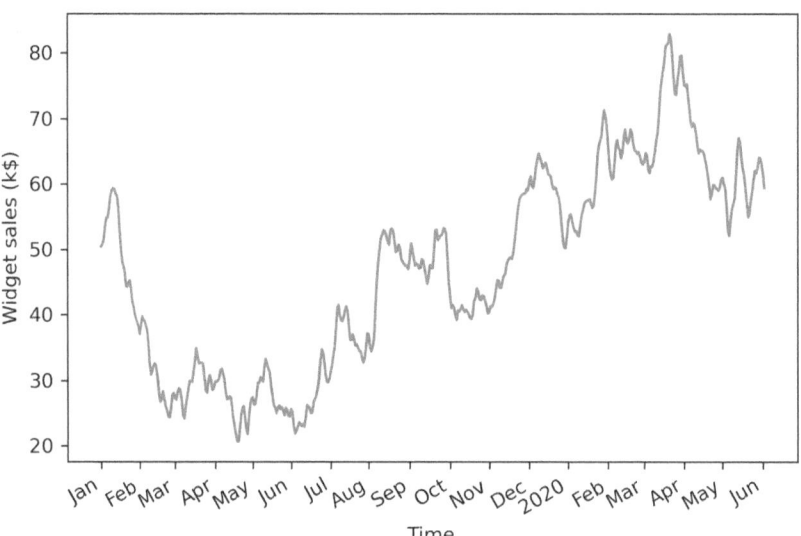

Figure 4.4   Volume of widget sales for the XYZ Widget Company over 500 days, starting on January 1, 2019

The next step is to test for stationarity. We intuitively know that the series is not stationary, since there is an observable trend in figure 4.4. Still, we will use the ADF test to make sure. Again, we'll use the `adfuller` function from the `statsmodels` library and extract the ADF statistic and p-value. If the ADF statistic is a large negative number and the p-value is smaller than 0.05, our series is stationary. Otherwise, we must apply transformations.

```
from statsmodels.tsa.stattools import adfuller

ADF_result = adfuller(df['widget_sales'])

print(f'ADF Statistic: {ADF_result[0]}')
print(f'p-value: {ADF_result[1]}')
```

Run the ADF test on the volume of widget sales, which is stored in the widget_sales column.

Print the ADF statistic.

Print the p-value.

This results in an ADF statistic of –1.51 and a p-value of 0.53. Here, the ADF statistic is not a large negative number, and the p-value is greater than 0.05. Therefore, our time series is not stationary, and we must apply transformations to make it stationary.

In order to make our series stationary, we will try to stabilize the trend by applying a first-order differencing. We can do so by using the `diff` method from the `numpy` library. Remember that this method takes in a parameter n that specifies the order of differencing. In this case, because it is a first-order differencing, n will be equal to 1.

```
import numpy as np

widget_sales_diff = np.diff(df['widget_sales'], n=1)
```

Apply first-order differencing on our data and store the result in widget_sales_diff.

We can optionally plot the differenced series to see if we have stabilized the trend. Figure 4.5 shows the differenced series. We can see that we successfully removed the long-term trend component of our series, as values are hovering around 0 over the entire period.

> **Can you recreate figure 4.5?**
> While optional, it is a good idea to plot your series as you apply transformations. This will give you a better intuition as to whether a series is stationary or not after a particular transformation. Try recreating figure 4.5 on your own.

Now that a transformation has been applied to our series, we can test for stationarity again using the ADF test. This time, make sure to run the test on the differenced data stored in the `widget_sales_diff` variable.

```
ADF_result = adfuller(widget_sales_diff)

print(f'ADF Statistic: {ADF_result[0]}')
print(f'p-value: {ADF_result[1]}')
```

Run the ADF test on the differenced time series.

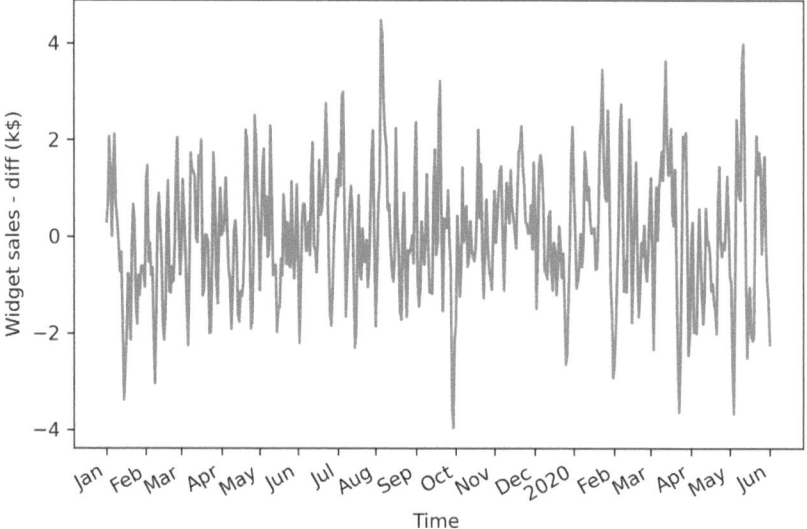

Widget sales - diff (k$)

Time

Figure 4.5 Differenced volume of widget sales. The trend component has been stabilized, since values are hovering around 0 over our entire sample.

This gives an ADF statistic of -10.6 and a p-value of 7×10^{-19}. Therefore, with a large negative ADF statistic and a p-value much smaller than 0.05, we can say that our series is stationary.

Our next step is to plot the autocorrelation function. The `statsmodels` library conveniently includes the `plot_acf` function. We simply pass in our differenced series and specify the number of lags in the `lags` parameter. Remember that the number of lags determines the range of values on the *x*-axis.

```
from statsmodels.graphics.tsaplots import plot_acf

plot_acf(widget_sales_diff, lags=30);    ←——  Plot the ACF of the
                                               differenced series.
plt.tight_layout()
```

The resulting ACF plot is shown in figure 4.6. You'll notice that there are significant coefficients up until lag 2. Then they abruptly become non-significant, as they remain in the shaded area of the plot. This means that we have a stationary moving average process of order 2. We can use a second-order moving average model, or MA(2) model, to forecast our stationary time series.

You can see how the ACF plot helps us determine the order of a moving average process. The ACF plot will show significant autocorrelation coefficients up until lag q, after which all coefficients will be non-significant. We can then conclude that we have a moving average process of order q, or an MA(q) process.

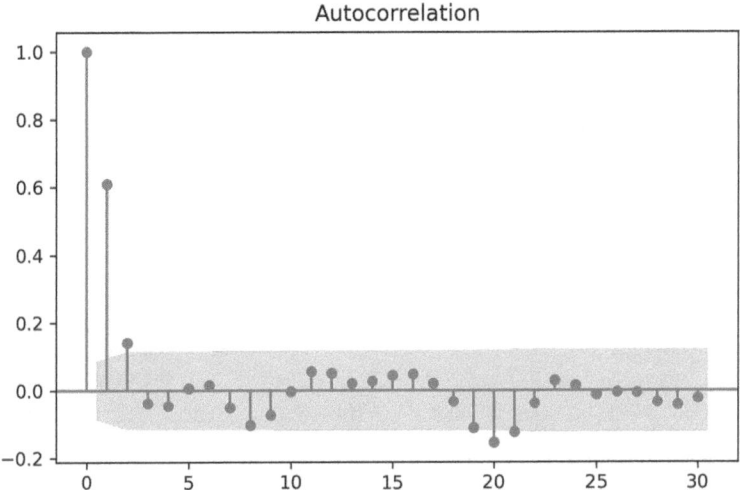

Figure 4.6   ACF plot of the differenced series. Notice how the coefficients are significant up until lag 2, and then they fall abruptly into the non-significance zone (shaded area) of the plot. There are some significant coefficients around lag 20, but this is likely due to chance, since they are non-significant between lags 3 and 20 and after lag 20.

4.2   Forecasting a moving average process

Once the order q of the moving average process is identified, we can fit the model to our training data and start forecasting. In our case, we discovered that the differenced volume of widget sales is a moving average process of order 2, or an MA(2) process.

The moving average model assumes stationarity, meaning that our forecasts must be done on a stationary time series. Therefore, we will train and test our model on the differenced volume of widget sales. We will try two naive forecasting techniques and fit a second-order moving average model. The naive forecasts will serve as baselines to evaluate the performance of the moving average model, which we expect to be better than the baselines, since we previously identified our process to be a moving average process of order 2. Once we obtain our forecasts for the stationary process, we will have to inverse-transform the forecasts, meaning that we must undo the process of differencing to bring the forecasts back to their original scale.

In this scenario, we will allocate 90% of the data to the train set and reserve the other 10% for the test set, meaning that we must forecast 50 timesteps into the future. We will assign our differenced data to a DataFrame and then split the data.

The first 90% of the data goes in the training set.   **Place the differenced data in a DataFrame.**

```
df_diff = pd.DataFrame({'widget_sales_diff': widget_sales_diff})

train = df_diff[:int(0.9*len(df_diff))]
test = df_diff[int(0.9*len(df_diff)):]
```

The last 10% of the data goes in the test set for prediction.

```
print(len(train))
print(len(test))
```

We've printed out the size of the train and test sets to remind you of the data point that we lose when we difference. The original dataset contained 500 data points, while the differenced series contains a total of 499 data points, since we differenced once.

Now we can visualize the forecasting period for the differenced and original series. Here we will make two subplots in the same figure. The result is shown in figure 4.7.

```
fig, (ax1, ax2) = plt.subplots(nrows=2, ncols=1, sharex=True)   ◁─────┐

ax1.plot(df['widget_sales'])                              Make two
ax1.set_xlabel('Time')                               subplots inside
ax1.set_ylabel('Widget sales (k$)')                   the same figure.
ax1.axvspan(450, 500, color='#808080', alpha=0.2)

ax2.plot(df_diff['widget_sales_diff'])
ax2.set_xlabel('Time')
ax2.set_ylabel('Widget sales - diff (k$)')
ax2.axvspan(449, 498, color='#808080', alpha=0.2)

plt.xticks(
    [0, 30, 57, 87, 116, 145, 175, 204, 234, 264, 293, 323, 352, 382, 409,
     439, 468, 498],
    ['Jan', 'Feb', 'Mar', 'Apr', 'May', 'Jun', 'Jul', 'Aug', 'Sep', 'Oct',
     'Nov', 'Dec', '2020', 'Feb', 'Mar', 'Apr', 'May', 'Jun'])

fig.autofmt_xdate()
plt.tight_layout()
```

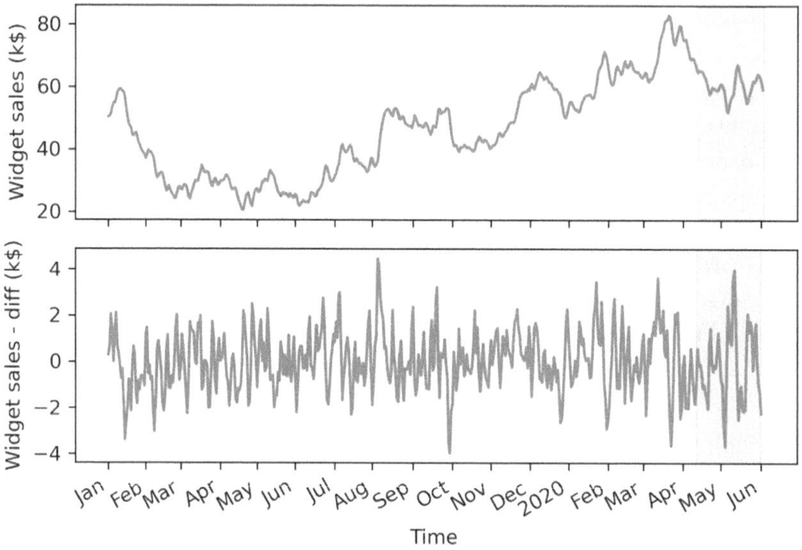

Figure 4.7   **Forecasting period for the original and differenced series. Remember that our differenced series has one less data point than in its original state.**

For the forecast horizon, the moving average model brings in a particularity. The MA(q) model does not allow us to forecast 50 steps into the future in one shot. Remember that the moving average model is linearly dependent on past error terms, and those terms are not observed in the dataset—they must therefore be recursively estimated. This means that for an MA(q) model, we can only forecast q steps into the future. Any prediction made beyond that point will not have past error terms, and the model will only predict the mean. Therefore, there is no added value in forecasting beyond q steps into the future, because the predictions will fall flat, as only the mean is returned, which is equivalent to a baseline model.

To avoid simply predicting the mean beyond two timesteps into the future, we need to develop a function that will predict two timesteps or less at a time, until 50 predictions are made, so that we can compare our predictions against the observed values of the test set. This method is called *rolling forecasts*. On the first pass, we will train on the first 449 timesteps and predict timesteps 450 and 451. Then, on the second pass, we will train on the first 451 timesteps, and predict timesteps 452 and 453. This is repeated until we finally predict the values at timesteps 498 and 499.

Forecasting using the MA(q) model

When using an MA(q) model, forecasting beyond q steps into the future will simply return the mean, because there are no error terms to estimate beyond q steps. We can use rolling forecasts to predict up to q steps at a time in order avoid predicting only the mean of the series.

We will compare our fitted MA(2) model to two baselines: the historical mean and the last value. That way, we can make sure that an MA(2) model will yield better predictions than naive forecasts, which should be the case, since we know the stationary process is an MA(2) process.

> **NOTE** You do not have to forecast two steps ahead when you perform rolling forecasts with an MA(2) model. You can forecast either one or two steps ahead repeatedly in order to avoid predicting only the mean. Similarly, with an MA(3) model, you could perform rolling forecasts with one-, two-, or three-step-ahead rolling forecasts.

To create these forecasts, we need a function that will repeatedly fit a model and generate forecasts over a certain window of time, until forecasts for the entire test set are obtained. This function is shown in listing 4.1.

First, we import the SARIMAX function from the statsmodels library. This function will allow us to fit an MA(2) model to our differenced series. Note that SARIMAX is a complex model that allows us to consider seasonal effects, autoregressive processes, non-stationary time series, moving average processes, and exogenous variables all in a single model. For now, we will disregard all factors except the moving average portion.

We will gradually build on the moving average model and eventually reach the SARIMAX model in later chapters:

- Next, we define our `rolling_forecast` function. It will take in a `DataFrame`, the length of the training set, the forecast horizon, a window size, and a method. The `DataFrame` contains the entire time series.
- The `train_len` parameter initializes the number of data points that can be used to fit a model. As predictions are done, we can update this to simulate the observation of new values and then use them to make the next sequence of forecasts.
- The `horizon` parameter is equal to the length of the test set and represents how many values must be predicted.
- The `window` parameter specifies how many timesteps are predicted at a time. In our case, because we have an MA(2) process, the window will be equal to 2.
- The `method` parameter specifies what model to use. The same function allows us to generate forecasts from the naive methods and the MA(2) model.

Note the use of type hinting in the function declaration. This will help us avoid passing parameters of an unexpected type, which might cause our function to fail.

Then, each forecasting method is run in a loop. The loop starts at the end of the training set and continues until `total_len`, exclusive, with steps of `window` (`total_len` is the sum of `train_len` and `horizon`). This loop generates a list of 25 values, [450,451,452,...,497], but each pass generates two forecasts, thus returning a list of 50 forecasts for the entire test set.

Listing 4.1   A function for rolling forecasts on a horizon

```python
from statsmodels.tsa.statespace.sarimax import SARIMAX

def rolling_forecast(df: pd.DataFrame, train_len: int, horizon: int,
    window: int, method: str) -> list:

    total_len = train_len + horizon

    if method == 'mean':
        pred_mean = []

        for i in range(train_len, total_len, window):
            mean = np.mean(df[:i].values)
            pred_mean.extend(mean for _ in range(window))

        return pred_mean

    elif method == 'last':
        pred_last_value = []

        for i in range(train_len, total_len, window):
            last_value = df[:i].iloc[-1].values[0]
            pred_last_value.extend(last_value for _ in range(window))
```

The function takes in a DataFrame containing the full simulated moving average process. We also pass in the length of the training set (800 in this case) and the horizon of the forecast (200). The next parameter specifies how many steps at a time we wish to forecast (2). Finally, we specify the method to use to make forecasts.

```
        return pred_last_value

    elif method == 'MA':
        pred_MA = []

        for i in range(train_len, total_len, window):
            model = SARIMAX(df[:i], order=(0,0,2))
            res = model.fit(disp=False)
            predictions = res.get_prediction(0, i + window - 1)
            oos_pred = predictions.predicted_mean.iloc[-window:]
            pred_MA.extend(oos_pred)

    return pred_MA
```

The predicted_mean method allows us to retrieve the actual value of the forecast as defined by the statsmodels library.

The MA(q) model is part of the more complex SARIMAX model.

Once it's defined, we can use our function and forecast using three methods: the historical mean, the last value, and the fitted MA(2) model.

First, we'll first create a `DataFrame` to hold our predictions and name it `pred_df`. We can copy the test set, to include the actual values in `pred_df`, making it easier to evaluate the performance of our models.

Then, we'll specify some constants. In Python, it is a good practice to name constants in capital letters. `TRAIN_LEN` is simply the length of our training set, `HORIZON` is the length of the test set, which is 50 days, and `WINDOW` can be 1 or 2 because we are using an MA(2) model. In this case we will use a value of 2.

Next, we'll use our `rolling_forecast` function to generate a list of predictions for each method. Each list of predictions is then stored in its own column in `pred_df`.

```
pred_df = test.copy()

TRAIN_LEN = len(train)
HORIZON = len(test)
WINDOW = 2

pred_mean = rolling_forecast(df_diff, TRAIN_LEN, HORIZON, WINDOW, 'mean')
pred_last_value = rolling_forecast(df_diff, TRAIN_LEN, HORIZON, WINDOW,
 'last')
pred_MA = rolling_forecast(df_diff, TRAIN_LEN, HORIZON, WINDOW, 'MA')

pred_df['pred_mean'] = pred_mean
pred_df['pred_last_value'] = pred_last_value
pred_df['pred_MA'] = pred_MA

pred_df.head()
```

Now we can visualize our predictions against the observed values in the test set. Keep in mind that we are still working with the differenced dataset, so our predictions are also differenced values.

For this figure, we will plot part of the training data to see the transition between the train and test sets. Our observed values will be a solid line, and we will label this curve as "actual." Then we'll plot the forecasts from the historical mean, those from the last observed value, and those from the MA(2) model. They will respectively be a dotted line, a dotted and dashed line, and a dashed line, with labels of "mean," "last," and "MA(2)." The result is shown in figure 4.8.

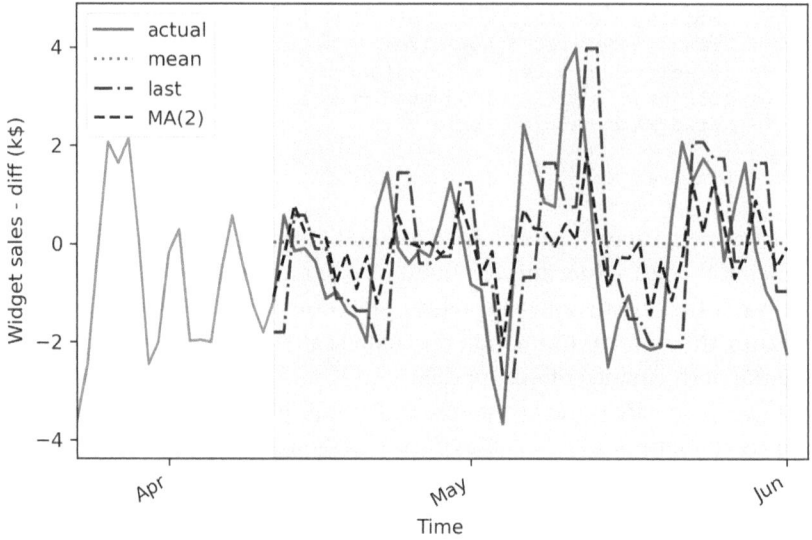

Figure 4.8   Forecasts of the differenced volume of widget sales. In a professional setting, it does not make sense to report differenced predictions. Therefore, we will undo the transformation later on.

In figure 4.8 you'll notice that the prediction coming from the historical mean, shown as a dotted line, is almost a straight line. This is expected; the process is stationary, so the historical mean should be stable over time.

The next step is to measure the performance of our models. To do so, we will calculate the mean squared error (MSE). Here we will use the mean_squared_error function from the sklearn package. We simply need to pass the observed values and the predicted values into the function.

```
from sklearn.metrics import mean_squared_error

mse_mean = mean_squared_error(pred_df['widget_sales_diff'],
⇒ pred_df['pred_mean'])
mse_last = mean_squared_error(pred_df['widget_sales_diff'],
⇒ pred_df['pred_last_value'])
mse_MA = mean_squared_error(pred_df['widget_sales_diff'],
⇒ pred_df['pred_MA'])

print(mse_mean, mse_last, mse_MA)
```

This prints out an MSE of 2.56 for the historical mean method, 3.25 for the last value method, and 1.95 for the MA(2) model. Here our MA(2) model is the best-performing forecasting method, since its MSE is the lowest of the three methods. This is expected, because we previously identified a second-order moving average process for the differenced volume of widget sales, thus resulting in a smaller MSE compared to the naive forecasting methods. We can visualize the MSE for all forecasting techniques in figure 4.9.

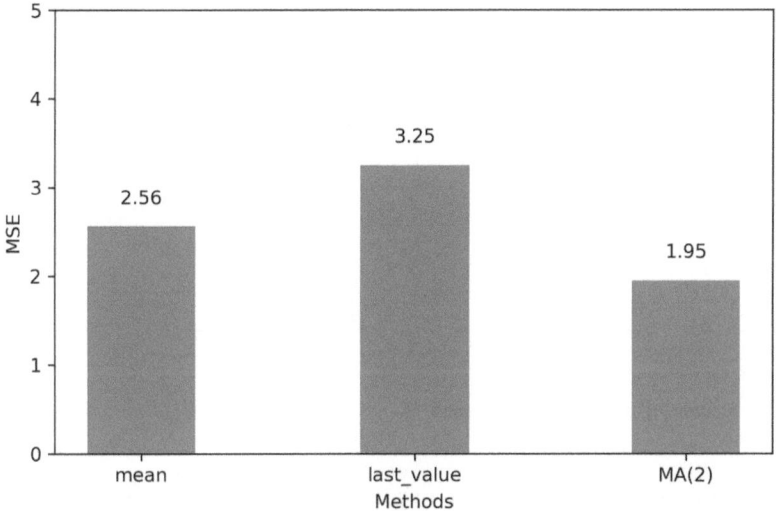

Figure 4.9 MSE for each forecasting method on the differenced volume of widget sales. Here the MA(2) model is the champion, since its MSE is the lowest.

Now that we have our champion model on the stationary series, we need to inverse-transform our predictions to bring them back to the original scale of the untransformed dataset. Recall that differencing is the result of the difference between a value at time t and its previous value, as shown in figure 4.10.

In order to reverse our first-order difference, we need to add an initial value y_0 to the first differenced value y'_1. That way, we can recover y_1 in its original scale. This is what is demonstrated in equation 4.4:

$$y_1 = y_0 + y'_1 = y_0 + y_1 - y_0 = y_1 \qquad \textbf{Equation 4.4}$$

Then y_2 can be obtained using a cumulative sum of the differenced values, as shown in equation 4.5.

$$y_2 = y_0 + y'_1 + y'_2 = y_0 + y_1 - y_0 + y_2 - y_1 = (y_0 - y_0) + (y_1 - y_1) + y_2 = y_2 \quad \textbf{Equation 4.5}$$

Applying the cumulative sum once will undo a first-order differencing. In the case where the series was differenced twice to become stationary, we would need to repeat this process.

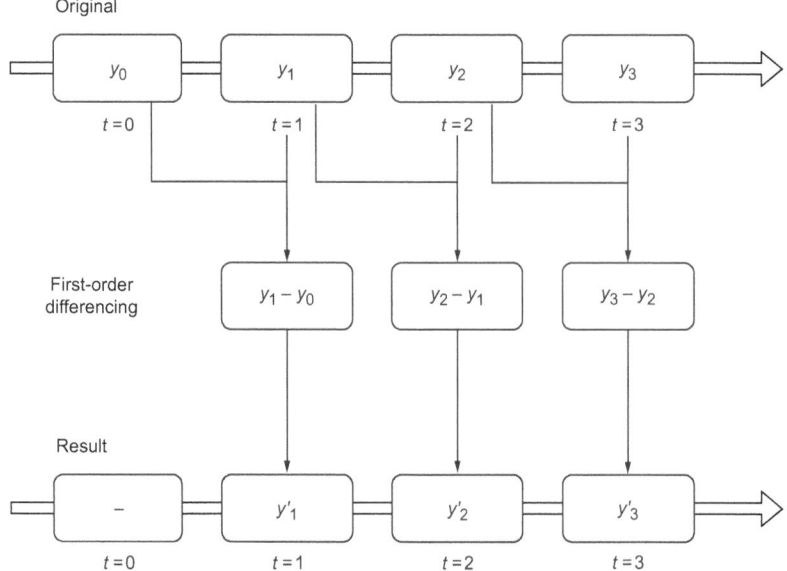

Original

$t = 0$ $t = 1$ $t = 2$ $t = 3$

First-order
differencing

Result

$t = 0$ $t = 1$ $t = 2$ $t = 3$

Figure 4.10 Visualizing a first-order difference

Thus, to obtain our predictions in the original scale of our dataset, we need to use the first value of the test as our initial value. Then we can perform a cumulative sum to obtain a series of 50 predictions in the original scale of the dataset. We will assign these predictions to the pred_widget_sales column.

```
df['pred_widget_sales'] = pd.Series()          ◁──┐  Initialize an empty column
df['pred_widget_sales'][450:] = df['widget_sales'].iloc[450] +   to hold our predictions.
➡ pred_df['pred_MA'].cumsum()     ◁──┐  Inverse-transform the predictions
                                       to bring them back to the original
                                       scale of the dataset.
```

Let's visualize our untransformed predictions against the recorded data. Remember that we are now using the original dataset stored in df.

```
fig, ax = plt.subplots()
                                                        Plot the actual
ax.plot(df['widget_sales'], 'b-', label='actual')   ◁──┘ values.
ax.plot(df['pred_widget_sales'], 'k--', label='MA(2)')   ◁──┐ Plot the inverse-
                                                              transformed
ax.legend(loc=2)                                              predictions.

ax.set_xlabel('Time')
ax.set_ylabel('Widget sales (K$)')

ax.axvspan(450, 500, color='#808080', alpha=0.2)
```

```
ax.set_xlim(400, 500)

plt.xticks(
    [409, 439, 468, 498],
    ['Mar', 'Apr', 'May', 'Jun'])

fig.autofmt_xdate()
plt.tight_layout()
```

You can see in figure 4.11 that our forecast curve, shown with a dashed line, follows the general trend of the observed values, although it does not predict bigger troughs and peaks.

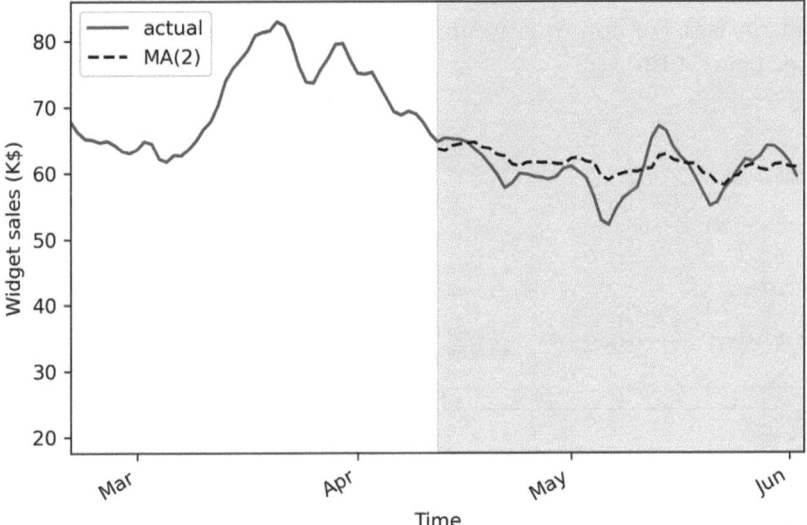

Figure 4.11 **Inverse-transformed MA(2) forecasts**

The final step is to report the MSE on the original dataset. In a professional setting, we would not report the differenced predictions, because they do not make sense from a business perspective; we must report values and errors in the original scale of the data.

We can measure the mean absolute error (MAE) using the mean_absolute_error function from sklearn. We'll use this metric because it is easy to interpret, as it returns the average of the absolute difference between the predicted and actual values, instead of a squared difference like the MSE.

```
from sklearn.metrics import mean_absolute_error

mae_MA_undiff = mean_absolute_error(df['widget_sales'].iloc[450:],
⇒ df['pred_widget_sales'].iloc[450:])

print(mae_MA_undiff)
```

This prints out an MAE of 2.32. Therefore, our predictions are, on average, off by $2,320, either above or below the actual value. Remember that our data has units of thousands of dollars, so we multiply the MAE by 1,000 to express the average absolute difference.

4.3   Next steps

In this chapter, we covered the moving average process and how it can be modeled by an MA(q) model, where q is the order. You learned that to identify a moving average process, you must study the ACF plot once it is stationary. The ACF plot will show significant peaks all the way to lag q, and the rest will not be significantly different from 0.

However, it is possible that when studying the ACF plot of a stationary process, you'll see a sinusoidal pattern, with negative coefficients and significant autocorrelation at large lags. For now you can simply accept that this is not a moving average process (see figure 4.12).

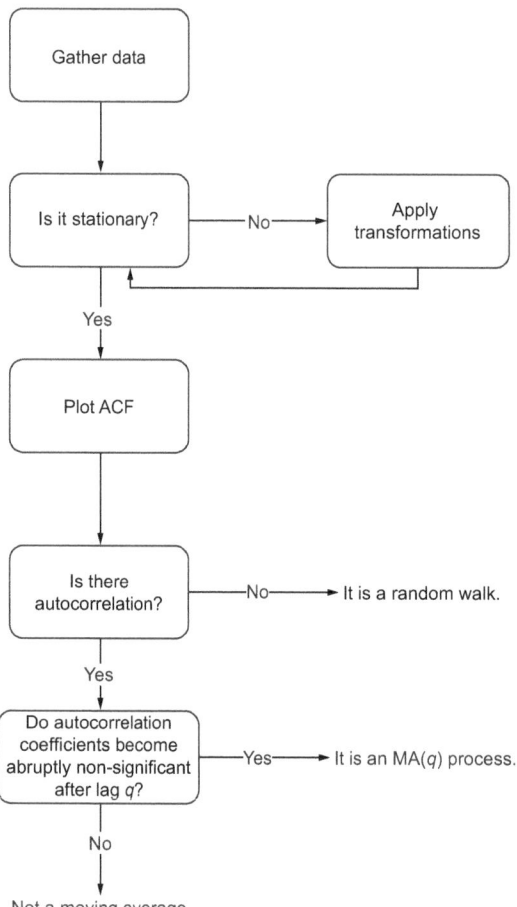

Figure 4.12   Steps to identify the underlying process of a stationary time series

When we see a sinusoidal pattern in the ACF plot of a stationary process, this is a hint that an autoregressive process is at play, and we must use an AR(p) model to produce our forecast. Just like the MA(q) model, the AR(p) model will require us to identify its order. This time we will have to plot the *partial* autocorrelation function and see at which lag the coefficients suddenly become non-significant. The next chapter will focus entirely on the autoregressive process, how to identify its order, and how to forecast such a process.

4.4 Exercises

Take some time to test your knowledge and mastery of the MA(q) model with these exercises. The full solutions are available on GitHub: https://github.com/marcopeix/TimeSeriesForecastingInPython/tree/master/CH04.

4.4.1 Simulate an MA(2) process and make forecasts

Simulate a stationary MA(2) process. To do so, use the `ArmaProcess` function from the `statsmodels` library and simulate the following process:

$$y_t = 0.9\theta_{t-1} + 0.3\theta_{t-2}$$

1 For this exercise, generate 1,000 samples.

```
from statsmodels.tsa.arima_process import ArmaProcess
import numpy as np

np.random.seed(42)          ◁────────  Set the seed for reproducibility.
                                       Change the seed if you want to
                                       experiment with different values.
ma2 = np.array([1, 0.9, 0.3])
ar2 = np.array([1, 0, 0])

MA2_process = ArmaProcess(ar2, ma2).generate_sample(nsample=1000)
```

2 Plot your simulated moving average.
3 Run the ADF test, and check if the process is stationary.
4 Plot the ACF, and see if there are significant coefficients after lag 2.
5 Separate your simulated series into train and test sets. Take the first 800 time-steps for the train set, and assign the rest to the test set.
6 Make forecasts over the test set. Use the mean, last value, and an MA(2) model. Make sure you repeatedly forecast 2 timesteps at a time using the `recursive_forecast` function we defined.
7 Plot your forecasts.
8 Measure the MSE, and identify your champion model.
9 Plot your MSEs in a bar plot.

4.4.2   Simulate an MA(q) process and make forecasts

Recreate the previous exercise, but simulate a moving average process of your choice. Try simulating a third-order or fourth-order moving average process. I recommend generating 10,000 samples. Be especially attentive to the ACF, and see if your coefficients become non-significant after lag q.

Summary

- A moving average process states that the present value is linearly dependent on the mean, present error term, and past error terms. The error terms are normally distributed.
- You can identify the order q of a stationary moving average process by studying the ACF plot. The coefficients are significant up until lag q only.
- You can predict up to q steps into the future because the error terms are not observed in the data and must be recursively estimated.
- Predicting beyond q steps into the future will simply return the mean of the series. To avoid that, you can apply rolling forecasts.
- If you apply a transformation to the data, you must undo it to bring your predictions back to the original scale of the data.
- The moving average model assumes the data is stationary. Therefore, you can only use this model on stationary data.

Modeling an autoregressive process

5

This chapter covers
- Illustrating an autoregressive process
- Defining the partial autocorrelation function (PACF)
- Using the PACF plot to determine the order of an autoregressive process
- Forecasting a time series using the autoregressive model

In the previous chapter, we covered the moving average process, also denoted as $MA(q)$, where q is the order. You learned that in a moving average process, the present value is linearly dependent on current and past error terms. Therefore, if you predict more than q steps ahead, the prediction will fall flat and will return only the mean of the series, because the error terms are not observed in the data and must be recursively estimated. Finally, you saw that you can determine the order of a stationary $MA(q)$ process by studying the ACF plot; the autocorrelation coefficients will be significant up until lag q. In the case where the autocorrelation coefficients slowly decay or exhibit a sinusoidal pattern, then you are possibly in the presence of an autoregressive process.

In this chapter, we will first define the autoregressive process. Then, we will define the partial autocorrelation function and use it to find the order of the underlying autoregressive process of a dataset. Finally, we will use the AR(p) model to produce forecasts.

5.1 *Predicting the average weekly foot traffic in a retail store*

Suppose that you want to forecast the average weekly foot traffic in a retail store so that the store manager can better manage the staff's schedule. If many people are expected to come to the store, more employees should be present to provide assistance. If fewer people are expected to visit the store, the manager can schedule fewer employees to work. That way the store can optimize its spending on salaries and ensure that employees are not overwhelmed or underwhelmed by store visitors.

For this example, we have 1,000 data points, each representing the average weekly foot traffic at a retail store starting in the year 2000. You can see the evolution of our data through time in figure 5.1.

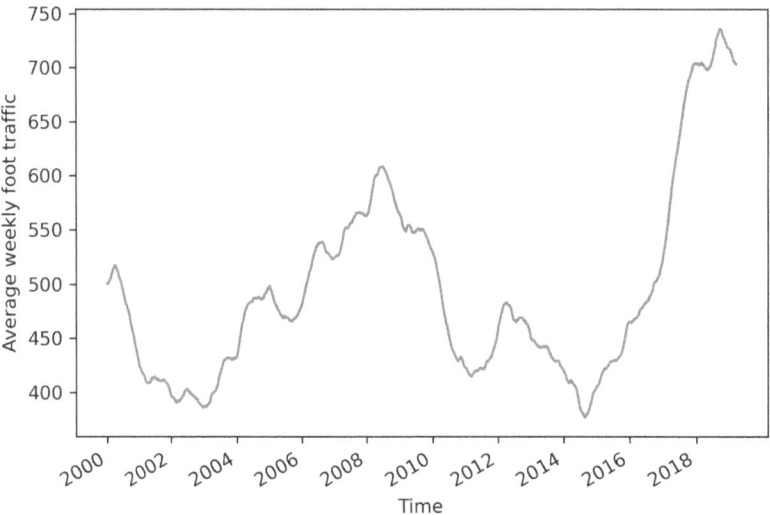

Figure 5.1   Average weekly foot traffic in a retail store. The dataset contains 1,000 data points, starting in the first week of 2000. Note that this is fictional data.

In figure 5.1 we can see a long-term trend with peaks and troughs along the way. We can intuitively say that this time series is not a stationary process, since we observe a trend over time. Furthermore, there is no apparent cyclical pattern in the data, so we can rule out any seasonal effects for now.

Again, in order to forecast the average weekly foot traffic, we need to identify the underlying process. Thus, we must apply the same steps that we covered in chapter 4. That way, we can verify whether we have a random walk or a moving average process at play. The steps are shown in figure 5.2.

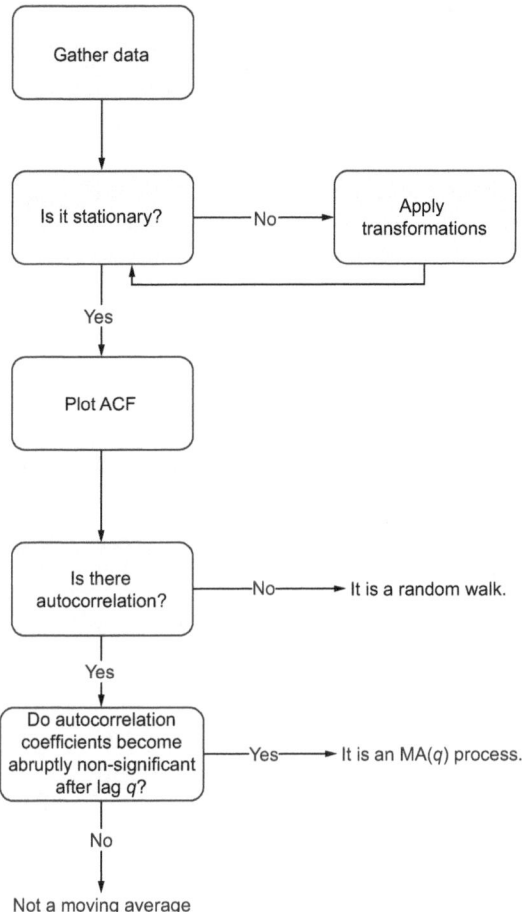

Figure 5.2 Steps to identify the underlying process of a stationary time series. So far we can identify a random walk or a moving average process.

In this example, the data is already collected, so we can move on to testing for stationarity. As mentioned previously, the presence of a trend over time means that our series is likely not stationary, so we will have to apply a transformation in order to make it stationary. Then we will plot the ACF. As we work through the chapter, you will see that not only is there autocorrelation, but the ACF plot will have a slowly decaying trend.

This is indicative of an autoregressive process of order p, also denoted as $AR(p)$. In this case, we must plot the *partial autocorrelation function* (PACF) to find the order p. Just like the coefficients on an ACF plot for an $MA(q)$ process, the coefficients on the PACF plot will become abruptly non-significant after lag p, hence determining the order of the autoregressive process.

Again, the order of the autoregressive process determines how many parameters must be included in the $AR(p)$ model. Then we will be ready to make forecasts. In this example, we wish to forecast next week's average foot traffic.

5.2   *Defining the autoregressive process*

An autoregressive process establishes that the output variable depends linearly on its own previous values. In other words, it is a regression of the variable against itself.

An *autoregressive process* is denoted as an AR(p) process, where p is the order. In such a process, the present value y_t is a linear combination of a constant C, the present error term ϵ_t, which is also white noise, and the past values of the series y_{t-p}. The magnitude of the influence of the past values on the present value is denoted as ϕ_p, which represents the coefficients of the AR(p) model. Mathematically, we express a general AR(p) model with equation 5.1.

$$y_t = C + \phi_1 y_{t-1} + \phi_2 y_{t-2} + \cdots \phi_p y_{t-p} + \epsilon_t \qquad \text{Equation 5.1}$$

Autoregressive process

An autoregressive process is a regression of a variable against itself. In a time series, this means that the present value is linearly dependent on its past values.

The autoregressive process is denoted as AR(p), where p is the order. The general expression of an AR(p) model is

$$y_t = C + \phi_1 y_{t-1} + \phi_2 y_{t-2} + \cdots + \phi_p y_{t-p} + \epsilon_t$$

Similar to the moving average process, the order p of an autoregressive process determines the number of past values that affect the present value. If we have a first-order autoregressive process, also denoted as AR(1), then the present value y_t is only dependent on a constant C, the value at the previous timestep $\phi_1 y_{t-1}$, and some white noise ϵ_t, as shown in equation 5.2.

$$y_t = C + \phi_1 y_{t-1} + \epsilon_t \qquad \text{Equation 5.2}$$

Looking at equation 5.2, you might notice that it is very similar to a random walk process, which we covered in chapter 3. In fact, if $\phi_1 = 1$, then equation 5.2 becomes

$$y_t = C + y_{t-1} + \epsilon_t$$

which is our random walk model. Therefore, we can say that the random walk is a special case of an autoregressive process, where the order p is 1 and ϕ_1 is equal to 1. Notice also that if C is not equal to 0, then we have a random walk with drift.

In the case of a second-order autoregressive process, or AR(2), the present value y_t is linearly dependent on a constant C, the value at the previous timestep $\phi_1 y_{t-1}$, the value two timesteps prior $\phi_2 y_{t-2}$, and the present error term ϵ_t, as shown in equation 5.3.

$$y_t = C + \phi_1 y_{t-1} + \phi_2 y_{t-2} + \epsilon_t \qquad \text{Equation 5.3}$$

We see how the order p influences the number of parameters that must be included in our model. As with a moving average process, we must find the right order of an autoregressive process in order to build the appropriate model. This means that if we identify an AR(3) process, we will use a third-order autoregressive model to make forecasts.

5.3   *Finding the order of a stationary autoregressive process*

Just like with the moving average process, there is a way to determine the order p of a stationary autoregressive process. We can extend the steps needed to identify the order of a moving average, as shown in figure 5.3.

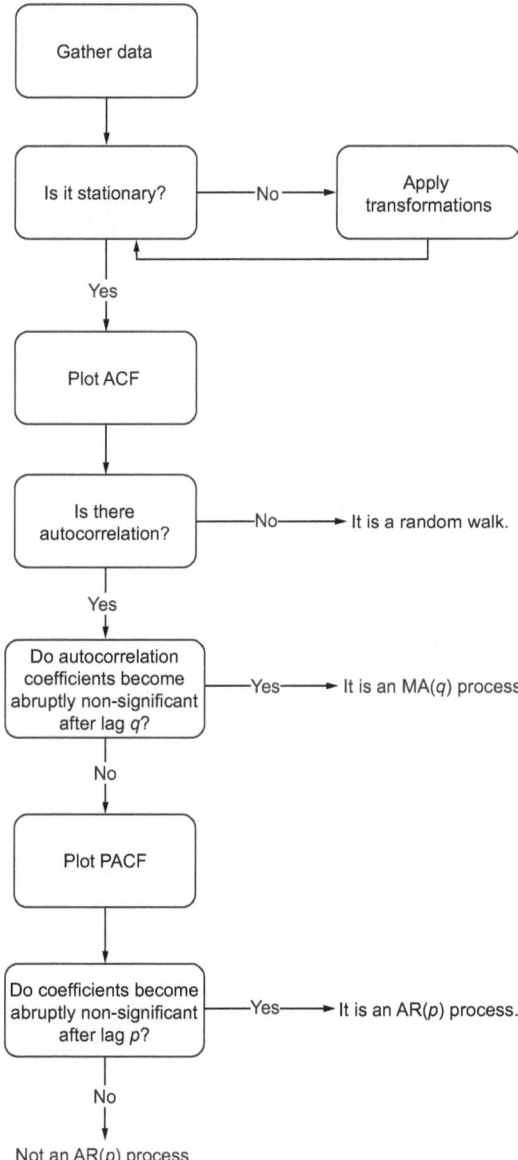

Figure 5.3   Steps to identify the order of an autoregressive process

The natural first step is to collect the data. Here we will work with the average weekly foot traffic dataset that you saw at the beginning of the chapter. We will read the data using pandas and store it as a DataFrame.

> **NOTE**   Feel free to consult the source code for this chapter on GitHub at any time: https://github.com/marcopeix/TimeSeriesForecastingInPython/tree/master/CH05.

```
import pandas as pd

df = pd.read_csv('../data/foot_traffic.csv')        ◁─── Read the CSV file into
                                                         a DataFrame.
df.head()        ◁─── Display the first five
                      rows of data.
```

You'll see that our data contains a single foot_traffic column in which the average weekly foot traffic at the retail store is recorded.

As always, we will plot our data to see if there are any observable patterns, such as a trend or seasonality. By now, you should be comfortable with plotting time series, so we will not dive deeply into the code that generates the graph. The result is the plot shown in figure 5.4.

```
import matplotlib.pyplot as plt        Plot the average weekly foot
                                       traffic at a retail store.
fig, ax = plt.subplots()
                                            Label the x-axis.
ax.plot(df['foot_traffic'])        ◁──┘
ax.set_xlabel('Time')        ◁────
ax.set_ylabel('Average weekly foot traffic')        ◁──── Label the y-axis.

plt.xticks(np.arange(0, 1000, 104), np.arange(2000, 2020, 2))        ◁──   Label the ticks
                                                                          on the x-axis.
fig.autofmt_xdate()        ◁───  Tilt the labels on the x-axis ticks
plt.tight_layout()        ◁──    so that they display nicely.

                                 Remove extra whitespace around the figure.
```

Looking at figure 5.4, you'll notice that there is no cyclical pattern, so we can rule out the presence of seasonality. As for the trend, it is sometimes positive and sometimes negative throughout the years, with the most recent trend being positive, since 2016.

The next step is to check for stationarity. As mentioned before, the presence of a trend means that our series is likely non-stationary. Let's verify that using the ADF test. Again, you should be comfortable running this without a detailed explanation of the code.

```
from statsmodels.tsa.stattools import adfuller        Run the ADF test on the average
                                                      weekly foot traffic, which is stored
ADF_result = adfuller(df['foot_traffic'])        ◁──  in the foot_traffic column.

                                                                     Print the ADF statistic.
print(f'ADF Statistic: {ADF_result[0]}')        ◁────────
print(f'p-value: {ADF_result[1]}')
```

Print the
p-value.

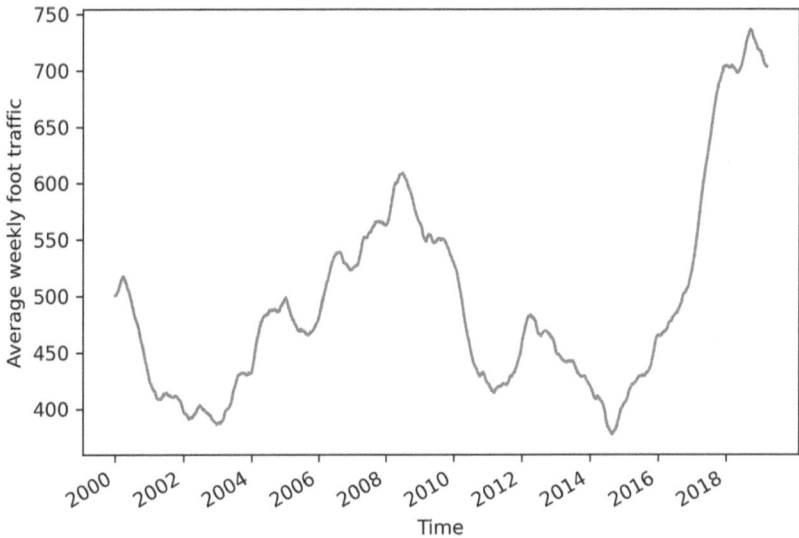

Figure 5.4   Average weekly foot traffic in a retail store. The dataset contains 1,000 data points, starting in the first week of 2000.

This prints out an ADF statistic of –1.18 along with a p-value of 0.68. Since the ADF statistic is not a large negative number, and it has a p-value greater than 0.05, we cannot reject the null hypothesis and our series is therefore non-stationary.

Hence, we must apply a transformation to make it stationary. To remove the effect of the trend and stabilize the mean of the series, we will use differencing.

```
import numpy as np
foot_traffic_diff = np.diff(df['foot_traffic'], n=1)
```

Apply a first-order differencing on the data and store the result in foot_traffic_diff.

Optionally, we could plot our differenced series `foot_traffic_diff` to see if we successfully removed the effect of the trend. The differenced series is shown in figure 5.5. We can see that we indeed removed the long-term trend, since the series starts and finishes roughly at the same value.

Can you recreate figure 5.5?

While optional, it is a good idea to plot your series as you apply transformations. This will give you a better intuition as to whether the series is stationary or not after a particular transformation. Try recreating figure 5.5 on your own.

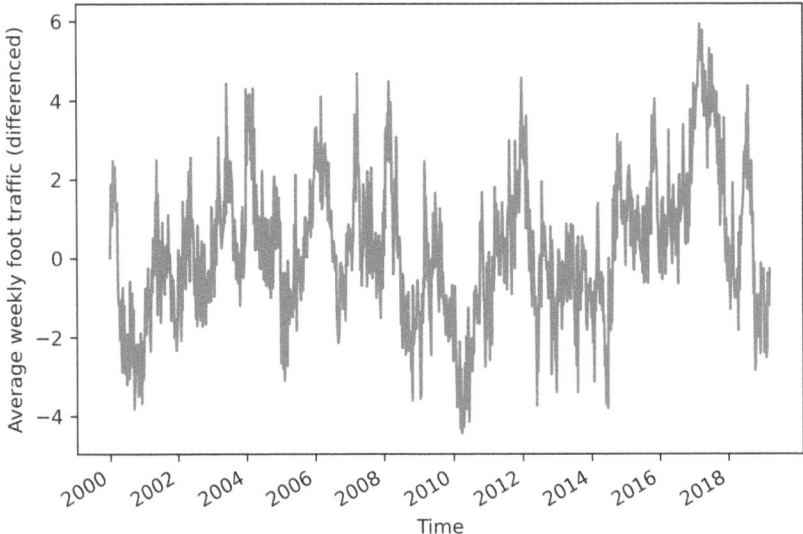

Figure 5.5   Differenced average weekly foot traffic at a retail store. Notice that the trend effect has been removed, since the series starts and ends at roughly the same value.

With a transformation applied to the series, we can verify whether the series is stationary by running the ADF test on the differenced series.

```
ADF_result = adfuller(foot_traffic_diff)        ⊲┐  Run the ADF test on the
                                                  │  differenced time series.
print(f'ADF Statistic: {ADF_result[0]}')
print(f'p-value: {ADF_result[1]}')
```

This prints out an ADF statistic of –5.27 and a p-value of $6.36{\times}10^{-6}$. With a p-value smaller than 0.05, we can reject the null hypothesis, meaning that we now have a stationary series.

The next step is to plot the ACF and see if there is autocorrelation and if the coefficients become abruptly non-significant after a certain lag. As we did in the two previous chapters, we will use the plot_acf function from statsmodels. The result is shown in figure 5.6.

```
from statsmodels.graphics.tsaplots import plot_acf

plot_acf(foot_traffic_diff, lags=20);            ⊲┐  Plot the ACF of the
                                                   │  differenced series.
plt.tight_layout()
```

Looking at figure 5.6, you'll notice that we have significant autocorrelation coefficients beyond lag 0. Therefore, we know that our process is not a random walk. Furthermore, you'll notice that the coefficients are decaying exponentially as the lag

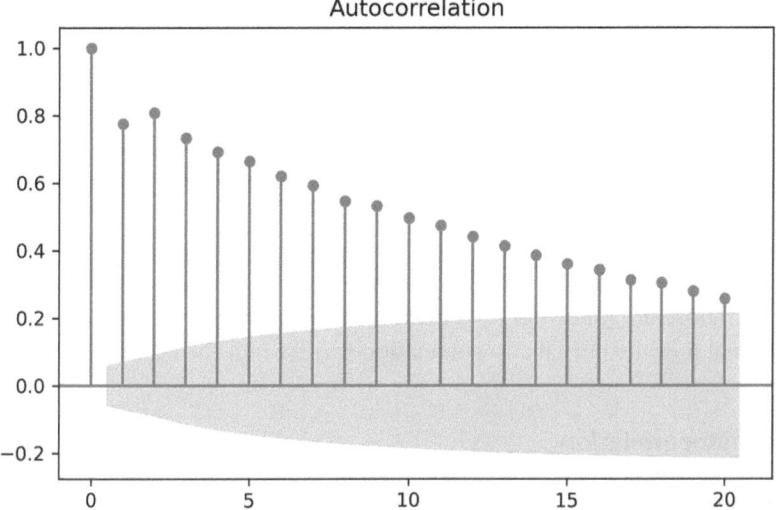

Figure 5.6   ACF plot of the differenced average weekly foot traffic at a retail store. Notice how the plot is slowly decaying. This is a behavior that we have not observed before, and it is indicative of an autoregressive process.

increases. Therefore, there is no lag at which the coefficients abruptly become non-significant. This means that we do not have a moving average process and that we are likely studying an autoregressive process.

When the ACF plot of a stationary process exhibits a pattern of exponential decay, we probably have an autoregressive process in play, and we must find another way to identify the order p of the AR(p) process. Specifically, we must turn our attention to the *partial autocorrelation function* (PACF) plot.

5.3.1   The partial autocorrelation function (PACF)

In an attempt to identify the order of a stationary autoregressive process, we used the ACF plot just as we did for a moving average process. Unfortunately, the ACF plot cannot give us this information, and we must turn to the *partial autocorrelation function* (PACF).

Remember that the autocorrelation measures the linear relationship between lagged values of a time series. Consequently, the autocorrelation function measures how the correlation changes between two values as the lag is increased.

To understand the partial autocorrelation function, let's consider the following scenario. Suppose we have the following AR(2) process:

$$y_t = 0.33y_{t-1} + 0.50y_{t-2}$$ **Equation 5.4**

We wish to measure how y_t relates to y_{t-2}; in other words, we want to measure their correlation. This is done with the autocorrelation function (ACF). However, from the equation, we can see that y_{t-1} also has an influence on y_t. Even more important, it also has an impact on the value of y_{t-2}, since in an AR(2) process, each value depends on the previous two values. Therefore, when we measure the autocorrelation between y_t and y_{t-2} using the ACF, we are not taking into account the fact that y_{t-1} has an influence on both y_t and y_{t-2}. This means that we are not measuring the *true* impact of y_{t-2} on y_t. To do so, we must remove the effect of y_{t-1}. Thus, we are measuring the partial autocorrelation between y_t and y_{t-2}.

In more formal terms, the partial autocorrelation measures the correlation between lagged values in a time series when we remove the influence of correlated lagged values in between. Those are known as *confounding variables*. The partial autocorrelation function will reveal how the partial autocorrelation varies when the lag increases.

Partial autocorrelation

Partial autocorrelation measures the correlation between lagged values in a time series when we remove the influence of correlated lagged values in between. We can plot the partial autocorrelation function to determine the order of a stationary AR(p) process. The coefficients will be non-significant after lag p.

Let's verify whether plotting the PACF will reveal the order of the process shown in equation 5.4. We know from equation 5.4 that we have a second-order autoregressive process, or AR(2). We will simulate it using the `ArmaProcess` function from `statsmodels`. The function expects an array containing the coefficients of an MA(q) process and an array containing the coefficients for an AR(p) process. Since we are only interested in simulating an AR(2) process, we will set the coefficients of the MA(q) process to 0. Then, as specified by the `statsmodels` documentation, the coefficients of the AR(2) process must have opposite signs to those we wish to simulate. Therefore, the array will contain −0.33 and −0.50. In addition, the function requires us to include the coefficient at lag 0, which is the number that multiplies y_t. Here, that number is simply 1.

Once the arrays of coefficients are defined, we can feed them to the `ArmaProcess` function, and we will generate 1,000 samples. Make sure you set the random seed to 42 in order to reproduce the results shown here.

```
from statsmodels.tsa.arima_process import ArmaProcess
import numpy as np

np.random.seed(42)          ◁── Set the random seed to 42 in order to
                                reproduce the results shown here.

ma2 = np.array([1, 0, 0])   ◁──── Set the coefficients of the
ar2 = np.array([1, -0.33, -0.50])      MA(q) process to 0, since
                                       we are only interested in
                                       simulating an AR(2) process.
AR2_process = ArmaProcess(ar2, ma2).generate_sample(nsample=1000)   ◁──
```

Set the coefficients of the MA(q) process to 0, since we are only interested in simulating an AR(2) process. Note that the first coefficient is 1 for lag 0, and it must be provided as specified by the documentation.

Set the coefficients for the AR(2) process. Again, the coefficient at lag 0 is 1. Then, write the coefficients with opposite signs to what was defined in equation 5.4, as specified by the documentation.

Simulate the AR(2) process and generate 1,000 samples.

Now that we have a simulated AR(2) process, let's plot the PACF and see if the coefficients become abruptly non-significant after lag 2. If that is the case, we'll know that we can use the PACF plot to determine the order of a stationary autoregressive process, just as we can use the ACF plot to determine the order of a stationary moving average process.

The statsmodels library allows us to plot the PACF rapidly. We can use the plot_pacf function, which simply requires our series and the number of lags to display on the plot.

```
from statsmodels.graphics.tsaplots import plot_pacf

plot_pacf(AR2_process, lags=20);         ◁─┐   Plot the PACF of our
                                           │   simulated AR(2) process.
plt.tight_layout()
```

The resulting plot is shown in figure 5.7, and it shows that we have an autoregressive process of order 2.

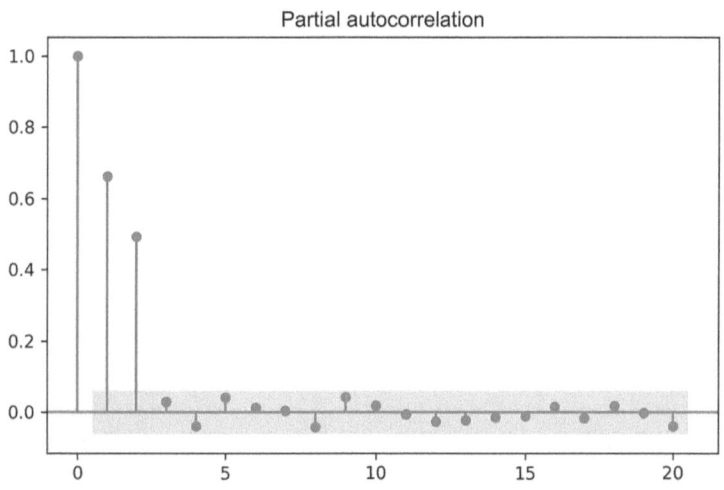

Figure 5.7 Plot of the PACF for our simulated AR(2) process. You can clearly see here that after lag 2, the partial autocorrelation coefficients are not significantly different from 0. Therefore, we can identify the order of a stationary AR(p) model using the PACF plot.

We now know that we can use the PACF plot to identify the order of a stationary AR(p) process. The coefficients in the PACF plot will be significant up until lag p. Afterward, they should not be significantly different from 0.

Let's see if we can apply the same strategy to our average weekly foot traffic dataset. We made the series stationary and saw that the ACF plot exhibited a slowly decaying trend. Let's plot the PACF to see if the lags become non-significant after a particular lag.

The process is exactly the same as what we just did, but this time we will plot the PACF of our differenced series stored in `foot_traffic_diff`. You can see the resulting plot in figure 5.8.

```
plot_pacf(foot_traffic_diff, lags=20);

plt.tight_layout()
```
◁—— **Plot the PACF of our differenced series.**

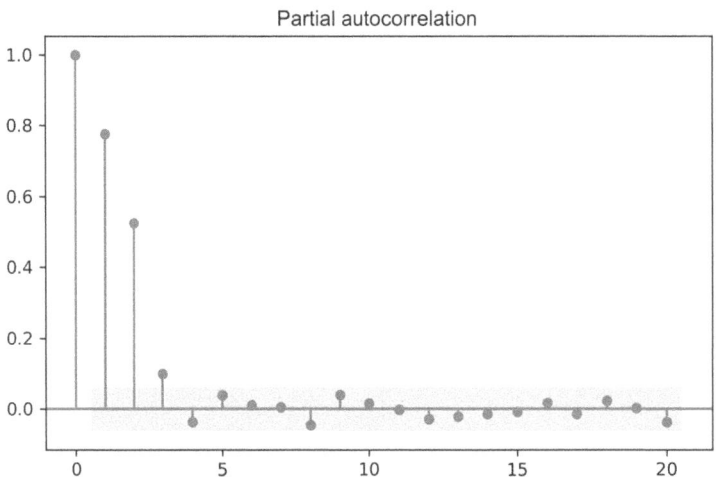

Figure 5.8   The PACF of our differenced average weekly foot traffic in a retail store. You can see that the coefficients are non-significant after lag 3. Therefore, we can say that our stationary process is a third-order autoregressive process, or an AR(3) process.

Looking at figure 5.8, you can see that there are no significant coefficients after lag 3. Therefore, the differenced average weekly foot traffic is an autoregressive process of order 3, which can also be denoted as AR(3).

5.4   *Forecasting an autoregressive process*

Once the order is determined, we can fit an autoregressive model to forecast our time series. In this case, the model is also termed AR(p), where p is still the order of the process.

We will forecast next week's average foot traffic in a retail store using the same dataset we have been working with. In order to evaluate our forecasts, we will hold out the last 52 weeks of data for our test set, while the rest will be used for training. That way, we can evaluate the performance of our forecast over a period of 1 year.

```
df_diff = pd.DataFrame({'foot_traffic_diff': foot_traffic_diff})

train = df_diff[:-52]
test = df_diff[-52:]

print(len(train))
print(len(test))
```

Create a DataFrame from the differenced foot traffic data.

The training set is all the data except the last 52 data points.

The test set is the last 52 data points.

Display how many data points are in the test set.

Display how many data points are in the train set.

You can see that our training set contains 947 data points, while the test set contains 52 data points as expected. Note that the sum of both sets gives 999, which is one less data point than our original series. This is normal, since we applied differencing to make the series stationary, and we know that differencing removes the first data point from the series.

Next, we will visualize the testing period for our scenario, in both the original series and the differenced series. The plot is shown in figure 5.9.

```
fig, (ax1, ax2) = plt.subplots(nrows=2, ncols=1, sharex=True,
    figsize=(10, 8))

ax1.plot(df['foot_traffic'])
ax1.set_xlabel('Time')
ax1.set_ylabel('Avg. weekly foot traffic')
ax1.axvspan(948, 1000, color='#808080', alpha=0.2)

ax2.plot(df_diff['foot_traffic_diff'])
ax2.set_xlabel('Time')
ax2.set_ylabel('Diff. avg. weekly foot traffic')
ax2.axvspan(947, 999, color='#808080', alpha=0.2)

plt.xticks(np.arange(0, 1000, 104), np.arange(2000, 2020, 2))

fig.autofmt_xdate()
plt.tight_layout()
```

Specify the figure's size using the figsize parameter. The first number is the height, and the second number is the width, both in inches.

Given that our objective is to forecast next week's average foot traffic at the retail store, we will perform rolling forecasts over our test set. Remember that our data was recorded over a weekly period, so predicting the next timestep means we're forecasting next week's average foot traffic.

We will forecast using three different methods. The historical mean method and the last known value method will act as baselines, and we will use an AR(3) model, since we previously established that we have a stationary third-order autoregressive process. As we did in the previous chapter, we will use the mean squared error (MSE) to evaluate the performance of each forecasting method.

Also, we will reuse the function we defined in the previous chapter to recursively forecast over the testing period. However, this time we must include a method to use an autoregressive model.

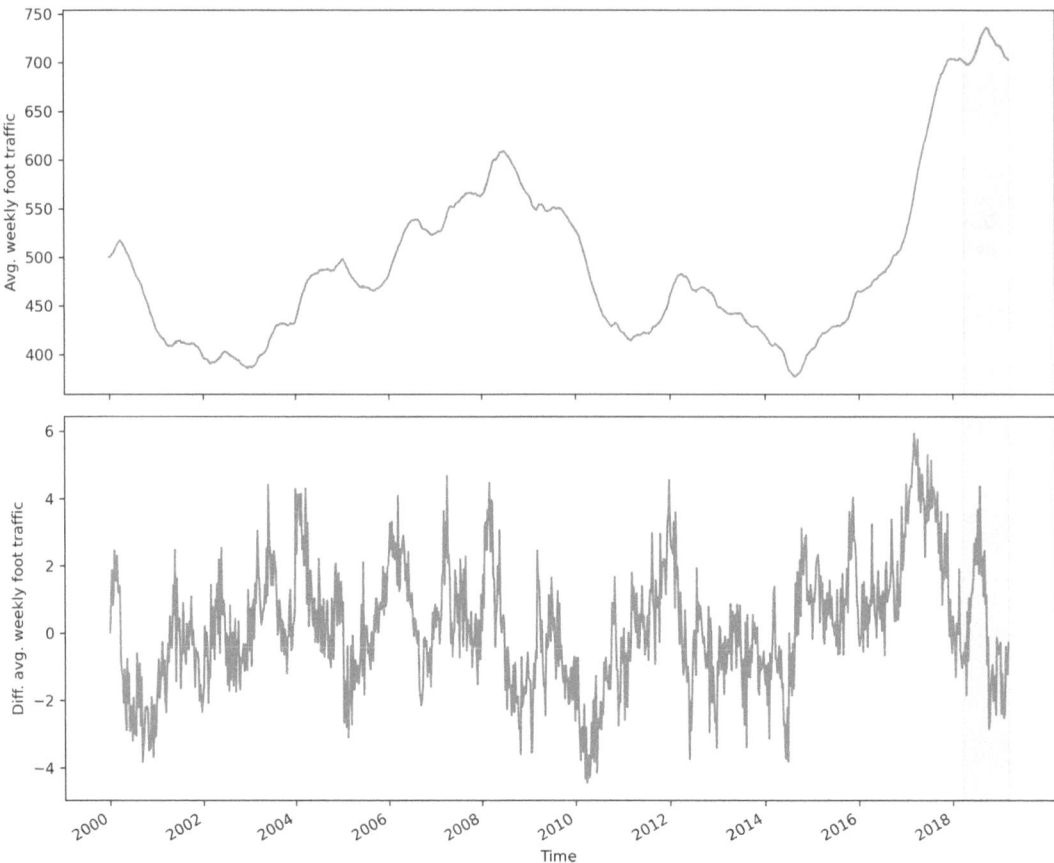

Figure 5.9   Testing period for our forecasts on the original and differenced series. Keep in mind that our differenced series has lost its first data point.

We will again use the SARIMAX function from `statsmodels`, as it encompasses an AR model. As mentioned previously, SARIMAX is a complex model that allows us to consider seasonal effects, autoregressive processes, non-stationary time series, moving average processes, and exogenous variables all in one single model. For now, we will disregard all factors except the moving autoregressive portion.

Listing 5.1   A function for rolling forecasts on a horizon

```
def rolling_forecast(df: pd.DataFrame, train_len: int, horizon: int,
    window: int, method: str) -> list:

    total_len = train_len + horizon
    end_idx = train_len
```

```
    if method == 'mean':
        pred_mean = []

        for i in range(train_len, total_len, window):
            mean = np.mean(df[:i].values)
            pred_mean.extend(mean for _ in range(window))

        return pred_mean

    elif method == 'last':
        pred_last_value = []

        for i in range(train_len, total_len, window):
            last_value = df[:i].iloc[-1].values[0]
            pred_last_value.extend(last_value for _ in range(window))

        return pred_last_value

    elif method == 'AR':
        pred_AR = []

        for i in range(train_len, total_len, window):
            model = SARIMAX(df[:i], order=(3,0,0))       ◁─── The order specifies
            res = model.fit(disp=False)                        an AR(3) model.
            predictions = res.get_prediction(0, i + window - 1)
            oos_pred = predictions.predicted_mean.iloc[-window:]
            pred_AR.extend(oos_pred)

        return pred_AR
```

Once our function is defined, we can use it to generate the predictions according to each method. We will assign them to their own column in test.

**Since we wish to predict the
next timestep, our window is 1.**

**Store the length of the training set.
Note that constants are usually in
capital letters in Python.**

```
    TRAIN_LEN = len(train)     ◁──
    HORIZON = len(test)        ◁──
    WINDOW = 1
```

**Store the length
of the test set.**

```
pred_mean = rolling_forecast(df_diff, TRAIN_LEN, HORIZON, WINDOW, 'mean')
pred_last_value = rolling_forecast(df_diff, TRAIN_LEN, HORIZON, WINDOW,
➥ 'last')
pred_AR = rolling_forecast(df_diff, TRAIN_LEN, HORIZON, WINDOW, 'AR')

test['pred_mean'] = pred_mean                    │  Store the predictions
test['pred_last_value'] = pred_last_value        │  in their respective
test['pred_AR'] = pred_AR                         │  columns in test.

test.head()
```

We can now visualize our predictions against the observed values in the test set. Note that we are working with the differenced series, so our predictions are also differenced values. The result is shown in figure 5.10.

```
fig, ax = plt.subplots()

ax.plot(df_diff['foot_traffic_diff'])
ax.plot(test['foot_traffic_diff'], 'b-', label='actual')
ax.plot(test['pred_mean'], 'g:', label='mean')
ax.plot(test['pred_last_value'], 'r-.', label='last')
ax.plot(test['pred_AR'], 'k--', label='AR(3)')

ax.legend(loc=2)

ax.set_xlabel('Time')
ax.set_ylabel('Diff. avg. weekly foot traffic')

ax.axvspan(947, 998, color='#808080', alpha=0.2)

ax.set_xlim(920, 999)

plt.xticks([936, 988],[2018, 2019])

fig.autofmt_xdate()
plt.tight_layout()
```

Plot part of the training set so we can see the transition from the training set to the test set.

Plot the values from the test set.

Plot the predictions from the historical mean method.

Plot the predictions from the last known value method.

Plot the predictions from the AR(3) model.

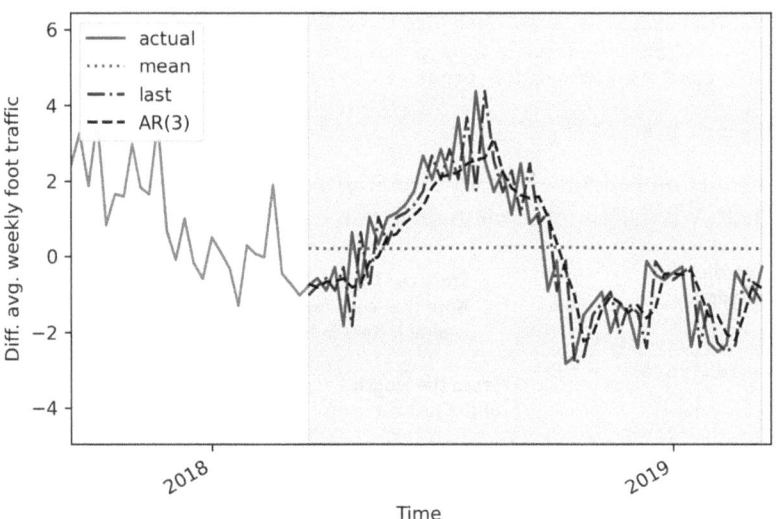

Figure 5.10 Forecasts of the differenced average weekly foot traffic in a retail store

Looking at figure 5.10, you'll see that, once again, using the historical mean produces a straight line, which is shown in the plot as a dotted line. As for the predictions from the AR(3) model and the last known value method, the curves are almost confounding with that of the test set, so we will have to measure the MSE to assess which method is the most performant. Again, we will use the `mean_squared_error` function from the `sklearn` library.

```
ffrom sklearn.metrics import mean_squared_error

mse_mean = mean_squared_error(test['foot_traffic_diff'], test['pred_mean'])
mse_last = mean_squared_error(test['foot_traffic_diff'],
➥ test['pred_last_value'])
mse_AR = mean_squared_error(test['foot_traffic_diff'], test['pred_AR'])

print(mse_mean, mse_last, mse_AR)
```

This prints out an MSE of 3.11 for the historical mean method, 1.45 for the last known value method, and 0.92 for the AR(3) model. Since the MSE for the AR(3) model is the lowest of the three, we conclude that the AR(3) model is the best-performing method for forecasting next week's average foot traffic. This is expected, since we established that our stationary process was a third-order autoregressive process. It makes sense that modeling using an AR(3) model will yield the best predictions.

Since our forecasts are differenced values, we need to reverse the transformation in order to bring our forecasts back to the original scale of the data; otherwise, our predictions will not make sense in a business context. To do this, we can take the cumulative sum of our predictions and add it to the last value of our training set in the original series. This point occurs at index 948, since we are forecasting the last 52 weeks in a dataset containing 1,000 points.

```
df['pred_foot_traffic'] = pd.Series()
df['pred_foot_traffic'][948:] = df['foot_traffic'].iloc[948] +
➥ pred_df['pred_AR'].cumsum()        ◁──┐  Assign the undifferenced
                                         predictions to the pred_foot_traffic
                                         column in df.
```

Now we can plot our undifferenced predictions against the observed values in the test set of the original series in its original scale.

```
fig, ax = plt.subplots()

ax.plot(df['foot_traffic'])
ax.plot(df['foot_traffic'], 'b-', label='actual')      ◁──┐  Plot the actual values.
ax.plot(df['pred_foot_traffic'], 'k--', label='AR(3)')  ◁──┐
                                                            Plot the
                                                            undifferenced
ax.legend(loc=2)                                            predictions.

ax.set_xlabel('Time')
ax.set_ylabel('Average weekly foot traffic')

ax.axvspan(948, 1000, color='#808080', alpha=0.2)

ax.set_xlim(920, 1000)
ax.set_ylim(650, 770)

plt.xticks([936, 988],[2018, 2019])

fig.autofmt_xdate()
plt.tight_layout()
```

In figure 5.11 you can see that our model (shown as a dashed line) follows the general trend of the observed values in the test set.

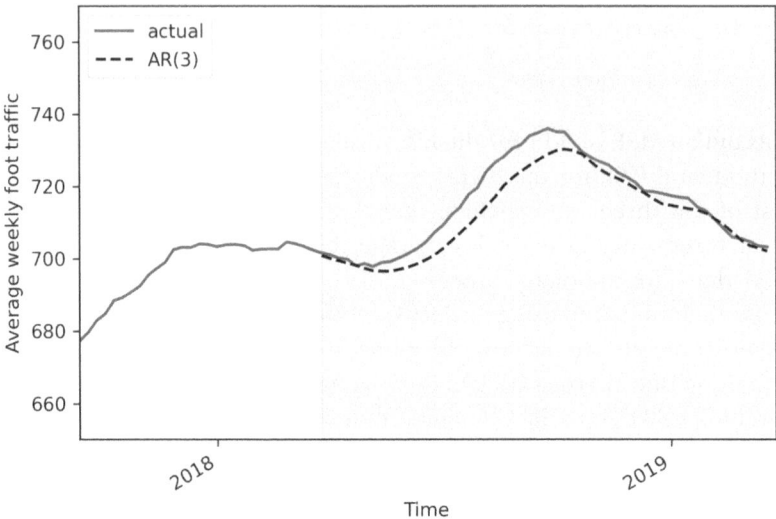

Figure 5.11   Undifferenced forecasts from the AR(3) model

Now we can measure the mean absolute error (MAE) on the original dataset to get its meaning in a business context. We'll simply measure the MAE using the undifferenced predictions.

```
from sklearn.metrics import mean_absolute_error

mae_AR_undiff = mean_absolute_error(df['foot_traffic'][948:],
    df['pred_foot_traffic'][948:])

print(mae_AR_undiff)
```

This prints out a mean absolute error of 3.45. This means that our predictions are off by 3.45 people on average, either above or below the actual value for the week's foot traffic. Note that we report the MAE because it has a simple business meaning that is easy to understand and interpret.

5.5   *Next steps*

In this chapter, we covered the autoregressive process and how it can be modeled by an AR(p) model, where p is the order, and it determines how many lagged values are included in the model. We also saw how plotting the ACF cannot help us determine the order of a stationary AR(p) process. Instead, we must plot the PACF, in which the partial autocorrelation coefficients will be significant up until lag p only.

However, there might be a situation where neither the ACF nor PACF gives us information. What if both the ACF and PACF plots exhibit a slow decay or a sinusoidal pattern? In that case, there is no order for the MA(q) or AR(p) process that can be inferred. This means that we are facing a more complex process that is likely a combination of both an AR(p) process and an MA(q) process. This is called an *autoregressive moving average* (ARMA) process, or ARMA(p,q), and it will the subject of the next chapter.

5.6   Exercises

Test your knowledge and mastery of the AR(p) model with these exercises. The solutions to all exercises are available on GitHub: https://github.com/marcopeix/Time SeriesForecastingInPython/tree/master/CH05.

5.6.1   Simulate an AR(2) process and make forecasts

Simulate a stationary AR(2) process. Use the `ArmaProcess` function from the statsmodels library and simulate this process:

$$y_t = 0.33y_{t-1} + 0.50y_{t-2}$$

1 For this exercise, generate 1,000 samples.

```
from statsmodels.tsa.arima_process import ArmaProcess
import numpy as np

np.random.seed(42)         ◁———  Set the seed for reproducibility.
                                 Change the seed if you want to
                                 experiment with different values.
ma2 = np.array([1, 0, 0])
ar2 = np.array([1, -0.33, -0.50])

AR2_process = ArmaProcess(ar2, ma2).generate_sample(nsample=1000)
```

2 Plot your simulated autoregressive process.
3 Run the ADF test and check if the process is stationary. If not, apply differencing.
4 Plot the ACF. Is it slowly decaying?
5 Plot the PACF. Are there significant coefficients after lag 2?
6 Separate your simulated series into train and test sets. Take the first 800 timesteps for the train set and assign the rest to the test set.
7 Make forecasts over the test set. Use the historical mean method, last known value method, and an AR(2) model. Use the `rolling_forecast` function, and use a `window` length of 2.
8 Plot your forecasts.
9 Measure the MSE, and identify your champion model.
10 Plot your MSEs in a bar plot.

5.6.2   *Simulate an AR(p) process and make forecasts*

Recreate the previous exercise but simulate an AR(p) process of your choice. Experiment with a third- or fourth-order autoregressive process. I would recommend generating 10,000 samples.

When forecasting, experiment with different values for the `window` parameter of your `rolling_forecast` function. How does it affect the model's performance? Is there a value that minimizes the MSE?

Summary

- An autoregressive process states that the present value is linearly dependent on its past values and an error term.
- If the ACF plot of a stationary process shows a slow decay, then you likely have an autoregressive process.
- The partial autocorrelation measures the correlation between two lagged values of a time series when you remove the effect of the other autocorrelated lagged values.
- Plotting the PACF of a stationary autoregressive process will show the order p of the process. The coefficients will be significant up until lag p only.

Modeling
complex time series
6

This chapter covers

- Examining the autoregressive moving average model or ARMA(p,q)
- Experimenting with the limitations of the ACF and PACF plots
- Selecting the best model with the Akaike information criterion (AIC)
- Analyzing a time series model using residual analysis
- Building a general modeling procedure
- Forecasting using the ARMA(p,q) model

In chapter 4 we covered the moving average process, denoted as MA(q), where q is the order. You learned that in a moving average process, the present value is linearly dependent on the mean, the current error term, and past error terms. The order q can be inferred using the ACF plot, where autocorrelation coefficients will be significant up until lag q only. In the case where the ACF plot shows a slowly decaying pattern or a sinusoidal pattern, it is possible that you are in the presence of an autoregressive process instead of a moving average process.

This led us to chapter 5, in which we covered the autoregressive process, denoted as AR(p), where p is the order. In the autoregressive process, the present value is linearly dependent on its own past value. In other words, it is a regression of the variable against itself. You saw that we can infer the order p using the PACF plot, where the partial autocorrelation coefficients will be significant up until lag p only. We are therefore at a point where we can identify, model, and predict a random walk, a pure moving average process, and a pure autoregressive process.

The next step is learning how to treat time series where you cannot infer an order from the ACF plot or from the PACF plot. This means that both figures exhibit a slowly decaying pattern or a sinusoidal pattern. In such a case, we are in the presence of an autoregressive moving average (ARMA) process. This denotes the combination of both the autoregressive and moving average processes that we covered in the two previous chapters.

In this chapter, we will examine the autoregressive moving average process, ARMA(p,q), where p denotes the order of the autoregressive portion and q denotes the order of the moving average portion. Furthermore, using the ACF and PACF plots to determine the orders q and p, respectively, becomes difficult, as both plots will show either a slowly decaying or sinusoidal pattern. Thus, we will define a general modeling procedure that will allow us to model such complex time series. This procedure involves model selection using the *Akaike information criterion* (AIC), which will determine the optimal combination of p and q for our series. Then we must evaluate the model's validity using residual analysis by studying the correlogram, Q-Q plot, and density plot of the model's residuals to assess if they closely resemble white noise. If that is the case, we can move on to forecasting our time series using the ARMA(p,q) model.

This chapter will introduce foundational knowledge for forecasting complex time series. All the concepts introduced here will be reused in further chapters when we start modeling non-stationary time series and incorporating seasonality and exogenous variables.

6.1 *Forecasting bandwidth usage for data centers*

Suppose that you are tasked with predicting bandwidth usage for a large data center. Bandwidth is defined as the maximum rate of data that can be transferred. Its base unit is bits per second (bps).

Forecasting bandwidth usage allows data centers to better manage their computing resources. In the case where less bandwidth usage is expected, they can shut down some of their computing resources. This in turns reduces expenses and allows for maintenance. On the other hand, if bandwidth usage is expected to increase, they can dedicate the required resources to sustain the demand and ensure low latency, thus keeping their customers satisfied.

For this situation, there are 10,000 data points representing the hourly bandwidth usage starting in January 1, 2019. Here the bandwidth is measured in megabits per second (Mbps), which is equivalent to 10^6 bps. We can visualize our time series in figure 6.1.

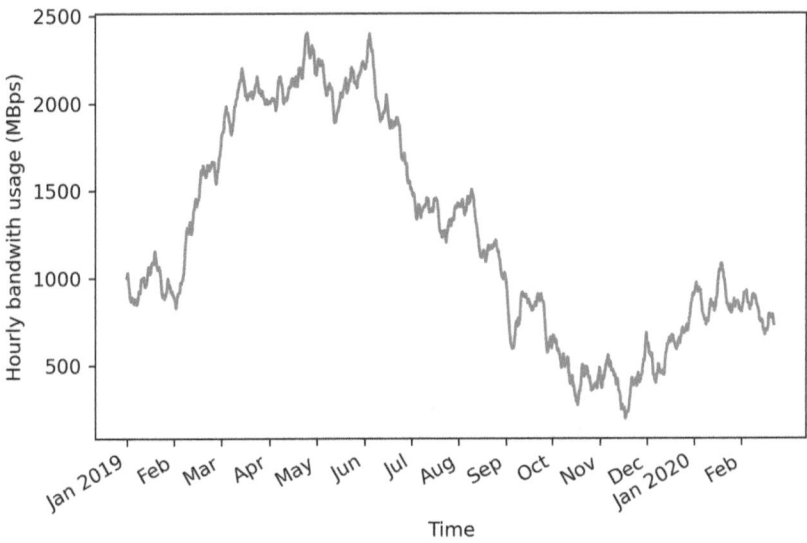

Figure 6.1   Hourly bandwidth usage in a data center since January 1, 2019. The dataset contains 10,000 points.

Looking at figure 6.1, you can see long-term trends over time, meaning that this series is likely not stationary, so we need to apply a transformation. Also, there seems to be no cyclical behavior, so we can rule out the presence of seasonality in our series.

In order to forecast bandwidth usage, we need to identify the underlying process in our series. Thus, we'll follow the steps that we defined in chapter 5. That way, we can verify whether we have a random walk, a moving average process, or an autoregressive process. The steps are shown in figure 6.2.

The first step is to collect the data, which is already done in this case. Then we must determine if our series is stationary or not. The presence of a trend in the plot hints that our series is not stationary. Nevertheless, we will apply the ADF test to check for stationarity and apply a transformation accordingly.

Then we will plot the ACF function and find that there are significant autocorrelation coefficients after lag 0, which means it is not a random walk. However, we will observe that coefficients slowly decay. They do not become abruptly non-significant after a certain lag, which means that it is not a purely moving average process.

We'll then move on to plotting the PACF function. This time we will notice a sinusoidal pattern, meaning that coefficients do not become abruptly non-significant after a certain lag. This will lead us to the conclusion that it is not a purely autoregressive process either.

Therefore, it must be a combination of autoregressive and moving average processes, resulting in an autoregressive moving average process that can be modeled with the ARMA(p,q) model, where p is the order of the autoregressive process and q is

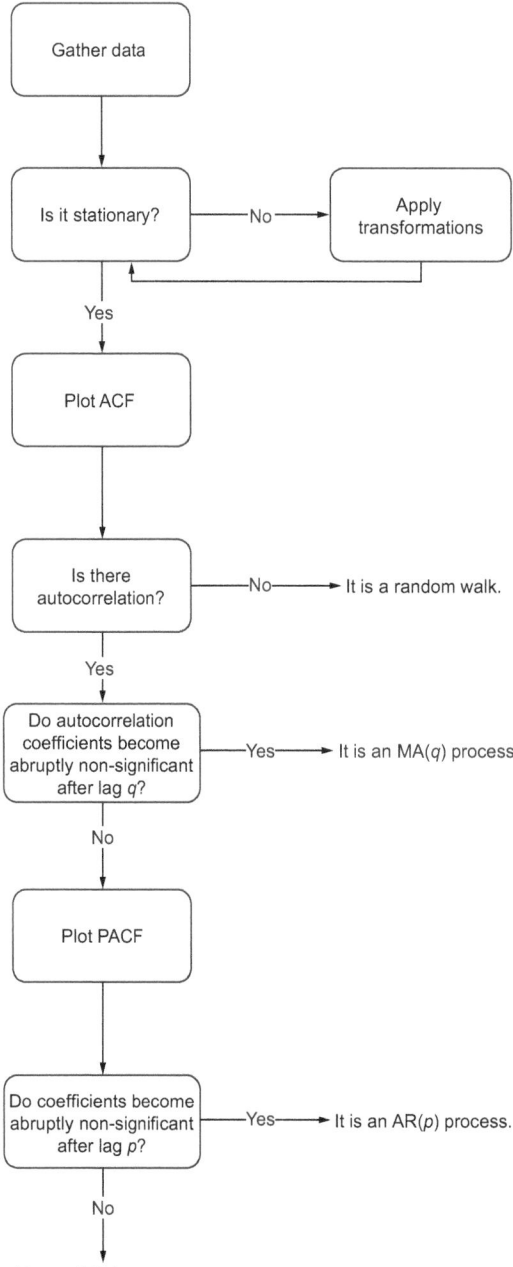

Figure 6.2   Steps to identify a random walk, a moving average process, and an autoregressive process

the order of the moving average process. It is difficult to use the ACF and PACF plots to respectively find p and q, so we will fit many ARMA(p,q) models with different combinations of values for p and q. We will then select a model according to the Akaike information criterion and assess its viability by analyzing its residuals. Ideally, the residuals of a model will have characteristics similar to white noise. Then we will be able to use this model to make forecasts. For this example, we will forecast the hourly bandwidth usage over the next two hours.

6.2 Examining the autoregressive moving average process

The *autoregressive moving average process* is a combination of the autoregressive process and the moving average process. It states that the present value is linearly dependent on its own previous values and a constant, just like in an autoregressive process, as well as on the mean of the series, the current error term, and past error terms, like in a moving average process.

The autoregressive moving average process is denoted as ARMA(p,q), where p is the order of the autoregressive portion, and q is the order of the moving average portion. Mathematically, the ARMA(p,q) process is expressed as a linear combination of a constant C, the past values of the series y_{t-p}, the mean of the series μ, past error terms ϵ_{t-q}, and the current error term ϵ_t, as shown in equation 6.1.

$$y_t = C + \phi_1 y_{t-1} + \phi_2 y_{t-2} + \cdots + \phi_p y_{t-p} + \epsilon_t + \theta_1 \epsilon_{t-1} + \theta_2 \epsilon_{t-2} + \cdots + \theta_q \epsilon_{t-q} \quad \text{Equation 6.1}$$

> **Autoregressive moving average process**
>
> The autoregressive moving average process is a combination of the autoregressive process and the moving average process.
>
> It is denoted as ARMA(p,q), where p is the order of the autoregressive process, and q is the order of the moving average process. The general equation of the ARMA(p,q) model is
>
> $$y_t = C + \phi_1 y_{t-1} + \phi_2 y_{t-2} + \cdots + \phi_p y_{t-p} + \mu + \epsilon_t + \theta_1 \epsilon_{t-1} + \theta_2 \epsilon_{t-2} + \cdots + \theta_q \epsilon_{t-q}$$
>
> An ARMA(0,q) process is equivalent to an MA(q) process, since the order $p = 0$ cancels the AR(p) portion. An ARMA(p,0) process is equivalent to an AR(p) process, since the order $q = 0$ cancels the MA(q) portion.

Again, the order p determines the number of past values that affect the present value. Similarly, the order q determines the number of past error terms that affect the present value. In other words, the orders p and q dictate the number of parameters for the autoregressive and moving average portions, respectively.

Thus, if we have an ARMA(1,1) process, we are combining an autoregressive process of order 1, or AR(1), with a moving average process of order 1, or MA(1). Recall that a first-order autoregressive process is a linear combination of a constant C, the value of the series at the previous timestep $\phi_1 y_{t-1}$, and white noise ϵ_t, as shown in equation 6.2.

$$AR(1) := y_t = C + \phi_1 y_{t-1} + \epsilon_t \quad \text{Equation 6.2}$$

Also recall that a first-order moving average process, or MA(1), is a linear combination of the mean of the series μ, the current error term ϵ_t, and the error term at the previous timestep $\theta_1\epsilon_{t-1}$, as shown in equation 6.3.

$$MA(1) := y_t = \mu + \epsilon_t + \theta_1\epsilon_{t-1}$$ **Equation 6.3**

We can combine the AR(1) and MA(1) processes to obtain an ARMA(1,1) process as shown in equation 6.4, which combines the effects of equations 6.2 and 6.3.

$$ARMA(1,1) := y_t = C + \phi_1 y_{t-1} + \epsilon_t + \theta_1\epsilon_{t-1}$$ **Equation 6.4**

If we have an ARMA(2,1) process, we are combining a second-order autoregressive process with a first-order moving average process. We know that we can express an AR(2) process as equation 6.5, while the MA(1) process from equation 6.3 remains the same.

$$AR(2) := y_t = C + \phi_1 y_{t-1} + \phi_2 y_{t-2} + \epsilon_t$$ **Equation 6.5**

Thus, an ARMA(2,1) process can be expressed as the combination of the AR(2) process defined in equation 6.5 and the MA(1) process defined in equation 6.3. This is shown in equation 6.6.

$$ARMA(2,1) := y_t = C + \phi_1 y_{t-1} + \phi_2 y_{t-2} + \mu + \epsilon_t + \theta_1\epsilon_{t-1}$$ **Equation 6.6**

In the case where $p = 0$, we have an ARMA(0,q) process, which is equivalent to a pure MA(q) process as seen in chapter 4. Similarly, if $q = 0$, we have an ARMA(p,0) process, which is equivalent to a pure AR(p) process, as seen in chapter 5.

We can see now how the order p only affects the autoregressive portion of the process by determining the number of past values to include in the equation. Similarly, the order q only affects the moving average portion of the process by determining the number of past error terms to include in the equation of ARMA(p,q). Of course, the higher the orders p and q, the more terms that are included, and the more complex our process becomes.

In order to model and forecast an ARMA(p,q) process, we need to find the orders p and q. That way, we can use an ARMA(p,q) model to fit the available data and produce forecasts.

6.3 *Identifying a stationary ARMA process*

Now that we've defined the autoregressive moving average process and seen how the orders p and q affect the model's equation, we need to determine how to identify such an underlying process in a given time series.

We'll extend the steps that we defined in chapter 5 to include the final possibility that we have an ARMA(p,q) process, as shown in figure 6.3.

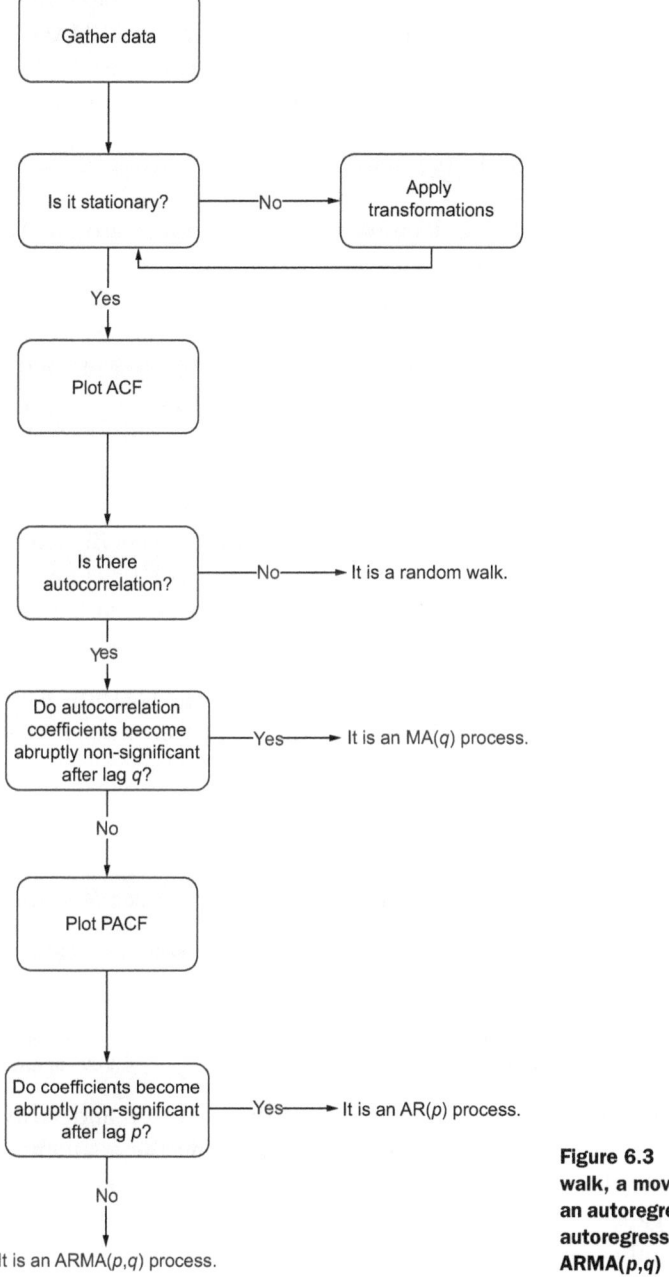

Figure 6.3   Steps to identify a random walk, a moving average process MA(q), an autoregressive process AR(p), and an autoregressive moving average process ARMA(p,q)

In figure 6.3 you'll notice that if neither of the ACF and PACF plots shows a clear cut-off between significant and non-significant coefficients, then we have an ARMA(p,q) process. To verify that, let's simulate our own ARMA process.

We'll simulate an ARMA(1,1) process. This is equivalent to combining an MA(1) process with an AR(1) process. Specifically, we will simulate the ARMA(1,1) process defined in equation 6.7. Notice that the constant C and mean µ are both equal to 0 here. The coefficients 0.33 and 0.9 are subjective choices for this simulation.

$$y_t = 0.33y_{t-1} + 0.9\epsilon_{t-1} + \epsilon_t \qquad \textbf{Equation 6.7}$$

The objective of this simulation is to demonstrate that we cannot use the ACF plot to identify the order q of an ARMA(p,q) process, which in this case is 1, nor can we use the PACF plot to identify the order p of an ARMA(p,q) process, which in this case is 1 also.

We'll use the `ArmaProcess` function from the `statsmodels` library to simulate our ARMA(1,1) process. As in previous chapters, we'll define the array of coefficients for the AR(1) process, as well as for the MA(1) process. From equation 6.7, we know our AR(1) process will have a coefficient of 0.33. However, keep in mind that the function expects to have the coefficient of the autoregressive process with its opposite sign, as this is how it is implemented in the `statsmodels` library. Therefore, we input it as –0.33. For the moving average portion, equation 6.7 specifies that the coefficient is 0.9. Also recall that when defining your arrays of coefficients, the first coefficient is always equal to 1, as specified by the library, which represents the coefficient at lag 0. Once our coefficients are defined, we will generate 1,000 data points.

> **NOTE**   The source code for this chapter is available on GitHub: https://github.com/marcopeix/TimeSeriesForecastingInPython/tree/master/CH06.

```
from statsmodels.tsa.arima_process import ArmaProcess
import numpy as np

np.random.seed(42)

ar1 = np.array([1, -0.33])
ma1 = np.array([1, 0.9])

ARMA_1_1 = ArmaProcess(ar1, ma1).generate_sample(nsample=1000)
```

Define the coefficients for the AR(1) portion. Remember that the first coefficient is always 1, as specified by the documentation. Also, we must write the coefficient of the AR portion with the opposite sign of what is defined in equation 6.7.

Define the coefficients for the MA(1) portion. The first coefficient is 1, for lag 0, as specified by the documentation.

Generate 1,000 samples.

With our simulated data ready, we can move on to the next step and verify whether our process is stationary or not. We can do this by running the augmented Dickey-Fuller (ADF) test. We'll print out the ADF statistic as well as the p-value. If the ADF statistic is a large negative number, and if we have a p-value smaller than 0.05, we can reject the null hypothesis and conclude that we have a stationary process.

```
from statsmodels.tsa.stattools import adfuller

ADF_result = adfuller(ARMA_1_1)

print(f'ADF Statistic: {ADF_result[0]}')
print(f'p-value: {ADF_result[1]}')
```

Run the ADF test on the simulated ARMA(1,1) data.

This returns an ADF statistic of –6.43 and a p-value of $1.7{\times}10^{-8}$. Since we have a large negative ADF statistic and a p-value that's much smaller than 0.05, we can conclude that our simulated ARMA(1,1) process is stationary.

Following the steps outlined in figure 6.3, we'll plot the ACF and see if we can infer the order of the moving average portion of our simulated ARMA(1,1) process. Again, we'll use the `plot_acf` function from `statsmodels` to generate figure 6.4.

```
from statsmodels.graphics.tsaplots import plot_acf

plot_acf(ARMA_1_1, lags=20);

plt.tight_layout()
```

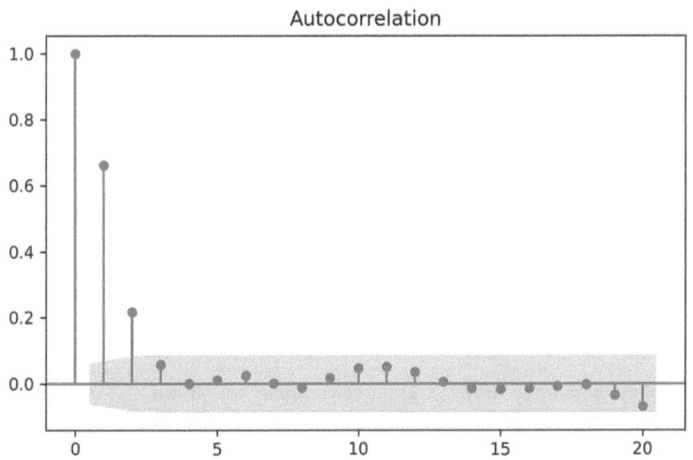

Figure 6.4   ACF plot of our simulated ARMA(1,1) process. Notice the sinusoidal pattern on the plot, meaning that an AR(p) process is in play. Also, the last significant coefficient is at lag 2, which suggests that $q = 2$. However, we know that we simulated an ARMA(1,1) process, so q must be equal to 1! Therefore, the ACF plot cannot be used to infer the order q of an ARMA(p,q) process.

In figure 6.4 you'll notice a sinusoidal pattern in the plot, which indicates the presence of an autoregressive process. This is expected, since we simulated an ARMA(1,1) process and we know of the existence of the autoregressive portion. Furthermore, you'll notice that the last significant coefficient is at lag 2. However, we know that our simulated data has an MA(1) process, so we would expect to have significant coefficients up to lag 1 only. We can thus conclude that the ACF plot does not reveal any useful information about the order q of our ARMA(1,1) process.

We can now move on to the next step outlined in figure 6.3 and plot the PACF. In chapter 5 you learned that the PACF can be used to find the order of a stationary AR(p) process. We will now verify whether we can find the order p of our simulated

ARMA(1,1) process, where p = 1. We'll use the `plot_pacf` function to generate figure 6.5.

```
from statsmodels.graphics.tsaplots import plot_pacf
```

```
plot_pacf(ARMA_1_1, lags=20);
```

```
plt.tight_layout()
```

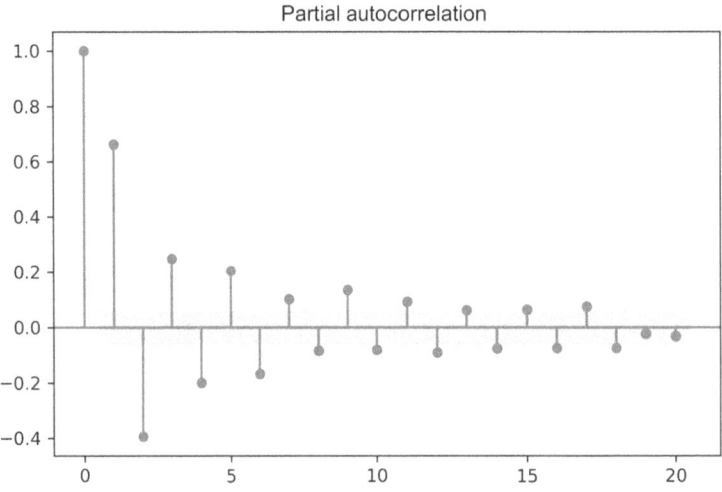

Figure 6.5   PACF plot of our simulated ARMA(1,1) process. Again, we have a sinusoidal pattern with no clear cutoff between significant and non-significant coefficients. From this plot, we cannot infer that p = 1 in our simulated ARMA(1,1) process, meaning that we cannot determine the order *p* of an ARMA(*p*,*q*) process using a PACF plot.

In figure 6.5 we can see a clear sinusoidal pattern, meaning that we cannot infer a value for the order *p*. We know that we simulated an ARMA(1,1) process, but we cannot determine that value from the PACF plot in figure 6.5, since we have significant coefficients past lag 1. Therefore, the PACF plot cannot be used to find the order *p* of an ARMA(*p*,*q*) process.

According to figure 6.3, since there is no clear cutoff between significant and non-significant coefficients in both the ACF and PACF plots, we can conclude that we have an ARMA(*p*,*q*) process, which is indeed the case.

> ### Identifying a stationary ARMA(*p*,*q*) process
> If your process is stationary and both the ACF and PACF plots show a decaying or sinusoidal pattern, then it is a stationary ARMA(*p*,*q*) process.

We know that determining the order of our process is key in modeling and forecasting, since the order will dictate how many parameters must be included in our model. Since the ACF and PACF plots are not useful in the case of an ARMA(p,q) process, we must thus devise a general modeling procedure that will allow us to find the appropriate combination of (p,q) for our model.

6.4 Devising a general modeling procedure

In the previous section, we covered the steps for identifying a stationary ARMA(p,q) process. We saw that if both the ACF and PACF plots display a sinusoidal or decaying pattern, our time series can be modeled by an ARMA(p,q) process. However, neither plot was useful for determining the orders p and q. With our simulated ARMA(1,1) process, we noticed that coefficients were significant after lag 1 in both plots.

Therefore, we must devise a procedure that allows us to find the orders p and q. This procedure will have the advantage that it can also be applied in situations where our time series is non-stationary and has seasonal effects. Furthermore, it will also be suitable for cases where p or q are equal to 0, meaning that we can move away from plotting the ACF and PACF and rely entirely on a model selection criterion and residual analysis. The steps are shown in figure 6.6.

In figure 6.6 you can see that this new modeling procedure completely removes the plotting of the ACF and PACF. It allows us to select a model based entirely on statistical tests and numerical criteria, instead of relying on the qualitative analysis of the ACF and PACF plots.

The first few steps remain unchanged from those we gradually built up until chapter 5, as we must still gather the data, test for stationarity, and apply transformations accordingly. Then we list different possible values of p and q—note that they only take positive integers. With a list of possible values, we can fit every unique combination of ARMA(p,q) to our data.

Once that's done, we can compute the *Akaike information criterion* (AIC), which is discussed at length in sections 6.4.1 and 6.4.2. This quantifies the quality of each model in relation to each other. The model with the lowest AIC is then selected.

From there, we can analyze the model's residuals, which is the difference between the actual and predicted values of the model. Ideally, the residuals will look like white noise, which would mean that any difference between the predicted values and actual values is due to randomness. Therefore, the residuals must be uncorrelated and independently distributed. We can assess those properties by studying the *quantile-quantile plot* (Q-Q plot) and running the *Ljung-Box test*, which we'll explore in section 6.4.3. If the analysis leads us to conclude that the residuals are completely random, we have a model ready for forecasting. Otherwise, we must try a different set of values for p and q and start the process over.

A lot of new concepts and techniques will be introduced as we work through our new general modeling procedure. We will dive into each step in detail in future sections

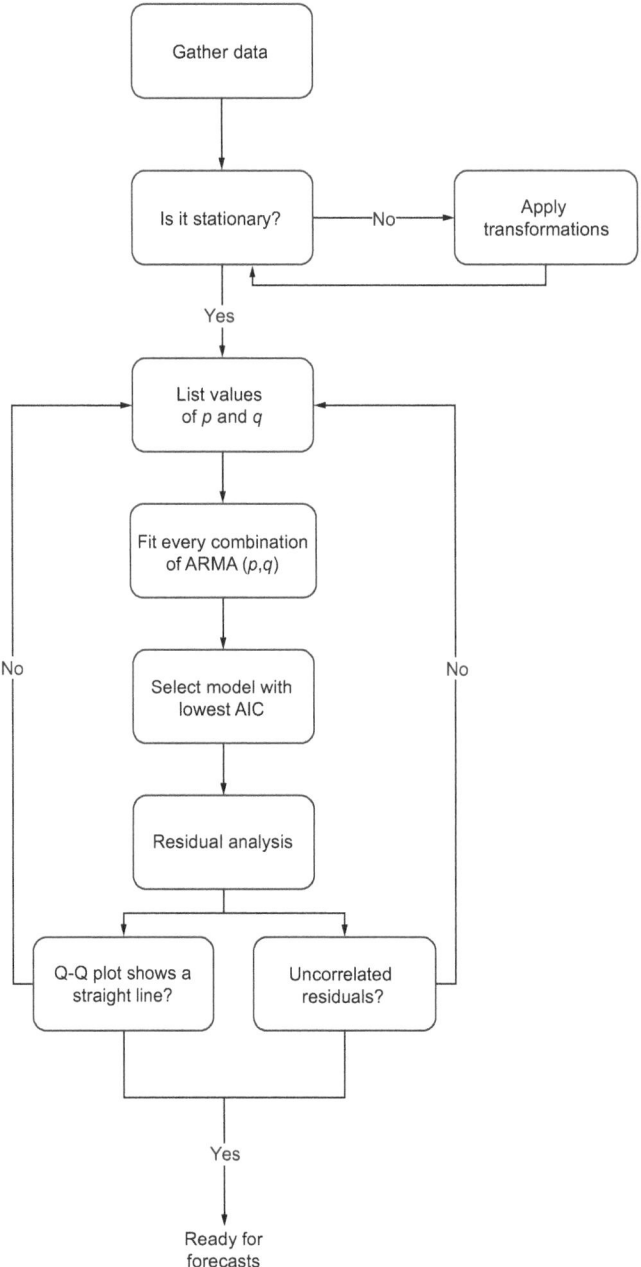

Figure 6.6 **General modeling procedure for an ARMA(p,q) process. The first steps are to gather the data, test for stationarity, and apply transformations accordingly. Then we define a list of possible values for p and q. We then fit every combination of ARMA(p,q) to our data and select the model with the lowest AIC. Then we perform the residual analysis by looking at the Q-Q plot and the residual correlogram. If they approach that of white noise, the model can be used for forecasts. Otherwise, we must try different values for p and q.**

and work with our simulated ARMA(1,1) process. Then we will apply the same procedure to model bandwidth usage.

6.4.1   *Understanding the Akaike information criterion (AIC)*

Before covering the steps outlined in figure 6.6, we need to determine how we will choose the best model of all the models that we will fit. Here we will use the Akaike information criterion (AIC) to select the optimal model.

The AIC estimates the quality of a model relative to other models. Given that there will be some information lost when a model is fitted to the data, the AIC quantifies the relative amount of information lost by the model. The less information lost, the lower the AIC value and the better the model.

The AIC is a function of the number of estimated parameters k and the maximum value of the likelihood function for the model $\hat{L}$, as shown in equation 6.8.

$$\text{AIC} = 2k - 2\ln(\hat{L})$$

Equation 6.8

> **Akaike information criterion (AIC)**
>
> The Akaike information criterion (AIC) is a measure of the quality of a model in relation to other models. It is used for model selection.
>
> The AIC is a function of the number of parameters k in a model and the maximum value of the likelihood function $\hat{L}$:
>
> $$\text{AIC} = 2k - 2\ln(\hat{L})$$
>
> The lower the value of the AIC, the better the model. Selecting according to the AIC allows us to keep a balance between the complexity of a model and its goodness of fit to the data.

The number of estimated parameters k is directly related to the order (p,q) of an ARMA(p,q) model. If we fit an ARMA(2,2) model, then we have $2 + 2 = 4$ parameters to estimate. If we fit an ARMA(3,4) model, then we have $3 + 4 = 7$ parameters to estimate. You can see how fitting a more complex model can penalize the AIC score: as the order (p,q) increases, the number of parameters k increases, and so the AIC increases.

The likelihood function measures the goodness of fit of a model. It can be viewed as the opposite of the distribution function. Given a model with fixed parameters, the distribution function will measure the probability of observing a data point. The likelihood function flips the logic. Given a set of observed data, it will estimate how likely it is that different model parameters will generate the observed data.

For example, consider the situation where we roll a six-sided die. The distribution function tells us that there is a $1/6$ probability that we'll observe one of these values: [1,2,3,4,5,6]. Now let's flip this logic to explain the likelihood function. Suppose that you roll a die 10 times and you obtain the following values: [1,5,3,4,6,2,4,3,2,1]. The likelihood function will determine how likely it is that the die has six sides. Applying this logic to the context of AIC, we can think of the likelihood function as an answer to the question "How likely is it that my observed data is coming from an ARMA(1,1) model?" If it is very likely, meaning that $\hat{L}$ is large, then the ARMA(1,1) model fits the data well.

Therefore, if a model fits the data really well, the maximum value of the likelihood will be high. Since the AIC subtracts the natural logarithm of the maximum value of the likelihood, represented by $\hat{L}$ in equation 6.8, then a large value of $\hat{L}$ will lower the AIC.

You can see how the AIC keeps a balance between underfitting and overfitting. Remember that the lower the AIC, the better the model relative to other models. Therefore, an overfitting model would have a very good fit, meaning that $\hat{L}$ is large and AIC decreases. However, the number of parameters k would be large as well, which penalizes the AIC. An underfitting model would have a small number of parameters, so k would be small. However, the maximum value of the likelihood function would also be small due to the poor fit, meaning again that the AIC is penalized. Thus, the AIC allows us to find a balance between the number of parameters in a model and a good fit to the training data.

Finally, we must keep in mind that the AIC quantifies the quality of a model in relation to other models only. It is therefore a relative measure of quality. In the event that we fit only poor models to our data, the AIC will simply help us determine the best from that group of models.

Now let's use the AIC to help us select an appropriate model for our simulated ARMA(1,1) process.

6.4.2   *Selecting a model using the AIC*

We'll now cover the steps of the general modeling procedure outlined in figure 6.6 using our simulated ARMA(1,1) process.

In section 6.3 we tested for stationarity and concluded that our simulated process is already stationary. Therefore, we can move on to defining a list of possible values for p and q. While we know the values of both orders from the simulation, let's consider the following steps as a demonstration that the general modeling procedure works.

We will allow the values of p and q to vary from 0 to 3. Note that this range is arbitrary, and you may try a larger range of values if you wish. We will create a list of all possible combinations of (p,q), using the `product` function from `itertools`. Since there four possible values for p and q, this will generate a list of 16 unique combinations of (p,q).

```
from itertools import product

ps = range(0, 4, 1)          ◁─── Create a list of possible values for p starting from 0 inclusively to 4 exclusively, with steps of 1.
qs = range(0, 4, 1)          ◁─── Create a list of possible values for q starting from 0 inclusively to 4 exclusively, with steps of 1.

order_list = list(product(ps, qs))   ◁─── Generate a list containing all unique combinations of (p,q).
```

With our list of possible values created, we must now fit all unique 16 ARMA(p,q) models to our simulated data. To do so, we'll define an `optimize_ARMA` function that takes the data and the list of unique (p,q) combinations as input. Inside the function, we'll initialize an empty list to store each (p,q) combination and its corresponding AIC. Then we'll iterate over each (p,q) combination and fit an ARMA(p,q) model to our data. We'll compute the AIC and store the result. Then we'll create a `DataFrame` and sort it by AIC value in ascending order, since the lower the AIC, the better the model. Our function will finally output the ordered `DataFrame` so we can select the appropriate model. The `optimize_ARMA` function is shown in the following listing.

Listing 6.1 Function to fit all unique ARMA(*p,q*) models

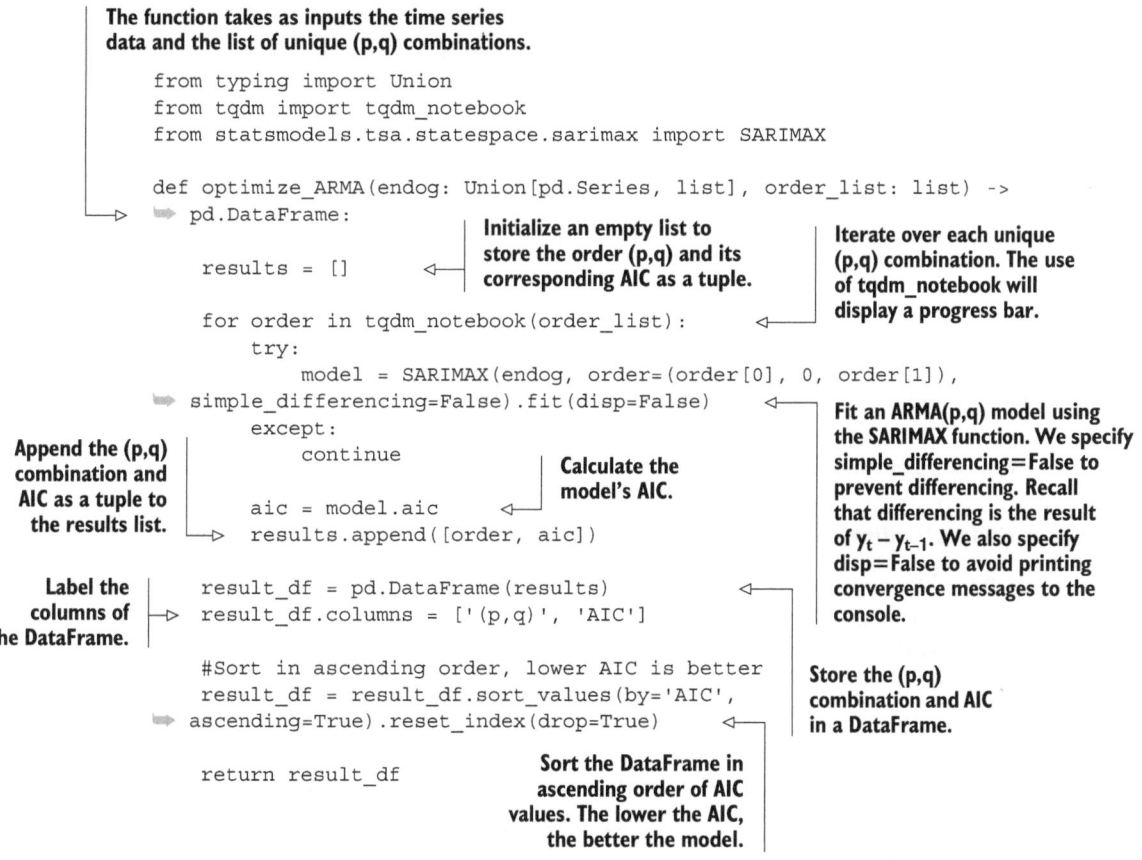

The function takes as inputs the time series data and the list of unique (p,q) combinations.

```
from typing import Union
from tqdm import tqdm_notebook
from statsmodels.tsa.statespace.sarimax import SARIMAX

def optimize_ARMA(endog: Union[pd.Series, list], order_list: list) ->
    pd.DataFrame:

    results = []

    for order in tqdm_notebook(order_list):
        try:
            model = SARIMAX(endog, order=(order[0], 0, order[1]),
    simple_differencing=False).fit(disp=False)
        except:
            continue

        aic = model.aic
        results.append([order, aic])

    result_df = pd.DataFrame(results)
    result_df.columns = ['(p,q)', 'AIC']

    #Sort in ascending order, lower AIC is better
    result_df = result_df.sort_values(by='AIC',
    ascending=True).reset_index(drop=True)

    return result_df
```

Initialize an empty list to store the order (p,q) and its corresponding AIC as a tuple.

Iterate over each unique (p,q) combination. The use of tqdm_notebook will display a progress bar.

Fit an ARMA(p,q) model using the SARIMAX function. We specify simple_differencing=False to prevent differencing. Recall that differencing is the result of $y_t - y_{t-1}$. We also specify disp=False to avoid printing convergence messages to the console.

Append the (p,q) combination and AIC as a tuple to the results list.

Calculate the model's AIC.

Label the columns of the DataFrame.

Store the (p,q) combination and AIC in a DataFrame.

Sort the DataFrame in ascending order of AIC values. The lower the AIC, the better the model.

With our function defined, we can now use it and fit the different ARMA(p,q) models. The output is shown in figure 6.7. You'll see that the model with the lowest AIC corresponds to an ARMA(1,1) model, which is exactly the process that we simulated.

```
result_df = optimize_ARMA(ARMA_1_1, order_list)
result_df
```

Fit the different ARMA(p,q) models on the simulated ARMA(1,1) data.

Display the resulting DataFrame.

	(p,q)	AIC
0	(1, 1)	2801.407785
1	(2, 1)	2802.906070
2	(1, 2)	2802.967762
3	(0, 3)	2803.666793
4	(1, 3)	2804.524027
5	(3, 1)	2804.588567
6	(2, 2)	2804.822282
7	(3, 3)	2805.947168
8	(2, 3)	2806.175380
9	(3, 2)	2806.894930
10	(0, 2)	2812.840730
11	(0, 1)	2891.869245
12	(3, 0)	2981.643911
13	(2, 0)	3042.627787
14	(1, 0)	3207.291261
15	(0, 0)	3780.418416

Figure 6.7   Resulting `DataFrame` from fitting all ARMA(p,q) models to the simulated ARMA(1,1) data. We can see that the model with the lowest AIC corresponds to an ARMA(1,1) model, meaning that we successfully identified the order of our simulated data.

As mentioned in the previous section, the AIC is a measure of relative quality. Here we can say that an ARMA(1,1) model is the best model relative to all other models that we fit to our data. Now we need an absolute measure of the model's quality. This brings us to the next step of our modeling procedure, which is residual analysis.

6.4.3   *Understanding residual analysis*

Up to this point, we have fit different ARMA(p,q) models to our simulated ARMA(1,1) process. Using the AIC as a model selection criterion, we found that an ARMA(1,1) model is the best model relative to all others that were fit. Now we must measure its absolute quality by performing an analysis on the model's residuals.

This brings us to the last steps before forecasting, which is residual analysis and answering the two questions in figure 6.8: does the Q-Q plot show a straight line, and are the residuals uncorrelated? If the answer to both questions is yes, then we have a model that's ready to make forecasts. Otherwise, we must try different combinations of (p,q) and restart the process.

The residuals of a model are simply the difference between the predicted values and the actual values. Consider our simulated ARMA(1,1) process expressed in equation 6.9.

$$y_t = 0.33y_{t-1} + 0.9\epsilon_{t-1} + \epsilon_t$$ **Equation 6.9**

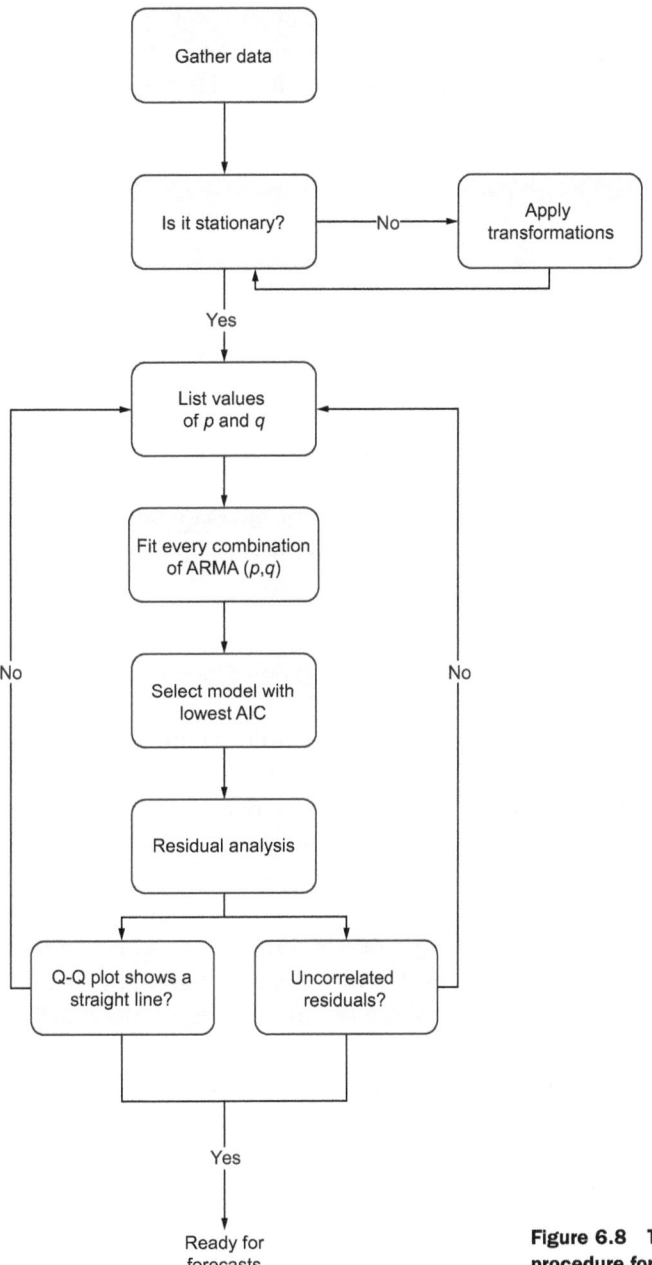

Figure 6.8   **The general modeling procedure for an ARMA(p,q) process**

Now suppose that we fit an ARMA(1,1) model to our process, and we estimate the model's coefficients perfectly, such that the model is expressed as equation 6.10.

$$\widehat{y_t} = 0.33y_{t-1} + 0.9\epsilon_{t-1}$$

Equation 6.10

The residuals will be the difference between the values coming from our model and the observed values from our simulated process. In other words, the residuals are the difference between equation 6.9 and equation 6.10. The result is shown in equation 6.11.

$$\text{residuals} = 0.33y_{t-1} + 0.9\epsilon_{t-1} + \epsilon_t - (0.33y_{t-1} + 0.9)$$

$$\text{residuals} = \epsilon_t \qquad \text{\textbf{Equation 6.11}}$$

As you can see in equation 6.11, in a perfect situation the residuals of a model are white noise. This indicates that the model has captured all predictive information, and there is only a random fluctuation left that cannot be modeled. Thus, the residuals must be uncorrelated and have a normal distribution in order for us to conclude that we have a good model for making forecasts.

There are two aspects to residual analysis: a qualitative analysis and a quantitative analysis. The qualitative analysis focuses on studying the Q-Q plot, while the quantitative analysis determines whether our residuals are uncorrelated.

QUALITATIVE ANALYSIS: STUDYING THE Q-Q PLOT

The first step in residual analysis is the study of the *quantile-quantile plot* (Q-Q plot). The Q-Q plot is a graphical tool for verifying our hypothesis that the model's residuals are normally distributed.

The Q-Q plot is constructed by plotting the quantiles of our residuals on the *y*-axis against the quantiles of a theoretical distribution, in this case the normal distribution, on the *x*-axis. This results in a scatterplot. We are comparing the distribution to a normal distribution because we want the residuals to be similar to white noise, which is normally distributed.

If both distributions are similar, meaning that the distribution of the residuals is close to a normal distribution, the Q-Q plot will display a straight line that approximately lies on *y* = *x*. This in turn means that our model is a good fit for our data. You can see an example of a Q-Q plot where the residuals are normally distributed in figure 6.9.

On the other hand, a Q-Q plot of residuals that are not close to a normal distribution will generate a curve that departs from *y* = *x*. In figure 6.10 you can see that the thick line is not straight and not lying on *y* = *x*. If we get this sort of result, we can conclude that the distribution of our residuals does not resemble a normal distribution, which is a sign that our model is not a good fit for our data. Therefore, we must try a different range of values for *p* and *q*, fit the models, select the one with the lowest AIC, and perform residual analysis on the new model.

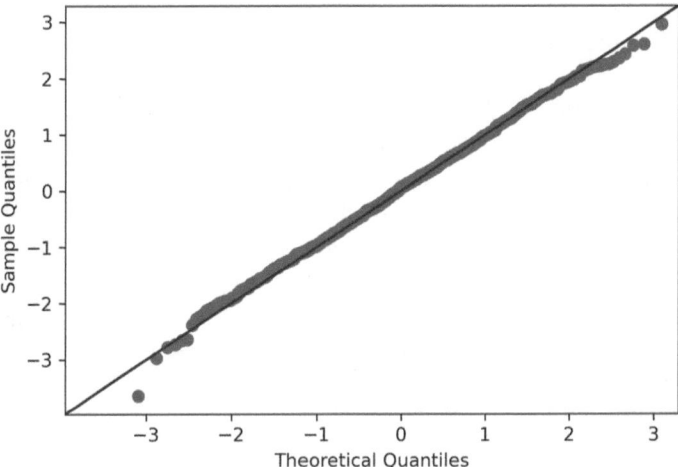

Figure 6.9   A Q-Q plot of randomly distributed residuals. On the *y*-axis, we have the quantiles coming from the residuals. On the *x*-axis, we have the quantiles coming from a theoretical normal distribution. You can see a straight line approximately lying on *y* = *x*. This is an indication that our residuals are very close to a normal distribution.

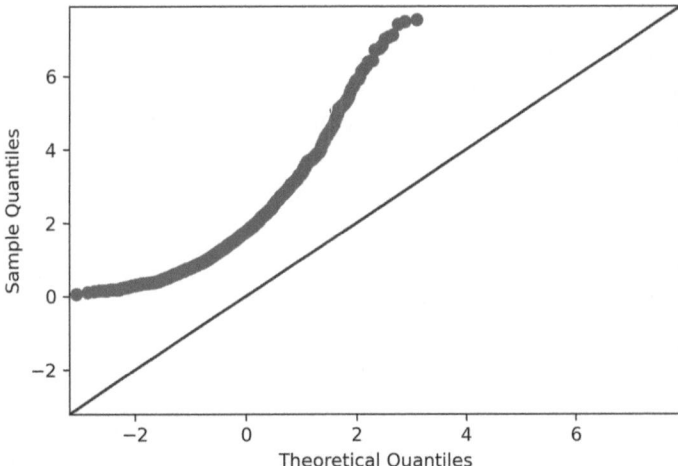

Figure 6.10   A Q-Q plot of residuals that are not close to a normal distribution. You can clearly see that the thick line is curved, and it is not lying on *y* = *x*. Therefore, the distribution of the residuals is very different from a normal distribution.

Quantile-quantile plot (Q-Q plot)

A Q-Q plot is a plot of the quantiles of two distributions against each other. In time series forecasting, we plot the distribution of our residuals on the *y*-axis against the theoretical normal distribution on the *x*-axis.

This graphical tool allows to us to assess the goodness of fit of our model. If the distribution of our residuals is similar to a normal distribution, we will see a straight line lying on *y* = *x*. This means that our model is a good fit, because the residuals are similar to white noise.

On the other hand, if the distribution of our residuals is different from a normal distribution, we will see a curved line. We can then conclude that our model is not a good fit, since the residuals' distribution is not close to a normal distribution, and therefore the residuals are not similar to white noise.

You can see how the Q-Q plot can help us. We know that if a model is a good fit to our data, the residuals will be similar to white noise and therefore will have similar properties. This means that they should be normally distributed. Hence, if the Q-Q plot displays a straight line, we have a good model. Otherwise, our model must be discarded, and we must try to fit a better model.

While the Q-Q plot is a fast method for assessing the quality of our model, this analysis remains subjective. Thus, we will further support our residual analysis with a quantitative method by applying the Ljung-Box test.

QUANTITATIVE ANALYSIS: APPLYING THE LJUNG-BOX TEST

Once we have analyzed the Q-Q plot and determined that our residuals are approximately normally distributed, we can then apply the Ljung-Box test to demonstrate that the residuals are uncorrelated. Remember that a good model has residuals that are similar to white noise, so the residuals should be normally distributed and uncorrelated.

The Ljung-Box test is a statistical test that tests if the autocorrelation of a group of data is significantly different from 0. In our case, we will apply the Ljung-Box test to the model's residuals to assess whether they are correlated or not. The null hypothesis states that the data is independently distributed, meaning that there is no autocorrelation.

Ljung-Box test

The Ljung-Box test is a statistical test that determines whether the autocorrelation of a group of data is significantly different from 0.

In time series forecasting, we apply the Ljung-Box test on the model's residuals to test whether they are similar to white noise. The null hypothesis states that the data is independently distributed, meaning that there is no autocorrelation. If the p-value is larger than 0.05, we cannot reject the null hypothesis, meaning that the residuals are independently distributed. Therefore, there is no autocorrelation, the residuals are similar to white noise, and the model can be used for forecasting.

> If the p-value is less than 0.05, we reject the null hypothesis, meaning that our resid-
> uals are not independently distributed and are correlated. The model cannot be used
> for forecasting.

The test will return the Ljung-Box statistic and a p-value. If the p-value is less than 0.05, we reject the null hypothesis, meaning that the residuals are not independently distributed, which in turn means that there is autocorrelation. In such a situation, the residuals do not approximate the properties of white noise, and the model must be discarded.

If the p-value is larger than 0.05, we cannot reject the null hypothesis, meaning that our residuals are independently distributed. Thus, there is no autocorrelation, and the residuals are similar to white noise. This means that we can move on with our model and make forecasts.

Now that you understand the concepts of residual analysis, let's apply these techniques to our simulated ARMA(1,1) process.

6.4.4 *Performing residual analysis*

We will now resume the modeling procedure for our simulated ARMA(1,1) process. We have successfully selected a model with the lowest AIC, which was expectedly an ARMA(1,1) model. Now, as you can see in figure 6.11, we need to perform residual analysis to assess whether our model is a good fit to the data.

We know that our ARMA(1,1) model must be good, since we simulated an ARMA(1,1) process, but this section will demonstrate that our modeling procedure works. We are not likely to be modeling and forecasting simulated data in a business context, so it is important to cover the entire modeling procedure on a known process first, to convince ourselves that it works, before applying it on real-life data.

To perform residual analysis, we need to fit our model and store the residuals in a variable for easy access. Using statsmodels, we will first define an ARMA(1,1) model before fitting it to our simulated data. Then we can access the residuals with the resid property.

```
model = SARIMAX(ARMA_1_1, order=(1,0,1), simple_differencing=False)
model_fit = model.fit(disp=False)
residuals = model_fit.resid      ◁——— Store the model's residuals.
```

The next step is to plot the Q-Q plot, and we'll use the qqplot function from stats-models to display our residuals against a normal distribution. The function simply requires the data, and it will by default compare its distribution to a normal distribution. We'll also need to display the line $y = x$ in order to assess the similarity of both distributions.

```
from statsmodels.graphics.gofplots import qqplot

qqplot(residuals, line='45');    ◁——| Plot the Q-Q plot of the residuals.
                                     | Specify the display of the line y = x.
```

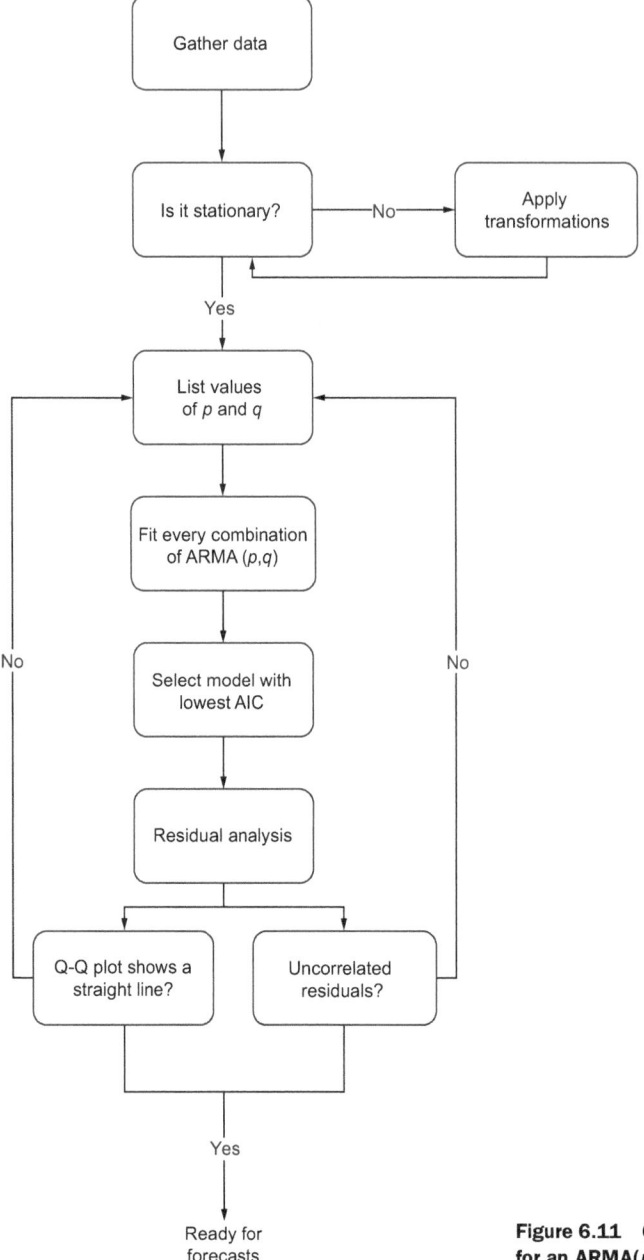

Figure 6.11   General modeling procedure for an ARMA(*p,q*) process

The result is shown in figure 6.12. You will see a thick straight line that approximately lies on *y* = *x*. Therefore, from a qualitative standpoint, the model's residuals seem to be normally distributed, just like white noise, which is an indication that our model fits the data well.

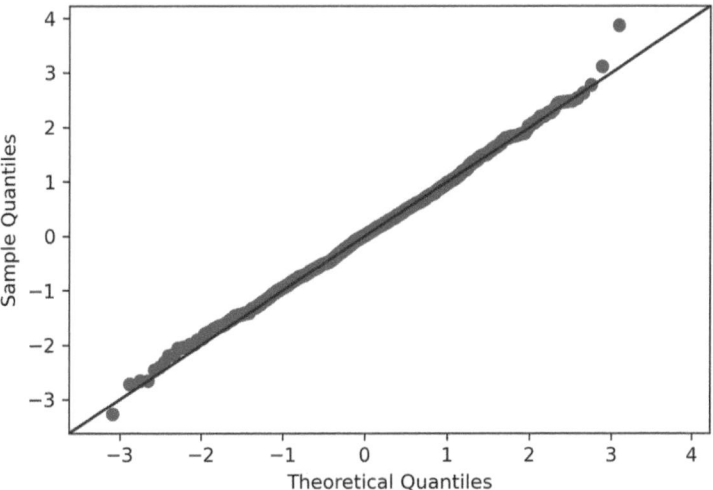

Figure 6.12 Q-Q plot of our ARMA(1,1) residuals. You can see a thick straight line lying on *y* = *x*. This means that our residuals are normally distributed, just like white noise.

We'll extend our qualitative analysis by using the `plot_diagnostics` method. This generates a figure containing four different plots, including a Q-Q plot.

```
model_fit.plot_diagnostics(figsize=(10, 8));
```

The result is shown in figure 6.13. You can see how `statsmodels` makes it easy for us to qualitatively analyze the residuals.

The top-left plot shows the residuals across the entire dataset. You can see that there is no trend, and the mean seems stable over time, which is indicative of stationarity, just like white noise.

The top-right plot shows a histogram of the residuals. You can see the shape of a normal distribution on this plot, which again indicates that the residuals are close to white noise, as white noise is normally distributed as well.

At the bottom left, we have the Q-Q plot, which is identical to figure 6.12, and therefore leads us to the same conclusion.

Finally, the bottom-right plot shows the autocorrelation function of our residuals. You can see that there is only a significant peak at lag 0, and no significant coefficients otherwise. This means that the residuals are not correlated, which further supports the conclusion that they are similar to white noise, which is what we expect from a good model.

The final step in residual analysis is applying the Ljung-Box test. This allows us to quantitatively assess whether our residuals are indeed uncorrelated. We will use the `acorr_ljungbox` function from `statsmodels` to perform the Ljung-Box test on the residuals. The function takes as input the residuals as well as a list of lags. Here we will compute the Ljung-Box statistic and p-value for 10 lags.

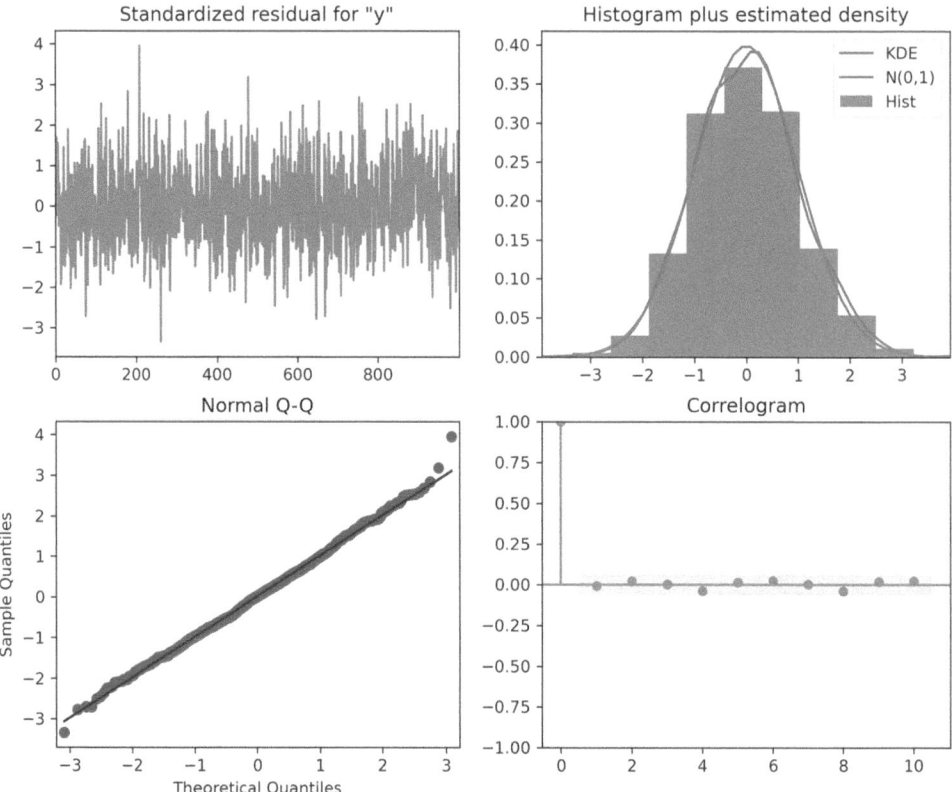

Figure 6.13 Model diagnostics from `statsmodels`. The top-left plot displays the residuals, the histogram of the residuals is at the top right, the Q-Q plot of the residuals is at the bottom left, and the bottom right shows the ACF plot of the residuals.

```
from statsmodels.stats.diagnostic import acorr_ljungbox

lbvalue, pvalue = acorr_ljungbox(residuals, np.arange(1, 11, 1))
```

`print(pvalue)` ◀— **Display the p-value for each lag.**   **Apply the Ljung-Box test on the residuals, on 10 lags.**

The resulting list of p-values shows that each is above 0.05. Therefore, at each lag, the null hypothesis cannot be rejected, meaning that the residuals are independently distributed and uncorrelated.

We can conclude from our analysis that the residuals are similar to white noise. The Q-Q plot showed a straight line, meaning that the residuals are normally distributed. Furthermore, the Ljung-Box test shows that the residuals are uncorrelated, just like white noise. Thus, the residuals are completely random, meaning that we have a model that fits our data well.

Now let's apply the same modeling procedure to the bandwidth dataset.

6.5 *Applying the general modeling procedure*

We now have a general modeling procedure that allows us to model and forecast a general ARMA(p,q) model, as outlined in figure 6.14. We applied this procedure to our simulated ARMA(1,1) process and found that the best fit was an ARMA(1,1) model, as expected.

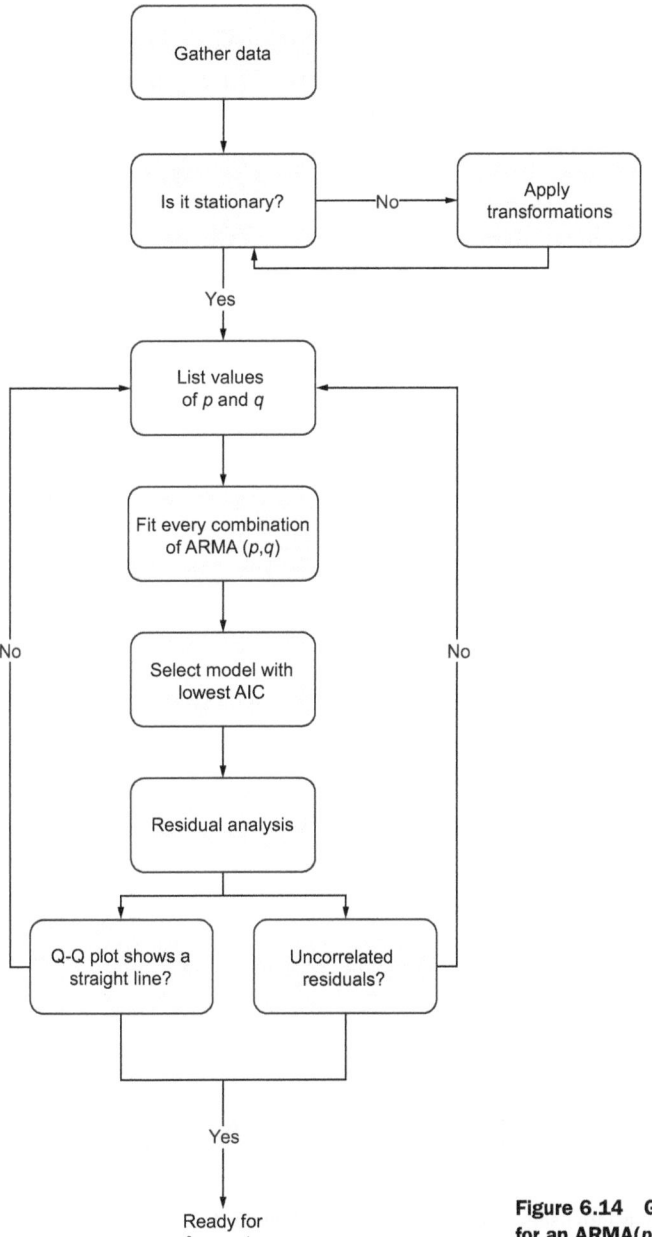

Figure 6.14   General modeling procedure for an ARMA(p,q) process

Now we can apply the same procedure on the bandwidth dataset to obtain the best model possible for this situation. Recall that our objective is to forecast bandwidth usage for the next 2 hours.

The first step is to gather and load the data using pandas:

```
import pandas as pd

df = pd.read_csv('data/bandwidth.csv')
```

We can then plot our time series and look for a trend or a seasonal pattern. By now, you should be comfortable with plotting your time series. The result is shown in figure 6.15.

```
import matplotlib.pyplot as plt

fig, ax = plt.subplots()

ax.plot(df.hourly_bandwidth)
ax.set_xlabel('Time')
ax.set_ylabel('Hourly bandwith usage (MBps)')

plt.xticks(
    np.arange(0, 10000, 730),
    ['Jan', 'Feb', 'Mar', 'Apr', 'May', 'Jun', 'Jul', 'Aug', 'Sep', 'Oct',
➡  'Nov', 'Dec', '2020', 'Feb'])

fig.autofmt_xdate()
plt.tight_layout()
```

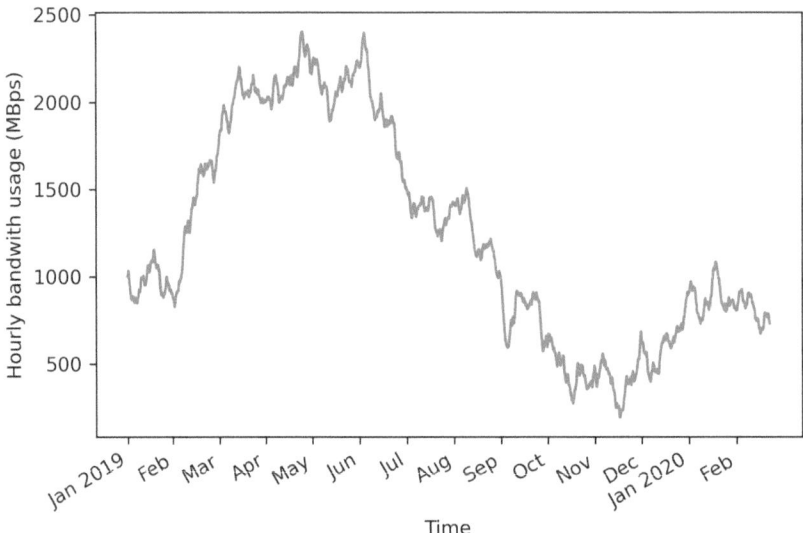

Figure 6.15   Hourly bandwidth usage in a data center since January 1, 2019. The dataset contains 10,000 points.

With the data plotted in figure 6.15, you can see that there is no periodic pattern in the data. However, you'll notice the presence of a long-term trend, meaning that our data is likely not stationary. Let's apply the ADF test to verify our hypothesis. Again, we'll use the adfuller function from statsmodels and print out the ADF statistic and the p-value.

```
from statsmodels.tsa.stattools import adfuller

ADF_result = adfuller(df['hourly_bandwidth'])

print(f'ADF Statistic: {ADF_result[0]}')
print(f'p-value: {ADF_result[1]}')
```

This prints out an ADF statistic of –0.8 and a p-value of 0.80. Therefore, we cannot reject the null hypothesis, meaning that our time series is not stationary.

   We must apply a transformation to our data in order to make it stationary. Let's apply a first-order differencing using numpy.

```
import numpy as np

bandwidth_diff = np.diff(df.hourly_bandwidth, n=1)
```

With this done, we can apply the ADF test again, this time on the differenced data, in order to test for stationarity.

```
ADF_result = adfuller(bandwidth_diff)

print(f'ADF Statistic: {ADF_result[0]}')
print(f'p-value: {ADF_result[1]}')
```

This returns an ADF statistic of –20.69 and a p-value of 0.0. With a large, negative ADF statistic and a p-value that is much smaller than 0.05, we can say that our differenced series is stationary.

   We are now ready to start modeling our stationary process using an $ARMA(p,q)$ model. We'll split our series into train and test sets. Here we'll keep the last 7 days of data for the test set. Since our forecasts are for the next 2 hours, the test set thus contains 84 periods of 2 hours on which to evaluate our models' performance, since 7 days of hourly data totals 168 hours.

```
df_diff = pd.DataFrame({'bandwidth_diff': bandwidth_diff})

train = df_diff[:-168]
test = df_diff[-168:]          ◁────┐  There are 168 hours in a week,
                                     │  so we will assign the last 168
print(len(train))                    │  data points to the test set.
print(len(test))
```

We can print out the length of the train and test sets as a sanity check, and sure enough, the test set has 168 data points, and the train set has 9,831 data points.

   Now let's visualize our train set and test set for both the differenced and original series. The resulting plot is shown in figure 6.16.

```
fig, (ax1, ax2) = plt.subplots(nrows=2, ncols=1, sharex=True, figsize=(10,
➥  8))

ax1.plot(df.hourly_bandwidth)
ax1.set_xlabel('Time')
ax1.set_ylabel('Hourly bandwidth')
ax1.axvspan(9831, 10000, color='#808080', alpha=0.2)

ax2.plot(df_diff.bandwidth_diff)
ax2.set_xlabel('Time')
ax2.set_ylabel('Hourly bandwidth (diff)')
ax2.axvspan(9830, 9999, color='#808080', alpha=0.2)

plt.xticks(
    np.arange(0, 10000, 730),
    ['Jan', 'Feb', 'Mar', 'Apr', 'May', 'Jun', 'Jul', 'Aug', 'Sep', 'Oct',
➥  'Nov', 'Dec', '2020', 'Feb'])

fig.autofmt_xdate()
plt.tight_layout()
```

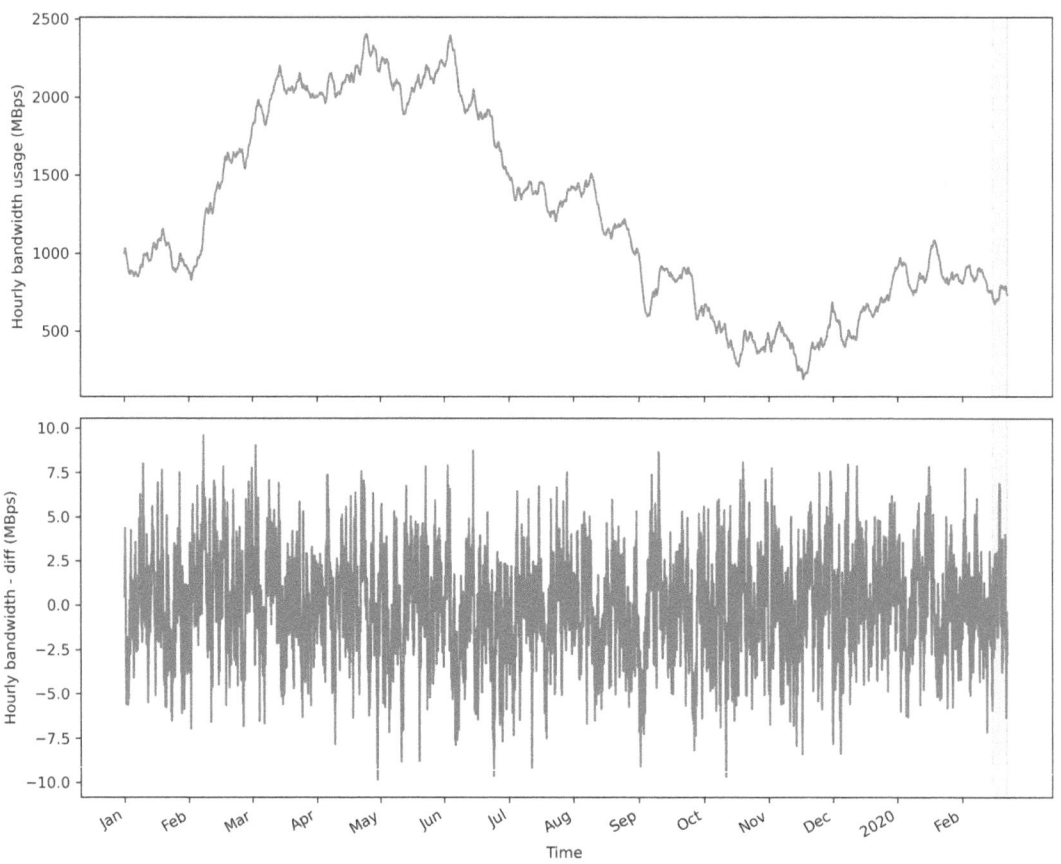

Figure 6.16 Train and test sets for the original and differenced series

With our train set ready, we can now fit different ARMA(p,q) models using the optimize_ ARMA function that we defined earlier. Remember that the function takes the data and the list of unique (p,q) combinations as input. Inside the function, we initialize an empty list to store each (p,q) combination and its corresponding AIC. Then we iterate over each (p,q) combination and fit an ARMA(p,q) model on our data. We compute the AIC and store the result. Then we create a DataFrame and sort it by AIC value in ascending order, since the lower the AIC, the better the model. Our function finally outputs the ordered DataFrame so we can select the appropriate model. The optimize_ ARMA function is shown in the following listing.

Listing 6.2 Function to fit all unique ARMA(p,q) models

The function takes as inputs the time series
data and the list of unique (p,q) combinations.

```
from typing import Union
from tqdm import tqdm_notebook
from statsmodels.tsa.statespace.sarimax import SARIMAX

def optimize_ARMA(endog: Union[pd.Series, list], order_list: list) ->
    pd.DataFrame:

        results = []          ◁──  Initialize an empty list to store the order
                                    (p,q) and its corresponding AIC as a tuple.

        for order in tqdm_notebook(order_list):          ◁──  Iterate over each unique
            try:                                              (p,q) combination. The use
                model = SARIMAX(endog, order=(order[0], 0, order[1]),   of tqdm_notebook will
        simple_differencing=False).fit(disp=False)        ◁──  display a progress bar.
            except:
                continue                                       Fit an ARMA(p,q) model
                                                               using the SARIMAX
            aic = model.aic          ◁──  Calculate the      function. We specify
            results.append([order, aic])   model's AIC.      simple_differencing=False
                                                             to prevent differencing. We
        result_df = pd.DataFrame(results)        ◁──         also specify disp=False to
        result_df.columns = ['(p,q)', 'AIC']                avoid printing convergence
                                                            messages to the console.
        #Sort in ascending order, lower AIC is better
        result_df = result_df.sort_values(by='AIC',         Store the (p,q)
    ascending=True).reset_index(drop=True)     ◁──          combination and AIC
                                                            in a DataFrame.
        return result_df
```

Append the (p,q)
combination and
AIC as a tuple to
the results list.

Label the
columns of the
DataFrame.

Sort the DataFrame in ascending
order of AIC value. The lower the
AIC, the better the model.

Here we will try values for p and q ranging from 0 to 3 inclusively. This means that we will fit 16 unique ARMA(p,q) models to our training set and select the one with the lowest AIC. Feel free to change the range of values for p and q, but keep in mind that a larger range will result in more models being fit and a longer computation time. Also, you don't need to worry about overfitting—we are selecting our model using the AIC, which will prevent us from selecting a model that overfits.

```
ps = range(0, 4, 1)        ◁──────┐  The order p can have the values {0,1,2,3}.
qs = range(0, 4, 1)        ◁──────┤
                                  │  The order q can have the values {0,1,2,3}.

order_list = list(product(ps, qs))    ◁───┐  Generate the unique (p,q) combinations.
```

With this step done, we can pass in our training set and the list of unique (p,q) combinations to the `optimize_ARMA` function.

```
result_df = optimize_ARMA(train['bandwidth_diff'], order_list)
result_df
```

The resulting `DataFrame` is shown in figure 6.17. You'll notice that the first three models all have an AIC of 27,991, with only slight differences. Therefore, I would argue that the ARMA(2,2) model is the model that should be selected. Its AIC value is very close to the ARMA(3,2) and ARMA(2,3) models, while being less complex, since it has four parameters to be estimated instead of five. Therefore, we'll select the ARMA(2,2) model and move on to the next steps, which is the analysis of the model's residuals.

	(p,q)	AIC
0	(3, 2)	27991.063879
1	(2, 3)	27991.287509
2	(2, 2)	27991.603598
3	(3, 3)	27993.416924
4	(1, 3)	28003.349550
5	(1, 2)	28051.351401
6	(3, 1)	28071.155496
7	(3, 0)	28095.618186
8	(2, 1)	28097.250766
9	(2, 0)	28098.407664
10	(1, 1)	28172.510044
11	(1, 0)	28941.056983
12	(0, 3)	31355.802141
13	(0, 2)	33531.179284
14	(0, 1)	39402.269523
15	(0, 0)	49035.184224

Figure 6.17 A `DataFrame` ordered by ascending value of AIC, resulting from fitting different ARMA(p,q) models on the differenced bandwidth dataset. Notice how the first three models all have an AIC value of 27,991.

To perform the residual analysis, we'll fit the ARMA(2,2) model on our training set. Then we'll use the `plot_diagnostics` method to study the Q-Q plot, as well as the other accompanying plots. The result is shown in figure 6.18.

```
model = SARIMAX(train['bandwidth_diff'], order=(2,0,2),
⮕ simple_differencing=False)
model_fit = model.fit(disp=False)model_fit = best_model.fit(disp=False)
model_fit.plot_diagnostics(figsize=(10, 8));
```

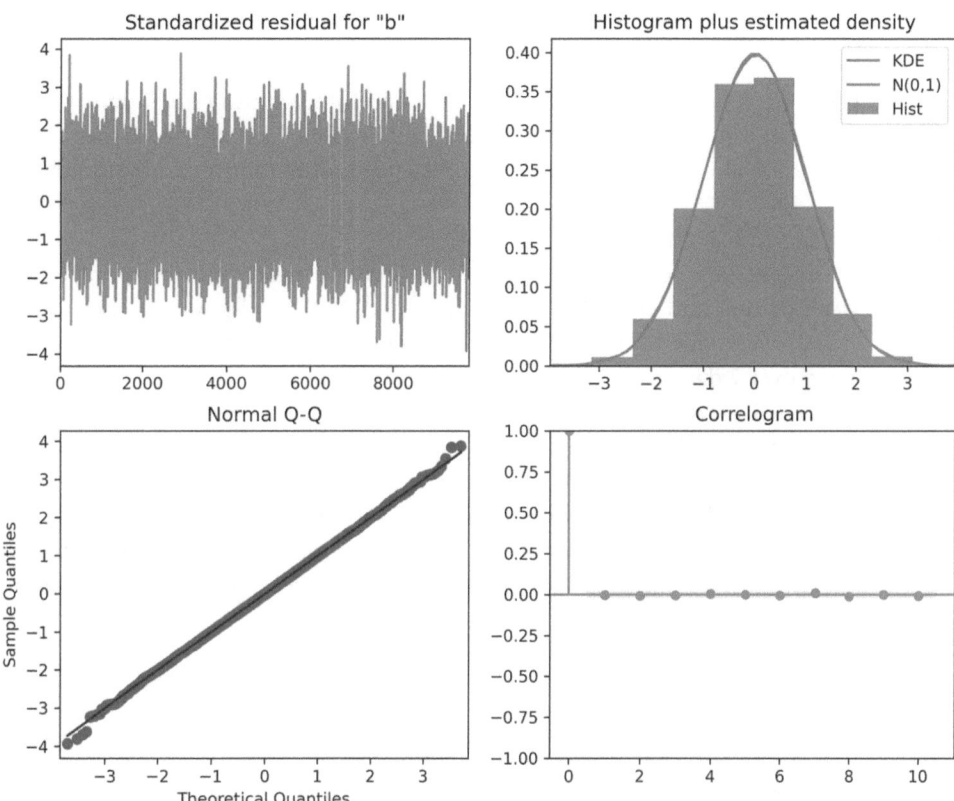

Figure 6.18   Model diagnostics from `statsmodels`. **The top-left plot displays the residuals, the histogram of the residuals is at the top right, the Q-Q plot of the residuals is at the bottom left, and the bottom right shows the ACF plot of the residuals.**

In figure 6.18 you can see that the top-left plot shows no trend, and the mean seems constant over time, meaning that our residuals are likely stationary. The top right displays a density plot with a shape similar to that of a normal distribution. The Q-Q plot at the bottom left shows a thick straight line that is very close to *y* = *x*. Finally, the ACF plot at the bottom right shows no autocorrelation after lag 0. Thus, figure 6.18 indicates that our residuals clearly resemble white noise, since they are normally distributed and uncorrelated.

Our last step is to run the Ljung-Box test on the residuals for the first 10 lags. If the returned p-values exceed 0.05, we cannot reject the null hypothesis, which means that our residuals are uncorrelated and independently distributed, just like white noise.

```
residuals = model_fit.resid

lbvalue, pvalue = acorr_ljungbox(residuals, np.arange(1, 11, 1))

print(pvalue)
```

The returned p-values all exceed 0.05. Therefore, we can conclude that our residuals are indeed uncorrelated. Our ARMA(2,2) model has passed all the checks on the residual analysis, and we are ready to use this model to forecast bandwidth usage.

6.6   *Forecasting bandwidth usage*

In the previous section, we applied the general modeling procedure on the bandwidth dataset and concluded than an ARMA(2,2) model was the best model for our data. Now we will use the ARMA(2,2) model to forecast the next 2 hours of bandwidth usage over 7 days.

We will reuse the `rolling_forecast` function that we defined and used in chapters 4 and 5, as shown in listing 6.3. Recall that this function allows us to forecast a few timesteps at a time, until we have forecasts for the entire horizon. This time, of course, we'll fit an ARMA(2,2) model to our differenced data. Also, we'll compare the model's performance to two benchmarks: the mean and the last known value. This will allow us to make sure that an ARMA(2,2) model performs better than naive forecasting methods.

Listing 6.3   A function to perform a rolling forecast on a horizon

```
def rolling_forecast(df: pd.DataFrame, train_len: int, horizon: int,
➡ window: int, method: str) -> list:

    total_len = train_len + horizon
    end_idx = train_len

    if method == 'mean':
        pred_mean = []

        for i in range(train_len, total_len, window):
            mean = np.mean(df[:i].values)
            pred_mean.extend(mean for _ in range(window))

        return pred_mean

    elif method == 'last':
        pred_last_value = []

        for i in range(train_len, total_len, window):
            last_value = df[:i].iloc[-1].values[0]
            pred_last_value.extend(last_value for _ in range(window))
```

```
        return pred_last_value

    elif method == 'ARMA':
        pred_ARMA = []

        for i in range(train_len, total_len, window):
            model = SARIMAX(df[:i], order=(2,0,2))
            res = model.fit(disp=False)
            predictions = res.get_prediction(0, i + window - 1)
            oos_pred = predictions.predicted_mean.iloc[-window:]
            pred_ARMA.extend(oos_pred)

    return pred_ARMA
```

> **The order specifies an ARMA(2,2) model.**

With `rolling_forecast` defined, we can use it to evaluate the performance of the different forecasting methods. We'll first create a `DataFrame` to hold the actual values of the test set as well as the predictions from the different methods. Then we'll specify the size of the train and test sets. We will predict two steps at a time, because we have an ARMA(2,2) model, meaning that there is an MA(2) component. We know from chapter 4 that predicting beyond q steps into the future with an MA(q) model will simply return the mean, so the predictions will remain flat. We'll therefore avoid this situation by setting the window to 2. We can then forecast on the test set using the mean method, the last known value method, and the ARMA(2,2) model, and store each forecast in its appropriate column in `test`.

```
pred_df = test.copy()

TRAIN_LEN = len(train)
HORIZON = len(test)
WINDOW = 2

pred_mean = recursive_forecast(df_diff, TRAIN_LEN, HORIZON, WINDOW, 'mean')
pred_last_value = recursive_forecast(df_diff, TRAIN_LEN, HORIZON, WINDOW,
➡ 'last')
pred_ARMA = recursive_forecast(df_diff, TRAIN_LEN, HORIZON, WINDOW, 'ARMA')

test.loc[:, 'pred_mean'] = pred_mean
test.loc[:, 'pred_last_value'] = pred_last_value
test.loc[:, 'pred_ARMA'] = pred_ARMA

pred_df.head()
```

We can then plot and visualize the forecasts for each method.

```
fig, ax = plt.subplots()

ax.plot(df_diff['bandwidth_diff'])
ax.plot(test['bandwidth_diff'], 'b-', label='actual')
ax.plot(test['pred_mean'], 'g:', label='mean')
ax.plot(test['pred_last_value'], 'r-.', label='last')
ax.plot(test['pred_ARMA'], 'k--', label='ARMA(2,2)')
ax.legend(loc=2)
```

```
ax.set_xlabel('Time')
ax.set_ylabel('Hourly bandwidth (diff)')

ax.axvspan(9830, 9999, color='#808080', alpha=0.2)

ax.set_xlim(9800, 9999)

plt.xticks(
    [9802, 9850, 9898, 9946, 9994],
    ['2020-02-13', '2020-02-15', '2020-02-17', '2020-02-19', '2020-02-21'])

fig.autofmt_xdate()
plt.tight_layout()
```

Assign a gray background for the testing period.

Zoom in on the testing period.

The results are shown in figure 6.19. I've zoomed in on the testing period for a better visualization.

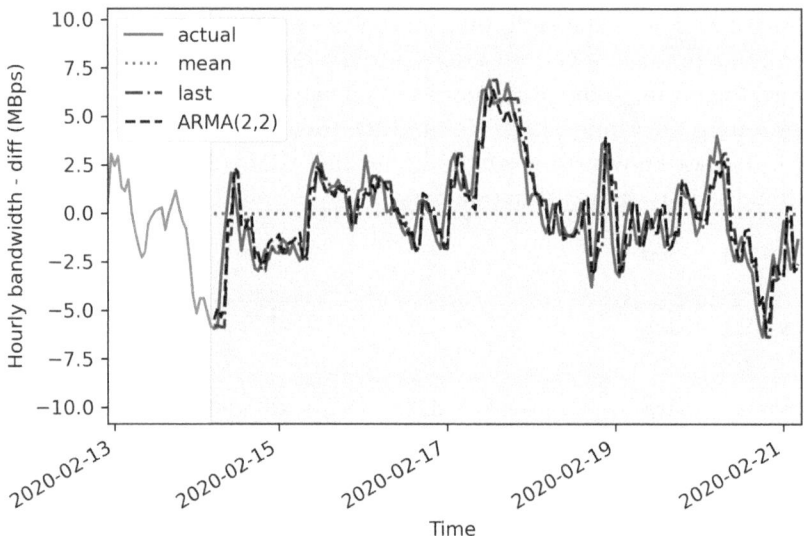

Figure 6.19 Forecasts of the differenced hourly bandwidth usage using the mean, the last known value, and an ARMA(2,2) model. You can see how the ARMA(2,2) forecasts and last known value forecasts almost coincide with the actual values of the test set.

In figure 6.19 you can see that the ARMA(2,2) forecasts, shown as a dashed line, almost coincide with the actual values of the test set. The same can be said of the forecasts from the last known value method, shown as a dashed and dotted line. Of course, the forecasts using the mean, shown as a dotted line, are completely flat over the testing period.

We'll now measure the mean squared error (MSE) to evaluate the performance of each model. The model with the lowest MSE is the best-performing model.

```
mse_mean = mean_squared_error(test['bandwidth_diff'], test['pred_mean'])
mse_last = mean_squared_error(test['bandwidth_diff'],
➥ test['pred_last_value'])
mse_ARMA = mean_squared_error(test['bandwidth_diff'], test['pred_ARMA'])

print(mse_mean, mse_last, mse_ARMA)
```

This returns an MSE of 6.3 for the mean method, 2.2 for the last known value method, and 1.8 for the ARMA(2,2) model. The ARMA(2,2) model outperforms the benchmarks, meaning that we have a well-performing model.

The final step is to reverse the transformation of our forecast in order to bring it to the same scale as our original data. Remember that we differenced the original data to make it stationary. The ARMA(2,2) model was then applied on the stationary dataset and produced forecasts that are differenced.

To reverse the differencing transformation, we can apply a cumulative sum, just as we did in chapters 4 and 5.

```
df['pred_bandwidth'] = pd.Series()
df['pred_bandwidth'][9832:] = df['hourly_bandwidth'].iloc[9832] +
➥ pred_df['pred_ARMA'].cumsum()
```

We can then plot the forecasts on the original scale of the data.

```
fig, ax = plt.subplots()

ax.plot(df['hourly_bandwidth'])
ax.plot(df['hourly_bandwidth'], 'b-', label='actual')
ax.plot(df['pred_bandwidth'], 'k--', label='ARMA(2,2)')

ax.legend(loc=2)

ax.set_xlabel('Time')
ax.set_ylabel('Hourly bandwith usage (MBps)')

ax.axvspan(9831, 10000, color='#808080', alpha=0.2)

ax.set_xlim(9800, 9999)

plt.xticks(
    [9802, 9850, 9898, 9946, 9994],
    ['2020-02-13', '2020-02-15', '2020-02-17', '2020-02-19', '2020-02-21'])

fig.autofmt_xdate()
plt.tight_layout()
```

Looking at the results in figure 6.20, you can see that our forecasts, shown as a dashed line, closely follow the actual values of the test set, and the two lines almost coincide.

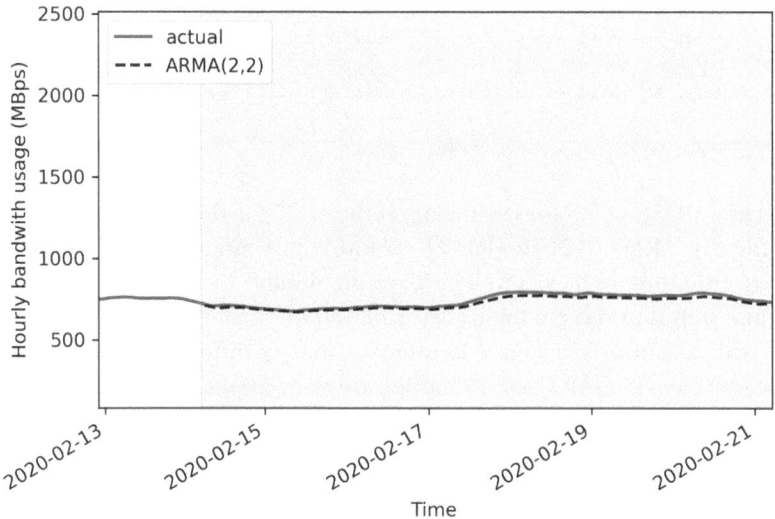

Figure 6.20   Undifferenced predictions of hourly bandwidth usage. Notice how the dashed line representing our predictions almost coincides with the solid line representing the actual values. This means that our predictions are very close to the actual values, indicating a performant model.

We can measure the mean absolute error (MAE) of the undifferenced ARMA(2,2) predictions to understand how far apart the predictions are from the actual values. We'll use the MAE simply because it is easy to interpret.

```
mae_ARMA_undiff = mean_absolute_error(df['hourly_bandwidth'][9832:],
    df['pred_bandwidth'][9832:])

print(mae_ARMA_undiff)
```

This returns an MAE of 14, meaning that, on average, our forecasts are 14 Mbps above or below the actual bandwidth usage.

6.7   *Next steps*

In this chapter, we covered the ARMA(p,q) model and how it effectively combines an AR(p) model with an MA(q) model to model and forecast more complex time series. This required us to define an entirely new modeling procedure that does not rely on the qualitative study of the ACF and PACF plots. Instead, we fit many ARMA(p,q) models with different (p,q) combinations and selected the model with the lowest AIC. Then we analyzed the model's residuals to make sure that their properties were similar to white noise: normally distributed, stationary, and uncorrelated. This analysis is both qualitative, because we can study the Q-Q plot to evaluate whether the residuals are normally distributed, as well as quantitative, since we can apply the Ljung-Box test to determine whether the residuals are correlated or not. If the model's residuals have the properties of a random variable, like white noise, the model can be used for forecasting.

So far we have covered different models for stationary time series: mainly the MA(q) model, AR(p) model, and ARMA(p,q) model. Each model required us to transform our data to make it stationary before we could forecast. Furthermore, we had to reverse the transformation on our forecast to obtain predictions in the original scale of the data.

However, there is a way to model non-stationary time series without having to transform them and reverse the transformation on the predictions. Specifically, we can model *integrated* time series using the *autoregressive integrated moving average* model or ARIMA(p,d,q). This will be the subject of the next chapter.

6.8   Exercises

It is time to test your knowledge and apply the general modeling procedure with these exercises. The solutions are available on GitHub: https://github.com/marcopeix/TimeSeriesForecastingInPython/tree/master/CH06.

6.8.1   Make predictions on the simulated ARMA(1,1) process

1 Reusing the simulated ARMA(1,1) process, split it into train and test sets. Assign 80% of the data to the train set and the remaining 20% to the test set.
2 Use the `rolling_forecast` function to make predictions using the ARMA(1,1) model, the mean method, and the last known value method.
3 Plot your forecasts.
4 Evaluate each method's performance using the MSE. Which method performed best?

6.8.2   Simulate an ARMA(2,2) process and make forecasts

Simulate a stationary ARMA(2,2) process. Use the `ArmaProcess` function from statsmodels and simulate this:

$$y_t = 0.33y_{t-1} + 0.50y_{t-2} + 0.9\epsilon_{t-1} + 0.3\epsilon_{t-2}$$

1 Simulate 10,000 samples.

```
from statsmodels.tsa.arima_process import ArmaProcess
import numpy as np                          Set the seed for reproducibility.
                                            Change the seed if you want
np.random.seed(42)          ◁───────────    to experiment with different
                                            values.
ma2 = np.array([1, 0.9, 0.3])
ar2 = np.array([1, -0.33, -0.5])

ARMA_2_2 = ArmaProcess(ar2, ma2).generate_sample(nsample=10000)
```

2 Plot your simulated process.

3 Test for stationarity using the ADF test.

4 Split your data into train and test sets. The test set must contain the last 200 timesteps. The rest is for the train set.

5 Define a range of values for p and q, and generate all unique combinations of orders (p,q).

6 Use the `optimize_ARMA` function to fit all unique ARMA(p,q) models, and select the one with the lowest AIC. Is the ARMA(2,2) model the one with the lowest AIC?

7 Select the best model according to the AIC, and store the residuals in a variable called `residuals`.

8 Perform a qualitative analysis of the residuals with the `plot_diagnostics` method. Does the Q-Q plot show a straight line that lies on $y = x$? Does the correlogram show significant coefficients?

9 Perform a quantitative analysis of the residuals by applying the Ljung-Box test on the first 10 lags. Are all returned p-values above 0.05? Are the residuals correlated or not?

10 Use the `rolling_forecast` function to make predictions using the selected ARMA(p,q) model, the mean method, and the last known value method.

11 Plot your forecasts.

12 Evaluate each method's performance using the MSE. Which method performed best?

Summary

- The autoregressive moving average model, denoted as ARMA(p,q), is the combination of the autoregressive model AR(p) and the moving average model MA(q).

- An ARMA(p,q) process will display a decaying pattern or a sinusoidal pattern on both the ACF and PACF plots. Therefore, they cannot be used to estimate the orders p and q.

- The general modeling procedure does not rely on the ACF and PACF plots. Instead, we fit many ARMA(p,q) models and perform model selection and residual analysis.

- Model selection is done with the Akaike information criterion (AIC). It quantifies the information loss of a model, and it is related to the number of parameters in a model and its goodness of fit. The lower the AIC, the better the model.

- The AIC is relative measure of quality. It returns the best model among other models. For an absolute measure of quality, we perform residual analysis.

- Residuals of a good model must approximate white noise, meaning that they must be uncorrelated, normally distributed, and independent.

- The Q-Q plot is a graphical tool for comparing two distributions. We use it to compare the distribution of the residuals against a theoretical normal distribution.

If the plot shows a straight line that lies on $y = x$, then both distributions are similar. Otherwise, it means that the residuals are not normally distributed.

- The Ljung-Box test allows us to determine whether the residuals are correlated or not. The null hypothesis states that the data is independently distributed and uncorrelated. If the returned p-values are larger than 0.05, we cannot reject the null hypothesis, meaning that the residuals are uncorrelated, just like white noise.

Forecasting
non-stationary time series

This chapter covers

- Examining the autoregressive integrated moving average model, or ARIMA(p,d,q)
- Applying the general modeling procedure for non-stationary time series
- Forecasting using the ARIMA(p,d,q) model

In chapters 4, 5, and 6 we covered the moving average model, MA(q); the autoregressive model, AR(p); and the ARMA model, ARMA(p,q). We saw how these models can only be used for stationary time series, which required us to apply transformations, mainly differencing, and test for stationarity using the ADF test. In the examples that we covered, the forecasts from each model returned differenced values, which required us to reverse this transformation in order to bring the values back to the scale of the original data.

Now we'll add another component to the ARMA(p,q) model so we can forecast non-stationary time series. This component is the *integration order*, which is denoted by the variable *d*. This leads us to the *autoregressive integrated moving average* (ARIMA) model, or ARIMA(p,d,q). Using this model, we can take into account non-stationary time series and avoid the steps of modeling on differenced data and having to inverse transform the forecasts.

In this chapter, we'll define the ARIMA(p,d,q) model and the order of integration d. Then we'll add a step to our general modeling procedure. Figure 7.1 shows the general modeling procedure as defined in chapter 6. We must add a step to determine the order of integration in order to use this procedure with the ARIMA(p,d,q) model.

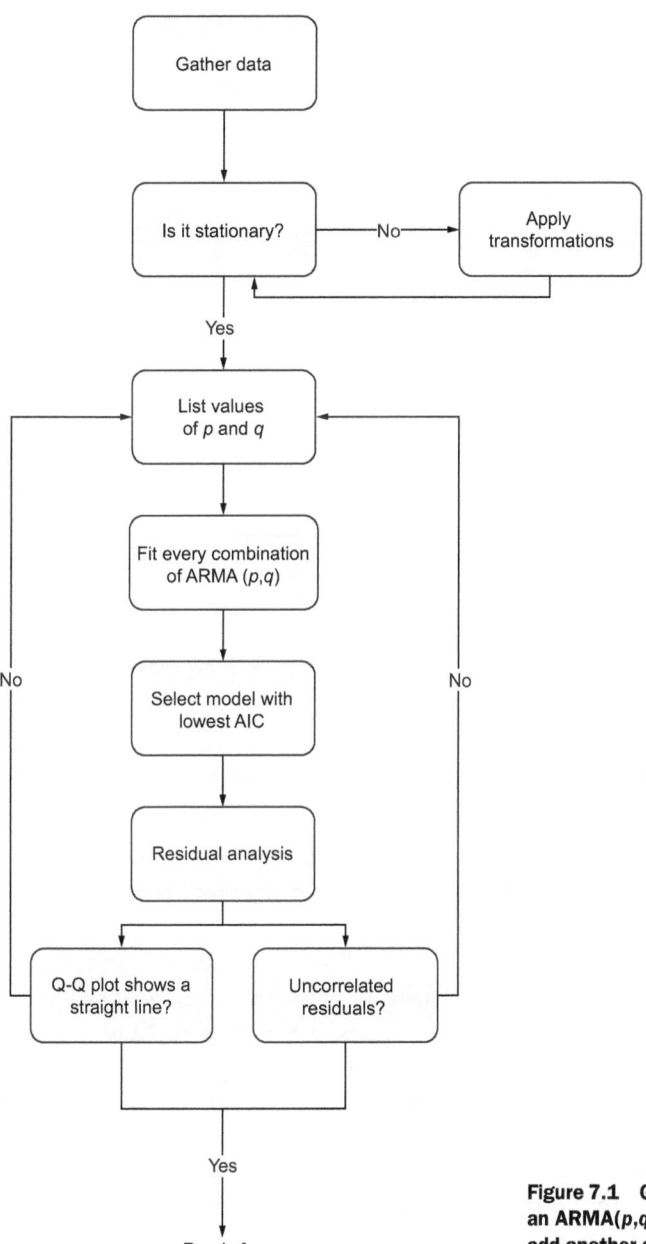

Figure 7.1 **General modeling procedure using an ARMA(p,q) model. In this chapter, we will add another step to this procedure in order to accommodate the ARIMA(p,d,q) model.**

Then we'll apply our modified procedure to forecast a non-stationary time series, meaning that the series has a trend, or its variance is not constant over time. Specifically, we'll revisit the dataset of Johnson & Johnson's quarterly earnings per share (EPS) between 1960 and 1980, which we first studied in chapters 1 and 2. The series is shown in figure 7.2. We'll apply the ARIMA(p,d,q) model to forecast the quarterly EPS for 1 year.

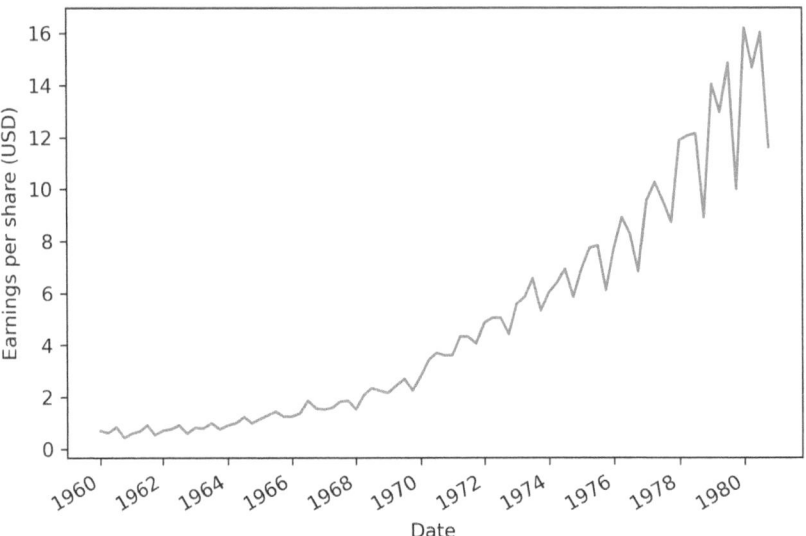

Figure 7.2   Quarterly earnings per share (EPS) of Johnson & Johnson from 1960 to 1980. We worked with the same dataset in chapters 1 and 2.

7.1   *Defining the autoregressive integrated moving average model*

An *autoregressive integrated moving average process* is the combination of an autoregressive process AR(p), integration I(d), and the moving average process MA(q).

Just like the ARMA process, the ARIMA process states that the present value is dependent on past values, coming from the AR(p) portion, and past errors, coming from the MA(q) portion. However, instead of using the original series, denoted as y_t, the ARIMA process uses the differenced series, denoted as y_t'. Note that y_t' can represent a series that has been differenced more than once.

Therefore, the mathematical expression of the ARIMA(p,d,q) process states that the present value of the differenced series y_t' is equal to the sum of a constant C, past values of the differenced series $\varphi_p y_{t-p}'$, the mean of the differenced series μ, past error terms $\theta_q \epsilon_{t-q}$, and a current error term ϵ_t, as shown in equation 7.1.

$$y_t' = C + \varphi_1 y_{t-1}' + \cdots \varphi_p y_{t-p}' + \theta_1 \epsilon_{t-1}' + \cdots + \theta_q \epsilon_{t-q}' + \epsilon_t$$ **Equation 7.1**

Just like in the ARMA process, the order p determines how many lagged values of the series are included in the model, while the order q determines how many lagged error terms are included in the model. However, in equation 7.1 you'll notice that there is no order d explicitly displayed.

Here, the order d is defined as the order of integration. Integration is simply the reverse of differencing. The order of integration is thus equal to the number of times a series has been differenced to become stationary.

If we difference a series once and it becomes stationary, then $d = 1$. If a series is differenced twice to become stationary, then $d = 2$.

Autoregressive integrated moving average model

An *autoregressive integrated moving average* (ARIMA) process is the combination of the AR(p) and MA(q) processes, but in terms of the differenced series.

It is denoted as ARIMA(p,d,q), where p is the order of the AR(p) process, d is the order of integration, and q is the order of the MA(q) process.

Integration is the reverse of differencing, and the order of integration d is equal to the number of times the series has been differenced to be rendered stationary.

The general equation of the ARIMA(p,d,q) process is

$$y'_t = C + \varphi_1 y'_{t-1} + \cdots \varphi_p\, y'_{t-p} + \theta_1 \epsilon'_{t-1} + \cdots + \theta_q \epsilon'_{t-q} + \epsilon_t$$

Note that y'_t represents the differenced series, and it may have been differenced more than once.

A time series that can be rendered stationary by applying differencing is said to be an *integrated* series. In the presence of a non-stationary integrated time series, we can use the ARIMA(p,d,q) model to produce forecasts.

Thus, in simple terms, the ARIMA model is simply an ARMA model that can be applied on non-stationary time series. Whereas the ARMA(p,q) model requires the series to be stationary before fitting an ARMA(p,q) model, the ARIMA(p,d,q) model can be used on non-stationary series. We must simply find the order of integration d, which corresponds to the minimum number of times a series must be differenced to become stationary.

Therefore, we must add the step of finding the order of integration to our general modeling procedure before we apply it to forecast the quarterly EPS of Johnson & Johnson.

7.2 Modifying the general modeling procedure to account for non-stationary series

In chapter 6 we built a general modeling procedure that allowed us to model more complex time series, meaning that the series has both an autoregressive and a moving average component. This procedure involves fitting many ARMA(p,q) models and selecting the one with the lowest AIC. Then we study the model's residuals to verify that they resemble white noise. If that is the case, the model can be used for forecasting. We can visualize the general modeling procedure in its present state in figure 7.3.

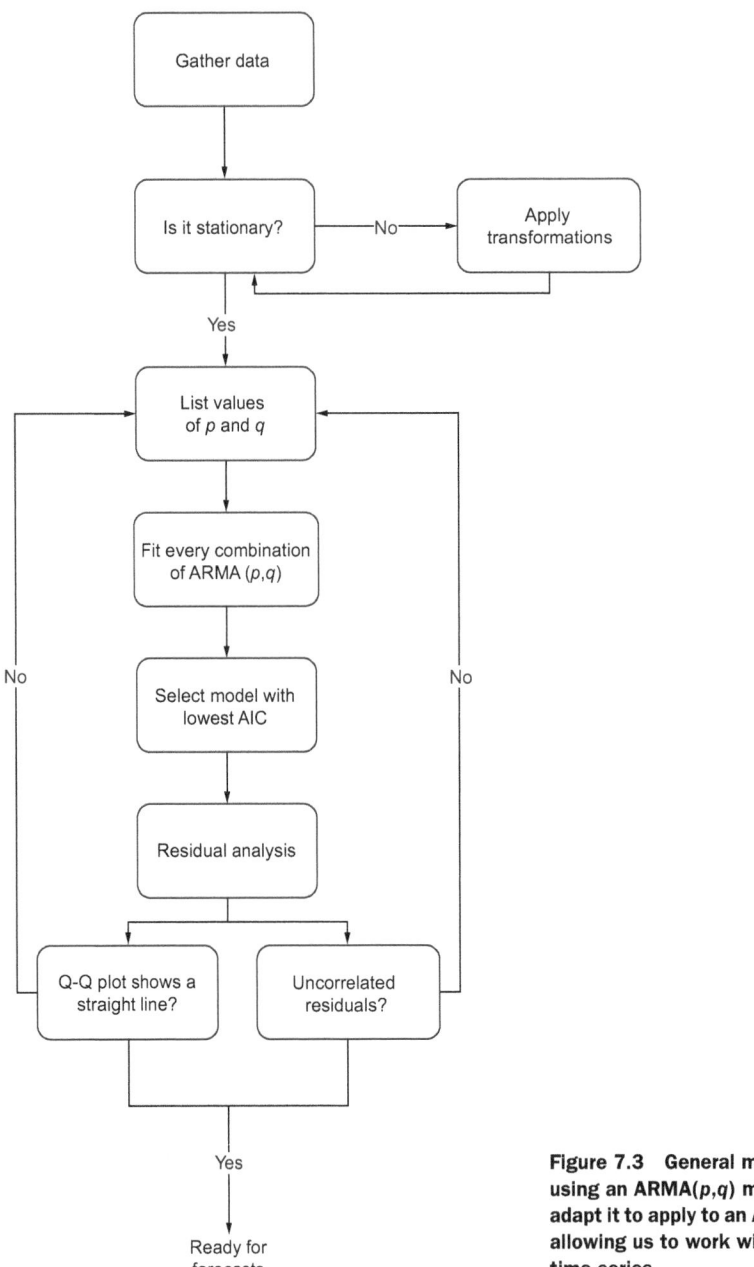

Figure 7.3   General modeling procedure using an ARMA(p,q) model. Now we must adapt it to apply to an ARIMA(p,d,q) model, allowing us to work with non-stationary time series.

The next iteration of the general modeling procedure will include a step to determine the order of integration d. That way, we can apply the same procedure but using an ARIMA(p,d,q) model, which will allow us to forecast non-stationary time series.

From the previous section, we know that the order of integration d is simply the minimum number of times a series must be differenced to become stationary. Therefore, if a series is stationary after being differenced once, then $d = 1$. If it is stationary after being differenced twice, then $d = 2$. In my experience, a time series rarely needs to be differenced more than twice to become stationary.

We can add a step such that when transformations are applied to the series, we set the value of d to the number of times the series was differenced. Then, instead of fitting many ARMA(p,q) models, we fit many ARIMA(p,d,q) models. The rest of the procedure remains the same, as we still use the AIC to select the best model and study its residuals. The resulting procedure is shown in figure 7.4.

Note that in the case where $d = 0$, it is equivalent to an ARMA(p,q) model. This also means that the series did not need to be differenced to be stationary. It must also be specified that the ARMA(p,q) model can only be applied on a stationary series, whereas the ARIMA(p,d,q) model can be applied on a series that has not been differenced.

Let's apply our new general modeling procedure to forecast the quarterly earnings per share of Johnson & Johnson.

7.3   *Forecasting a non-stationary times series*

We are now going to apply the general modeling procedure displayed in figure 7.4 to forecast the quarterly earnings per share (EPS) of Johnson & Johnson. We'll use the same dataset that was introduced in chapters 1 and 2. We will forecast 1 year's quarterly EPS, meaning that we must forecast four timesteps into the future, since there are four quarters in a year. The dataset covers the period between 1960 and 1980.

As always, the first step is to collect our data. Here it is done for us, so we can simply load it and display the series. The result is shown in figure 7.5.

> **NOTE**   At any time, feel free to refer to the source for this chapter on GitHub: https://github.com/marcopeix/TimeSeriesForecastingInPython/tree/master/CH07.

```
df = pd.read_csv('../data/jj.csv')

fig, ax = plt.subplots()

ax.plot(df.date, df.data)
ax.set_xlabel('Date')
ax.set_ylabel('Earnings per share (USD)')

plt.xticks(np.arange(0, 81, 8), [1960, 1962, 1964, 1966, 1968, 1970, 1972,
➥ 1974, 1976, 1978, 1980])

fig.autofmt_xdate()
plt.tight_layout()
```

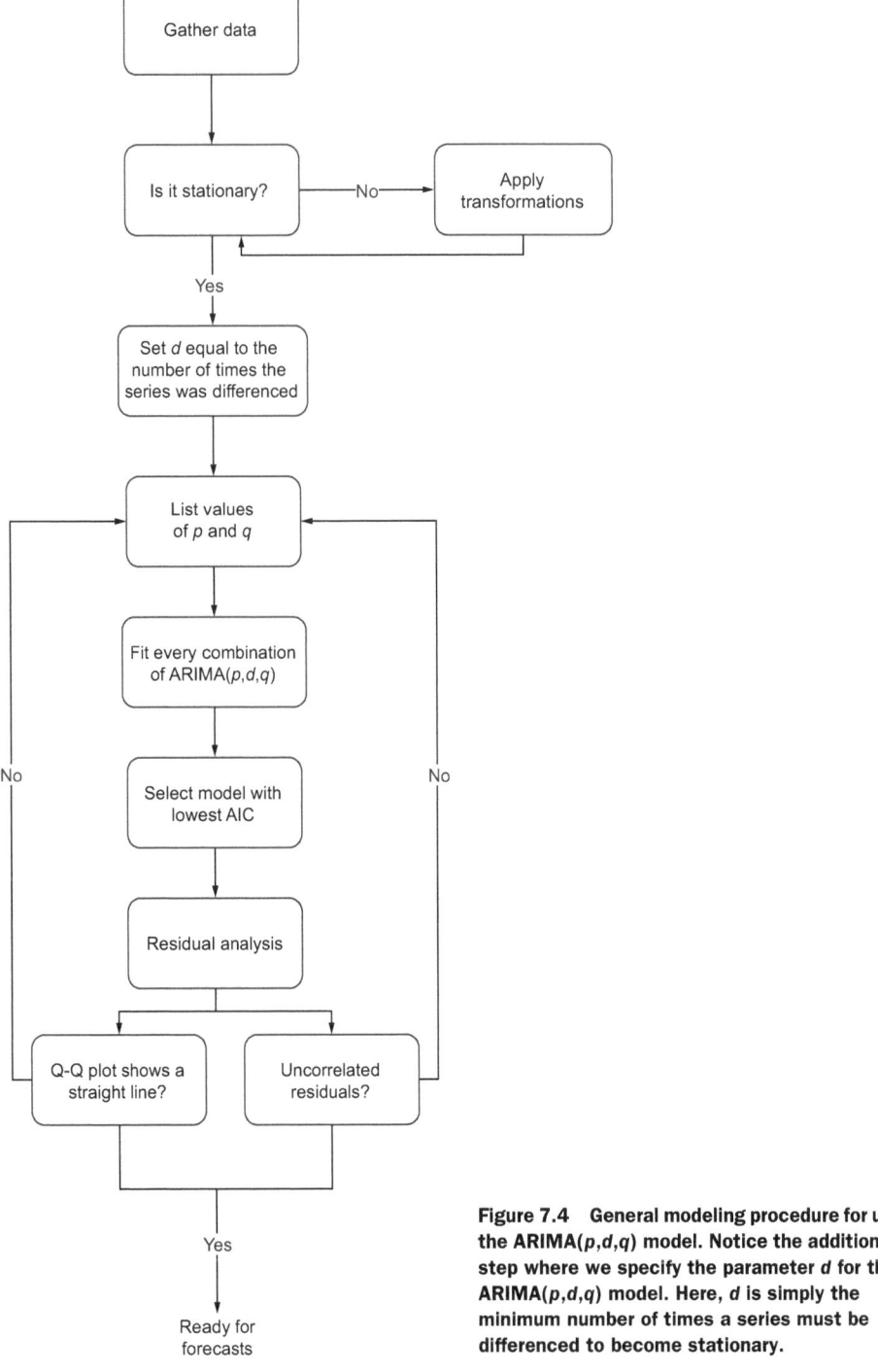

Figure 7.4   General modeling procedure for using the ARIMA(p,d,q) model. Notice the addition of a step where we specify the parameter d for the ARIMA(p,d,q) model. Here, d is simply the minimum number of times a series must be differenced to become stationary.

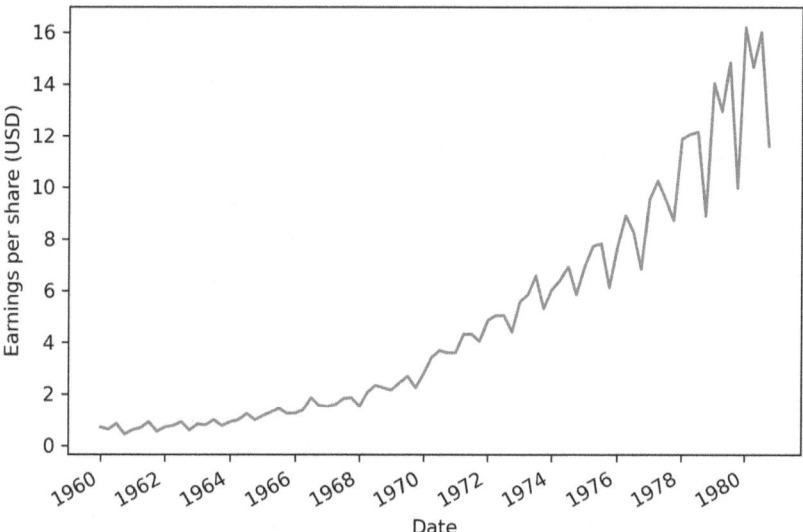

Figure 7.5   Quarterly earnings per share (EPS) of Johnson & Johnson between 1960 and 1980

Following our procedure, we must check if the data is stationary. Figure 7.5 shows a positive trend, as the quarterly EPS tends to increase over time. Nevertheless, we can apply the augmented Dickey-Fuller (ADF) test to determine if it is stationary or not. By now you should be very comfortable with these steps, so they will be accompanied by minimal comments.

```
ad_fuller_result = adfuller(df['data'])

print(f'ADF Statistic: {ad_fuller_result[0]}')
print(f'p-value: {ad_fuller_result[1]}')
```

This block of code returns an ADF statistic of 2.74 with a p-value of 1.0. Since the ADF statistic is not a large negative number, and the p-value is larger than 0.05, we cannot reject the null hypothesis, meaning that our series is not stationary.

We need to determine how many times the series must be differenced to become stationary. This will then set the order of integration *d*. We can apply a first-order differencing and test for stationarity.

```
eps_diff = np.diff(df['data'], n=1)        ◁──┤ Apply first-order
                                               │ differencing.

ad_fuller_result = adfuller(eps_diff)      ◁───┐ Test for
                                               │ stationarity.
print(f'ADF Statistic: {ad_fuller_result[0]}')
print(f'p-value: {ad_fuller_result[1]}')
```

This results in an ADF statistic of –0.41 and a p-value of 0.9. Again, the ADF statistic is not a large negative number, and the p-value is larger than 0.05. Therefore, we cannot reject the null hypothesis and we must conclude that after a first-order differencing, the series is not stationary.

Let's try differencing again to see if the series becomes stationary:

```
eps_diff2 = np.diff(eps_diff, n=1)        ◁───┤ Take the differenced series
                                               and difference it again.

ad_fuller_result = adfuller(eps_diff2)    ◁────────┐ Test for
                                                     stationarity.
print(f'ADF Statistic: {ad_fuller_result[0]}')
print(f'p-value: {ad_fuller_result[1]}')
```

This results in an ADF statistic of –3.59 and a p-value of 0.006. Now that we have a p-value smaller than 0.05 and a large negative ADF statistic, we can reject the null hypothesis and conclude that our series is stationary. It took two rounds of differencing to make our data stationary, which means that our order of integration is 2, so $d = 2$.

Before we move on to fitting different combinations of ARIMA(p,d,q) models, we must separate our data into train and test sets. We will hold out the last year of data for testing. This means that we will fit the model with data from 1960 to 1979 and predict the quarterly EPS in 1980 to evaluate the quality of our model against the observed values in 1980. In figure 7.6 the testing period is the shaded area.

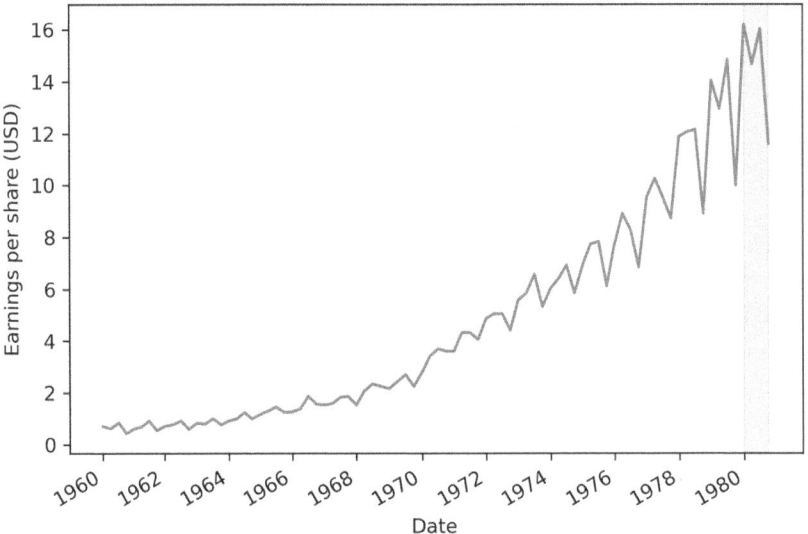

Figure 7.6   The train and test sets. The training period spans the years 1960 to 1979 inclusively, while the test set is the quarterly EPS reported in 1980. This test set corresponds to the last four data points of the dataset.

To fit the many ARIMA(p,d,q) models, we'll define the `optimize_ARIMA` function. It is almost identical to the `optimize_ARMA` function that we defined in chapter 6, only this time we'll add the order of integration d as an input to the function. The remainder of the function stays the same, as we fit the different models and order them by ascending AIC in order to select the model with the lowest AIC. The `optimize_ARIMA` function is shown in the following listing.

> **Listing 7.1 Function to fit all unique ARIMA(p,d,q) models**

The function takes as inputs the time series data, the list of unique (p,q) combinations, and the order of integration d.

```
from typing import Union
from tqdm import tqdm_notebook
from statsmodels.tsa.statespace.sarimax import SARIMAX

def optimize_ARIMA(endog: Union[pd.Series, list], order_list: list, d: int)
        -> pd.DataFrame:

    results = []

    for order in tqdm_notebook(order_list):
        try:
            model = SARIMAX(endog, order=(order[0], d, order[1]),
simple_differencing=False).fit(disp=False)
        except:
            continue

        aic = model.aic
        results.append([order, aic])

    result_df = pd.DataFrame(results)
    result_df.columns = ['(p,q)', 'AIC']

    #Sort in ascending order, lower AIC is better
    result_df = result_df.sort_values(by='AIC',
ascending=True).reset_index(drop=True)

    return result_df
```

Initialize an empty list to store each order (p,q) and its corresponding AIC as a tuple.

Iterate over each unique (p,q) combination. The use of tqdm_notebook will display a progress bar.

Fit an ARIMA(p,d,q) model using the SARIMAX function. We specify simple_differencing =False to prevent differencing. We also specify disp=False to avoid printing convergence messages to the console.

Append the (p,q) combination and AIC as a tuple to the results list.

Calculate the model's AIC.

Label the columns of your DataFrame.

Store the (p,q) combination and AIC in a DataFrame.

Sort the DataFrame in ascending order of AIC values. The lower the AIC, the better the model.

With the function in place, we can define a list of possible values for the orders p and q. In this case, we'll try the values 0, 1, 2, and 3 for both orders and generate the list of unique (p,q) combinations.

```
from itertools import product

ps = range(0, 4, 1)
qs = range(0, 4, 1)
d = 2

order_list = list(product(ps, qs))
```

Create a list of possible values for p from 0 inclusively to 4 exclusively, with steps of 1.

Create a list of possible values for q from 0 inclusively to 4 exclusively, with steps of 1.

Set d to 2, as the series needed to be differenced twice to become stationary.

Generate a list containing all unique combinations of (p,q).

Note that we do not give a range of values for the parameter d because it has a very specific definition: it is the number of times a series must be differenced to become stationary. Hence, it must be set to a specific value, which in this case is 2.

Furthermore, d must be constant in order to compare models using the AIC. Varying d would change the likelihood function used in the calculation of the AIC value, so comparing models using the AIC as a criterion would not be valid anymore.

We can now run the `optimize_ARIMA` function using the training set. The function returns a `DataFrame` with the model that has the lowest AIC at the top.

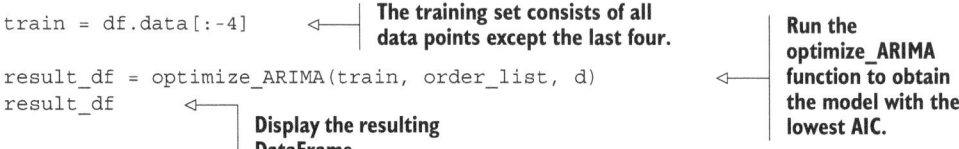

```
train = df.data[:-4]            ◁―|  The training set consists of all
                                     data points except the last four.

result_df = optimize_ARIMA(train, order_list, d)     ◁―  Run the
result_df   ◁―|                                           optimize_ARIMA
                |  Display the resulting                   function to obtain
                   DataFrame.                              the model with the
                                                           lowest AIC.
```

The returned `DataFrame` shows that a value of 3 for both p and q results in the lowest AIC. Therefore, an ARIMA(3,2,3) model seems to be the most suitable for this situation. Now let's assess the validity of the model by studying its residuals.

To do so, we'll fit an ARIMA(3,2,3) model on the training set and display the residuals' diagnostics using the `plot_diagnostics` method. The result is shown in figure 7.7.

```
model = SARIMAX(train, order=(3,2,3), simple_differencing=False)     ◁―|
model_fit = model.fit(disp=False)
                                                   Fit an ARIMA(3,2,3)
model_fit.plot_diagnostics(figsize=(10,8));   ◁―  model on the training
                                                   set, since this model
                          Display the residuals'   has the lowest AIC.
                          diagnostics.
```

In figure 7.7, the top-left plot shows the residuals over time. While there is no trend in the residuals, the variance does not seem to be constant, which is a discrepancy in comparison to white noise. At the top right is the distribution of the residuals. We can see it is fairly close to a normal distribution. The Q-Q plot leads us to the same conclusion, as it displays a line that is fairly straight, meaning that the residuals' distribution is close to a normal distribution. Finally, by looking at the correlogram at the bottom right, we can see that a coefficient seems to be significant at lag 3. However, since it is not preceded by any significant autocorrelation coefficients, we can assume that this is due to chance. Therefore, we can say that the correlogram shows no significant coefficients after lag 0, just like white noise.

Thus, from a qualitative standpoint, it seems that our residuals are close to white noise, which is a good sign, as it means that the model's errors are random.

The last step is to evaluate the residuals from a quantitative standpoint. We'll thus apply the Ljung-Box test to determine whether the residuals are correlated. We'll apply the test on the first 10 lags and study the p-values. If all p-values are greater than

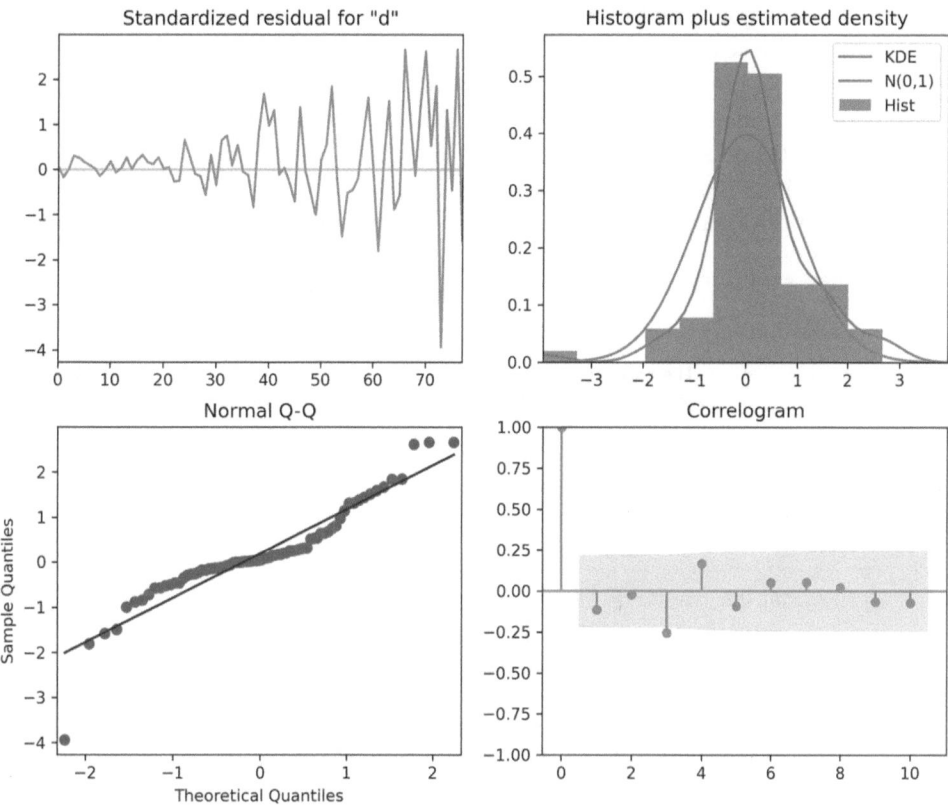

Figure 7.7 Diagnostics of the ARIMA(3,2,3) residuals. The Q-Q plot at the bottom left displays a fairly straight line with some deviation at the extremities.

0.05, we cannot reject the null hypothesis and we'll conclude that the residuals are not correlated, just like white noise.

```
from statsmodels.stats.diagnostic import acorr_ljungbox

residuals = model_fit.resid

lbvalue, pvalue = acorr_ljungbox(residuals, np.arange(1, 11, 1))

print(pvalue)
```

Store the model's residuals in a variable.

Apply the Ljung-Box test on the first 10 lags.

Running the Ljung-Box test on the first 10 lags of the model's residuals returns a list of p-values that are all larger than 0.05. Therefore, we do not reject the null hypothesis, and we conclude that the residuals are not correlated, just like white noise.

Our ARIMA(3,2,3) model has passed all the checks, and it can now be used for forecasting. Remember that our test set is the last four data points, corresponding to the four quarterly EPS reported in 1980. As a benchmark for our model, we will use the naive seasonal method. This means that we'll take the EPS of the first quarter of 1979 and use it as a forecast for the EPS of the first quarter of 1980. Then the EPS of the second quarter of 1979 will be used as a forecast for the EPS of the second quarter of 1980, and so on. Remember that we need a benchmark, or a baseline model, when modeling to determine whether the model we develop is better than a naive method. The performance of a model must always be assessed relative to a baseline model.

```
test = df.iloc[-4:]                              ◁───  The test set corresponds to
                                                       the last four data points.

test['naive_seasonal'] = df['data'].iloc[76:80].values      ◁───
```

The naive seasonal forecast is implemented by selecting the quarterly EPS reported in 1979 and using the same values as a forecast for the year 1980.

With our baseline in place, we can now make forecasts using the ARIMA(3,2,3) model and store the results in the ARIMA_pred column.

```
ARIMA_pred = model_fit.get_prediction(80, 83).predicted_mean      ◁───

test['ARIMA_pred'] = ARIMA_pred      ◁───
```

Get the predicted values for the year 1980.

Assign the forecasts to the ARIMA_pred column.

Let's visualize our forecasts to see how close the predictions from each method are to the observed values. The resulting plot is shown in figure 7.8.

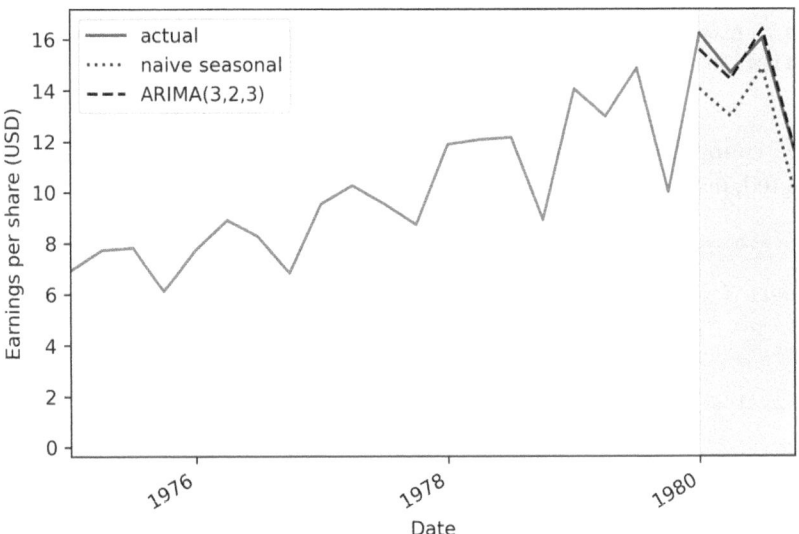

Figure 7.8   Forecasts of the quarterly EPS of Johnson & Johnson in 1980. We can see that the predictions coming from the ARIMA(3,2,3) model, shown as a dashed line, almost perfectly overlap the observed data in 1980.

In figure 7.8 we can see the naive seasonal forecast as a dotted line and the ARIMA(3,2,3) forecasts as a dashed line. The ARIMA(3,2,3) model predicted the quarterly EPS with a very small error.

We can quantify that error by measuring the mean absolute percentage error (MAPE) and display the metric for each forecasting method in a bar plot, as shown in figure 7.9.

```
def mape(y_true, y_pred):          ◁─┘ Define a function to
    return np.mean(np.abs((y_true - y_pred) / y_true)) * 100     compute the MAPE.

mape_naive_seasonal = mape(test['data'], test['naive_seasonal'])     ◁─────
mape_ARIMA = mape(test['data'], test['ARIMA_pred'])     ◁───

fig, ax = plt.subplots()

x = ['naive seasonal', 'ARIMA(3,2,3)']
y = [mape_naive_seasonal, mape_ARIMA]

ax.bar(x, y, width=0.4)
ax.set_xlabel('Models')
ax.set_ylabel('MAPE (%)')
ax.set_ylim(0, 15)

for index, value in enumerate(y):
    plt.text(x=index, y=value + 1, s=str(round(value,2)), ha='center')

plt.tight_layout()
```

Define a function to compute the MAPE.

Compute the MAPE for the ARIMA(3,2,3) model.

Compute the MAPE for the naive seasonal method.

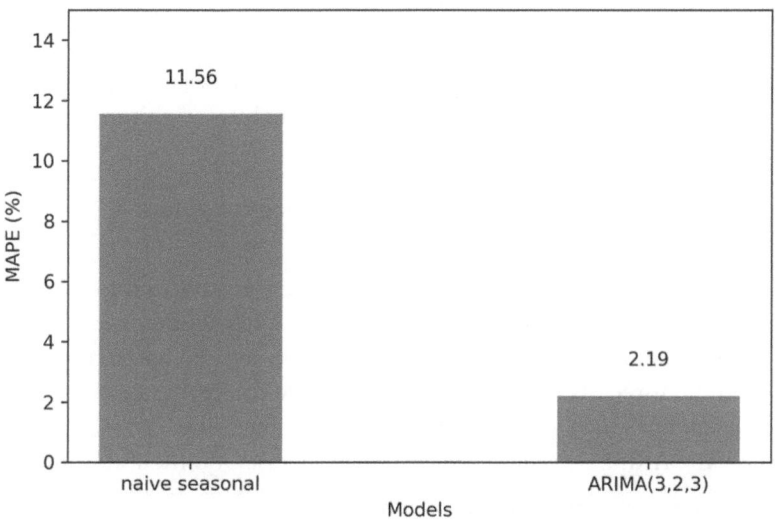

Figure 7.9   The MAPE for both forecasting methods. You can see that the ARIMA model has an error metric that is one fifth of the baseline.

In figure 7.9, you can see that the MAPE for the naive seasonal forecast is 11.56%, while the MAPE for the ARIMA(3,2,3) model is 2.19%, which roughly one fifth of the benchmark value. This means that our predictions are on average 2.19% off from the actual values. The ARIMA(3,2,3) model is clearly a better model than the naive seasonal method.

7.4   Next steps

In this chapter, we covered the ARIMA(p,d,q) model, which allows us to model and forecast non-stationary time series.

The order of integration d defines how many times a series must be differenced to become stationary. This parameter then allows us to fit the model on the original series and get a forecast in the same scale, unlike the ARMA(p,q) model, which required the series to be stationary for the model to be applied and required us to reverse the transformations on the forecasts.

To apply the ARIMA(p,d,q) model, we added an extra step to our general modeling procedure, which simply involves finding the value for the order of integration. This corresponds to the minimum number of times a series must be differenced to become stationary.

Now we can add another layer to the ARIMA(p,d,q) model that allows us to consider yet another property of time series: seasonality. We have studied the Johnson & Johnson dataset enough times to realize that there are clear cyclical patterns in the series. To integrate the seasonality of a series in a model, we must use the *seasonal autoregressive integrated moving average* (SARIMA) model, or SARIMA(p,d,q)(P,D,Q)$_m$. This will be the subject of the next chapter.

7.5   Exercises

Now is the time to apply the ARIMA model on previous datasets that we have explored. The full solution to this exercise is available on GitHub: https://github.com/marcopeix/TimeSeriesForecastingInPython/tree/master/CH07.

7.5.1   Apply the ARIMA(p,d,q) model on the datasets from chapters 4, 5, and 6

In chapters 4, 5, and 6, non-stationary time series were introduced to show you how to apply the MA(q), AR(p), and ARMA(p,q) models. In each chapter, we transformed the series to make it stationary, fit the model, made forecasts, and had to reverse the transformation on the forecasts to bring them back to the original scale of the data.

Now that you know how to account for non-stationary time series, revisit each dataset and apply the ARIMA(p,d,q) model. For each dataset, do the following:

1   Apply the general modeling procedure.
2   Is an ARIMA(0,1,2) model suitable for the dataset in chapter 4?
3   Is an ARIMA(3,1,0) model suitable for the dataset in chapter 5?
4   Is an ARIMA(2,1,2) model suitable for the dataset in chapter 6?

Summary

- The autoregressive integrated moving average model, denoted as ARIMA(p,d,q), is the combination of the autoregressive model AR(p), the order of integration d, and the moving average model MA(q).
- The ARIMA(p,d,q) model can be applied on non-stationary time series and has the added advantage of returning forecasts in the same scale as the original series.
- The order of integration d is equal to the minimum number of times a series must be differenced to become stationary.
- An ARIMA$(p,0,q)$ model is equivalent to an ARMA(p,q) model.

Accounting
for seasonality

This chapter covers

- Examining the seasonal autoregressive integrated moving average model, SARIMA(p,d,q)(P,D,Q)$_m$
- Analyzing seasonal patterns in a time series
- Forecasting using the SARIMA(p,d,q)(P,D,Q)$_m$ model

In the previous chapter, we covered the autoregressive integrated moving average model, ARIMA(p,d,q), which allows us to model non-stationary time series. Now we'll add another layer of complexity to the ARIMA model to include seasonal patterns in time series, leading us to the SARIMA model.

The *seasonal autoregressive integrated moving average* (SARIMA) model, or SARIMA (p,d,q) (P,D,Q) $_m$, adds another set of parameters that allows us to take into account periodic patterns when forecasting a time series, which is not always possible with an ARIMA(p,d,q) model.

In this chapter, we'll examine the SARIMA(p,d,q) (P,D,Q) $_m$ model and adapt our general modeling procedure to account for the new parameters. We'll also determine how to identify seasonal patterns in a time series and apply the SARIMA model to forecast a seasonal time series. Specifically, we'll apply the model to forecast the total number of monthly passengers for an airline. The data was recorded from January 1949 to December 1960. The series is shown in figure 8.1.

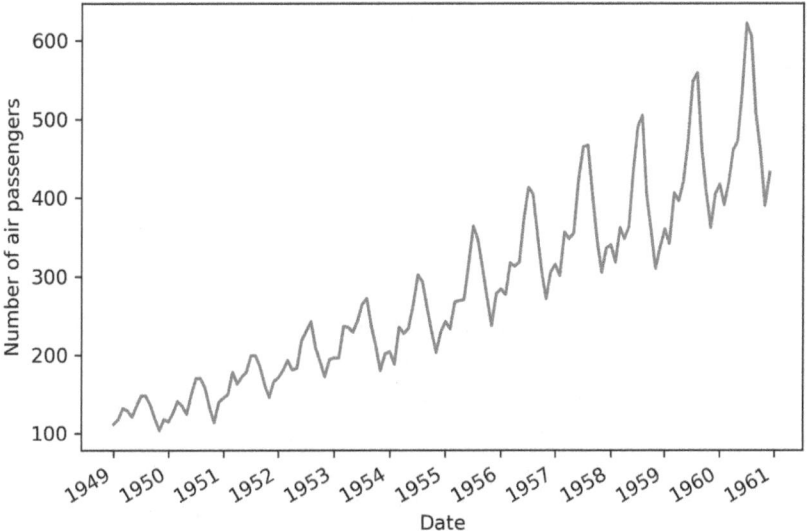

Figure 8.1   Monthly total number of air passengers for an airline, from January 1949 to December 1960. You'll notice a clear seasonal pattern in the series, with peak traffic occurring toward the middle of each year.

In figure 8.1 we can see a clear seasonal pattern in the series. The number of air passengers is lower at the beginning and end of the year, and it spikes up during the months of June, July, and August. Our objective is to forecast the number of monthly air passengers for the one year. It is important for an airline company to forecast the number of air passengers so they can better price their tickets and schedule flights to meet the demand for a given month.

8.1   Examining the SARIMA(p,d,q)(P,D,Q)$_m$ model

The SARIMA(p,d,q) (P,D,Q) $_m$ model expands on the ARIMA(p,d,q) model from the previous chapter by adding seasonal parameters. You'll notice four new parameters in the model: P, D, Q, and m. The first three have the same meaning as in the ARIMA(p,d,q) model, but they are their seasonal counterparts. To understand the meaning of these parameters and how they affect the final model, we must first define m.

The parameter m stands for the frequency. In the context of a time series, the frequency is defined as the number of observations per cycle. The length of the cycle will depend on the dataset. For data that was recorded every year, quarter, month, or week, the length of a cycle is considered to be 1 year. If the data was recorded annually, $m = 1$ since there is only one observation per year. If the data was recorded quarterly, $m = 4$ since there are four quarters in a year, and therefore four observations per year. Of course, if the data was recorded monthly, $m = 12$. Finally, for weekly data, $m = 52$. Table 8.1 indicates the appropriate value of m depending on the frequency at which the data was collected.

Table 8.1   Appropriate frequency *m* depending on the data

Data collection	Frequency *m*
Annual	1
Quarterly	4
Monthly	12
Weekly	52

When data is collected on a daily or sub-daily basis, there are multiple ways of interpreting the frequency. For example, daily data can have a weekly seasonality. In that case, the frequency is $m = 7$ because there would be seven observations in a full cycle of 1 week. It could also have a yearly seasonality, meaning that $m = 365$. Thus, you can see that daily and sub-daily data can have a different cycle length, and therefore a different frequency m. Table 8.2 provides the appropriate value of m depending on the seasonal cycle for daily and sub-daily data.

Table 8.2   Appropriate frequency *m* for daily and sub-daily data

Data collection	Frequency *m*				
	Minute	Hour	Day	Week	Year
Daily				7	365
Hourly			24	168	8766
Every minute		60	1440	10080	525960
Every second	60	3600	86400	604800	31557600

Now that you understand the parameter m, the meanings of P, D, and Q become intuitive. As mentioned before, they are the seasonal counterparts of the p, d, and q parameters that you know from the ARIMA(p,d,q) model.

Seasonal autoregressive integrated moving average (SARIMA) model

The *seasonal autoregressive integrated moving average* (SARIMA) model adds seasonal parameters to the ARIMA(p,d,q) model.

It is denoted as SARIMA$(p,d,q)(P,D,Q)_m$, where P is the order of the seasonal AR(P) process, D is the seasonal order of integration, Q is the order of the seasonal MA(Q) process, and m is the frequency, or the number of observations per seasonal cycle.

Note that a SARIMA$(p,d,q)(0,0,0)_m$ model is equivalent to an ARIMA(p,d,q) model.

Let's consider an example where $m = 12$. If $P = 2$, this means that we are including two past values of the series at a lag that is a multiple of m. Therefore, we'll include the values at y_{t-12} and y_{t-24}.

Similarly, if $D = 1$, this means that a seasonal difference makes the series stationary. In this case, a seasonal difference would be expressed as equation 8.1.

$$y'_t = y_t - y_{t-12}$$

Equation 8.1

In a situation where $Q = 2$, we'll include past error terms at lags that are a multiple of m. Therefore, we'll include the errors ϵ_{t-12} and ϵ_{t-24}.

Let's put this into perspective using the airline's total monthly air passengers dataset. We know that this is monthly data, which means that $m = 12$. Also, we can see that the months of July and August usually have the highest numbers of air passengers in the year, as shown by the round markers in figure 8.2. Therefore, if we are to forecast the month of July in 1961, the information coming from the month of July in prior years is likely going to be useful, since we can intuitively expect the number of air passengers to be at its highest point in the month of July 1961. The parameters P, D, Q, and m allow us to capture that information from the previous seasonal cycle to help us forecast our time series.

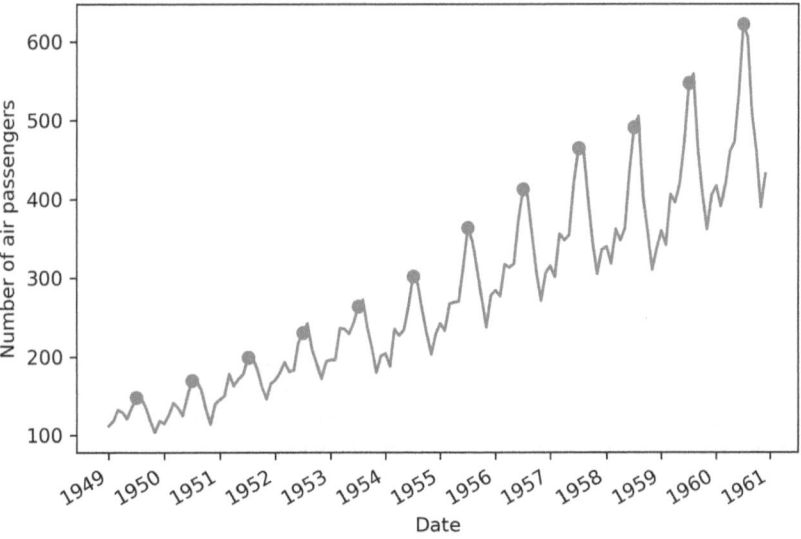

Figure 8.2 **Marking the month of July of each year. You can see how the month of July has the highest number of air passengers. Therefore, it would make sense if July of the following year also saw the highest number of air passengers in the year. That kind of information is captured by the seasonal parameters P, Q, Q, and m of the SARIMA$(p,d,q)(P,D,Q)_m$ model.**

Now that we have examined the SARIMA model and you understand how it expands on the ARIMA model, let's move on to identifying the presence of seasonal patterns in a time series.

8.2   *Identifying seasonal patterns in a time series*

Intuitively, we know that it makes sense to apply the SARIMA model on data that exhibits a seasonal pattern. Therefore, it is important to determine ways to identify seasonality in time series.

Usually, plotting the time series data is enough to observe periodic patterns. For example, looking at the total monthly air passengers in figure 8.3, it is easy for us to identify a repeating pattern every year, with a high number of passengers being recorded during June, July, and August of each year, and fewer passengers in November, December, and January of each year.

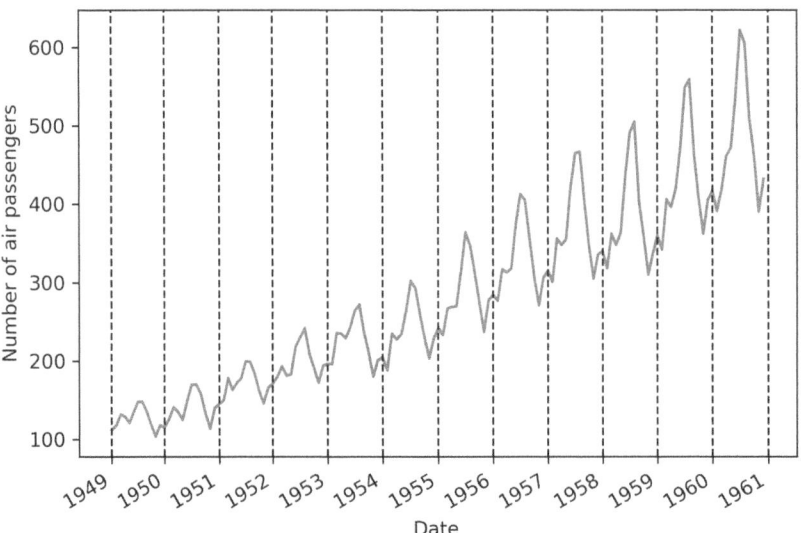

Figure 8.3   Highlighting the seasonal pattern in the monthly number of air passengers. The dashed vertical lines separate periods of twelve months. We can clearly see how a peak occurs in the middle of each year, and there is a very similar pattern for the beginning and end of each year. This observation is usually enough to determine that the dataset is seasonal.

Another way of identifying seasonal patterns in a time series is using time series decomposition, a method that we first used in chapter 1. Time series decomposition is a statistical task that separates the time series into its three main components: a trend component, a seasonal component, and the residuals.

The trend component represents the long-term change in the time series. This component is responsible for time series that increase or decrease over time. The seasonal component is, of course, the seasonal pattern in the time series. It represents repeated fluctuations that occur over a fixed period of time. Finally, the residuals, or the noise, express any irregularity that cannot be explained by the trend or the seasonal component.

> ## Time series decomposition
>
> *Time series decomposition* is a statistical task that separates the time series into its three main components: a trend component, a seasonal component, and the residuals.
>
> The trend component represents the long-term change in the time series. This component is responsible for time series that increase or decrease over time. The seasonal component is the periodic pattern in the time series. It represents repeated fluctuations that occur over a fixed period of time. Finally, the residuals, or the noise, express any irregularity that cannot be explained by the trend or the seasonal component.

NOTE The source code for this chapter is available on GitHub: https://github .com/marcopeix/TimeSeriesForecastingInPython/tree/master/CH08.

With time series decomposition, we can clearly identify and visualize the seasonal component of a time series. We can decompose the dataset for air passengers using the STL function from the statsmodels library to generate figure 8.4.

```
from statsmodels.tsa.seasonal import STL

decomposition = STL(df['Passengers'], period=12).fit()          ◁──────

fig, (ax1, ax2, ax3, ax4) = plt.subplots(nrows=4, ncols=1, sharex=True,
➥  figsize=(10,8))                          ◁─┐ Plot each
                                               │ component
ax1.plot(decomposition.observed)              │ in a figure.
ax1.set_ylabel('Observed')

ax2.plot(decomposition.trend)
ax2.set_ylabel('Trend')

ax3.plot(decomposition.seasonal)
ax3.set_ylabel('Seasonal')

ax4.plot(decomposition.resid)
ax4.set_ylabel('Residuals')

plt.xticks(np.arange(0, 145, 12), np.arange(1949, 1962, 1))

fig.autofmt_xdate()
plt.tight_layout()
```

Decompose the series using the STL function. The period is equal to the frequency m. Since we have monthly data, the period is 12.

In figure 8.4 you can see each component of our time series. You'll notice that the *y*-axis for the plots of the trend, seasonal, and residuals components are all slightly different

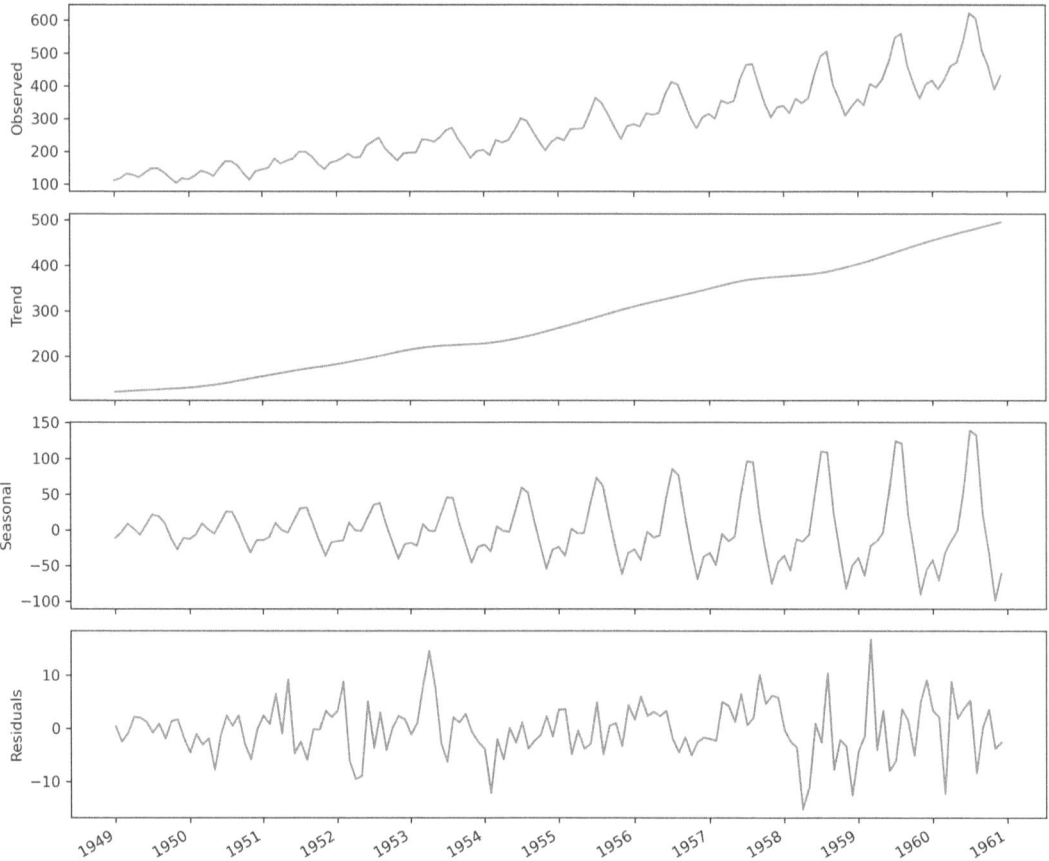

Figure 8.4   Decomposing the dataset for air passengers. The first plot shows the observed data. The second plot shows the trend component, which tells us that the number of air passengers is increasing over time. The third plot displays the seasonal component, and we can clearly see a repeating pattern through time. Finally, the last plot shows the residuals, which are variations in the data that cannot be explained by the trend or the seasonal component.

from the observed data. This is because each plot shows the magnitude of change that is attributed to that particular component. That way, the sum of the trend, seasonal, and residuals components results in the observed data shown in the top plot. This explains why the seasonal component is sometimes in the negative values and other times in the positive values, as it creates the peaks and troughs in the observed data.

In a situation where we have a time series with no seasonal pattern, the decomposition process will display a flat horizontal line at 0 for the seasonal component. To demonstrate that, I simulated a linear time series and decomposed it into its three components using the method you just saw. The result is shown in figure 8.5.

You can see how time series decomposition can help us determine if our data is seasonal or not. This is a graphical method and not a statistical test, but it is enough to

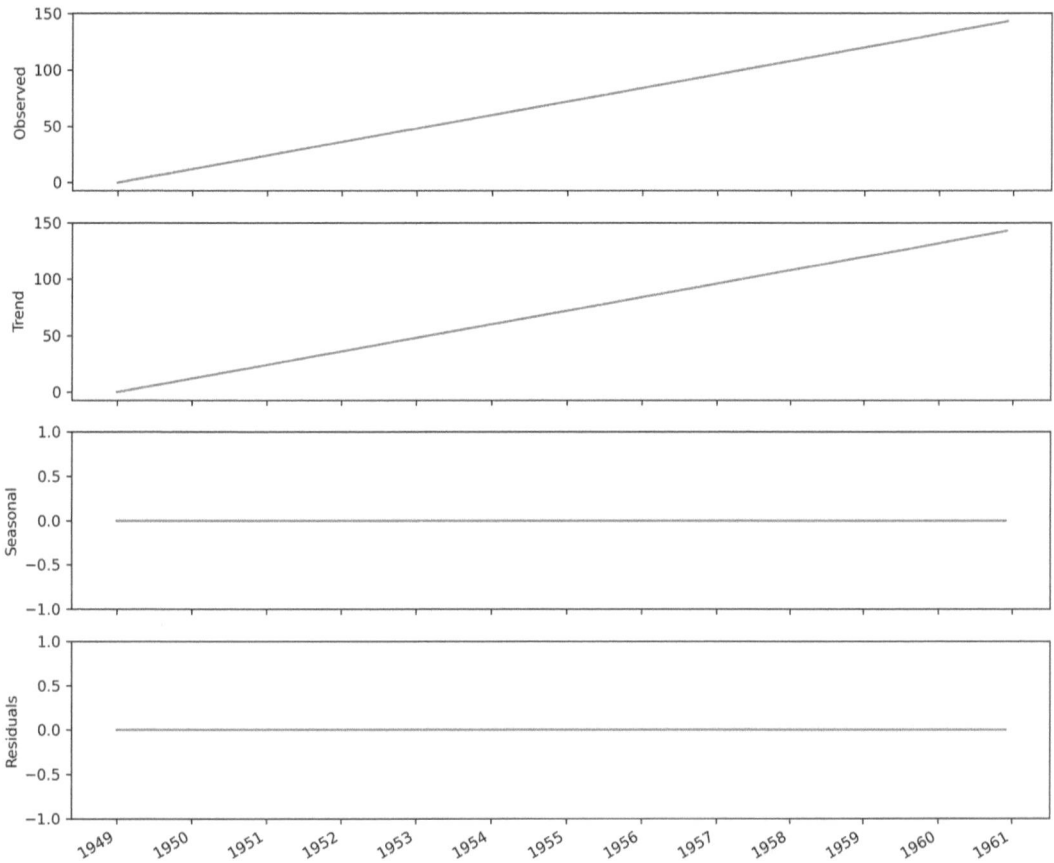

Figure 8.5   Time series decomposition of a simulated linear series. The top plot shows the observed data, and you'll notice that I simulated a perfectly linear series. The second plot shows the trend component, which is expected to be the same as the observed data, since the series is linearly increasing over time. Since there is no seasonal pattern, the seasonal component is a flat horizontal line at 0. Here the residuals are also 0, because I simulated a perfectly linear series.

determine whether a series is seasonal or not, so that we can apply the appropriate model for forecasting. In fact, there are no statistical tests to identify seasonality in time series.

Now that you know how to identify seasonal patterns in a series, we can move on to adapting the general modeling procedure to include the new parameters of the SARIMA$(p,d,q)(P,D,Q)_m$ model and forecast the number of monthly air passengers.

8.3   Forecasting the number of monthly air passengers

In the previous chapter, we adapted our general modeling procedure to account for the new parameter *d* in the ARIMA model that allows us to forecast non-stationary time series. The steps are outlined in figure 8.6. Now we must modify it again to account for the new parameters of the SARIMA model, which are *P*, *D*, *Q*, and *m*.

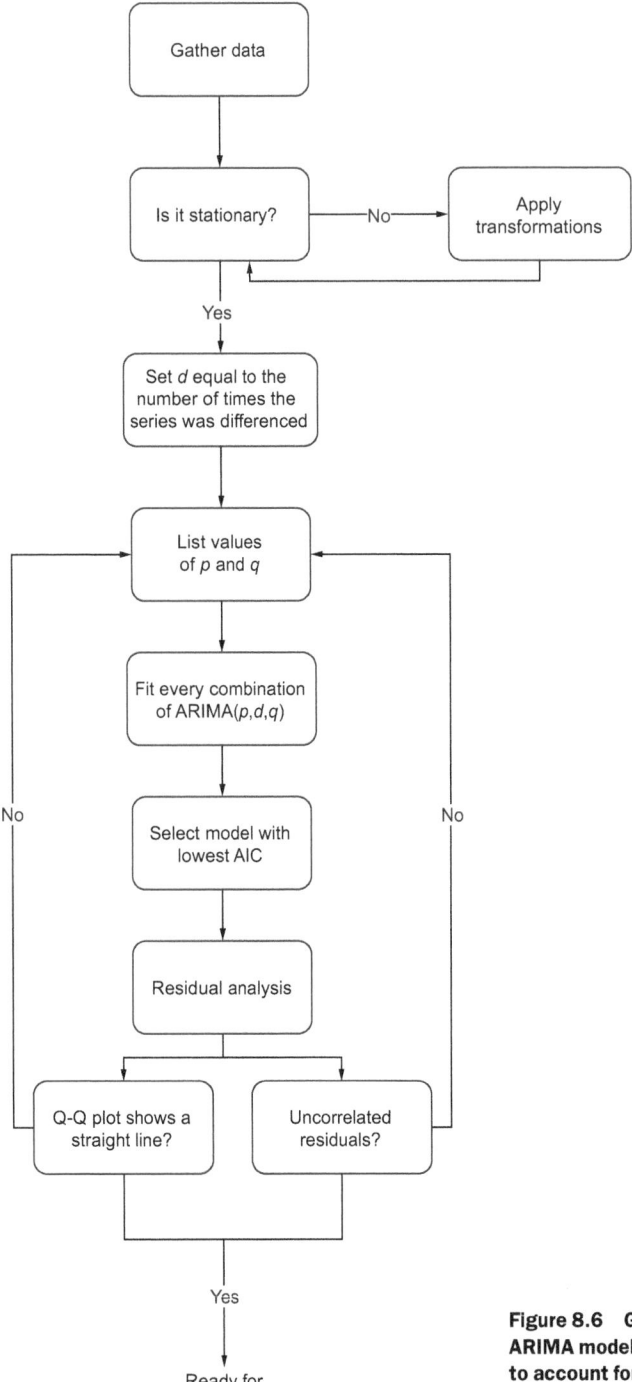

Figure 8.6   **General modeling procedure for an ARIMA model. We now need to adapt the steps to account for the parameters *P*, *D*, *Q*, and *m* of the SARIMA model.**

The first step of gathering data remains untouched. Then we still check for stationarity and apply transformation in order to set the parameter *d*. However, we can also perform seasonal differencing to make the series stationary, and *D* will be equal to the minimum number of times we applied seasonal differencing.

Then we set a range of possible values for *p*, *q*, *P*, and *Q*, as the SARIMA model can also incorporate the order of the seasonal autoregressive and seasonal moving average processes. Note that the addition of these two new parameters will increase the number of unique combinations of SARIMA$(p,d,q)(P,D,Q)_m$ models we can fit, so this step will take longer to complete. The rest of the procedure remains the same, as we still need to select the model with the lowest AIC and perform residual analysis before using the model for forecasting. The resulting modeling procedure is shown in figure 8.7.

With our new modeling procedure defined, we are now ready to forecast the total number of monthly air passengers. For this scenario, we wish to forecast 1 year of monthly air passengers, so we will use the data from 1960 as the test set, as shown in figure 8.8.

The baseline model will be the naive seasonal forecast, and we will use both the ARIMA(p,d,q) and SARIMA$(p,d,q)(P,D,Q)_m$ models to verify whether the addition of seasonal components will yield better forecasts.

8.3.1   Forecasting with an ARIMA(p,d,q) model

We'll first model the dataset using an ARIMA(p,d,q) model. That way, we can compare its performance to the SARIMA$(p,d,q)(P,D,Q)_m$ model.

Following the general modeling procedure we outlined before, we'll first test for stationarity. Again, we use the ADF test.

```
ad_fuller_result = adfuller(df['Passengers'])

print(f'ADF Statistic: {ad_fuller_result[0]}')
print(f'p-value: {ad_fuller_result[1]}')
```

This prints out an ADF statistic of 0.82 and a p-value of 0.99. Therefore, we cannot reject the null hypothesis and the series is not stationary. We'll difference the series and test for stationarity again.

```
df_diff = np.diff(df['Passengers'], n=1)      ⟵  First-order
                                                  differencing
ad_fuller_result = adfuller(df_diff)

print(f'ADF Statistic: {ad_fuller_result[0]}')
print(f'p-value: {ad_fuller_result[1]}')
```

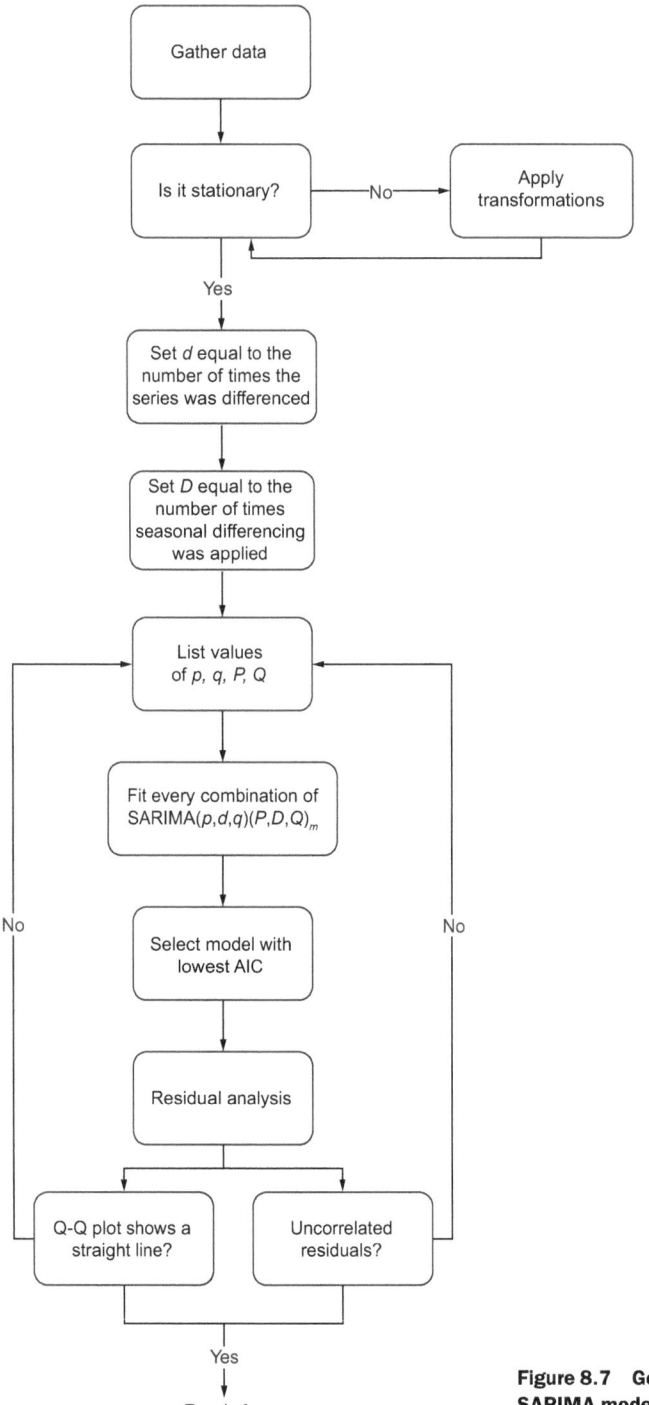

Figure 8.7   **General modeling procedure for the SARIMA model. Note that we can set *P*, *D*, and *Q* to 0 to obtain an ARIMA(*p*,*d*,*q*) model.**

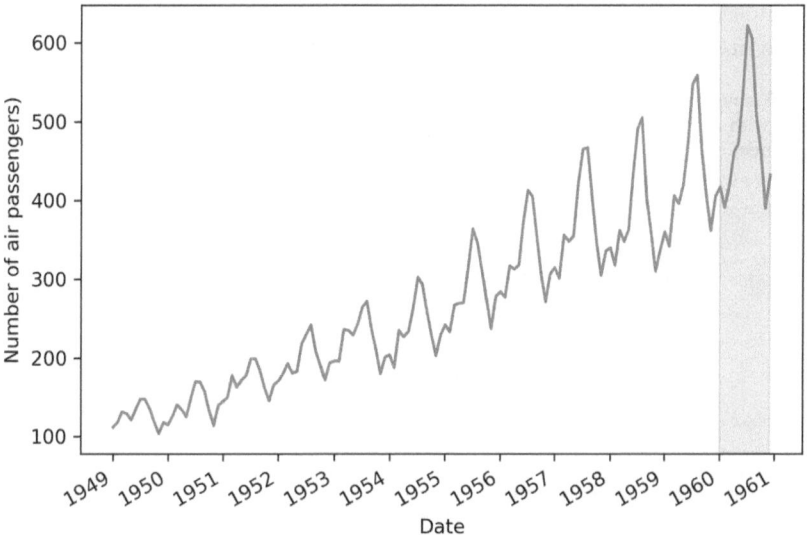

Figure 8.8 Train set and test set split for the air passengers dataset. The shaded area represents the testing period, which corresponds to the full year of 1960, as our goal is to forecast a year of monthly air passengers.

This returns an ADF statistic of –2.83 and a p-value of 0.054. Again, we cannot reject the null hypothesis, and differencing the series once did not make it stationary. Therefore, we'll difference it again and test for stationarity.

```
df_diff2 = np.diff(df_diff, n=1)          ◁──┐  Series is now
                                             │  differenced
ad_fuller_result = adfuller(df_diff2)        │  twice

print(f'ADF Statistic: {ad_fuller_result[0]}')
print(f'p-value: {ad_fuller_result[1]}')
```

This returns an ADF statistic of –16.38 and a p-value of 2.73×10^{-29}. Now we can reject the null hypothesis, and our series is considered to be stationary. Since the series was differenced twice to become stationary, $d = 2$.

Now we can define a range of possible values for the parameters p and q and fit all unique ARIMA(p,d,q) models. We'll specifically choose a range from 0 to 12 to allow the ARIMA model to go back 12 timesteps in time. Since the data is sampled monthly and we know it is seasonal, we can hypothesize that the number of air passengers in January of a given year is likely predictive of the number of air passengers in January of the following year. Since these two points are 12 timesteps apart, we'll allow the values of p and q to vary from 0 to 12 in order to potentially capture this seasonal information in the ARIMA(p,d,q) model. Finally, since we are working with an ARIMA model, we'll set P, D, and Q to 0. Note the use of the parameter s in the following code, which is equivalent to *m*. The implementation of SARIMA in `statsmodels` simply uses s instead of *m*—they both denote the frequency.

Set P and Q to 0, since we are working with an ARIMA(p,d,q) model.

Allow p and q to vary from 0 to 12 in order to capture seasonal information.

```
ps = range(0, 13, 1)
qs = range(0, 13, 1)
Ps = [0]
Qs = [0]

d = 2
D = 0
s = 12

ARIMA_order_list = list(product(ps, qs, Ps, Qs))
```

Set the parameter d to the number of times the series was differenced to become stationary.

D is set to 0 because we are working with an ARIMA(p,d,q) model.

Generate all possible combinations of (p,d,q)(0,0,0).

The parameter s is equivalent to m. They both denote the frequency. This is simply how the SARIMA model is implemented in the statsmodels library.

You'll notice that we set the parameters *P*, *D*, *Q*, and *m*, even though we are working with an ARIMA model. This is because we are going to define an `optimize_SARIMA` function that will then be reused in the next section. We set *P*, *D*, and *Q* to 0 because a SARIMA(*p,d,q*)(0,0,0)$_m$ model is equivalent to an ARIMA(*p,d,q*) model.

The `optimize_SARIMA` function builds on the `optimize_ARIMA` function that we defined in the previous chapter. This time, we'll integrate the possible values of *P* and *Q*, as well as add the seasonal order of integration *D* and the frequency *m*. The function is shown in the following listing.

Listing 8.1   Defining a function to select the best SARIMA model

```
from typing import Union
from tqdm import tqdm_notebook
from statsmodels.tsa.statespace.sarimax import SARIMAX

def optimize_SARIMA(endog: Union[pd.Series, list], order_list: list, d:
    int, D: int, s: int) -> pd.DataFrame:

    results = []

    for order in tqdm_notebook(order_list):
        try:
            model = SARIMAX(
                endog,
                order=(order[0], d, order[1]),
                seasonal_order=(order[2], D, order[3], s),
                simple_differencing=False).fit(disp=False)
        except:
            continue
```

The order_list parameter now includes p, q, P, and Q orders. We also add the seasonal order of differencing D and the frequency. Remember that the frequency m in the SARIMA model is denoted as s in the implementation in the statsmodels library.

Loop over all unique SARIMA(p,d,q)(P,D,Q)$_m$ models, fit them, and store the AICs.

```
        aic = model.aic
        results.append([order, aic])

    result_df = pd.DataFrame(results)
    result_df.columns = ['(p,q,P,Q)', 'AIC']

    #Sort in ascending order, lower AIC is better
    result_df = result_df.sort_values(by='AIC',
➡  ascending=True).reset_index(drop=True)

    return result_df
```
◄──┐ **Return the sorted DataFrame,**
    │ **starting with the lowest AIC.**

With the function ready, we can launch it using the train set and get the ARIMA model with the lowest AIC. Despite the fact that we are using the `optimize_SARIMA` function, we are still fitting an ARIMA model because we specifically set *P*, *D*, and *Q* to 0. For the train set, we'll take all data points but the last twelve, as they will be used for the test set.

The train set consists of all data points but the last 12, as the last year of data is used for the test set.

```
train = df['Passengers'][:-12]
```
◄─┘

```
ARIMA_result_df = optimize_SARIMA(train, ARIMA_order_list, d, D, s)    ◄──────┐
ARIMA_result_df    ◄──┐
```
Display the sorted   **Run the**
DataFrame in increasing   **optimize_SARIMA**
order of AIC.   **function.**

This returns a `DataFrame` where the model with the lowest AIC is a SARIMA(11,2,3)(0,0,0)$_{12}$ model, which is equivalent to an ARIMA(11,2,3) model. As you can see, allowing the order *p* to vary from 0 to 12 was beneficial for the model, as the model with the lowest AIC takes into account the past 11 values of the series, since *p* = 11. We will see if this is enough to capture seasonal information from the series, and we will compare the performance of the ARIMA model to the SARIMA model in the next section.

For now, we'll focus on performing residual analysis. We can fit the ARIMA(11,2,3) model obtained previously and plot the residuals' diagnostics.

```
ARIMA_model = SARIMAX(train, order=(11,2,3), simple_differencing=False)
ARIMA_model_fit = ARIMA_model.fit(disp=False)

ARIMA_model_fit.plot_diagnostics(figsize=(10,8));
```

The result is shown in figure 8.9. Based on the qualitative analysis, the residuals are close to white noise, meaning that the errors are random.

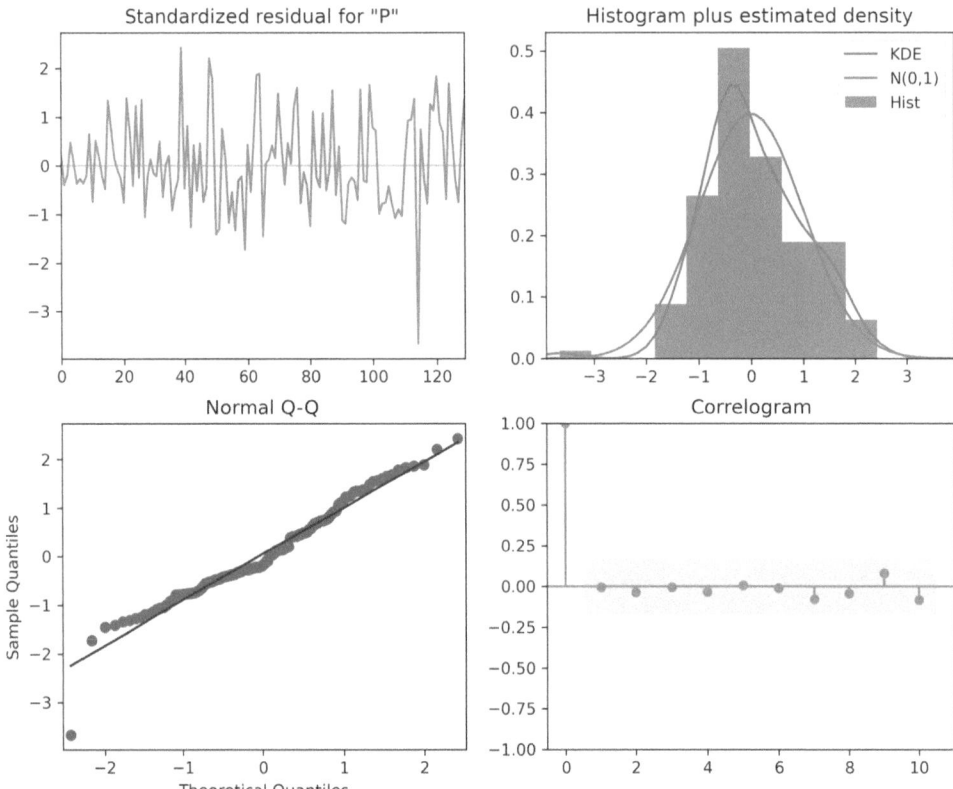

Figure 8.9   Residuals' diagnostics of the ARIMA(11,2,3) model. In the top-left plot, the residuals have no trend with a variance that seems fairly constant over time, which resembles the behavior of white noise. The top-right plot shows the distribution of the residuals, which approaches a normal distribution, despite the unusual peak. This is further confirmed by the Q-Q plot at the bottom left, which displays a fairly straight line that lies on *y = x*. Finally, the correlogram in the bottom-right plot shows no significant autocorrelation coefficients after lag 0, which is exactly like white noise. From this analysis, the residuals resemble white noise.

The next step is to run the Ljung-Box test on the residuals to make sure that they are independent and uncorrelated.

```
from statsmodels.stats.diagnostic import acorr_ljungbox

residuals = ARIMA_model_fit.resid

lbvalue, pvalue = acorr_ljungbox(residuals, np.arange(1, 11, 1))

print(pvalue)
```

The returned p-values are all greater than 0.05 except for the first two values. This means that, according to the Ljung-Box test, we reject the null hypothesis with a 5% chance of being wrong, since we set our significance boundary to 0.05. However, the third value and onwards are all greater than 0.05, so we reject the null hypothesis, concluding that the residuals are uncorrelated starting at lag 3.

This is an interesting situation to dissect, because the graphical analysis of the residuals leads us to conclude that they resemble white noise, but the Ljung-Box test points to some correlation at lags 1 and 2. This means that our ARIMA model is not capturing all the information from the data.

In this case, we'll move forward with the model, because we know that we are modeling seasonal data with a non-seasonal model. Therefore, the Ljung-Box test is really telling us that our model is not perfect, but that's okay, because part of this exercise is to compare the performance of ARIMA and SARIMA and demonstrate that SARIMA is the way to go when dealing with seasonal data.

As previously mentioned, we wish to predict a full year of monthly air passengers, using the last 12 months of data as our test set. The baseline model is the naive seasonal forecast, where we simply use the number of air passengers for each month of 1959 as a forecast for each month of 1960.

Create the test set. It corresponds to the last 12 data points, which is the data for 1960.

The naive seasonal forecast simply reuses the data from 1959 as a forecast for 1960.

```
test = df.iloc[-12:]

test['naive_seasonal'] = df['Passengers'].iloc[120:132].values
```

We can append the forecasts from our ARIMA(11,2,3) model to the `test` DataFrame.

```
ARIMA_pred = ARIMA_model_fit.get_prediction(132, 143).predicted_mean

test['ARIMA_pred'] = ARIMA_pred
```

Append predictions to test.

Get predictions for each month of 1960.

With forecasts from the ARIMA model stored in `test`, we will now use a SARIMA model and later compare the performance of both models to see if the SARIMA model actually performs better than the ARIMA model when applied on a seasonal time series.

8.3.2 Forecasting with a SARIMA(p,d,q)(P,D,Q)$_m$ model

In the previous section, we used an ARIMA(11,2,3) model to forecast the number of monthly air passengers. Now we'll fit a SARIMA model and see if it performs better than the ARIMA model. Hopefully the SARIMA model will perform better, since it can capture seasonal information, and we know that our dataset exhibits clear seasonality, as shown in figure 8.10.

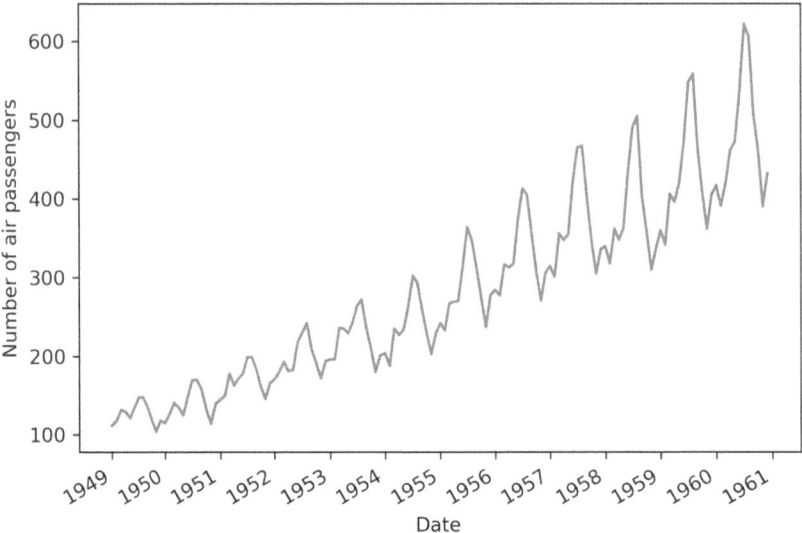

Figure 8.10 Monthly total number of air passengers for an airline, from January 1949 to December 1960. You can see a clear seasonal pattern in the series, with peak traffic occurring toward the middle of the year.

Following the steps in our general modeling procedure (figure 8.11), we'll first check for stationarity and apply the required transformations.

```
ad_fuller_result = adfuller(df['Passengers'])

print(f'ADF Statistic: {ad_fuller_result[0]}')
print(f'p-value: {ad_fuller_result[1]}')
```

The ADF test on the dataset returns an ADF statistic of 0.82 and a p-value of 0.99. Therefore, we cannot reject the null hypothesis and the series is not stationary. We can apply a first-order differencing and test for stationarity.

```
df_diff = np.diff(df['Passengers'], n=1)

ad_fuller_result = adfuller(df_diff)

print(f'ADF Statistic: {ad_fuller_result[0]}')
print(f'p-value: {ad_fuller_result[1]}')
```

This returns an ADF statistic of −2.83 and a p-value of 0.054. Since the p-value is greater than 0.05, we cannot reject the null hypothesis, and the series is still non-stationary. Therefore, let's apply a seasonal difference and test for stationarity.

```
df_diff_seasonal_diff = np.diff(df_diff, n=12)      ◁───

ad_fuller_result = adfuller(df_diff_seasonal_diff)

print(f'ADF Statistic: {ad_fuller_result[0]}')
print(f'p-value: {ad_fuller_result[1]}')
```

Seasonal differencing. Since we have monthly data, m = 12, so the seasonal difference is the difference between two values that are 12 timesteps apart.

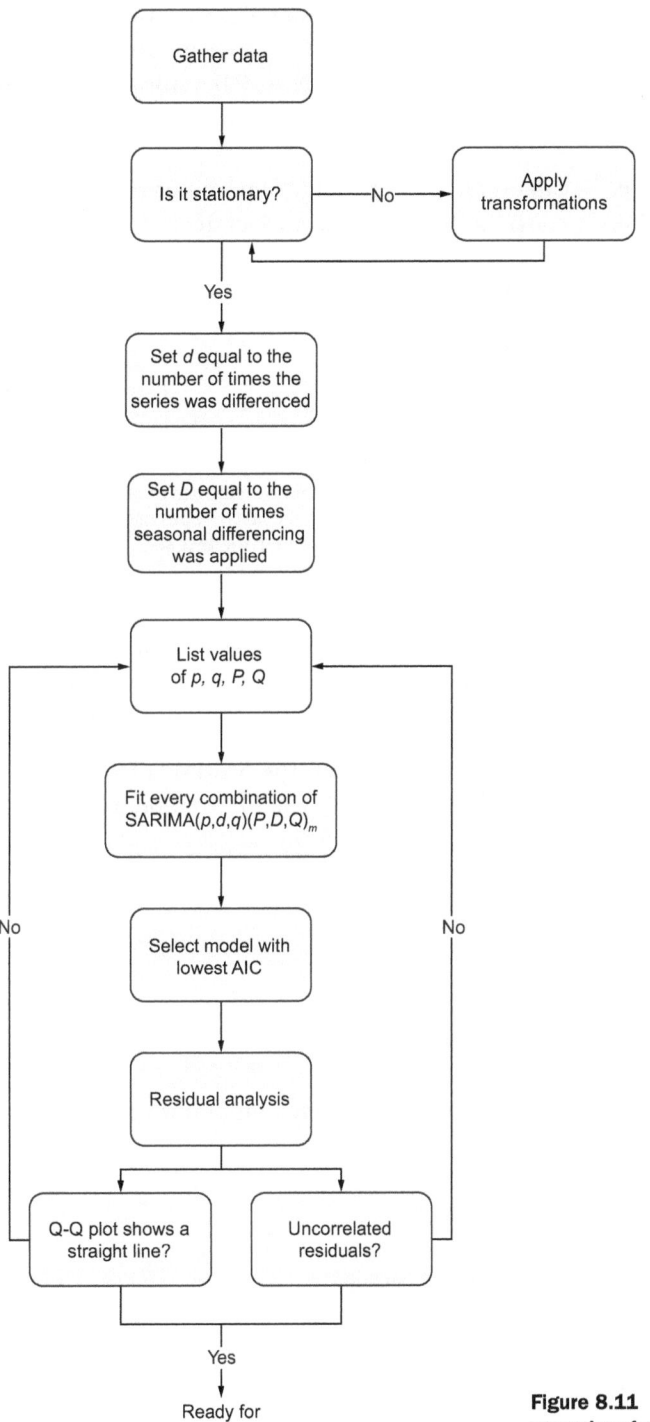

Figure 8.11 General modeling procedure for the SARIMA model

This returns an ADF statistic of –17.63 and a p-value of 3.82×10^{-30}. With a large and negative ADF statistic and a p-value smaller than 0.05, we can reject the null hypothesis and consider the transformed series as stationary. Therefore, we performed one round of differencing, meaning that $d = 1$, and one round of seasonal differencing, meaning that $D = 1$.

With this step done, we can now define the range of possible values for p, q, P, and Q, fit each unique SARIMA$(p,d,q)(P,D,Q)_m$ model, and select the one with the lowest AIC.

```
ps = range(0, 4, 1)        ◁──┐   We try values of
qs = range(0, 4, 1)           │   [0,1,2,3] for p, q,
Ps = range(0, 4, 1)           │   P, and Q.
Qs = range(0, 4, 1)        ───┘
                                         Generate the unique
                                         combinations of
SARIMA_order_list = list(product(ps, qs, Ps, Qs))   ◁──┘  orders.


train = df['Passengers'][:-12]   ◁──┐  The train set consists of all the data
                                     │  except the last 12 data points, which
d = 1                                │  are used for the test set.
D = 1
s = 12

SARIMA_result_df = optimize_SARIMA(train, SARIMA_order_list, d, D, s)   ◁──┐
SARIMA_result_df   ◁──┐                                                     │
                      │  Display the                 Fit all SARIMA models  │
                      └  result.                     on the training set. ──┘
```

Once the function is done running, we find that the SARIMA$(2,1,1)(1,1,2)_{12}$ model has the lowest AIC, which is a value of 892.24. We can fit this model again on the training set to perform residual analysis.

We'll start by plotting the residuals' diagnostics in figure 8.12.

```
SARIMA_model = SARIMAX(train, order=(2,1,1), seasonal_order=(1,1,2,12),
➡ simple_differencing=False)
SARIMA_model_fit = SARIMA_model.fit(disp=False)

SARIMA_model_fit.plot_diagnostics(figsize=(10,8));
```

The results show that our residuals are completely random, which is exactly what we are looking for in a good model.

The final test to determine whether we can use this model for forecasting or not is the Ljung-Box test.

```
from statsmodels.stats.diagnostic import acorr_ljungbox

residuals = SARIMA_model_fit.resid

lbvalue, pvalue = acorr_ljungbox(residuals, np.arange(1, 11, 1))

print(pvalue)
```

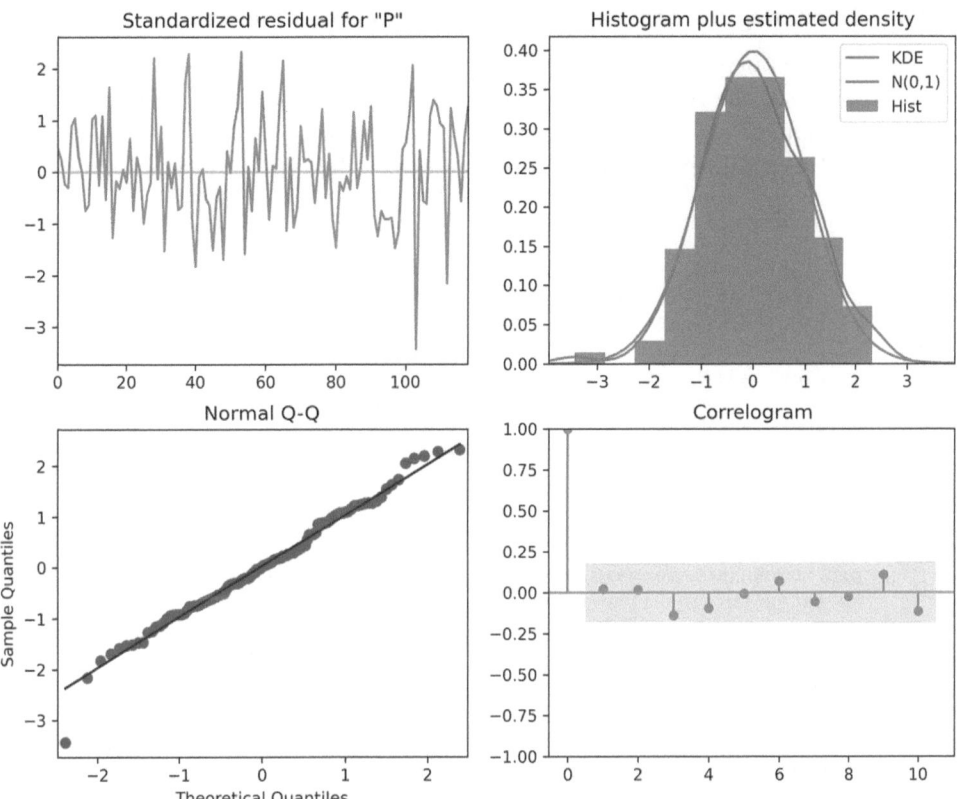

Figure 8.12   Residuals' diagnostics of the SARIMA(2,1,1)(1,1,2)$_{12}$ model. The top-left plot shows that the residuals do not exhibit a trend or a change in variance. The top-right plot shows that the residuals' distribution is very close to a normal distribution. This is further supported by the Q-Q plot at the bottom left, which displays a fairly straight line that lies on y = x. Finally, the correlogram at the bottom right shows no significant coefficients after lag 0. Therefore, everything leads to the conclusion that the residuals resemble white noise.

The returned p-values are all greater than 0.05. Therefore, we do not reject the null hypothesis, and we conclude that the residuals are independent and uncorrelated, just like white noise.

Our model has passed all the tests from the residuals analysis, and we are ready to use it for forecasting. Again, we'll forecast the number of monthly air passengers for the year of 1960 to compare the predicted values to the observed values in the test set.

```
SARIMA_pred = SARIMA_model_fit.get_prediction(132, 143).predicted_mean

test['SARIMA_pred'] = SARIMA_pred
```

Forecast the number of monthly air passengers for the year 1960.

Now that we have the results, we can compare the performance of each model and determine the best forecasting method for our problem.

8.3.3   *Comparing the performance of each forecasting method*

We can now compare the performance of each forecasting method: the naive seasonal forecasts, the ARIMA model, and the SARIMA model. We'll use the mean absolute percentage error (MAPE) to evaluate each model.

We can first visualize the forecasts against the observed values of the test set.

```
fig, ax = plt.subplots()

ax.plot(df['Month'], df['Passengers'])
ax.plot(test['Passengers'], 'b-', label='actual')
ax.plot(test['naive_seasonal'], 'r:', label='naive seasonal')
ax.plot(test['ARIMA_pred'], 'k--', label='ARIMA(11,2,3)')
ax.plot(test['SARIMA_pred'], 'g-.', label='SARIMA(2,1,1)(1,1,2,12)')

ax.set_xlabel('Date')
ax.set_ylabel('Number of air passengers')
ax.axvspan(132, 143, color='#808080', alpha=0.2)

ax.legend(loc=2)

plt.xticks(np.arange(0, 145, 12), np.arange(1949, 1962, 1))
ax.set_xlim(120, 143)        ⟵————  Zoom in on
                                    the test set
fig.autofmt_xdate()
plt.tight_layout()
```

The plot is shown in figure 8.13. The lines from the ARIMA and SARIMA models sit almost on top of the observed data, meaning that the predictions are very close to the observed data.

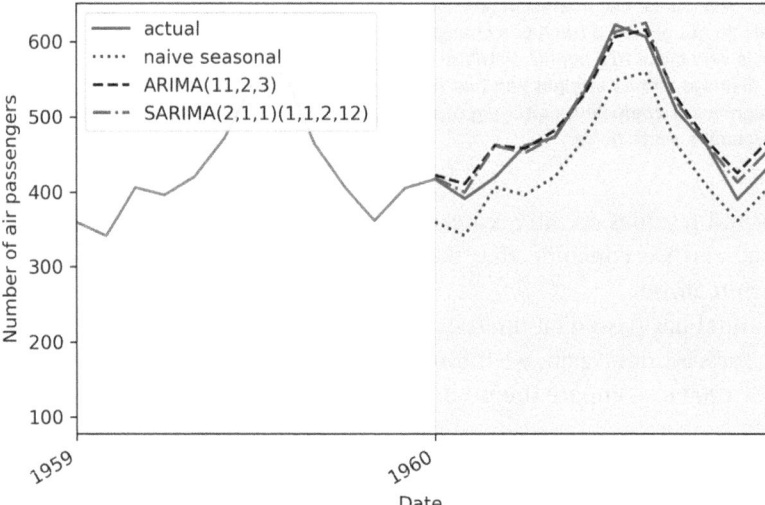

Figure 8.13   Forecasts of the number of monthly air passengers. The shaded area designates the test set. You can see that the curves coming from the ARIMA and SARIMA models almost obscure the observed data, which is indicative of good predictions.

We can measure the MAPE of each model and display it in a bar plot, as shown in figure 8.14.

```
def mape(y_true, y_pred):          ← Define a function to
    return np.mean(np.abs((y_true - y_pred) / y_true)) * 100   compute the MAPE.
```

Compute the MAPE for each forecasting method.

```
mape_naive_seasonal = mape(test['Passengers'], test['naive_seasonal'])   ←
mape_ARIMA = mape(test['Passengers'], test['ARIMA_pred'])
mape_SARIMA = mape(test['Passengers'], test['SARIMA_pred'])

fig, ax = plt.subplots()          ← Plot the MAPE
                                    on a bar plot.

x = ['naive seasonal', 'ARIMA(11,2,3)', 'SARIMA(2,1,1)(1,1,2,12)']
y = [mape_naive_seasonal, mape_ARIMA, mape_SARIMA]

ax.bar(x, y, width=0.4)
ax.set_xlabel('Models')
ax.set_ylabel('MAPE (%)')
ax.set_ylim(0, 15)                 ← Display the MAPE as
                                     text in the bar plot.

for index, value in enumerate(y):  ←
    plt.text(x=index, y=value + 1, s=str(round(value,2)), ha='center')

plt.tight_layout()
```

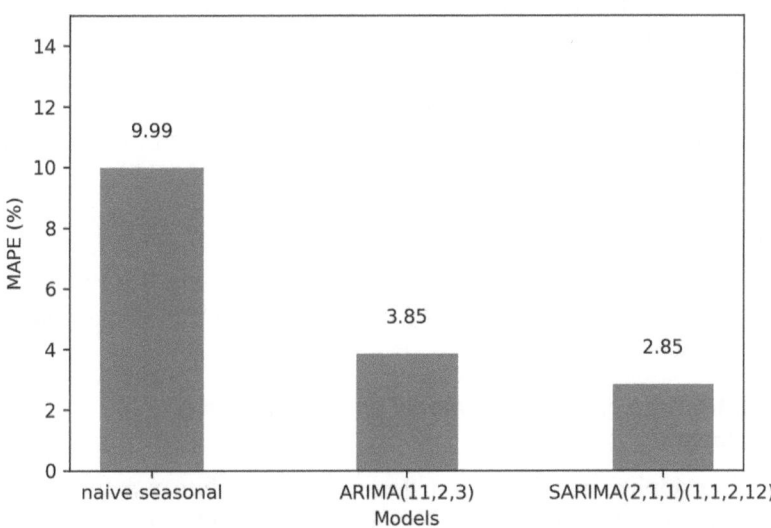

Figure 8.14   The MAPE of all forecasting methods. You can see that the best-performing model is the SARIMA model, since it has the lowest MAPE of all methods.

In figure 8.14 you can see that our baseline achieves a MAPE of 9.99%. The ARIMA model produced forecasts with a MAPE of 3.85%, and the SARIMA model scored a MAPE of 2.85%. A MAPE closer to 0 is indicative of better predictions, so the SARIMA model is the best-performing method for this situation. This makes sense, since our dataset had clear seasonality, and the SARIMA model is built to use the seasonal properties of time series to make forecasts.

8.4   Next steps

In this chapter, we covered the $SARIMA(p,d,q)(P,D,Q)_m$ model, which allows us to model non-stationary seasonal time series.

The addition of the parameters P, D, Q, and m allows us to include the seasonal properties of a time series in a model and use them to produce forecasts. Here, P is the order of the seasonal autoregressive process, D is the order of seasonal integration, Q is the order of the seasonal moving average process, and m is the frequency of the data.

We looked at how to first detect seasonal patterns using time series decomposition, and we adapted our general modeling procedure to also test values for P and Q.

In chapters 4 through 8, we have slowly built a more general and complex model, starting with the $MA(q)$ and $AR(p)$ models, combining them into the $ARMA(p,q)$ model, which led us to the $ARIMA(p,d,q)$ model, and finally to the $SARIMA(p,d,q)(P,D,Q)_m$ model. These models only consider the values of the time series itself. However, it would make sense that external variables are also predictive of our time series. For example, if we wish to model a country's total spending over time, looking at interest rates or the debt level could likely be predictive. How can we include those external variables in a model?

This leads us to the *SARIMAX* model. Notice the addition of *X*, which stands for *exogenous variables*. This model will combine everything that we have learned so far and further expand on it by adding the effect of external variables to predict our target. This will be the subject of the next chapter.

8.5   Exercises

Take the time to experiment with the SARIMA model using this exercise. The full solution is on GitHub: https://github.com/marcopeix/TimeSeriesForecastingInPython/tree/master/CH08.

8.5.1   Apply the SARIMA(p,d,q)(P,D,Q)$_m$ model on the Johnson & Johnson dataset

In chapter 7 we applied an $ARIMA(p,d,q)$ model to the Johnson & Johnson dataset to forecast the quarterly EPS over a year. Now use the $SARIMA(p,d,q)(P,D,Q)_m$ model on the same dataset, and compare its performance to the ARIMA model.

1   Use time series decomposition to identify the presence of a periodic pattern.
2   Use the `optimize_SARIMA` function and select the model with the lowest AIC.
3   Perform residual analysis.
4   Forecast the EPS for the last year, and measure the performance against the ARIMA model. Use the MAPE. Is it better?

Summary

- The seasonal autoregressive integrated moving average model, denoted as SARIMA$(p,d,q)(P,D,Q)_m$, adds seasonal properties to the ARIMA(p,d,q) model.
- P is the order of the seasonal autoregressive process, D is the order of seasonal integration, Q is the order of the seasonal moving average process, and m is the frequency of the data.
- The frequency m corresponds to the number of observations in a cycle. If the data is collected every month, then $m = 12$. If data is collected every quarter, then $m = 4$.
- Time series decomposition can be used to identify seasonal patterns in a time series.

Adding external variables to our model

This chapter covers

- Examining the SARIMAX model
- Exploring the use of external variables for forecasting
- Forecasting using the SARIMAX model

In chapters 4 through 8, we have increasingly built a general model that allows us to consider more complex patterns in time series. We started our journey with the autoregressive and moving average processes before combining them into the ARMA model. Then we added a layer of complexity to model non-stationary time series, leading us to the ARIMA model. Finally, in chapter 8 we added yet another layer to ARIMA that allows us to consider seasonal patterns in our forecasts, which resulted in the SARIMA model.

So far, each model that we have explored and used to produce forecasts has considered only the time series itself. In other words, past values of the time series were used as predictors of future values. However, it is possible that external variables also have an impact on our time series and can therefore be good predictors of future values.

This brings us to the *SARIMAX* model. You'll notice the addition of the *X* term, which denotes exogenous variables. In statistics the term *exogenous* is used to describe predictors or input variables, while *endogenous* is used to define the target variable—what we are trying to predict. With the SARIMAX model, we can now consider external variables, or exogenous variables, when forecasting a time series.

As a guiding example, we'll use a macroeconomics dataset from the United States, collected quarterly from 1959 to 2009, to forecast the real gross domestic product (GDP), as shown in figure 9.1.

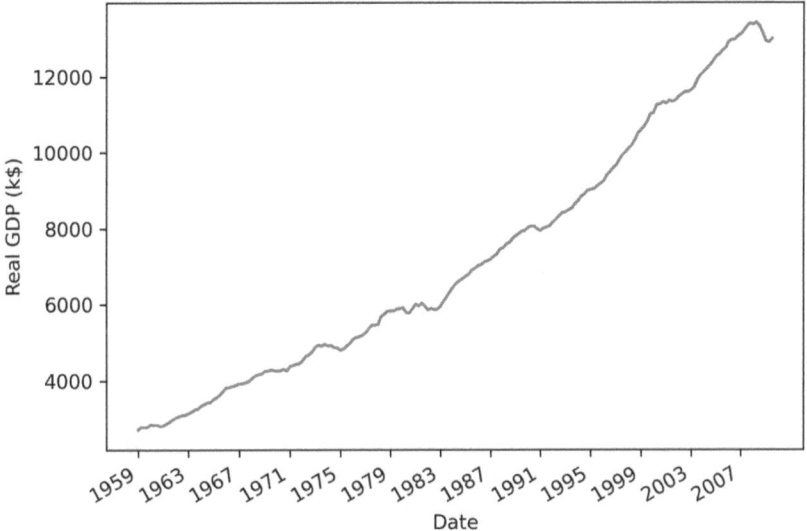

Figure 9.1 Real gross domestic product (GDP) of the United States from 1959 to 2009. The data was collected quarterly and is expressed in thousands of US dollars. Notice the clear positive trend over the years with no cyclical pattern, suggesting that seasonality is not present in the series.

The GDP is the total market value of all the finished goods and services produced within a country. The *real* GDP is an inflation-adjusted measure that removes the impact of inflation on the market value of goods. Inflation or deflation can respectively increase or decrease the monetary value of goods and services, hence increasing or decreasing the GDP. By removing the effect of inflation, we can better determine whether an economy saw an expansion of production.

Without diving into the technicalities of measuring the GDP, we'll define the GDP as the sum of consumption C, government spending G, investments I, and net exports NX, as shown in equation 9.1.

$$GDP = C + G + I + NX$$
Equation 9.1

Each element of equation 9.1 is likely affected by some external variable. For example, consumption is likely impacted by the unemployment rate, because if fewer people are employed, consumption is likely to decrease. Interest rates can also have an impact, because if they go up, it is harder to borrow money, and spending decreases as a result. We can also think of currency exchange rates as having an impact on net exports. A weaker local currency will generally stimulate exports and make imports more expensive. Thus, we can see how many exogenous variables can likely impact the real GDP of the United States.

In this chapter, we'll first examine the SARIMAX model and explore an important caveat when using it to produce forecasts. Then we'll apply the model to forecast the real GDP of the United States.

9.1   *Examining the SARIMAX model*

The SARIMAX model further extends the SARIMA$(p,d,q)(P,D,Q)_m$ model by adding the effect of exogenous variables. Therefore, we can express the present value y_t simply as a SARIMA$(p,d,q)(P,D,Q)_m$ model to which we add any number of exogenous variables X_t as shown in equation 9.2.

$$y_t = SARIMA(p, d, q)(P, D, Q)_m + \sum_{i=1}^{n} \beta_i X_t^i$$

Equation 9.2

The SARIMA model is a linear model, as it is a linear combination of past values of the series and error terms. Here we add another linear combination of different exogenous variables, resulting in SARIMAX being a linear model as well. Note that in SARIMAX you can include categorical variables as exogenous variables, but make sure you encode them (give them numerical values or binary flags) just like you would do for traditional regression tasks.

We have been using the `SARIMAX` function from `statsmodels` since chapter 4 to implement different models. This is because SARIMAX is the most general function for forecasting a time series. You now understand how a SARIMAX model without exogenous variables is a SARIMA model. Similarly, a model with no seasonality but with exogenous variables can be denoted as an ARIMAX model, and a model with no seasonality and no exogenous variables becomes an ARIMA model. Depending on the problem, different combinations of each portion of the general SARIMAX model will be used.

SARIMAX model

The SARIMAX model simply adds a linear combination of exogenous variables to the SARIMA model. This allows us to model the impact of external variables on the future value of a time series.

We can loosely define the SARIMAX model as follows:

$$y_t = SARIMA(p, d, q)(P, D, Q)_m + \sum_{i=1}^{n} \beta_i X_t^i$$

> The SARIMAX model is the most general model for forecasting time series. You can see that if you have no seasonal patterns, it becomes an ARIMAX model. With no exogenous variables, it is a SARIMA model. With no seasonality or exogenous variables, it becomes an ARIMA model.

Theoretically, this sums up the SARIMAX model. Chapters 4 through 8 were purposely ordered in such a way that we incrementally developed the SARIMAX model, making the addition of exogenous variables easy to understand. To reinforce your learning, let's explore the exogenous variables of our dataset.

9.1.1 Exploring the exogenous variables of the US macroeconomics dataset

Let's load the US macroeconomics dataset and explore the different exogenous variables available to us to forecast the real GDP. This dataset is available with the `statsmodels` library, meaning that you do not need to download and read an external file. You can load the dataset using the `datasets` module of `statsmodels`.

NOTE The full source code for this chapter is available on GitHub: https://github.com/marcopeix/TimeSeriesForecastingInPython/tree/master/CH09.

```
import statsmodels.api as sm

macro_econ_data = sm.datasets.macrodata.load_pandas().data     ◄──── Load the US
macro_econ_data     ◄──── Display the                                 macroeconomics dataset.
                           DataFrame.
```

This displays the entire `DataFrame` containing the US macroeconomics dataset. Table 9.1 describes the meaning of each variable. We have our target variable, or endogenous variable, which is the real GDP. Then we have 11 exogenous variables that can be used for forecasting, such as personal and federal consumption expenditures, interest rate, inflation rate, population, and others.

Table 9.1 Description of all variables in the US macroeconomics dataset

Variable	Description
realgdp	Real gross domestic product (the target variable or endogenous variable)
realcons	Real personal consumption expenditure
realinv	Real gross private domestic investment
realgovt	Real federal consumption expenditure and investment
realdpi	Real private disposable income
cpi	Consumer price index for the end of the quarter

Table 9.1   Description of all variables in the US macroeconomics dataset *(continued)*

Variable	Description
m1	M1 nominal money stock
tbilrate	Quarterly monthly average of the monthly 3-month treasury bill
unemp	Unemployment rate
pop	Total population at the end of the quarter
infl	Inflation rate
realint	Real interest rate

Of course, each of these variables may or may not be a good predictor of the real GDP. We do not have to perform feature selection because the linear model will attribute a coefficient close to 0 for exogenous variables that are not significant in predicting the target.

For the sake of simplicity and clarity, we will only work with six variables in this chapter: the real GDP, which is our target, and the next five variables listed in table 9.1 (`realcons` to `cpi`) as our exogenous variables.

We can visualize how each variable behaves through time to see if we can discern any distinctive patterns. The result is shown in figure 9.2.

```
fig, axes = plt.subplots(nrows=3, ncols=2, dpi=300, figsize=(11,6))

for i, ax in enumerate(axes.flatten()[:6]):          ← Iterate for six variables.
    data = macro_econ_data[macro_econ_data.columns[i+2]]   ←┐ Skip the year and
                                                            │ quarter columns.
    ax.plot(data, color='black', linewidth=1)              │ That way, we can
    ax.set_title(macro_econ_data.columns[i+2])         ←───┘ start at realgdp.
    ax.xaxis.set_ticks_position('none')
    ax.yaxis.set_ticks_position('none')                  Display the variable's
    ax.spines['top'].set_alpha(0)                        name at the top of
    ax.tick_params(labelsize=6)                          the plot.

plt.setp(axes, xticks=np.arange(0, 208, 8), xticklabels=np.arange(1959,
➥ 2010, 2))
fig.autofmt_xdate()
plt.tight_layout()
```

There are two ways to work with exogenous variables for time series forecasting. First, we could train multiple models with various combinations of exogenous variables, and see which model generates the best forecasts. Alternatively, we can simply include all exogenous variables and stick to model selection using the AIC, as we know this yields a good-fitting model that does not overfit.

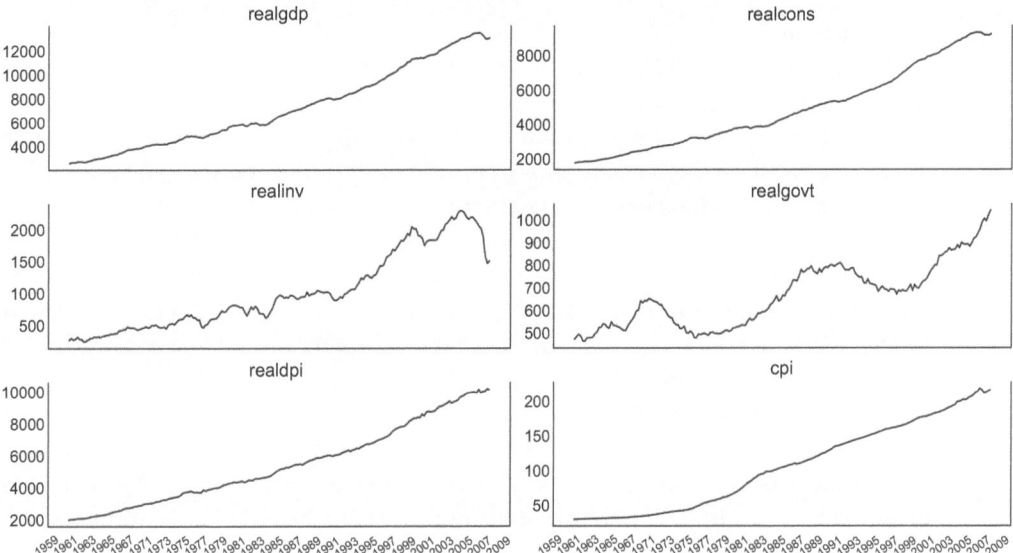

Figure 9.2 Evolution of the real GDP and five exogenous variables from 1959 to 2009. You'll notice that `realgdp`, `realcons`, `realdpi`, and `cpi` all have a similar shape, which means that `realcons`, `realdpi`, and `cpi` are potentially good predictors, although a graphical analysis is not sufficient to confirm that idea. On the other hand, `realgovt` has peaks and troughs that do not appear in `realgdp`, so we can hypothesize that `realgovt` is a weaker predictor.

Why disregard the p-value in regression analysis?

The SARIMAX implementation in `statsmodels` comes with a regression analysis using the `summary` method. This is shown later in the chapter.

In that analysis, we can see the p-value associated with each coefficient of each predictor of the SARIMAX model. Often the p-value is misused as a way to perform feature selection. Many incorrectly interpret the p-value as a way to determine if a predictor is correlated with the target.

In fact, the p-value tests whether the coefficient is significantly different from 0 or not. If the p-value is less than 0.05, then we reject the null hypothesis and conclude that the coefficient is significantly different from 0. It does not determine whether a predictor is useful for forecasting.

Therefore, you should not remove predictors based on their p-values. Selecting the model by minimizing the AIC takes care of that step.

To learn more, I recommend reading Rob Hyndman's "Statistical tests for variable selection" blog post: https://robjhyndman.com/hyndsight/tests2/.

9.1.2 Caveat for using SARIMAX

There is an important caveat that comes with the use of the SARIMAX model. Including external variables can potentially be beneficial, as you may find strong predictors for your target. However, you might encounter issues when forecasting multiple time-steps into the future.

Recall that the SARIMAX model uses the SARIMA(p,d,q) $(P,D,Q)_m$ model and a linear combination of exogenous variables to predict one timestep into the future. But what if you wish to predict two timesteps into the future? While this is possible with a SARIMA model, the SARIMAX model requires us to forecast the exogenous variables too.

To illustrate this idea, let's assume that `realcons` is a predictor of `realgdp` (this will be verified later in the chapter). Assume also that we have a SARIMAX model where `realcons` is used as an input feature to predict `realgdp`. Now suppose that we are at the end of 2009 and must predict the real GDP for 2010 and 2011. The SARIMAX model allows us to use the `realcons` of 2009 to predict the real GDP for 2010. However, predicting the real GDP for 2011 will require us to predict `realcons` for 2010, unless we wait to observe the value at the end of 2010.

Because the `realcons` variable is a time series itself, it can be forecast using a version of the SARIMA model. Nevertheless, we know that our forecast always has some error associated with it. Therefore, having to forecast an exogenous variable to forecast our target variable can magnify the prediction error of our target, meaning that our predictions can quickly degrade as we predict more timesteps into the future.

The only way to avoid that situation is to predict only one timestep into the future and wait to observe the exogenous variable before predicting the target for another timestep into the future.

On the other hand, if your exogenous variable is *easy* to predict, meaning that it follows a known function that can be accurately predicted, there is no harm in forecasting the exogenous variable and using these forecasts to predict the target.

In the end, there is no clear recommendation to predict only one timestep. It is dependent on the situation and the exogenous variables available. This is where your expertise as a data scientist and rigorous experimenting come into play. If you determine that your exogenous variable can be accurately predicted, you can recommend forecasting many timesteps into the future. Otherwise, your recommendation must be to predict one timestep at a time and justify your decision by explaining that errors will accumulate as more predictions are made, meaning that the forecasts will lose accuracy.

Now that we have explored the SARIMAX model in depth, let's apply it to forecast the real GDP.

9.2   *Forecasting the real GDP using the SARIMAX model*

We are now ready to use the SARIMAX model to forecast the real GDP. Having explored the exogenous variables of the dataset, we will incorporate them into our forecasting model.

Before diving in, we must reintroduce the general modeling procedure. There are no major changes to the procedure. The only modification is that we will now fit a SARIMAX model. All the other steps remain the same, as shown in figure 9.3.

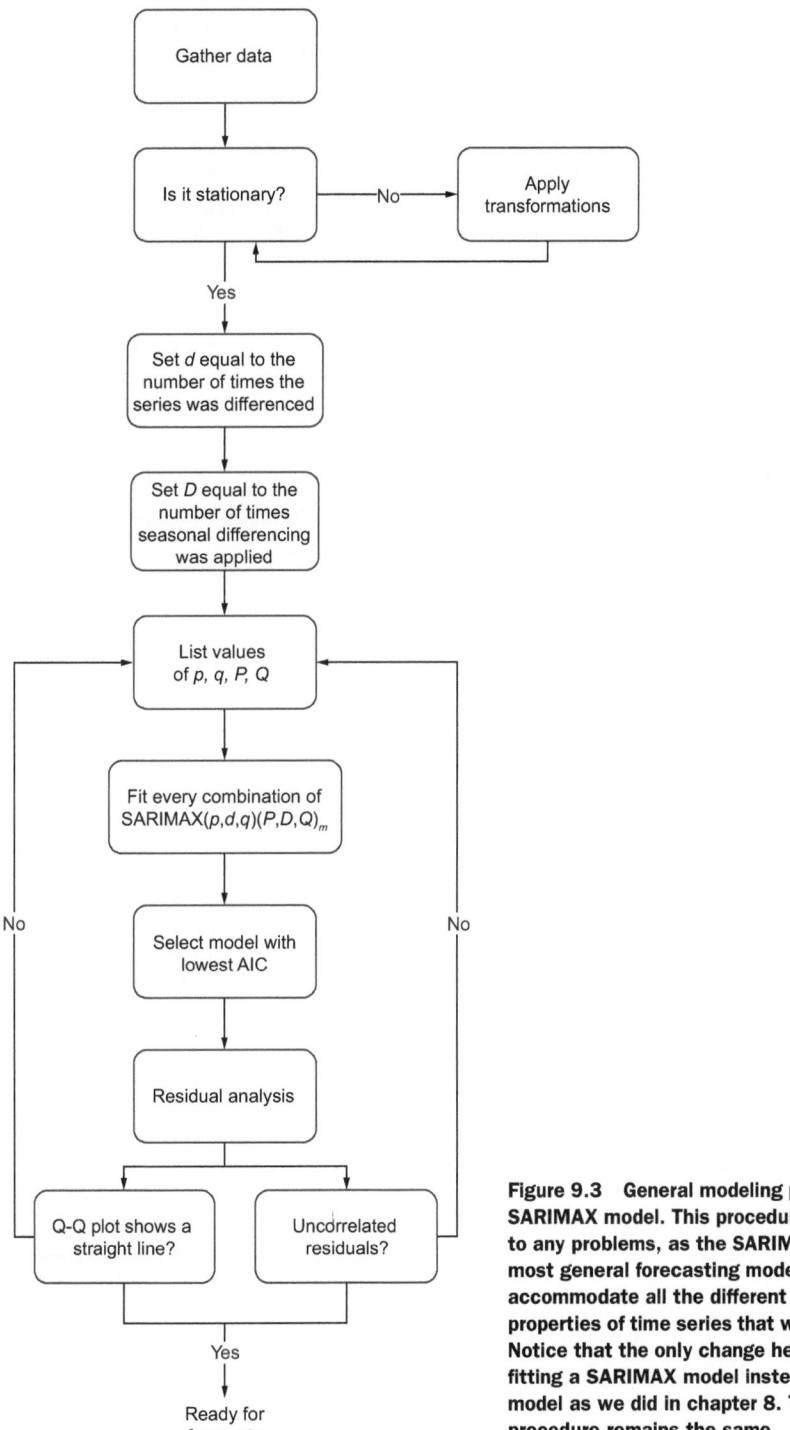

Figure 9.3   General modeling procedure for the SARIMAX model. This procedure can be applied to any problems, as the SARIMAX model is the most general forecasting model and can accommodate all the different processes and properties of time series that we have explored. Notice that the only change here is that we are fitting a SARIMAX model instead of a SARIMA model as we did in chapter 8. The rest of the procedure remains the same.

Following the modeling procedure of figure 9.3, we'll first check for the stationarity of our target using the augmented Dickey-Fuller (ADF) test.

```
target = macro_econ_data['realgdp']          ⟵⌐  Define the target variable. In
exog = macro_econ_data[['realcons', 'realinv', 'realgovt', 'realdpi',   this case, it is the real GDP.
⇒ 'cpi']]                                    ⟵⌐  Define the exogenous
                                                  variables. Here we limit it to
ad_fuller_result = adfuller(target)               five variables for simplicity.

print(f'ADF Statistic: {ad_fuller_result[0]}')
print(f'p-value: {ad_fuller_result[1]}')
```

This returns an ADF statistic of 1.75 and a p-value of 1.00. Since the ADF statistic is not a large negative number, and the p-value is larger than 0.05, we cannot reject the null hypothesis and conclude that the series is not stationary.

Therefore, we must apply a transformation and test for stationarity again. Here we will difference the series once:

```
target_diff = target.diff()       ⟵⌐  Difference
                                       the series.
ad_fuller_result = adfuller(target_diff[1:])

print(f'ADF Statistic: {ad_fuller_result[0]}')
print(f'p-value: {ad_fuller_result[1]}')
```

This now returns an ADF statistic of -6.31 and p-value of 3.32×10^{-8}. With a large negative ADF statistic and a p-value smaller than 0.05, we can reject the null hypothesis and conclude that the series is now stationary. Therefore, we know that $d = 1$. Since we did not need to take a seasonal difference to make the series stationary, $D = 0$.

We will now define the `optimize_SARIMAX` function, which will fit all unique combinations of the model and return a `DataFrame` in ascending order of AIC.

Listing 9.1   Function to fit all unique SARIMAX models

```
from typing import Union
from tqdm import tqdm_notebook
from statsmodels.tsa.statespace.sarimax import SARIMAX

def optimize_SARIMAX(endog: Union[pd.Series, list], exog: Union[pd.Series,
⇒ list], order_list: list, d: int, D: int, s: int) -> pd.DataFrame:

    results = []

    for order in tqdm_notebook(order_list):
        try:
            model = SARIMAX(
                endog,
```

Notice the addition of the exogenous variables when fitting the model.

```
                  exog,
                  order=(order[0], d, order[1]),
                  seasonal_order=(order[2], D, order[3], s),
                  simple_differencing=False).fit(disp=False)
        except:
            continue

        aic = model.aic
        results.append([order, aic])

    result_df = pd.DataFrame(results)
    result_df.columns = ['(p,q,P,Q)', 'AIC']

    #Sort in ascending order, lower AIC is better
    result_df = result_df.sort_values(by='AIC',
ascending=True).reset_index(drop=True)

    return result_df
```

Next we'll define the range of possible values for the orders p, q, P, and Q. We'll try values from 0 to 3, but feel free to try a different set of values. Also, since the data is collected quarterly, $m = 4$.

```
p = range(0, 4, 1)
d = 1
q = range(0, 4, 1)
P = range(0, 4, 1)
D = 0
Q = range(0, 4, 1)
s = 4
```

Remember that s in the implementation of SARIMAX from statsmodels is equivalent to m.

```
parameters = product(p, q, P, Q)
parameters_list = list(parameters)
```

To train the model, we will use the first 200 instances of both the target and exogenous variables. We'll then run the `optimize_SARIMAX` function and select the model with the lowest AIC.

```
target_train = target[:200]
exog_train = exog[:200]

result_df = optimize_SARIMAX(target_train, exog_train, parameters_list, d,
    D, s)
result_df
```

Once it's completed, the function returns the verdict that the $SARIMAX(3,1,3)(0,0,0)_4$ model is the model with the lowest AIC. Notice that the seasonal component of the model has only orders of 0. This makes sense, as there is no visible seasonal pattern in the plot of real GDP, as shown in figure 9.4. Therefore, the seasonal component is null, and we have an ARIMAX(3,1,3) model.

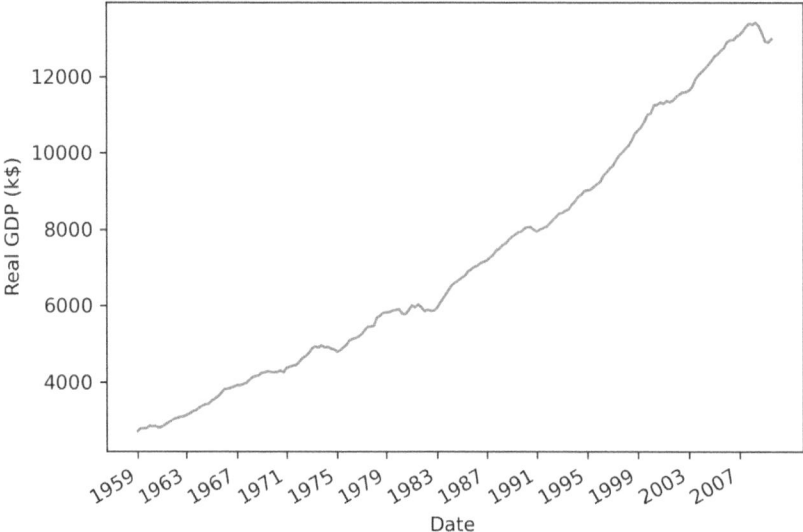

Figure 9.4   Real gross domestic product (GDP) of the United States between 1959 and 2009. The data is collected quarterly and is expressed in thousands of US dollars. Notice the clear positive trend over the years with no cyclical pattern, suggesting that seasonality is not present in the series.

Now we can fit the selected model and display a summary table to see the coefficients associated with our exogenous variables. The result is shown in figure 9.5.

```
best_model = SARIMAX(target_train, exog_train, order=(3,1,3),
➥ seasonal_order=(0,0,0,4), simple_differencing=False)
best_model_fit = best_model.fit(disp=False)

print(best_model_fit.summary())        ◁─────┤ Display the summary
                                              │ table of the model.
```

In figure 9.5 you'll notice that all exogenous variables have a p-value smaller than 0.05, except for `realdpi`, which has a p-value of 0.712. This means that the coefficient of `realdpi` is not significantly different from 0. You'll also notice that its coefficient is 0.0091. However, the coefficient is kept in the model, as the p-value does not determine the relevance of this predictor in forecasting our target.

```
                              SARIMAX Results
==============================================================================
Dep. Variable:                 realgdp   No. Observations:             200
Model:               SARIMAX(3, 1, 3)   Log Likelihood            -859.431
Date:                Fri, 06 Aug 2021   AIC                       1742.863
Time:                        17:02:59   BIC                       1782.382
Sample:                             0   HQIC                      1758.857
                              - 200
Covariance Type:                  opg
==============================================================================
                 coef    std err          z      P>|z|      [0.025      0.975]
------------------------------------------------------------------------------
realcons       0.9652      0.044     21.693      0.000       0.878       1.052
realinv        1.0142      0.033     30.944      0.000       0.950       1.078
realgovt       0.7249      0.127      5.717      0.000       0.476       0.973
realdpi        0.0091      0.025      0.369      0.712      -0.039       0.058
cpi            5.8671      1.311      4.476      0.000       3.298       8.436
ar.L1          1.0648      0.399      2.671      0.008       0.283       1.846
ar.L2          0.4895      0.701      0.698      0.485      -0.885       1.864
ar.L3         -0.6718      0.337     -1.995      0.046      -1.332      -0.012
ma.L1         -1.1035      0.430     -2.565      0.010      -1.947      -0.260
ma.L2         -0.3196      0.767     -0.417      0.677      -1.823       1.184
ma.L3          0.6457      0.403      1.601      0.109      -0.145       1.436
sigma2       328.9706     30.395     10.823      0.000     269.397     388.545
==============================================================================
Ljung-Box (L1) (Q):                   0.00   Jarque-Bera (JB):            13.55
Prob(Q):                              0.95   Prob(JB):                     0.00
Heteroskedasticity (H):               3.57   Skew:                         0.32
Prob(H) (two-sided):                  0.00   Kurtosis:                     4.11
==============================================================================

Warnings:
[1] Covariance matrix calculated using the outer product of gradients (complex-step).
```

Figure 9.5 Summary table of the selected model. You can see that our exogenous variables were assigned coefficients. You can also see their p-values under the column P>|z|.

Moving on with the modeling procedure, we'll now study the residuals of the model, which are shown in figure 9.6. Everything points to the residuals being completely random, just like white noise. Our model passes the visual check.

```
best_model_fit.plot_diagnostics(figsize=(10,8));
```

Now we'll apply the Ljung-Box test to make sure the residuals are not correlated. We therefore want to see p-values that are greater than 0.05, since the null hypothesis of the Ljung-Box test is that residuals are independent and uncorrelated.

```
residuals = best_model_fit.resid

lbvalue, pvalue = acorr_ljungbox(residuals, np.arange(1, 11, 1))

print(pvalue)
```

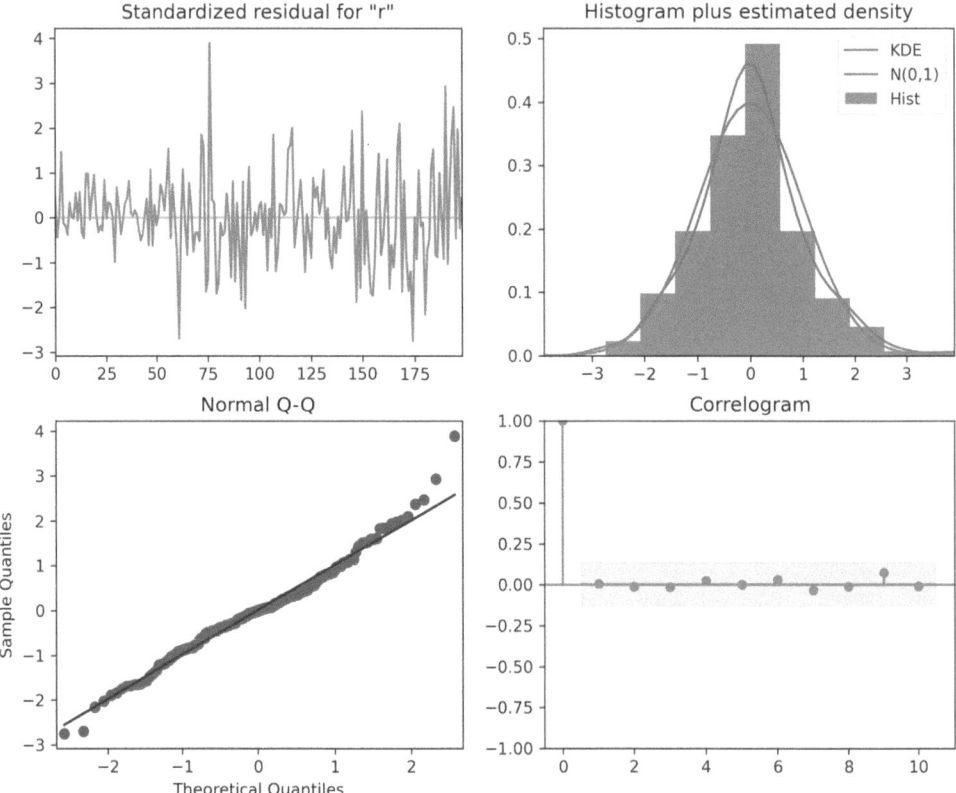

Figure 9.6   Residual analysis of the selected model. You can see that the residuals have no trend and a fairly constant variance over time, just like white noise. In the top-right plot, the distribution of residuals is very close to a normal distribution. This is further supported by the Q-Q plot at the bottom left, which shows a fairly straight line that lies on y = x. Finally, the correlogram shows no significant coefficients after lag 0, just like white noise. Therefore, from a graphical analysis, the residuals of this model resemble white noise.

All the p-values are greater than 0.05. Therefore, we do not reject the null hypothesis, and we conclude that the residuals are independent and uncorrelated. Having passed both residual checks, our model can be used for forecasting.

As mentioned before, the caveat of using a SARIMAX model is that it is reasonable to predict only the next timestep, to avoid predicting the exogenous variables as well, which would lead us to accumulate prediction errors in the final forecast.

Instead, to test our model, we predict the next timestep multiple times and average the errors of each prediction. This is done using the `rolling_forecast` function, which we defined and worked with in chapters 4–6. As a baseline model, we will use the last known value method.

Listing 9.2 Function to forecast the next timestep multiple times

```
def rolling_forecast(endog: Union[pd.Series, list], exog:
➡ Union[pd.Series, list], train_len: int, horizon: int, window: int,
➡ method: str) -> list:

    total_len = train_len + horizon

    if method == 'last':
        pred_last_value = []

        for i in range(train_len, total_len, window):
            last_value = endog[:i].iloc[-1]
            pred_last_value.extend(last_value for _ in range(window))

        return pred_last_value

    elif method == 'SARIMAX':
        pred_SARIMAX = []

        for i in range(train_len, total_len, window):
            model = SARIMAX(endog[:i], exog[:i], order=(3,1,3),
➡ seasonal_order=(0,0,0,4), simple_differencing=False)
            res = model.fit(disp=False)
            predictions = res.get_prediction(exog=exog)
            oos_pred = predictions.predicted_mean.iloc[-window:]
            pred_SARIMAX.extend(oos_pred)

        return pred_SARIMAX
```

The `recursive_forecast` function allows us to predict the next timestep over a certain period of time. Specifically, we will use it to forecast the next timestep starting in 2008 and going to the third quarter of 2009.

```
target_train = target[:196]        ←⌐ We fit the model on the data
target_test = target[196:]         ←   from 1959 to the end of 2007.

pred_df = pd.DataFrame({'actual': target_test})

TRAIN_LEN = len(target_train)
HORIZON = len(target_test)
WINDOW = 1                         ←

pred_last_value = recursive_forecast(target, exog, TRAIN_LEN, HORIZON,
➡ WINDOW, 'last')
pred_SARIMAX = recursive_forecast(target, exog, TRAIN_LEN, HORIZON, WINDOW,
➡ 'SARIMAX')

pred_df['pred_last_value'] = pred_last_value
pred_df['pred_SARIMAX'] = pred_SARIMAX

pred_df
```

> **We fit the model on the data from 1959 to the end of 2007.**

> **The test set contains the values starting in 2008 to the third quarter of 2009. There is a total of seven values to predict.**

> **This specifies that we predict the next timestep only.**

With the predictions done, we can visualize which model has the lowest mean absolute percentage error (MAPE). The result is shown in figure 9.7.

```
def mape(y_true, y_pred):
    return np.mean(np.abs((y_true - y_pred) / y_true)) * 100

mape_last = mape(pred_df.actual, pred_df.pred_last_value)
mape_SARIMAX = mape(pred_df.actual, pred_df.pred_SARIMAX)

fig, ax = plt.subplots()

x = ['naive last value', 'SARIMAX']
y = [mape_last, mape_SARIMAX]

ax.bar(x, y, width=0.4)
ax.set_xlabel('Models')
ax.set_ylabel('MAPE (%)')
ax.set_ylim(0, 1)

for index, value in enumerate(y):
    plt.text(x=index, y=value + 0.05, s=str(round(value,2)), ha='center')

plt.tight_layout()
```

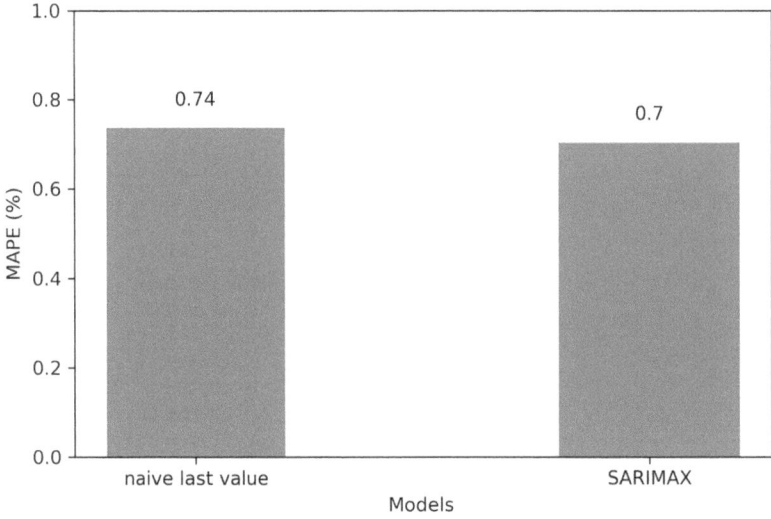

Figure 9.7   The mean absolute percentage error (MAPE) of the forecasts of each method. You can see that the SARIMAX model only has a slightly smaller MAPE than the baseline. This highlights the importance of using a baseline, as a MAPE of 0.70% is extremely good, but a naive forecast achieves a MAPE of 0.74%, meaning that the SARIMAX model only has a small advantage.

In figure 9.7 you'll see that the SARIMAX model is the winning model by only 0.04%. You'll appreciate the importance of a baseline here, as both methods achieve an extremely low MAPE, showing that the SARIMAX model is only slightly better than simply predicting the last value. This is where the business context comes into play. In our case, since we are predicting the real GDP of the United States, a difference of 0.04% represents thousands of dollars. This difference might be relevant in this particular context, justifying the use of the SARIMAX model, even though it is only slightly better than the baseline.

9.3   *Next steps*

In this chapter, we covered the SARIMAX model, which allows us to include external variables when forecasting our target time series.

   The addition of exogenous variables comes with a caveat: if we need to predict many timesteps into the future, we must also predict the exogenous variables, which can magnify the prediction error on the target. To avoid that, we must only predict the next timestep.

   In considering exogenous variables for predicting real GDP, we can also hypothesize that real GDP can be a predictor for other variables. For example, the variable cpi was a predictor for realgdp, but we could also show that realgdp can predict cpi.

   In a situation where we wish to show that two variables varying in time can impact one another, we must use the *vector autoregression* (VAR) model. This model allows for multivariate time series forecasting, unlike the SARIMAX model, which is for univariate time series forecasting. In the next chapter we will explore the VAR model in detail, and you'll see that it can also be extended to become a *VARMA* model and a *VARMAX* model.

9.4   *Exercises*

Take the time to test your knowledge with this exercise. The full solution is on GitHub: https://github.com/marcopeix/TimeSeriesForecastingInPython/tree/master/CH09.

9.4.1   *Use all exogenous variables in a SARIMAX model to predict the real GDP*

In this chapter we limited the number of exogenous variables when forecasting for the real GDP. This exercise is an occasion to fit a SARIMAX model using all exogenous variables and to verify if you can achieve better performance.

   1 Use all exogenous variables in the SARIMAX model.
   2 Perform residual analysis.
   3 Produce forecasts for the last seven timesteps in the dataset.
   4 Measure the MAPE. Is it better, worse, or identical to what was achieved with a limited number of exogenous variables?

Summary

- The SARIMAX model allows you to include external variables, also termed exogenous variables, to forecast your target.
- Transformations are applied only on the target variable, not on the exogenous variables.
- If you wish to forecast multiple timesteps into the future, the exogenous variables must also be forecast. This can magnify the errors on the final forecast. To avoid that, you must predict only the next timestep.

Forecasting multiple time series

10

This chapter covers

- Examining the VAR model
- Exploring Granger causality to validate the use of the VAR model
- Forecasting multiple time series using the VAR model

In the last chapter, you saw how the SARIMAX model can be used to include the impact of exogenous variables on a time series. With the SARIMAX model, the relationship is unidirectional: we assume that the exogenous variable has an impact on the target only.

However, it is possible that two time series have a bidirectional relationship, meaning that time series t1 is a predictor of time series t2, and time series t2 is also a predictor for time series t1. In such a case, it would be useful to have a model that can take this bidirectional relationship into account and output predictions for *both* time series simultaneously.

This brings us to the *vector autoregression* (VAR) model. This particular model allows us to capture the relationship between multiple time series as they change over time. That, in turn, allows us to produce forecasts for many time series simultaneously, therefore performing multivariate forecasting.

Throughout this chapter, we will use the same US macroeconomics dataset as in chapter 9. This time we'll explore the relationship between real disposable income and real consumption, as shown in figure 10.1.

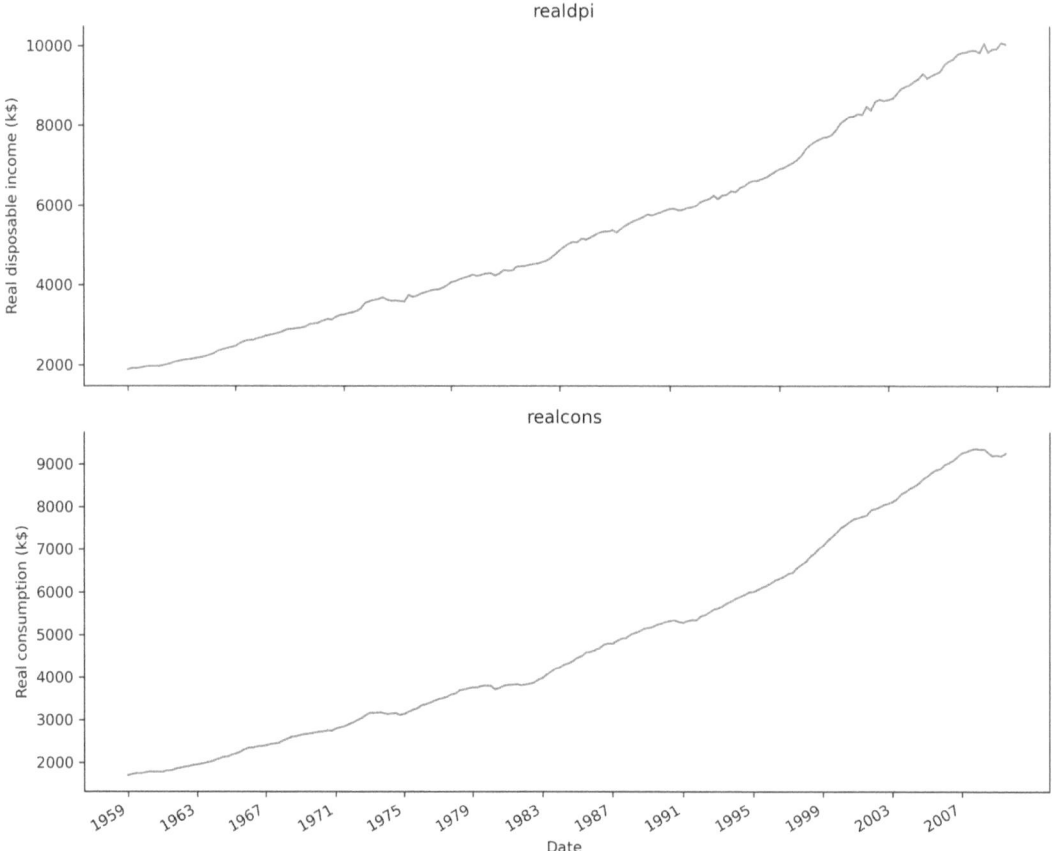

Figure 10.1   Real disposable income (`realdpi`) and real consumption (`realcons`) in the United States from 1959 to 2009. The data is collected quarterly and is expressed in thousands of US dollars. Both series have a similar shape and trend over time.

Real consumption expresses how much money people spend, while real disposable income represents how much money is available to spend. Therefore, it is a reasonable hypothesis that a higher amount of disposable income could signal higher consumption. The opposite can also be true, with higher consumption meaning that more income is available for spending. This bidirectional relationship can be captured by a VAR model.

In this chapter, we'll first explore the VAR model in detail. Then, we'll introduce the Granger-causality test, which will help us validate the hypothesis that two time series have an impact on one another. Finally, we'll apply the VAR model to produce forecasts for both real consumption and real disposable income.

10.1   *Examining the VAR model*

The vector autoregression (VAR) model captures the relationship between multiple series as they change over time. In this model, each series has an impact on the other, unlike the SARIMAX model where the exogenous variable had an impact on the target, but not the other way around. Recall in chapter 9 that we used the variables `real-cons`, `realinv`, `realgovt`, `realdpi`, `cpi`, `m1`, and `tbilrate` as predictors for `realgdp`, but we did not consider how `realgdp` can affect any of those variables. That is why we used the SARIMAX model in that case.

You might have noticed the return of *autoregression*, which brings us back to the $AR(p)$ model of chapter 5. This is a good intuition, as the VAR model can be seen as a generalization of the $AR(p)$ model to allow for the forecast of multiple time series. Therefore, we can also denote the VAR model as $VAR(p)$, where p is the order and has the same meaning as in the $AR(p)$ model.

Recall that $AR(p)$ expressed the value of a time series as a linear combination of a constant C, the present error term ϵ_t, which is also white noise, and the past values of the series y_{t-p}. The magnitude of the influence of the past values on the present value is denoted as ϕ_p, which represents the coefficients of the $AR(p)$ model, as shown in equation 10.1.

$$y_t = C + \phi_1 y_{t-1} + \phi_2 y_{t-2} + \cdots + \phi_p y_{t-p} + \epsilon_t \qquad \textbf{Equation 10.1}$$

We can simply extend equation 10.1 to allow for multiple time series to be modeled, where each has an impact on the others.

For simplicity, let's consider a system with two time series, denoted as $y_{1,t}$ and $y_{2,t}$, and an order of 1, meaning that $p = 1$. Then, using matrix notation, the VAR(1) model can be expressed as equation 10.2.

$$\begin{bmatrix} y_{1,t} \\ y_{2,t} \end{bmatrix} = \begin{bmatrix} C_1 \\ C_2 \end{bmatrix} + \begin{bmatrix} \phi_{1,1} & \phi_{1,2} \\ \phi_{2,1} & \phi_{2,2} \end{bmatrix} \begin{bmatrix} y_{1,t-1} \\ y_{2,t-1} \end{bmatrix} + \begin{bmatrix} \epsilon_{1,t} \\ \epsilon_{2,t} \end{bmatrix} \qquad \textbf{Equation 10.2}$$

Carrying out the matrix multiplication, the mathematical expression for $y_{1,t}$ is shown in equation 10.3, and that for $y_{2,t}$ is shown in equation 10.4.

$$y_{1,t} = C_1 + \phi_{1,1} y_{1,t-1} + \phi_{1,2} y_{2,t-1} + \epsilon_{1,t} \qquad \textbf{Equation 10.3}$$

$$y_{2,t} = C_2 + \phi_{2,1} y_{1,t-1} + \phi_{2,2} y_{2,t-1} + \epsilon_{2,t} \qquad \textbf{Equation 10.4}$$

In equation 10.3 you'll notice that the expression for $y_{1,t}$ includes the past value of $y_{2,t}$. Similarly, in equation 10.4, the expression for $y_{2,t}$ includes the past value of $y_{1,t}$. Hence, you can see how the VAR model captures the impact of each series on the other.

We can extend equation 10.3 to express a general VAR(p) model that considers p lagged values, resulting in equation 10.5. Note that the superscript does not represent an exponent but is used for indexing. For simplicity, we'll again consider only two time series.

$$\begin{bmatrix} y_{1,t} \\ y_{2,t} \end{bmatrix} = \begin{bmatrix} C_1 \\ C_2 \end{bmatrix} + \begin{bmatrix} \phi_{1,1}^1 & \phi_{1,2}^1 \\ \phi_{2,1}^1 & \phi_{2,2}^1 \end{bmatrix} \begin{bmatrix} y_{1,t-1} \\ y_{2,t-1} \end{bmatrix} + \begin{bmatrix} \phi_{1,1}^2 & \phi_{1,2}^2 \\ \phi_{2,1}^2 & \phi_{2,2}^2 \end{bmatrix} \begin{bmatrix} y_{1,t-2} \\ y_{2,t-2} \end{bmatrix} + \cdots$$

$$+ \begin{bmatrix} \phi_{1,1}^p & \phi_{1,2}^p \\ \phi_{2,1}^p & \phi_{2,2}^p \end{bmatrix} \begin{bmatrix} y_{1,t-p} \\ y_{2,t-p} \end{bmatrix} + \begin{bmatrix} \epsilon_{1,t} \\ \epsilon_{2,t} \end{bmatrix}$$

Equation 10.5

Just like with the AR(p) model, the VAR(p) model requires each time series to be stationary.

Vector autoregression model

The vector autoregression model VAR(p) models the relationship of two or more time series. In this model, each time series has an impact on the others. This means that past values of one time series affect the other time series, and vice versa.

The VAR(p) model can be seen as a generalization of the AR(p) model that allows for multiple time series. Just like in the AR(p) model, the order p of the VAR(p) model determines how many lagged values impact the present value of a series. In this model, however, we also include lagged values of other time series.

For two time series, the general equation for the VAR(p) model is a linear combination of a vector of constants, past values of both time series, and a vector of error terms:

$$\begin{bmatrix} y_{1,t} \\ y_{2,t} \end{bmatrix} = \begin{bmatrix} C_1 \\ C_2 \end{bmatrix} + \begin{bmatrix} \phi_{1,1}^1 & \phi_{1,2}^1 \\ \phi_{2,1}^1 & \phi_{2,2}^1 \end{bmatrix} \begin{bmatrix} y_{1,t-1} \\ y_{2,t-1} \end{bmatrix} + \begin{bmatrix} \phi_{1,1}^2 & \phi_{1,2}^2 \\ \phi_{2,1}^2 & \phi_{2,2}^2 \end{bmatrix} \begin{bmatrix} y_{1,t-2} \\ y_{2,t-2} \end{bmatrix} + \cdots$$

$$+ \begin{bmatrix} \phi_{1,1}^p & \phi_{1,2}^p \\ \phi_{2,1}^p & \phi_{2,2}^p \end{bmatrix} \begin{bmatrix} y_{1,t-p} \\ y_{2,t-p} \end{bmatrix} + \begin{bmatrix} \epsilon_{1,t} \\ \epsilon_{2,t} \end{bmatrix}$$

Note that the time series must be stationary to apply the VAR model.

You have seen how the VAR(p) model is expressed mathematically, with their lagged values included in each expression, as shown in equations 10.3 and 10.4. This should give you a sense of how each series has an impact on the others. The VAR(p) model is only valid if both series are useful in predicting one another. Looking at the general shape of the series over time is not sufficient to support that hypothesis. Instead, we must apply the *Granger causality* test, which is a statistical hypothesis test to determine whether one time series is predictive of another. Only upon the success of this test can we apply the VAR model to make predictions. This is an important step in our modeling procedure when using a VAR model.

10.2 Designing a modeling procedure for the VAR(p) model

The VAR(p) model requires a slightly modified version of the modeling procedure we have been using. The most notable modification is the addition of the Granger causality test, since the VAR model assumes that past values of both time series are significantly predictive of the other time series.

The complete modeling procedure for the VAR(p) model is shown in figure 10.2. As you can see, the modeling procedure for the VAR(p) model is very similar to the modeling procedures we have been using since the introduction of the ARMA(p,q) model.

The main difference here is that we list values only for the order p, since we are fitting different VAR(p) models on the data. Then, once the model with the lowest AIC has been selected, we perform the Granger causality test. This test determines whether past values of a time series are statistically significant in forecasting another time series. It is important to test for this relationship because the VAR(p) model uses past values of one time series to forecast another.

If the Granger causality test fails, we cannot say that past values of one time series are predictive of the other time series. In that case, the VAR(p) model becomes invalid, and we must revert to using a variation of the SARIMAX model to forecast the time series. On the other hand, if the Granger causality test passes, we can resume the procedure with residual analysis. As before, if the residuals are close to white noise, we can use the selected VAR(p) model to make forecasts.

Before we move on to applying this modeling procedure, it is worth spending some time exploring the Granger causality test in more detail.

10.2.1 Exploring the Granger causality test

As shown in the previous section, the VAR(p) model assumes that each time series has an impact on another. Therefore, it is important to test if this relationship actually exists. Otherwise, we would be assuming a relationship that does not exist, which would introduce mistakes in the model and make our predictions invalid and unreliable.

Hence, we use the Granger causality test. This is a statistical test that helps us determine if past values of a time series $y_{2,t}$ can help forecast time series $y_{1,t}$. If that is the case, then we say that $y_{2,t}$ *Granger-causes* $y_{1,t}$.

Note that the Granger causality test is restricted to predictive causality, as we are only determining whether past values of a time series are statistically significant in predicting another time series. Furthermore, the test requires both time series to be

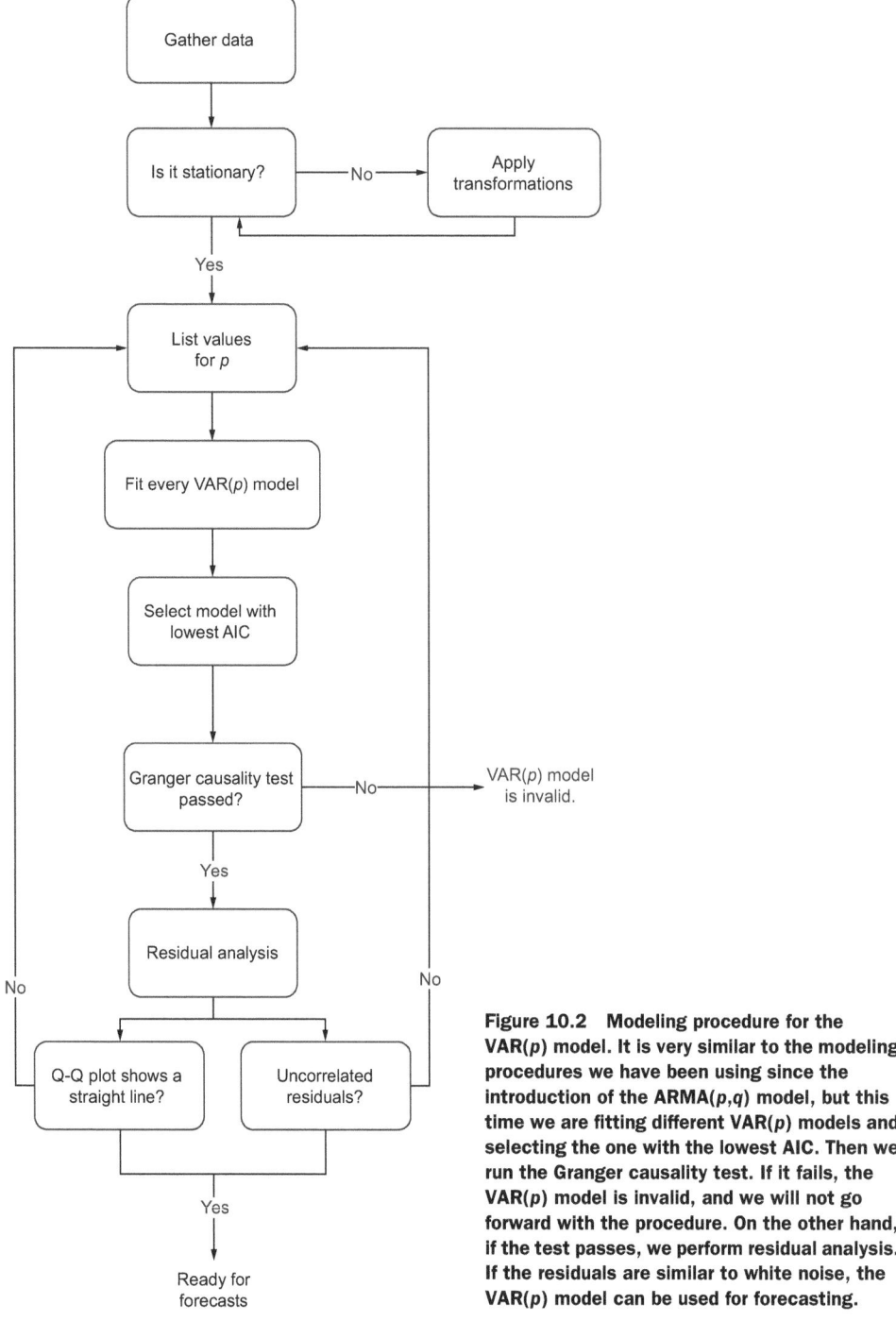

Figure 10.2   Modeling procedure for the VAR(p) model. It is very similar to the modeling procedures we have been using since the introduction of the ARMA(p,q) model, but this time we are fitting different VAR(p) models and selecting the one with the lowest AIC. Then we run the Granger causality test. If it fails, the VAR(p) model is invalid, and we will not go forward with the procedure. On the other hand, if the test passes, we perform residual analysis. If the residuals are similar to white noise, the VAR(p) model can be used for forecasting.

stationary in order for the results to be valid. Also, the Granger causality test tests causality only in one direction; we must repeat the test to verify that $y_{1,t}$ also Granger-causes $y_{2,t}$ in order for the VAR model to be valid. Otherwise, we must resort to the SARIMAX model and predict each time series separately.

The null hypothesis for this test states that $y_{2,t}$ does not Granger-cause $y_{1,t}$. Again, we will use the p-value with a critical value of 0.05 to determine whether we will reject the null hypothesis or not. In the case where the returned p-value of the Granger causality test is less than 0.05, we can reject the null hypothesis and say that $y_{2,t}$ Granger-causes $y_{1,t}$.

You saw that the Granger causality test is performed after the VAR(p) model is selected. This is because the test requires us to specify the number of lags to include in the test, which is equivalent to the order of the model. For example, if the selected VAR(p) model is of order 3, the Granger causality test will determine if the past three values of a time series are statistically significant in forecasting the other time series.

The `statsmodels` library conveniently includes the Granger causality test, which we will apply in the next section when we forecast both real consumption and real disposable income.

10.3 Forecasting real disposable income and real consumption

Having examined the VAR(p) model and designed a modeling procedure for it, we are now ready to apply it to forecasting both the real disposable income and real consumption in the United States. We will use the same dataset as in the previous chapter, which contains the macroeconomics data between 1959 and 2009.

> **NOTE** The source code for this chapter is available on GitHub: https://github.com/marcopeix/TimeSeriesForecastingInPython/tree/master/CH10.

```
macro_econ_data = sm.datasets.macrodata.load_pandas().data
macro_econ_data
```

We can now plot our two variables of interest, which are real disposable income, denoted as `realdpi` in the dataset, and real consumption, denoted as `realcons`. The result is shown in figure 10.3.

```
fig, (ax1, ax2) = plt.subplots(nrows=2, ncols=1, figsize=(10,8))

ax1.plot(macro_econ_data['realdpi'])
ax1.set_xlabel('Date')
ax1.set_ylabel('Real disposable income (k$)')
ax1.set_title('realdpi')
ax1.spines['top'].set_alpha(0)

ax2.plot(macro_econ_data['realcons'])
ax2.set_xlabel('Date')
ax2.set_ylabel('Real consumption (k$)')
```

```
ax2.set_title('realcons')
ax2.spines['top'].set_alpha(0)

plt.xticks(np.arange(0, 208, 16), np.arange(1959, 2010, 4))

fig.autofmt_xdate()
plt.tight_layout()
```

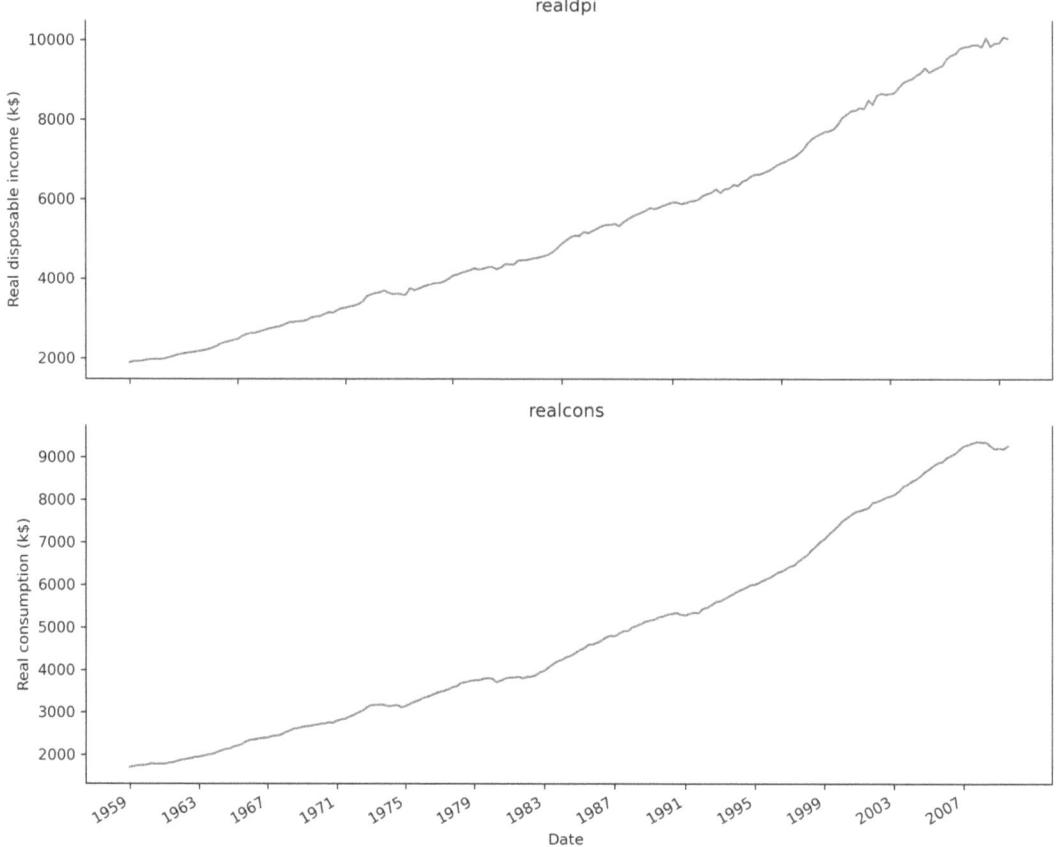

Figure 10.3 Real disposable income and real consumption in the United States, between 1959 and 2009. The data was collected quarterly and is expressed in thousands of US dollars. You can see that both curves have a similar shape through time.

In figure 10.3 you can see that both curves have a very similar shape through time, which intuitively makes them good candidates for a VAR(p) model. It is reasonable to think that with a higher disposable income, consumption is likely to be high, just as higher consumption can be a sign of higher disposable income. Of course, this hypothesis will have to be tested using the Granger causality test later in the modeling procedure.

We have gathered the data, so now we must determine if the time series are stationary. In figure 10.3 both of them exhibit a positive trend through time, meaning that they are non-stationary. Nevertheless, we'll apply the augmented Dickey-Fuller (ADF) test to make sure.

```
ad_fuller_result_1 = adfuller(macro_econ_data['realdpi'])
print('realdpi')                                              ADF test
print(f'ADF Statistic: {ad_fuller_result_1[0]}')             for realdpi
print(f'p-value: {ad_fuller_result_1[1]}')


print('\n--------------------\n')


ad_fuller_result_2 = adfuller(macro_econ_data['realcons'])

print('realcons')                                             ADF test for realcons. Note
print(f'ADF Statistic: {ad_fuller_result_2[0]}')             that both time series must
print(f'p-value: {ad_fuller_result_2[1]}')                   be stationary before they are
                                                              used in the VAR(p) model.
```

For both variables, the ADF test outputs a p-value of 1.0. Therefore, we cannot reject the null hypothesis, and we conclude that both time series are not stationary, as expected.

We'll apply a transformation to make them stationary. Specifically, we'll difference both series and test for stationarity again.

```
ad_fuller_result_1 = adfuller(macro_econ_data['realdpi'].diff()[1:])

print('realdpi')                                              First-order
print(f'ADF Statistic: {ad_fuller_result_1[0]}')             differencing
print(f'p-value: {ad_fuller_result_1[1]}')                   for realdpi


print('\n--------------------\n')


ad_fuller_result_2 = adfuller(macro_econ_data['realcons'].diff()[1:])

print('realcons')                                             First-order
print(f'ADF Statistic: {ad_fuller_result_2[0]}')             differencing
print(f'p-value: {ad_fuller_result_2[1]}')                   for realcons
```

The ADF test for realdpi returns a p-value of 1.45×10^{-14}, while the ADF test for realcons returns a p-value of 0.0006. In both cases, the p-value is smaller than 0.05. Therefore, we reject the null hypothesis and conclude that both time series are stationary. As mentioned before, the VAR(p) model requires the time series to be stationary. We can thus use the transformed series for modeling, and we will need to integrate the forecasts to bring them back to their original scales.

We are now at the step of fitting many VAR(p) models to select the one with the smallest Akaike information criterion (AIC). We'll write a function, optimize_VAR, to fit many VAR(p) models while varying the order p. This function will return an ordered DataFrame in ascending order of AIC. This function is shown in the following listing.

Listing 10.1   Function to fit many VAR(*p*) models and select the one with the lowest AIC

```
from typing import Union
from tqdm import tqdm_notebook
from statsmodels.tsa.statespace.varmax import VARMAX

def optimize_VAR(endog: Union[pd.Series, list]) -> pd.DataFrame:

    results = []
                                                        Vary the order
    for i in tqdm_notebook(range(15)):        ◁—┘      p from 0 to 14.
        try:
            model = VARMAX(endog, order=(i, 0)).fit(dips=False)
        except:
            continue

        aic = model.aic
        results.append([i, aic])

    result_df = pd.DataFrame(results)
    result_df.columns = ['p', 'AIC']

    result_df = result_df.sort_values(by='AIC',
  ➛  ascending=True).reset_index(drop=True)

    return result_df
```

We can now use this function to select the order *p* that minimizes the AIC.

First, though, we must define the train and test sets. In this case, we'll use 80% of the data for training and 20% for testing. This means that the last 40 data points will be used for testing, and the rest is used for training. Remember that the VAR(*p*) model requires both series to be stationary. Therefore, we'll split on the differenced dataset and feed the differenced training set to the optimize_VAR function.

Select only realdpi and realcons, as they are   **Difference both series,**
the only two variables of interest in this case.   **as the ADF test shows that**
                                                              a first-order differencing
                                                              makes them stationary.

```
 └─▷ endog = macro_econ_data[['realdpi', 'realcons']]

    endog_diff = macro_econ_data[['realdpi', 'realcons']].diff()[1:]    ◁─┘

    train = endog_diff[:162]    ◁─         The first 162 data points go
 ─▷ test = endog_diff[162:]                for training. This is roughly
                                           80% of the dataset.
    result_df = optimize_VAR(train)   ◁─┐
    result_df                          Run the optimize_VAR function using
                                       the differenced data stored in train.
The last 40 data points go for the test   This is required for the VAR(p) model.
set. This is roughly 20% of the dataset.
```

Running the function returns a DataFrame in which we see that *p* = 3 has the lowest AIC value of all. Therefore, the selected model is a VAR(3) model, meaning that the past three values of each time series are used to forecast the other time series.

Following the modeling procedure, we must now use the Granger causality test Recall that the VAR model assumes that past values of realcons are useful in predicting realdpi and that past values of realdpi are useful in predicting realcons. This relationship must be tested. If the Granger causality test returns a p-value greater than 0.05, we cannot reject the null hypothesis, meaning that the variables do not Granger-cause each other, and the model is invalid. On the other hand, a p-value smaller than 0.05 will allow us to reject the null hypothesis, thus validating the VAR(3) model, meaning that we can move on with the modeling procedure.

We'll run the Granger causality test for both variables, using the grangercausalitytests function from the statsmodels library. Remember that the series must be stationary for the Granger causality test, which is why they are differenced when passed in to the function. Also, we specify the number of lags for the test, which in this case is 3, since the model selection step returned $p = 3$.

The function tests if the second variable Granger-causes the first one. Here we thus test if realcons Granger-causes realdpi. We then pass the number of lags in a list, which in our case is 3. Note that the series are differenced to make them stationary.

```
print('realcons Granger-causes realdpi?\n')
print('------------------')
granger_1 = grangercausalitytests(macro_econ_data[['realdpi',
  'realcons']].diff()[1:], [3])

print('\nrealdpi Granger-causes realcons?\n')
print('------------------')
granger_2 = grangercausalitytests(macro_econ_data[['realcons',
  'realdpi']].diff()[1:], [3])
```

Here we test if realdpi Granger-causes realcons.

Running the Granger causality test for both variables returns a p-value smaller than 0.05 in both cases. Therefore, we can reject the null hypothesis and conclude that realdpi Granger-causes realcons, and realcons Granger-causes realdpi. Our VAR(3) model is thus valid. In the event that one variable does not Granger-cause the other, the VAR(p) model becomes invalid, and it cannot be used. In that case, we must use the SARIMAX model and predict each time series individually.

We can now move on to residual analysis. For this step, we first fit the VAR(3) model on our train set.

```
best_model = VARMAX(train, order=(3,0))
best_model_fit = best_model.fit(disp=False)
```

Then we can use the plot_diagnostics function to plot a histogram of the residuals, the Q-Q plot, and the correlogram. However, we must study the residuals of two variables here, since we are modeling both realdpi and realcons.

Let's focus on the residuals for realdpi first.

Passing variable=0 specifies that we want plots for the residuals of realdpi, since it is the first variable that was passed to the VAR model.

```
best_model_fit.plot_diagnostics(figsize=(10,8), variable=0);
```

The output in figure 10.4 shows that the residuals are close to white noise.

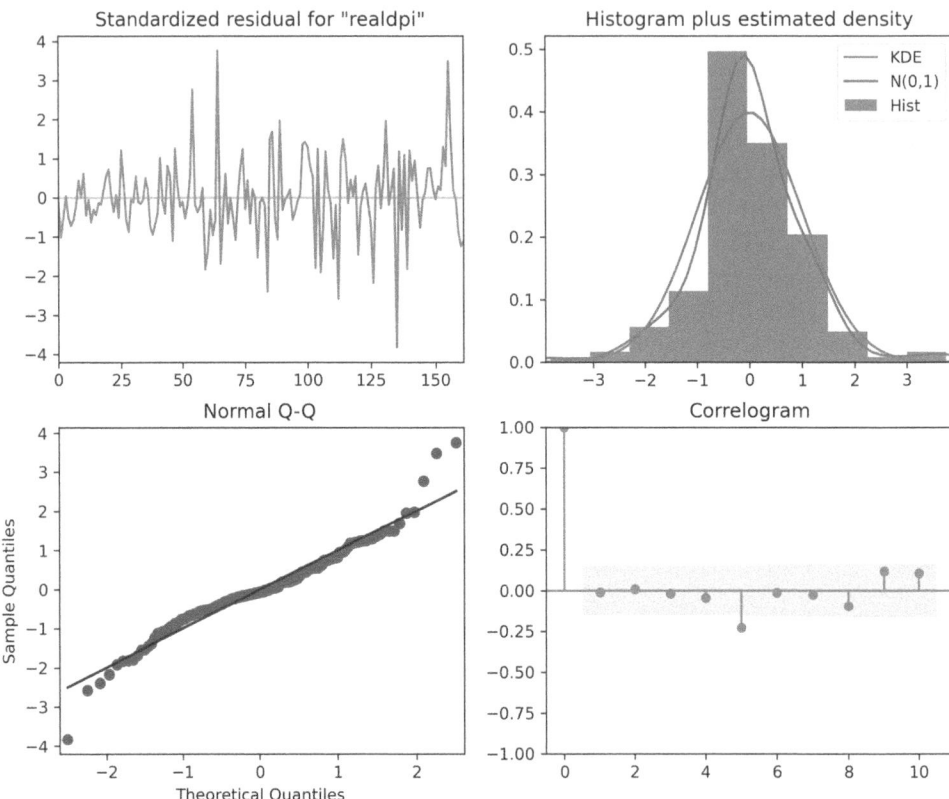

Figure 10.4   Residuals analysis of `realdpi`. The standardized residuals seem to have no trend and constant variance, which is in line with white noise. The histogram also closely resembles the shape of a normal distribution. This is further supported by the Q-Q plot, which shows a fairly straight line that lies on y = x, although we can see some curvature at the extremities. Finally, the correlogram shows no significant coefficients except at lag 5. However, this is likely due to chance, since there are no preceding significant coefficients. Thus, we can conclude that the residuals are close to white noise.

Now we can move on to analyzing the residuals of `realcons`.

> **Passing variable=1 specifies that we want the plots of the residuals for realcons, since it was the second variable passed in the model.**

```
best_model_fit.plot_diagnostics(figsize=(10,8), variable=1);
```

The output in figure 10.5 shows that the residuals of `realcons` closely resemble white noise.

Once the qualitative analysis is done, we can move on to the quantitative analysis using the Ljung-Box test. Recall that the null hypothesis of the Ljung-Box test states

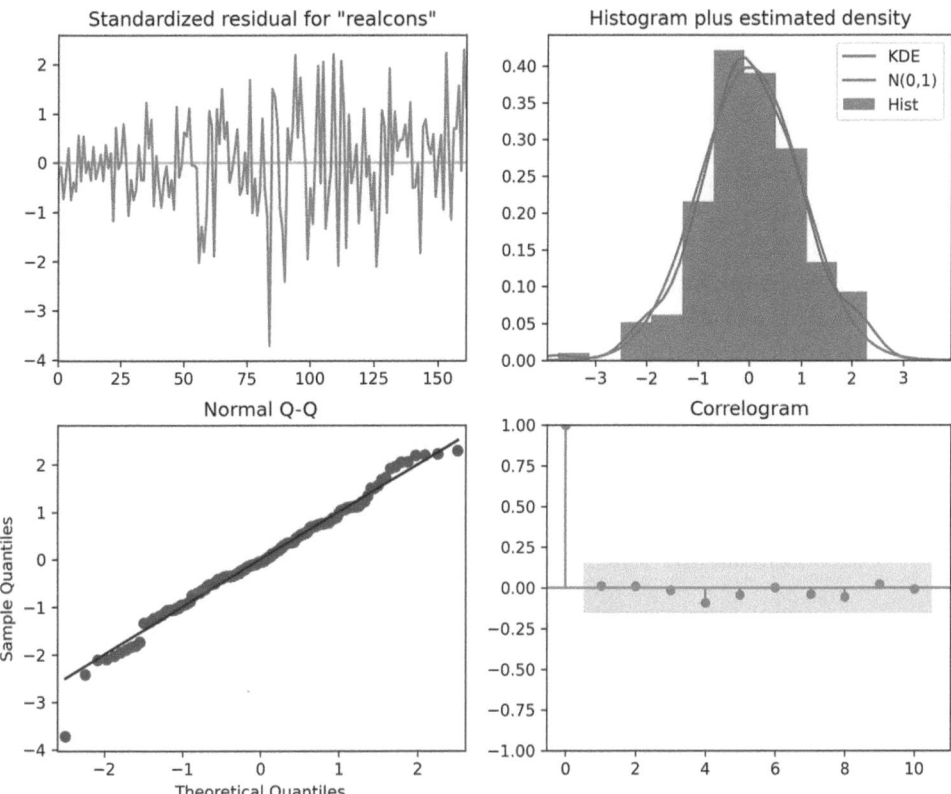

Figure 10.5   Residuals analysis of `realcons`. The top-left plot shows the residuals over time, and you can see that there is no trend and constant variance, which is in line with the behavior of white noise. At the top right, the distribution is very close to a normal distribution. This is further supported by the Q-Q plot at the bottom left, which displays a fairly straight line that lies on y = x. Finally, the correlogram at the bottom right shows that there are no significant autocorrelation coefficients after lag 0. Therefore, the residuals are close to white noise.

that the residuals are independent and uncorrelated. Therefore, for the residuals to behave like white noise, the test must return p-values that are larger than 0.05, in which case we do not reject the null hypothesis.

The test must be applied on both `realdpi` and `realcons`:

```
realgdp_residuals = best_model_fit.resid['realdpi']

lbvalue, pvalue = acorr_ljungbox(realgdp_residuals, np.arange(1, 11, 1))

print(pvalue)
```

Running the Ljung-Box test on the residuals of `realdpi` returns p-values that are all larger than 0.05. Thus, we do not reject the null hypothesis, meaning that the residuals are uncorrelated and independent, just like white noise.

```
realcons_residuals = best_model_fit.resid['realcons']

lbvalue, pvalue = acorr_ljungbox(realcons_residuals, np.arange(1, 11, 1))

print(pvalue)
```

Next, we'll run the test on the residuals of `realcons`. This test returns p-values that are all greater than 0.05. Again, we do not reject the null hypothesis, meaning that the residuals are not correlated and independent, just like white noise.

Since the model passed both the qualitative and quantitative aspects of residual analysis, we can move on to forecasting `realcons` and `realdpi` using a VAR(3) model. We will compare the VAR(3) model to a baseline that simply predicts the last observed value. We'll forecast four steps into the future, which is equivalent to forecasting one full year as the data is sampled quarterly. We'll thus perform a rolling forecast four steps into the future over the entire length of the test set.

To do so, we'll use the `rolling_forecast` function that we have defined many times over the last several chapters. This time, we'll apply some slight modifications to accommodate the VAR(3) model. It will need to output predictions for both `realdpi` and `realcons`, so we must return two lists containing forecasts. The following listing shows the code for the `rolling_forecast` function.

Listing 10.2   Function for rolling forecasts over a test set

```
def rolling_forecast(df: pd.DataFrame, train_len: int, horizon: int,
➥ window: int, method: str) -> list:

    total_len = train_len + horizon
    end_idx = train_len

    if method == 'VAR':                          Initialize two empty lists
                                                 to hold the predictions for
        realdpi_pred_VAR = []        ◁——         realdpi and realcons.
        realcons_pred_VAR = []

        for i in range(train_len, total_len, window):
            model = VARMAX(df[:i], order=(3,0))
Extract the     res = model.fit(disp=False)
predictions     predictions = res.get_prediction(0, i + window - 1)
for realdpi.
            oos_pred_realdpi = predictions.predicted_mean.iloc[-
➥ window:]['realdpi']
            oos_pred_realcons = predictions.predicted_mean.iloc[-
➥ window:]['realcons']
                                                         Extend the lists with
Extract the     realdpi_pred_VAR.extend(oos_pred_realdpi)   ◁——  the new predictions
predictions     realcons_pred_VAR.extend(oos_pred_realcons)        for each variable.
for realcons.
        return realdpi_pred_VAR, realcons_pred_VAR   ◁——

                                      Return both lists of predictions
                                        for realdpi and realcons.
```

```
elif method == 'last':
    realdpi_pred_last = []
    realcons_pred_last = []

    for i in range(train_len, total_len, window):

        realdpi_last = df[:i].iloc[-1]['realdpi']
        realcons_last = df[:i].iloc[-1]['realcons']

        realdpi_pred_last.extend(realdpi_last for _ in range(window))
        realcons_pred_last.extend(realcons_last for _ in range(window))

    return realdpi_pred_last, realcons_pred_last
```

> For the baseline, we'll also use two lists to hold the predictions for each variable and return them at the end.

We can now use this function to produce the forecasts for `realdpi` and `realcons` using the VAR(3) model.

```
TRAIN_LEN = len(train)
HORIZON = len(test)
WINDOW = 4
```

> The window is 4, since we want to forecast four time steps into the future at a time, which is equivalent to 1 year.

```
realdpi_pred_VAR, realcons_pred_VAR = rolling_forecast(endog_diff,
    TRAIN_LEN, HORIZON, WINDOW, 'VAR')
```

Recall that the VAR(3) model requires the series to be stationary, meaning that we have transformed forecasts. We must then integrate them using the cumulative sum to bring them back to the original scale of the data.

```
test = endog[163:]

test['realdpi_pred_VAR'] = pd.Series()
test['realdpi_pred_VAR'] = endog.iloc[162]['realdpi'] +
    np.cumsum(realdpi_pred_VAR)

test['realcons_pred_VAR'] = pd.Series()
test['realcons_pred_VAR'] = endog.iloc[162]['realcons'] +
    np.cumsum(realcons_pred_VAR)

test
```

> Integrate the forecasts using the cumulative sum.

> Display the test DataFrame.

At this point, `test` contains the actual values of the test set and the predictions from the VAR(3) model. We can now add the forecasts from our baseline method, which simply predicts the last known value for the next four timesteps.

```
realdpi_pred_last, realcons_pred_last = rolling_forecast(endog,
    TRAIN_LEN, HORIZON, WINDOW, 'last')

test['realdpi_pred_last'] = realdpi_pred_last
test['realcons_pred_last'] = realcons_pred_last

test
```

> Use rolling_forecast to obtain the baseline predictions using the last known value method.

> Display the test DataFrame.

Now test holds the actual values of the test set, the predictions from the VAR(3) model, and the predictions from the baseline method. Everything is set for us to visualize the forecasts and evaluate the forecasting methods using the mean absolute percentage error (MAPE). The forecasts are shown in figure 10.6.

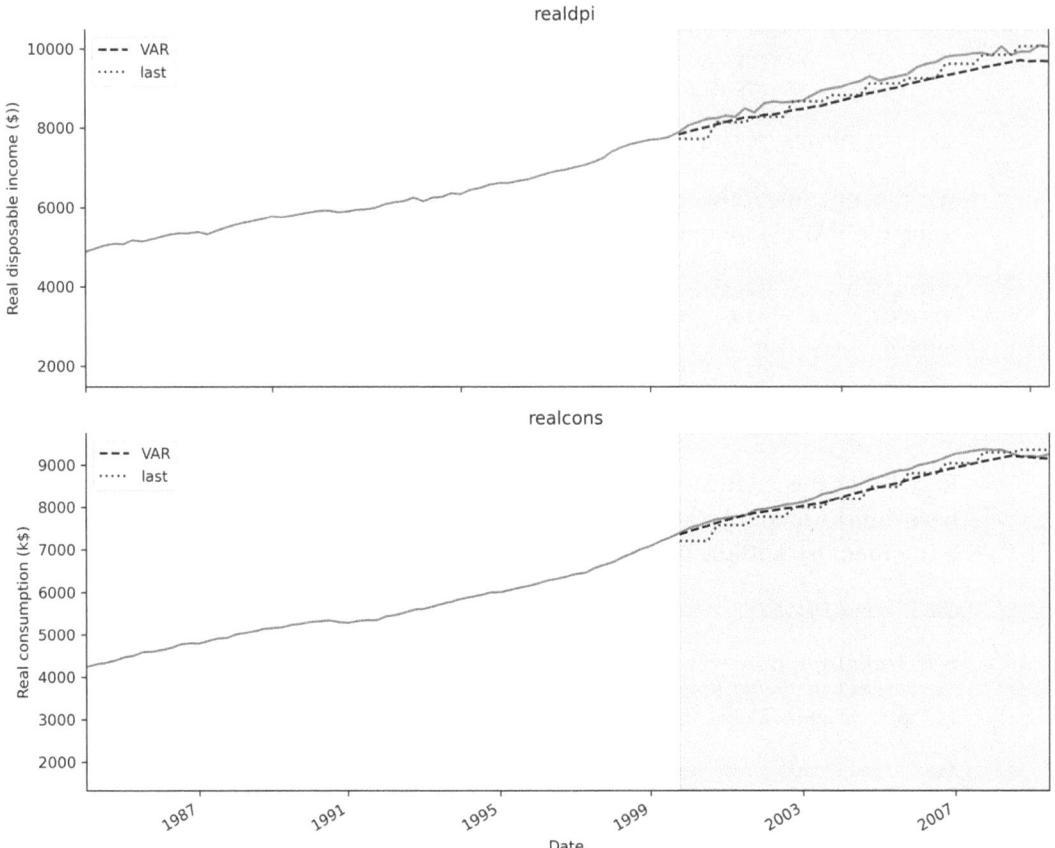

Figure 10.6 Forecasts of realdpi and realcons. You can see that the predictions from the VAR(3) model, shown as a dashed line, closely follow the actual values of the test set. You'll also notice that the dotted curve from the baseline method shows little steps, which makes sense since we are forecasting a constant value over four timesteps.

In figure 10.6 the dashed line represents the forecasts from the VAR(3) model, and the dotted line shows the predictions from the last known value method. You can see that both lines are very close to the actual values of the test set, making it hard for us to visually determine which method is better.

We will now calculate the MAPE. The result is shown in figure 10.7.

```
def mape(y_true, y_pred):
    return np.mean(np.abs((y_true - y_pred) / y_true)) * 100

mape_realdpi_VAR = mape(test['realdpi'], test['realdpi_pred_VAR'])
mape_realdpi_last = mape(test['realdpi'], test['realdpi_pred_last'])

mape_realcons_VAR = mape(test['realcons'], test['realcons_pred_VAR'])
mape_realcons_last = mape(test['realcons'], test['realcons_pred_last'])
```

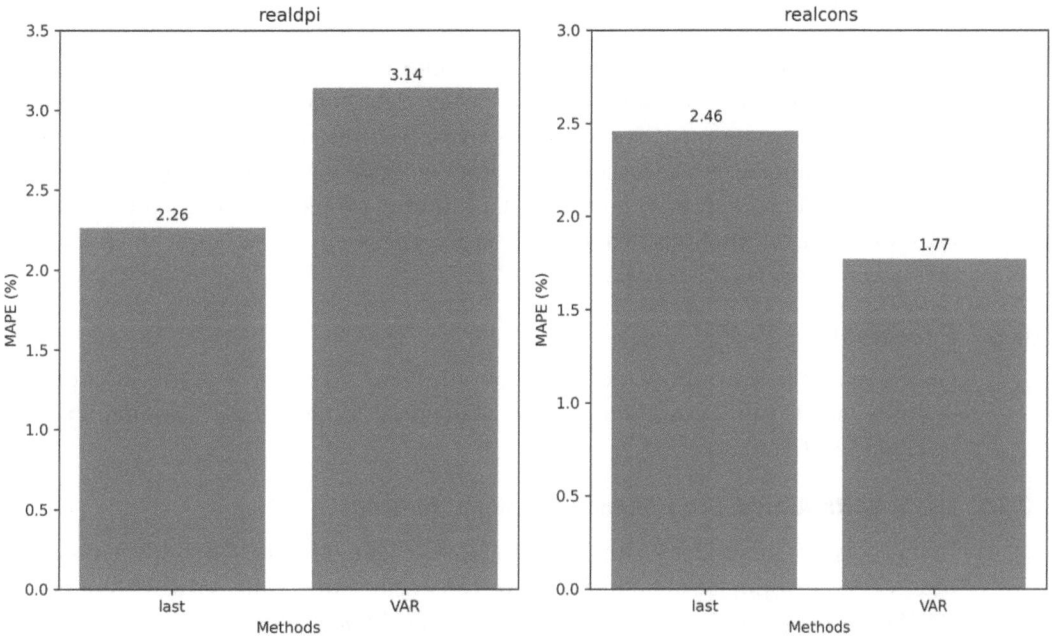

Figure 10.7   The MAPE of the forecast for `realdpi` and `realcons`. You can see that the VAR(3) model performs worse than the baseline in the case of `realdpi`. However, the VAR(3) model performs better than the baseline for `realcons`.

In figure 10.7 you can see that the VAR(3) model performs worse than the baseline in the case of `realdpi` but better than the baseline for `realcons`. This is an ambiguous situation. There is no clear result, since the model does not outperform the baseline in both situations.

We can hypothesize that in the case of `realdpi`, `realcons` is not predictive enough to make more accurate forecasts than the baseline, even though the Granger causality test passed. Therefore, we should resort to using a variation of the SARIMAX model to predict `realdpi`. Thus, I would conclude that the VAR(3) model is not sufficient to accurately forecast `realdpi` and `realcons`. I would suggest using two separate models, which could include `realdpi` and `realcons` as exogenous variables, while also potentially including moving average terms.

10.4   Next steps

In this chapter, we covered the VAR(p) model, which allows us to forecast multiple time series at once.

The VAR(p) model stands for vector autoregression, and it assumes that the past values of some time series are predictive of the future values of other time series. This bidirectional relationship is tested using the Granger causality test. If the test fails, meaning that the returned p-values are larger than 0.05, the VAR(p) model is invalid, and it cannot be used.

Congratulations on making it this far—we have covered a wide array of statistical methods for forecasting time series! These statistical methods are great for smaller datasets with low dimensionality. However, when datasets start getting large, starting at 10,000 data points or more, and they have many features, deep learning can be a great tool for obtaining accurate forecasts and leveraging all the available data.

In the next chapter, we'll go through a capstone project to consolidate our knowledge of statistical methods. Then we'll start a new section and apply deep learning forecasting models on large datasets.

10.5   Exercises

Go above and beyond the VAR(p) model with these exercises. The full solutions are available on GitHub: https://github.com/marcopeix/TimeSeriesForecastingInPython/ tree/master/CH10.

10.5.1   Use a VARMA model to predict realdpi and realcons

In this chapter, we used a VAR(p) model. However, we used the `VARMAX` function from `statsmodels` to do so, meaning that we can easily extend the VAR(p) model to a VARMA(p,q) model. In this exercise, use a VARMA(p,q) model to forecast `realdpi` and `realcons`.

1   Use the same train and test sets as in this chapter.
2   Generate a list of unique (p,q) combinations.
3   Rename the `optimize_VAR` function to `optimize_VARMA`, and adapt it to loop over all unique (p,q) combinations.
4   Select the model with the lowest AIC, and perform the Granger causality test. Pass in the largest order among (p,q). Is the VARMA(p,q) model valid?
5   Perform residual analysis.
6   Make forecasts on a four-step window over the test set. Use the last known value method as a baseline.
7   Calculate the MAPE. Is it lower or higher than that of our VAR(3) model?

10.5.2 *Use a VARMAX model to predict realdpi and realcons*

Again, since we used the `VARMAX` function from `statsmodels`, we know that we can also add exogenous variables to the model, just like in SARIMAX. In this exercise, use the VARMAX model to forecast `realdpi` and `realcons`.

1 Use the same train and test sets as in this chapter.
2 Generate a list of unique (p,q) combinations.
3 Rename the `optimize_VAR` function to `optimize_VARMAX`, and adapt it to loop over all the unique (p,q) combinations and exogenous variables.
4 Select the model with the lowest AIC, and perform the Granger causality test. Pass in the largest order among (p,q). Is the VARMAX (p,q) model valid?
5 Perform residual analysis.
6 Make forecasts on a one-step window over the test set. Use the last known value method as a baseline.
7 Calculate the MAPE. Did the model perform better than the baseline?

Summary

- The vector autoregression model, VAR(p), captures the relationship between multiple series as they change over time. In this model, each series has an impact on the others.
- A VAR(p) model is valid only if each time series Granger-causes the others. This is determined using the Granger causality test.
- The null hypothesis of the Granger causality test states that one time series does not Granger-cause the other. If the p-value is less than 0.05, we reject the null hypothesis and conclude that the first time series Granger-causes the other.

Capstone: Forecasting the number of antidiabetic drug prescriptions in Australia

11

This chapter covers

- Developing a forecasting model to predict the number of antidiabetic drug prescriptions in Australia
- Applying the modeling procedure with a SARIMA model
- Evaluating our model against a baseline
- Determining the champion model

We have covered a lot of statistical models for time series forecasting. Back in chapters 4 and 5, you learned how to model moving average processes and autoregressive processes. We then combined these models to form the ARMA model and added a parameter to forecast non-stationary time series, leading us to the ARIMA model. We then added a seasonal component with the SARIMA model. Adding the effect of exogenous variables culminated in the SARIMAX model. Finally, we covered multivariate time series forecasting using the VAR model. Thus, you now have access to many statistical models that allow you to forecast a wide variety of time series, from simple to more complex. This is a good time to consolidate your learning and put your knowledge into practice with a capstone project.

The objective of the project in this chapter is forecasting the number of antidiabetic drug prescriptions in Australia, from 1991 to 2008. In a professional setting, solving this problem would allow us to gauge the production of antidiabetic drugs, such as to produce enough to meet the demand and but also avoid overproduction. The data we'll use was recorded by the Australian Health Insurance Commission. We can visualize the time series in figure 11.1.

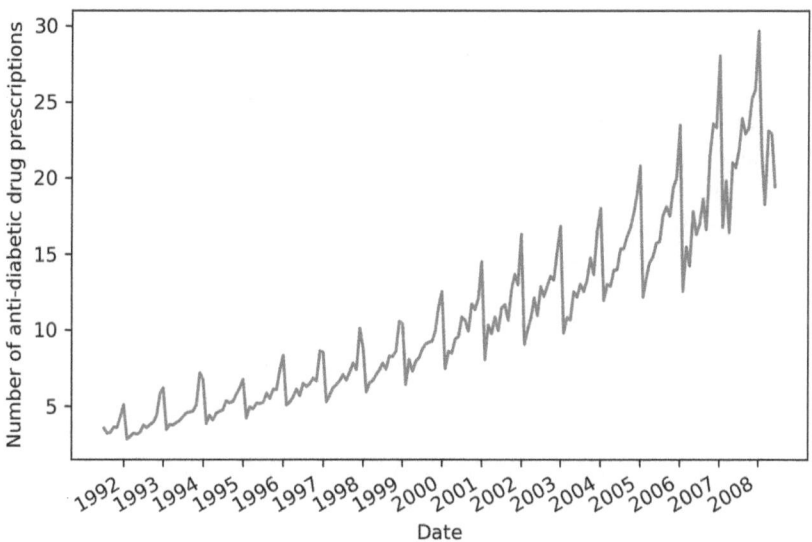

Figure 11.1   Monthly number of antidiabetic drug prescriptions in Australia between 1991 and 2008.

In figure 11.1 you'll see a clear trend in the time series, as the number of prescriptions increases over time. Furthermore, you'll observe strong seasonality, as each year seems to start at a low value and end at a high value. By now, you should intuitively know which model is potentially the most suitable for solving this problem.

To solve this problem, refer to the following steps:

1   The objective is to forecast 12 months of antidiabetic drug prescriptions. Use the last 36 months of the dataset as a test set to allow for rolling forecasts.
2   Visualize the time series.
3   Use time series decomposition to extract the trend and seasonal components.
4   Based on your exploration, determine the most suitable model.
5   Model the series with the usual steps:
    a   Apply transformations to make it stationary
    b   Set the values of d and D. Set the value of m.

  c Find the optimal $(p,d,q)(P,D,Q)_m$ parameters.

  d Perform residual analysis to validate your model.

 6 Perform rolling forecasts of 12 months on the test set.

 7 Visualize your forecasts.

 8 Compare the model's performance to a baseline. Select an appropriate baseline and error metric.

 9 Conclude whether the model should be used or not.

To get the most out of this capstone project, you are highly encouraged to complete it on your own by referring to the preceding steps. This will help you assess your autonomy in the modeling process and your understanding.

If you ever feel stuck or want to validate your reasoning, the rest of this chapter walks through the completion of this project. Also, the full solution is available on GitHub if you wish to refer to the code directly: https://github.com/marcopeix/TimeSeriesForecastingInPython/tree/master/CH11.

I wish you luck on this project!

11.1 *Importing the required libraries and loading the data*

The natural first step is to import the libraries that will be needed to complete the project. We can then load the data and store it in a `DataFrame` to be used throughout the project.

Thus, we'll import the following libraries and specify the magic function `%matplotlib inline` to display the plots in the notebook:

```
from sklearn.metrics import mean_squared_error, mean_absolute_error
from statsmodels.graphics.tsaplots import plot_acf, plot_pacf
from statsmodels.tsa.seasonal import seasonal_decompose, STL
from statsmodels.stats.diagnostic import acorr_ljungbox
from statsmodels.tsa.statespace.sarimax import SARIMAX
from statsmodels.tsa.arima_process import ArmaProcess
from statsmodels.graphics.gofplots import qqplot
from statsmodels.tsa.stattools import adfuller
from tqdm import tqdm_notebook
from itertools import product
from typing import Union

import matplotlib.pyplot as plt
import statsmodels.api as sm
import pandas as pd
import numpy as np

import warnings
warnings.filterwarnings('ignore')

%matplotlib inline
```

Once the libraries are imported, we can read the data and store it in a `DataFrame`. We can also display the shape of the `DataFrame` to determine the number of data points.

```
df = pd.read_csv('data/AusAnti-diabeticDrug.csv')
print(df.shape)
```

Displays the shape of a DataFrame. The first value is the number of rows, and the second value is the number of columns.

The data is now ready to be used throughout the project.

11.2 *Visualizing the series and its components*

With the data loaded, we can now easily visualize the series. This essentially recreates figure 11.1.

```
fig, ax = plt.subplots()

ax.plot(df.y)
ax.set_xlabel('Date')
ax.set_ylabel('Number of anti-diabetic drug prescriptions')

plt.xticks(np.arange(6, 203, 12), np.arange(1992, 2009, 1))

fig.autofmt_xdate()
plt.tight_layout()
```

Next we can perform decomposition to visualize the different components of the time series. Remember that time series decomposition allows us to visualize the trend component, seasonal component, and the residuals.

```
decomposition = STL(df.y, period=12).fit()

fig, (ax1, ax2, ax3, ax4) = plt.subplots(nrows=4, ncols=1, sharex=True,
    figsize=(10,8))

ax1.plot(decomposition.observed)
ax1.set_ylabel('Observed')

ax2.plot(decomposition.trend)
ax2.set_ylabel('Trend')

ax3.plot(decomposition.seasonal)
ax3.set_ylabel('Seasonal')

ax4.plot(decomposition.resid)
ax4.set_ylabel('Residuals')

plt.xticks(np.arange(6, 203, 12), np.arange(1992, 2009, 1))

fig.autofmt_xdate()
plt.tight_layout()
```

Column y holds the number of monthly antidiabetic prescriptions. Also, the period is set to 12, since we have monthly data.

The result is shown in figure 11.2. Everything seems to suggest that a SARIMA(p,d,q) $(P,D,Q)_m$ model would be the optimal solution for forecasting this time series. We have a

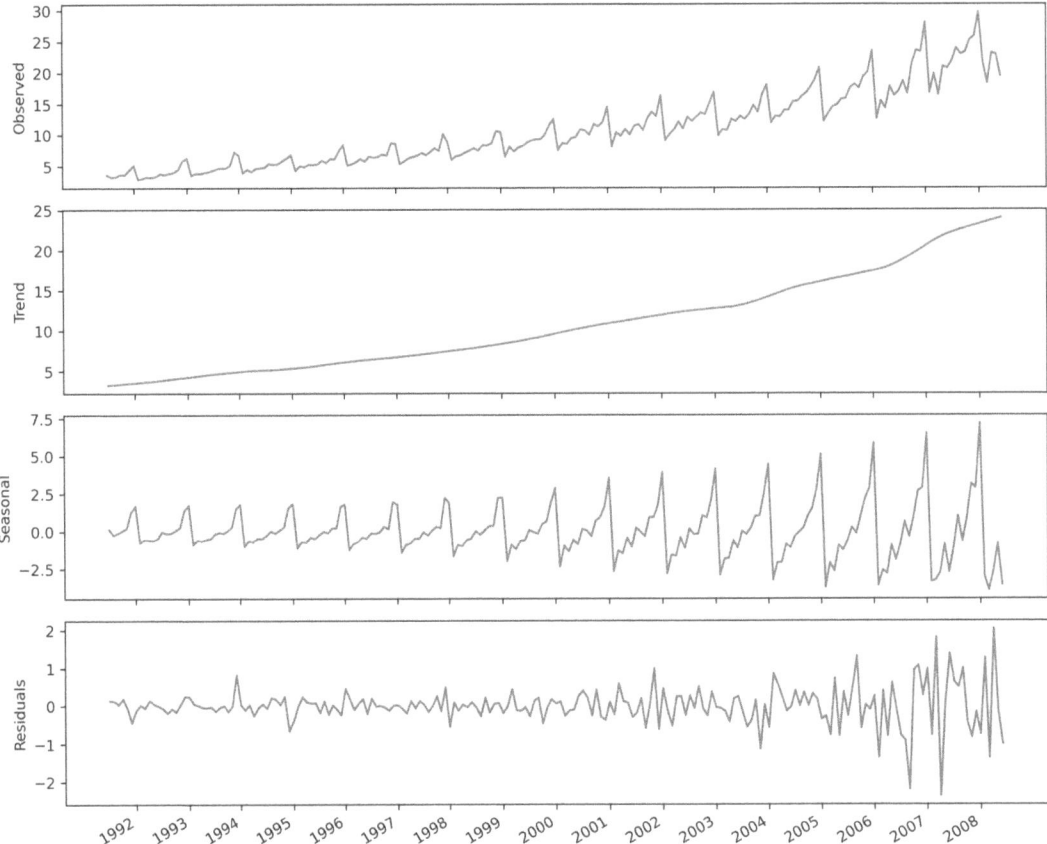

Figure 11.2 Time series decomposition on the antidiabetic drug prescriptions dataset. The first plot shows the observed data. The second plot shows the trend component, which tells us that the number of antidiabetic drug prescriptions is increasing over time. The third plot shows the seasonal component, where we can see a repeating pattern over time, indicating the presence of seasonality. The last plot shows the residuals, which are variations that are not explained by the trend of the seasonal component.

trend as well as clear seasonality. Plus, we do not have any exogenous variables to work with, so the SARIMAX model cannot be applied. Finally, we wish to predict only one target, meaning that a VAR model is also not relevant in this case.

11.3 Modeling the data

We've decided that a SARIMA(p,d,q) $(P,D,Q)_m$ model is the most suitable for modeling and forecasting this time series. Therefore, we'll follow the general modeling procedure for a SARIMAX model, as a SARIMA model is a special case of the SARIMAX model. The modeling procedure is shown in figure 11.3.

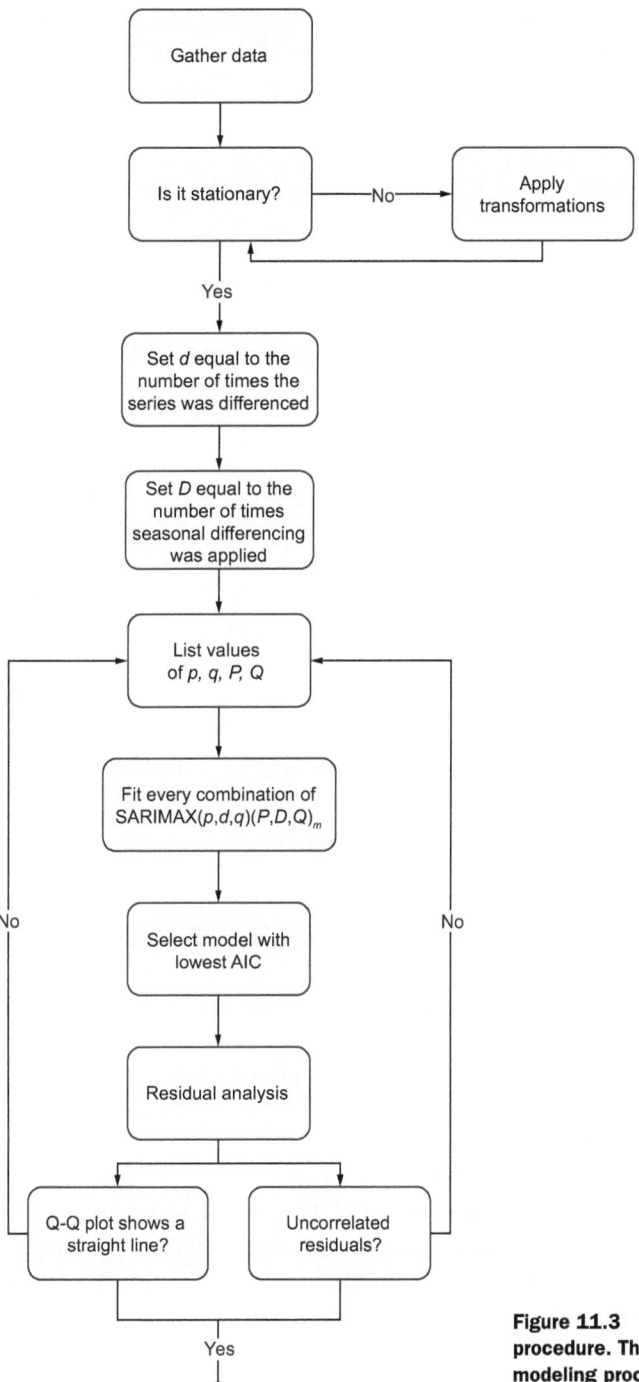

Figure 11.3   The SARIMA modeling procedure. This procedure is the most general modeling procedure, and it can be used for a SARIMA, ARIMA, or ARMA model, as they are simply special cases of the SARIMAX model.

Following the modeling procedure outlined in figure 11.3, we'll first determine whether the series is stationary using the augmented Dickey-Fuller (ADF) test.

```
ad_fuller_result = adfuller(df.y)

print(f'ADF Statistic: {ad_fuller_result[0]}')
print(f'p-value: {ad_fuller_result[1]}')
```

This returns a p-value of 1.0, meaning that we cannot reject the null hypothesis, and we conclude that the series is not stationary. Thus, we must apply transformations to make it stationary.

We'll first apply a first-order differencing on the data and test for stationarity again.

```
y_diff = np.diff(df.y, n=1)

ad_fuller_result = adfuller(y_diff)

print(f'ADF Statistic: {ad_fuller_result[0]}')
print(f'p-value: {ad_fuller_result[1]}')
```

This returns a p-value of 0.12. Again, the p-value is greater than 0.05, meaning that the series is not stationary. Let's try applying a seasonal difference, since we noticed a strong seasonal pattern in the data. Recall that we have monthly data, meaning that $m = 12$. Thus, a seasonal difference subtracts values that are 12 timesteps apart.

```
y_diff_seasonal_diff = np.diff(y_diff, n=12)    ◁──┐  We have monthly
                                                   │  data, so n = 12.
ad_fuller_result = adfuller(y_diff_seasonal_diff)  ┘

print(f'ADF Statistic: {ad_fuller_result[0]}')
print(f'p-value: {ad_fuller_result[1]}')
```

The returned p-value is 0.0. Thus, we can reject the null hypothesis and conclude that our time series is stationary.

Since we differenced the series once and took one seasonal difference, $d = 1$ and $D = 1$. Also, since we have monthly data, we know that $m = 12$. Therefore, we know that our final model will be a $\text{SARIMA}(p,1,q)(P,1,Q)_{12}$ model.

11.3.1　*Performing model selection*

We have established that our model will be a $\text{SARIMA}(p,1,q)(P,1,Q)_{12}$ model. Now we need to find the optimal values of p, q, P, and Q. This is the model selection step where we choose the parameters that minimize the Akaike information criterion (AIC).

To do so, we'll first split the data into train and test sets. As specified in the steps in the chapter introduction, the test set will consist of the last 36 months of data.

```
train = df.y[:168]
test = df.y[168:]        Print out the length of the
                         test set to make sure that it
print(len(test))    ◁──┘ contains the last 36 months.
```

With our split done, we can now use the `optimize_SARIMAX` function to find the values of p, q, P, and Q that minimize the AIC. Note that we can use `optimize_SARIMAX` here because SARIMA is a special case of the more general SARIMAX model. The function is shown in the following listing.

Listing 11.1   Function to find the values of *p*, *q*, *P*, and *Q* that minimize the AIC

```
from typing import Union
from tqdm import tqdm_notebook
from statsmodels.tsa.statespace.sarimax import SARIMAX

def optimize_SARIMAX(endog: Union[pd.Series, list], exog: Union[pd.Series,
➥ list], order_list: list, d: int, D: int, s: int) -> pd.DataFrame:

    results = []

    for order in tqdm_notebook(order_list):
        try:
            model = SARIMAX(
                endog,
                exog,
                order=(order[0], d, order[1]),
                seasonal_order=(order[2], D, order[3], s),
                simple_differencing=False).fit(disp=False)
        except:
            continue

        aic = model.aic
        results.append([order, model.aic])

    result_df = pd.DataFrame(results)
    result_df.columns = ['(p,q,P,Q)', 'AIC']

    #Sort in ascending order, lower AIC is better
    result_df = result_df.sort_values(by='AIC',
➥ ascending=True).reset_index(drop=True)

    return result_df
```

With the function defined, we can now decide on the range of values to try for p, q, P, and Q. Then we'll generate a list of unique combinations of parameters. Feel free to test a different range of values than I've used here. Simply note that the larger the range, the longer it will take to run the `optimize_SARIMAX` function.

```
ps = range(0, 5, 1)
qs = range(0, 5, 1)
Ps = range(0, 5, 1)
Qs = range(0, 5, 1)

order_list = list(product(ps, qs, Ps, Qs))
```

```
d = 1
D = 1
s = 12
```

We can now run the `optimize_SARIMAX` function. In this example, 625 unique combinations are tested, since we have 5 possible values for 4 parameters.

```
SARIMA_result_df = optimize_SARIMAX(train, None, order_list, d, D, s)
SARIMA_result_df
```

Once the function is finished, the result shows that the minimum AIC is achieved with $p = 2$, $q = 3$, $P = 1$, and $Q = 3$. Therefore, the optimal model is a SARIMA$(2,1,3)(1,1,3)_{12}$ model.

11.3.2 Conducting residual analysis

Now that we have the optimal model, we must analyze its residuals to determine whether the model can be used or not. This will depend on the residuals, which should behave like white noise. If that is the case, the model can be used for forecasting.

We can fit the model and use the `plot_diagnostics` method to qualitatively analyze its residuals.

```
SARIMA_model = SARIMAX(train, order=(2,1,3),
    seasonal_order=(1,1,3,12), simple_differencing=False)
SARIMA_model_fit = SARIMA_model.fit(disp=False)

SARIMA_model_fit.plot_diagnostics(figsize=(10,8));
```

The result is shown in figure 11.4, and we can conclude from this qualitative analysis that the residuals closely resemble white noise.

The next step is to perform the Ljung-Box test, which determines whether the residuals are independent and uncorrelated. The null hypothesis of the Ljung-Box test states that the residuals are uncorrelated, just like white noise. Thus, we want the test to return p-values larger than 0.05. In that case, we cannot reject the null hypothesis and conclude that our residuals are independent, and therefore behave like white noise.

```
residuals = SARIMA_model_fit.resid

lbvalue, pvalue = acorr_ljungbox(residuals, np.arange(1, 11, 1))

print(pvalue)
```

In this case, all the p-values are above 0.05, so we do not reject the null hypothesis, and we conclude that the residuals are independent and uncorrelated. We can conclude that the model can used for forecasting.

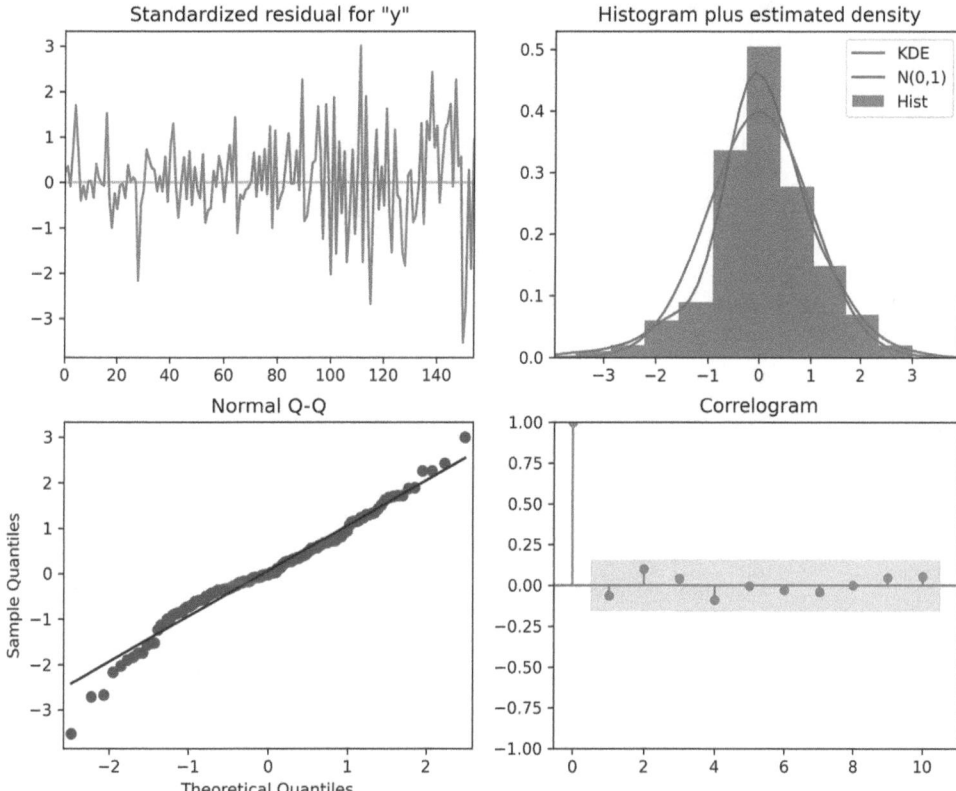

Figure 11.4   Visual diagnostics of the residuals. In the top-left plot, the residuals have no trend over time, and the variance seems constant. At the top right, the distribution of the residuals is very close to a normal distribution. This is further supported by the Q-Q plot at the bottom left, which displays a fairly straight line that sits on y = x. Finally, the correlogram at the bottom right shows no significant coefficients after lag 0, just like white noise.

11.4   *Forecasting and evaluating the model's performance*

We have a model that can be used for forecasting, so we'll now perform rolling forecasts of 12 months over the test set of 36 months. That way we'll have a better evaluation of our model's performance, as testing on fewer data points might lead to skewed results. We'll use the naive seasonal forecast as a baseline; it will simply take the last 12 months of data and use them as forecasts for the next 12 months.

We'll first define the `rolling_forecast` function to generate the predictions over the entire test set with a window of 12 months. The function is shown in the following listing.

> **Listing 11.2   Function to perform a rolling forecast over a horizon**

```
def rolling_forecast(df: pd.DataFrame, train_len: int, horizon: int,
    window: int, method: str) -> list:
```

```
    total_len = train_len + horizon
    end_idx = train_len

    if method == 'last_season':
        pred_last_season = []

        for i in range(train_len, total_len, window):
            last_season = df['y'][i-window:i].values
            pred_last_season.extend(last_season)

        return pred_last_season

    elif method == 'SARIMA':
        pred_SARIMA = []

        for i in range(train_len, total_len, window):
            model = SARIMAX(df['y'][:i], order=(2,1,3),
➥ seasonal_order=(1,1,3,12), simple_differencing=False)
            res = model.fit(disp=False)
            predictions = res.get_prediction(0, i + window - 1)
            oos_pred = predictions.predicted_mean.iloc[-window:]
            pred_SARIMA.extend(oos_pred)

        return pred_SARIMA
```

Next, we'll create a `DataFrame` to hold the predictions as well as the actual values. This is simply a copy of the test set.

```
pred_df = df[168:]
```

Now we can define the parameters to be used for the `rolling_forecast` function. The dataset contains 204 rows, and the test set contains 36 data points, which means the length of the training set is 204 – 36 = 168. The horizon is 36, since our test set contains 36 months of data. Finally, the window is 12 months, as we are forecasting 12 months at a time.

With those values set, we can record the predictions coming from our baseline, which is a naive seasonal forecast. It simply takes the last 12 months of observed data and uses them as forecasts for the next 12 months.

```
TRAIN_LEN = 168
HORIZON = 36
WINDOW = 12

pred_df['last_season'] = rolling_forecast(df, TRAIN_LEN, HORIZON, WINDOW,
➥ 'last_season')
```

Next, we'll compute the forecasts from the SARIMA model.

```
pred_df['SARIMA'] = rolling_forecast(df, TRAIN_LEN, HORIZON, WINDOW,
➥ 'SARIMA')
```

At this point, `pred_df` contains the actual values, the forecasts from the naive seasonal method, and the forecasts from the SARIMA model. We can use this to visualize our forecasts against the actual values. For clarity, we'll limit the *x*-axis to zoom in on the test period. The resulting plot is shown in figure 11.5.

```
fig, ax = plt.subplots()

ax.plot(df.y)
ax.plot(pred_df.y, 'b-', label='actual')
ax.plot(pred_df.last_season, 'r:', label='naive seasonal')
ax.plot(pred_df.SARIMA, 'k--', label='SARIMA')
ax.set_xlabel('Date')
ax.set_ylabel('Number of anti-diabetic drug prescriptions')
ax.axvspan(168, 204, color='#808080', alpha=0.2)

ax.legend(loc=2)

plt.xticks(np.arange(6, 203, 12), np.arange(1992, 2009, 1))
plt.xlim(120, 204)

fig.autofmt_xdate()
plt.tight_layout()
```

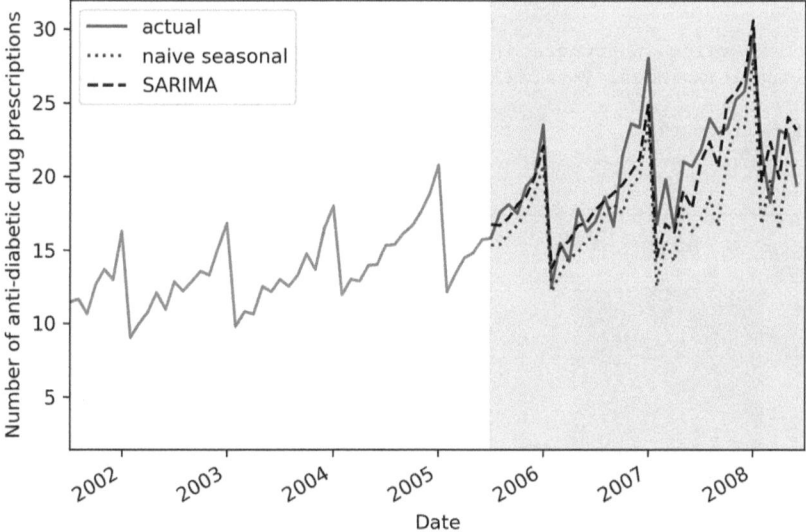

Figure 11.5   Forecasts of the number of antidiabetic drug prescriptions in Australia. The predictions from the baseline are shown as a dotted line, while the predictions from the SARIMA model are shown as a dashed line.

In figure 11.5 you can see that the predictions from the SARIMA model (the dashed line) follow the actual values more closely than the naive seasonal forecasts (the dotted line). We can therefore intuitively expect the SARIMA model to have performed better than the baseline method.

To evaluate the performance quantitatively, we'll use the mean absolute percentage error (MAPE). The MAPE is easy to interpret, as it returns a percentage error.

```
def mape(y_true, y_pred):
    return np.mean(np.abs((y_true - y_pred) / y_true)) * 100

mape_naive_seasonal = mape(pred_df.y, pred_df.last_season)
mape_SARIMA = mape(pred_df.y, pred_df.SARIMA)

print(mape_naive_seasonal, mape_SARIMA)
```

This prints out a MAPE of 12.69% for the baseline and 7.90% for the SARIMA model. We can optionally plot the MAPE of each model in a bar chart for a nice visualization, as shown in figure 11.6.

```
fig, ax = plt.subplots()

x = ['naive seasonal', 'SARIMA(2,1,3)(1,1,3,12)']
y = [mape_naive_seasonal, mape_SARIMA]

ax.bar(x, y, width=0.4)
ax.set_xlabel('Models')
ax.set_ylabel('MAPE (%)')
ax.set_ylim(0, 15)

for index, value in enumerate(y):
    plt.text(x=index, y=value + 1, s=str(round(value,2)), ha='center')

plt.tight_layout()
```

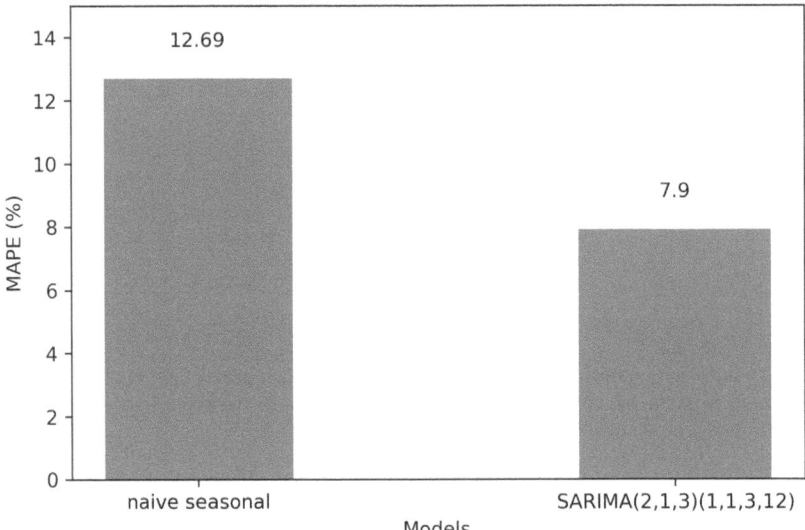

Figure 11.6 The MAPE for the naive seasonal forecast and the SARIMA model. Since the MAPE of the SARIMA model is lower than the MAPE of the baseline, we can conclude that the SARIMA model should be used to forecast the number of antidiabetic drug prescriptions.

Since the SARIMA model achieves the lowest MAPE, we can conclude that the SARIMA$(2,1,3)(1,1,3)_{12}$ model should be used to forecast the monthly number of antidiabetic drug prescriptions in Australia.

Next steps

Congratulations on completing this capstone project. I hope that you were able to complete it on your own and that you now feel confident in your skills and knowledge of time series forecasting using statistical models.

Of course, practice makes perfect, so I highly encourage you to find other time series datasets and practice modeling and forecasting them. This will help you build your intuition and hone your skills.

In the next chapter, we'll start a new section where we'll use deep learning models to model and forecast complex time series with high dimensionality.

Part 3

Large-scale forecasting with deep learning

Statistical models have their limitations, especially when a dataset is large and has many features and nonlinear relationships. In such cases, deep learning is the perfect tool for time series forecasting. In this part of the book, we'll work with a massive dataset and apply different deep learning architectures, such as long short-term memory (LSTM), a convolutional neural network (CNN), and an autoregressive deep neural network, to predict the future of our series. Again, we'll conclude this part with a capstone project to test your skills.

Deep learning is a subset of machine learning, and it is therefore possible to use more traditional machine learning algorithms for time series forecasting, such as gradient-boosted trees. To keep this section reasonable, we won't cover those techniques specifically, although data windowing is required to forecast time series with machine learning, and we'll apply this concept numerous times.

Introducing deep learning for time series forecasting

12

This chapter covers

- Using deep learning for forecasting
- Exploring different types of deep learning models
- Getting ready to apply deep learning to time series forecasting

In the last chapter, we concluded the part of the book on time series forecasting using statistical models. Those models work particularly well when you have small datasets (usually less than 10,000 data points), and when the seasonal period is monthly, quarterly, or yearly. In situations where you have daily seasonality or where the dataset is very large (more than 10,000 data points), those statistical models become very slow, and their performance degrades.

Thus, we turn to deep learning. *Deep learning* is a subset of machine learning that focuses on building models on the neural network architecture. Deep learning has the advantage that it tends to perform better as more data is available, making it a great choice for forecasting high-dimensional time series.

In this part of the book, we'll explore various model architectures so you'll have a set of tools for tackling virtually any time series forecasting problem. Note that I'll assume you have some familiarity with deep learning, so topics such as activation functions, loss functions, batches, layers, and epochs should be known. This part of the book will not serve as an introduction to deep learning, but rather focuses on applying deep learning to time series forecasting. Of course, each model architecture will be thoroughly explained, and you will gain an intuition as to why a particular architecture might work better than another in particular situations. Throughout these chapters, we will use TensorFlow, or more specifically Keras, to build different deep learning models.

In this chapter specifically, we identify the conditions that justify the use of deep learning and explore the different types of models that can be built, such as single-step, multi-step, and multi-output models. We'll conclude the chapter with the initial setup that will get us ready to apply deep learning models in the following chapters. Finally, we'll explore the data, perform feature engineering, and split the data into training, validation, and testing sets.

12.1   *When to use deep learning for time series forecasting*

Deep learning shines when we have large complex datasets. In those situations, deep learning can leverage all the available data to infer relationships between each feature and the target, usually resulting in good forecasts.

In the context of time series, a dataset is considered to be large when we have more than 10,000 data points. Of course, this is an approximation rather than a hard-set limit, so if you have 8,000 data points, deep learning could be a viable option. When the size of the dataset is large, any declination of the SARIMAX model will take a long time to fit, which is not ideal for model selection, as we usually fit many models during that step.

If your data has multiple seasonal periods, the SARIMAX model cannot be used. For example, suppose you must forecast the hourly temperature. It is reasonable to assume that there will be daily seasonality, as temperature tends to be lower at night and higher during the day, but there is also yearly seasonality, due to temperatures being lower in winter and higher during summer. In such a case, deep learning can be used to leverage the information from both seasonal periods to make forecasts. In fact, from experience, fitting a SARIMA model in such a case will usually result in residuals that are not normally distributed and still correlated, meaning that the model cannot be used at all.

Ultimately, deep learning is used either when statistical models take too much time to fit or when they result in correlated residuals that do not approximate white noise. This can be due to the fact that there is another seasonal period that cannot be considered in the model, or simply because there is a nonlinear relationship between the features and the target. In those cases, deep learning models can be used to capture this nonlinear relationship, and they have the added advantage of being very fast to train.

12.2   *Exploring the different types of deep learning models*

There are three main types of deep learning models that we can build for time series forecasting: single-step models, multi-step models, and multi-output models.

The single-step model is the simplest of the three. Its output is a single value representing the forecast of one variable one step into the future. The model therefore simply returns a scalar, as shown in figure 12.1.

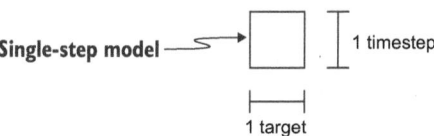

Single-step model — 1 timestep

1 target

Figure 12.1   The single-step model outputs the value of one target one timestep into the future. The output is therefore a scalar.

Single-step model
The single-step model outputs a single value representing the prediction for the next timestep. The input can be of any length, but the output remains a single prediction for the next timestep.

Next we can have a multi-step model, meaning that we output the value for one target, but for many timesteps into the future. For example, given hourly data, we may want to forecast the next 24 hours. In that case, we have a multi-step model, since we are forecasting 24 timesteps into the future. The output is a 24 × 1 matrix, as shown in figure 12.2.

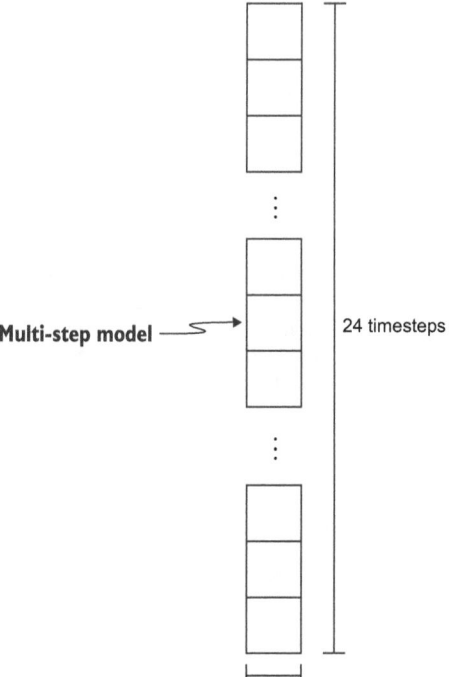

Multi-step model — 24 timesteps

1 target

Figure 12.2   A multi-step model outputs the predictions for 1 variable multiple timesteps into the future. This example predicts 24 timesteps, resulting in a 24 x 1 output matrix.

Multi-step model

In a multi-step model, the output of the model is a sequence of values representing predictions for many timesteps into the future. For example, if the model predicts the next 6 hours, 24 hours, or 12 months, it is a multi-step model.

Finally, the multi-output model generates predictions for more than one target. For example, if we were to predict both the temperature and humidity, we would use a multi-output model. This model can output as many timesteps as desired. In figure 12.3, a multi-output model returning predictions for two features for the next 24 timesteps is shown. In that particular case, the output is a 24 x 2 matrix.

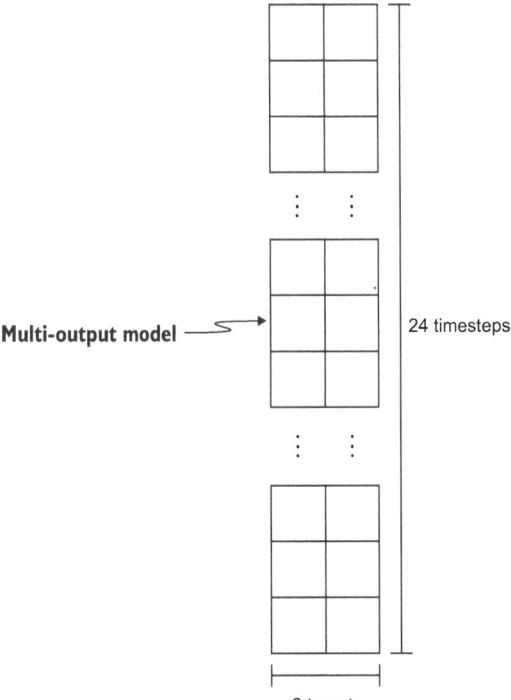

Multi-output model

24 timesteps

2 targets

Figure 12.3   A multi-output model makes predictions for more than one target for one or more timesteps in the future. Here the model outputs predictions for two targets for the next 24 timesteps.

Multi-output model

A multi-output model generates predictions for more than one target. For example, if we forecast the temperature and wind speed, it is a multi-output model.

Each of these models can have different architectures. For example, a convolutional neural network can be used as a single-step model, a multi-step model, or a multi-output model. In the following chapters, we will implement different model architectures and apply them for all three model types.

This brings us to the stage where we'll do the initial setup for the different deep learning models we'll implement in the next five chapters.

12.3 Getting ready to apply deep learning for forecasting

From here through chapter 17, we will use the metro interstate traffic volume dataset available on the UCI machine learning repository. The original dataset recorded the hourly westbound traffic on I-94 between Minneapolis and St. Paul in Minnesota, from 2012 to 2018. For the purpose of learning how to apply deep learning for time series forecasting, the dataset has been shortened and cleaned to get rid of missing values. While the cleaning steps are not covered in this chapter, you can still consult the preprocessing code in the GitHub repository for this chapter. Our main forecasting goal is to predict the hourly traffic volume. In the case of multi-output models, we will also forecast the hourly temperature. In this initial setup for the next several chapters, we'll load the data, perform feature engineering, and split it into training, validation, and testing sets.

We will use TensorFlow, or more specifically Keras, in this part of the book. At the time of writing, the latest stable version of TensorFlow was 2.6.0, which is what I'll use in this and the following chapters.

> **NOTE** The full source code for this chapter is available on GitHub: https://github.com/marcopeix/TimeSeriesForecastingInPython/tree/master/CH12.

12.3.1 Performing data exploration

We will first load the data using `pandas`.

```
df =
➥ pd.read_csv('../data/metro_interstate_traffic_volume_preprocessed.csv')
df.head()
```

As mentioned, this dataset is a shortened and cleaned version of the original dataset available on the UCI machine learning repository. In this case, the dataset starts on September 29, 2016, at 5 p.m. and ends on September 30, 2018, at 11 p.m. Using `df.shape`, we can see that we have a total of six features and 17,551 rows.

The features include the date and time, the temperature, the amount of rain and snow, the cloud coverage, as well as the traffic volume. Table 12.1 describes each column in more detail.

Table 12.1   The variables in the metro interstate traffic volume dataset

Feature	Description
date_time	Date and time of the data, recorded in the CST time zone. The format is YYYY-MM-DD HH:MM:SS.
temp	Average temperature recorded in the hour, expressed in Kelvin.
rain_1h	Amount of rain that occurred in the hour, expressed in millimeters.
snow_1h	Amount of snow that occurred in the hour, expressed in millimeters.
clouds_all	Percentage of cloud cover during the hour.
traffic_volume	Volume of traffic reported westbound on I-94 during the hour.

Now, let's visualize the evolution of the traffic volume over time. Since our dataset is very large, with more than 17,000 records, we'll plot only the first 400 data points, which is roughly equivalent to two weeks of data. The result is shown in figure 12.4.

```
fig, ax = plt.subplots()

ax.plot(df['traffic_volume'])
ax.set_xlabel('Time')
ax.set_ylabel('Traffic volume')

plt.xticks(np.arange(7, 400, 24), ['Friday', 'Saturday', 'Sunday',
➥ 'Monday', 'Tuesday', 'Wednesday', 'Thursday', 'Friday', 'Saturday',
➥ 'Sunday', 'Monday', 'Tuesday', 'Wednesday', 'Thursday', 'Friday',
➥ 'Saturday', 'Sunday'])
plt.xlim(0, 400)

fig.autofmt_xdate()
plt.tight_layout()
```

In figure 12.4 you'll notice clear daily seasonality, since the traffic volume is lower at the start and end of each day. You'll also see a smaller traffic volume during the weekends. As for the trend, two weeks of data is likely insufficient to draw a reasonable conclusion, but it seems that the volume is neither increasing nor decreasing over time in the figure.

We can also plot the hourly temperature, as it will be a target for our multi-output models. Here, we'll expect to see both yearly and daily seasonality. The yearly seasonality should be due to the seasons in the year, while the daily seasonality will be due to the fact that temperatures tend to be lower at night and higher during the day.

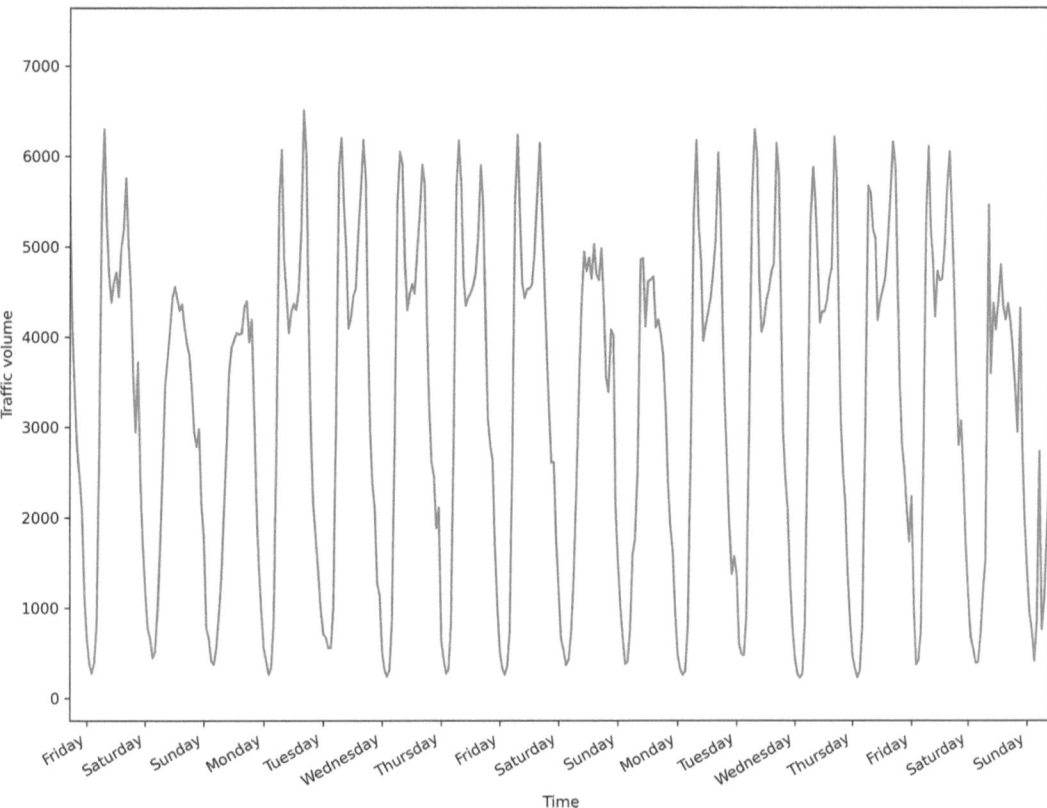

Figure 12.4   Westbound traffic volume on I-94 between Minneapolis and St. Paul in Minnesota, starting on September 29, 2016, at 5 p.m. You'll notice clear daily seasonality, with traffic being lower at the start and end of each day.

Let's first visualize the hourly temperature over the entire dataset to see if we can identify any yearly seasonality. The result is shown in figure 12.5.

```
fig, ax = plt.subplots()

ax.plot(df['temp'])
ax.set_xlabel('Time')
ax.set_ylabel('Temperature (K)')

plt.xticks([2239, 10999], [2017, 2018])

fig.autofmt_xdate()
plt.tight_layout()
```

In figure 12.5 you'll see a yearly seasonal pattern in the hourly temperature, since temperatures are lower at the end and beginning of the year (winter in Minnesota), and

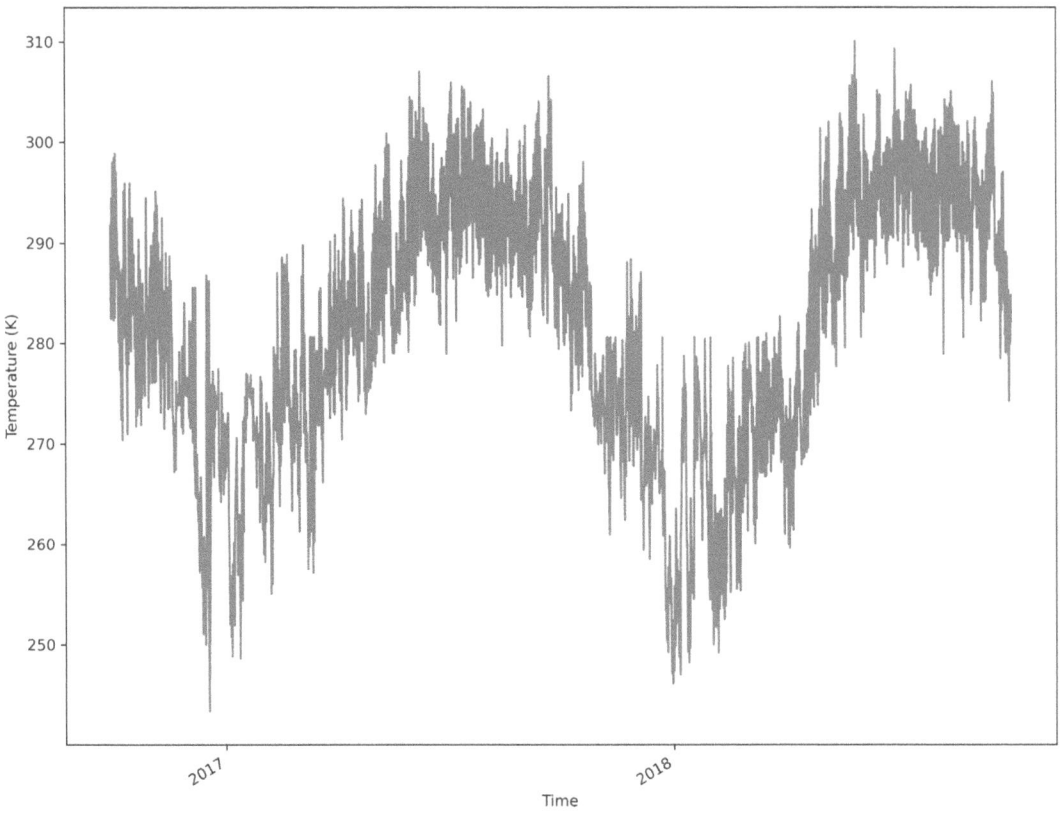

Figure 12.5   Hourly temperature (in Kelvin) from September 29, 2016, to September 30, 2018. Although there is noise, we can see a yearly seasonal pattern.

higher in the middle of the year (summer). Thus, as expected, the temperature has yearly seasonality.

Now let's verify whether we can observe daily seasonality in temperature. The result is shown in figure 12.6.

```
fig, ax = plt.subplots()

ax.plot(df['temp'])
ax.set_xlabel('Time')
ax.set_ylabel('Temperature (K)')

plt.xticks(np.arange(7, 400, 24), ['Friday', 'Saturday', 'Sunday',
➥ 'Monday', 'Tuesday', 'Wednesday', 'Thursday', 'Friday', 'Saturday',
➥ 'Sunday', 'Monday', 'Tuesday', 'Wednesday', 'Thursday', 'Friday',
➥ 'Saturday', 'Sunday'])
plt.xlim(0, 400)
```

```
fig.autofmt_xdate()
plt.tight_layout()
```

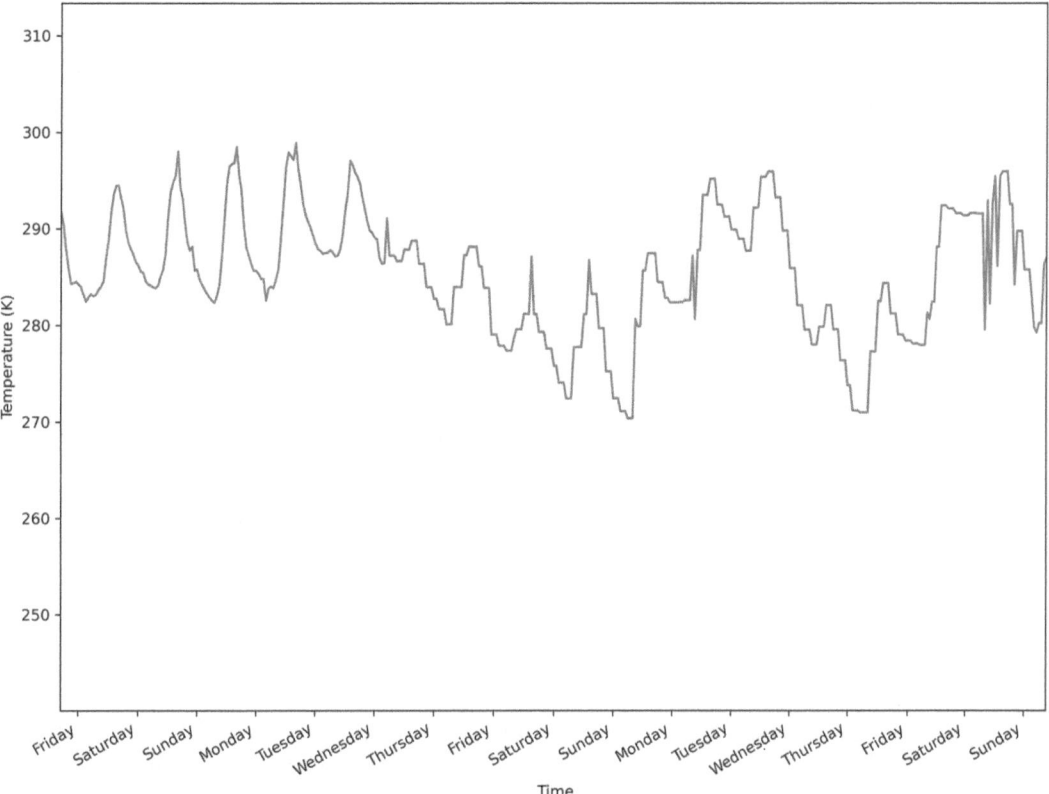

Figure 12.6   Hourly temperature (in Kelvin) starting on September 29, 2016, at 5 p.m. CST. Although it is a bit noisy, we can see that temperatures are indeed lower at the start and end of each day and peak during midday, suggesting daily seasonality.

In figure 12.6 you'll notice that the temperature is indeed lower at the start and end of each day and peaks toward the middle of each day. This suggests daily seasonality, just as we observed for traffic volume in figure 12.4.

12.3.2 Feature engineering and data splitting

With our data exploration done, we'll move on to feature engineering and data splitting. In this section, we will study each feature and create new ones that will help our models forecast the traffic volume and hourly temperature. Finally, we'll split the data and save each set as a CSV file for later use.

A great way to study the features of a dataset is to use the describe method from pandas. This method returns the number of records for each feature, allowing us to quickly identify missing values, the mean, standard deviation, quartiles, and maximum and minimum values for each feature.

```
df.describe().transpose()
```
◁——— **The transpose method puts each feature on its own row.**

From the output, you'll notice that `rain_1h` is mostly 0 throughout the dataset, as its third quartile is still at 0. Since at least 75% of the values for `rain_1h` are 0, it is unlikely that it is a strong predictor of traffic volume. Thus, this feature will be removed.

Looking at `snow_1h`, you'll notice that this variable is at 0 through the entire dataset. This is easily observable, since its minimum and maximum values are both 0. Thus, this is not predictive of the variation in traffic volume over time. This feature will also be removed from the dataset.

```
cols_to_drop = ['rain_1h', 'snow_1h']
df = df.drop(cols_to_drop, axis=1)
```

Now we reach the interesting problem of encoding time as a usable feature for our deep learning models. Right now, the `date_time` feature is not usable by our models, since it is a `datetime` string. We will thus convert it into a numerical value.

A simple way to do that is to express the date as a number of seconds. This is achieved through the use of the `timestamp` method from the `datetime` library.

```
timestamp_s =
  pd.to_datetime(df['date_time']).map(datetime.datetime.timestamp)
```

Unfortunately, we are not done, as this simply expresses each date in seconds, as shown in figure 12.7. This leads us to losing the cyclical nature of time, because the number of seconds simply increases linearly with time.

Therefore, we must apply a transformation to recover the cyclical behavior of time. A simple way to do that is to apply a sine transformation. We know that the sine function is cyclical, bounded between –1 and 1. This will help us regain part of the cyclical property of time.

The timestamp is in seconds, so we must calculate the number of seconds in a day before applying the sine transformation.

Application of the sine transformation. Notice that we use radians in the sine function.

```
day = 24 * 60 * 60                                      ◁
df['day_sin'] = (np.sin(timestamp_s * (2*np.pi/day))).values    ◁
```

With a single sine transformation, we regain some of the cyclical property that was lost when converting to seconds. However, at this point, 12 p.m. is equivalent to 12 a.m., and 5 p.m. is equivalent to 5 a.m. This is undesired, as we want to distinguish between morning and afternoon. Thus, we'll apply a cosine transformation. We know that cosine is out of phase with the sine function. This allows us to distinguish between

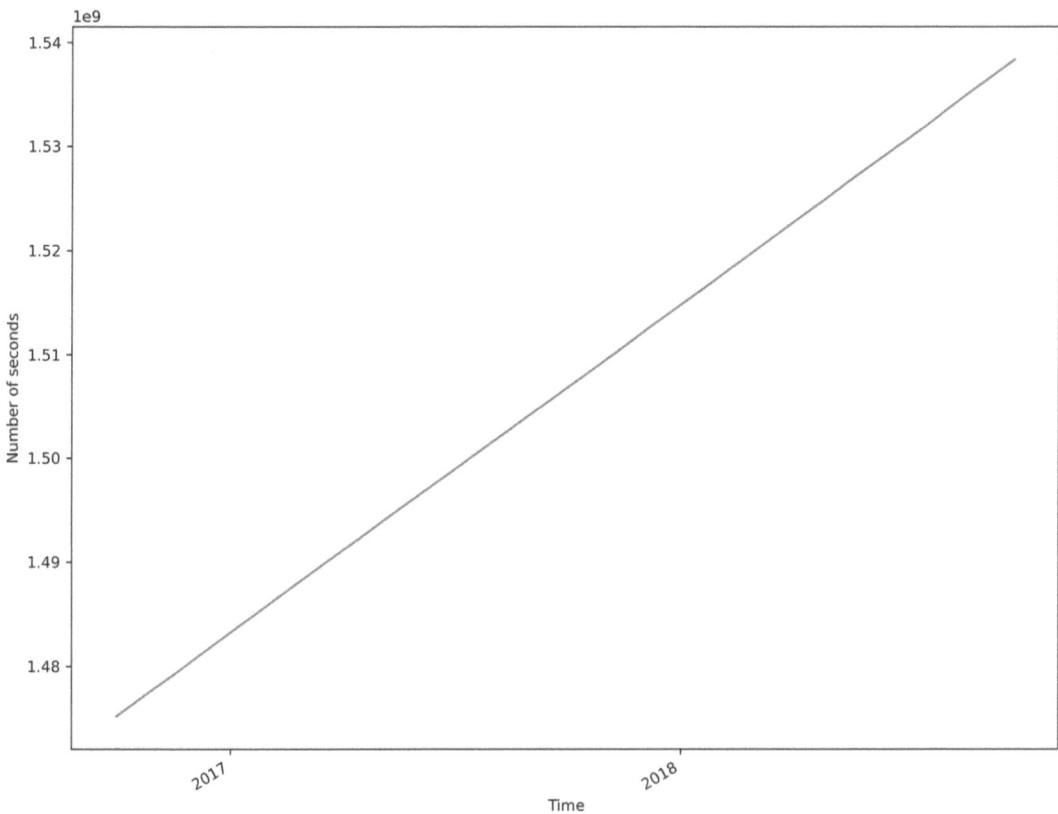

Figure 12.7   Number of seconds expressing each date in the dataset. The number of seconds linearly increases with time, meaning that we lose the cyclical property of time.

5 a.m. and 5 p.m., expressing the cyclical nature of time in a day. At this point, we can remove the date_time column from the DataFrame.

```
df['day_cos'] = (np.cos(timestamp_s * (2*np.pi/day))).values      ◁─────────
df = df.drop(['date_time'], axis=1)                                Apply the cosine
                                                                   transformation to the
Remove the                                                         timestamp in seconds.
date_time column.
```

We can quickly convince ourselves that these transformations worked by plotting a sample of day_sin and day_cos. The result is shown in figure 12.8.

```
df.sample(50).plot.scatter('day_sin', 'day_cos').set_aspect('equal');
```

In figure 12.8 you'll notice that the points form a circle, just like a clock. Therefore, we have successfully expressed each timestamp as a point on the clock, meaning that we now have numerical values that retain the cyclical nature of time in a day, and this

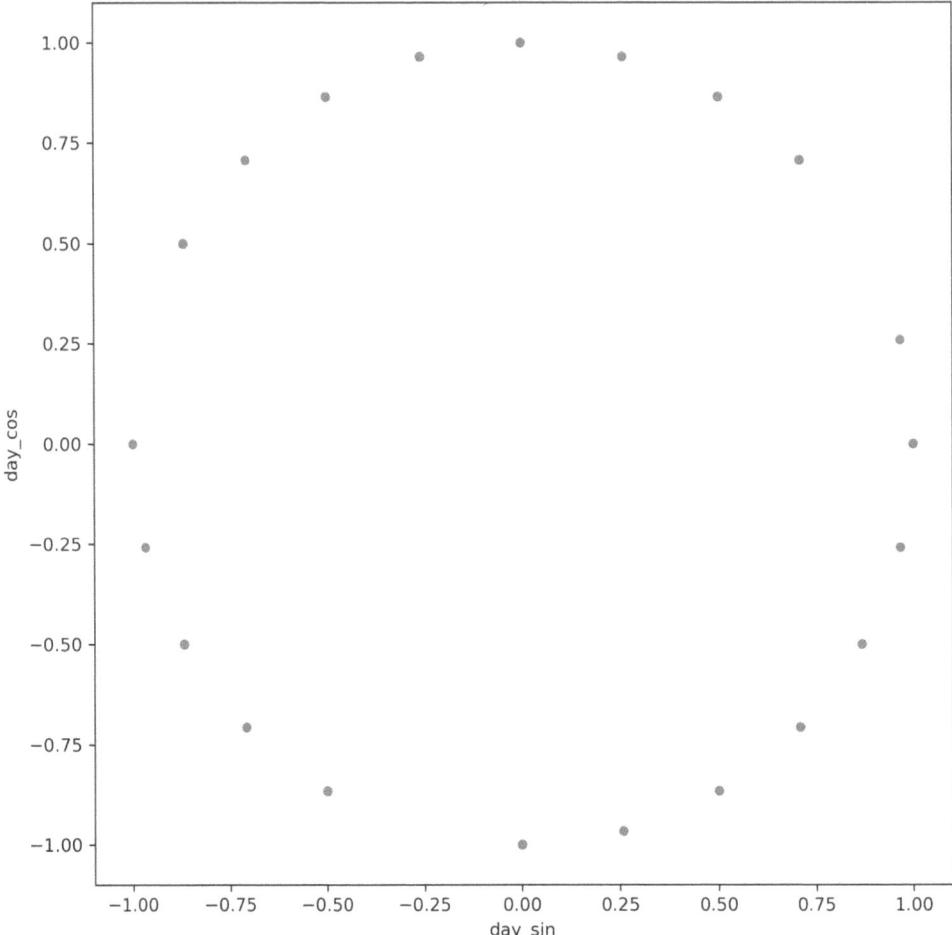

Figure 12.8   **Plot of a sample of the** `day_sin` **and** `day_cos` **encoding. We have successfully encoded the time as a numerical value while keeping the daily cycle.**

can be used in our deep learning models. This will be useful since we observed daily seasonality for both the temperature and the volume of traffic.

With the feature engineering complete, we can now split our data train, validation, and test sets. The train set is the sample of data used to fit the model. The validation set is a bit like a test set that the model can peek at to tune its hyperparameters and improve its performance during the model's training. The test set is completely separate from the model's training procedure and is used for an unbiased evaluation of the model's performance.

Here we'll use a simple 70:20:10 split for the train, validation, and test sets. While 10% of the data seems like a small portion for the test set, remember that we have more than 17,000 records, meaning that we will evaluate the model on more than 1,000 data points, which is more than enough.

```
n = len(df)

# Split 70:20:10 (train:validation:test)
train_df = df[0:int(n*0.7)]
val_df = df[int(n*0.7):int(n*0.9)]
test_df = df[int(n*0.9):]
```

First 70% goes to the train set.

Next 20% goes to the validation set.

The remaining 10% goes to the test set.

Before saving the data, we must scale it so all values are between 0 and 1. This decreases the time required for training deep learning models, and it improves their performance. We'll use `MinMaxScaler` from `sklearn` to scale our data.

Note that we will fit the `scaler` on the training set to avoid data leakage. That way, we are simulating the fact that we only have the training data available when we're using the model, and no future information is known by the model. The evaluation of the model remains unbiased.

```
from sklearn.preprocessing import MinMaxScaler

scaler = MinMaxScaler()
scaler.fit(train_df)
```

Fit only on the training set.

```
train_df[train_df.columns] = scaler.transform(train_df[train_df.columns])
val_df[val_df.columns] = scaler.transform(val_df[val_df.columns])
test_df[test_df.columns] = scaler.transform(test_df[test_df.columns])
```

It is worth mentioning why the data is scaled and not normalized. Scaling and normalization can be confusing terms for data scientists, as they are often used interchangeably. In short, scaling the data affects only its *scale* and not its *distribution*. Thus, it simply forces the values into a certain range. In our case, we force the values to be between 0 and 1.

Normalizing the data, on the other hand, affects its *distribution* and its *scale*. Thus, normalizing the data would force it to have a normal distribution or a Gaussian distribution. The original range would also change, and plotting the frequency of each value would generate a classic bell curve.

Normalizing the data is only useful when the models we use require the data to be normal. For example, linear discriminant analysis (LDA) is derived from the assumption of a normal distribution, so it is better to normalize data before using LDA. However, in the case of deep learning, no assumptions are made, so normalizing is not required.

Finally, we'll save each set as a CSV file for use in the following chapters.

```
train_df.to_csv('../data/train.csv')
val_df.to_csv('../data/val.csv')
test_df.to_csv('../data/test.csv')
```

12.4   Next steps

In this chapter, we looked at the use of deep learning for forecasting and covered the three main types of deep learning models. We then explored the data we'll be using and performed feature engineering so the data is ready to be used in the next chapter, where we'll apply deep learning models to forecast traffic volume.

In the next chapter, we will start by implementing baseline models that will serve as benchmarks for more complex deep learning architectures. We will also implement linear models, the simplest models that can be built, followed by deep neural networks, which have at least one hidden layer. Baselines, linear models, and deep neural networks will be implemented as single-step models, multi-step models, and multi-output models. You should be excited for the next chapter, as we'll start modeling and forecasting using deep learning.

12.5   Exercise

As an exercise, we will prepare some data for use in deep learning exercises in chapters 12 through 18. This data will be used to develop a deep learning model to forecast the air quality in Beijing at the Aotizhongxin station.

Specifically, for univariate modeling, we will ultimately predict the concentration of nitrogen dioxide (NO_2). For the multivariate problem, we will predict the concentration of nitrogen dioxide and temperature.

> **NOTE** Predicting the concentration of air pollutants is an important problem, as they can have negative health effects on a population, such as coughing, wheezing, inflammation, and reduced lung function. Temperature also plays an important role, because hot air tends to rise, creating a convection effect and moving pollutants from the ground to higher altitudes. With accurate models, we can better manage air pollution and better inform the population to take the right precautions.

The original dataset is available in the UCI Machine Learning Repository: https://archive.ics.uci.edu/ml/datasets/Beijing+Multi-Site+Air-Quality+Data. It has been preprocessed and cleaned to treat missing data and make it easy to work with (the preprocessing steps are available on GitHub). You will find the data in a CSV file on GitHub: https://github.com/marcopeix/TimeSeriesForecastingInPython/tree/master/CH12.

The objective of this exercise is to prepare the data for deep learning. Follow these steps:

1. Read the data.
2. Plot the target.
3. Remove unnecessary columns.
4. Identify whether there is daily seasonality and encode the time accordingly.
5. Split your data into training, validation, and testing sets.
6. Scale the data using `MinMaxScaler`.
7. Save the train, validation, and test sets to be used later.

Summary

- Deep learning for forecasting is used when:
  - The dataset is large (more than 10,000 data points).
  - Declination of the SARIMAX model takes a long time to fit.
  - The residuals of the statistical model still show some correlation.
  - There is more than one seasonal period.
- There are three types of models for forecasting:
  - Single-step model: Predicts one step into the future for one variable.
  - Multi-step model: Predicts many steps into the future for one variable.
  - Multi-output model: Predicts many variables one or more steps into the future.

Data windowing
and creating baselines
for deep learning

This chapter covers

- Creating windows of data
- Implementing baseline models for deep learning

In the last chapter, I introduced deep learning for forecasting by covering the situations where deep learning is ideal and by outlining the three main types of deep learning models: single-step, multi-step, and multi-output. We then proceeded with data exploration and feature engineering to remove useless features and create new features that will help us forecast traffic volume. With that setup done, we are now ready to implement deep learning to forecast our target variable, which is the traffic volume.

In this chapter, we'll build a reusable class that will create windows of data. This step is probably the most complicated and most useful topic in this part of the book on deep learning. Applying deep learning for forecasting relies on creating appropriate time windows and specifying the inputs and labels. Once that is done, you will see that implementing different models becomes incredibly easy, and this framework can be reused for different situations and datasets.

Once you know how to create windows of data, we'll move on to implement baseline models, linear models, and deep neural networks. This will let us measure the performance of these models, and we can then move on to more complex architectures in the following chapters.

13.1 Creating windows of data

We'll start off by creating the DataWindow class, which will allow us to format the data appropriately to be fed to our deep learning models. We'll also add a plotting method to this class so that we can visualize the predictions and the actual values.

Before diving into the code and building the DataWindow class, however, it is important to understand why we must perform data windowing for deep learning. Deep learning models have a particular way of fitting on data, which we'll explore in the next section. Then we'll move on and implement the DataWindow class.

13.1.1 Exploring how deep learning models are trained for time series forecasting

In the first half of this book, we fit statistical models, such as SARIMAX, on training sets and made predictions. We were, in reality, fitting a set of predefined functions of a certain order (p,d,q) $(P,D,Q)_m$, and finding out which order resulted in the best fit.

For deep learning models, we do not have a set of functions to try. Instead, we let the neural network derive its own function such that when it takes the inputs, it generates the best predictions possible. To achieve that, we perform what is called *data windowing*. This is a process in which we define a sequence of data points on our time series and define which are inputs and which are labels. That way, the deep learning model can fit on the inputs, generate predictions, compare them to the labels, and repeat this process until it cannot improve the accuracy of its predictions.

Let's walk through an example of data windowing. Our data window will use 24 hours of data to predict the next 24 hours. You probably wonder why are we using just 24 hours of data to generate predictions. After all, deep learning is data hungry and is used for large datasets. The key lies in the data window. A single window has 24 timesteps as input to generate an output of 24 timesteps. However, the entire training set is separated into multiple windows, meaning that we have many windows with inputs and labels, as shown in figure 13.1.

In figure 13.1 you can see the first 400 timesteps of our training set for traffic volume. Each data window consists of 24 input timesteps and 24 label timesteps (as shown in figure 13.2), giving us a total length of 48 timesteps. We can generate many data windows with the training set, so we are, in fact, leveraging this large quantity of data.

As you can see in figure 13.2, the data window's total length is the sum of the lengths of each sequence. In this case, since we have 24 timesteps as input and 24 labels, the total length of the data window is 48 timesteps.

You might think that we are wasting a lot of training data, since in figure 13.2 timesteps 24 to 47 are labels. Are those never going to be used as inputs? Of course, they will be. The DataWindow class that we'll implement in the next section generates data windows with inputs starting at $t = 0$. Then it will create another set of data windows, but this time starting at $t = 1$. Then it will start at $t = 2$. This goes on until it

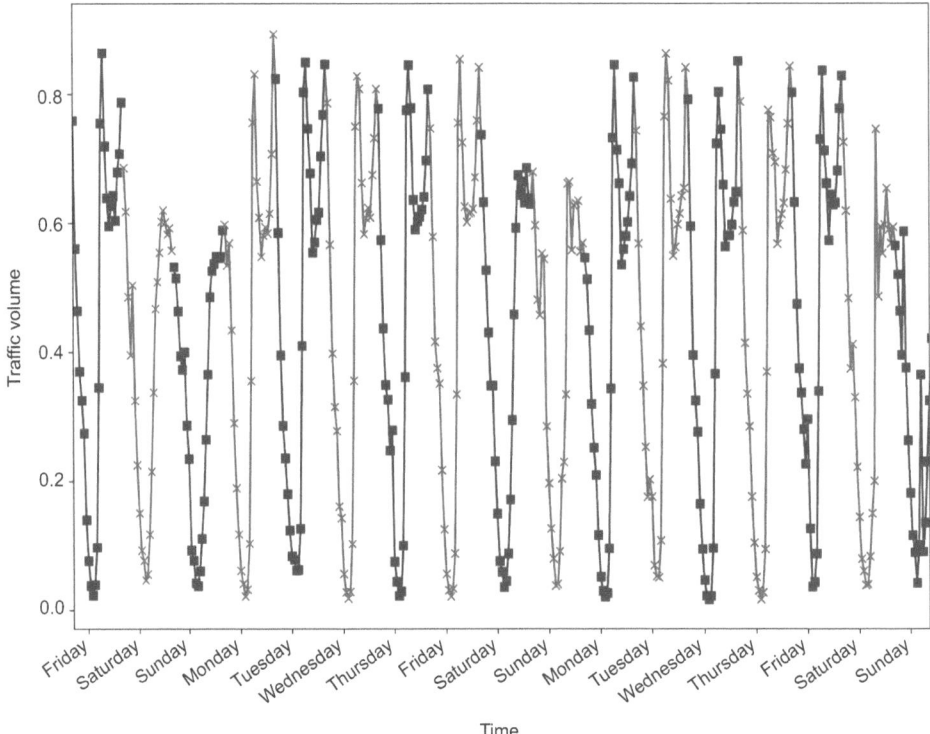

Figure 13.1   Visualizing the data windows on the training set. The inputs are shown with square markers, and the labels are shown with crosses. Each data window consists of 24 timesteps with square markers followed by 24 labels with crosses.

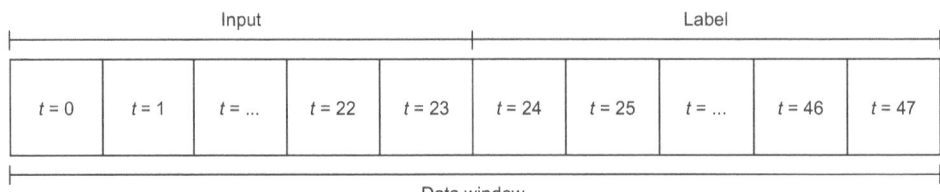

Figure 13.2   An example of a data window. Our data window has 24 timesteps as input and 24 timesteps as output. The model will then use 24 hours of input to generate 24 hours of predictions. The total length of the data window is the sum of the length of inputs and labels. In this case, we have a total length of 48 timesteps.

cannot have a sequence of 24 consecutive labels in the training set, as illustrated in figure 13.3.

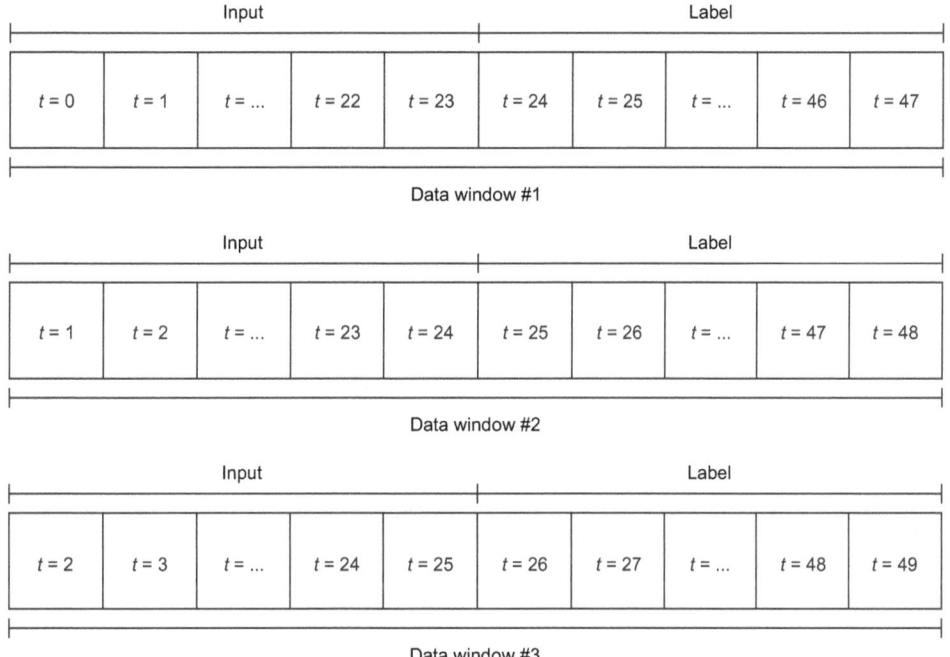

Figure 13.3   Visualizing the different data windows that are generated by the `DataWindow` class. You can see that by repeatedly shifting the starting point by one timestep, we use as much of the training data as possible to fit our deep learning models.

To make computation more efficient, deep learning models are trained with *batches*. A batch is simply a collection of data windows that are fed to the model for training, as shown in figure 13.4.

Figure 13.4 shows an example of a batch with a batch size of 32. That means that 32 data windows are grouped together and used to train the model. Of course, this is only one batch—the `DataWindow` class generates as many batches as possible with the given training set. In our case, we have a training set with 12,285 rows. If each batch has 32 data windows, that means that we will have 12285/32 = 384 batches.

Training the model on all 384 batches once is called one *epoch*. One epoch often does not result in an accurate model, so the model will train for as many epochs as necessary until it cannot improve the accuracy of its predictions.

The final important concept in data windowing for deep learning is *shuffling*. I mentioned in the very first chapter of this book that time series data cannot be shuffled. Time series data has an order, and that order must be kept, so why are we shuffling the data here?

In this context, shuffling occurs at the batch level, not inside the data window— the order of the time series itself is maintained within each data window. Each data window is independent of all others. Therefore, in a batch, we can shuffle the data

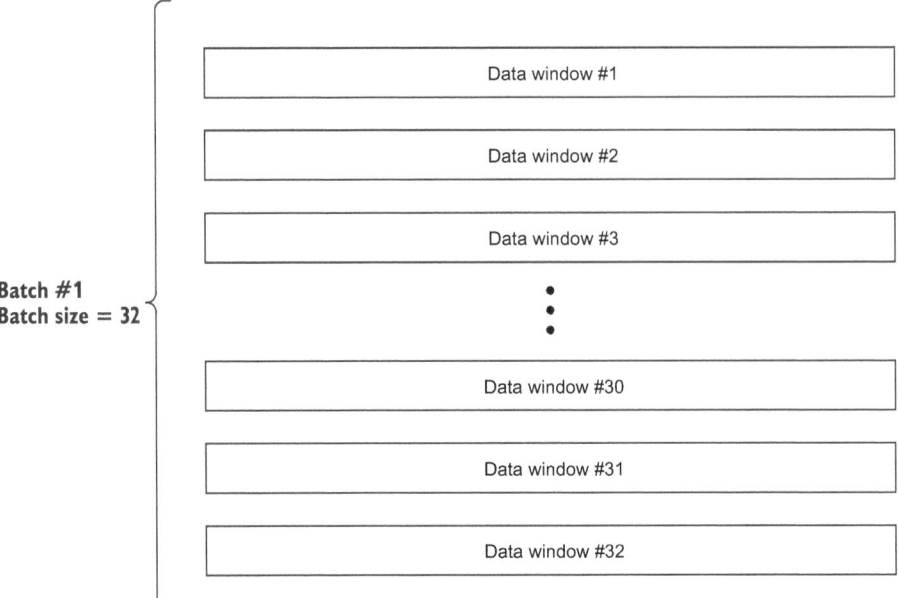

Figure 13.4   A batch is simply a collection of data windows that are used for training the deep learning model.

windows and still keep the order of our time series, as shown in figure 13.5. Shuffling the data is not essential, but it is recommended as it tends to make more robust models.

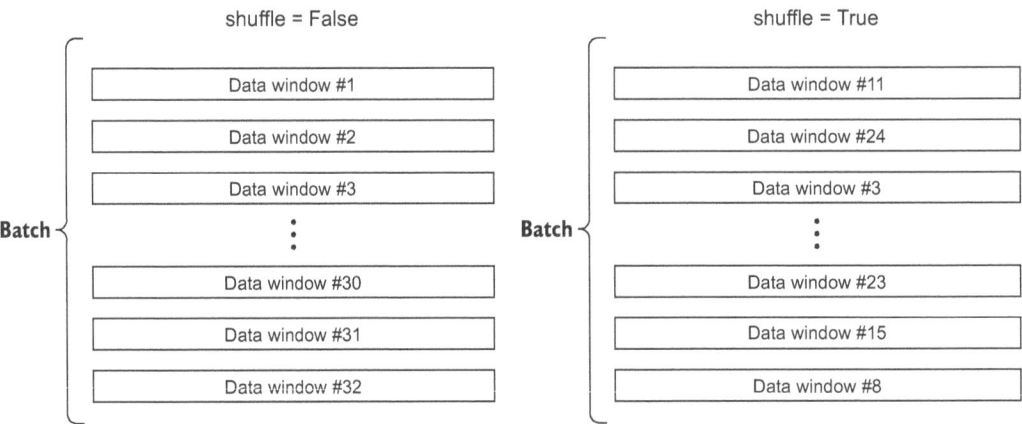

Figure 13.5   Shuffling the data windows in a batch. Each data window is independent of all others, so it is safe to shuffle the data windows within a batch. Note that the order of the time series is maintained within each data window.

Now that you understand the inner working of data windowing and how it is used for training deep learning models, let's implement the DataWindow class.

13.1.2 *Implementing the DataWindow class*

We are now ready to implement the DataWindow class. This class has the advantage of being flexible, meaning that you can use it in a wide variety of scenarios to apply deep learning. The full code is available on GitHub: https://github.com/marcopeix/ TimeSeriesForecastingInPython/tree/master/CH13%26CH14.

The class is based on the width of the input, the width of the label, and the shift. The width of the input is simply the number of timesteps that are fed into the model to make predictions. For example, given that we have hourly data in our dataset, if we feed the model with 24 hours of data to make a prediction, the input width is 24. If we feed only 12 hours of data, the input width is 12.

The label width is equivalent to the number of timesteps in the predictions. If we predict only one timestep, the label width is 1. If we predict a full day of data (with hourly data), the label width is 24.

Finally, the shift is the number of timesteps separating the input and the predictions. If we predict the next timestep, the shift is 1. If we predict the next 24 hours (with hourly data), the shift is 24.

Let's visualize some windows of data to better understand these parameters. Figure 13.6 shows a window of data where the model predicts the next data point, given a single data point.

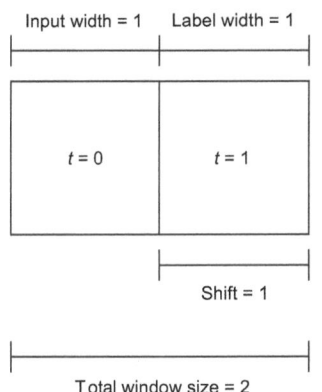

Figure 13.6 **A data window where the model predicts one timestep in the future, given a single point of data. The input width is 1, since the model takes only 1 data point as input. The label width is also only 1, since the model outputs the prediction for 1 timestep only. Since the model predicts the next timestep, the shift is also 1. Finally, the total window size is the sum of the shift and the input widths, which equals 2.**

Now let's consider the situation where we feed 24 hours of data to the model in order to predict the next 24 hours. The data window in that situation is shown in figure 13.7. Now that you understand the concept of input width, label width, and shift, we can create the DataWindow class and define its initialization function in listing 13.1. The function will also take in the training, validation, and test sets, as the windows of data will come from our dataset. Finally, we'll allow the target column to be specified.

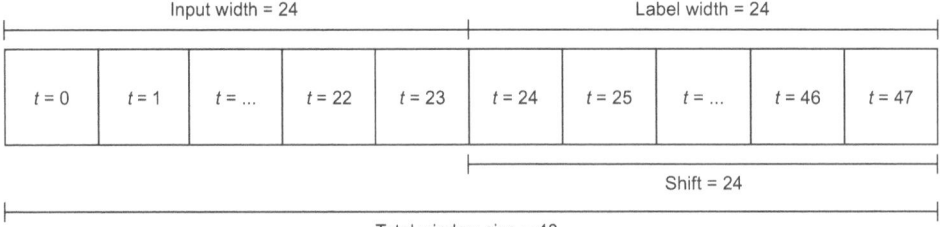

Figure 13.7   Data window where the model predicts the next 24 hours using the last 24 hours of data. The input width is 24 and the label width is also 24. Since there are 24 timesteps separating the inputs and the predictions, the shift is also 24. This gives a total window size of 48 timesteps.

Note that the following listing reuses code from the official TensorFlow documentation's website (https://www.tensorflow.org/tutorials/structured_data/time_series). This method of creating windows of data is viewed by the community as the best and easiest way of predicting time series data with deep learning models. It is also the best way to extend the capabilities of TensorFlow's native function `timeseries_dataset_from_array`, such that we can apply deep learning models in any forecasting scenario.

The full implementation of the data windowing technique is shown in code listing 13.3. All code is reused within the terms of the Apache 2.0 License (https://www.apache.org/licenses/LICENSE-2.0), which you can consult in the GitHub repository (https://github.com/marcopeix/TimeSeriesForecastingInPython) for this book.

The examples that follow in the book build upon the code from the documentation, to make it more reusable in any scenario you might encounter outside of this book.

> **Listing 13.1   Defining the initialization function of `DataWindow`**

Create a dictionary with the name and index of the label column. This will be used for plotting.

```
class DataWindow():
    def __init__(self, input_width, label_width, shift,
                 train_df=train_df, val_df=val_df, test_df=test_df,
                 label_columns=None):

        self.train_df = train_df
        self.val_df = val_df
        self.test_df = test_df

        self.label_columns = label_columns
        if label_columns is not None:
            self.label_columns_indices = {name: i for i, name in
    enumerate(label_columns)}
        self.column_indices = {name: i for i, name in
    enumerate(train_df.columns)}

        self.input_width = input_width
        self.label_width = label_width
```

Name of the column that we wish to predict

Create a dictionary with the name and index of each column. This will be used to separate the features from the target variable.

Assign indices to the inputs. These are useful for plotting.

```
self.shift = shift

self.total_window_size = input_width + shift

self.input_slice = slice(0, input_width)
self.input_indices =
np.arange(self.total_window_size)[self.input_slice]
```

The slice function returns a slice object that specifies how to slice a sequence. In this case, it says that the input slice starts at 0 and ends when we reach the input_width.

```
self.label_start = self.total_window_size - self.label_width
self.labels_slice = slice(self.label_start, None)
self.label_indices =
np.arange(self.total_window_size)[self.labels_slice]
```

Get the index at which the label starts. In this case, it is the total window size minus the width of the label.

The same steps that were applied for the inputs are applied for labels.

In listing 13.1 you can see that the initialization function basically assigns the variables and manages the indices of the inputs and the labels. Our next step is to split our window between inputs and labels, so that our models can make predictions based on the inputs and measure an error metric against the labels. The following `split_to_inputs_labels` function is defined within the `DataWindow` class.

Slice the window to get the labels using the labels_slice defined in __init__.

Slice the window to get the inputs using the input_slice defined in __init__.

```
def split_to_inputs_labels(self, features):
    inputs = features[:, self.input_slice, :]
    labels = features[:, self.labels_slice, :]
    if self.label_columns is not None:
        labels = tf.stack(
            [labels[:,:,self.column_indices[name]] for name in
self.label_columns],
            axis=-1
        )
    inputs.set_shape([None, self.input_width, None])
    labels.set_shape([None, self.label_width, None])

    return inputs, labels
```

If we have more than one target, we stack the labels.

The shape will be [batch, time, features]. At this point, we only specify the time dimension and allow the batch and feature dimensions to be defined later.

The `split_to_inputs_labels` function will separate the big data window into two windows: one for the inputs and the other for the labels, as shown in figure 13.8.

Next we'll define a function to plot the input data, the predictions, and the actual values (listing 13.2). Since we will be working with many time windows, we'll show only the plot of three time windows, but this parameter can easily be changed. Also, the default label will be traffic volume, but we can change that by specifying any column we choose. Again, this function should be included in the `DataWindow` class.

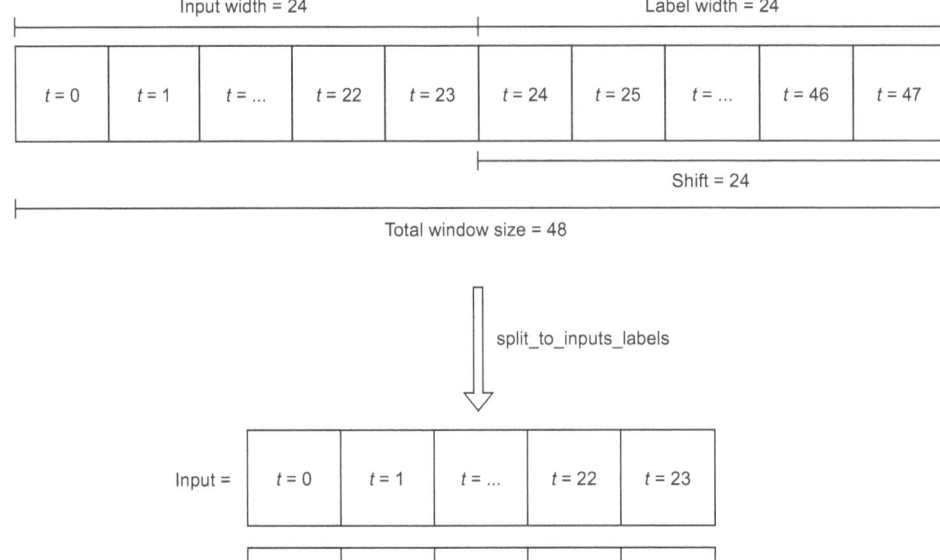

Figure 13.8 The `split_to_inputs_labels` function simply separates the big data window into two windows, where one contains the inputs and the other the labels.

Listing 13.2   Method to plot a sample of data windows

```
def plot(self, model=None, plot_col='traffic_volume', max_subplots=3):
    inputs, labels = self.sample_batch

    plt.figure(figsize=(12, 8))
    plot_col_index = self.column_indices[plot_col]
    max_n = min(max_subplots, len(inputs))

    for n in range(max_n):
        plt.subplot(3, 1, n+1)
        plt.ylabel(f'{plot_col} [scaled]')
        plt.plot(self.input_indices, inputs[n, :, plot_col_index],
                label='Inputs', marker='.', zorder=-10)

        if self.label_columns:
            label_col_index = self.label_columns_indices.get(plot_col,
    None)
        else:
            label_col_index = plot_col_index

        if label_col_index is None:
            continue

        plt.scatter(self.label_indices, labels[n, :, label_col_index],
                    edgecolors='k', marker='s', label='Labels',
```

> **Plot the inputs. They will appear as a continuous blue line with dots.**

```
        c='green', s=64)
            if model is not None:
                predictions = model(inputs)
                plt.scatter(self.label_indices, predictions[n, :,
    label_col_index],
                        marker='X', edgecolors='k', label='Predictions',
                            c='red', s=64)

            if n == 0:
                plt.legend()

        plt.xlabel('Time (h)')
```

Plot the labels or actual values. They will appear as green squares.

Plot the predictions. They will appear as red crosses.

We are almost done building the `DataWindow` class. The last main piece of logic will format our dataset into tensors so that they can be fed to our deep learning models. TensorFlow comes with a very handy function called `timeseries_dataset_from_array`, which creates a dataset of sliding windows, given an array.

Pass in the data. This corresponds to our training set, validation set, or test set.

Targets are set to None, as they are handled by the split_to_input_labels function.

```
def make_dataset(self, data):
    data = np.array(data, dtype=np.float32)
    ds = tf.keras.preprocessing.timeseries_dataset_from_array(
        data=data,
        targets=None,
        sequence_length=self.total_window_size,
        sequence_stride=1,
        shuffle=True,
        batch_size=32
    )

    ds = ds.map(self.split_to_inputs_labels)
    return ds
```

Define the total length of the array, which is equal to the total window length.

Define the number of timesteps separating each sequence. In our case, we want the sequences to be consecutive, so sequence_stride=1.

Define the number of sequences in a single batch.

Shuffle the sequences. Keep in mind that the data is still in chronological order. We are simply shuffling the order of the sequences, which makes the model more robust.

Remember that we are shuffling the sequences in a batch. This means that within each sequence, the data is in chronological order. However, in a batch of 32 sequences, we can and should shuffle them to make our model more robust and less prone to overfitting.

We'll conclude our `DataWindow` class by defining some properties to apply the `make_dataset` function on the training, validation, and testing sets. We'll also create a sample batch that we'll cache within the class for plotting purposes.

```
@property
def train(self):
    return self.make_dataset(self.train_df)

@property
def val(self):
    return self.make_dataset(self.val_df)

@property
def test(self):
    return self.make_dataset(self.test_df)

@property
def sample_batch(self):      ◁─────────
    result = getattr(self, '_sample_batch', None)
    if result is None:
        result = next(iter(self.train))
        self._sample_batch = result
    return result
```

Get a sample batch of data for plotting purposes. If the sample batch does not exist, we'll retrieve a sample batch and cache it.

Our DataWindow class is now complete. The full class with all methods and properties is shown in listing 13.3.

Listing 13.3   The complete DataWindow class

```
class DataWindow():
    def __init__(self, input_width, label_width, shift,
                 train_df=train_df, val_df=val_df, test_df=test_df,
                 label_columns=None):

        self.train_df = train_df
        self.val_df = val_df
        self.test_df = test_df

        self.label_columns = label_columns
        if label_columns is not None:
            self.label_columns_indices = {name: i for i, name in
⇒ enumerate(label_columns)}
        self.column_indices = {name: i for i, name in
⇒ enumerate(train_df.columns)}

        self.input_width = input_width
        self.label_width = label_width
        self.shift = shift

        self.total_window_size = input_width + shift

        self.input_slice = slice(0, input_width)
        self.input_indices =
⇒ np.arange(self.total_window_size)[self.input_slice]

        self.label_start = self.total_window_size - self.label_width
        self.labels_slice = slice(self.label_start, None)
```

```python
        self.label_indices =
np.arange(self.total_window_size)[self.labels_slice]


    def split_to_inputs_labels(self, features):
        inputs = features[:, self.input_slice, :]
        labels = features[:, self.labels_slice, :]
        if self.label_columns is not None:
            labels = tf.stack(
                [labels[:,:,self.column_indices[name]] for name in
self.label_columns],
                axis=-1
            )
        inputs.set_shape([None, self.input_width, None])
        labels.set_shape([None, self.label_width, None])

        return inputs, labels


    def plot(self, model=None, plot_col='traffic_volume', max_subplots=3):
        inputs, labels = self.sample_batch

        plt.figure(figsize=(12, 8))
        plot_col_index = self.column_indices[plot_col]
        max_n = min(max_subplots, len(inputs))

        for n in range(max_n):
            plt.subplot(3, 1, n+1)
            plt.ylabel(f'{plot_col} [scaled]')
            plt.plot(self.input_indices, inputs[n, :, plot_col_index],
                     label='Inputs', marker='.', zorder=-10)

            if self.label_columns:
                label_col_index = self.label_columns_indices.get(plot_col,
None)
            else:
                label_col_index = plot_col_index

            if label_col_index is None:
                continue

            plt.scatter(self.label_indices, labels[n, :, label_col_index],
                        edgecolors='k', marker='s', label='Labels',
c='green', s=64)
            if model is not None:
                predictions = model(inputs)
                plt.scatter(self.label_indices, predictions[n, :,
label_col_index],
                            marker='X', edgecolors='k', label='Predictions',
                            c='red', s=64)

            if n == 0:
                plt.legend()

        plt.xlabel('Time (h)')
```

```
    def make_dataset(self, data):
        data = np.array(data, dtype=np.float32)
        ds = tf.keras.preprocessing.timeseries_dataset_from_array(
            data=data,
            targets=None,
            sequence_length=self.total_window_size,
            sequence_stride=1,
            shuffle=True,
            batch_size=32
        )

        ds = ds.map(self.split_to_inputs_labels)
        return ds

@property
def train(self):
    return self.make_dataset(self.train_df)

@property
def val(self):
    return self.make_dataset(self.val_df)

@property
def test(self):
    return self.make_dataset(self.test_df)

@property
def sample_batch(self):
    result = getattr(self, '_sample_batch', None)
    if result is None:
        result = next(iter(self.train))
        self._sample_batch = result
    return result
```

For now, the DataWindow class might seem a bit abstract, but we will soon use it to apply baseline models. We will be using this class in all the chapters in this deep learning part of the book, so you will gradually tame this code and appreciate how easy it is to test different deep learning architectures.

13.2   *Applying baseline models*

With the DataWindow class complete, we are ready to use it. We will apply baseline models as single-step, multi-step, and multi-output models. You will see that their implementation is similar and incredibly simple when we have the right data windows.

Recall that a baseline is used as a benchmark to evaluate more complex models. A model is performant if it compares favorably to another, so building a baseline is an important step in modeling.

13.2.1   *Single-step baseline model*

We'll first implement a single-step model as a baseline. In a single-step model, the input is one timestep and the output is the prediction of the next timestep.

The first step is to generate a window of data. Since we are defining a single-step model, the input width is 1, the label width is 1, and the shift is also 1, since the model predicts the next timestep. Our target variable is the volume of traffic.

```
single_step_window = DataWindow(input_width=1, label_width=1, shift=1,
  label_columns=['traffic_volume'])
```

For plotting purposes, we'll also define a wider window so we can visualize many predictions of our model. Otherwise, we could only visualize one input data point and one output prediction, which is not very interesting.

```
wide_window = DataWindow(input_width=24, label_width=24, shift=1,
  label_columns=['traffic_volume'])
```

In this situation, the simplest prediction we can make is the last observed value. Basically, the prediction is simply the input data point. This is implemented by the class `Baseline`. As you can see in the following listing, the `Baseline` class can also be used for a multi-output model. For now, we'll solely focus on a single-step model.

Listing 13.4 Class to return the input data as a prediction

```
class Baseline(Model):
    def __init__(self, label_index=None):
        super().__init__()
        self.label_index = label_index         If no target is specified, we
                                               return all columns. This is useful
                                               for multi-output models where
    def call(self, inputs):                    all columns are to be predicted.
        if self.label_index is None:    ◁───┘
            return inputs

        elif isinstance(self.label_index, list):    ◁───┐ If we specify a list of targets, it
            tensors = []                                 will return only the specified
            for index in self.label_index:              columns. Again, this is used
                result = inputs[:, :, index]            for multi-output models.
                result = result[:, :, tf.newaxis]
                tensors.append(result)
            return tf.concat(tensors, axis=-1)

                                                    ┐ Return the input for a
                                                    │ given target variable.
        result = inputs[:, :, self.label_index]   ◁─┘
        return result[:,:,tf.newaxis]
```

With the class defined, we can now initialize the model and compile it to generate predictions. To do so, we'll find the index of our target column, traffic_volume, and pass it in to `Baseline`. Note that TensorFlow requires us to provide a loss function and a metric of evaluation. In this case, and throughout the deep learning chapters, we'll use the mean squared error (MSE) as a loss function—it penalizes large errors, and it generally yields well-fitted models. For the evaluation metric, we'll use the mean absolute error (MAE) for its ease of interpretation.

```
column_indices = {name: i for i, name in enumerate(train_df.columns)}    ◁
```

```
baseline_last = Baseline(label_index=column_indices['traffic_volume'])    ◁
```

```
baseline_last.compile(loss=MeanSquaredError(),
    ⇨ metrics=[MeanAbsoluteError()])    ◁
```

Pass the index of the target column in the Baseline class.

Compile the model to generate the predictions.

Generate a dictionary with the name and index of each column in the training set.

We'll now evaluate the performance of our baseline on both the validation and test sets. Models built with TensorFlow conveniently come with the `evaluate` method, which allows us to compare the predictions to the actual values and calculate the error metric.

Create a dictionary to hold the MAE of a model on the validation set.

Create a dictionary to hold the MAE of a model on the test set.

```
val_performance = {}    ◁
performance = {}    ◁
```

```
val_performance['Baseline - Last'] =
    ⇨ baseline_last.evaluate(single_step_window.val)    ◁
performance['Baseline - Last'] =
    ⇨ baseline_last.evaluate(single_step_window.test, verbose=0)    ◁
```

Store the MAE of the baseline on the validation set.

Store the MAE of the baseline on the test set.

Great, we have successfully built a baseline that predicts the last known value and evaluated it. We can visualize the predictions using the `plot` method of the `DataWindow` class. Remember to use the `wide_window` to see more than just two data points.

```
wide_window.plot(baseline_last)
```

In figure 13.9 the labels are squares and the predictions are crosses. The crosses at each timestep are simply the last known value, meaning that we have a baseline that functions as expected. Your plot may differ from figure 13.9, as the cached sample batch changes every time a data window is initialized.

We can optionally print the MAE of our baseline on the test set.

```
print(performance['Baseline - Last'][1])
```

This returns an MAE of 0.081. More complex models should perform better than the baseline, resulting in a smaller MAE.

13.2.2 *Multi-step baseline models*

In the previous section, we built a single-step baseline model that simply predicted the last known value. For multi-step models, we'll predict more than one timestep into the future. In this case, we'll forecast the traffic volume for the next 24 hours of data given an input of 24 hours.

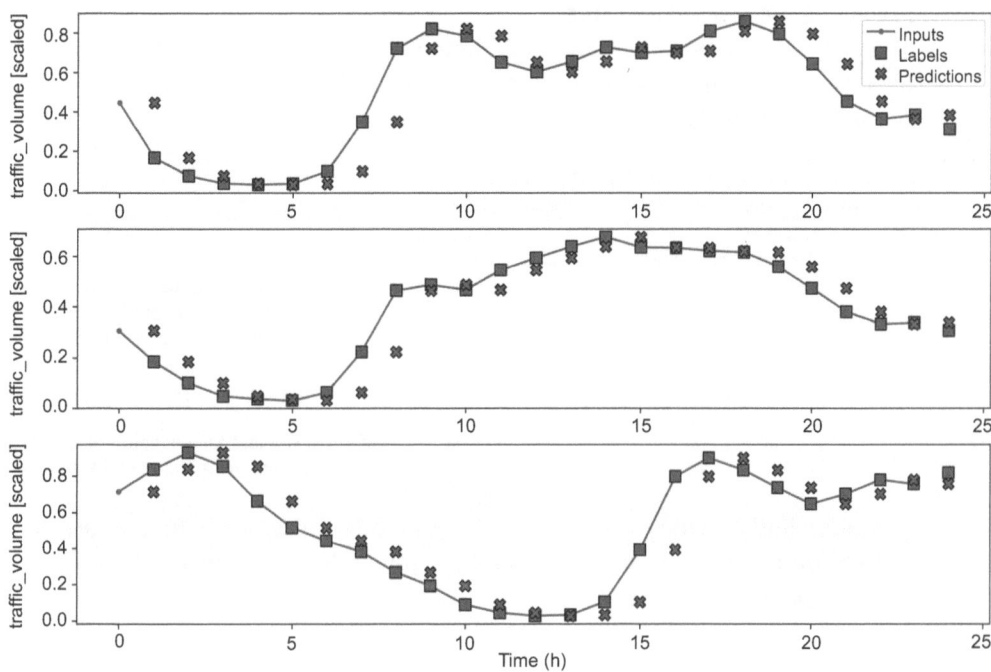

Figure 13.9 Predictions of our baseline single-step model on three sequences from the sample batch. The prediction at each timestep is the last known value, meaning that our baseline works as expected.

Again, the first step is to generate the appropriate window of data. Because we wish to predict 24 timesteps into the future with an input of 24 hours, the input width is 24, the label width is 24, and the shift is also 24.

```
multi_window = DataWindow(input_width=24, label_width=24, shift=24,
➥ label_columns=['traffic_volume'])
```

With the data window generated, we can now focus on implementing the baseline models. In this situation, there are two reasonable baselines:

- Predict the last known value for the next 24 timesteps.
- Predict the last 24 timesteps for the next 24 timesteps.

With that in mind, let's implement the first baseline, where we'll simply repeat the last known value over the next 24 timesteps.

To predict the last known value, we'll define a `MultiStepLastBaseline` class that simply takes in the input and repeats the last value of the input sequence over 24 timesteps. This acts as the prediction of the model.

```
class MultiStepLastBaseline(Model):
    def __init__(self, label_index=None):
        super().__init__()
        self.label_index = label_index

    def call(self, inputs):
        if self.label_index is None:
            return tf.tile(inputs[:, -1:, :], [1, 24, 1])
        return tf.tile(inputs[:, -1:, self.label_index:], [1, 24, 1])
```

> **If no target is specified, return the last known value of all columns over the next 24 timesteps.**

> **Return the last known value of the target column over the next 24 timesteps.**

Next we'll initialize the class and specify the target column. We'll then repeat the same steps as in the previous section, compiling the model and evaluating it on the validation set and test set.

```
ms_baseline_last =
⮡ MultiStepLastBaseline(label_index=column_indices['traffic_volume'])

ms_baseline_last.compile(loss=MeanSquaredError(),
⮡ metrics=[MeanAbsoluteError()])

ms_val_performance = {}
ms_performance = {}

ms_val_performance['Baseline - Last'] =
⮡ ms_baseline_last.evaluate(multi_window.val)
ms_performance['Baseline - Last'] =
⮡ ms_baseline_last.evaluate(multi_window.test, verbose=0)
```

We can now visualize the predictions using the `plot` method of `DataWindow`. The result is shown in figure 13.10.

```
multi_window.plot(ms_baseline_last)
```

Again, we can optionally print the baseline's MAE. From figure 13.10, we can expect it to be fairly high, since there is a large discrepancy between the labels and the predictions.

```
print(ms_performance['Baseline - Last'][1])
```

This gives an MAE of 0.347. Now let's see if we can build a better baseline by simply repeating the input sequence.

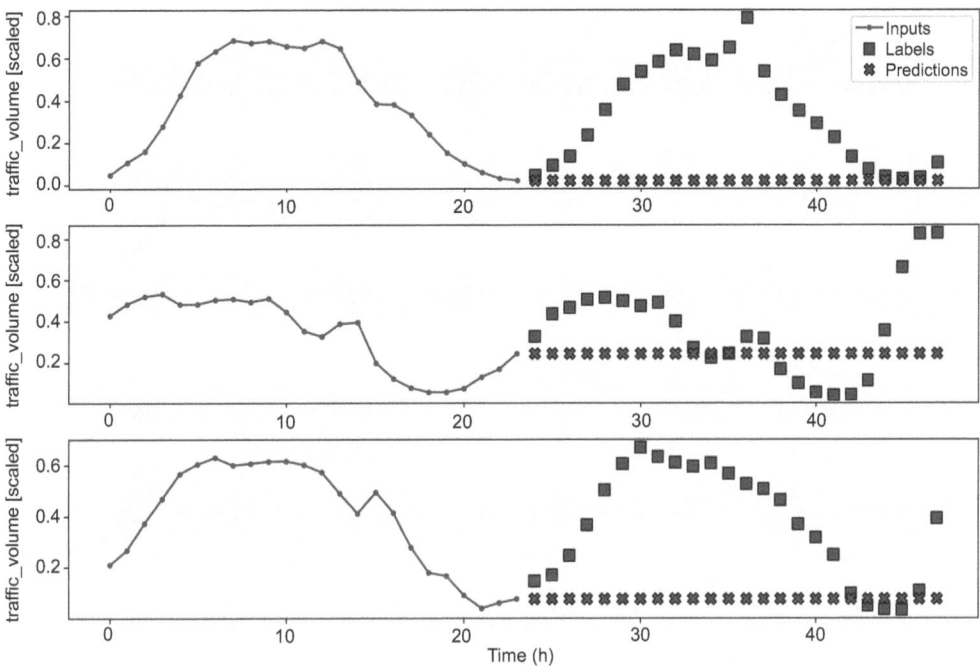

Figure 13.10 Predicting the last known value for the next 24 timesteps. We can see that the predictions, shown as crosses, correspond to the last value of the input sequence, so our baseline behaves as expected.

REPEATING THE INPUT SEQUENCE

Let's implement a second baseline for multi-step models, which simply returns the input sequence. This means that the prediction for the next 24 hours will simply be the last known 24 hours of data. This is implemented through the RepeatBaseline class.

```
class RepeatBaseline(Model):
    def __init__(self, label_index=None):
        super().__init__()
        self.label_index = label_index

    def call(self, inputs):
        return inputs[:, :, self.label_index:]
```

Return the input sequence for the given target column.

Now we can initialize the baseline model and generate predictions. Note that the loss function and evaluation metric remain the same.

```
ms_baseline_repeat =
⮕ RepeatBaseline(label_index=column_indices['traffic_volume'])

ms_baseline_repeat.compile(loss=MeanSquaredError(),
⮕ metrics=[MeanAbsoluteError()])

ms_val_performance['Baseline - Repeat'] =
⮕ ms_baseline_repeat.evaluate(multi_window.val)
```

```
ms_performance['Baseline - Repeat'] =
➥ ms_baseline_repeat.evaluate(multi_window.test, verbose=0)
```

Next we can visualize the predictions. The result is shown in figure 13.11.

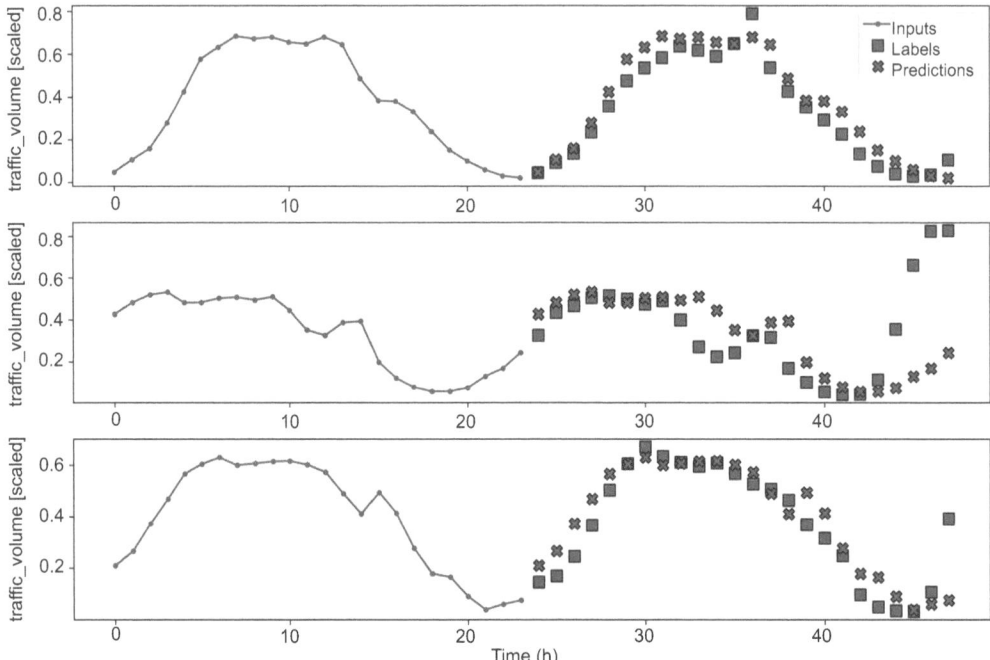

Figure 13.11 Repeating the input sequence as the predictions. You'll see that the predictions (represented as crosses) match exactly the input sequence. You'll also notice that many predictions overlap the labels, which indicates that this baseline performs quite well.

This baseline performs well. This is to be expected, since we identified daily seasonality in the previous chapter. This baseline is the equivalent to predicting the last known season.

Again, we can print the MAE on the test set to verify that we indeed have a better baseline than simply predicting the last known value.

```
print(ms_performance['Baseline - Repeat'][1])
```

This gives an MAE of 0.341, which is lower than the MAE obtained by predicting the last known value. We have therefore successfully built a better baseline.

13.2.3 *Multi-output baseline model*

The final type of model we'll cover is the multi-output model. In this situation, we wish to predict the traffic volume and the temperature for the next timestep using a single input data point. Essentially, we're applying the single-step model on both the traffic volume and temperature, making it a multi-output model.

Again, we'll start off by defining the window of data, but here we'll define two windows: one for training and the other for visualization. Since the model takes in one data point and outputs one prediction, we want to initialize a wide window of data to visualize many predictions over many timesteps.

```
mo_single_step_window = DataWindow(input_width=1, label_width=1, shift=1,
    label_columns=['temp','traffic_volume'])
mo_wide_window = DataWindow(input_width=24, label_width=24, shift=1,
    label_columns=['temp','traffic_volume'])
```

Notice that we pass in both temp and traffic_volume, as those are our two targets for the multi-output model.

Then we'll use the `Baseline` class that we defined for the single-step model. Recall that this class can output the last known value for a list of targets.

Listing 13.5   Class to return the input data as a prediction

```
class Baseline(Model):
    def __init__(self, label_index=None):
        super().__init__()
        self.label_index = label_index

    def call(self, inputs):
        if self.label_index is None:        ◁── If no target is specified, we
            return inputs                        return all columns. This is useful
                                                 for multi-output models where
                                                 all columns are to be predicted.
        elif isinstance(self.label_index, list):   ◁──┐  If we specify a list of
            tensors = []                                 targets, it will return only
            for index in self.label_index:               these specified columns.
                result = inputs[:, :, index]             Again, this is used for
                result = result[:, :, tf.newaxis]        multi-output models.
                tensors.append(result)
            return tf.concat(tensors, axis=-1)

        result = inputs[:, :, self.label_index]   ◁──┐ Return the input for a
        return result[:,:,tf.newaxis]                   given target variable.
```

In the case of the multi-output model, we must simply pass the indexes of the temp and traffic_volume columns to output the last known value for the respective variables as a prediction.

```
print(column_indices['traffic_volume'])    ◁──┘  Prints out 2
print(column_indices['temp'])    ◁──┐ Prints out 0

mo_baseline_last = Baseline(label_index=[0, 2])
```

With the baseline initialized with our two target variables, we can now compile the model and evaluate it.

```
mo_val_performance = {}
mo_performance = {}

mo_val_performance['Baseline - Last'] =
➥  mo_baseline_last.evaluate(mo_wide_window.val)
mo_performance['Baseline - Last'] =
➥  mo_baseline_last.evaluate(mo_wide_window.test, verbose=0)
```

Finally, we can visualize the predictions against the actual values. By default, our plot method will show the traffic volume on the *y*-axis, allowing us to quickly display one of our targets, as shown in figure 13.12.

```
mo_wide_window.plot(mo_baseline_last)
```

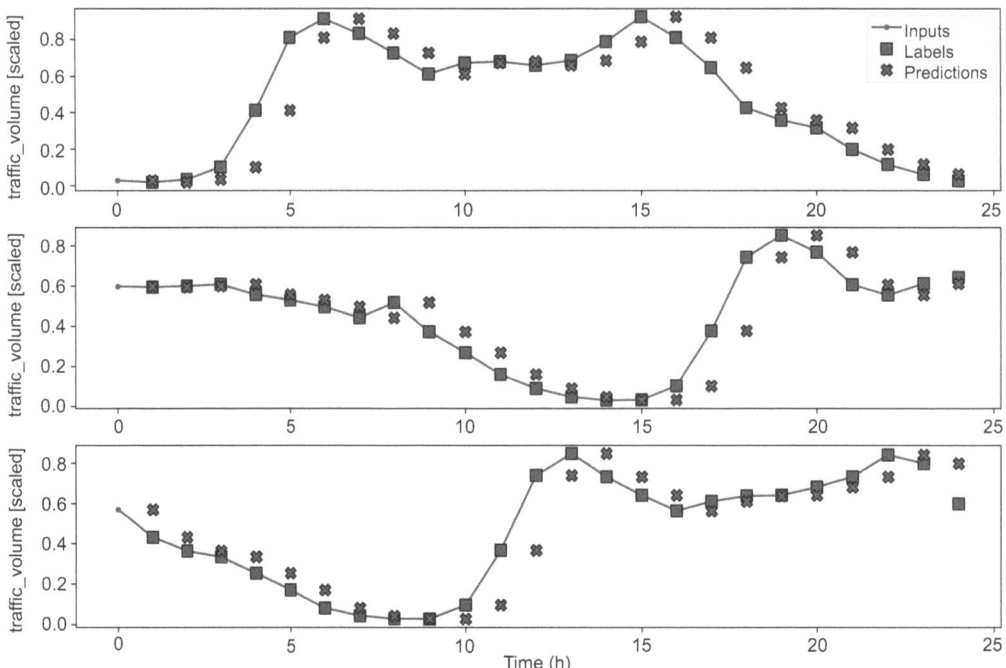

Figure 13.12   Predicting the last known value for traffic volume

Figure 13.12 does not show anything surprising, as we already saw these results when we built a single-step baseline model. The particularity of the multi-output model is that we also have predictions for the temperature. Of course, we can also visualize the predictions for the temperature by specifying the target in the plot method. The result is shown in figure 13.13.

```
mo_wide_window.plot(model=mo_baseline_last, plot_col='temp')
```

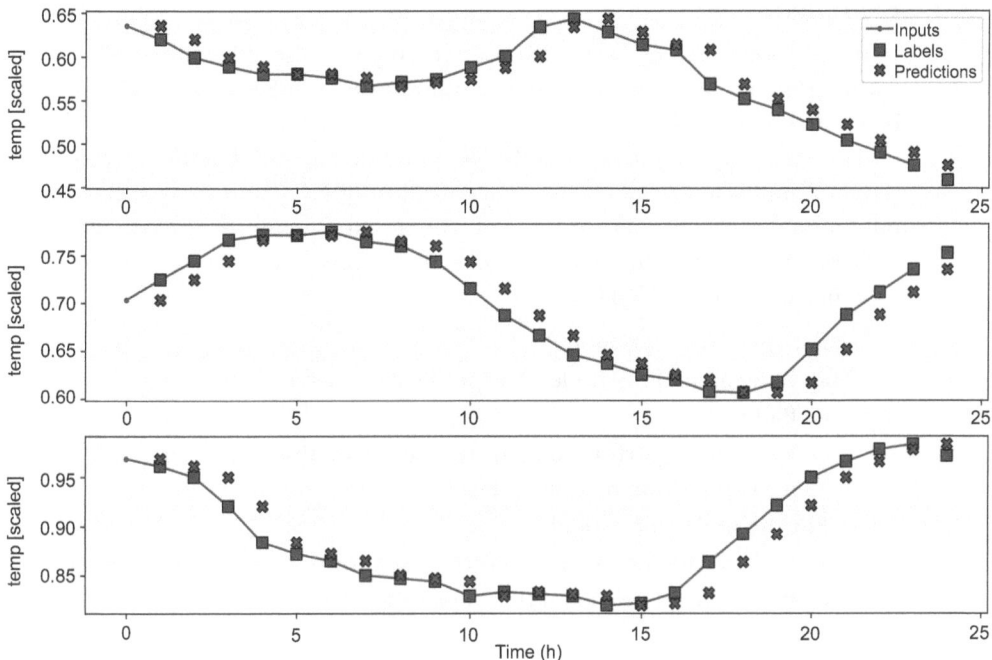

Figure 13.13 Predicting the last known value for the temperature. The predictions (crosses) are equal to the previous data point, so our baseline model behaves as expected.

Again, we can print the MAE of our baseline model.

```
print(mo_performance['Baseline - Last'])
```

We obtain an MAE of 0.047 on the test set. In the next chapter, we'll start building more complex models, and they should result in a lower MAE, as they will be trained to fit the data.

13.3 Next steps

In this chapter, we covered the crucial step of creating data windows, which will allow us to quickly build any type of model. We then proceeded to build baseline models for each type of model, so that we have benchmarks we can compare to when we build our more complex models in later chapters.

Of course, building baseline models is not an application of deep learning just yet. In the next chapter, we will implement linear models and deep neural networks, and see if those models are already more performant than the simple baselines.

13.4   Exercises

In the previous chapter, as an exercise, we prepared the air pollution dataset for deep learning modeling. Now we'll use the training set, validation set, and test set to build baseline models and evaluate them.

For each type of model, follow the steps outlined. Recall that the target for the single-step and multi-step model is the concentration of NO_2, and the targets for the multi-output model are the concentration of NO_2 and temperature. The complete solution is available on GitHub: https://github.com/marcopeix/TimeSeriesForecastingInPython/tree/master/CH13%26CH14.

1 For the single-step model
   a Build a baseline model that predicts the last known value.
   b Plot it.
   c Evaluate its performance using the mean absolute error (MAE) and store it for comparison in a dictionary.
2 For the multi-step model
   a Build a baseline that predicts the last known value over a horizon of 24 hours.
   b Build a baseline model that repeats the last 24 hours.
   c Plot the predictions of both models.
   d Evaluate both models using the MAE and store their performance.
3 For the multi-output model
   a Build a baseline model that predicts the last known value.
   b Plot it.
   c Evaluate its performance using the MAE and store it for comparison in a dictionary.

Summary

- Data windowing is essential in deep learning to format the data as inputs and labels for the model.
- The `DataWindow` class can easily be used in any situation and can be extended to your liking. Make use of it in your own projects.
- Deep learning models require a loss function and an evaluation metric. In our case, we chose the mean squared error (MSE) as the loss function, because it penalizes large errors and tends to yield better-fit models. The evaluation metric is the mean absolute error (MAE), chosen for its ease of interpretation.

Baby steps with deep learning

This chapter covers

- Implementing linear models
- Enacting deep neural networks

In the last chapter, we implemented the `DataWindow` class, which allows us to quickly create windows of data for building single-step models, multi-step models, and multi-output models. With this crucial component in place, we then developed the baseline models that will serve as benchmarks for our more complex models, which we'll start building in this chapter.

Specifically, we'll implement linear models and deep neural networks. A *linear model* is a special case of a neural network, where there is no hidden layer. This model simply calculates weights for each input variable in order to output a prediction for the target. In contrast, a *deep neural network* has at least one hidden layer, allowing us to start modeling nonlinear relationships between the features and the target, usually resulting in better forecasts.

In this chapter, we'll continue the work we started in chapter 13. I recommend that you continue coding in the same notebook or Python scripts as in the last chapter, so that you can compare the performance of these linear models and deep neural networks to that of the baseline models from chapter 13. We'll also keep working with the same dataset as previously, and our target variable will remain the traffic volume for both the single-step and multi-step models. For the multi-output model, we'll keep the temperature and traffic volume as our targets.

14.1 *Implementing a linear model*

A *linear model* is the simplest architecture we can implement in deep learning. In fact, we might argue that it is not deep learning at all, since the model has no hidden layer. Each input feature is simply given a weight, and they are combined to output a prediction for the target, just like in a traditional linear regression.

Let's consider a single-step model as an example. Recall that we have the following features in our dataset: temperature, cloud coverage, traffic volume, and day_sin and day_cos, which encode the time of day as numerical values. A linear model simply takes all the features, calculates a weight for each of them, and sums them to output a prediction for the next timestep. This process is illustrated in figure 14.1.

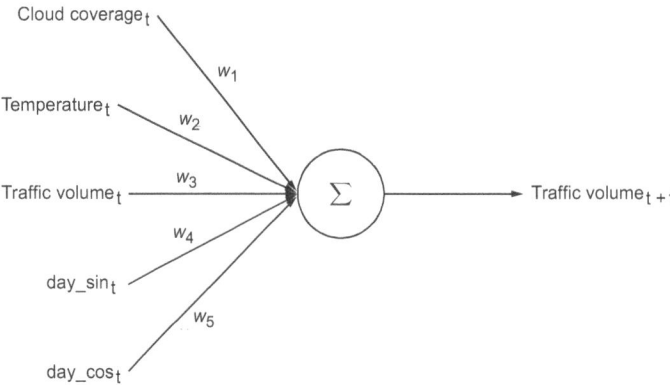

Figure 14.1 An example of a linear model as a single-step model. Each feature at time *t* is assigned a weight (w_1 to w_5). They are then summed to calculate an output for the traffic volume at the next timestep, t+1. This is similar to a linear regression.

The model in figure 14.1 can be mathematically expressed as equation 14.1, where x_1 is cloud coverage, x_2 is temperature, x_3 is traffic volume, x_4 is day_sin, and x_5 is day_cos.

$$\text{traffic volume}_{t+1} = w_1 x_{1,t} + w_2 x_{2,t} + w_3 x_{3,t} + w_4 x_{4,t} + w_5 x_{5,t}$$ **Equation 14.1**

We can easily recognize equation 14.1 as being a simple multivariate linear regression. During training, the model tries multiple values for w_1 to w_5 in order to minimize the mean squared error (MSE) between the prediction and actual value of the traffic volume at the next timestep.

Now that you understand the concept of a linear model in deep learning, let's implement it as a single-step model, multi-step model, and multi-output model.

14.1.1 *Implementing a single-step linear model*

A single-step linear model is one of the simplest models to implement, as it is exactly as described in figure 14.1 and equation 14.1. We simply take all the inputs, assign a weight to each, take the sum, and generate a prediction. Remember that we are using the traffic volume as a target.

Assuming that you are working in the same notebook or Python script as in the last chapter, you should have access to the `single_step_window` for training and `wide_window` for plotting. Recall also that the performance of the baseline is stored in `val_performance` and `performance`.

Unlike a baseline model, a linear model actually requires training. Thus, we'll define a `compile_and_fit` function that configures the model for training and then fits the model on the data, as shown in the following listing.

> **NOTE** You can consult the source code for this chapter on GitHub: https://github.com/marcopeix/TimeSeriesForecastingInPython/tree/master/CH13%26CH14.

As in chapter 13, the following code block follows the terminology and best practices highlighted in the official TensorFlow documentation. Every model built in TensorFlow must be compiled before training. It is also very common when working with TensorFlow to assign the outputs of the model's training to the variable history. This code is again reused within the terms of the Apache 2.0 License.

Listing 14.1   Function to configure a deep learning model and fit it on data

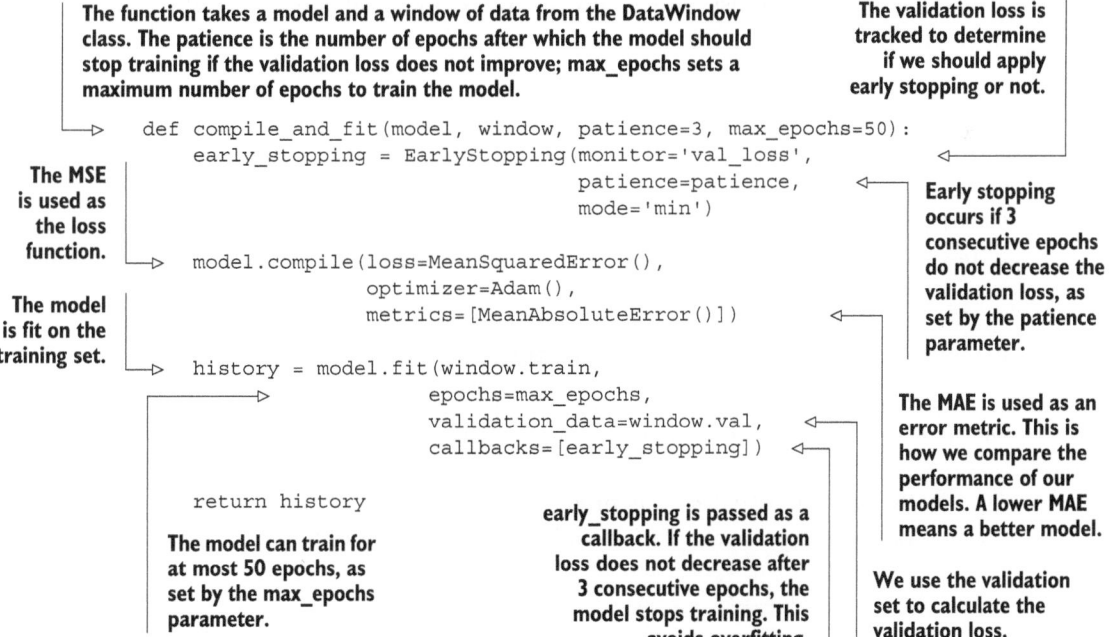

The function takes a model and a window of data from the DataWindow class. The patience is the number of epochs after which the model should stop training if the validation loss does not improve; max_epochs sets a maximum number of epochs to train the model.

The validation loss is tracked to determine if we should apply early stopping or not.

```
def compile_and_fit(model, window, patience=3, max_epochs=50):
    early_stopping = EarlyStopping(monitor='val_loss',
                                   patience=patience,
                                   mode='min')

    model.compile(loss=MeanSquaredError(),
                  optimizer=Adam(),
                  metrics=[MeanAbsoluteError()])

    history = model.fit(window.train,
                        epochs=max_epochs,
                        validation_data=window.val,
                        callbacks=[early_stopping])

    return history
```

The MSE is used as the loss function.

The model is fit on the training set.

Early stopping occurs if 3 consecutive epochs do not decrease the validation loss, as set by the patience parameter.

The MAE is used as an error metric. This is how we compare the performance of our models. A lower MAE means a better model.

We use the validation set to calculate the validation loss.

The model can train for at most 50 epochs, as set by the max_epochs parameter.

early_stopping is passed as a callback. If the validation loss does not decrease after 3 consecutive epochs, the model stops training. This avoids overfitting.

This piece of code will be reused throughout the deep learning chapters, so it's important to understand what is happening. The `compile_and_fit` function takes in a deep learning model, a window of data from the `DataWindow` class, the `patience` parameter, and the `max_epochs` parameter. The `patience` parameter is used in the `early_stopping` function, which allows us to stop the model from training if there are no improvements in the validation loss, as specified by the `monitor` parameter. That way, we avoid useless training time and overfitting.

Then the model is compiled. In Keras, this simply configures the model to specify the loss function to be used, the optimizer, and metrics of evaluation. In our case, we'll use the MSE as the loss function because the error is squared, meaning that the model is heavily penalized for large differences between the predicted and actual values. We'll use the Adam optimizer because it is a fast and efficient optimizer. Finally, we'll use the MAE as an evaluation metric to compare the performance of our models because we used it to evaluate our baseline models in the previous chapter, and it is easy to interpret.

The model is then fit on the training data for up to 50 epochs, as set by the `max_epochs` parameter. The validation is performed on the validation set, and we pass in `early_stopping` as a callback. That way, Keras will apply early stopping if it sees that the validation loss has not decreased after 3 consecutive epochs.

With `compile_and_fit` in place, we can move on to actually building our linear model. We'll use the `Sequential` model from Keras, as it allows us to stack different layers. Since we are building a linear model here, we only have one layer—a `Dense` layer, which is the most basic layer in deep learning. We'll specify the number of units as 1, since the model must output only one value: the prediction for traffic volume at the next timestep.

```
linear = Sequential([
    Dense(units=1)
])
```

Clearly, Keras makes it very easy to build models. With this step complete, we can then train the model using `compile_and_fit` and store the performance to later compare it to the baseline.

```
history = compile_and_fit(linear, single_step_window)

val_performance['Linear'] = linear.evaluate(single_step_window.val)
performance['Linear'] = linear.evaluate(single_step_window.test, verbose=0)
```

Optionally, we can visualize the predictions of our linear model using the `plot` method of the `wide_window`. The result is shown in figure 14.2.

```
wide_window.plot(linear)
```

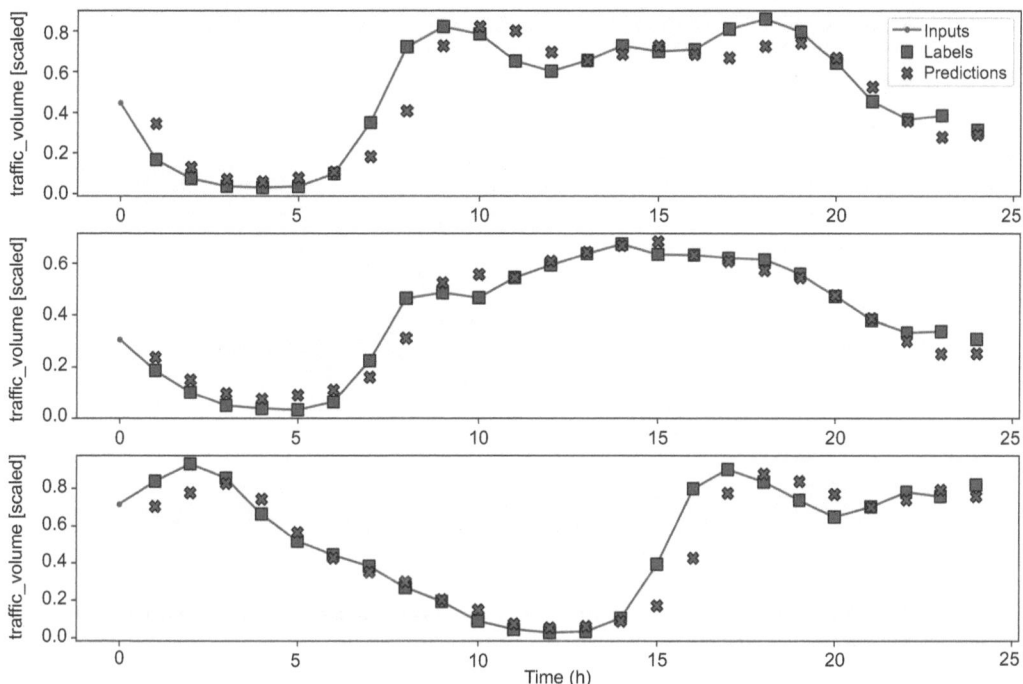

Figure 14.2   Predictions of traffic volume using the linear model as a single-step model. The predictions (shown as crosses) are fairly accurate, with some predictions overlapping the actual values (shown as squares).

Our model makes fairly good predictions, as we can observe some overlap between the forecasts and the actual values. We will wait until the end of the chapter to compare the performance of our models to the baselines. For now, let's move on to implementing the multi-step linear and multi-output linear models.

14.1.2 Implementing a multi-step linear model

Our single-step linear model is built, and we can now extend it to a multi-step linear model. Recall that in the multi-step situation, we wish to predict the next 24 hours of data using an input window of 24 hours of data. Our target remains the traffic volume.

This model will greatly resemble the single-step linear model, but this time we'll use 24 hours of input and output 24 hours of predictions. The multi-step linear model is illustrated in figure 14.3. As you can see, the model takes in 24 hours of each feature, combines them in a single layer, and outputs a tensor containing the forecast for the next 24 hours.

Implementing the model is easy, as our model only contains a single `Dense` layer. We can optionally initialize the weights to 0, which makes the training procedure slightly faster. We then compile and fit the model before storing its evaluation metrics in `ms_val_performance` and `ms_performance`.

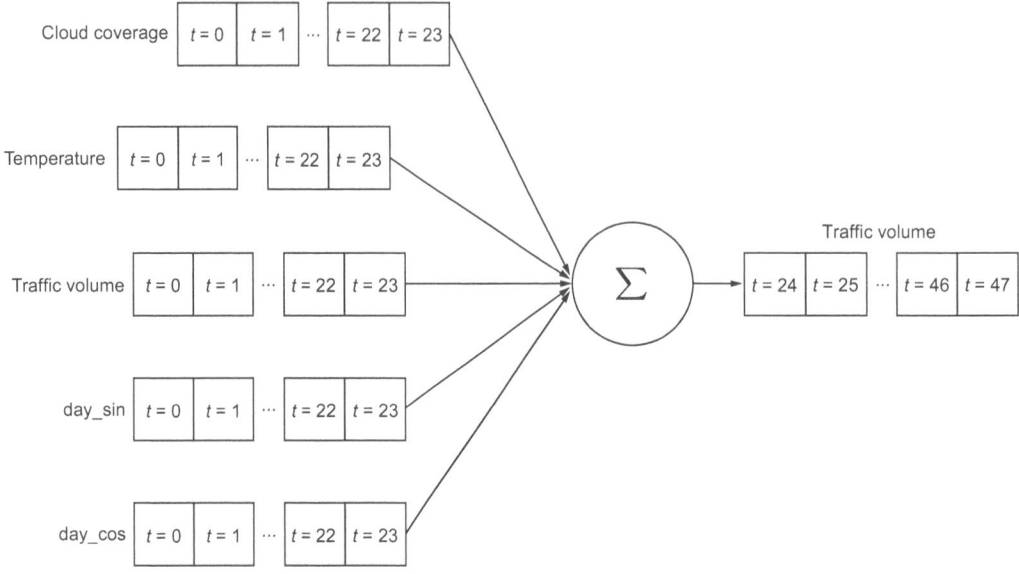

Figure 14.3   The multi-step linear model. We'll take 24 hours of each feature, combine them in a single layer, and immediately output predictions for the next 24 hours.

```
ms_linear = Sequential([
    Dense(1, kernel_initializer=tf.initializers.zeros)
])

history = compile_and_fit(ms_linear, multi_window)

ms_val_performance['Linear'] = ms_linear.evaluate(multi_window.val)
ms_performance['Linear'] = ms_linear.evaluate(multi_window.test, verbose=0)
```

Initializing the weights to 0 makes training slightly faster.

We have just built a multi-step linear model. You might feel underwhelmed, since the code is almost identical to the single-step linear model. This is due to our work building the DataWindow class and properly windowing our data. With that step done, building models becomes extremely easy.

Next we'll implement a multi-output linear model.

14.1.3 *Implementing a multi-output linear model*

The multi-output linear model will return predictions for the traffic volume and the temperature. The input is the present timestep, and the predictions are for the next timestep.

The model's architecture is shown in figure 14.4. There, you can see that our multi-output linear model will take all the features at $t = 0$, combine them in a single layer, and output both the temperature and traffic volume at the next timestep.

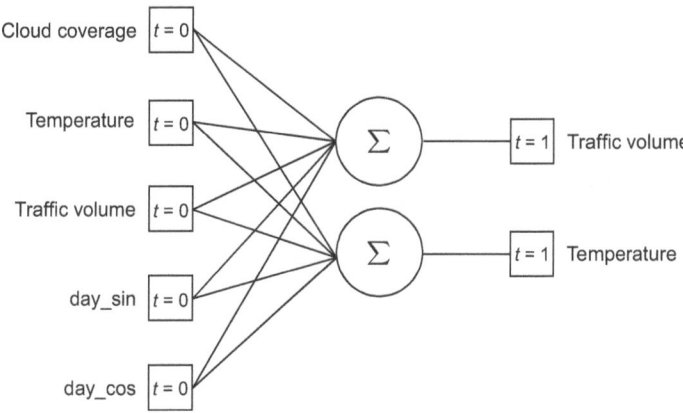

Figure 14.4 A multi-output linear model. In this case, the model takes the present timestep of all features and produces a forecast for the temperature and traffic volume at the next timestep.

Up to this point, we have only predicted the traffic volume, meaning that we had only one target, so we used the layer Dense(units=1). In this case, since we must output a prediction for two targets, our layer will be Dense(units=2). As before, we'll train the model and store its performance to compare it later to the baseline and deep neural network.

```
mo_linear = Sequential([          We set units equal to the number
    Dense(units=2)         ◁───   of targets we are predicting in
])                                the output layer.

history = compile_and_fit(mo_linear, mo_single_step_window)

mo_val_performance['Linear'] =
➥ mo_linear.evaluate(mo_single_step_window.val)
mo_performance['Linear'] = mo_linear.evaluate(mo_single_step_window.test,
➥ verbose=0)
```

Again, you can see how easy it is to build a deep learning model in Keras, especially when we have the proper data window as input.

With our single-step, multi-step, and multi-output linear models done, we can now move on to implementing a more complex architecture: a deep neural network.

14.2 *Implementing a deep neural network*

With our three types of linear models implemented, it is time to move on to deep neural networks. It has been empirically shown that adding hidden layers in neural networks helps achieve better results. Furthermore, we'll introduce a nonlinear activation function to capture nonlinear relationships in the data.

Linear models have no hidden layers; the model had an input layer and an output layer. In a deep neural network (DNN), we'll add more layers between the input and output layers, called *hidden layers*. This difference in architecture is highlighted in figure 14.5.

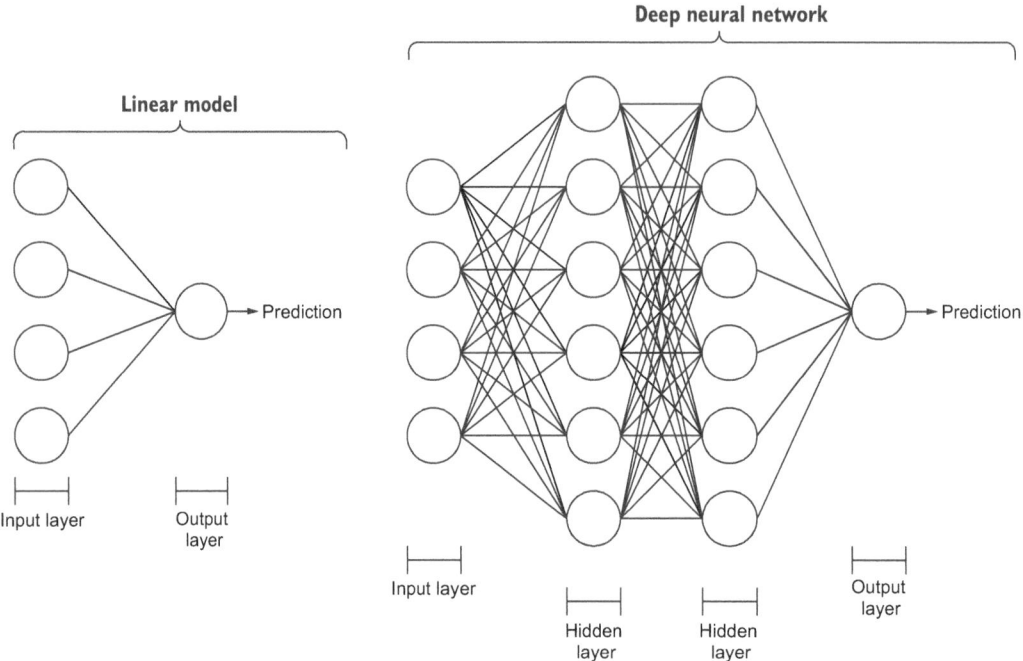

Figure 14.5   Comparing a linear model to a deep neural network. In the linear model, the input layer is directly connected to an output layer that returns a prediction. Therefore, only a linear relationship is derived. A deep neural network contains hidden layers. These layers allow it to model nonlinear relationships between inputs and predictions, generally resulting in better models.

The idea behind adding layers to the network is that it gives the model more opportunities to learn, which usually results in the model generalizing better on unseen data, thus improving its performance. Of course, with added layers, the model necessarily trains for a longer time and is thus supposed to learn better.

Each circle in a hidden layer represents a neuron, and each neuron has an activation function. The number of neurons is equal to the number of units that is passed as an argument in the Dense layer in Keras. Usually we set the number of units, or neurons, as a power of 2, as it is more computationally efficient—calculations in the CPU and GPU happen in batch sizes that are also powers of 2.

Before implementing a DNN, we need to address the *activation function* in each neuron of the hidden layers. The activation function defines the output of each neuron based on the input. Therefore, if we wish to model nonlinear relationships, we need to use a nonlinear activation function.

> **Activation function**
>
> The activation function is in each neuron of the neural network and is responsible for generating an output from the input data.
>
> If a linear activation function is used, the model will only model linear relationships. Therefore, to model nonlinear relationships in the data, we must use a nonlinear activation function. Examples of nonlinear activation functions are ReLU, softmax, or tanh.

In our case, we'll use the Rectified Linear Unit (ReLU) activation function. This nonlinear activation function basically returns either the positive part of its input or 0, as defined by equation 14.2.

$$f(x) = x^+ = \max(0, x)$$ **Equation 14.2**

This activation function comes with many advantages, such as better gradient propagation, more efficient computation, and scale-invariance. For all those reasons, it is now the most widely used activation function in deep learning, and we'll use it whenever we have a Dense layer that is a hidden layer.

We are now ready to implement a deep neural network in Keras.

14.2.1 *Implementing a deep neural network as a single-step model*

We are now back to the single-step model, but this time we'll implement a deep neural network. The DNN takes in the features at the current timestep to output the prediction for traffic volume at the next timestep.

The model still makes use of the Sequential model, as we'll stack Dense layers in order to build a deep neural network. In this case, we'll use two hidden layers with 64 neurons each. As mentioned before, we'll specify the activation function to be ReLU. The last layer is the output layer, which in this case only returns one value representing the prediction for traffic volume.

```
dense = Sequential([
    Dense(units=64, activation='relu'),      ← First hidden layer with 64
    Dense(units=64, activation='relu'),        neurons. Specify the activation
    Dense(units=1)         ←                    function to be ReLU.
])                           The output layer has only one neuron,
                             as we output only one value.
```

With the model defined, we can now compile it, train it, and record its performance to compare it to the baseline and the linear model.

```
history = compile_and_fit(dense, single_step_window)

val_performance['Dense'] = dense.evaluate(single_step_window.val)
performance['Dense'] = dense.evaluate(single_step_window.test, verbose=0)
```

Of course, we can take a look at the model's predictions using the `plot` method, as shown in figure 14.6. Our deep neural network seems to be making quite accurate predictions.

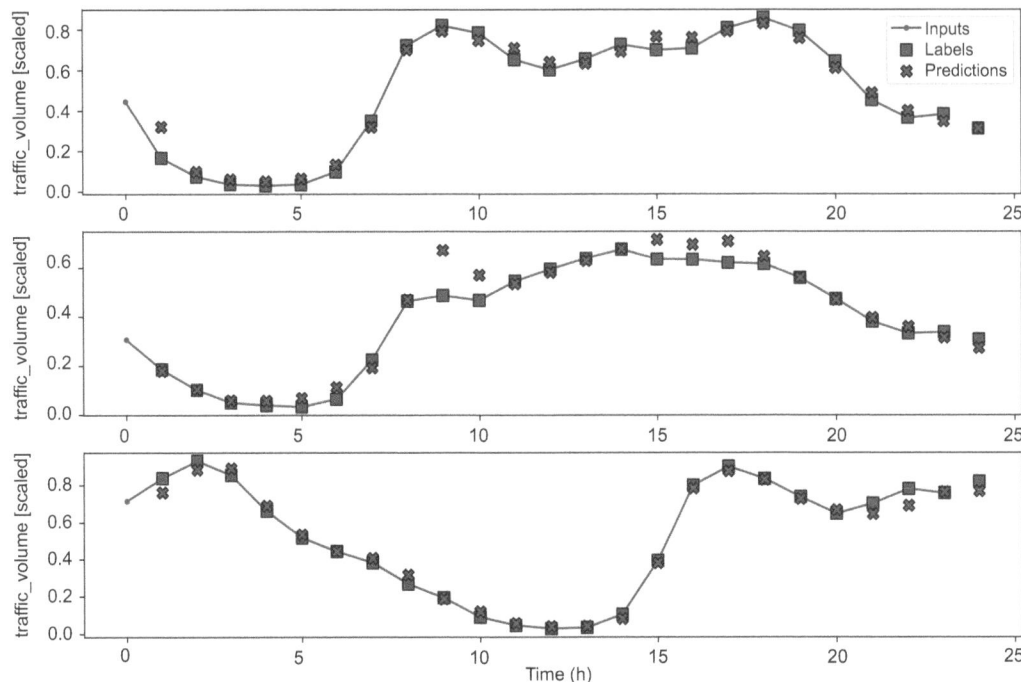

Figure 14.6 Predicting the traffic volume using a deep neural network as a single-step model. Here even more predictions (shown as crosses) overlap with the actual values (shown as squares), suggesting that the model is making very accurate predictions.

Let's compare the MAE of the DNN with the linear model and the baseline that we built in chapter 13. The result is shown in figure 14.7.

```
mae_val = [v[1] for v in val_performance.values()]
mae_test = [v[1] for v in performance.values()]

x = np.arange(len(performance))

fig, ax = plt.subplots()
ax.bar(x - 0.15, mae_val, width=0.25, color='black', edgecolor='black',
⮑ label='Validation')
ax.bar(x + 0.15, mae_test, width=0.25, color='white', edgecolor='black',
⮑ hatch='/', label='Test')
ax.set_ylabel('Mean absolute error')
ax.set_xlabel('Models')
```

```
for index, value in enumerate(mae_val):
    plt.text(x=index - 0.15, y=value+0.0025, s=str(round(value, 3)),
➥ ha='center')

for index, value in enumerate(mae_test):
    plt.text(x=index + 0.15, y=value+0.0025, s=str(round(value, 3)),
➥ ha='center')

plt.ylim(0, 0.1)
plt.xticks(ticks=x, labels=performance.keys())
plt.legend(loc='best')
plt.tight_layout()
```

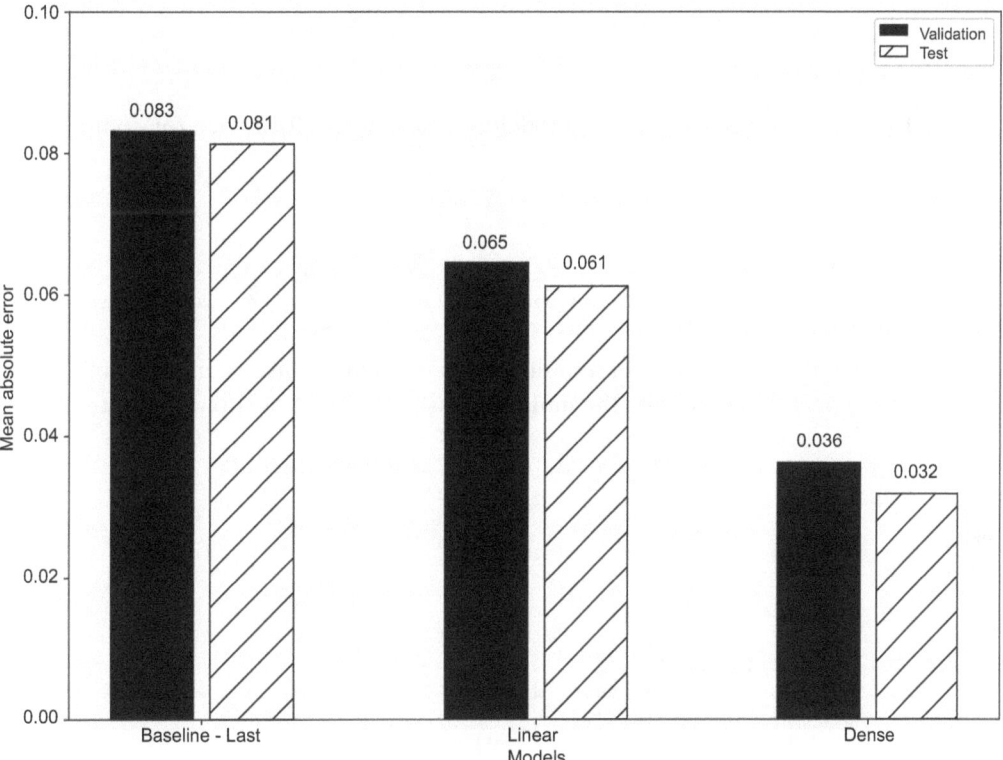

Figure 14.7 The MAE for all of the single-step models so far. The linear model performs better than the baseline, which only predicts the last known value. The dense model outperforms both models, since it has the lowest MAE.

In figure 14.7 the MAE is highest for the baseline. It decreases with the linear model and decreases again with the deep neural network. Thus, both models outperformed the baseline, with the deep neural network having the best performance.

14.2.2   *Implementing a deep neural network as a multi-step model*

Now let's implement a deep neural network as a multi-step model. In this case, we want to predict the next 24 hours of traffic volume based on the last 24 hours of recorded data.

Again we'll use two hidden layers with 64 neurons each, and we'll use the ReLU activation function. Since we have a data window with 24 hours of input, the model will also output 24 hours of predictions; the output layer simply has one neuron because we are predicting traffic volume only.

```
ms_dense = Sequential([
    Dense(64, activation='relu'),
    Dense(64, activation='relu'),
    Dense(1, kernel_initializer=tf.initializers.zeros),
])
```

Then we'll compile, train the model, and save its performance for comparison with the linear and baseline models.

```
history = compile_and_fit(ms_dense, multi_window)

ms_val_performance['Dense'] = ms_dense.evaluate(multi_window.val)
ms_performance['Dense'] = ms_dense.evaluate(multi_window.test, verbose=0)
```

Just like that, we have built a multi-step deep neural network model. Let's see which model performed best for the multi-step task. The result is shown in figure 14.8.

```
ms_mae_val = [v[1] for v in ms_val_performance.values()]
ms_mae_test = [v[1] for v in ms_performance.values()]


x = np.arange(len(ms_performance))


fig, ax = plt.subplots()
ax.bar(x - 0.15, ms_mae_val, width=0.25, color='black', edgecolor='black',
➥ label='Validation')
ax.bar(x + 0.15, ms_mae_test, width=0.25, color='white', edgecolor='black',
➥ hatch='/', label='Test')
ax.set_ylabel('Mean absolute error')
ax.set_xlabel('Models')


for index, value in enumerate(ms_mae_val):
    plt.text(x=index - 0.15, y=value+0.0025, s=str(round(value, 3)),
➥ ha='center')


for index, value in enumerate(ms_mae_test):
    plt.text(x=index + 0.15, y=value+0.0025, s=str(round(value, 3)),
➥ ha='center')


plt.ylim(0, 0.4)
plt.xticks(ticks=x, labels=ms_performance.keys())
```

```
plt.legend(loc='best')
plt.tight_layout()
```

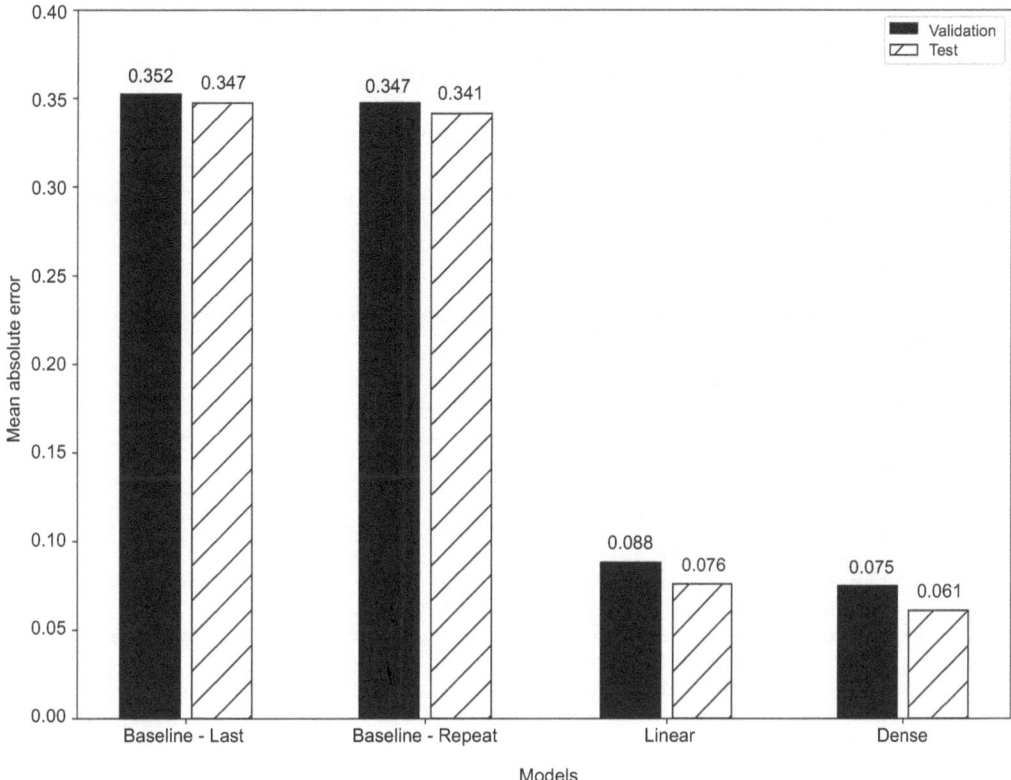

Figure 14.8 **The MAE for all of the multi-step models so far. The linear model performs better than both baselines. The dense model outperforms all models.**

In figure 14.8 you'll see that the linear model and deep neural network both outperform the two baselines that we built for the multi-step task in chapter 13. Again, the deep neural network has the lowest MAE of all, meaning that it is the most performant model for now.

14.2.3 *Implementing a deep neural network as a multi-output model*

Finally, we'll implement a deep neural network as a multi-output model. In this case, we'll use the features at the present timestep to forecast both the traffic volume and temperature at the next timestep.

As for the previous DNNs that we implemented, we'll use two hidden layers of 64 neurons each. This time, because we are forecasting two targets, our output layer has two neurons or units.

```
mo_dense = Sequential([
    Dense(units=64, activation='relu'),
    Dense(units=64, activation='relu'),
    Dense(units=2)
])
```

◁─┐ **The output layer has two neurons,
     since we are forecasting two targets.**

Next we'll compile and fit the model and store its performance for comparison.

```
history = compile_and_fit(mo_dense, mo_single_step_window)

mo_val_performance['Dense'] = mo_dense.evaluate(mo_single_step_window.val)
mo_performance['Dense'] = mo_dense.evaluate(mo_single_step_window.test,
    verbose=0)
```

Let's see which model performed best at the multi-output task. Note that the reported MAE is averaged for both targets.

```
mo_mae_val = [v[1] for v in mo_val_performance.values()]
mo_mae_test = [v[1] for v in mo_performance.values()]

x = np.arange(len(mo_performance))

fig, ax = plt.subplots()
ax.bar(x - 0.15, mo_mae_val, width=0.25, color='black', edgecolor='black',
    label='Validation')
ax.bar(x + 0.15, mo_mae_test, width=0.25, color='white', edgecolor='black',
    hatch='/', label='Test')
ax.set_ylabel('Mean absolute error')
ax.set_xlabel('Models')

for index, value in enumerate(mo_mae_val):
    plt.text(x=index - 0.15, y=value+0.0025, s=str(round(value, 3)),
    ha='center')

for index, value in enumerate(mo_mae_test):
    plt.text(x=index + 0.15, y=value+0.0025, s=str(round(value, 3)),
    ha='center')

plt.ylim(0, 0.06)
plt.xticks(ticks=x, labels=mo_performance.keys())
plt.legend(loc='best')
plt.tight_layout()
```

As you can see in figure 14.9, our models outperform the baseline, with the deep learning model being the most performant.

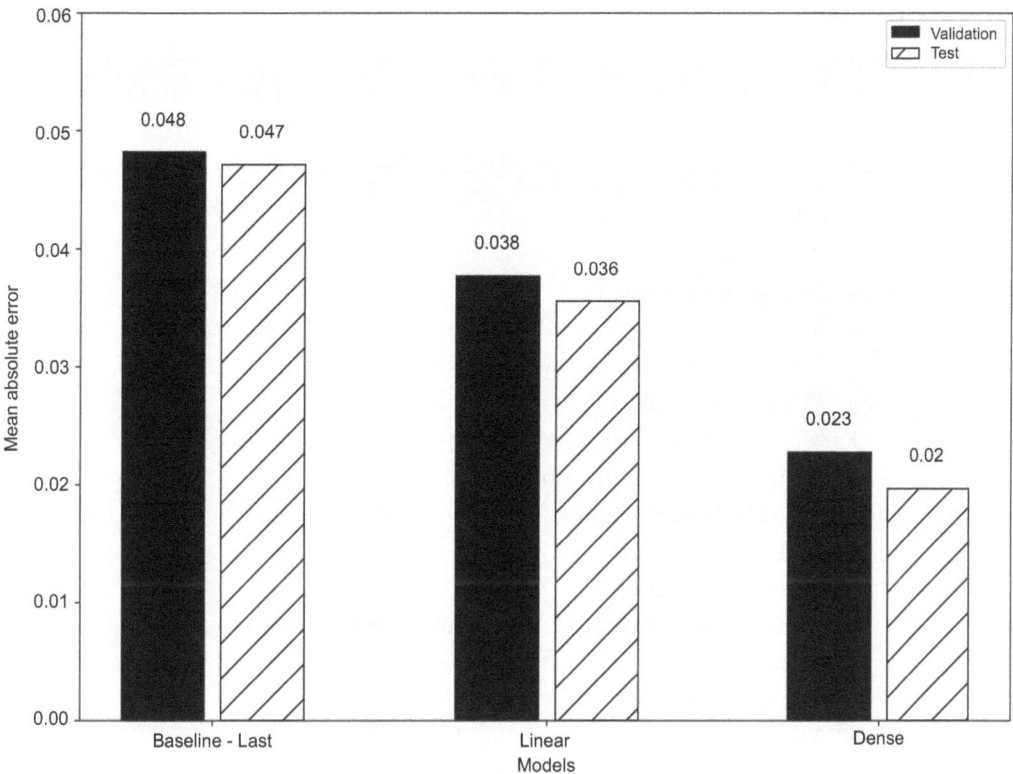

Figure 14.9   The MAE for all of the multi-output models built so far. Again, the baseline has the highest MAE, while the deep neural network achieves the lowest error metric.

14.3   *Next steps*

In this chapter, we implemented both linear models and deep neural networks to make single-step, multi-step, and multi-output predictions. In all cases, the deep neural network outperformed the other models. This is generally the case, as DNNs can map nonlinear relationships between the features and the targets, which generally leads to more accurate predictions.

This chapter only brushed the surface of what deep learning can achieve in time series forecasting. In the next chapter, we'll explore a more complex architecture: the *long short-term memory* (LSTM). This architecture is widely used to process sequences of data. Since a time series is a sequence of points equally spaced in time, it makes sense to apply an LSTM for time series forecasting. We will then test whether the LSTM outperforms the DNN or not.

14.4   Exercises

In the last chapter, as an exercise, you built baseline models to forecast the concentration of NO_2 and temperature. Now you'll build linear models and deep neural networks. The full solutions to these exercises are available on GitHub: https://github .com/marcopeix/TimeSeriesForecastingInPython/tree/master/CH13%26CH14.

1 For the single-step model:
   a Build a linear model.
   b Plot its predictions.
   c Measure its performance using the mean absolute error (MAE) and store it.
   d Build a deep neural network (DNN).
   e Plot its predictions.
   f Measure its performance using the MAE and store it.
   g Which model performs best?
2 For the multi-step model:
   a Build a linear model.
   b Plot its predictions.
   c Measure its performance using the MAE and store it.
   d Build a DNN.
   e Plot its predictions.
   f Measure its performance using the MAE and store it.
   g Which model performs best?
3 For the multi-output model:
   a Build a linear model.
   b Plot its predictions.
   c Measure its performance using the MAE and store it.
   d Build a DNN.
   e Plot its predictions.
   f Measure its performance using the MAE and store it.
   g Which model performs best?

At any point, feel free to run your own experiments with the deep neural networks. Add layers, change the number of neurons, and see how those changes impact the performance of the model.

Summary

- A linear model is the simplest architecture in deep learning. It has an input layer and an output layer, with no activation function.
- A linear model can only derive linear relationships between the features and the target.

- A deep neural network (DNN) has hidden layers, which are layers between the input and output layers. Adding more layers usually improves the performance of the model, as it allows it more time to train and learn the data.
- To model nonlinear relationships from the data, you must use a nonlinear activation function in the network. Examples of nonlinear activation functions are ReLU, softmax, tanh, sigmoid, etc.
- The number of neurons in a hidden layer is usually a power of 2, to make computation more efficient.
- The Rectified Linear Unit (ReLU) is a popular nonlinear activation function that does not vary with scale and allows for efficient model training.

Remembering
the past with LSTM

This chapter covers

- Examining the long short-term memory (LSTM) architecture
- Implementing an LSTM with Keras

In the last chapter, we built our first models in deep learning, implementing both linear and deep neural network models. In the case of our dataset, we saw that both models outperformed the baselines we built in chapter 13, with the deep neural network being the best model for single-step, multi-step, and multi-output tasks.

Now we'll explore a more advanced architecture called *long short-term memory* (LSTM), which is a particular case of a *recurrent neural network* (RNN). This type of neural network is used to process sequences of data, where the order matters. One common application of RNN and LSTM is in natural language processing. Words in a sentence have an order, and changing that order can completely change the meaning of a sentence. Thus, we often find this architecture behind text classification and text generation algorithms.

Another situation where the order of data matters is time series. We know that time series are sequences of data equally spaced in time, and that their order cannot be changed. The data point observed at 9 a.m. must come before the data point at 10 a.m. and after the data point at 8 a.m. Thus, it makes sense to apply the LSTM architecture for forecasting time series.

In this chapter, we'll first explore the general architecture of a recurrent neural network, and then we'll dive deep into the LSTM architecture and examine its unique features and inner workings. Then we'll implement an LSTM using Keras to produce single-step, multi-step, and multi-output models. We'll finally compare the performance of LSTM against all the models we've built, from the baselines to the deep neural networks.

15.1   Exploring the recurrent neural network (RNN)

A recurrent neural network (RNN) is a deep learning architecture especially adapted to processing sequences of data. It denotes a set of networks that share a similar architecture: long short-term memory (LSTM) and gated recurrent unit (GRU) are subtypes of RNNs. In this chapter, we'll solely focus on the LSTM architecture.

To understand the inner workings of an RNN, we'll start with figure 15.1, which shows a compact illustration of an RNN. Just like in a deep neural network (DNN), we have an input, denoted as x_t, and an output, denoted as y_t. Here x_t is an element of a sequence. When it is fed to the RNN, it computes a hidden state, denoted as h_t. This hidden state acts as memory. It is computed for each element of the sequence and fed back to the RNN as an input. That way, the network effectively uses past information computed for previous elements of the sequence to inform the output for the next element of the sequence.

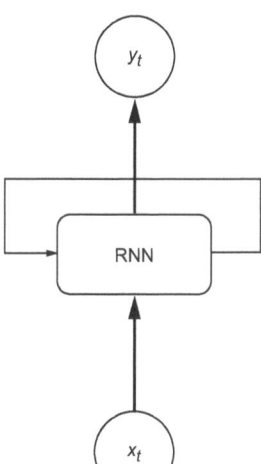

Figure 15.1   A compact illustration of an RNN. It computes a hidden state h_t, which is looped back in the network and combined with the next input of the sequence. This is how RNNs keep information from past elements of a sequence and use them to process the next element of a sequence.

Figure 15.2 shows an expanded illustration of an RNN. You can see how the hidden state is first computed at $t = 0$ and then is updated and passed on as each element of the sequence is processed. This is how the RNN effectively replicates the concept of memory and uses past information to produce a new output.

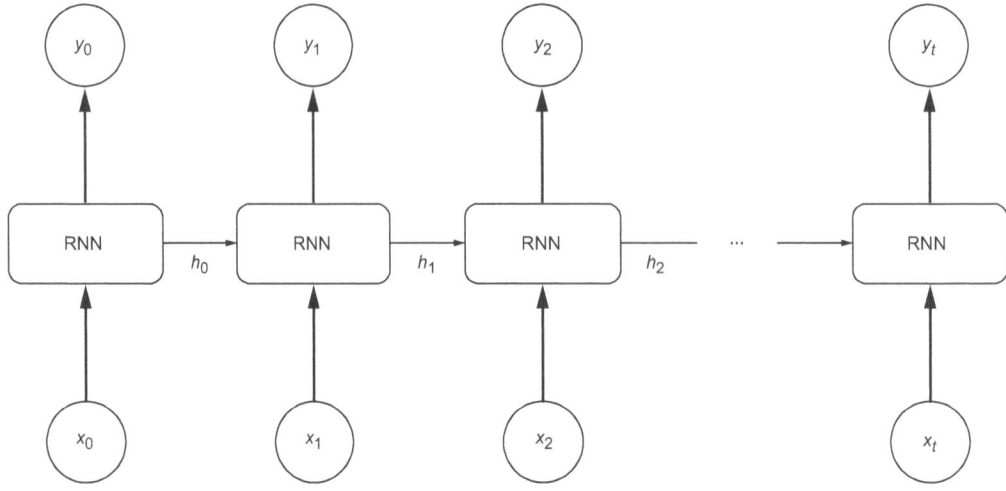

Figure 15.2   Expanded illustration of an RNN. Here you can see how the hidden state is updated and passed on to the next element of the sequence as an input.

Recurrent neural network

A recurrent neural network (RNN) is especially adapted to processing sequences of data. It uses a hidden state that is fed back into the network so it can use past information as an input when processing the next element of a sequence. This is how it replicates the concept of memory.

However, RNNs suffer from short-term memory, meaning that information from an early element in the sequence will stop having an impact further into the sequence.

However, the basic RNNs that we have examined come with a drawback: they suffer from short-term memory due to the vanishing gradient. The gradient is simply the function that tells the network how to change the weights. If the change in gradient is large, the weights change by a large magnitude. On the other hand, if the change in gradient is small, the weights do not change significantly. The vanishing gradient problem refers to what happens when the change in gradient becomes very small, sometimes close to 0. This in turn means that the weights of the network do not get updated, and the network stops learning.

In practice, this means the RNN forgets about past information that is far away in the sequence. It therefore suffers from a short-term memory. For example, if an RNN is processing 24 hours of hourly data, the points at hours 9, 10, and 11 might still impact the output at hour 12, but any point prior to hour 9 might not contribute at all to the network's learning, because the gradient gets very small for those early data points.

Therefore, we must find a way to retain the importance of past information in our network. This brings us to the long short-term memory (LSTM) architecture, which uses the cell state as an additional way of keeping past information in memory for a long time.

15.2 *Examining the LSTM architecture*

The *long short-term memory* (LSTM) architecture adds a cell state to the RNN architecture to avoid the vanishing gradient problem, where past information ceases to impact the learning of the network. This allows the network to keep past information in memory for a longer time.

The LSTM architecture is shown in figure 15.3, and you can see that it is more complex than the basic RNN architecture. You'll notice the addition of the cell state, denoted as *C*. This cell state is what allows the network to keep past information in the network for a longer time, thus resolving the vanishing gradient problem. Note that this is unique to the LSTM architecture. We still have an element of a sequence being processed, shown as x_t, and a hidden state is also computed, denoted as h_t. In this case, both the cell state C_t and the hidden h_t are passed on to the next element of the sequence, making sure that past information is used as an input for the next element in the sequence being processed.

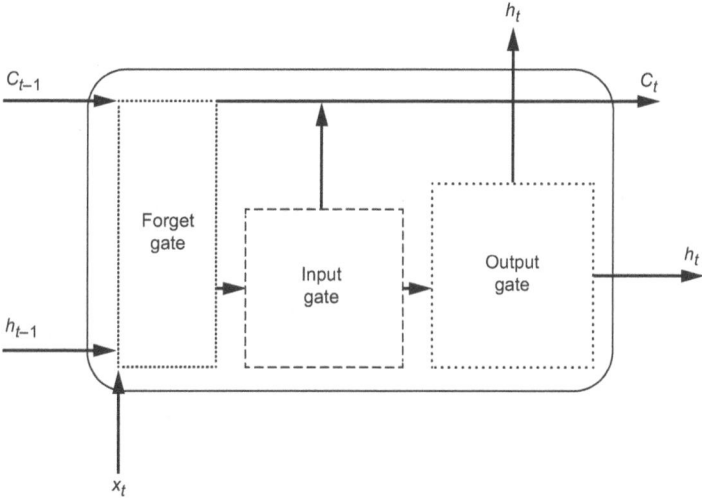

Figure 15.3   The architecture of an LSTM neuron. The cell state is denoted as *C*, while the input is *x* and the hidden state is *h*.

You'll also notice the presence of three gates: the forget gate, the input gate, and the output gate. Each has its specific function in the LSTM, so let's explore each one in detail.

Long short-term memory

Long short-term memory (LSTM) is a deep learning architecture that is a subtype of RNN. LSTM addresses the problem of short-term memory by adding the cell state. This allows for past information to flow through the network for a longer period of time, meaning that the network still carries information from early values in the sequence.

The LSTM is made up of three gates:

- The *forget gate* determines what information from past steps is still relevant.
- The *input gate* determines what information from the current step is relevant.
- The *output gate* determines what information is passed on to the next element of the sequence or as a result to the output layer.

15.2.1 *The forget gate*

The *forget gate* is the first gate in an LSTM cell. Its role is to determine what information, from both the past values and the current value of the sequence, should be forgotten or kept in the network.

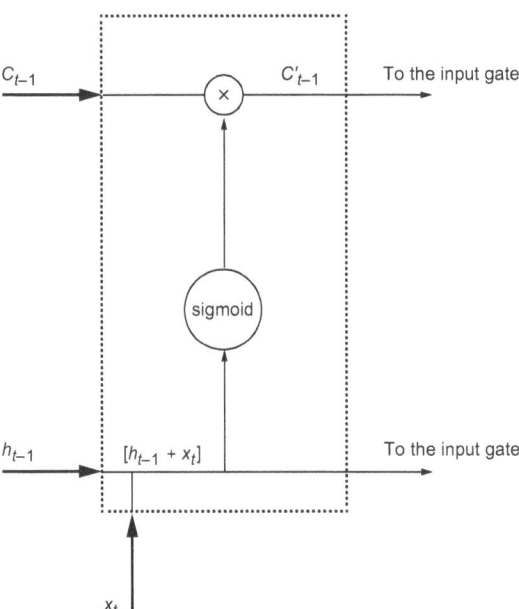

Figure 15.4   **The forget gate in an LSTM cell. The present element of a sequence, x_t, and past information, h_{t-1}, are first combined. They are duplicated, and one is sent to the input gate while the other goes through the sigmoid activation function. The sigmoid outputs a value between 0 and 1, and if the output is close to 0, this means that information must be forgotten. If it is close to 1, the information is kept. The output is then combined with the past cell state using pointwise multiplication, generating an updated cell state C'_{t-1}.**

Looking at figure 15.4, we can see how the different inputs flow through the forget gate. First, the past hidden state h_{t-1} and the present value of a sequence x_t are fed into the forget gate. Recall that the past hidden state carries information from past values. Then, h_{t-1} and x_t are combined and duplicated. One copy goes straight to the input gate, which we'll study in the next section. The other copy is sent through a sigmoid activation function, which is expressed as equation 15.1 and is shown in figure 15.5.

$$f(x) = \frac{1}{1 - e^{-x}}$$ **Equation 15.1**

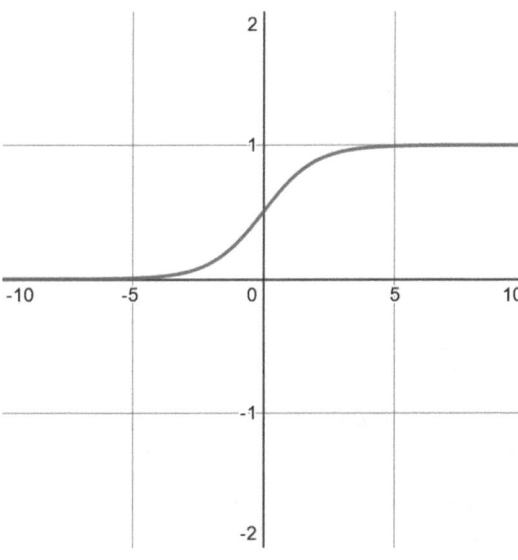

Figure 15.5   The sigmoid function outputs values between 0 and 1. In the context of the forget gate, if the output of the sigmoid function is close to 0, the output is information that is forgotten. If the output is close to 1, it is information that must be kept.

The sigmoid function determines which information to keep or to forget. That output is then combined with the previous cell state C_{t-1} using pointwise multiplication. This results in an updated cell state that we call C'_{t-1}.

Once this is done, two things are sent to the input gate: an updated cell state, and a copy of the combination of the past hidden state and the current element of the sequence.

15.2.2 The input gate

Once information has passed through the forget gate, it proceeds to the input gate. This is the step where the network determines which information is relevant from the current element of the sequence. The cell state is updated again here, resulting in the final cell state.

Again, let's zoom in on the input gate using figure 15.6. The combination of the past hidden state and the current element of a sequence $[h_{t-1} + x_t]$ coming from the forget gate is fed into the input gate and it is again duplicated. One copy goes out the input gate toward the output gate, which we'll explore in the next section. Another copy is sent through the sigmoid activation function to determine if the information will be kept or forgotten. Another copy is sent through the hyperbolic tangent (tanh) function, which is shown in figure 15.7.

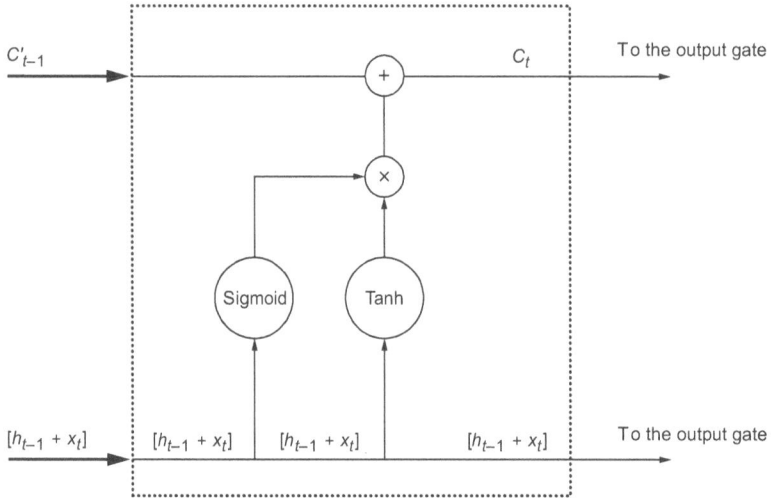

Figure 15.6   The input gate of an LSTM. The past hidden state and current element of the sequence are duplicated again and sent through a sigmoid activation function and a hyperbolic tangent (tanh) activation function. Again, the sigmoid determines what information is kept or discarded, while the tanh function regulates the network to keep it computationally efficient. The results of both operations are combined using pointwise multiplication, and the result is used to update the cell state using pointwise addition, resulting in the final cell state C_t. This final cell state is then sent to the output gate. Meanwhile, the same combination, $[h_{t-1} + x_t]$, is sent to the output gate too.

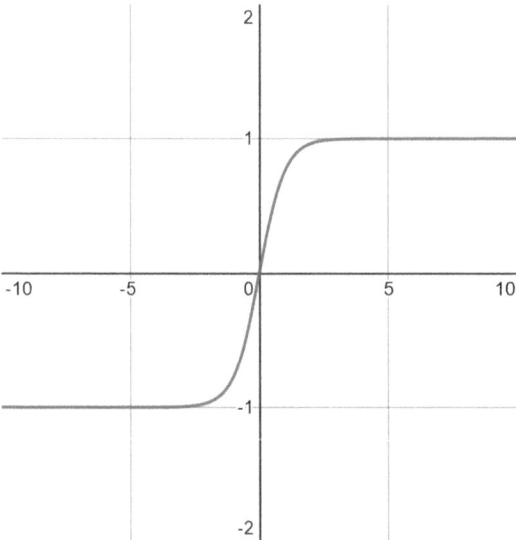

Figure 15.7   The hyperbolic tangent (tanh) function outputs values between –1 and 1. In the context of the LSTM, this serves as a way to regulate the network, making sure that values do not get very large and ensuring that computation remains efficient.

The outputs of the sigmoid and tanh functions are combined using pointwise multiplication, and the result is combined with the updated cell state coming from the forget gate C'_{t-1} using pointwise addition. This operation generates the final cell state C_t.

Therefore, it is in the input gate that we add information from the current element in the sequence to the long memory of the network. This newly updated cell state is then sent to the output gate.

15.2.3 *The output gate*

Information has now passed from the forget gate to the input gate, and now it arrives at the output gate. It is in this gate that past information contained in the network's memory, represented by the cell state C_t, is finally used to process the current element of the sequence. This is also where the network either outputs a result to the output layer or computes new information to be sent to the processing of the next element in the sequence.

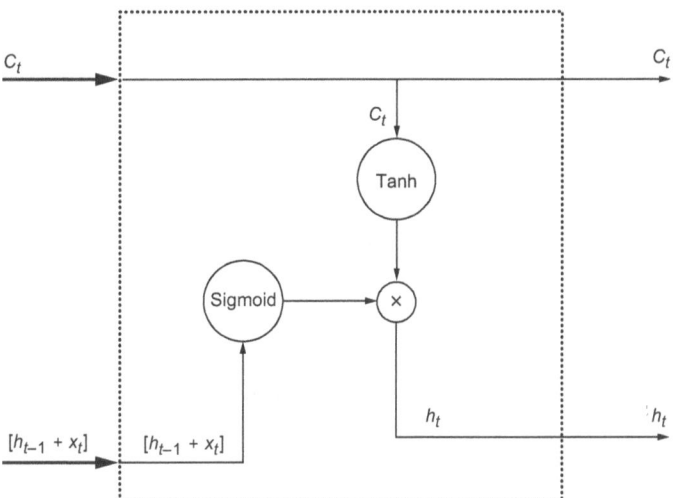

Figure 15.8   The output gate of an LSTM. The past hidden state and current element of a sequence [h_{t-1} + x_t] are passed through the sigmoid function to determine if information will be kept or discarded. Then the cell state is passed through the tanh function and combined with the output of the sigmoid using pointwise multiplication. This is the step where past information is used to process the current element of a sequence. We then output a new hidden state h_t, which is passed to the next LSTM neuron or to the output layer. The cell state is also output.

In figure 15.8 the past hidden state and current element of a sequence are sent through the sigmoid function. In parallel, the cell state goes through the tanh function.

The resulting values from the tanh and sigmoid functions are then combined using pointwise multiplication, generating an updated hidden state h_t. This is the step where past information, represented by the cell state C_t, is used to process the information of the present element of the sequence.

The current hidden state is then sent out of the output gate. This will either be sent to the output layer of the network or to the next LSTM neuron treating the next element of the sequence. The same applies for the cell state C_t.

In summary, the forget gate determines which information from the past is kept or discarded. The input gate determines which information from the current step is kept to update the network's memory or is discarded. Finally, the output gate uses the information from the past stored in the network's memory to process the current element of a sequence.

Having examined the inner workings of the LSTM architecture, we can now implement it for our interstate traffic dataset.

15.3 *Implementing the LSTM architecture*

We'll now implement the LSTM architecture for the interstate traffic dataset we have been working with since chapter 12. Recall that the main target of our scenario is the traffic volume. For the multi-output model, the targets are traffic volume and temperature.

We'll implement LSTM as a single-step model, a multi-step model, and a multi-output model. The single-step model will predict the traffic volume for the next timestep only, the multi-step model will predict the traffic volume for the next 24 hours, and the multi-output model will predict the temperature and traffic volume for the next timestep.

Make sure you have the `DataWindow` class and the `compile_and_fit` function (from chapters 13 and 14) in your notebook or Python script, as we'll use these pieces of code to create windows of data and train the LSTM model.

The other prerequisite is to read the training set, the validation set, and the test set, so let's do that right now:

```
train_df = pd.read_csv('../data/train.csv', index_col=0)
val_df = pd.read_csv('../data/val.csv', index_col=0)
test_df = pd.read_csv('../data/test.csv', index_col=0)
```

NOTE   At any point, feel free to consult the source code for this chapter on GitHub: https://github.com/marcopeix/TimeSeriesForecastingInPython/tree/master/CH15.

15.3.1 *Implementing an LSTM as a single-step model*

We'll start by implementing the LSTM architecture as a single-step model. In this case, we'll use 24 hours of data as an input to predict the next timestep. That way, there is a sequence of time that can be processed by the LSTM, allowing us to leverage past information to make a future prediction.

First we need to create a data window to train the model. This will be a wide window, with 24 hours of data as input. For plotting purposes, the `label_width` is also 24, so that we can compare the predictions to the actual values over 24 timesteps. Note that this is still a single-step model, so over 24 hours the model will only predict one timestep at a time, just like a rolling forecast.

```
wide_window = DataWindow(input_width=24, label_width=24, shift=1,
➥ label_columns=['traffic_volume'])
```

Then we need to define our LSTM model in Keras. Again we'll use the `Sequential` model to allow us to stack different layers in our network. Keras conveniently comes with the `LSTM` layer, which implements an LSTM. We'll set `return_sequences` to `True`, as this signals Keras to use past information from the sequence, in the form of the hidden state and cell state, which we covered earlier. Finally, we'll define the output layer, which is simply a `Dense` layer with one unit because we are forecasting the traffic volume only.

```
lstm_model = Sequential([                    Set return_sequences to True to
    LSTM(32, return_sequences=True),    ◄─┤  make sure that past information
    Dense(units=1)                            is being used by the network.
])
```

It is as simple as that. We can now train the model using the `compile_and_fit` function and store its performance on the validation and test sets.

```
history = compile_and_fit(lstm_model, wide_window)

val_performance = {}
performance = {}

val_performance['LSTM'] = lstm_model.evaluate(wide_window.val)
performance['LSTM'] = lstm_model.evaluate(wide_window.test, verbose=0)
```

Optionally, we can visualize the predictions of our model on three sampled sequences using the `plot` method of our data window. The result is shown in figure 15.9.

```
wide_window.plot(lstm_model)
```

Figure 15.9 shows that we have a performant model generating accurate predictions. Of course, this visualization is only three sampled sequences of 24 hours, so let's visualize the model's performance on the entire validation and test sets and compare it to the previous models we have built so far.

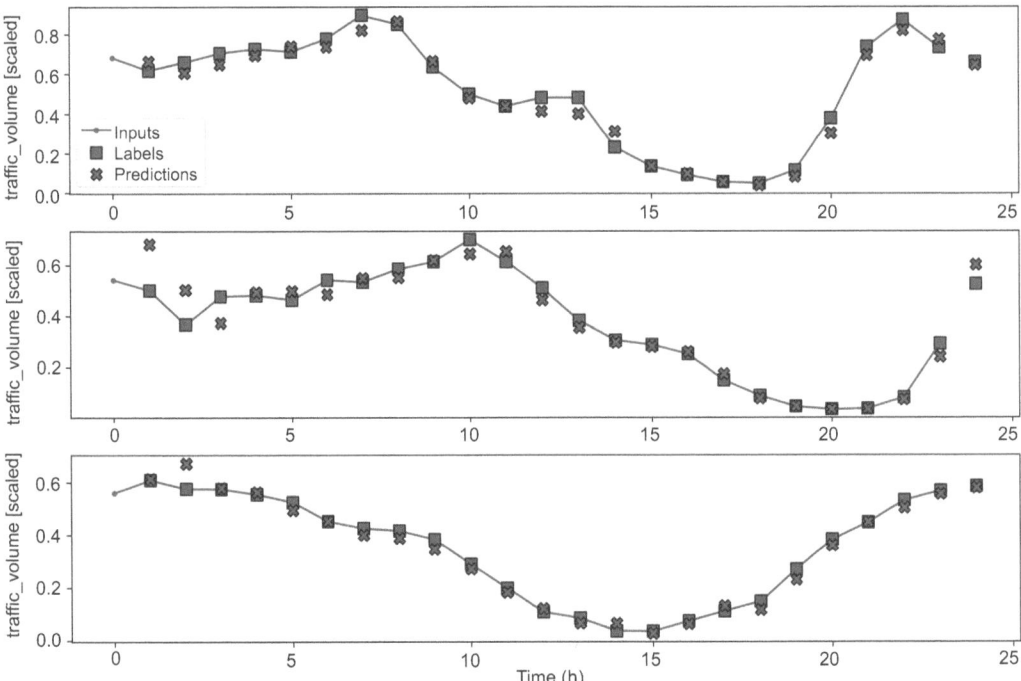

Figure 15.9   Predicting traffic volume using an LSTM as a single-step model. Many predictions (shown as crosses) overlap the labels (shown as squares), suggesting we have a performant model with accurate predictions.

Figure 15.10 shows that the LSTM is the winning model, since it has the lowest MAE on both the validation and test sets, meaning that it generated the most accurate predictions of all the models.

15.3.2 *Implementing an LSTM as a multi-step model*

We'll move on to implementing the LSTM architecture as a multi-step model. In this case, we wish to predict traffic volume for next 24 hours, using an input window of 24 hours.

First, we'll define the time window to feed our model. The `input_width` and `label_width` are both 24, since we want to input 24 hours of data and evaluate the predictions on 24 hours of data as well. This time the `shift` is also 24, specifying that the model must output predictions for the next 24 hours in a single shot.

```
multi_window = DataWindow(input_width=24, label_width=24, shift=24,
    label_columns=['traffic_volume'])
```

Next, we'll define our model in Keras. From chapter 14, you might recall that the process of defining the multi-step model and single-step model was exactly the same. The

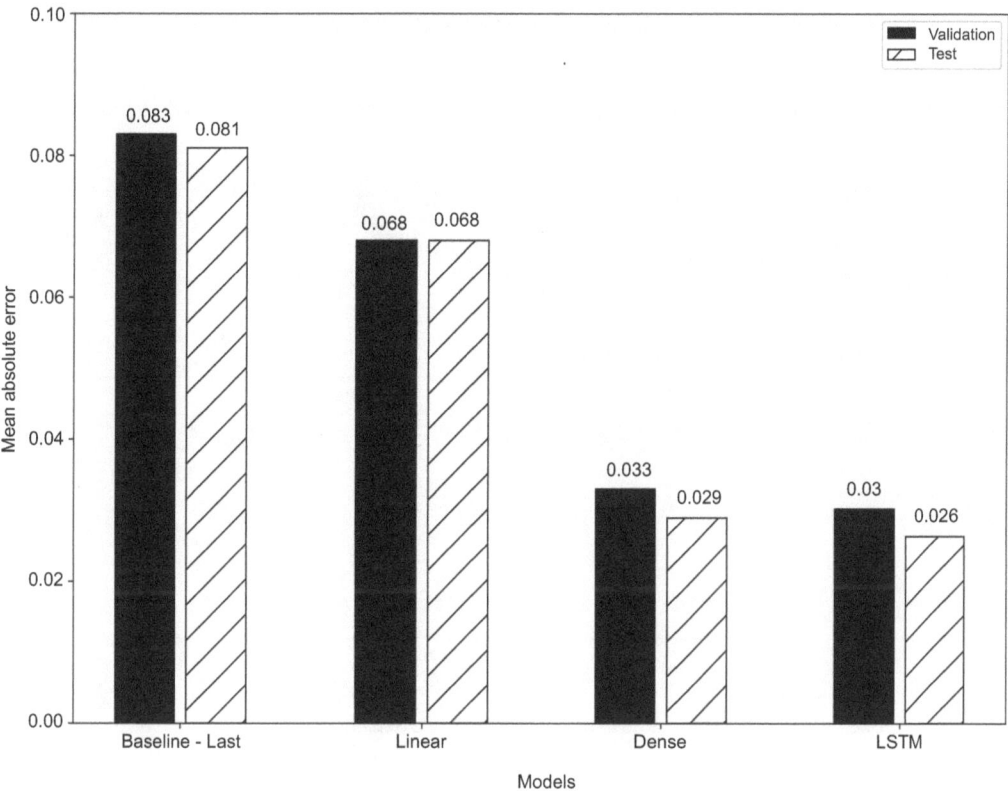

Figure 15.10 Mean absolute error (MAE) of all single-step models built so far. For now, the LSTM is the winning model, since it has the lowest MAE on both the validation and test sets.

same is true here. We still use the `Sequential` model, along with the `LSTM` layer and a `Dense` output layer with one unit.

```
ms_lstm_model = Sequential([
    LSTM(32, return_sequences=True),
    Dense(1, kernel_initializer=tf.initializers.zeros),
])
```

Once it's defined, we'll train the model and store its evaluation metrics for comparison. By now, you should be comfortable with this workflow.

```
history = compile_and_fit(ms_lstm_model, multi_window)

ms_val_performance = {}
ms_performance = {}

ms_val_performance['LSTM'] = ms_lstm_model.evaluate(multi_window.val)
ms_performance['LSTM'] = ms_lstm_model.evaluate(multi_window.test,
➥ verbose=0)
```

We can visualize the predictions of the model using the plot method, as shown in figure 15.11.

```
multi_window.plot(ms_lstm_model)
```

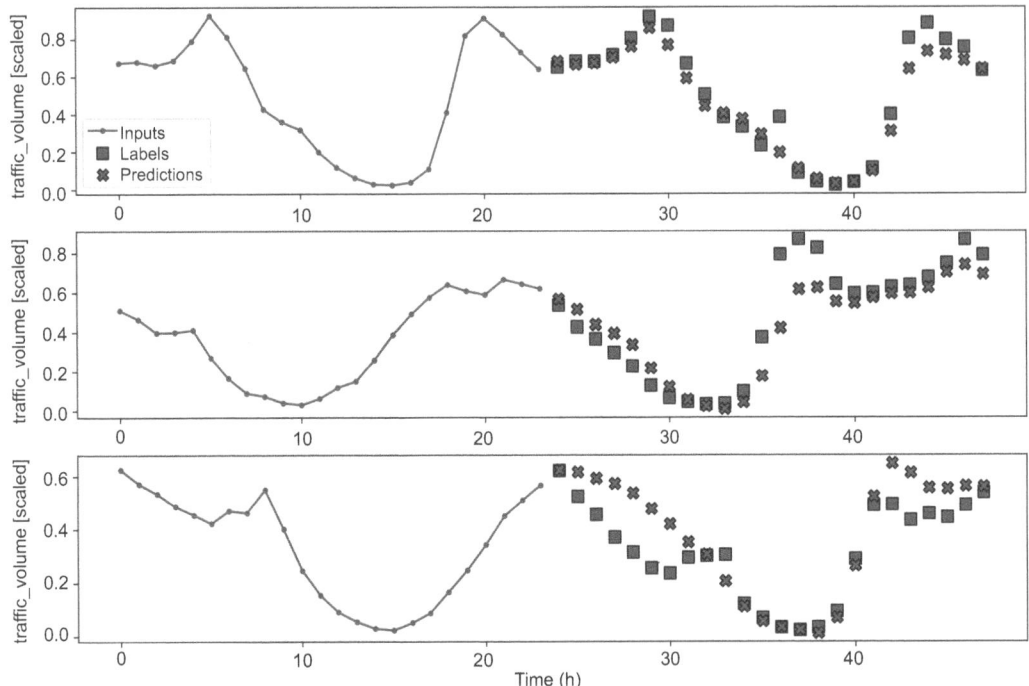

Figure 15.11 Predicting the traffic volume over the next 24 hours using a multi-step LSTM model. We can see some discrepancies between the predictions and the labels. Of course, this visual inspection is not enough to assess the performance of the model.

In figure 15.11 you'll see that the predictions for the top sequence are very good, as most predictions overlap the actual values. However, there are some discrepancies between the output and labels in the bottom two sequences. Let's compare its MAE to that of the other multi-step models we have built.

As you can see in figure 15.12, the LSTM is our most accurate model so far, as it achieved the lowest MAE on both the validation and test sets.

15.3.3 Implementing an LSTM as a multi-output model

Finally, we'll implement an LSTM as a multi-output model. Again, we'll use 24 hours of input data, so that the network can process a sequence of data points and use past information to produce forecasts. The predictions will be for both the traffic volume and temperature at the next timestep.

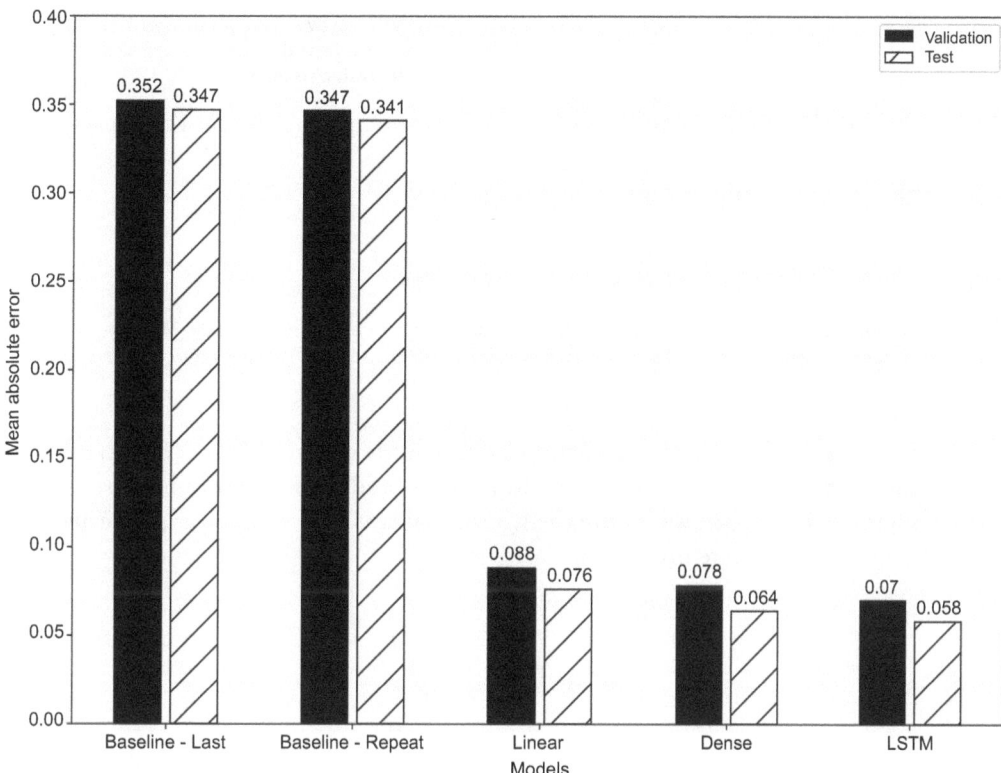

Figure 15.12   The MAE of all the multi-step models built so far. Again, the LSTM is the winning model, since it achieves the lowest MAE on both the validation and test sets.

In this situation, the data window consists of an input of 24 timesteps and 24 timesteps of labels. The shift is 1, as we want to produce forecasts for the next timestep only. Thus, our model will be creating rolling forecasts to generate predictions one time-step at a time, over 24 timesteps. We'll specify temp and traffic_volume as our target columns.

```
mo_wide_window = DataWindow(input_width=24, label_width=24, shift=1,
    label_columns=['temp','traffic_volume'])
```

The next step is to define our LSTM model. Just as before, we'll use the Sequential model to stack an LSTM layer and a Dense output layer with two units, since we have two targets.

```
mo_lstm_model = Sequential([
    LSTM(32, return_sequences=True),
```

```
    Dense(units = 2)
])
```

> We have two units because we have
> two targets: the temperature and
> the traffic volume.

Then we'll train the model and store its performance metrics for comparison.

```
history = compile_and_fit(mo_lstm_model, mo_wide_window)

mo_val_performance = {}
mo_performance = {}

mo_val_performance['LSTM'] = mo_lstm_model.evaluate(mo_wide_window.val)
mo_performance['LSTM'] = mo_lstm_model.evaluate(mo_wide_window.test,
    verbose=0)
```

We can now visualize the prediction for the traffic volume (figure 15.13) and temperature (figure 15.14). Both figures show many predictions (shown as crosses) overlapping the labels (shown as squares), which means that we have a performant model generating accurate predictions.

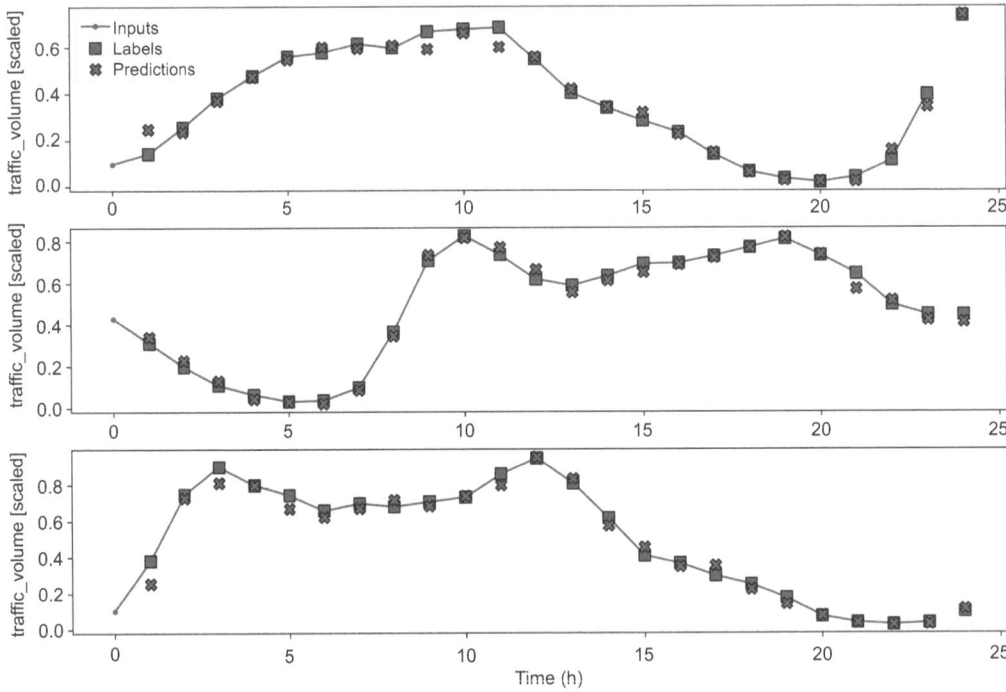

Figure 15.13 Predicting the traffic volume with an LSTM as a multi-output model. Many predictions (shown as crosses) overlap the labels (shown as squares), suggesting very accurate predictions for the traffic volume.

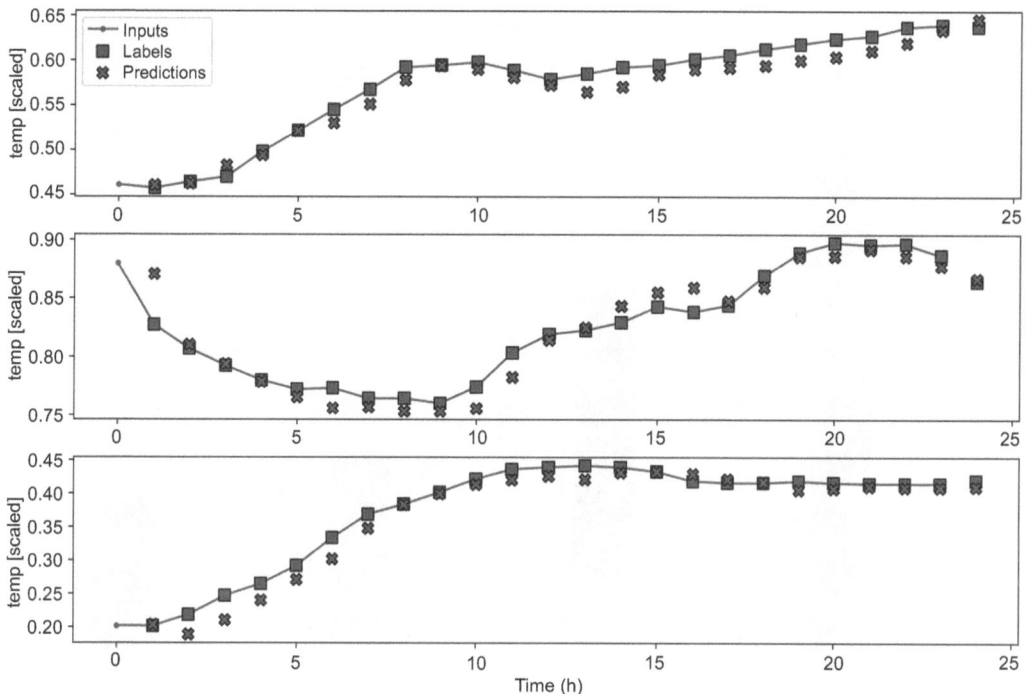

Figure 15.14   Predicting the temperature using an LSTM as a multi-output model. Again, we see a lot of overlap between the predictions (shown as crosses) and the labels (shown as squares), indicating accurate predictions.

Let's compare our LSTM model's performance to the other multi-output models built so far. Figure 15.15 again shows the LSTM as the winning model, since it achieves the lowest MAE on the validation and test sets. Thus, it generated the most accurate predictions so far for both our targets.

15.4   Next steps

In this chapter, we examined the long short-term memory (LSTM) architecture. You learned that it is a subtype of RNN, and you saw how it uses a cell state to overcome the problem of short-term memory that occurs in a basic RNN that uses only the hidden state.

We also studied the three gates of the LSTM. The forget gate determines which information from the past and present must be kept, the input gate determines the relevant information from the current element of a sequence, and the output gate uses the information stored in memory to generate a prediction.

We then implemented the LSTM as a single-step model, multi-step model, and multi-output model. In all cases, the LSTM was the winning model, as it achieved the lowest MAE of all models built so far.

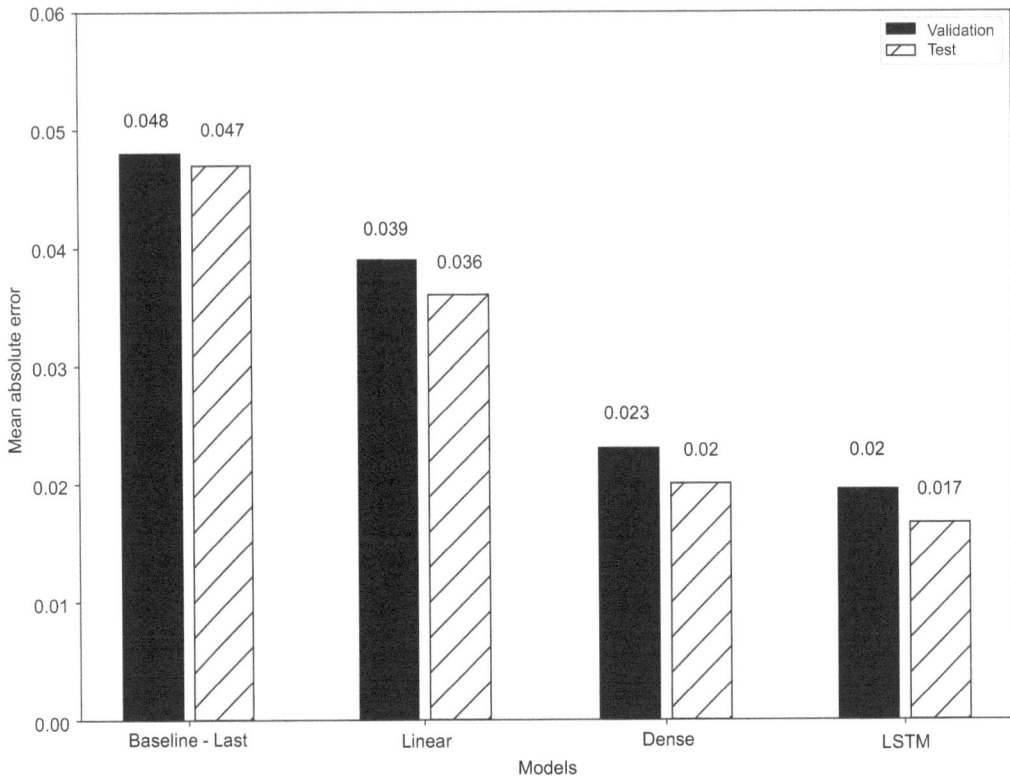

Figure 15.15   The MAE of all the multi-output models built so far. Again, the winning model is the LSTM, as it achieved the lowest MAE of all.

The deep learning architecture that we will explore in the next chapter is the *convolutional neural network* (CNN). You might have come across a CNN, especially in computer vision, as it is a very popular architecture for analyzing pictures. We will apply it for time series forecasting, as CNNs are faster to train than LSTMs, they are robust to noise, and they are good feature extractors.

15.5   Exercises

In the last chapter, we built linear models and deep neural networks to forecast the air quality. Now we'll try LSTM models and see if there is a gain in performance. The solution to these exercises can be found on GitHub: https://github.com/marcopeix/TimeSeriesForecastingInPython/tree/master/CH15.

1   For the single-step model:
   a   Build an LSTM model.
   b   Plot its predictions.

    c Evaluate it using the MAE and store the MAE.

    d Is it the most performant model?

2 For the multi-step model:

    a Build an LSTM model.

    b Plot its predictions.

    c Evaluate it using the MAE and store the MAE.

    d Is it the most performant model?

3 For the multi-output model:

    a Build an LSTM model.

    b Plot its predictions.

    c Evaluate it using the MAE and store the MAE.

    d Is it the most performant model?

At any point, try to experiment with the following ideas:

- Add more `LSTM` layers.
- Change the number of units in the `LSTM` layer.
- Set `return_sequences` to `False`.
- Experiment with different initializers in the output `Dense` layer.
- Run as many experiments as you want, and see how they impact the error metric.

Summary

- A recurrent neural network (RNN) is a deep learning architecture especially adapted to processing sequences of data like a time series.
- RNNs use a hidden state to store information in memory. However, this is only short-term memory due to the vanishing gradient problem.
- Long short-term memory (LSTM) is a type of RNN that addresses the short-term memory problem. It uses a cell state to store information for a longer time, giving the network a *long* memory.
- The LSTM is made of three gates:
  - The forget gate determines what information from the past and present must be kept.
  - The input gate determines what information from the present must be kept.
  - The output gate uses information stored in memory to process the current element of a sequence.

16

Filtering a time series with CNN

This chapter covers

- Examining the CNN architecture
- Implementing a CNN with Keras
- Combining a CNN with an LSTM

In the last chapter, we examined and implemented a long short-term memory (LSTM) network, which is a type of recurrent neural network (RNN) that processes sequences of data especially well. Its implementation was the top performing architecture for the single-step model, multi-step model, and multi-output model.

Now we're going to explore the *convolutional neural network* (CNN). CNNs are mostly applied in the field of computer vision, and this architecture is behind many algorithms for image classification and image segmentation.

Of course, this architecture can also be used for time series analysis. It turns out that CNNs are noise resistant and can effectively filter out the noise in a time series with the *convolution* operation. This allows the network to produce a set of robust features that do not include abnormal values. In addition, CNNs are usually faster to train than LSTMs, as their operations can be parallelized.

In this chapter, we'll first explore the CNN architecture and understand how the network filters a time series and creates a unique set of features. Then we'll implement a CNN using Keras to produce forecasts. We'll also combine the CNN architecture with the LSTM architecture to see if we can further improve the performance of our deep learning models.

16.1 Examining the convolutional neural network (CNN)

A convolutional neural network is a deep learning architecture that makes use of the convolution operation. The convolution operation allows the network to create a reduced set of features. Therefore, it is a way of regularizing the network, preventing overfitting, and effectively filtering the inputs. Of course, for this to make sense, you must first understand the convolution operation and how it impacts the inputs.

In mathematical terms, a convolution is an operation on two functions that generates a third function that expresses how the shape of one function is changed by the other. In a CNN, this operation occurs between the inputs and a *kernel* (also known as a *filter*). The kernel is simply a matrix that is placed on top of the feature matrix. In figure 16.1, the kernel is slid along the time axis, taking the dot product between the kernel and the features. This results in a reduced set of features, achieving regularization and the filtering of abnormal values.

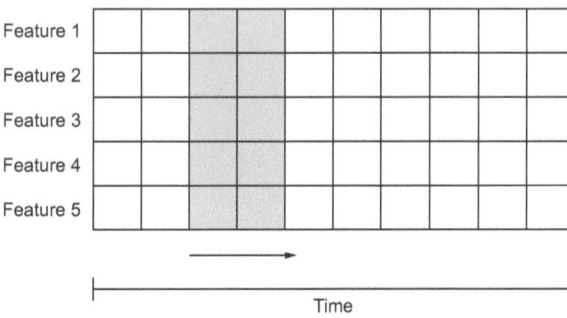

Figure 16.1   Visualizing the kernel and the feature map. The kernel is the light gray matrix that is applied on top of the feature map. Each row corresponds to a feature of the dataset, while the length is the time axis.

To better understand the convolution operation, let's consider a simple example with only one feature and one kernel, as shown in figure 16.2. To make things simple, we'll consider only one row of features. Keep in mind that the horizontal axis remains the time dimension. The kernel is a smaller vector that is used to perform the convolution operation. Do not worry about the values used inside the kernel and the feature vector. They are arbitrary values. The values of the kernel are optimized and will change as the network is trained.

| Feature | 2 | 3 | 12 | 0 | 3 | 1 |

| Kernel | 1 | 0 | 1 |

Figure 16.2   A simple example of one row of features and one kernel.

We can visualize the convolution operation and its result in figure 16.3. At first, the kernel is aligned with the beginning of the feature vector and the dot product is taken between the kernel and the values of the feature vector that are aligned with it. Once this is done, the kernel shifts one timestep to the right—this is also called a *stride* of one timestep. The dot product is again taken between the kernel and the feature vector, again only with the values that are aligned with the kernel. The kernel again shifts one timestep to the right, and the process is repeated until the kernel reaches the end of the feature vector. This happens when the kernel cannot be shifted any further with all of its values having an aligned feature value.

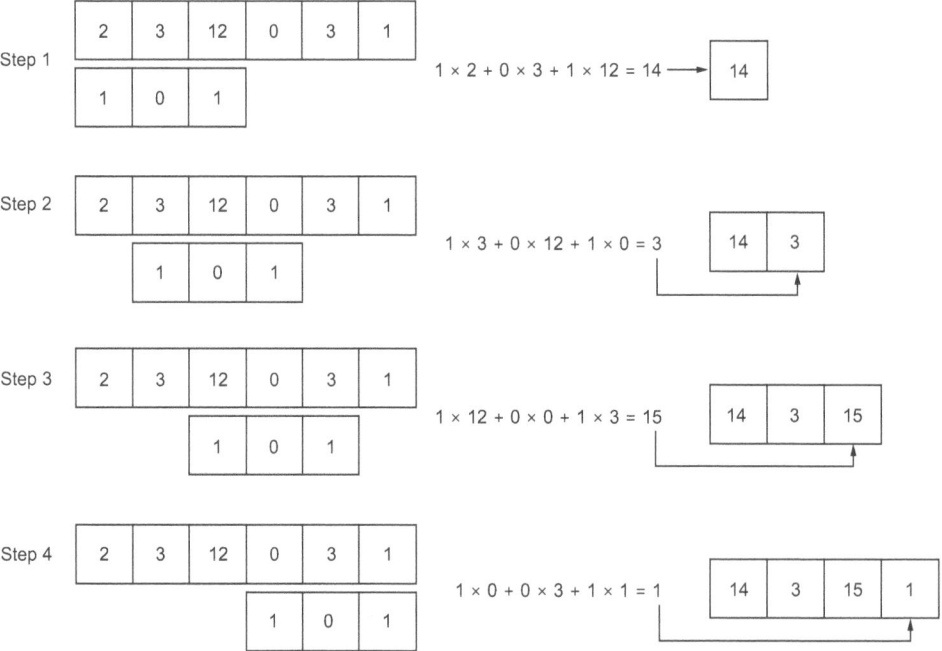

Figure 16.3   The full convolution operation. The operation starts with the kernel aligned at the beginning of the feature vector in step 1. The dot product is computed as shown by the intermediary equation of step 1, resulting in the first value in our output vector. In step 2, the kernel shifts one timestep to the right, and the dot product is taken again, resulting in the second value in the output vector. The process is repeated two more times until the kernel reaches the end of the feature vector.

In figure 16.3 you can see that using a feature vector of length 6 and a kernel of length 3, we obtain an output vector of length 4. Thus, in general, the length of the output vector of a convolution is given by equation 16.1.

$$\text{output length} = \text{input length} - \text{kernel length} + 1 \qquad \text{Equation 16.1}$$

Note that since the kernel is moving only in one direction (to the right), this is a *1D convolution*. Luckily, Keras comes with the Conv1D layer, allowing us to easily implement it in Python. This is mostly used for time series forecasting, as the kernel can only move in the time dimension. For image processing, you'll often see 2D or 3D convolutions, but that is outside of the scope of this book.

A convolution layer reduces the length of the set of features, and performing many convolutions will keep reducing the feature space. This can be problematic, as it limits the number of layers in the network, and we might lose too much information in the process. A common technique to prevent that is *padding*. Padding simply means adding values before and after the feature vector to keep the output length equivalent to the input length. Padding values are often zeros. You can see this in action in figure 16.4, where the output of the convolution is the same length as the input.

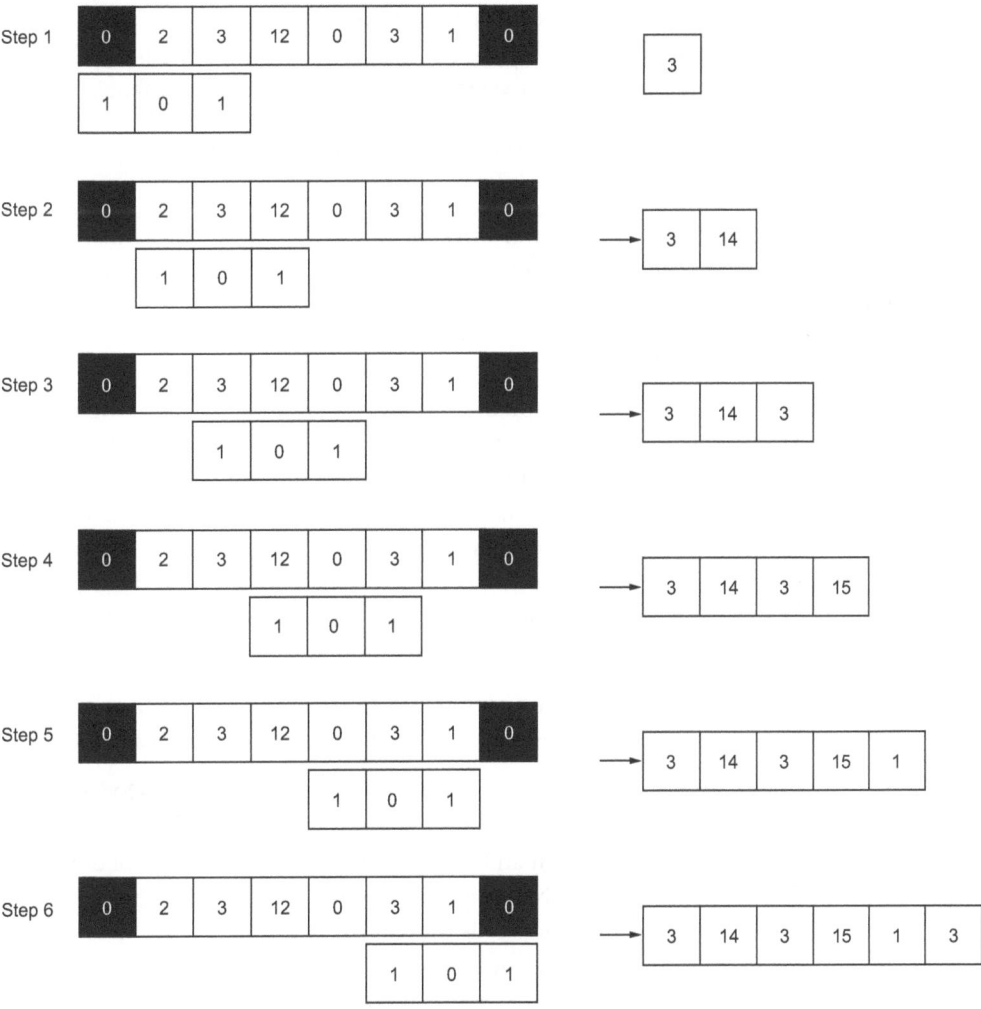

Figure 16.4   Convolution with padding. Here we padded the original input vector with zeros, as shown by the black squares. The output of the convolution thus has a length of 6, just like the original feature vector.

You can thus see how padding keeps the dimension of the output constant, allowing us to stack more convolution layers, and allowing the network to process features for a longer time. We use zeroes for padding because a multiplication by 0 is ignored. Thus, using zeroes as padding values is usually a good initial option.

Convolutional neural network (CNN)

A convolutional neural network (CNN) is a deep learning architecture that uses the convolution operation. This allows the network to reduce the feature space, effectively filtering the inputs and preventing overfitting.

The convolution is performed with a kernel, which is also trained during model fitting. The stride of the kernel determines the number of steps it shifts at each step of the convolution. In time series forecasting, only 1D convolution is used.

To avoid reducing the feature space too quickly, we can use padding, which adds zeros before and after the input vector. This keeps the output dimension the same as the original feature vector, allowing us to stack more convolution layers, which in turn allows the network to process the features for a longer time.

Now that you understand the inner working of a CNN, we can implement it with Keras and see if a CNN can produce more accurate predictions than the models we have built so far.

16.2 *Implementing a CNN*

As in previous chapters, we'll implement the CNN architecture as a single-step model, a multi-step model, and a multi-output model. The single-step model will predict the traffic volume for the next timestep only, the multi-step model will predict the traffic volume for the next 24 hours, and the multi-output model will predict the temperature and traffic volume at the next timestep.

Make sure you have the `DataWindow` class and the `compile_and_fit` function (from chapters 13 to 15) in your notebook or Python script, as we'll use both pieces of code to create windows of data and train the CNN model.

> **NOTE** The source code for this chapter is available on GitHub: https://github .com/marcopeix/TimeSeriesForecastingInPython/tree/master/CH16.

In this chapter, we'll also combine the CNN architecture with the LSTM architecture. It can be interesting to see if filtering our time series with a convolution layer and then processing the filtered sequence with an LSTM will improve the accuracy of our predictions. Thus, we'll implement both a CNN only, and the combination of a CNN with an LSTM.

Of course, the other prerequisite is to read the training set, the validation set, and the test set, so let's do that right now.

```
train_df = pd.read_csv('../data/train.csv', index_col=0)
val_df = pd.read_csv('../data/val.csv', index_col=0)
test_df = pd.read_csv('../data/test.csv', index_col=0)
```

Finally, we'll use a kernel length of three timesteps in our CNN implementation. This is an arbitrary value, and you will have a chance to experiment with various kernel lengths in this chapter's exercises and see how they impact the model's performance. However, your kernel should have a length greater than 1; otherwise, you are simply multiplying the feature space by a scalar, and no filtering will be achieved.

16.2.1 *Implementing a CNN as a single-step model*

We'll start by implementing a CNN as a single-step model. Recall that the single-step model outputs a prediction for traffic volume at the next timestep using the last known feature.

In this case, however, it does not make sense to provide the CNN model with only one timestep as an input because we want to run a convolution. We will instead use three input values to generate a prediction for the next timestep. That way we'll have a sequence of data on which we can run a convolution operation. Furthermore, our input sequence must have a length at least equal to the kernel's length, which in our case is 3. Recall that we expressed the relationship between the input length, kernel length, and output length in equation 16.1:

$$\text{output length} = \text{input length} - \text{kernel length} + 1$$

In this equation, no length can be equal to 0, since that would mean that no data is being processed or output. The condition that no length can be 0 is only satisfied if the input length is greater than or equal to the kernel length. Therefore, our input sequence must have at least three timesteps.

We can thus define the data window that will be used to train the model.

```
KERNEL_WIDTH = 3

conv_window = DataWindow(input_width=KERNEL_WIDTH, label_width=1, shift=1,
➥ label_columns=['traffic_volume'])
```

For plotting purposes, we would like to see the predictions of the model over a period of 24 hours. That way, we can evaluate the rolling forecasts of the model 1 timestep at a time, over 24 timesteps. Thus, we need to define another data window with a `label_width` of 24. The `shift` remains 1, as the model only predicts the next time-step. The input length is obtained by rearranging equation 16.1 as equation 16.2.

$$\text{output length} = \text{input length} - \text{kernel length} + 1$$

$$\text{input length} = \text{output length} + \text{kernel length} - 1 \qquad \textbf{Equation 16.2}$$

We can now simply compute the required input length to generate predictions over a sequence of 24 timesteps. In this case, the input length is $24 + 3 - 1 = 26$. That way, we avoid using padding. Later, in the exercises, you'll be able to try using padding instead of a longer input sequence to accommodate the output length.

We can now define our data window for plotting the predictions of the model.

```
LABEL_WIDTH = 24
INPUT_WIDTH = LABEL_WIDTH + KERNEL_WIDTH - 1
```
From equation
16.2

```
wide_conv_window = DataWindow(input_width=INPUT_WIDTH,
    label_width=LABEL_WIDTH, shift=1, label_columns=['traffic_volume'])
```

With all the data windows ready, we can define our CNN model. Again, we'll use the `Sequential` model from Keras to stack different layers. Then we'll use the `Conv1D` layer, as we are working with time series, and the kernel only moves in the temporal dimension. The `filters` parameter is equivalent to the `units` parameter of the `Dense` layer, and it simply represents the number of neurons in the convolutional layer. We'll set the `kernel_size` to the width of our kernel, which is 3. We don't need to specify the other dimensions, as Keras will automatically take the right shape to accommodate the inputs. Then we'll pass the output of the CNN to a `Dense` layer. That way, the model will be learning on a reduced set of features that were previously filtered by the convolutional step. We'll finally output a prediction with a `Dense` layer of only one unit, as we are forecasting only the traffic volume for the next timestep.

```
cnn_model = Sequential([
    Conv1D(filters=32,
           kernel_size=(KERNEL_WIDTH,),
           activation='relu'),
    Dense(units=32, activation='relu'),
    Dense(units=1)
])
```

The filters parameter is equivalent to the units parameter of the Dense layer; it defines the number of neurons in the convolutional layer.

The width of the kernel is specified, but the other dimensions are left out, as Keras automatically adapts to the shape of the inputs.

Next, we'll compile and fit the model, and we'll store its performance metrics for comparison later.

```
history = compile_and_fit(cnn_model, conv_window)

val_performance = {}
performance = {}

val_performance['CNN'] = cnn_model.evaluate(conv_window.val)
performance['CNN'] = cnn_model.evaluate(conv_window.test, verbose=0)
```

We can visualize the predictions against the labels using the `plot` method of our data window. The result is shown in figure 16.5.

```
wide_conv_window.plot(cnn_model)
```

As you can see in figure 16.5, many predictions overlap labels, meaning that we have fairly accurate predictions. Of course, we must compare this model's performance metrics to those of the other models to properly assess its performance.

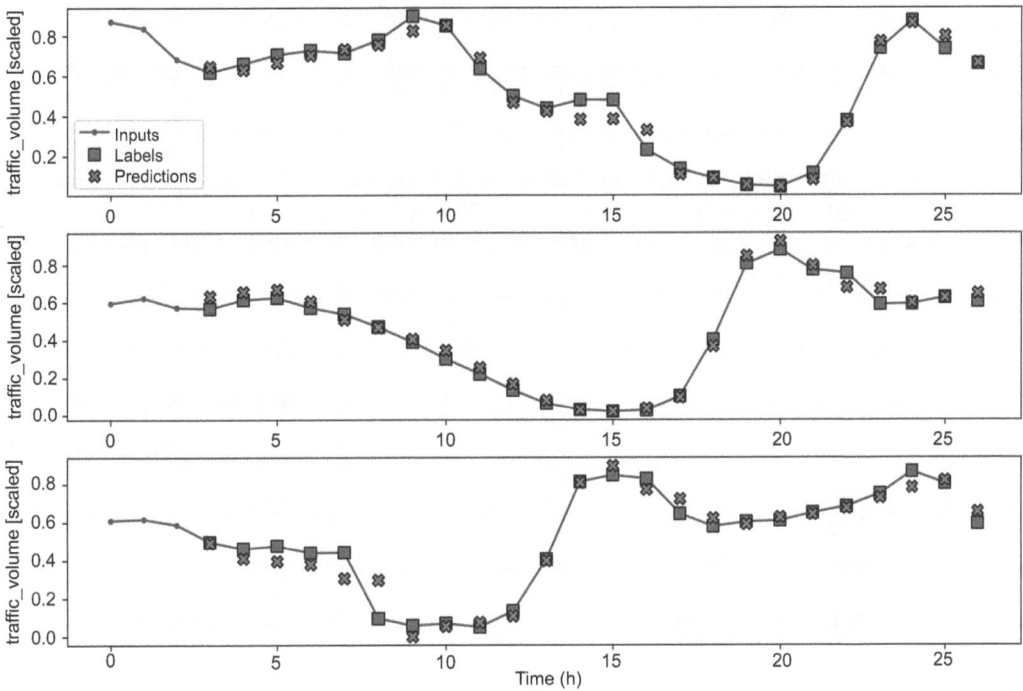

Figure 16.5 **Predicting traffic volume with a CNN as a single-step model. The model takes three values as an input, which is why we only see a prediction at the fourth timestep. Again, many predictions (shown as crosses) overlap labels (shown as squares), meaning that the model is fairly accurate.**

Before doing that, let's combine the CNN and LSTM architectures into a single model. You saw in the previous chapter how the LSTM architecture resulted in the best-performing models so far. Thus, it is a reasonable hypothesis that filtering our input sequence before feeding it to an LSTM might improve the performance.

Thus, we'll follow the Conv1D layer with two LSTM layers. This is an arbitrary choice, so make sure you experiment with it later on. There is rarely only one good way of building models, so it is important to showcase what is possible.

```
cnn_lstm_model = Sequential([
    Conv1D(filters=32,
           kernel_size=(KERNEL_WIDTH,),
           activation='relu'),
    LSTM(32, return_sequences=True),
    LSTM(32, return_sequences=True),
    Dense(1)
])
```

We'll then fit the model and store its evaluation metrics.

```
history = compile_and_fit(cnn_lstm_model, conv_window)

val_performance['CNN + LSTM'] = cnn_lstm_model.evaluate(conv_window.val)
performance['CNN + LSTM'] = cnn_lstm_model.evaluate(conv_window.test,
➥  verbose=0)
```

With both models built and evaluated, we can look at the MAE of our newly built models in figure 16.6. As you can see, the CNN model did not perform any better than the LSTM, and the combination of CNN and LSTM resulted in a slightly higher MAE than the CNN alone.

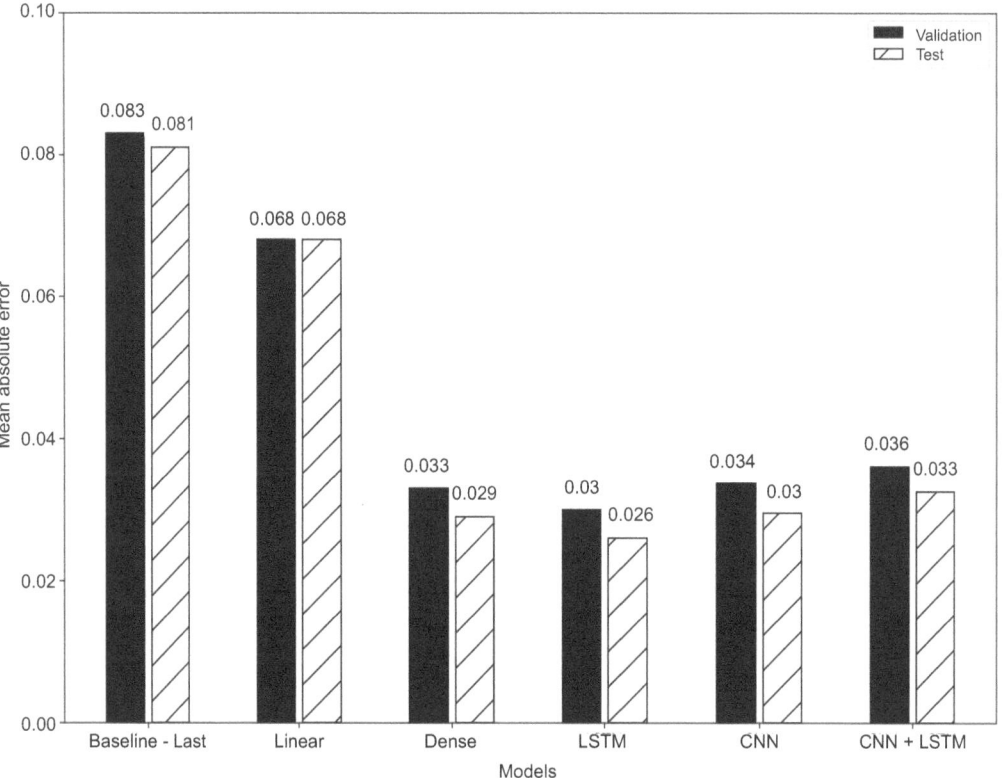

Figure 16.6   The MAE of all the single-step models built so far. You can see that the CNN did not improve upon the LSTM performance. Combining the CNN with an LSTM did not help either, and the combination even performed slightly worse than the CNN.

These results might be explained by the length of the input sequence. The model is given only an input sequence of three values, which might not be sufficient for the CNN to extract valuable features for predictions. While a CNN is better than the baseline model and the linear model, the LSTM remains the best-performing single-step model for now.

16.2.2 *Implementing a CNN as a multi-step model*

We'll now move on to the multi-step model. Here we'll use the last known 24 hours to forecast the traffic volume over the next 24 hours.

Again, keep in mind that the convolution reduces the length of the features, but we still expect the model to generate 24 predictions in a single shot. Therefore, we'll reuse equation 16.2 and feed the model an input sequence with a length of 26 to make sure that we get an output of length 24. This, of course, means that we'll keep the kernel length of 3. We can thus define our data window for the multi-step model.

```
KERNEL_WIDTH = 3
LABEL_WIDTH = 24
INPUT_WIDTH = LABEL_WIDTH + KERNEL_WIDTH - 1

multi_window = DataWindow(input_width=INPUT_WIDTH, label_width=LABEL_WIDTH,
➡ shift=24, label_columns=['traffic_volume'])
```

Next, we'll define the CNN model. Again, we'll use the Sequential model, in which we'll stack the Conv1D layer, followed by a Dense layer with 32 neurons, and then a Dense layer with one unit, since we are predicting only traffic volume.

```
ms_cnn_model = Sequential([
    Conv1D(32, activation='relu', kernel_size=(KERNEL_WIDTH)),
    Dense(units=32, activation='relu'),
    Dense(1, kernel_initializer=tf.initializers.zeros),
])
```

We can then train the model and store its performance metrics for comparison later.

```
history = compile_and_fit(ms_cnn_model, multi_window)

ms_val_performance = {}
ms_performance = {}

ms_val_performance['CNN'] = ms_cnn_model.evaluate(multi_window.val)
ms_performance['CNN'] = ms_cnn_model.evaluate(multi_window.test, verbose=0)
```

Optionally, we can visualize the forecasts of the model using multi_window .plot(ms_cnn_model). For now, let's skip this and combine the CNN architecture with the LSTM architecture as previously. Here we'll simply replace the intermediate Dense layer with an LSTM layer. Once the model is defined, we can fit it and store its performance metrics.

```
ms_cnn_lstm_model = Sequential([
    Conv1D(32, activation='relu', kernel_size=(KERNEL_WIDTH)),
    LSTM(32, return_sequences=True),
    Dense(1, kernel_initializer=tf.initializers.zeros),
])

history = compile_and_fit(ms_cnn_lstm_model, multi_window)
```

```
ms_val_performance['CNN + LSTM'] =
↪ ms_cnn_lstm_model.evaluate(multi_window.val)
ms_performance['CNN + LSTM'] =
↪ ms_cnn_lstm_model.evaluate(multi_window.test, verbose=0)
```

With the two new models trained, we can evaluate their performance against all the multi-step models built so far. As you can see in figure 16.7, the CNN model did not improve upon the LSTM model. However, combining both models resulted in the lowest MAE of all the multi-step models, meaning that it generates the most accurate predictions. The LSTM model is thus dethroned, and we have a new winning model.

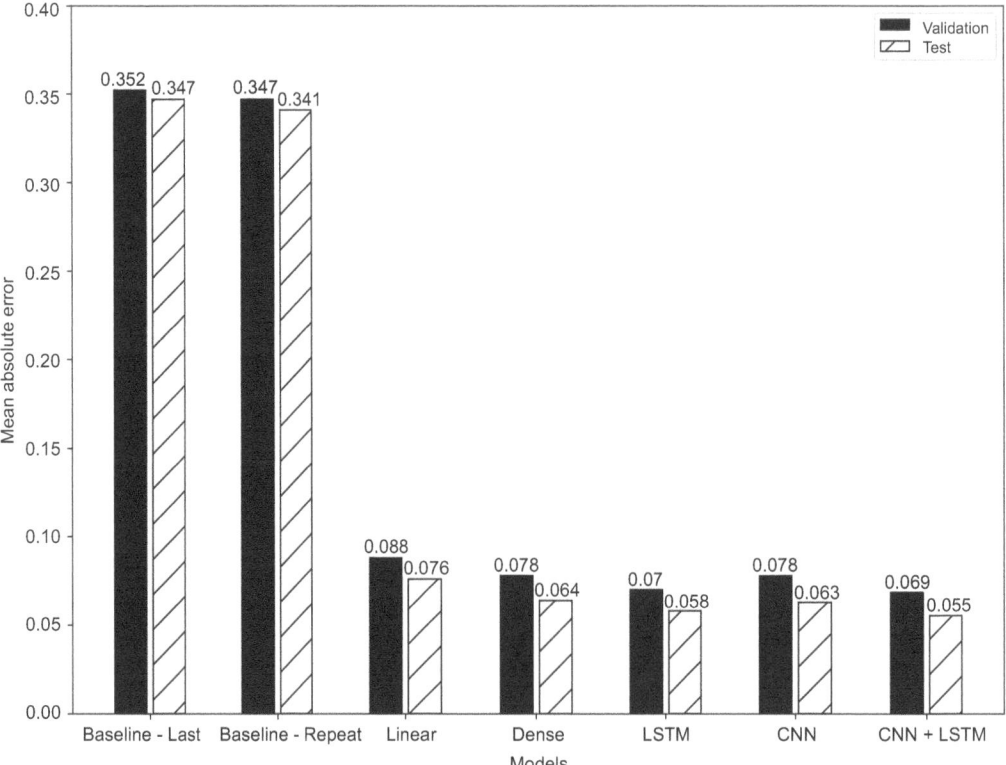

Figure 16.7   The MAE of all multi-step models built so far. The CNN model is worse than the LSTM model, since it has a higher MAE. However, combining the CNN with an LSTM resulted in the lowest MAE of all.

16.2.3   Implementing a CNN as a multi-output model

Finally, we'll implement the CNN architecture as a multi-output model. In this case, we wish to forecast the temperature and traffic volume for the next timestep only.

We have seen that giving an input sequence of length 3 was not sufficient for the CNN model to extract meaningful features, so we will use the same input length as for the multi-step model. This time, however, we are forecasting one timestep at a time over 24 timesteps.

We'll define our data window as follows:

```
KERNEL_WIDTH = 3
LABEL_WIDTH = 24
INPUT_WIDTH = LABEL_WIDTH + KERNEL_WIDTH - 1

wide_mo_conv_window = DataWindow(input_width=INPUT_WIDTH, label_width=24,
➥ shift=1, label_columns=['temp', 'traffic_volume'])
```

By now you should be comfortable building models with Keras, so defining the CNN architecture as a multi-output model should be straightforward. Again, we'll use the Sequential model, in which we'll stack a Conv1D layer, followed by a Dense layer, allowing the network to learn on a set of filtered features. The output layer will have two neurons, since we're forecasting both the temperature and the traffic volume. Next we'll fit the model and store its performance metrics.

```
mo_cnn_model = Sequential([
    Conv1D(filters=32, kernel_size=(KERNEL_WIDTH,), activation='relu'),
    Dense(units=32, activation='relu'),
    Dense(units=2)
])

history = compile_and_fit(mo_cnn_model, wide_mo_conv_window)

mo_val_performance = {}
mo_performance = {}

mo_val_performance['CNN'] = mo_cnn_model.evaluate(wide_mo_conv_window.val)
mo_performance['CNN'] = mo_cnn_model.evaluate(wide_mo_conv_window.test,
➥ verbose=0)
```

We can also combine the CNN architecture with the LSTM architecture as done previously. We'll simply replace the intermediate Dense layer with an LSTM layer, fit the model, and store its metrics.

```
mo_cnn_lstm_model = Sequential([
    Conv1D(filters=32, kernel_size=(KERNEL_WIDTH,), activation='relu'),
    LSTM(32, return_sequences=True),
    Dense(units=2)
])

history = compile_and_fit(mo_cnn_lstm_model, wide_mo_conv_window)

mo_val_performance['CNN + LSTM'] =
➥ mo_cnn_model.evaluate(wide_mo_conv_window.val)
mo_performance['CNN + LSTM'] =
➥ mo_cnn_model.evaluate(wide_mo_conv_window.test, verbose=0)
```

As usual, we'll compare the performance of the new models with the previous multi-output models in figure 16.8. You'll notice that the CNN, and the combination of

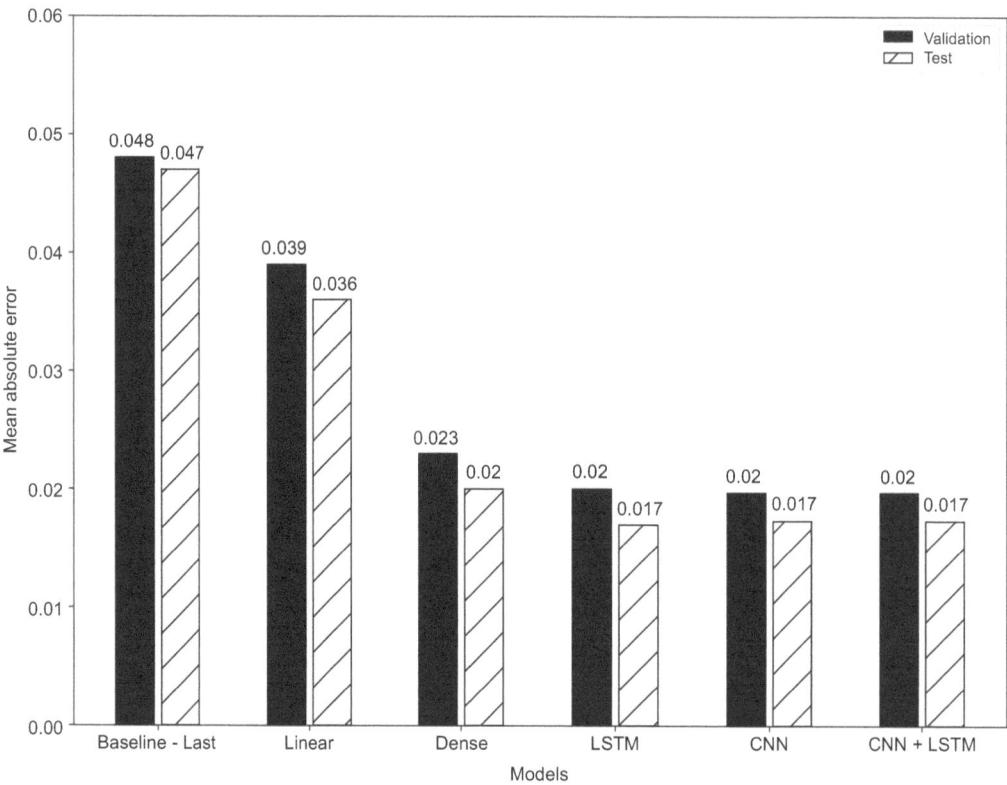

Figure 16.8 The MAE of all multi-output models built so far. As you can see, the CNN and the combination of CNN and LSTM did not result in improvements over the LSTM model.

CNN and LSTM, did not result in an improvement over the LSTM. In fact, all three models achieve the same MAE.

Explaining this behavior is hard, as deep learning models are black boxes, meaning that they are hard to interpret. While they can be very performant, the tradeoff lies in their explicability. Methods to interpret neural network models do exist, but they are outside of the scope of this book. If you want to learn more, take a look at Christof Molnar's book, *Interpretable Machine Learning, Second Edition* (https://christophm .github.io/interpretable-ml-book/).

16.3   *Next steps*

In this chapter, we examined the architecture of the CNN. We observed how the convolution operation is used in the network and how it effectively filters the input sequence with the use of a kernel. We then implemented the CNN architecture and combined it with the LSTM architecture to produce two new single-step models, multi-step models, and multi-output models.

In the case of the single-step models, using a CNN did not improve the results. In fact, it performed worse than the LSTM alone. For the multi-step models, we observed a slight performance boost and obtained the best-performing multi-step model with the combination of a CNN and an LSTM. In the case of the multi-output model, the use of a CNN resulted in constant performance, so we have a tie between the CNN, the LSTM, and the combination of CNN and LSTM. Thus, we can see that a CNN does not necessarily result in the best-performing model. In one situation it did, in another it did not, and in another there was no difference.

It is important to consider the CNN architecture as a tool in your toolset when it comes to modeling with deep learning. Models will perform differently depending on the dataset and the forecasting goal. The key lies in windowing your data correctly, as is done by the `DataWindow` class, and in following a testing methodology, as we have done by keeping the training set, validation set, and testing set constant and evaluating all models using the MAE against baseline models.

The last deep learning architecture that we are going to explore specifically concerns the multi-step models. Up until now, all multi-step models have output predictions for the next 24 hours in a single shot. However, it is possible to gradually predict the next 24 hours and feed a past prediction back into the model to output the next prediction. This is especially done with the LSTM architecture, resulting in an *autoregressive LSTM* (ARLSTM). This will be the subject of the next chapter.

16.4 Exercises

In the previous chapter's exercises, you built LSTM models. Now you'll experiment with a CNN and a combination of CNN and LSTM to see if you can gain in performance. The solutions to these exercises are available on GitHub: https://github.com/marcopeix/TimeSeriesForecastingInPython/tree/master/CH16.

1 For the single-step model:
   a Build a CNN model. Set the kernel width to 3.
   b Plot its predictions.
   c Evaluate the model using the mean absolute error (MAE) and store the MAE.
   d Build a CNN + LSTM model.
   e Plot its predictions.
   f Evaluate the model using the MAE and store the MAE.
   g Which model performs best?
2 For the multi-step model:
   a Build a CNN model. Set the kernel width to 3.
   b Plot its predictions.
   c Evaluate the model using the MAE and store the MAE.
   d Build a CNN+LSTM model.
   e Plot its predictions.

     f Evaluate the model using the MAE and store the MAE.

     g Which model performs best?

  3 Multi-output model:

     a Build a CNN model. Set the kernel width to 3.

     b Plot its predictions.

     c Evaluate the model using the MAE and store the MAE.

     d Build a CNN + LSTM model.

     e Plot its predictions.

     f Evaluate the model using the MAE and store the MAE.

     g Which model performs best?

As always, this is an occasion to experiment. You can explore the following:

- Add more layers.
- Change the number of units.
- Pad the sequence instead of increasing the input length. This is done in the `Conv1D` layer using the parameter `padding="same"`. In that case, your input sequence must have a length of 24.
- Use different layer initializers.

Summary

- The convolutional neural network (CNN) is a deep learning architecture that makes use of the convolution operation.
- The convolution operation is performed between a kernel and the feature space. It is simply the dot product between the kernel and the feature vector.
- Running a convolution operation results in an output sequence that is shorter than the input sequence. Running many convolutions can therefore decrease the output length quickly. Padding can be used to prevent that.
- In time series forecasting, the convolution is performed in one dimension only: the temporal dimension.
- The CNN is just another model in your toolbox and may not always be the best-performing model. Make sure you window your data correctly with `DataWindow`, and keep your testing methodology valid by keeping each set of data constant, building baseline models, and evaluating all models with the same error metric.

17
Using predictions to make more predictions

This chapter covers
- Examining the autoregressive LSTM (ARLSTM) architecture
- Discovering the caveat of the ARLSTM
- Implementing an ARLSTM

In the last chapter, we examined and built a convolutional neural network (CNN). We even combined it with the LSTM architecture to test whether we could outperform the LSTM models. The results were mixed, as the CNN models performed worse as single-step models, performed best as multi-step models, and performed equally well as multi-output models.

Now we'll focus entirely on the multi-step models, as all of them output the entire sequence of predictions in a single shot. We're going to modify that behavior and gradually output the prediction sequence, using past predictions to make new predictions. That way, the model will create rolling forecasts, but using its own predictions to inform the output.

This architecture is commonly used with LSTM and is called *autoregressive LSTM* (ARLSTM). In this chapter, we'll first explore the general architecture of the ARLSTM model, and then we'll build it in Keras to see if we can build a new top-performing multi-step model.

17.1 *Examining the ARLSTM architecture*

We have built many multi-step models that all output predictions for traffic volume in the next 24 hours. Each model has generated the entire prediction sequence in a single shot, meaning that we get 24 values from the model right away.

For illustration purposes, let's consider a simple model with only an LSTM layer. Figure 17.1 shows the general architecture of the multi-step models we have built so far. Each of them had inputs coming in, passing through a layer, whether it is LSTM, Dense, or Conv1D, and resulting in a sequence of 24 values. This type of architecture forces an output of 24 values.

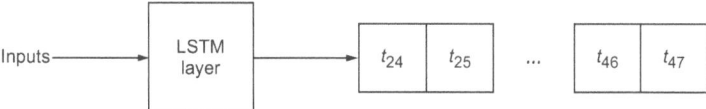

Figure 17.1   Illustrating a single-shot multi-step model with an LSTM layer. All multi-step models that we have built have had this general architecture. The LSTM layer can easily be replaced by a CNN layer or a dense layer.

But what if we want a longer sequence? Or a shorter sequence? What if we wish to forecast the next 8 hours only, or forecast the next 48 hours? In that case, we must redo our data windows and retrain the models, which might represent quite a bit of work.

Instead, we can opt for an autoregressive deep learning model. As you can see in figure 17.2, each prediction is sent back into the model, allowing it to generate the next prediction. This process is repeated until we obtain a sequence of the desired length.

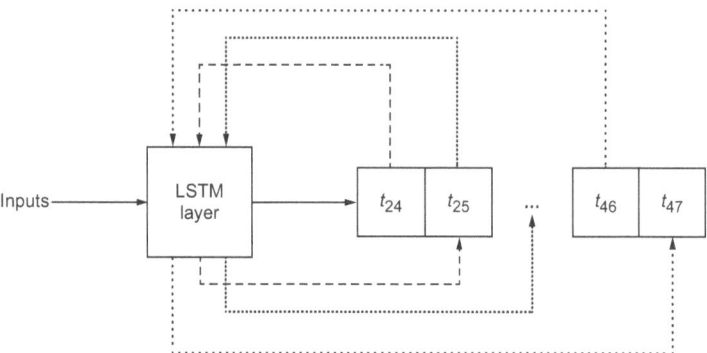

Figure 17.2   An autoregressive LSTM model. This model returns a first prediction at t_{24}, and it is sent back into the model to generate the prediction at t_{25}. This process is repeated until the desired output length is obtained. Again, an LSTM layer is shown, but it could be a CNN or a dense layer.

You can see how easy it becomes to generate any sequence length using an autoregressive deep learning architecture. This approach has the added advantage of allowing us to forecast time series with different scales, such as hours, days, or months, while avoiding having to retrain a new model. This is the type of architecture built by Google Deep-Mind to create WaveNet (https://deepmind.com/blog/article/wavenet-generative-model-raw-audio), a model that generates raw audio sequences. In the context of time series, DeepAR (http://mng.bz/GEoV) is a methodology that also uses an autoregressive recurrent neural network to achieve state-of-the-art results.

Nevertheless, autoregressive deep learning models come with a major caveat, which is the accumulation of error. We have forecast many time series, and we know that there is always some discrepancy between our predictions and the actual values. That error accumulates as it is fed back into the model, meaning that later predictions will have a larger error than earlier predictions. Thus, while the autoregressive deep learning architecture seems powerful, it might not be the best solution for a particular problem. Hence the importance of using a rigorous testing protocol, which is really what we have developed since chapter 13.

Still, it is good to have this model in your toolbox of time series forecasting methods. In the next section, we'll code an autoregressive LSTM model to produce forecasts for the next 24 hours. We'll compare its performance to that of our previous multi-step models.

17.2 Building an autoregressive LSTM model

We are now ready to code our own autoregressive deep learning model in Keras. Specifically, we'll code an ARLSTM model, since our experiments have shown that the LSTM model achieves the best performance of the multi-step models. Thus we'll try to further improve this model by making it autoregressive.

As always, make sure that you have the `DataWindow` class and the `compile_and_fit` function accessible in your notebook or Python script. They are the same versions that we developed in chapter 13.

> **NOTE**   At any time, feel free to consult the source code for this chapter on GitHub: https://github.com/marcopeix/TimeSeriesForecastingInPython/tree/master/CH17.

The first step is to read the training, validation, and test sets.

```
train_df = pd.read_csv('../data/train.csv', index_col=0)
val_df = pd.read_csv('../data/val.csv', index_col=0)
test_df = pd.read_csv('../data/test.csv', index_col=0)
```

Next, we'll define our window of data. In this case, we'll reuse the window of data we used for the LSTM model. The input and label sequences will each have 24 timesteps.

We'll specify a shift of 24 so that the model outputs 24 predictions. Our target remains the traffic volume.

```
multi_window = DataWindow(input_width=24, label_width=24, shift=24,
➥ label_columns=['traffic_volume'])
```

Now we'll wrap our model in a class called AutoRegressive, which inherits from the Model class in Keras. This is what allows us to access inputs and outputs. That way, we'll be able to specify that the output should become an input at each prediction step.

We'll start by defining the __init__ function in our AutoRegressive class. This function takes three parameters:

- self—References the instance of the AutoRegressive class.
- units—Represents the number of neurons in a layer.
- out_steps—Represents the length of the prediction sequence. In this case, it is 24.

Then we'll make use of three different Keras layers: the Dense layer, the RNN layer, and the LSTMCell layer. The LSTMCell layer is a lower-level layer than the LSTM layer. It allows us to access more granular information, such as state and predictions, which we can then manipulate to feed an output back into the model as an input. As for the RNN layer, this is used to train the LSTMCell layer on the input data. Its output is then passed through the Dense layer to generate a prediction. This is the complete __init__ function:

```
class AutoRegressive(Model):
    def __init__(self, units, out_steps):
        super().__init__()
        self.out_steps = out_steps
        self.units = units
        self.lstm_cell = LSTMCell(units)
        self.lstm_rnn = RNN(self.lstm_cell, return_state=True)
        self.dense = Dense(train_df.shape[1])
```

The number of neurons in a layer is defined by units, and the length of the prediction sequence is defined by out_steps.

The LSTMCell layer is a lower-level class that allows us to access more granular information, such as state and outputs.

The RNN layer wraps the LSTMCell layer so it is easier to train the LSTM on the data.

The prediction comes from this Dense layer.

With the initialization done, the next step is to define a function that outputs the very first prediction. Since this is an autoregressive model, that prediction is then fed back into the model as an input to generate the next prediction. We must therefore have a method to capture that very first forecast before entering the autoregressive loop.

Thus, we'll define the warmup function, which replicates a single-step LSTM model. We'll simply pass the inputs into the lstm_rnn layer, get the prediction from the Dense layer, and return both the prediction and the state.

```
def warmup(self, inputs):
    x, *state = self.lstm_rnn(inputs)
    prediction = self.dense(x)

    return prediction, state
```

Pass the inputs through the LSTM layer. The output is sent to the Dense layer.

Get a prediction from the Dense layer.

Now that we have a way to capture the first prediction, we can define the `call` function, which will run a loop to generate the sequence of predictions with a length of `out_steps`. Note that the function must be named `call` because it is called implicitly by Keras; naming it differently would result in an error.

Since we are using the `LSTMCell` class, which is a low-level class, we must manually pass in the previous state. Once the loop is finished, we stack our predictions and make sure they have the right output shape using the `transpose` method.

```
def call(self, inputs, training=None):
    predictions = []
    prediction, state = self.warmup(inputs)

    predictions.append(prediction)

    for n in range(1, self.out_steps):
        x = prediction
        x, state = self.lstm_cell(x, states=state, training=training)

        prediction = self.dense(x)
        predictions.append(prediction)

    predictions = tf.stack(predictions)
    predictions = tf.transpose(predictions, [1, 0, 2])

    return predictions
```

Initialize an empty list to collect all the predictions.

The first prediction is obtained from the warmup function.

Place the first prediction in the list of predictions.

The prediction becomes an input for the next one.

Generate a new prediction using the previous one as an input.

Use transpose to get the needed shape of (batch, time, features).

Stack all the predictions. At this point, we have a shape (time, batch, features). It must be changed to (batch, time, features).

The complete class is shown in the following listing. This code listing reuses the implementation found in the official TensorFlow documentation. This is again reused within the terms of the Apache 2.0 License. No modifications were made to this code snippet, as it follows all best practices of TensorFlow.

Listing 17.1 Defining a class to implement an ARLSTM model

```
class AutoRegressive(Model):
    def __init__(self, units, out_steps):
        super().__init__()
        self.out_steps = out_steps
        self.units = units
        self.lstm_cell = LSTMCell(units)
```

```
        self.lstm_rnn = RNN(self.lstm_cell, return_state=True)
        self.dense = Dense(train_df.shape[1])

    def warmup(self, inputs):
        x, *state = self.lstm_rnn(inputs)
        prediction = self.dense(x)

        return prediction, state

    def call(self, inputs, training=None):
        predictions = []
        prediction, state = self.warmup(inputs)

        predictions.append(prediction)

        for n in range(1, self.out_steps):
            x = prediction
            x, state = self.lstm_cell(x, states=state, training=training)

            prediction = self.dense(x)
            predictions.append(prediction)

        predictions = tf.stack(predictions)
        predictions = tf.transpose(predictions, [1, 0, 2])

        return predictions
```

We have now defined our AutoRegressive class, which implements an autoregressive LSTM model. We can use it and train a model on our data. We'll initialize it with 32 units and an output sequence length of 24 timesteps, since the objective of the multi-step model is to forecast the next 24 hours.

```
AR_LSTM = AutoRegressive(units=32, out_steps=24)
```

Next, we'll compile the model, train it, and store its performance metrics.

```
history = compile_and_fit(AR_LSTM, multi_window)

ms_val_performance = {}
ms_performance = {}

ms_val_performance['AR - LSTM'] = AR_LSTM.evaluate(multi_window.val)
ms_performance['AR - LSTM'] = AR_LSTM.evaluate(multi_window.test,
    verbose=0)
```

We can visualize the predictions of our model against the actual values by using the plot method from our DataWindow class.

```
multi_window.plot(AR_LSTM)
```

In figure 17.3 many predictions are very close to the actual values, sometimes even overlapping them. This indicates that we have a fairly accurate model.

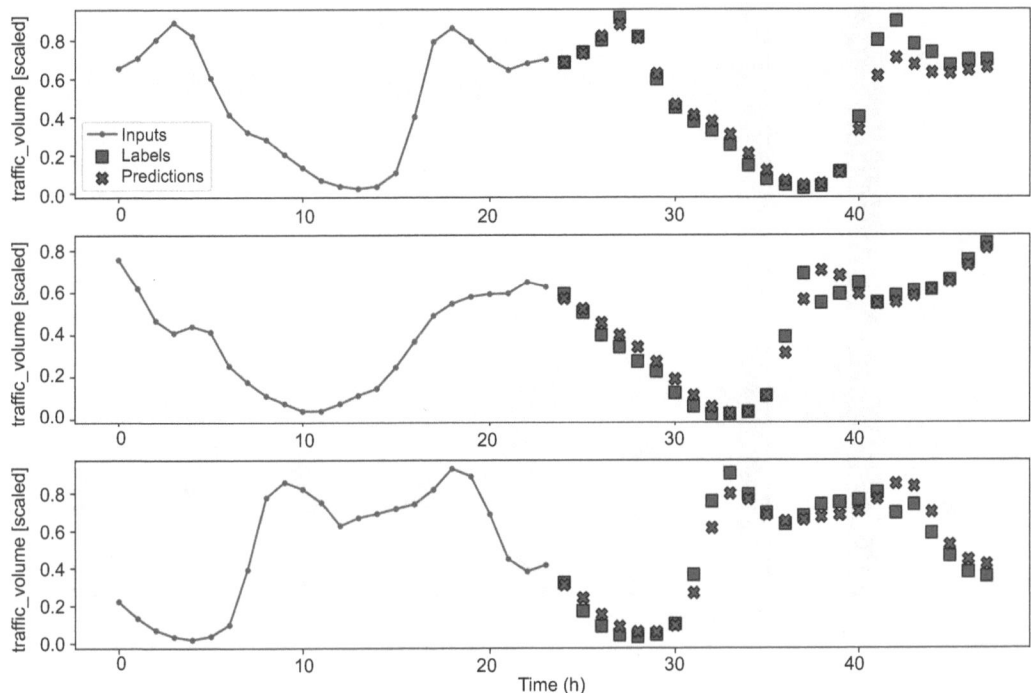

Figure 17.3   Forecasting traffic volume for the next 24 hours using an ARLSTM model. Many predictions (shown as crosses) overlap the actual values (shown as squares), which means that we have a fairly accurate model.

This visual inspection is not sufficient to determine whether we have a new top-performing model, so we'll display its MAE against that of all previous multi-step models. The result is shown in figure 17.4, which shows that our autoregressive LSTM model achieves an MAE of 0.063 on the validation set and 0.049 on the test set. This is a better score than the CNN, and the CNN + LSTM models, as well as the simple LSTM model. Thus, the ARLSTM model becomes the top-performing multi-step model.

Always keep in mind that the performance of each model depends on the problem at stake. The takeaway here is not that the ARLSTM is always the best model, but that it is the best-performing model for this situation. For another problem, you might find another champion model. If you have been completing the exercises since chapter 13, you can already see this happening. Keep in mind that each model we have built since chapter 13 is meant to be another tool in your toolbox to help you maximize the chances of solving a time series forecasting problem.

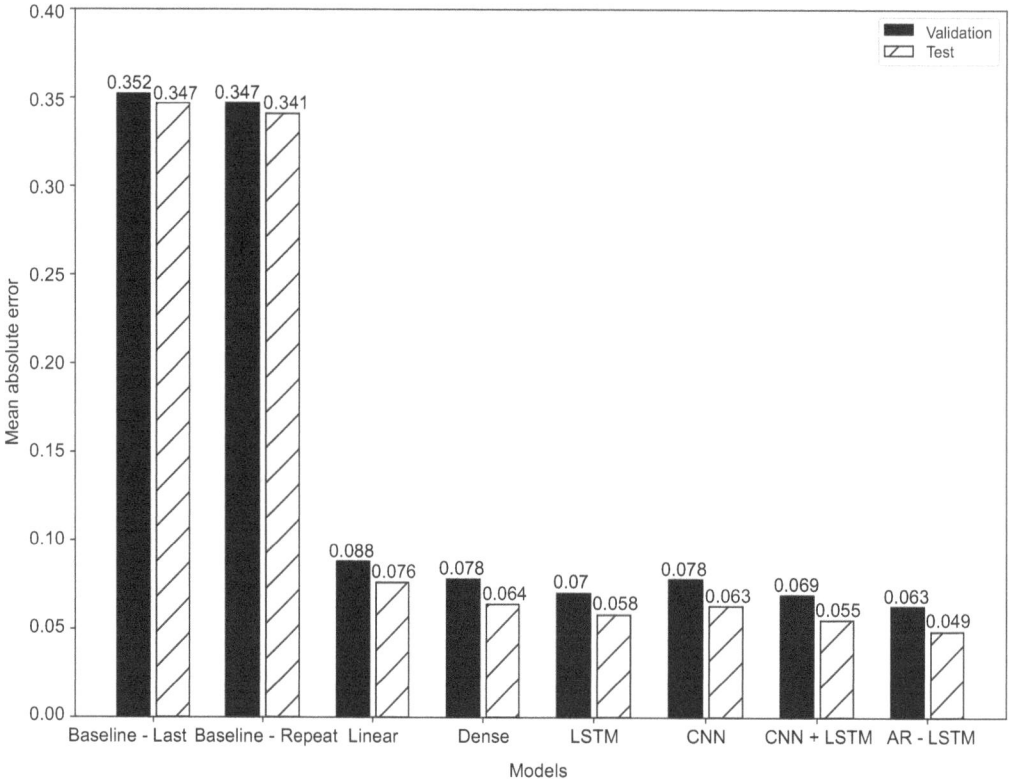

Figure 17.4   The MAE of all our multi-step models on the validation and test sets. The ARLSTM model achieves a lower MAE than the CNN and the CNN + LSTM models and the simple LSTM model.

17.3   Next steps

This is a rather short chapter, as it builds on concepts that we have already covered, such as the LSTM architecture and data windowing.

The autoregressive LSTM model outperformed the simple LSTM multi-step model in our example, and it performed better than a CNN model. Again, this does not mean that an ARLSTM model will always outperform a CNN model or a simple LSTM model. Each problem is unique, and a different architecture might result in the best performance for a different problem. The important thing is that you now have a wide array of models you can test and adapt to each problem in order to find the best solution possible.

This brings the deep learning part of the book almost to a conclusion. In the next chapter, we'll apply our knowledge of deep learning methods for time series forecasting in a capstone project. As before, a problem and dataset will be provided, and we must produce a forecasting model to solve the problem.

17.4 Exercises

In the exercises since chapter 13, we have built many models to forecast the air quality in Beijing using all three types of models (single-step, multi-step, and multi-output). Now we'll build one last multi-step model using an ARLSTM model. The solution can be found on GitHub: https://github.com/marcopeix/TimeSeriesForecastingInPython/tree/master/CH17.

1 For the multi-step model:
   a Build an ARLSTM model.
   b Plot its predictions.
   c Evaluate the model using the mean absolute error (MAE) and store the MAE for comparison.
   d Is the ARLSTM model the champion model?

Of course, feel free to experiment further. For example, you can vary the number of units to see how it impacts the model's performance.

Summary

- The autoregressive architecture in deep learning has given birth to state-of-the-art models, such as WaveNet and DeepAR.
- An autoregressive deep learning model generates a sequence of predictions, but each prediction is fed back into the model as an input.
- A caveat regarding autoregressive deep learning models is that errors accumulate as the length of the sequence increases. Therefore, an early bad prediction can have a large effect on a late prediction.

Capstone: Forecasting the electric power consumption of a household

This chapter covers

- Developing deep learning models to predict a household's electric power consumption
- Comparing various multi-step deep learning models
- Evaluating the mean absolute error and selecting the champion model

Congratulations on making it this far! In chapters 12 to 17, we dove headfirst into deep learning for time series forecasting. You learned that statistical models become inefficient or unusable when you have large datasets, which usually means more than 10,000 data points, with many features. We must then revert to using deep learning models, which can leverage all the available information while remaining computationally efficient, to produce forecasting models.

Just as we had to design a new forecasting procedure in chapter 6 when we started modeling time series with the $ARMA(p,q)$ model, modeling with deep learning techniques required us to use yet another modeling procedure: creating windows of data with the DataWindow class. This class plays a vital role in modeling with deep learning, as it allows us to format our data appropriately to create a set of inputs and labels for our models, as shown in figure 18.1.

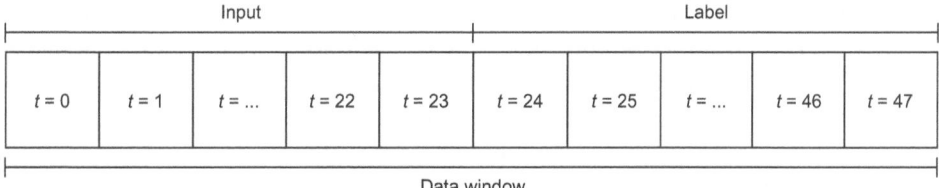

Figure 18.1   Example of a data window. This data window has 24 timesteps as input and 24 timesteps as output. The model will then use 24 hours of input to generate 24 hours of predictions. The total length of the data window is the sum of the lengths of inputs and labels. In this case, we have a total length of 48 timesteps.

This data windowing step allows us to produce a wide variety of models, from simple linear models to deep neural networks, long short-term memory (LSTM) networks, and convolutional neural networks (CNNs). Furthermore, data windowing can be used for different scenarios, allowing to us create single-step models where we predict only the next timestep, multi-step models where we predict a sequence of future steps, and multi-output models where we predict more than one target variable.

Having worked with deep learning in the last several chapters, it's time to apply our knowledge to a capstone project. In this chapter, we'll walk through the steps of a forecasting project using deep learning models. We'll first look at the project and describe the data that we'll use. Then we'll cover the data wrangling and preprocessing steps. Although those steps do not relate directly to time series forecasting, they are crucial steps in any machine learning project. We'll then focus on the modeling steps, where we'll try a set of deep learning models to uncover the best performer.

18.1   Understanding the capstone project

For this project, we'll use a dataset that tracks the electric power consumption of a household. The "Individual household electric power consumption" dataset is openly available from the UC Irvine Machine Learning Repository: https://archive.ics.uci .edu/ml/datasets/Individual+household+electric+power+consumption.

Forecasting electric energy consumption is a common task with worldwide applications. In developing countries, it can help in planning the construction of power grids. In countries where the grid is already developed, forecasting energy consumption ensures that the grid can provide enough energy to power all households efficiently. With accurate forecasting models, energy companies can better plan the load on the grid, ensuring that they are producing enough energy during peak times or have sufficient energy reserves to meet the demand. Also, they can avoid producing too much electricity, which, if it's not stored, could cause an imbalance in the grid, posing a risk of disconnection. Thus, forecasting electric energy consumption is an important problem that has consequences in our daily lives.

To develop our forecasting model, we'll use the power consumption dataset mentioned previously, which contains the electric consumption for a house in Sceaux,

France, between December 2006 and November 2010. The data spans 47 months and was recorded at every minute, meaning that we have more than two million data points.

The dataset contains a total of nine columns, listed in table 18.1. The main target is the global active power, as it represents the real power used in a circuit. This is the component that is used by the appliances. Reactive power, on the other hand, moves between the source and the load of a circuit, so it does not produce any useful work.

Table 18.1 Description of the columns in the dataset

Column name	Description
Date	Date in the following format: dd/mm/yyyy
Time	Time in the following format: hh:mm:ss
Global_active_power	The global active power in kilowatts
Global_reactive_power	The global reactive power in kilowatts
Voltage	Voltage in volts
Global_intensity	The current intensity in amperes
Sub_metering_1	Energy consumed in the kitchen by a dishwasher, oven, and microwave in watt-hours
Sub_metering_2	Energy consumed in the laundry room by a washing machine, tumble-dryer, refrigerator, and light in watt-hours
Sub_metering_3	Energy consumed by a water heater and air conditioner in watt-hours

This dataset does not include any weather information, which could potentially be a strong predictor of energy consumption. We can safely expect that during hot summer days, the air conditioning unit will function for longer, thus requiring more electrical power. The same can be expected during cold winter days, because heating a house requires a large amount of energy. This data is not available here, but in a professional setting we could request this type of data to augment our dataset and potentially produce better models.

Now that you have a general understanding of the problem and the dataset, let's define the objective of this project and the steps we'll take to achieve it.

18.1.1 *Objective of this capstone project*

The objective of this capstone project is to create a model that can forecast the next 24 hours of global active power. If you feel confident, this objective should be sufficient for you to download the dataset, work it on your own, and compare your process to the one presented in this chapter.

Otherwise, here are the steps that need to be done:

1 Data wrangling and preprocessing. This step is optional. It is not directly linked to time series forecasting, but it is an important step in any machine

learning project. You can safely skip this step and start at step 2 with a clean dataset:

  a Calculate the number of missing values.

  b Impute the missing values.

  c Express each variable as a numerical value (all data is originally stored as strings).

  d Combine the Date and Time columns into a `DateTime` object.

  e Determine whether the data sampled at every minute is usable for forecasting.

  f Resample the data by hour.

  g Remove any incomplete hours.

2 Feature engineering:

  a Identify any seasonality.

  b Encode the time with a sine and cosine transformation.

  c Scale the data.

3 Split the data:

  a Make a 70:20:10 split to create training, validation, and test sets.

4 Prepare for deep learning modeling:

  a Implement the `DataWindow` class.

  b Define the `compile_and_fit` function.

  c Create a dictionary of column indices and column names.

5 Model with deep learning:

  a Train at least one baseline model.

  b Train a linear model.

  c Train a deep neural network.

  d Train an LSTM.

  e Train a CNN.

  f Train a combination of LSTM and CNN.

  g Train an autoregressive LSTM.

  h Select the best-performing model.

You now have all the steps required to successfully complete this capstone project. I highly recommend that you try it on your own first, as that will reveal what you have mastered and what you need to review. At any point, you can refer to the following sections for a detailed walkthrough of each step.

The entire solution is available on GitHub: https://github.com/marcopeix/ TimeSeriesForecastingInPython/tree/master/CH18. Note that the data files were too large to be included in the repository, so you'll need to download the dataset separately. Good luck!

18.2 *Data wrangling and preprocessing*

Data wrangling is the process of transforming data into a form that is easily usable for modeling. This step usually involves exploring missing data, filling in blank values, and ensuring that the data has the right type, meaning that numbers are numerical values and not strings. This is a complex step, and it's probably the most vital one in any machine learning project. Having poor quality data at the start of a forecasting project is a guarantee that you'll have poor quality forecasts. You can skip this section of the chapter if you wish to focus solely on time series forecasting, but I highly recommend that you go through it, as it will really help you become comfortable with the dataset.

> **NOTE**   If you have not done so already, you can download the "Individual household electric power consumption" dataset from the UC Irvine Machine Learning Repository: https://archive.ics.uci.edu/ml/datasets/Individual+household +electric+power+consumption.

To perform this data wrangling, you can start by importing libraries that will be useful for data manipulation and visualization into a Python script or Jupyter Notebook.

```
import datetime

import numpy as np
import pandas as pd
import tensorflow as tf
import matplotlib.pyplot as plt

import warnings
warnings.filterwarnings('ignore')
```

Whenever numpy and TensorFlow are used, I like to set a random seed to ensure that the results can be reproduced. If you do not set a seed, your results might vary, and if you set a seed that's different than mine, your results will differ from those shown here.

```
tf.random.set_seed(42)
np.random.seed(42)
```

The next step is to read the data file into a DataFrame. We are working with a raw text file, but we can still use the read_csv method from pandas. We simply need to specify the separator, which is a semicolon in this case.

```
df = pd.read_csv('../data/household_power_consumption.txt', sep=';')
```
We can use this method with a .txt file as long as we specify the separator.

We can optionally display the first five rows with df.head() and the last five rows with df.tail(). This will show us that our data starts on December 16, 2006, at 5:24 p.m. and ends on November 26, 2010, at 9:02 p.m. and that the data was collected at every minute. We can also display the shape of our data with df.shape, showing us that we have 2,075,529 rows and 9 columns.

18.2.1 Dealing with missing data

Now let's check for missing values. We can do this by chaining the isna() method with the sum() method. This returns the sum of missing values for each column of our dataset.

```
df.isna().sum()
```

From the output shown in figure 18.2, only the Sub_metering_3 column has missing values. In fact, about 1.25% of its values are missing, according to the documentation of the data.

```
Date                      0
Time                      0
Global_active_power       0
Global_reactive_power     0
Voltage                   0
Global_intensity          0
Sub_metering_1            0
Sub_metering_2            0
Sub_metering_3        25979
dtype: int64
```

Figure 18.2 Output of the total number of missing values in our dataset. You can see that only the Sub_metering_3 column has missing values.

There are two options we can explore for dealing with the missing values. First, we could simply delete this column, since no other features have missing values. Second, we could fill in the missing values with a certain value. This process is called *imputing*.

   We'll first check whether there are many consecutive missing values. If that is the case, it is preferable to get rid of the column, as imputing many consecutive values will likely introduce a nonexistent trend in our data. Otherwise, if the missing values are dispersed across time, it is reasonable to fill them. The following code block outputs the length of the longest sequence of consecutive missing values:

```
na_groups =
    df['Sub_metering_3'].notna().cumsum()[df['Sub_metering_3'].isna()]
len_consecutive_na = na_groups.groupby(na_groups).agg(len)

longest_na_gap = len_consecutive_na.max()
```

This outputs a length of 7,226 consecutive minutes of missing data, which is equivalent to roughly 5 days. In this case, the gap is definitely too large to fill with missing values, so we'll remove this column from the dataset.

```
df = df.drop(['Sub_metering_3'], axis=1)
```

We no longer have any missing data in our dataset, so we can move on to the next step.

18.2.2 Data conversion

Now let's check if our data has the right type. We should be studying numerical data, as our dataset is a collection of sensor readings.

We can output the type of each column using df.dtypes, which shows us that each column is of object type. In pandas this means that our data is mostly text, or a mix of numeric and non-numeric values.

We can convert each column to a numerical value with the to_numeric function from pandas. This is essential, as our models expect numerical data. Note that we will not convert the date and time columns to numerical values—these will be processed in a later step.

```
cols_to_convert = df.columns[2:]

df[cols_to_convert] = df[cols_to_convert].apply(pd.to_numeric,
⮡ errors='coerce')
```

We can optionally check the type of each column again using df.dtypes to make sure that the values were converted correctly. This will show that every column from Global_active_power to Sub_metering_2 is now a float64 as expected.

18.2.3 Data resampling

The next step is to check if data sampled every minute is appropriate for modeling. It is possible that data sampled every minute is too noisy to build a performant predictive model.

To check this, we'll simply plot our target to see what it looks like. The resulting plot is shown in figure 18.3.

```
fig, ax = plt.subplots(figsize=(13,6))

ax.plot(df['Global_active_power'])
ax.set_xlabel('Time')
ax.set_xlim(0, 2880)

fig.autofmt_xdate()
plt.tight_layout()
```

Figure 18.3 shows that the data is very noisy, with large oscillations or flat sequences occurring at every minute. This kind of pattern is difficult to forecast using a deep learning model, since it seems to move at random. Also, we could question the need to forecast electricity consumption by the minute, as changes to the grid cannot occur in such short amounts of time.

Thus, we definitely need to resample our data. In this case, we'll resample by the hour. That way, we'll hopefully smooth out the data and uncover a pattern that may be easier to predict with a machine learning model.

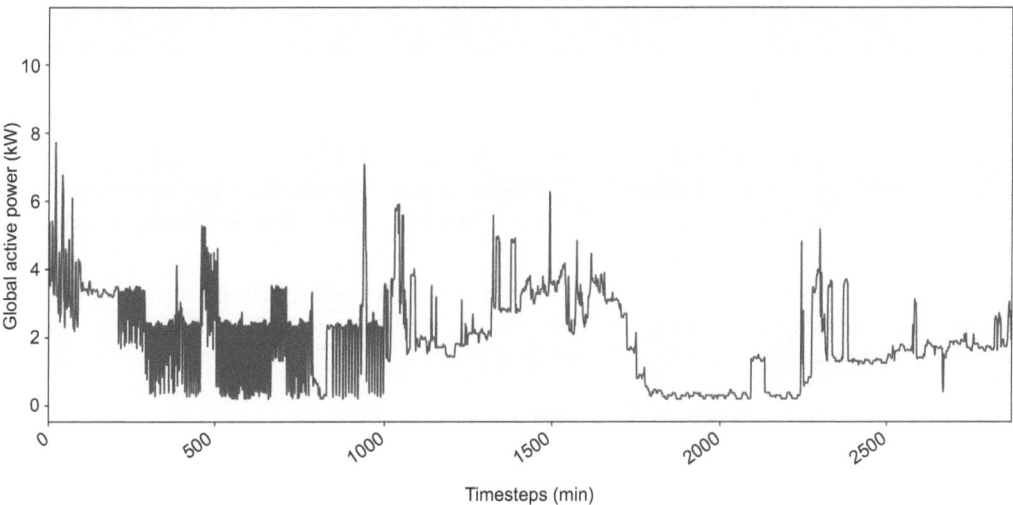

Figure 18.3   The first 24 hours of recorded global active power sampled every minute. You can see that the data is quite noisy.

To do this, we'll need a `datetime` data type. We can combine the Date and Time columns to create a new column that holds the same information with a `datetime` data type.

```
df.loc[:,'datetime'] = pd.to_datetime(df.Date.astype(str) + ' ' +
    df.Time.astype(str))                          ◁─────┐ This step will take a long time. Do
                                                         │ not worry if it seems like your
df = df.drop(['Date', 'Time'], axis=1)                   │ code is hanging.
```

Now we can resample our data. In this case, we'll take an hourly sum of each variable. That way we'll know the total electrical power consumed by the household every hour.

```
hourly_df = df.resample('H', on='datetime').sum()
```

Remember that our data started on December 16, 2006, at 5:24 p.m. and ended on November 26, 2010, at 9:02 p.m. With the new resampling, we now have a sum of each column per hour, which means that we have data that starts on December 16, 2006, at 5 p.m. and ends on November 26, 2010, at 9 p.m. However, the first and last rows of data do not have a full 60 minutes in their sum. The first row computed the sum from 5:24 p.m. to 5:59 p.m., which is 35 minutes. The last row computed the sum from 9:00 p.m. to 9:02 p.m., which is only 2 minutes. Therefore, we'll remove the first and last rows of data so that we are working only with sums over full hours.

```
hourly_df = hourly_df.drop(hourly_df.tail(1).index)
hourly_df = hourly_df.drop(hourly_df.head(1).index)
```

Finally, this process has changed the index. I personally prefer to have the index as integers and the dates as a column, so we'll simply reset the index of our `DataFrame`.

```
hourly_df = hourly_df.reset_index()
```

We can optionally check the shape of our data using `hourly_df.shape`, and we would see that we now have 34,949 rows of data. This is a drastic drop from the original two million rows. Nevertheless, a dataset of this size is definitely suitable for deep learning methods.

Let's plot our target again to see if resampling our data generated a discernible pattern that can be forecast. Here we'll plot the first 15 days of global active power sampled hourly:

```
fig, ax = plt.subplots(figsize=(13,6))

ax.plot(hourly_df['Global_active_power'])
ax.set_xlabel('Time')
ax.set_xlim(0, 336)

plt.xticks(np.arange(0, 360, 24), ['2006-12-17', '2006-12-18',
    '2006-12-19', '2006-12-20', '2006-12-21', '2006-12-22', '2006-12-23',
    '2006-12-24', '2006-12-25', '2006-12-26', '2006-12-27', '2006-12-28',
    '2006-12-29', '2006-12-30', '2006-12-31'])

fig.autofmt_xdate()
plt.tight_layout()
```

As you can see in figure 18.4, we now have a smoother pattern of global active power. Furthermore, we can discern daily seasonality, although it is not as apparent as previous examples in this book.

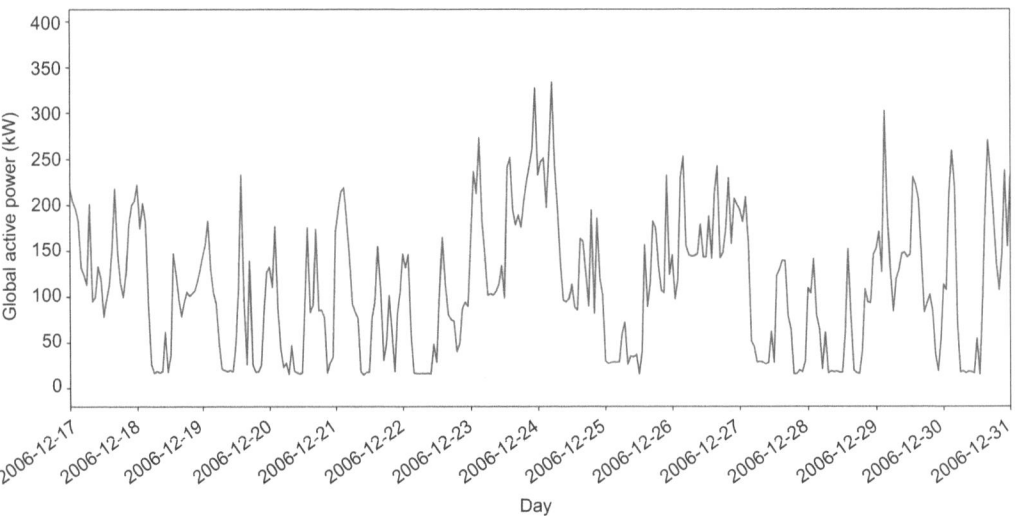

Figure 18.4   Total global active power sampled every hour. We now have a smoother pattern with daily seasonality. This is ready to be forecast with a deep learning model.

With the data wrangling done, we can save our dataset as a CSV file so we have a clean version of our data. This will be our starting file for the next section.

```
hourly_df.to_csv('../data/clean_household_power_consumption.csv',
header=True, index=False)
```

18.3   Feature engineering

At this point, we have a clean dataset with no missing values and a smoothed pattern that will be easier to predict using deep learning techniques. Whether you followed along with the last section or not, you can read a clean version of the data and start working on the feature engineering.

```
hourly_df = pd.read_csv('../data/clean_household_power_consumption.csv')
```

18.3.1   Removing unnecessary columns

The first step in feature engineering is to display the basic statistics for each column. This is especially useful for detecting whether there are any variables that do not vary greatly. Such variables should be removed, since if they are almost constant over time, they are not predictive of our target.

We can get a description of each column using the describe method from pandas:

```
hourly_df.describe().transpose()
```

As you can see in figure 18.5, Sub_metering_1 is likely not a good predictor for our target, since its constant value will not explain the variations in global active power. We can safely remove this column and keep the rest.

```
hourly_df = hourly_df.drop(['Sub_metering_1'], axis=1)
```

	count	mean	std	min	25%	50%	75%	max
Global_active_power	34949.0	64.002817	54.112103	0.0	19.974	45.868	93.738	393.632
Global_reactive_power	34949.0	7.253838	4.113238	0.0	4.558	6.324	8.884	46.460
Voltage	34949.0	14121.298311	2155.548246	0.0	14340.300	14454.060	14559.180	15114.120
Global_intensity	34949.0	271.331557	226.626113	0.0	88.400	196.600	391.600	1703.000
Sub_metering_1	34949.0	65.785430	210.107036	0.0	0.000	0.000	0.000	2902.000
Sub_metering_2	34949.0	76.139861	248.978569	0.0	0.000	19.000	39.000	2786.000

Figure 18.5   A description of each column in our dataset. You'll notice that Sub_metering_1 has a value of 0 for 75% of the time. Because this variable doesn't vary much over time, it can be removed from the set of features.

18.3.2 *Identifying the seasonal period*

With our target being global active power in a household, it is likely that we'll have some seasonality. We can expect that at night, less electrical power will be used. Similarly, there may be a peak in consumption when people come back from work during the week. Thus, it is reasonable to assume that there will be some seasonality in our target.

We can plot our target to see if we can visually detect the period.

```
fig, ax = plt.subplots(figsize=(13,6))

ax.plot(hourly_df['Global_active_power'])
ax.set_xlabel('Time')
ax.set_xlim(0, 336)

plt.xticks(np.arange(0, 360, 24), ['2006-12-17', '2006-12-18',
    '2006-12-19', '2006-12-20', '2006-12-21', '2006-12-22', '2006-12-23',
    '2006-12-24', '2006-12-25', '2006-12-26', '2006-12-27', '2006-12-28',
    '2006-12-29', '2006-12-30', '2006-12-31'])

fig.autofmt_xdate()
plt.tight_layout()
```

In figure 18.6 you can see that our target has some cyclical behavior, but the seasonal period is hard to determine from the graph. While our hypothesis about daily seasonality makes sense, we need to make sure that it is present in our data. One way to do it is with a Fourier transform.

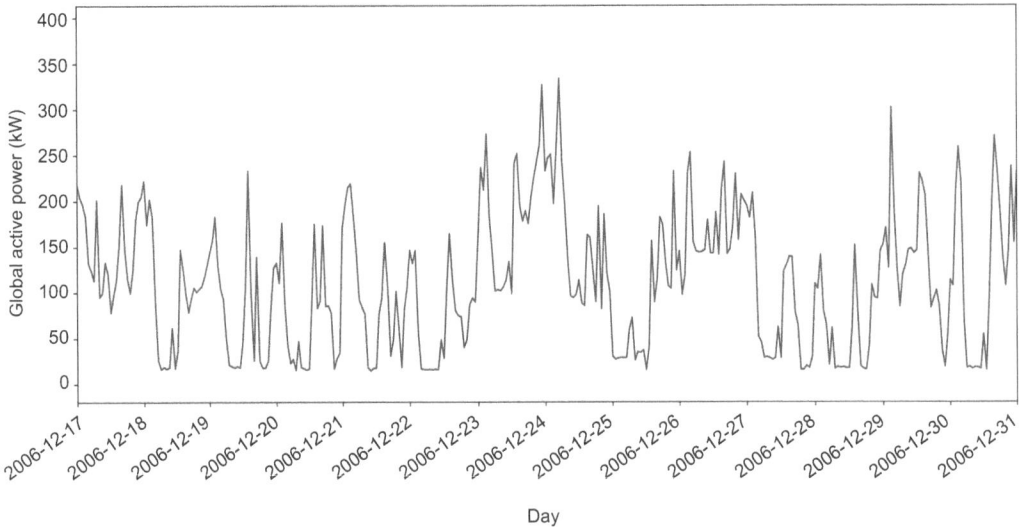

Figure 18.6 Total global active power in the first 15 days. While there is clear cyclical behavior, the seasonal period is hard to determine from the graph only.

Without diving into the details, a Fourier transform basically allows us to visualize the frequency and amplitude of a signal. Hence, we can treat our time series as a signal, apply a Fourier transform, and find the frequencies with large amplitudes. Those frequencies will determine the seasonal period. The great advantage of this method is that it is independent of the seasonal period. It can identify yearly, weekly, and daily seasonality, or any specific period we wish to test.

> **NOTE** For more information about Fourier transforms, I suggest reading Lakshay Akula's "Analyzing seasonality with Fourier transforms using Python & SciPy" blog post, which does a great job of gently introducing Fourier transforms for analyzing seasonality: http://mng.bz/7y2Q.

For our situation, let's test for weekly and daily seasonality.

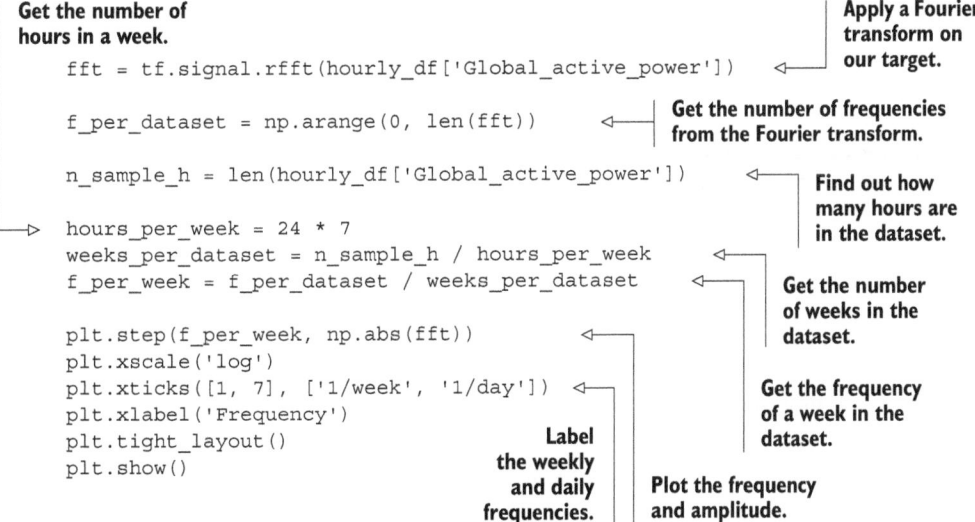

In figure 18.7 you can see the amplitude of the weekly and daily frequencies. The weekly frequency does not show any visible peak, meaning that its amplitude is very small. Therefore, there is no weekly seasonality.

Looking at the daily frequency, however, you'll notice a clear peak in the figure. This tells us that we indeed have daily seasonality in our data. Thus, we will encode our timestamp using a sine and cosine transformation to express the time while keeping its daily seasonal information. We did the same thing in chapter 12 when preparing our data for modeling with deep learning.

```
timestamp_s =
➥ pd.to_datetime(hourly_df.datetime).map(datetime.datetime.timestamp)

day = 24 * 60 * 60

hourly_df['day_sin'] = (np.sin(timestamp_s * (2*np.pi/day))).values
hourly_df['day_cos'] = (np.cos(timestamp_s * (2*np.pi/day))).values

hourly_df = hourly_df.drop(['datetime'], axis=1)
```

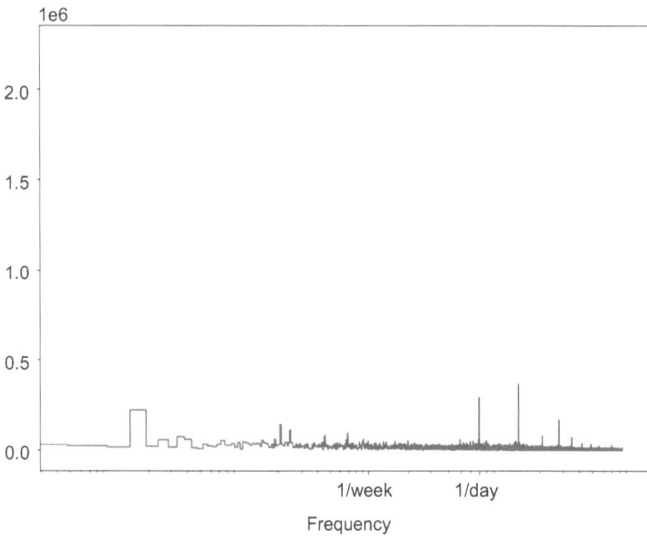

**Figure 18.7   Amplitude of the weekly and daily seasonality in our target.
You can see that the amplitude of the weekly seasonality is close to 0,
while there is a visible peak for the daily seasonality. Therefore, we
indeed have daily seasonality for our target.**

Our feature engineering is complete, and the data is ready to be scaled and split into training, validation, and test sets.

18.3.3 Splitting and scaling the data

The final step is to split the dataset into training, validation, and test sets, and to scale the data. Note that we'll first split the data, so that we scale it using only the information from the training set, thus avoiding information leakage. Scaling the data will decrease training time and improve the performance of our models.

We'll split the data 70:20:10 for the training, validation, and test sets respectively.

```
n = len(hourly_df)

# Split 70:20:10 (train:validation:test)
train_df = hourly_df[0:int(n*0.7)]
val_df = hourly_df[int(n*0.7):int(n*0.9)]
test_df = hourly_df[int(n*0.9):]
```

Next, we'll fit the scaler to the training set only, and scale each individual set.

```
from sklearn.preprocessing import MinMaxScaler

scaler = MinMaxScaler()
scaler.fit(train_df)

train_df[train_df.columns] = scaler.transform(train_df[train_df.columns])
val_df[val_df.columns] = scaler.transform(val_df[val_df.columns])
test_df[test_df.columns] = scaler.transform(test_df[test_df.columns])
```

We can now save each set to be used later for modeling.

```
train_df.to_csv('../data/ch18_train.csv', index=False, header=True)
val_df.to_csv('../data/ch18_val.csv', index=False, header=True)
test_df.to_csv('../data/ch18_test.csv', index=False, header=True)
```

We are now ready to move on to the modeling step.

18.4 Preparing for modeling with deep learning

In the last section, we produced the three sets of data required for training deep learning models. Recall that the objective of this project is to predict the global active power consumption in the next 24 hours. This means that we must build a univariate multi-step model, since we are forecasting only one target 24 timesteps into the future.

We will build two baselines, a linear model, a deep neural network model, a long short-term memory (LSTM) model, a convolutional neural network (CNN), a combination of CNN and LSTM, and finally an autoregressive LSTM. In the end, we will use the mean absolute error (MAE) to determine which model is the best. The one that achieves the lowest MAE on the test set will be the top-performing model.

Note that we'll use the MAE as our evaluation metric and the mean squared error (MSE) as the loss function, just as we have since chapter 13.

18.4.1 Initial setup

Before moving on to modeling, we first need to import the required libraries, as well as define our `DataWindow` class and a function to train our models.

We'll start off by importing the necessary Python libraries for modeling.

```
import numpy as np
import pandas as pd
import tensorflow as tf
import matplotlib.pyplot as plt

from tensorflow.keras import Model, Sequential

from tensorflow.keras.optimizers import Adam
from tensorflow.keras.callbacks import EarlyStopping
from tensorflow.keras.losses import MeanSquaredError
from tensorflow.keras.metrics import MeanAbsoluteError

from tensorflow.keras.layers import Dense, Conv1D, LSTM, Lambda, Reshape,
➥ RNN, LSTMCell

import warnings
warnings.filterwarnings('ignore')
```

Make sure you have TensorFlow 2.6 installed, as this is the latest version at the time of writing. You can check the version of TensorFlow using `print(tf.__version__)`.

Optionally, you can set parameters for the plots. In this case, I prefer to specify a size and remove the grid on the axes.

```
plt.rcParams['figure.figsize'] = (10, 7.5)
plt.rcParams['axes.grid'] = False
```

Then you can set a random seed. This ensures constant results when training models. Recall that the initialization of deep learning models is random, so training the same model twice in a row might result in slightly different performance. Thus, to ensure reproducibility, we set a random seed.

```
tf.random.set_seed(42)
np.random.seed(42)
```

Next, we need to read the training set, validation set, and test set so they are ready for modeling.

```
train_df = pd.read_csv('../data/ch18_train.csv')
val_df = pd.read_csv('../data/ch18_val.csv')
test_df = pd.read_csv('../data/ch18_test.csv')
```

Finally, we'll build a dictionary to store the column names and their corresponding indexes. This will be useful later on for building the baseline models and creating windows of data.

```
column_indices = {name: i for i, name in enumerate(train_df.columns)}
```

We'll now move on to defining the `DataWindow` class.

18.4.2 *Defining the DataWindow class*

The `DataWindow` class allows us to quickly create windows of data for training deep learning models. Each window of data contains a set of inputs and a set of labels. The model is then trained to produce predictions as close as possible to the labels using the inputs.

An entire section of chapter 13 was dedicated to implementing the `DataWindow` class step by step, and we have been using it ever since, so we will go straight to its implementation. The only change here will be the name of the default column to plot when we visualize the predictions against the labels.

> **Listing 18.1   Implementation of class to create windows of data**

```
class DataWindow():
    def __init__(self, input_width, label_width, shift,
                 train_df=train_df, val_df=val_df, test_df=test_df,
                 label_columns=None):

        self.train_df = train_df
        self.val_df = val_df
        self.test_df = test_df
```

```
        self.label_columns = label_columns
        if label_columns is not None:
            self.label_columns_indices = {name: i for i, name in
➡ enumerate(label_columns)}
        self.column_indices = {name: i for i, name in
➡ enumerate(train_df.columns)}

        self.input_width = input_width
        self.label_width = label_width
        self.shift = shift

        self.total_window_size = input_width + shift

        self.input_slice = slice(0, input_width)
        self.input_indices =
➡ np.arange(self.total_window_size)[self.input_slice]

        self.label_start = self.total_window_size - self.label_width
        self.labels_slice = slice(self.label_start, None)
        self.label_indices =
➡ np.arange(self.total_window_size)[self.labels_slice]

    def split_to_inputs_labels(self, features):
        inputs = features[:, self.input_slice, :]
        labels = features[:, self.labels_slice, :]
        if self.label_columns is not None:
            labels = tf.stack(
                [labels[:,:,self.column_indices[name]] for name in
➡ self.label_columns],
                axis=-1
            )
        inputs.set_shape([None, self.input_width, None])
        labels.set_shape([None, self.label_width, None])

        return inputs, labels

    def plot(self, model=None, plot_col='Global_active_power',
➡ max_subplots=3):
        inputs, labels = self.sample_batch
```

◁─── **Set the default name of our target to be the global active power.**

```
        plt.figure(figsize=(12, 8))
        plot_col_index = self.column_indices[plot_col]
        max_n = min(max_subplots, len(inputs))

        for n in range(max_n):
            plt.subplot(3, 1, n+1)
            plt.ylabel(f'{plot_col} [scaled]')
            plt.plot(self.input_indices, inputs[n, :, plot_col_index],
                    label='Inputs', marker='.', zorder=-10)

            if self.label_columns:
              label_col_index = self.label_columns_indices.get(plot_col,
➡ None)
            else:
              label_col_index = plot_col_index
```

```
          if label_col_index is None:
            continue

          plt.scatter(self.label_indices, labels[n, :, label_col_index],
                      edgecolors='k', marker='s', label='Labels',
  c='green', s=64)
          if model is not None:
            predictions = model(inputs)
            plt.scatter(self.label_indices, predictions[n, :,
  label_col_index],
                        marker='X', edgecolors='k', label='Predictions',
                        c='red', s=64)

          if n == 0:
            plt.legend()

      plt.xlabel('Time (h)')

  def make_dataset(self, data):
      data = np.array(data, dtype=np.float32)
      ds = tf.keras.preprocessing.timeseries_dataset_from_array(
          data=data,
          targets=None,
          sequence_length=self.total_window_size,
          sequence_stride=1,
          shuffle=True,
          batch_size=32
      )

      ds = ds.map(self.split_to_inputs_labels)
      return ds

  @property
  def train(self):
      return self.make_dataset(self.train_df)

  @property
  def val(self):
      return self.make_dataset(self.val_df)

  @property
  def test(self):
      return self.make_dataset(self.test_df)

  @property
  def sample_batch(self):
      result = getattr(self, '_sample_batch', None)
      if result is None:
          result = next(iter(self.train))
          self._sample_batch = result
      return result
```

With the `DataWindow` class defined, we only need a function to compile and train the different models we'll develop.

18.4.3 *Utility function to train our models*

Our final step before launching our experiments is to build a function that automates the training process. This is the `compile_and_fit` function that we have been using since chapter 13.

Recall that this function takes in a model and a window of data. Then it implements early stopping, meaning that the model will stop training if the validation loss does not change for three consecutive epochs. This is also the function in which we specify the loss function to be the MSE and the evaluation metric to be the MAE.

```
def compile_and_fit(model, window, patience=3, max_epochs=50):
    early_stopping = EarlyStopping(monitor='val_loss',
                                   patience=patience,
                                   mode='min')

    model.compile(loss=MeanSquaredError(),
                  optimizer=Adam(),
                  metrics=[MeanAbsoluteError()])

    history = model.fit(window.train,
                        epochs=max_epochs,
                        validation_data=window.val,
                        callbacks=[early_stopping])

    return history
```

At this point, we have everything we need to start developing models to forecast the next 24 hours of global active power.

18.5   *Modeling with deep learning*

The training, validation, and test sets are ready, as well as the `DataWindow` class and the function that will train our models. Everything is set for us to start building deep learning models.

We'll first implement two baselines, and then we'll train models with increasing complexity: a linear model, a deep neural network, an LSTM, a CNN, a CNN and LSTM model, and an autoregressive LSTM. Once all the models are trained, we'll select the best model by comparing the MAE on the test set. The model with the lowest MAE will be the one that we recommend.

18.5.1 *Baseline models*

Every forecasting project must start with a baseline model. Baselines serve as a benchmark for our more sophisticated models, as they can only be better in comparison to a certain benchmark. Building baseline models also allows us to assess whether the added complexity of a model really generates a significant benefit. It is possible that a complex model does not perform much better than a baseline, in which case implementing a complex model is hard to justify. In this case, we'll build two baseline models: one that repeats the last known value and another that repeats the last 24 hours of data.

We'll start by creating the window of data that will be used. Recall that the objective is to forecast the next 24 hours of global active power. Thus, the length of our label sequence is 24 timesteps, and the shift will also be 24 timesteps. We'll also use an input length of 24.

```
multi_window = DataWindow(input_width=24, label_width=24, shift=24,
➡ label_columns=['Global_active_power'])
```

Next, we'll implement a class that will repeat the last known value of the input sequence as a prediction for the next 24 hours.

```
class MultiStepLastBaseline(Model):
    def __init__(self, label_index=None):
        super().__init__()
        self.label_index = label_index

    def call(self, inputs):
        if self.label_index is None:
            return tf.tile(inputs[:, -1:, :], [1, 24, 1])
        return tf.tile(inputs[:, -1:, self.label_index:], [1, 24, 1])
```

We can now generate predictions using this baseline and store its performance in a dictionary. This dictionary will store the performance of each model so that we can compare them at the end. Note that we will not display the MAE of each model as we build them. We will compare the evaluation metrics once all the models are trained.

```
baseline_last =
➡ MultiStepLastBaseline(label_index=column_indices['Global_active_power'])

baseline_last.compile(loss=MeanSquaredError(),
➡ metrics=[MeanAbsoluteError()])

val_performance = {}
performance = {}

val_performance['Baseline - Last'] =
➡ baseline_last.evaluate(multi_window.val)
performance['Baseline - Last'] = baseline_last.evaluate(multi_window.test,
➡ verbose=0)
```

We can visualize the predictions using the `plot` method of the `DataWindow` class, as shown in figure 18.8. It will display three plots in the figure, as specified in the `Data-Window` class.

```
multi_window.plot(baseline_last)
```

In figure 18.8 we have a working baseline—the forecasts correspond to a flat line with the same value as the last input. You may get a slightly different plot, since the cached sample batch used to create the plots may not be the same. However, the model's metrics will be identical to what is shown here, as long as the random seeds are equal.

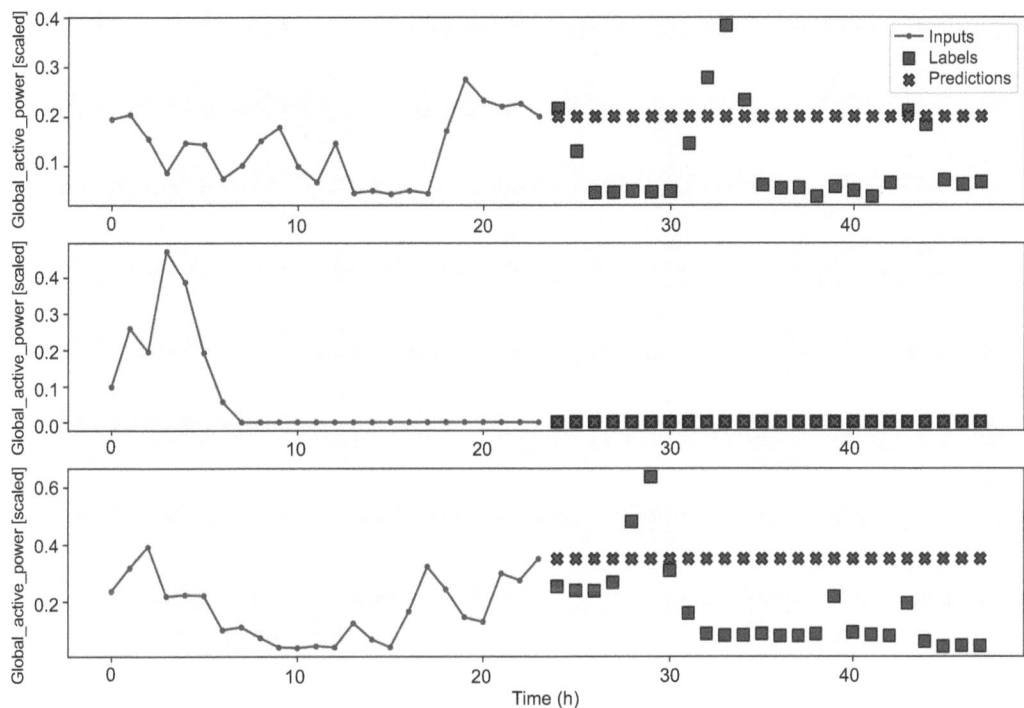

Figure 18.8 Predictions from the baseline model, which simply repeats the last known input value

Next, let's implement a baseline model that repeats the input sequence. Remember that we identified daily seasonality in our target, so this is equivalent to forecasting the last known season.

```
class RepeatBaseline(Model):
    def __init__(self, label_index=None):
        super().__init__()
        self.label_index = label_index

    def call(self, inputs):
        return inputs[:, :, self.label_index:]
```

Once it's defined, we can generate predictions and store the baseline's performance for comparison. We can also visualize the generated predictions, as shown in figure 18.9.

```
baseline_repeat =
➥ RepeatBaseline(label_index=column_indices['Global_active_power'])

baseline_repeat.compile(loss=MeanSquaredError(),
➥ metrics=[MeanAbsoluteError()])

val_performance['Baseline - Repeat'] =
➥ baseline_repeat.evaluate(multi_window.val)
performance['Baseline - Repeat'] =
➥ baseline_repeat.evaluate(multi_window.test, verbose=0)
```

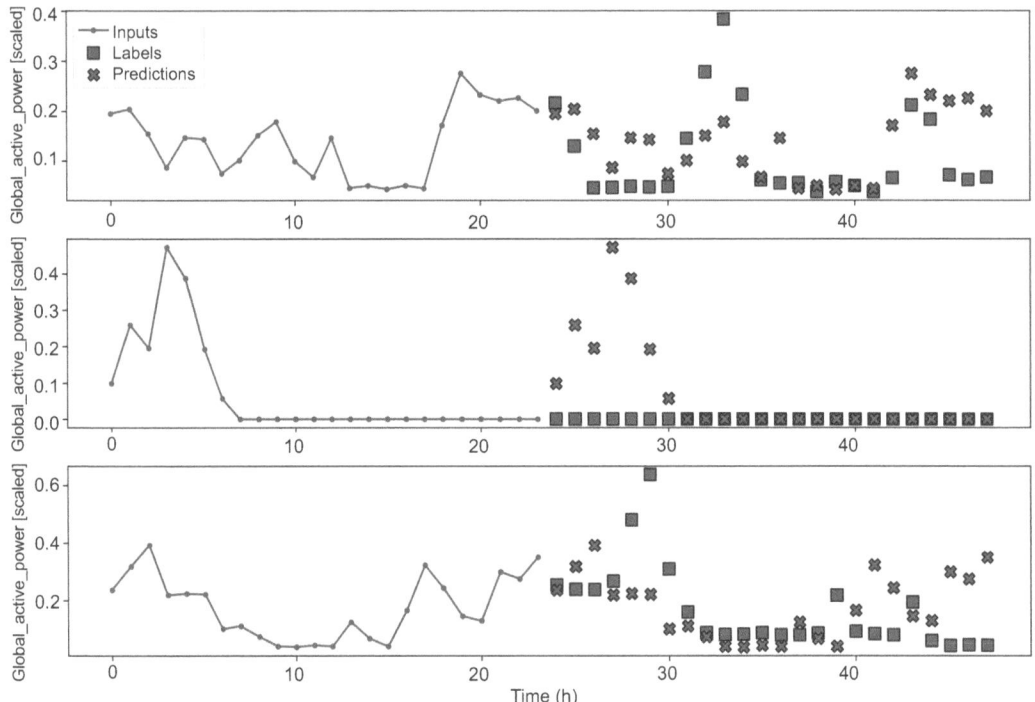

Figure 18.9   Predicting the last season as a baseline

In figure 18.9 you'll see that the predictions are equal to the input sequence, which is the expected behavior for this baseline model. Feel free to print out the MAE for each model as you build them. I'll display them at the end of the chapter in a bar chart to determine which model should be selected.

With the baseline models in place, we can move on to the slightly more complex linear model.

18.5.2   *Linear model*

One of the simplest models we can build is a linear model. This model consists of only an input layer and an output layer. Thus, only a sequence of weights is computed to generate predictions that are as close as possible to the labels.

In this case, we'll build a model with one Dense output layer that has only one neuron, since we are predicting only one target. We'll then train the model and store its performance.

```
label_index = column_indices['Global_active_power']
num_features = train_df.shape[1]

linear = Sequential([
    Dense(1, kernel_initializer=tf.initializers.zeros)
])
```

```
history = compile_and_fit(linear, multi_window)

val_performance['Linear'] = linear.evaluate(multi_window.val)
performance['Linear'] = linear.evaluate(multi_window.test, verbose=0)
```

As always, we can visualize the predictions using the `plot` method, as shown in figure 18.10.

```
multi_window.plot(linear)
```

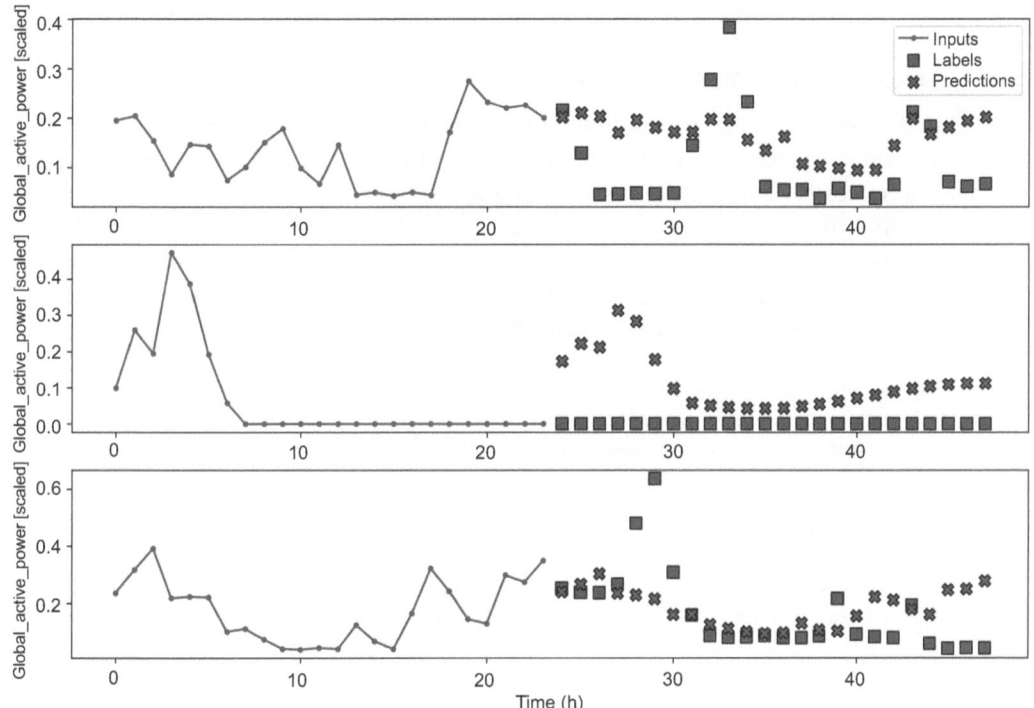

Figure 18.10   Predictions generated from a linear model

Now let's add hidden layers and implement a deep neural network.

18.5.3   Deep neural network

The previous linear model did not have any hidden layers; it was simply an input layer and an output layer. Now we'll add hidden layers, which will help us model nonlinear relationships in the data.

Here we'll stack two `Dense` layers with 64 neurons and use ReLU as the activation function. Then we'll train the model and store its performance for comparison.

```
dense = Sequential([
    Dense(64, activation='relu'),
```

```
    Dense(64, activation='relu'),
    Dense(1, kernel_initializer=tf.initializers.zeros),
])

history = compile_and_fit(dense, multi_window)

val_performance['Dense'] = dense.evaluate(multi_window.val)
performance['Dense'] = dense.evaluate(multi_window.test, verbose=0)
```

You can optionally visualize the predictions with `multi_window.plot(dense)`.

The next model we'll implement is the long short-term memory model.

18.5.4 *Long short-term memory (LSTM) model*

The main advantage of the long short-term memory (LSTM) model is that it keeps information from the past in memory. This makes it especially suitable for treating sequences of data, like time series. It allows us to combine information from the present and the past to produce a prediction.

We'll feed the input sequence through an LSTM layer before sending it to the output layer, which remains a Dense layer with one neuron. We'll then train the model and store its performance in the dictionary for comparison at the end.

```
lstm_model = Sequential([
    LSTM(32, return_sequences=True),
    Dense(1, kernel_initializer=tf.initializers.zeros),
])

history = compile_and_fit(lstm_model, multi_window)

val_performance['LSTM'] = lstm_model.evaluate(multi_window.val)
performance['LSTM'] = lstm_model.evaluate(multi_window.test, verbose=0)
```

We can visualize the predictions from the LSTM—they are shown in figure 18.11.

```
multi_window.plot(lstm_model)
```

Now let's implement a convolutional neural network.

18.5.5 *Convolutional neural network (CNN)*

A convolutional neural network (CNN) uses the convolution function to reduce the feature space. This effectively filters our time series and performs feature selection. Furthermore, a CNN is faster to train than an LSTM since the operations are parallelized, whereas the LSTM must treat one element of the sequence at a time.

Because the convolution operation reduces the feature space, we must provide a slightly longer input sequence to make sure that the output sequence contains 24 timesteps. How much longer it needs to be depends on the length of the kernel that

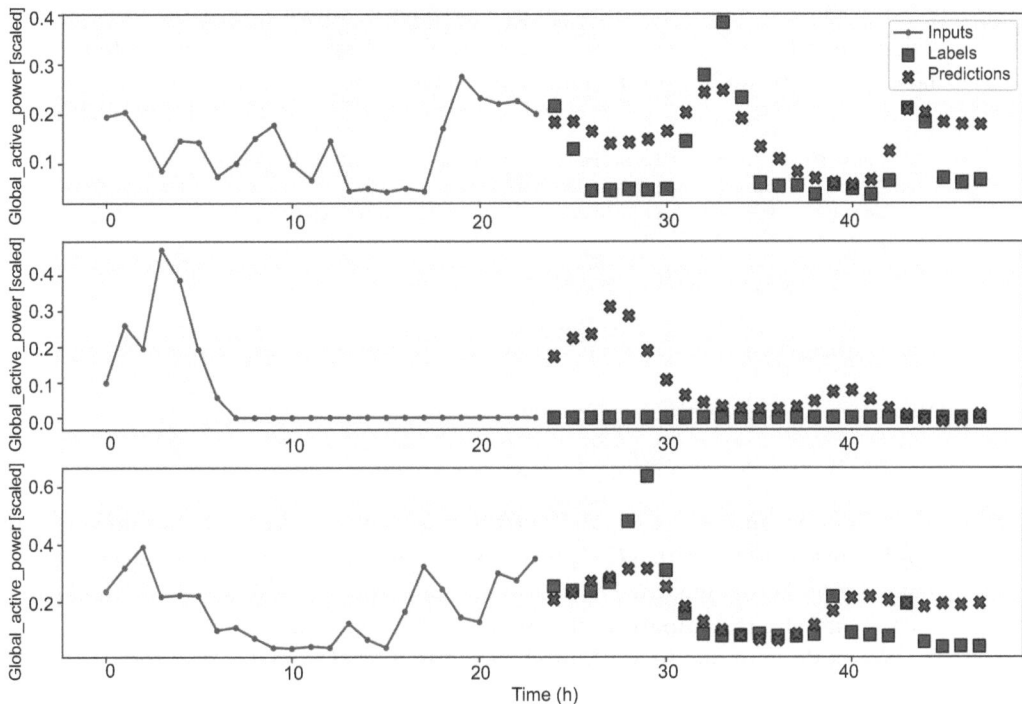

Figure 18.11 Predictions generated from the LSTM model

performs the convolution operation. In this case, we'll use a kernel length of 3. This is an arbitrary choice, so feel free to experiment with different values, although your results might differ from what is shown here. Given that we need 24 labels, we can calculate the input sequence using equation 18.1.

$$\text{input length} = \text{label length} + \text{kernel length} - 1 \qquad \textbf{Equation 18.1}$$

This forces us to define a window of data specifically for the CNN model. Note that since we are defining a new window of data, the sample batch used for plotting will differ from the one used so far.

We now have all the necessary information to define a window of data for the CNN model.

```
KERNEL_WIDTH = 3
LABEL_WIDTH = 24
INPUT_WIDTH = LABEL_WIDTH + KERNEL_WIDTH - 1

cnn_multi_window = DataWindow(input_width=INPUT_WIDTH,
➥ label_width=LABEL_WIDTH, shift=24,
➥ label_columns=['Global_active_power'])
```

Next, we'll send the input through a `Conv1D` layer, which filters the input sequence. Then it is fed to a `Dense` layer with 32 neurons for learning before going to the output layer. As always, we'll train the model and store its performance for comparison.

```
cnn_model = Sequential([
    Conv1D(32, activation='relu', kernel_size=(KERNEL_WIDTH)),
    Dense(units=32, activation='relu'),
    Dense(1, kernel_initializer=tf.initializers.zeros),
])

history = compile_and_fit(cnn_model, cnn_multi_window)

val_performance['CNN'] = cnn_model.evaluate(cnn_multi_window.val)
performance['CNN'] = cnn_model.evaluate(cnn_multi_window.test, verbose=0)
```

We can now visualize the predictions.

```
cnn_multi_window.plot(cnn_model)
```

You will notice in figure 18.12 that the input sequence differs from our previous methods because working with a CNN involves windowing the data again to account for the convolution kernel length. The training, validation, and test sets remain unchanged, so it is still valid to compare all the models' performance.

Now let's combine the CNN model with the LSTM model.

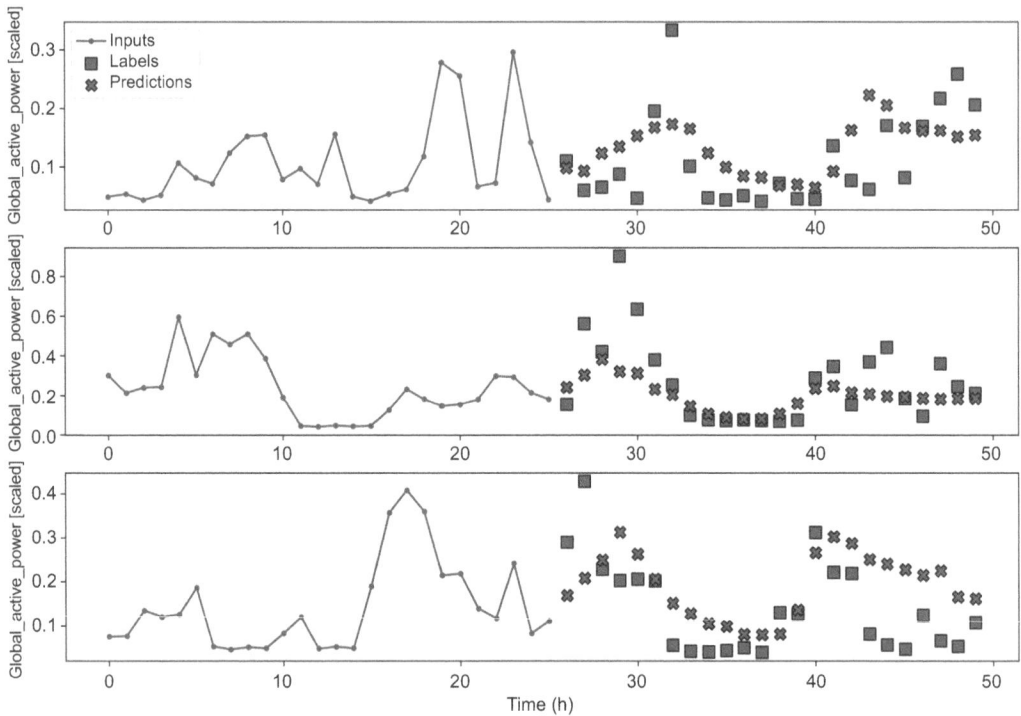

Figure 18.12   Predictions generated by the CNN model

18.5.6 *Combining a CNN with an LSTM*

We know that LSTM is good at treating sequences of data, while CNN can filter a sequence of data. Therefore, it is interesting to test whether filtering a sequence before feeding it to an LSTM can result in a better-performing model.

We'll feed the input sequence to a `Conv1D` layer, but use an LSTM layer for learning this time. Then we'll send the information to the output layer. Again, we'll train the model and store its performance.

```
cnn_lstm_model = Sequential([
    Conv1D(32, activation='relu', kernel_size=(KERNEL_WIDTH)),
    LSTM(32, return_sequences=True),
    Dense(1, kernel_initializer=tf.initializers.zeros),
])

history = compile_and_fit(cnn_lstm_model, cnn_multi_window)

val_performance['CNN + LSTM'] =
➥ cnn_lstm_model.evaluate(cnn_multi_window.val)
performance['CNN + LSTM'] = cnn_lstm_model.evaluate(cnn_multi_window.test,
➥ verbose=0)
```

The predictions are visualized in figure 18.13.

```
cnn_multi_window.plot(cnn_lstm_model)
```

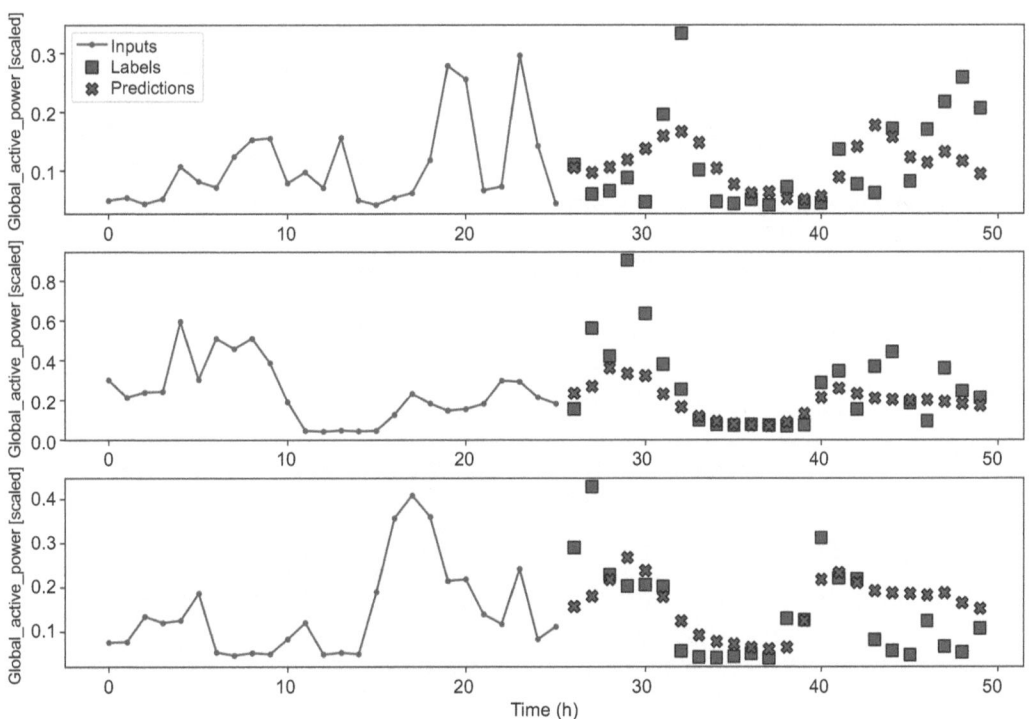

Figure 18.13 Predictions from a CNN combined with an LSTM model

Finally, let's implement an autoregressive LSTM model.

18.5.7 *The autoregressive LSTM model*

The final model that we'll implement is an autoregressive LSTM (ARLSTM) model. Instead of generating the entire output sequence in a single shot, the autoregressive model will generate one prediction at a time and use that prediction as an input to generate the next one. This kind of architecture is present in state-of-the-art forecasting models, but it comes with a caveat. If the model generates a very bad first prediction, this mistake will be carried on to the next predictions, which will magnify the errors. Nevertheless, it is worth testing this model to see if it works well in our situation.

The first step is defining the class that implements the ARLSTM model. This is the same class that we used in chapter 17.

Listing 18.2   Class to implement an ARLSTM model

```
class AutoRegressive(Model):
    def __init__(self, units, out_steps):
        super().__init__()
        self.out_steps = out_steps
        self.units = units
        self.lstm_cell = LSTMCell(units)
        self.lstm_rnn = RNN(self.lstm_cell, return_state=True)
        self.dense = Dense(train_df.shape[1])

    def warmup(self, inputs):
        x, *state = self.lstm_rnn(inputs)
        prediction = self.dense(x)

        return prediction, state

    def call(self, inputs, training=None):
        predictions = []
        prediction, state = self.warmup(inputs)

        predictions.append(prediction)

        for n in range(1, self.out_steps):
            x = prediction
            x, state = self.lstm_cell(x, states=state, training=training)

            prediction = self.dense(x)
            predictions.append(prediction)

        predictions = tf.stack(predictions)
        predictions = tf.transpose(predictions, [1, 0, 2])

        return predictions
```

We can then use this class to initialize our model. We'll train the model on the `multi_window` and store its performance for comparison.

```
AR_LSTM = AutoRegressive(units=32, out_steps=24)

history = compile_and_fit(AR_LSTM, multi_window)

val_performance['AR - LSTM'] = AR_LSTM.evaluate(multi_window.val)
performance['AR - LSTM'] = AR_LSTM.evaluate(multi_window.test, verbose=0)
```

We can then visualize the predictions of the autoregressive LSTM model, as shown in figure 18.14.

```
multi_window.plot(AR_LSTM)
```

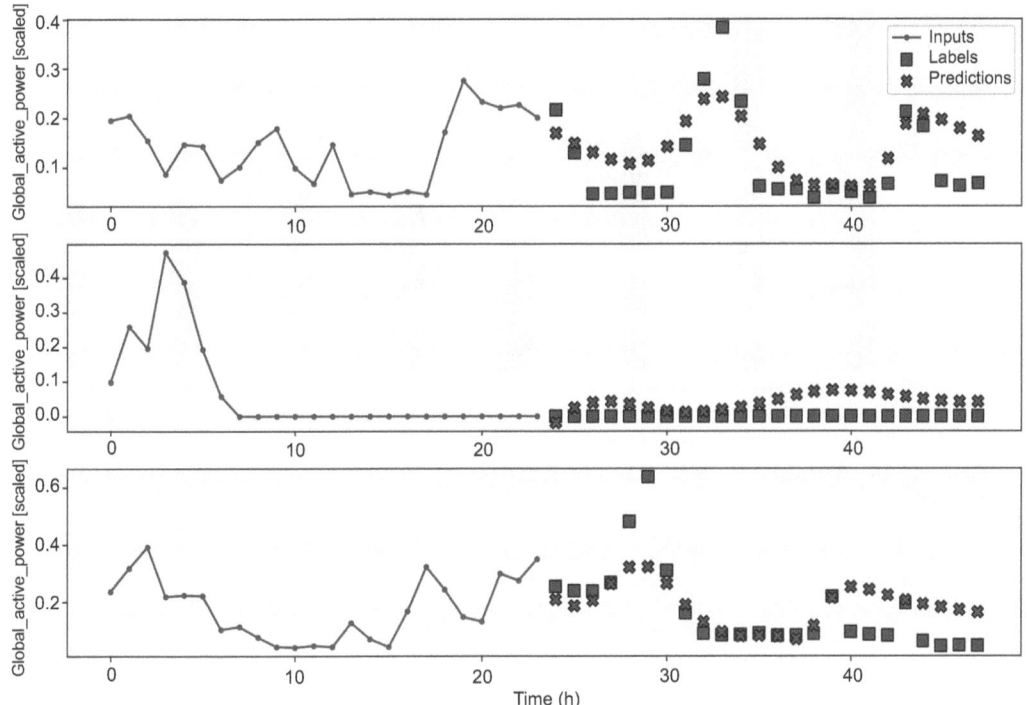

Figure 18.14 Predictions from the ARLSTM model

Now that we have built a wide variety of models, let's select the best one based on its MAE on the test set.

18.5.8 *Selecting the best model*

We have built many models for this project, from a linear model to an ARLSTM model. Now let's visualize the MAE of each model to determine the champion.

We'll plot the MAE on both the validation and test sets. The result is shown in figure 18.15.

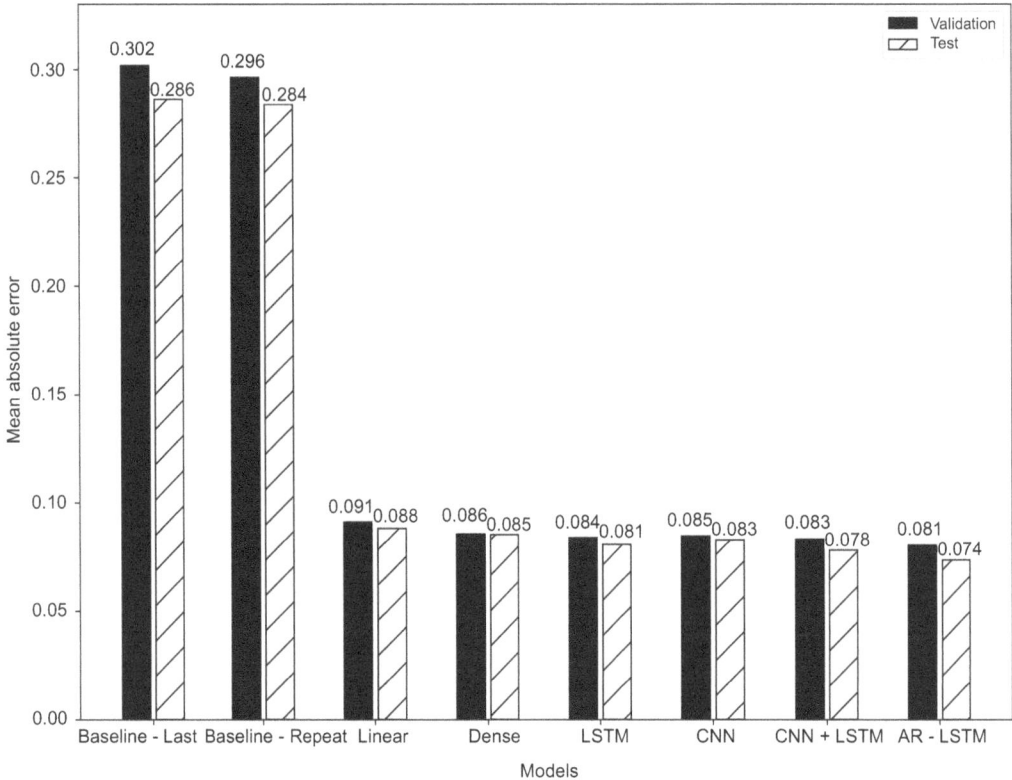

Figure 18.15   Comparing the MAE of all models tested. The ARLSTM model achieved the lowest MAE on the test set.

```
mae_val = [v[1] for v in val_performance.values()]
mae_test = [v[1] for v in performance.values()]

x = np.arange(len(performance))

fig, ax = plt.subplots()
ax.bar(x - 0.15, mae_val, width=0.25, color='black', edgecolor='black',
⮡ label='Validation')
ax.bar(x + 0.15, mae_test, width=0.25, color='white', edgecolor='black',
⮡ hatch='/', label='Test')
ax.set_ylabel('Mean absolute error')
ax.set_xlabel('Models')

for index, value in enumerate(mae_val):
    plt.text(x=index - 0.15, y=value+0.005, s=str(round(value, 3)),
⮡ ha='center')

for index, value in enumerate(mae_test):
    plt.text(x=index + 0.15, y=value+0.0025, s=str(round(value, 3)),
⮡ ha='center')
```

```
plt.ylim(0, 0.33)
plt.xticks(ticks=x, labels=performance.keys())
plt.legend(loc='best')
plt.tight_layout()
```

Figure 18.15 shows that all the models performed much better than the baselines. Furthermore, our champion is the ARLSTM model, since it achieved a MAE of 0.074 on the test set, which is the lowest MAE of all. Thus, we would recommend using this model to forecast the global active power over the next 24 hours.

18.6 *Next steps*

Congratulations on completing this capstone project! I hope that you were successful in completing it on your own and that you feel confident in your knowledge of forecasting time series using deep learning models.

I highly encourage you to make this project your own. You can turn this project into a multivariate forecasting problem by forecasting more than one target. You could also change the forecast horizon. In short, make changes and play around with the models and the data and see what you can achieve on your own.

In the next chapter, we'll start the final part of this book, where we'll automate the forecasting process. There are many libraries that can generate accurate predictions with minimal steps, and they are often used in the industry, making this an essential tool for time series forecasting. We'll look at a widely used library called Prophet.

Part 4

Automating
forecasting at scale

We have so far been building our models by hand. This has given us granular control over what is happening, but it can also be a lengthy process. Thus, it's time to explore some tools for automatic time series forecasting. These tools are widely used in the industry, as they are easy to use and enable quick experimentation. They also implement state-of-the-art models, making them easily accessible to any data scientist.

Here we'll explore the ecosystem of automatic forecasting tools and focus on Prophet, as it is one of the most popular libraries for automatic forecasting, and more recent libraries model their syntax on that of Prophet. This means that if you know how to work with Prophet, it is easy to work with another tool.

As in previous parts, we'll conclude with a capstone project.

Automating time series forecasting with Prophet

19

This chapter covers

- Assessing different libraries for automated forecasting
- Exploring the functionality of Prophet
- Forecasting with Prophet

Throughout this book, we have built models involving many manual steps. For declinations of the SARIMAX models, for example, we had to develop a function to select the best model according to the Akaike information criterion (AIC) and a function to perform rolling forecasts. In the deep learning portion of the book, we had to build a class to create windows of data, as well as define all the deep learning models, although this was greatly facilitated by the use of Keras.

While manually building and tweaking our models allows for great flexibility and total control over our forecasting techniques, it is also useful to automate most of the forecasting process, making it easier to forecast time series and accelerating experiments. Therefore, it is important to understand the automation tools, as they are a fast way to obtain predictions, and they often facilitate the use of state-of-the-art models.

In this chapter, we'll first look at the various libraries that automate the process of time series forecasting. Then we'll focus specifically on the Prophet library, which is arguably the most well-known and widely used forecasting library. We'll explore its functionality using a real-life dataset. Finally, we'll conclude this chapter with a forecasting project so we can see Prophet in action.

19.1 *Overview of the automated forecasting libraries*

The data science community and companies have developed many libraries to automate the forecasting process and make it easier. Some of the most popular libraries and their websites are listed here:

- *Pmdarima*—http://alkaline-ml.com/pmdarima/modules/classes.html
- *Prophet*—https://facebook.github.io/prophet
- *NeuralProphet*—https://neuralprophet.com/html/index.html
- *PyTorch Forecasting*—https://pytorch-forecasting.readthedocs.io/en/stable

This is by no means an exhaustive list, and I wish to remain impartial in their use. As a data scientist, you have the knowledge and capacity to assess whether a particular library is suitable for your needs in a particular context.

The pmdarima library is the Python implementation of the popular `auto.arima` library in R. Pmdarima is essentially a wrapper that generalizes many of the statistical models we have used, such as the ARMA, ARIMA, and SARIMA models. The main advantage of this library is that it provides an easy-to-use interface that automatically uses all the tools we've discussed for forecasting with statistical models, such as the augmented Dickey-Fuller (ADF) test to test for stationarity and selecting the orders p, q, P, and Q to minimize the AIC. It also comes with toy datasets, making it great for first-time learners to test different models on simple time series. This package is built and maintained by the community, but, most importantly, it is still being actively maintained at the time of writing.

Prophet is an open source package from Meta Open Source, meaning that it is built and maintained by Meta. This library was built specifically for business forecasting at scale. It arose from the internal need at Facebook to produce accurate forecasts quickly, and the library was then made freely available. Prophet is arguably the best-known forecasting library in the industry, as it can fit nonlinear trends and combine the effect of multiple seasonalities. The remainder of this chapter and the next one will focus entirely on this library, and we'll explore it in greater detail in the next section.

NeuralProphet builds on the Prophet library to automate the use of hybrid models for time series forecasting. This is a rather new project that is still in its beta phase at the time of writing. The library was built with the collaboration of people from different universities and Facebook. This package introduces a combination of classical models, such as ARIMA, and neural networks, to produce accurate forecasts. It uses PyTorch on the backend, meaning that experienced users can easily extend the library's functionality. Most importantly, it uses an API similar to Prophet's, so once you learn how to work with Prophet, you can seamlessly transition to working with NeuralProphet. To learn more, you can read their paper, "NeuralProphet: Explainable

Forecasting at Scale" (https://arxiv.org/abs/2111.15397). It provides greater detail on NeuralProphet's internal functions and performance benchmarks while still being an accessible article.

Finally, PyTorch Forecasting facilitates the use of state-of-the-art deep learning models for time series forecasting. It, of course, uses PyTorch, and it provides a simple interface to implement models such as DeepAR, N-Beats, LSTM, and more. This package is built by the community and, at the time of writing, is being actively maintained.

> **NOTE**   For more information about DeepAR, see David Salinas, Valentin Flunkert, Jan Gasthaus, Tim Januschowski, "DeepAR: Probabilistic forecasting with autoregressive recurrent networks," *International Journal of Forecasting* 36:3 (2020), http://mng.bz/z4Kr. For information about N-Beats, see Boris N. Oreshkin, Dmitri Carpov, Nicolas Chapados, Yoshua Bengio, "N-BEATS: Neural basis expansion analysis for interpretable time series forecasting," arXiv:1905.10437 (2019), https://arxiv.org/abs/1905.10437.

This gives you a brief overview of the automatic forecasting ecosystem. Note that this list is not exhaustive, as there are many more libraries for automated time series forecasting.

You do not need to learn how to use each of the libraries I've presented. This is meant to be an overview of the different tools available. Each time series forecasting problem can require a different set of tools, but knowing how to use one of the libraries usually makes it easier to use a new one. Thus, we'll focus on the Prophet library for the rest of this book.

As I mentioned, Prophet is a well-known and widely used library in the industry, and anyone doing time series forecasting will likely come across Prophet. In the next section, we'll explore the package in greater detail and learn about its advantages, limitations, and functionality before using it for forecasting.

19.2   Exploring Prophet

Prophet is an open source library created by Meta that implements a forecasting procedure taking into account nonlinear trends with multiple seasonal periods, such as yearly, monthly, weekly, and daily. The package is available for use with Python. It allows you forecast rapidly with minimal manual work. More advanced users, such as ourselves, can fine tune the model to ensure that we get the best results possible.

Under the hood, Prophet implements a general additive model where each time series $y(t)$ is modeled as the linear combination of a trend $g(t)$, a seasonal component $s(t)$, holiday effects $h(t)$, and an error term ϵ_t, which is normally distributed. Mathematically, this is expressed as equation 19.1.

$$y(t) = g(t) + s(t) + h(t) + \epsilon_t$$ **Equation 19.1**

The trend component models the non-periodic long-term changes in the time series. The seasonal component models the periodic change, whether it is yearly, monthly, weekly, or daily. The holiday effect occurs irregularly and potentially on more than one day. Finally, the error term represents any change in value that cannot be explained by the previous three components.

Notice that this model does not take into account the time dependence of the data, unlike the ARIMA(p,d,q) model, where future values are dependent on past values. Thus, this process is closer to fitting a curve to the data, rather than finding the underlying process. Although there is some loss of predictive information using this method, it comes with the advantage that it is very flexible, since it can accommodate multiple seasonal periods and changing trends. Also, it is robust to outliers and missing data, which is a clear advantage in a business context.

The inclusion of multiple seasonal periods was motivated by the observation that human behavior produced multi-period seasonal time series. For example, the five-day work week can produce a pattern that repeats every week, while school break can produce a pattern that repeats every year. Thus, to take multiple seasonal periods into account, Prophet uses the Fourier series to model multiple periodic effects. Specifically, the seasonal component $s(t)$ is expressed as equation 19.2, where P is the length of the seasonal period in days, and N is the number of terms in the Fourier series.

$$s(t) = \sum_{n=1}^{N} \left(a_n \cos\left(\frac{2\pi n t}{P}\right) + b_n \sin\left(\frac{2\pi n t}{P}\right) \right)$$ **Equation 19.2**

In equation 19.2, if we have a yearly seasonality, $P = 365.25$, as there are 365.25 days in a year. For a weekly seasonality, $P = 7$. N is simply the number of parameters we wish to use to estimate the seasonal component. This has the added benefit that the seasonal component's sensitivity can be tweaked depending on how many parameters N are estimated to model the seasonality. We'll look at this in section 19.4 when we explore the different functions of Prophet. By default, Prophet uses 10 terms to model the yearly seasonality and 3 terms to model the weekly seasonality.

Finally, this model allows us to consider the effect of holidays. Holidays are irregular events that can have a clear impact on a time series. For example, events such as Black Friday in the United States can dramatically increase the attendance in stores or the sales on an ecommerce website. Similarly, Valentine's Day is probably a strong indicator of an increase in sales of chocolates and flowers. Therefore, to model the impact of holidays in a time series, Prophet lets us define a list of holidays for a specific country. Holiday effects are then incorporated in the model, assuming that they are all independent. If a data point falls on a holiday date, a parameter K_i is calculated to represent the change in the time series at that point in time. The larger the change, the greater the holiday effect.

> **NOTE** For more information on the inner workings of Prophet, I highly suggest that you read the official paper, Sean J. Taylor and Benjamin Letham, "Forecasting at Scale," *PeerJ Preprints* 5:e3190v2 (2017), https://peerj.com/preprints/3190/. It contains a more detailed explanation of the library, including mathematical expressions and test results, while remaining accessible.

The flexibility of Prophet can make it an attractive choice for rapid and accurate forecasting. However, it must not be considered to be a one-size-fits-all solution. The documentation itself specifies that Prophet works best with time series that have a strong seasonal effect with several seasons of historical data. Therefore, there may be situations where Prophet is not the ideal choice, but that's okay, since you have a variety of statistical and deep learning models in your tool belt to produce forecasts.

Let's now dive deeper into Prophet and explore its functionality.

19.3 Basic forecasting with Prophet

To accompany our exploration of Prophet's functionality, we'll use a dataset containing the historical daily minimum temperature recorded in Melbourne, Australia, between 1981 and 1990. Besides predicting the weather, this dataset can also help us identify long-term climate trends and determine if the daily minimum temperature is, for example, increasing over time. Our forecast horizon will be 1 year or 365 days. We thus wish to build a model that forecasts the next year of daily minimum temperatures.

> **NOTE** At any time, feel free to consult the source code for this chapter on GitHub: https://github.com/marcopeix/TimeSeriesForecastingInPython/tree/master/CH19.

Prophet is as easy to install as any other Python package. It can then be imported in a Jupyter Notebook or Python script with the same syntax as when you use `pandas` or `numpy`.

```
import numpy as np
import pandas as pd
import matplotlib.pyplot as plt
from fbprophet import Prophet
```

A note on installing Prophet on Windows

If you are using a Windows machine, it is highly recommended that you use Anaconda to perform any data science task. Trying to install Prophet through Anaconda the first time might result in an error. This is because a compiler must be installed in order for the package to function correctly on Windows.

If you are using Anaconda, you can run the following commands in your Anaconda prompt to install Prophet successfully:

```
conda install libpython m2w64-toolchain -c msys2
conda install numpy cython matplotlib scipy pandas -c conda-forge
conda install -c conda-forge pystan
conda install -c conda-forge fbprophet
```

The next step is, of course, to read the CSV file.

```
df = pd.read_csv('../data/daily_min_temp.csv')
```

We can now plot our time series.

```
fig, ax = plt.subplots()

ax.plot(df['Temp'])
ax.set_xlabel('Date')
ax.set_ylabel('Minimum temperature (deg C)')

plt.xticks(np.arange(0, 3649, 365), np.arange(1981, 1991, 1))

fig.autofmt_xdate()
plt.tight_layout()
```

The result is shown in figure 19.1. You'll see a clear yearly seasonality, which is expected, as temperature is generally higher during summer and lower during winter. We thus have a fairly large dataset with 10 seasons of data, which is a perfect scenario for using Prophet, as the library performs best when there is a strong seasonal effect with many historical seasonal periods.

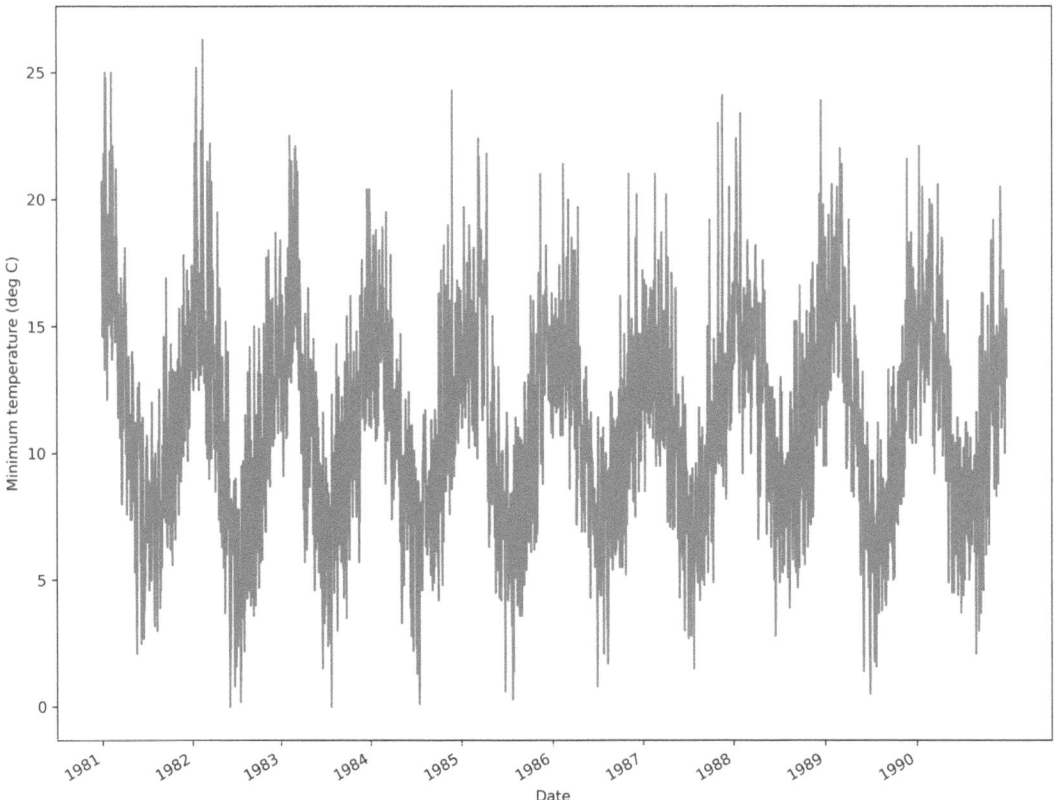

Figure 19.1   Daily minimum temperature recorded in Melbourne from 1981 to 1991. There is a yearly seasonality, as expected, since it is hotter in the summer and colder in the winter.

We can now move on to forecasting with Prophet. You will see how quickly you can obtain accurate forecasts using Prophet with very few manual steps.

The first step is to rename our columns. Prophet expects to have a `DataFrame` with two columns: a date column named ds and a value column named y. The date column must have a format accepted by `pandas`—usually YYYY-MM-DD or YYYY-MM-DD HH:MM:SS. The y column contains the values to be forecast, and those values must be numeric, whether float or integer. In our case, the dataset has only two columns that are already in the correct format, so we only need to rename them.

```
df.columns = ['ds', 'y']
```

Next, we'll split our data into train and test sets. We'll keep the last 365 days for the test set, as this represents a full year. We'll then take the first 9 years of data for training.

```
train = df[:-365]
test = df[-365:]
```

Prophet follows the `sklearn` API, where a model is initialized by creating an instance of the `Prophet` class, the model is trained using the `fit` method, and predictions are generated using the `predict` method. Therefore, we'll first initialize a Prophet model by creating an instance of the `Prophet` class. Note that throughout this chapter, we'll code using Prophet's naming convention.

```
m = Prophet()
```

Once it's initialized, we'll then fit the model on the train set.

```
m.fit(train);
```

We now have a model that is ready to produce forecasts, with only two lines of code.

The next step is to create a `DataFrame` to hold the predictions from Prophet. We'll use the `make_future_dataframe` method and specify the number of periods, which is the number of days in our forecast horizon. In this case, we want 365 days of forecast, so that they can be compared to the actual values observed in the test set.

```
future = m.make_future_dataframe(periods=365)
```

All that's left to do is to generate the forecast using the `predict` method.

```
forecast = m.predict(future)
```

Take some time to appreciate the fact that we trained a model and obtained predictions using only four lines of code. One of the main benefits of automated forecasting libraries is that we can experiment quickly and fine-tune the models later to tailor them to the task at hand.

However, our work is not done, since we wish to evaluate the model and measure its performance. The `forecast` `DataFrame` holds many columns with a lot of information, as shown in figure 19.2.

	ds	trend	yhat_lower	trend_lower	trend_upper	additive_terms	additive_terms_lower	additive_terms_upper	weekly
3656	1990-12-27	11.406616	11.234023	11.317184	11.505689	3.043416	3.043416	3.043416	-0.026441
3656	1990-12-28	11.406528	11.168300	11.316559	11.505902	3.120759	3.120759	3.120759	-0.009965
3647	1990-12-29	11.406441	11.235604	11.315997	11.506198	3.144845	3.144845	3.144845	-0.048854
3648	1990-12-30	11.406353	11.122686	11.315449	11.506547	3.069314	3.069314	3.069314	-0.188713
3649	1990-12-31	11.406265	11.540265	11.314879	11.506889	3.366551	3.366551	3.366551	0.043655

Figure 19.2 The `forecast` `DataFrame` containing the different components of the prediction. Note that if you add trend with additive_terms, you get the prediction yhat, which is hidden in the figure because the `DataFrame` has too many columns. Note also that additive_terms is the sum of weekly and yearly, indicating that we have both weekly and yearly seasonality.

We are only interested in these four columns: ds, yhat, yhat_lower, and yhat_upper. The ds column simply has the datestamp of the forecast. The yhat column contains the value of the forecast. You can see how Prophet uses y for the actual value and yhat for the predicted value as a naming convention. Then, yhat_lower and yhat_upper represent the lower and upper bounds of the 80% confidence interval of the forecast. This means that there is an 80% chance that the forecast will fall between yhat_lower and yhat_upper, with yhat being the value that we expect to obtain.

We can now join test and forecast together, to create a single `DataFrame` holding both the actual and predicted values.

```
test[['yhat', 'yhat_lower', 'yhat_upper']] = forecast[['yhat',
➥  'yhat_lower', 'yhat_upper']]
```

Before evaluating our mode, let's implement a baseline, as our model can only be better in relation to a certain benchmark. Here, let's apply the last season naive forecasting method, meaning that the last year of the training set is repeated as the forecast for next year.

```
test['baseline'] = train['y'][-365:].values
```

Everything is set up to easily evaluate our model. We'll use the mean absolute error (MAE) for its ease of interpretation. Note that the mean absolute percentage error (MAPE) is not suitable in this situation, because we have values that are close to 0, in which case the MAPE gets inflated.

```
from sklearn.metrics import mean_absolute_error

prophet_mae = mean_absolute_error(test['y'], test['yhat'])
baseline_mae = mean_absolute_error(test['y'], test['baseline'])
```

This returns a baseline MAE of 2.87, while the MAE achieved by the Prophet model is 1.94. Therefore, we achieve a lower MAE using Prophet, meaning that it is indeed better than the baseline. This means that, on average, our model predicts the daily minimum temperature with a difference of 1.94 degrees Celsius, either above or below the observed value.

We can optionally plot the forecasts, as well as the confidence interval from Prophet. The result is shown in figure 19.3.

```
fig, ax = plt.subplots()

ax.plot(train['y'])
ax.plot(test['y'], 'b-', label='Actual')
ax.plot(test['yhat'], color='darkorange', ls='--', lw=3, label='Predictions')
ax.plot(test['baseline'], 'k:', label='Baseline')

ax.set_xlabel('Date')
ax.set_ylabel('Minimum temperature (deg C)')

ax.axvspan(3285, 3649, color='#808080', alpha=0.1)

ax.legend(loc='best')

plt.xticks(
    [3224, 3254, 3285, 3316, 3344, 3375, 3405, 3436, 3466, 3497, 3528,
    3558, 3589, 3619],
    ['Nov', 'Dec', 'Jan 1990', 'Feb', 'Mar', 'Apr', 'May', 'Jun', 'Jul',
    'Aug', 'Sep', 'Oct', 'Nov', 'Dec'])
plt.fill_between(x=test.index, y1=test['yhat_lower'], y2=test['yhat_upper'],
    color='lightblue')
plt.xlim(3200, 3649)

fig.autofmt_xdate()
plt.tight_layout()
```

You'll see that the Prophet forecast looks more like a curve-fitting procedure, since its forecast, shown as a dashed line in figure 19.3, is a smooth curve that seems to filter the noisier fluctuations in the data.

Using Prophet allowed us to generate accurate forecasts with very few lines of code. However, we have only scratched the surface in terms of Prophet's functionality. This is only the basic workflow of using Prophet. In the next section, we'll explore more advanced Prophet functions, such as visualization techniques and fine-tuning procedures, as well as cross-validation and evaluation methods.

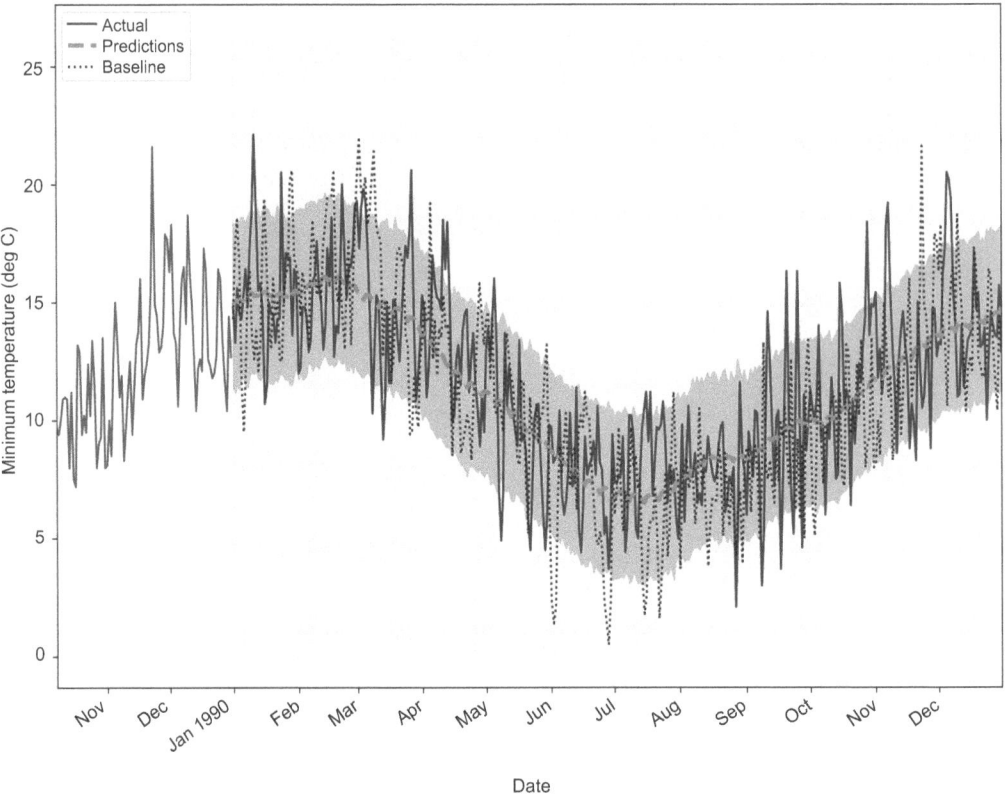

Figure 19.3   Forecasting the daily minimum temperature for the year 1990. We can see that the forecast from Prophet, shown as a dashed line, is smoother than the baseline, clearly demonstrating the curve-fitting property of Prophet.

19.4   *Exploring Prophet's advanced functionality*

We'll now explore Prophet's more advanced functionality. These advanced functions can be separated into three categories: visualization, performance diagnosis, and hyperparameter tuning. We'll work with the same dataset as in the previous section, and I highly recommend that you work in the same Jupyter Notebook or Python script as before.

19.4.1   *Visualization capabilities*

Prophet comes with many methods that allow us to quickly visualize a model's predictions or its different components.

First of all, we can quickly generate a plot of our forecasts simply by using the `plot` method. The result is shown in figure 19.4.

```
fig1 = m.plot(forecast)
```

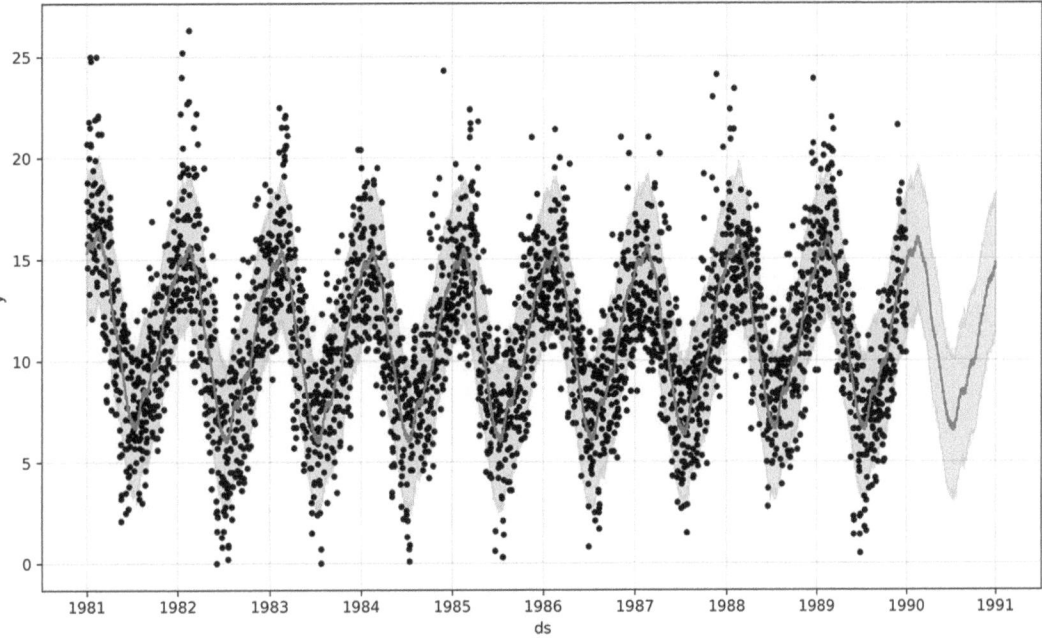

Figure 19.4 Plotting our predictions using Prophet. The black dots represent the training data, while the solid continuous line represents the model's predictions. The shaded band surrounding the line represents an 80% confidence interval.

We can also display the different components used in our model with the plot_components method.

```
fig2 = m.plot_components(forecast)
```

The resulting plot is shown in figure 19.5. The top plot shows the trend component, as well as the uncertainty in the trend for the forecast period. Looking closely, you'll see that the trend changes over time, with there being six different trends. We'll explore that in more detail later.

The two bottom plots in figure 19.5 show two different seasonal components: one with a weekly period and the other with a yearly period. The yearly seasonality makes sense, as the summer months (December to February, since Australia is in the southern hemisphere) see hotter temperatures than the winter months (June to August). However, the weekly seasonal component is rather odd. While it may help the model produce a better forecast, I doubt there is a meteorological phenomenon that can explain weekly seasonality in daily minimum temperatures. Thus, this component likely helps the model achieve a better fit and a better forecast, but it is hard to explain its presence.

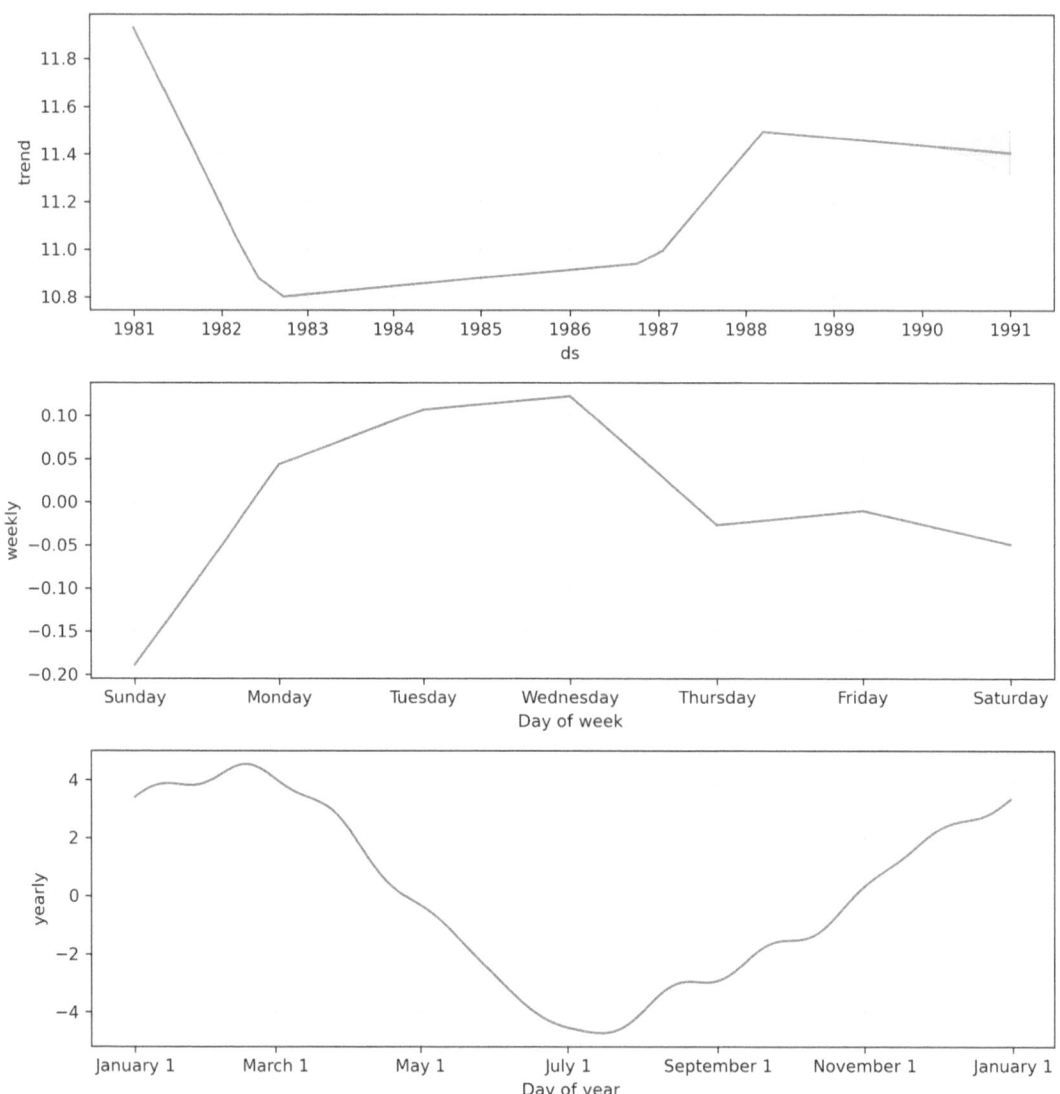

Figure 19.5   Displaying the components of our model. Here our model uses a trend component and two different seasonal components—one with a weekly period and the other with a yearly period.

Alternatively, Prophet allows us to plot only the seasonal component. Specifically, we can plot the weekly seasonality using the `plot_weekly` method or the yearly seasonality with the `plot_yearly` method. The result for the latter is shown in figure 19.6.

```
from fbprophet.plot import plot_yearly, plot_weekly

fig4 = plot_yearly(m)
```

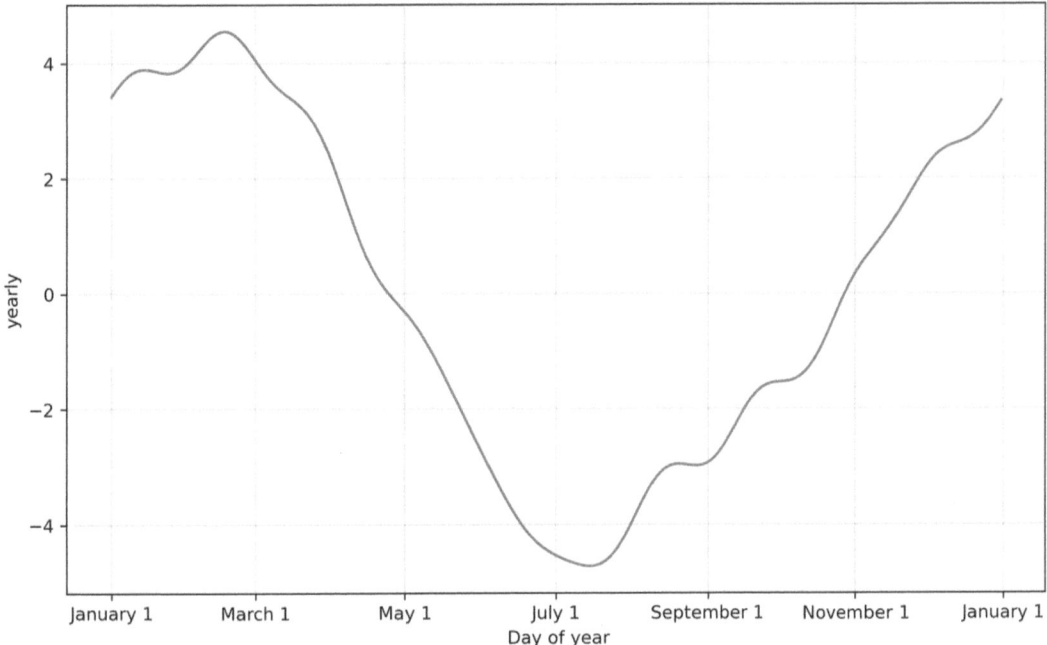

Figure 19.6 Plotting the yearly seasonal component of our data. This is equivalent to the third plot in figure 19.5.

You'll recognize the yearly seasonal component of our data, as it is the same plot as the third plot in figure 19.5. However, this method allows us to visualize how changing the number of terms to estimate the seasonal component can impact our model. Recall that Prophet uses 10 terms in the Fourier series to estimate the yearly seasonality. Now let's visualize the seasonal component if 20 terms are used for the estimation.

```
m2 = Prophet(yearly_seasonality=20).fit(train)

fig6 = plot_yearly(m2)
```

In figure 19.7 the yearly seasonal component shows more fluctuation than in figure 19.6, meaning that it is more sensitive. Tuning this parameter can lead to overfitting if too many terms are used, or to underfitting if we reduce the number of terms in the Fourier series. This parameter is rarely changed, but it is interesting to see that Prophet comes with this fine-tuning functionality.

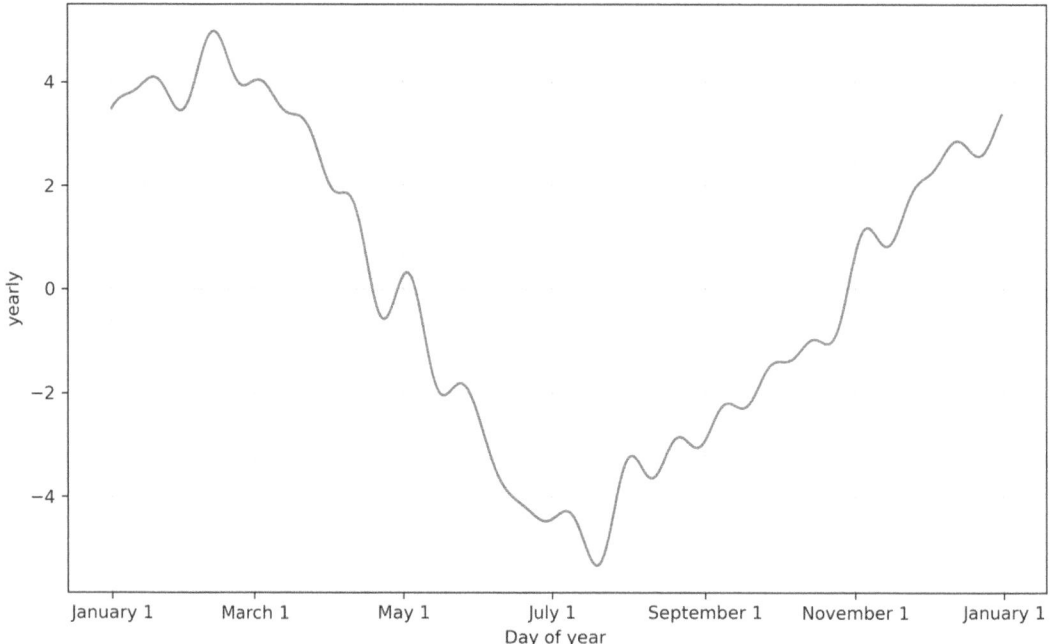

Figure 19.7 Using 20 terms to estimate the yearly seasonal component in our data. Compared to figure 19.6, this view of the seasonal component is more sensitive, since it shows more variation across time. This can potentially lead to overfitting.

Finally, we saw in figure 19.5 that the trend changed over time, and we could identify six unique trends. Prophet can identify these trend *changepoints*. We can visualize them using the add_changepoints_to_plot method.

```
from fbprophet.plot import add_changepoints_to_plot

fig3 = m.plot(forecast)
a = add_changepoints_to_plot(fig3.gca(), m, forecast)
```

The result is shown in figure 19.8. Notice that Prophet identifies points in time where the trend changes.

We've explored the most important visualization capabilities of Prophet, so let's move on to using cross-validation to diagnose our model in more detail.

19.4.2 *Cross-validation and performance metrics*

Prophet comes with an important cross-validation capability, allowing us to forecast over multiple periods in our dataset to ensure that we have a stable model. This is similar to a rolling forecast procedure.

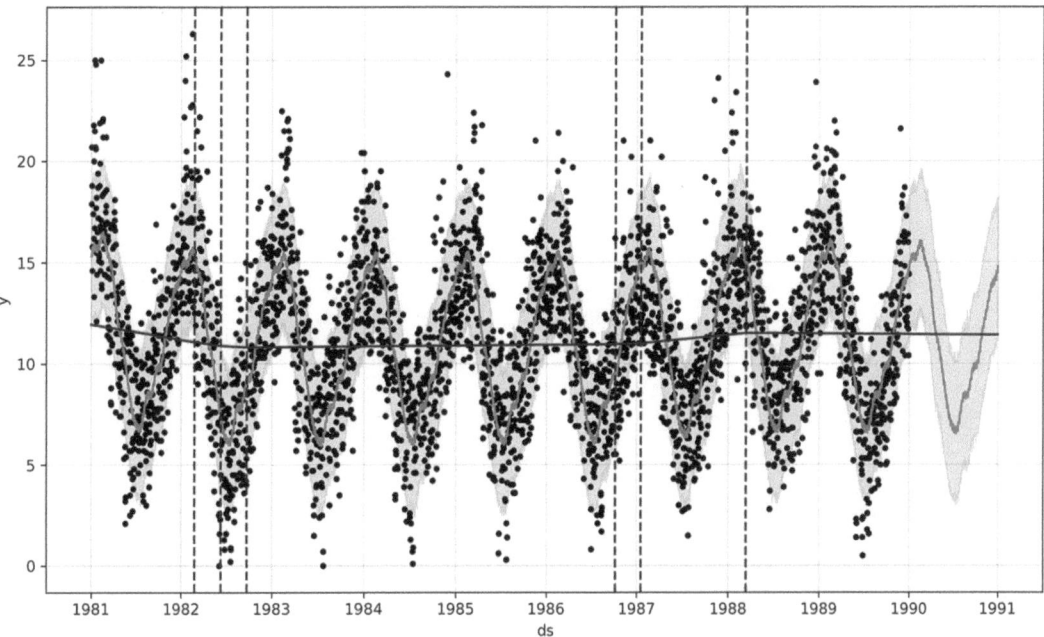

Figure 19.8   Showing trend changepoints in our model. Each point where the trend changes is identified by a vertical dashed line. Notice that there are six vertical dashed lines, matching the six different trend slopes in the top plot of figure 19.5.

Recall that with time series, the order of the data must remain the same. Therefore, cross-validation is performed by training the model on a subset of the training data and forecasting on a certain horizon. Figure 19.9 shows how we start by defining a subset within the training set and use it to fit the model and generate predictions. Then we add more data to the initial subset, and predict for another period of time. This process is repeated until the entire training set is used.

You'll notice the resemblance to rolling forecasts, but this time we are using this technique for cross-validation, to ensure that we have a stable model. A stable model is one with an evaluation metric that is fairly constant over each forecast period, keeping the horizon constant. In other words, the performance of our model should be constant, whether it must forecast 365 days starting in January or starting in July.

Prophet's `cross_validation` function requires a Prophet model that has been fit to training data. Then we must specify an initial length for the training set in the cross-validation process, denoted as `initial`. The next parameter is the length of time separating each cutoff date, denoted as `period`. Finally, we must specify the horizon of the forecast, denoted as `horizon`. These three parameters must have units that are compatible with the `pandas.Timedelta` class (https://pandas.pydata.org/docs/reference/api/pandas.Timedelta.html). In other words, the largest unit is days, and the

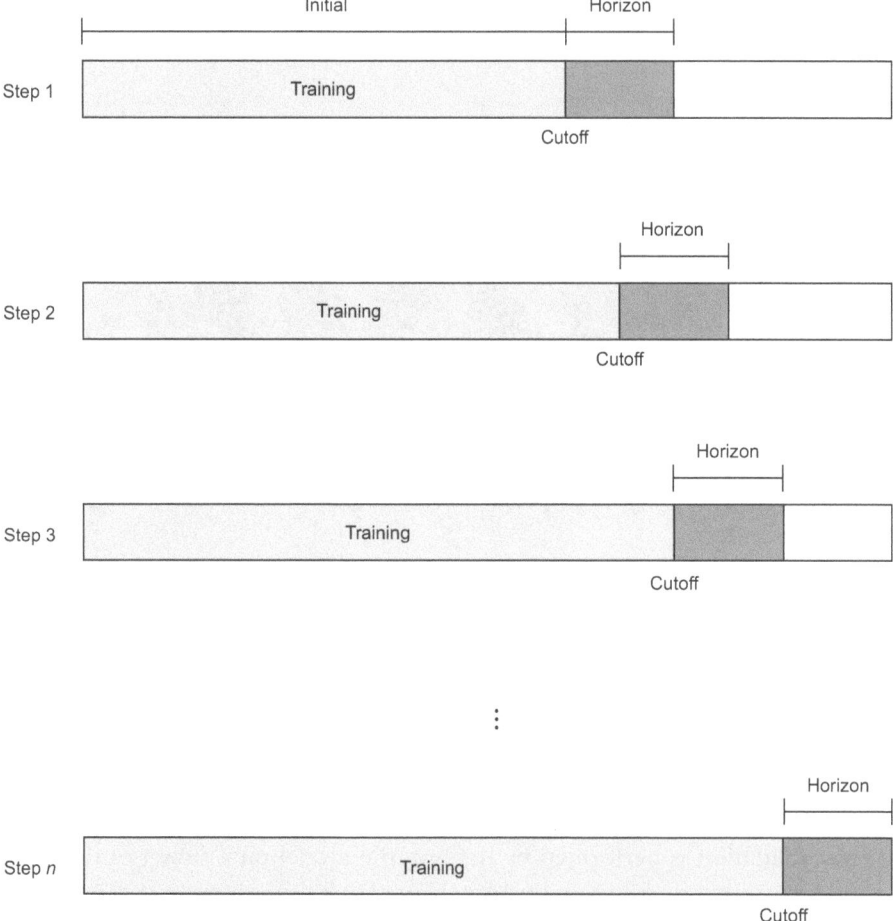

Figure 19.9 Illustrating the cross-validation procedure in Prophet. The entire rectangle represents the training set, and an initial subset of the set is identified to fit the model. At a certain cutoff date, the model produces a forecast over a set horizon. In the next step, more data is added to the training subset, and the model makes predictions over another period of time. The process is then repeated until the horizon exceeds the length of the training set.

smallest unit is nanoseconds. Anything in between, such as hours, minutes, seconds, or milliseconds, will work as well.

By default, Prophet uses `horizon` to determine the length of `initial` and `period`. It sets `initial` to three times the length of `horizon` and `period` to half the length of `horizon`. Of course, we can tweak this behavior to meet our needs.

Let's start with an initial training period of 730 days, which represents two years of data. The horizon will be 365 days, and each cutoff date will be separated by 180 days, which is roughly half a year. Given our training set size, our cross-validation procedure has 13 steps. The output of the procedure is a `DataFrame` with the datestamp, the forecast, its upper and lower bounds, the actual value, and the cutoff date, as shown in figure 19.10.

```
from fbprophet.diagnostics import cross_validation

df_cv = cross_validation(m, initial='730 days', period='180 days',
    horizon='365 days')

df_cv.head()
```

The initial training set has 2 years of data. Each cutoff date is separated by 180 days, or half a year. The forecast horizon is 365 days, which is a year.

	ds	yhat	yhat_lower	yhat_upper	y	cutoff
0	1983-02-02	15.156298	11.393460	18.821358	17.3	1983-02-01
1	1983-02-03	14.818082	11.443539	18.180941	13.0	1983-02-01
2	1983-02-04	15.212860	11.629483	18.580597	16.0	1983-02-01
3	1983-02-05	15.203778	11.808610	18.677870	14.9	1983-02-01
4	1983-02-06	15.250535	11.780555	18.771718	16.2	1983-02-01

Figure 19.10   The first five rows of our cross-validation `DataFrame`. We can see the predictions, the upper and lower bounds, as well as the cutoff date.

With cross-validation done, we can use the `performance_metrics` function to evaluate the performance of the model over the multiple forecasting periods. We pass in the output of cross-validation, which is `df_cv`, and we set the `rolling_window` parameter. This parameter determines the portion of data over which we want to compute the error metric. Setting it to 0 means that each evaluation metric is computed for each forecast point. Setting it to 1 averages the evaluation metrics over the entire horizon. Here, let's set it to 0.

```
from fbprophet.diagnostics import performance_metrics

df_perf = performance_metrics(df_cv, rolling_window=0)

df_perf.head()
```

The output of this procedure is shown in figure 19.11. The MAPE is not included, since Prophet automatically detected that we have values close to 0, which makes the MAPE an unsuitable evaluation metric.

Finally, we can visualize the evolution of an evaluation metric over the horizon. This allows us to determine whether the error increases as the model predicts further in time or if it remains relatively stable. Again, we'll use the MAE, as this is how we first evaluated our model.

```
from fbprophet.plot import plot_cross_validation_metric

fig7 = plot_cross_validation_metric(df_cv, metric='mae')
```

	horizon	mse	rmse	mae	mdape	coverage
0	1 days	6.350924	2.520104	2.070329	0.147237	0.846154
1	2 days	4.685452	2.164590	1.745606	1.139852	0.846154
2	3 days	10.049956	3.170167	2.661797	0.147149	0.769231
3	4 days	8.686183	2.947233	2.377724	0.195119	0.769231
4	5 days	8.250061	2.872292	2.569552	0.196067	0.692308

Figure 19.11 **The first five rows of the evaluation** `DataFrame`. **We can see different performance metrics over different horizons, allowing us to visualize how the performance varies according to the horizon.**

The result is shown in figure 19.12. Ideally, we will see a fairly flat line, like in figure 19.12, as it means that the error in our predictions does not increase as the model predicts further in time. If the error increases, we should revise the forecast horizon or make sure that we are comfortable with an increasing error.

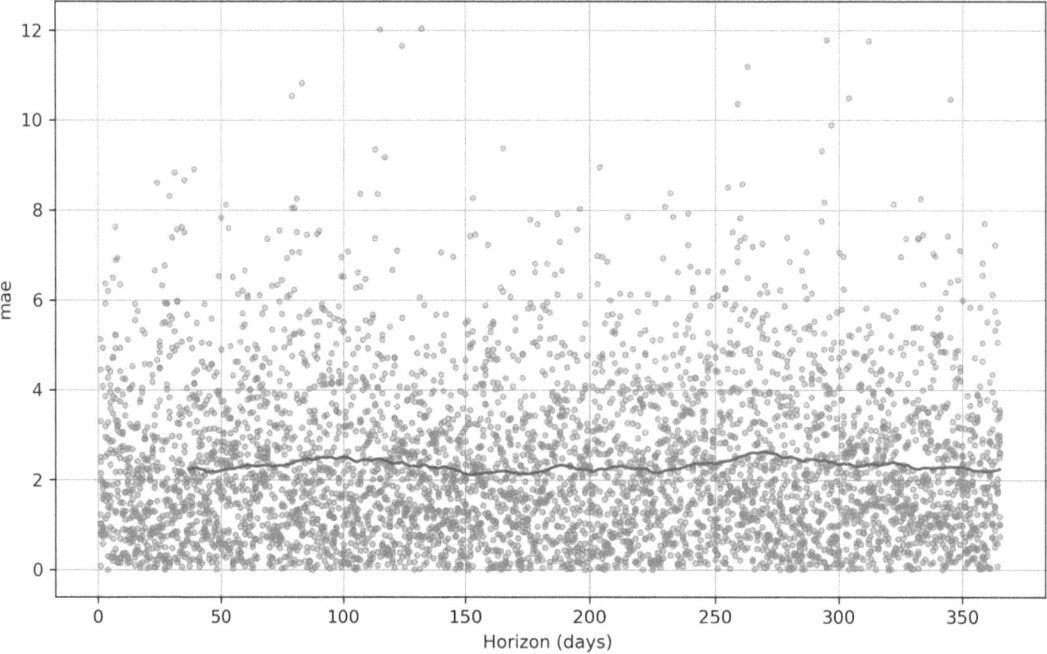

Figure 19.12 **Evolution of the MAE over the forecast horizon. Each dot represents the absolute error for one of the 13 forecast periods, while the solid line averages them over time. The line is fairly flat, meaning that we have a stable model where the error does not increase as it predicts further in time.**

Now that you've seen Prophet's cross-validation capability, we'll look at hyperparameter tuning. Combining the two will result in a robust way of finding an optimal model for our problem.

19.4.3 *Hyperparameter tuning*

We can combine hyperparameter tuning and cross-validation in Prophet to design a robust process that automatically identifies the best parameter combination to fit our data.

Prophet comes with many parameters that can be fine-tuned by more advanced users in order to produce better forecasts. Four parameters are usually tuned: changepoint_prior_scale, seasonality_prior_scale, holidays_prior_scale, and seasonality_mode. Other parameters can technically be changed, but they are often redundant forms of the preceding parameters:

- changepoint_prior_scale—The changepoint_prior_scale parameter is said to be the most impactful parameter in Prophet. It determines the flexibility of the trend, and particularly how much the trend changes at the trend change-points. If the parameter is too small, the trend will underfit, and the variance observed in the data will be treated as noise. If it is set too high, the trend will overfit to noisy fluctuations. Using the range [0.001, 0.01, 0.1, 0.5] is enough to have a well-fitted model.

- seasonality_prior_scale—The seasonality_prior_scale parameter sets the flexibility of the seasonality. A large value allows the seasonal component to fit smaller fluctuations, while a small value will result in a smoother seasonal component. Using the range [0.01, 0.1, 1.0, 10.0] generally works well to find a good model.

- holidays_prior_scale—The holidays_prior_scale parameter sets the flexibility of the holiday effects and works just like seasonality_prior_scale. It can be tuned using the same range, [0.01, 0.1, 1.0, 10.0].

- seasonality_mode—The seasonality_mode parameter can be either additive or multiplicative. By default, it is additive, but it can be set to multiplicative if you see that the seasonal fluctuation gets larger over time. This can be observed by plotting the time series, but when in doubt, you can include it in the hyper-parameter tuning process. Our current dataset of historical daily minimum temperature is a great example of additive seasonality, as the yearly fluctuations do not increase over time. An example of multiplicative seasonality is shown in figure 19.13.

Let's combine hyperparameter tuning and cross-validation to find the best model parameters for forecasting the daily minimum temperature. We'll use only change-point_prior_scale and seasonality_prior_scale in this example, since we do not have any holiday effects and our seasonal component is additive.

We'll first define the range of values to try for each parameter and generate a list of unique combinations of parameters. Then, for each unique combination of parameters, we'll train a model and perform cross-validation. We will then evaluate the model using a rolling_window of 1 to speed up the process and average the evaluation metric over the entire forecasting period. We'll finally store the parameter combinations

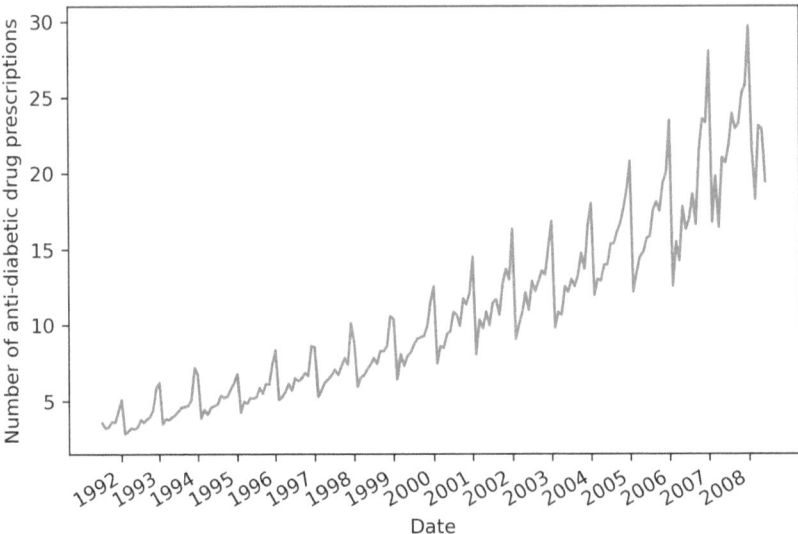

Figure 19.13 Example of multiplicative seasonality. This is taken from the capstone project in chapter 11, where we predicted the monthly volume of antidiabetic drug prescriptions in Australia. We not only saw a yearly seasonality, but we also noticed that the fluctuations get larger as we move through time.

and their associated MAE to find the best parameter combination. The combination with the lowest MAE will be deemed to be the best. We'll use the MAE because we have been using it since the beginning of this project.

```
from itertools import product

param_grid = {
    'changepoint_prior_scale': [0.001, 0.01, 0.1, 0.5],
    'seasonality_prior_scale': [0.01, 0.1, 1.0, 10.0]
}

all_params = [dict(zip(param_grid.keys(), v)) for v in
    product(*param_grid.values())]          ⟵  Create a list of unique
                                                 parameter combinations.
maes = []

                                             For each unique combination,
for params in all_params:          ⟵        do the next three steps.
    m = Prophet(**params).fit(train)
    df_cv = cross_validation(m, initial='730 days', period='180 days',
    horizon='365 days', parallel='processes')    ⟵   Perform cross-
    df_p = performance_metrics(df_cv, rolling_window=1)  ⟵   validation. We
    maes.append(df_p['mae'].values[0])                        can speed up the
                                                              process by using
tuning_results = pd.DataFrame(all_params)                     parallelization.
tuning_results['mae'] = maes
```

Fit a model. ── *(annotation pointing to the `m = Prophet(**params).fit(train)` line)*

Evaluate the model with a rolling_window of 1. This averages the performance over the entire forecast horizon.

Organize the results in a DataFrame.

The parameters achieving the lowest MAE can now be found:

```
best_params = all_params[np.argmin(maes)]
```

In this case, both `changepoint_prior_scale` and `seasonality_prior_scale` should be set to 0.01.

This concludes our exploration of Prophet's advanced functionality. We have mostly worked with them in discovery mode, so let's solidify what you've learned by designing and implementing a forecast that uses Prophet's more advanced functions, such as cross-validation and hyperparameter tuning, to automate the forecasting process.

19.5 Implementing a robust forecasting process with Prophet

Having explored Prophet's advanced functionality, we'll now design a robust and automated forecasting process with Prophet. This step-by-step system will allow us to automatically find the best model that Prophet can build for a particular problem.

Keep in mind that finding the best Prophet model does not mean that Prophet is the optimal solution to all problems. This process will simply identify the best possible outcome when using Prophet. It is recommended that you test various models, using either deep learning or statistical techniques, along with a baseline model, of course, to ensure that you find the best possible solution to your forecasting problem.

Figure 19.14 illustrates the forecasting process with Prophet to ensure that we obtain the optimal Prophet model. We'll first ensure that the columns are named and formatted correctly for Prophet. Then we'll combine cross-validation and hyperparameter tuning to obtain the best parameter combination, fit the model, and evaluate it on a test set. It is a fairly straightforward process, which is to be expected. Prophet does much of the heavy lifting for us, allowing us to quickly experiment and come up with a model.

Let's apply this procedure to yet another forecasting project. It involves monthly data, which Prophet handles in a particular way. Furthermore, we'll work with data that is potentially affected by holiday effects, giving us the opportunity to work with a function of Prophet that we have not explored yet.

19.5.1 Forecasting project: Predicting the popularity of "chocolate" searches on Google

For this project, we'll try to predict the popularity of the search term "chocolate" on Google. Predicting the popularity of search terms can help marketing teams better optimize their bidding for a particular keyword, which of course impacts the cost-per-click on an ad, ultimately affecting the entire return on investment of a marketing campaign. It can also give insight into consumer behavior. For example, if we know that next month is likely to see a surge in people searching for chocolate, it can make sense for a chocolate shop to offer discounts and ensure that they have enough supply to meet the demand.

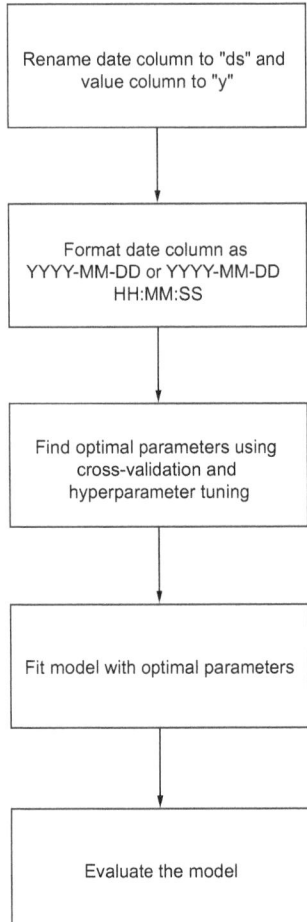

Figure 19.14   Forecasting process using Prophet. First, we'll ensure that the dataset has the right column names for Prophet and that the date is expressed correctly as a datestamp or a timestamp. Then, we'll combine hyperparameter tuning with cross-validation to obtain the optimal parameters for our model. We'll finally fit the model using the optimal parameters and evaluate it on a test set.

The data for this project comes directly from Google Trends (https://trends.google .com/trends/explore?date=all&geo=US&q=chocolate), and it shows the monthly popularity of the keyword "chocolate" in the United States, from 2004 to today. Note that this chapter was written before the end of 2021, so visiting the link now will not result in the exact same dataset. I have included the dataset I used as a CSV file on GitHub to ensure that you can recreate the work presented here.

We'll kick off this project by reading the data.

```
df = pd.read_csv('../data/monthly_chocolate_search_usa.csv')
```

The dataset contains 215 rows of data from January 2014 to December 2021. The dataset also has two columns: one with the year and month, and one with the measured popularity of "chocolate" searches. We can plot the evolution of the keyword searches over time—the result is shown in figure 19.15. The plot shows strongly seasonal data

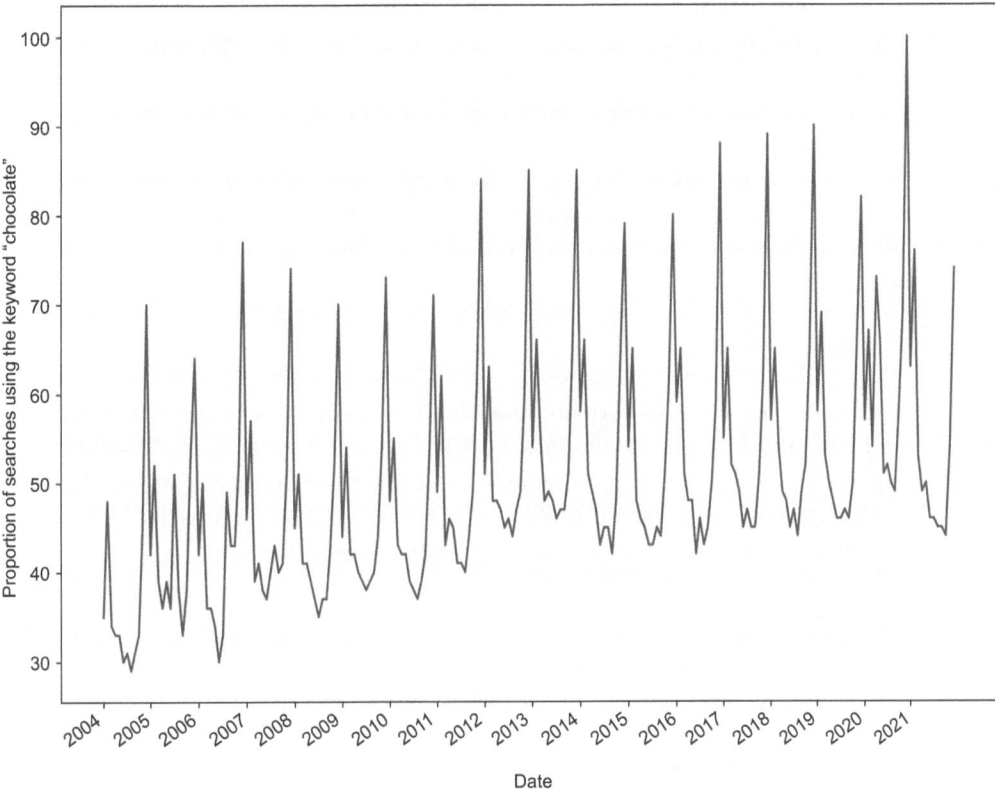

Figure 19.15   Popularity of the keyword "chocolate" in Google searches in the United States from January 2004 to December 2021. The values are expressed as a proportion relative to the period where the search term was the most popular, which occurs in December 2020 and has a value of 100. Therefore, a value of 50 for a particular month means that the keyword "chocolate" was searched for half as often, relative to the month of December 2020.

with repeated peaks every year. We can also see a clear trend, as the data increases over time.

```
fig, ax = plt.subplots()

ax.plot(df['chocolate'])
ax.set_xlabel('Date')
ax.set_ylabel('Proportion of searches using the keyword "chocolate"')

plt.xticks(np.arange(0, 215, 12), np.arange(2004, 2022, 1))

fig.autofmt_xdate()
plt.tight_layout()
```

There are two elements that make this dataset very interesting to model with Prophet. First, it is likely that we have holiday effects in action. For example, Christmas is a holiday in the United States, and it is quite common to offer chocolate for Christmas. The next element is that we have monthly data. While Prophet can be used to model monthly data, some tweaking must be done to ensure that we get good results. Out of the box, Prophet can work with daily and sub-daily data, but monthly data requires a bit of extra work.

Following our forecasting process with Prophet, shown earlier in figure 19.14, we'll start by renaming our columns following Prophet's naming convention. Recall that Prophet expects the date column to be named ds, while the value column must be named y.

```
df.columns = ['ds', 'y']
```

We can now move on to verifying that the date is correctly formatted. In this case, we only have the year and the month, which does not respect the YYYY-MM-DD format expected by Prophet for a datestamp. We'll therefore add a day to our date column. In this case, we have monthly data, which can only be obtained at the end of the month, so we'll add the last day of the month to the datestamp.

```
from pandas.tseries.offsets import MonthEnd

df['ds'] = pd.to_datetime(df['ds']) + MonthEnd(1)
```

Before we dive into hyperparameter tuning, we'll first split our data into train and test sets, so we can perform hyperparameter tuning on the training set only and avoid data leakage. In this case, we'll keep the last twelve months for the test set.

```
train = df[:-12]
test = df[-12:]
```

We'll now move on to the next step, where we'll combine hyperparameter tuning and cross-validation to find the optimal parameter combination for our model. Just as we did before, we'll define a range of values for each parameter we wish to tune and build a list containing each unique combination of values.

```
param_grid = {
    'changepoint_prior_scale': [0.001, 0.01, 0.1, 0.5],
    'seasonality_prior_scale': [0.01, 0.1, 1.0, 10.0]
}

params = [dict(zip(param_grid.keys(), v)) for v in
    product(*param_grid.values())]
```

> **NOTE** We will not optimize for holidays_prior_scale to save on time here, but feel free to add it as a tunable parameter with the following range of values: [0.01, 0.1, 1.0, 10.0].

Next, we'll create a list to hold the evaluation metric that we'll use to decide on the set of optimal parameters. We'll use the MSE, because it penalizes large errors during the fitting process.

```
mses = []
```

Now, because we are working with monthly data, we must define our own cutoff dates. Recall that the cutoff dates define the training and testing periods during cross-validation, as shown in figure 19.16. Therefore, when working with monthly data, we must define our own list of cutoff dates to specify the initial training period and forecasting period for each step during the cross-validation process. This is a workaround that allows us to work with monthly data using Prophet.

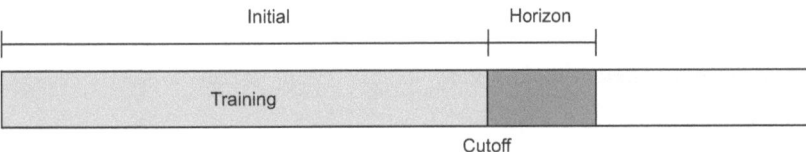

Figure 19.16   The cutoff date sets a boundary between the training period and the forecast horizon during cross-validation. By defining a list of cutoff dates, we can specify the initial training period and forecast period for each step during cross-validation.

Here we'll set the initial training period to be the first 5 years of data. Therefore, our first cutoff date will be 2009-01-31. The last cutoff date can be set as the last row of the training set, and we'll separate each cutoff date by 12 months, so that we have a model that forecasts a full year.

```
cutoffs = pd.date_range(start='2009-01-31', end='2020-01-31', freq='12M')   ◁─┐
```
> **The first cutoff date is 2009-01-31, giving us 5 years of initial training data on the first step of cross-validation. Each cutoff is separated by 12 months until the end of the training set, resulting in a forecast horizon of 1 year.**

With this step done, we can test each parameter combination using cross-validation and store their MSEs in a `DataFrame`. Note that we'll add the holidays effect with the simple `add_country_holidays` method, and we'll specify the country, which is the United States in this case.

```
for param in params:
    m = Prophet(**param)
    m.add_country_holidays(country_name='US')      ◁─┐  Add the dates of
    m.fit(train)                                         the holidays in the
                                                         United States.
    df_cv = cross_validation(model=m, horizon='365 days', cutoffs=cutoffs)
    df_p = performance_metrics(df_cv, rolling_window=1)
    mses.append(df_p['mse'].values[0])
```

```
tuning_results = pd.DataFrame(params)
tuning_results['mse'] = mses
```

The full code for hyperparameter tuning is shown in the following listing.

Listing 19.1   Hyperparameter tuning in Prophet with monthly data

```
param_grid = {
    'changepoint_prior_scale': [0.001, 0.01, 0.1, 0.5],
    'seasonality_prior_scale': [0.01, 0.1, 1.0, 10.0]
}

params = [dict(zip(param_grid.keys(), v)) for v in
⮞ product(*param_grid.values())]

mses = []

cutoffs = pd.date_range(start='2009-01-31', end='2020-01-31', freq='12M')

for param in params:
    m = Prophet(**param)
    m.add_country_holidays(country_name='US')
    m.fit(train)

    df_cv = cross_validation(model=m, horizon='365 days', cutoffs=cutoffs)
    df_p = performance_metrics(df_cv, rolling_window=1)
    mses.append(df_p['mse'].values[0])

tuning_results = pd.DataFrame(params)
tuning_results['mse'] = mses
```

Once this process is over, we can extract the optimal parameter combination.

```
best_params = params[np.argmin(mses)]
```

The result is that `changepoint_prior_scale` must be set to 0.01, and `seasonality_prior_scale` must be set to 0.01.

Now that we have the optimal values for each parameter, we can fit the model on the entire training set to evaluate it later on the test set.

```
m = Prophet(**best_params)
m.add_country_holidays(country_name='US')
m.fit(train);
```

The next step is to obtain the forecast of our model for the same period as the test set and merge them with the test set for easier evaluation and plotting.

```
future = m.make_future_dataframe(periods=12, freq='M')
forecast = m.predict(future)
```

```
test[['yhat', 'yhat_lower', 'yhat_upper']] = forecast[['yhat',
➡ 'yhat_lower', 'yhat_upper']]
```

Before evaluating our model, we must have a benchmark, so we'll use the last season as a baseline model.

```
test['baseline'] = train['y'][-12:].values
```

We are now ready to evaluate our model from Prophet. We'll use the MAE for its ease of interpretation.

```
prophet_mae = mean_absolute_error(test['y'], test['yhat'])
baseline_mae = mean_absolute_error(test['y'], test['baseline'])
```

Prophet achieves an MAE of 7.42, while our baseline gets an MAE of 10.92. Since the MAE of Prophet is lower, the model is better than the baseline.

We can optionally plot the forecasts, as shown in figure 19.17. Note that this plot also shows the confidence interval of the Prophet model.

```
fig, ax = plt.subplots()

ax.plot(train['y'])
ax.plot(test['y'], 'b-', label='Actual')
ax.plot(test['baseline'], 'k:', label='Baseline')
ax.plot(test['yhat'], color='darkorange', ls='--', lw=3, label='Predictions')

ax.set_xlabel('Date')
ax.set_ylabel('Proportion of searches using the keyword "chocolate"')

ax.axvspan(204, 215, color='#808080', alpha=0.1)

ax.legend(loc='best')

plt.xticks(np.arange(0, 215, 12), np.arange(2004, 2022, 1))
plt.fill_between(x=test.index, y1=test['yhat_lower'],
➡ y2=test['yhat_upper'], color='lightblue')      ◁──┐ Plot 80% confidence
plt.xlim(180, 215)                                   │ interval of the
                                                     │ Prophet model.
fig.autofmt_xdate()
plt.tight_layout()
```

In figure 19.17 it is clear that the forecast from Prophet, shown as a dashed line, is closer to the actual values than the forecast from the baseline model, shown as a dotted line. This translates to a lower MAE for Prophet.

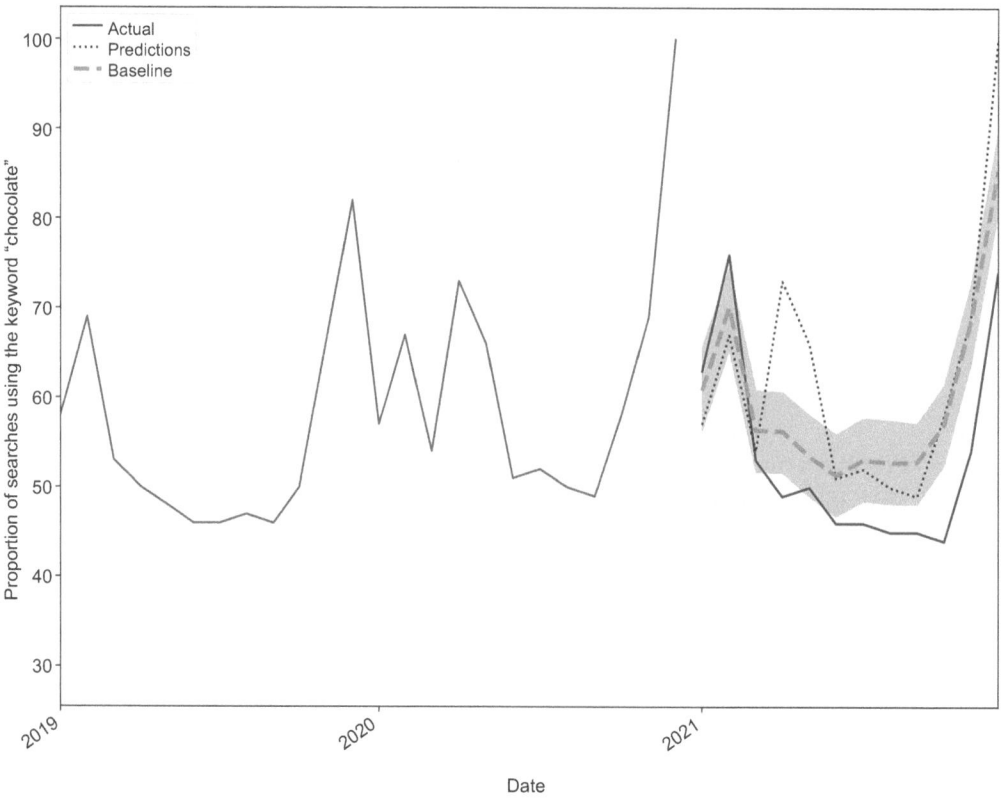

Figure 19.17   Forecasting the popularity of "chocolate" searches on Google in the United States. The forecast from Prophet, shown as a dashed line, is much closer to the actual values than the baseline model, shown as a dotted line.

We can further discover how Prophet modeled our data by plotting the components of the model, as shown in figure 19.18.

```
prophet_components_fig = m.plot_components(forecast)
```

In figure 19.18 you'll see that the trend component in the first plot increases over time, just as we noted when we first plotted our data. The second plot shows the holiday effects, which is interesting because there are troughs in the negative. This means that Prophet used the list of holidays to determine when "chocolate" searches were likely to decrease. This counters our first intuition when we thought that holidays might determine when chocolate would be more popular. Finally, the third plot shows the yearly seasonality, with peaks occurring toward the end and beginning of the year, which corresponds to Christmas, New Year, and Valentine's Day.

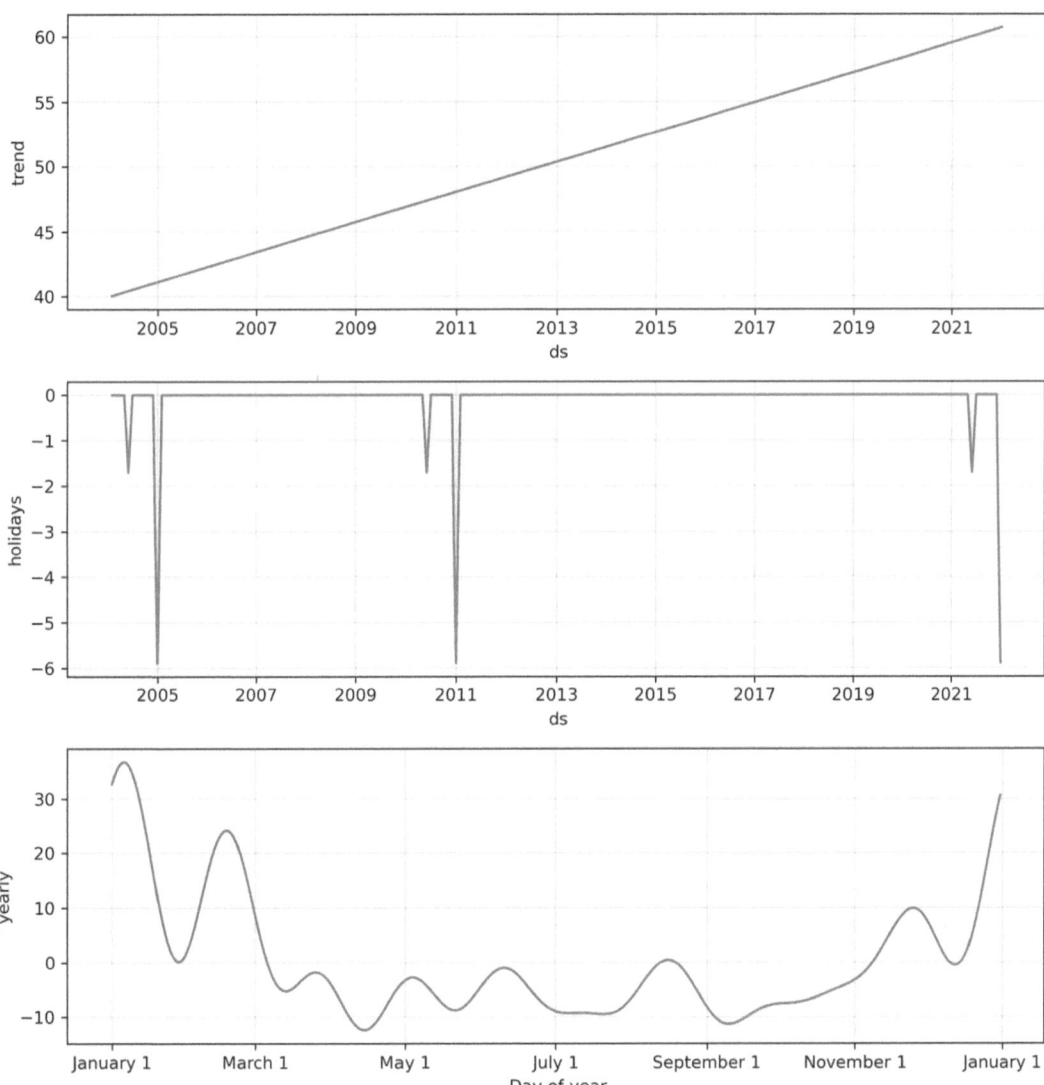

Figure 19.18 Components of the Prophet model. The trend component increases over time, as expected. We can also see the holidays component, which shows signals in the negatives. This is interesting, because it means that Prophet used holidays to determine when "chocolate" was not a popular search term. Finally, we have the yearly seasonal component, with peaks in January.

19.5.2 *Experiment: Can SARIMA do better?*

In the previous section, we used Prophet to forecast the popularity of searches on Google involving the keyword "chocolate" in the United States. Our model achieved a better performance than our baseline, but it would be interesting to see how a SARIMA model compares to Prophet in this situation. This section is optional, but it is a great occasion to revisit our modeling skills using statistical models, and it ultimately is a fun experiment.

Let's start by importing the libraries that we need.

```
from statsmodels.stats.diagnostic import acorr_ljungbox
from statsmodels.tsa.statespace.sarimax import SARIMAX
from statsmodels.tsa.stattools import adfuller
from tqdm import tqdm_notebook
from itertools import product
from typing import Union
```

Next, we'll check whether the data is stationary using the augmented Dickey-Fuller (ADF) test.

```
ad_fuller_result = adfuller(df['y'])

print(f'ADF Statistic: {ad_fuller_result[0]}')
print(f'p-value: {ad_fuller_result[1]}')
```

We get an ADF statistic of –2.03 and a p-value of 0.27. Since the p-value is greater than 0.05, we fail to reject the null hypothesis and conclude that our series is not stationary.

Let's difference our time series and test for stationarity again.

```
y_diff = np.diff(df['y'], n=1)

ad_fuller_result = adfuller(y_diff)

print(f'ADF Statistic: {ad_fuller_result[0]}')
print(f'p-value: {ad_fuller_result[1]}')
```

We now obtain an ADF statistic of –7.03 and a p-value that is much smaller than 0.05, so we reject the null hypothesis and conclude that our series is now stationary. Since we differenced only once and did not take a seasonal difference, we set $d = 1$ and $D = 0$. Also, since we have monthly data, the frequency is $m = 12$. As you can see, having seasonal data does not mean that we have to take a seasonal difference to make it stationary.

Now we'll use the `optimize_SARIMAX` function, as shown in listing 19.2, to find the values of p, q, P, and Q that minimize the Akaike information criterion (AIC). Note that although the function has SARIMAX in its name, we can use it to optimize any declination of the SARIMAX mode. In this case, we'll optimize a SARIMA model simply by setting the exogenous variables to `None`.

Listing 19.2   Function to minimize the AIC of a SARIMAX model

```
def optimize_SARIMAX(endog: Union[pd.Series, list],
➥ exog: Union[pd.Series, list],
➥ order_list: list, d: int, D: int, s: int) -> pd.DataFrame:

    results = []
```

```
for order in tqdm_notebook(order_list):
    try:
        model = SARIMAX(
            endog,
            exog,
            order=(order[0], d, order[1]),
            seasonal_order=(order[2], D, order[3], s),
            simple_differencing=False).fit(disp=False)
    except:
        continue

    aic = model.aic
    results.append([order, model.aic])

result_df = pd.DataFrame(results)
result_df.columns = ['(p,q,P,Q)', 'AIC']

result_df = result_df.sort_values(by='AIC',
ascending=True).reset_index(drop=True)

return result_df
```

To find the optimal parameters, we'll first define a range of values for each and create a list of unique combinations. We can then pass that list to the `optimize_SARIMAX` function.

```
ps = range(0, 4, 1)
qs = range(0, 4, 1)
Ps = range(0, 4, 1)
Qs = range(0, 4, 1)

order_list = list(product(ps, qs, Ps, Qs))

d = 1
D = 0
s = 12

SARIMA_result_df = optimize_SARIMAX(train['y'], None, order_list, d, D, s)
SARIMA_result_df
```

The resulting `DataFrame`, shown in figure 19.19, is interesting. The lowest AIC is 143.51 and the second-lowest AIC is 1,127.75. The difference is very large, which hints that something is wrong with the first p, d, P, Q values.

	(p,q,P,Q)	AIC
0	(1,0,1,3)	143.508936
1	(1,1,1,1)	1127.746591
2	(1,1,2,1)	1129.725199
3	(1,1,1,2)	1129.725695
4	(0,2,1,1)	1130.167369

Figure 19.19 Ordering the parameters (p, d, P, Q) in ascending order of AIC. We can see a large difference between the first two entries of the `DataFrame`. This indicates that something is wrong with the first set of parameters, and we should choose the second set.

We'll thus use the second set of values, which sets the values p, q, P, and Q to 1, resulting in a SARIMA$(1,1,1)(1,0,1)_{12}$ model. We can fit a model on the training set using those values and study its residuals, which are shown in figure 19.20.

```
SARIMA_model = SARIMAX(train['y'], order=(1,1,1),
➥    seasonal_order=(1,0,1,12), simple_differencing=False)
SARIMA_model_fit = SARIMA_model.fit(disp=False)

SARIMA_model_fit.plot_diagnostics(figsize=(10,8));
```

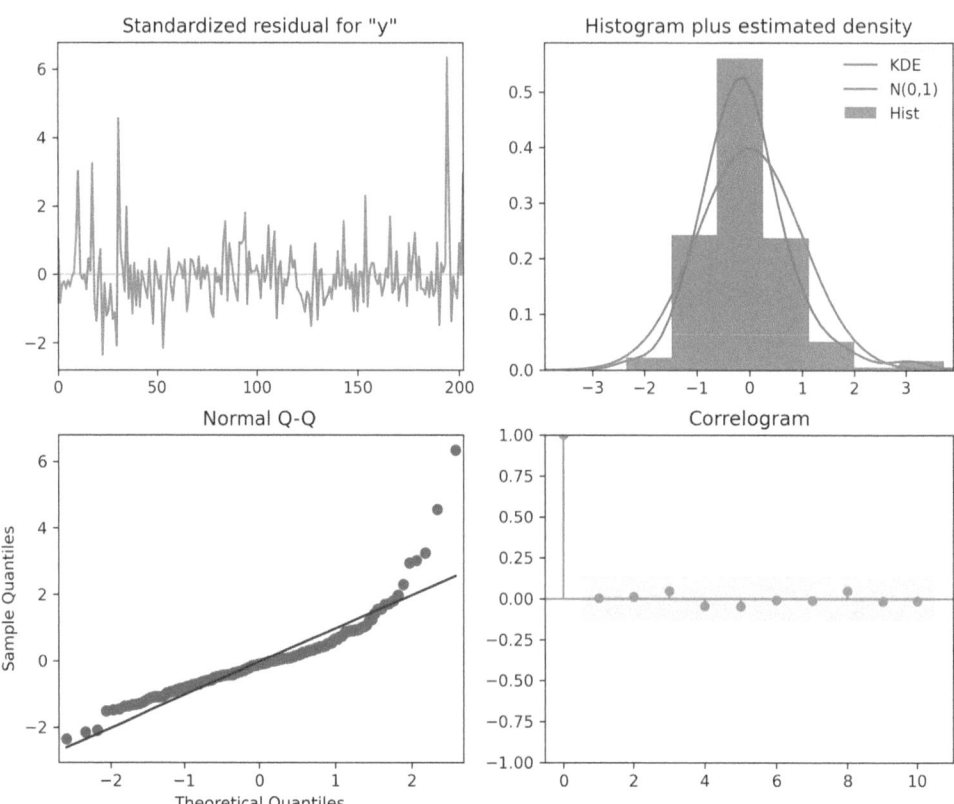

Figure 19.20   Residuals of the SARIMA$(1,1,1)(1,0,1)_{12}$ model. At the top left, you can see that the residuals are random, with no trend. At the top right, the distribution is close to a normal distribution, but there is some deviation on the right. This is further supported by the Q-Q plot at the bottom left, where we see a fairly straight line that lies on y = x, but there is a clear departure at the end. Finally, the correlogram at the bottom right shows no significant coefficients after lag 0, just like white noise.

At this point, it is hard to determine whether the residuals are close enough to white noise, so we'll use the Ljung-Box test to determine if the residuals are independent and uncorrelated.

```
residuals = SARIMA_model_fit.resid

lbvalue, pvalue = acorr_ljungbox(residuals, np.arange(1, 11, 1))
```

The returned p-values are all greater than 0.05, except the first one, which stands at 0.044. Since all other nine p-values are greater than 0.05, we'll assume we can reject the null hypothesis and conclude that this is as close as we can get our residuals to white noise.

Next, let's generate the predictions from the SARIMA model over the period of the test set.

```
SARIMA_pred = SARIMA_model_fit.get_prediction(204, 215).predicted_mean

test['SARIMA_pred'] = SARIMA_pred
```

Finally, we'll measure the MAE of the SARIMA model. Remember that our Prophet model had an MAE of 7.42, and the baseline achieved an MAE of 10.92.

```
SARIMA_mae = mean_absolute_error(test['y'], test['SARIMA_pred'])
```

Here, SARIMA achieves an MAE of 10.09. It is better than the baseline, but it does not perform better than Prophet in this case.

19.6 Next steps

In this chapter, we explored the use of the Prophet library for automatic time series forecasting. Prophet uses a general additive model that combines a trend component, a seasonal component, and holiday effects.

The main advantage of this library is that it allows us to quickly experiment and generate predictions. Many functions are available for visualizing and understanding our models, and more advanced functions are also available, allowing us to perform cross-validation and hyperparameter tuning.

While Prophet is widely used in the industry, it must not be considered a one-size-fits-all solution. Prophet works particularly well with strongly seasonal data that has many historical seasons. Thus, it is to be treated as another tool in our forecasting tool belt that can be tested along with other statistical or deep learning models.

We've explored the fundamentals of time series forecasting throughout this book, and now you've seen one way to automate most of the manual work we did with statistical and deep learning models. I highly encourage you to browse through Prophet's documentation for more granular information, as well as to explore the other libraries for automatic forecasting. Now that you know how to work with one library, transitioning to another is very easy.

In the next chapter, we'll work through a final capstone project and forecast the price of beef in Canada. This is a great occasion to apply the forecasting procedure we developed using Prophet, as well as to experiment with the other models you have learned so far to develop the best solution possible.

19.7   Exercises

Here we'll revisit problems from previous chapters but use Prophet to make forecasts. We can then compare the performance of Prophet to the previously built models. As always, the solution is available on GitHub: https://github.com/marcopeix/ TimeSeriesForecastingInPython/tree/master/CH19.

19.7.1   Forecast the number of air passengers

In chapter 8 we used a dataset that tracks the number of monthly air passengers between 1949 and 1960. We developed a SARIMA model that achieved a MAPE of 2.85%.

Use Prophet to forecast the last 12 months of the dataset:

- Does it make sense to add holiday effects?
- Looking at the data, is the seasonality additive or multiplicative?
- Use hyperparameter tuning and cross-validation to find the optimal parameters.
- Fit the model with the optimal parameters and evaluate its predictions for the last 12 months. Does it achieve a lower MAPE?

19.7.2   Forecast the volume of antidiabetic drug prescriptions

In chapter 11 we worked through a capstone project to predict the monthly volume of antidiabetic drug prescriptions in Australia. We developed a SARIMA model that achieved a MAPE of 7.9%.

Use Prophet to forecast the last 36 months of the dataset:

- Does it make sense to add holiday effects?
- Looking at the data, is the seasonality additive or multiplicative?
- Use hyperparameter tuning and cross-validation to find the optimal parameters.
- Fit the model with the optimal parameters and evaluate its predictions for the last 36 months. Does it achieve a lower MAPE?

19.7.3   Forecast the popularity of a keyword on Google Trends

Google Trends (https://trends.google.com/trends/) is a great place to generate time series datasets. This is where you can see the popular searches on Google around the world.

Choose a keyword and a country of your choice, and generate a time series dataset. Then use Prophet to predict its popularity in the future. This is a very open-ended project with no solutions to it. Take this opportunity to explore the Google Trends tool, and experiment with Prophet to learn what works and what does not.

Summary

- There are many libraries that automate the forecasting process, such as pmdarima, Prophet, NeuralProphet, and PyTorch Forecasting.
- Prophet is one of the most widely known and used libraries in the industry for automatic time series forecasting. Knowing how to use it is important for any data scientist doing time series forecasting.
- Prophet uses a general additive model that combines a trend component, a seasonal component, and holiday effects.
- Prophet is not the optimal solution to all problems. It works best on strongly seasonal data with multiple historical seasons for training. Therefore, it must be regarded as one of several tools for forecasting.

Capstone: Forecasting the monthly average retail price of steak in Canada

This chapter covers

- Developing a forecasting model to predict the monthly average retail price of steak in Canada
- Using Prophet's cross-validation functionality
- Developing a SARIMA model and comparing its performance to Prophet to determine the champion model

Again, congratulations on making it this far! We have come a long way since the beginning of this book. We first defined time series and learned how to forecast them using statistical models that generalize as the SARIMAX model. Then we turned to large, high-dimensional datasets and used deep learning for time series forecasting. In the previous chapter, we covered one of the most popular libraries for automating the entire forecasting process: Prophet. We developed two forecasting models using Prophet and saw how quick and easy it is to generate accurate predictions with few manual steps.

In this last capstone project, we'll use everything you have learned in this book to forecast the monthly average retail price of steak in Canada. At this point, we have a robust methodology and a wide array of tools to develop a performant forecasting model.

20.1 Understanding the capstone project

For this project, we'll use the historical monthly average retail price of food in Canada, from 1995 to today. Note that at the time of writing, the data for December 2021 and onward was not available. The dataset, titled "Monthly average retail prices for food and other selected products," is available for download from Statistics Canada here: www150.statcan.gc.ca/t1/tbl1/en/tv.action?pid=1810000201.

The price of a basket of goods is an important macroeconomic indicator. This is what composes the consumer price index (CPI), which is used to determine if there is an inflationary or deflationary period. This in turn allows analysts to assess the effectiveness of the economic policy, and it can of course impact programs of government assistance, such as social security. If the price of goods is expected to rise, the amount reserved for social security should technically increase.

The original dataset contains the monthly average retail price of 52 goods, from 1 kilogram of round steak to a dozen eggs, 60 grams of deodorant, and gasoline, to name a few. The price is reported in Canadian dollars for every month starting in 1995 to November 2021. For this project, we'll focus specifically on forecasting the price of 1 kg of round steak.

20.1.1 Objective of the capstone project

The objective of this capstone project is to create a model that can forecast the monthly average retail price of 1 kg of round steak over the next 36 months. If you feel confident, you can download the dataset and develop a forecasting model. Feel free to use Prophet.

If you feel you need a little more guidance, here are the steps that need to be completed:

1. Clean the data so you only have information regarding 1 kg of round steak.
2. Rename the columns according to Prophet's convention.
3. Format the date correctly. The datestamp only has the year and month, so the day must be added. Recall that we are working with monthly averages, so does it make sense to add the first day of the month, or the last day of the month?
4. Use cross-validation for hyperparameter tuning with Prophet.
5. Fit a Prophet model with the optimal parameters.
6. Forecast over the test set.
7. Evaluate your model using the mean absolute error (MAE).
8. Compare your model to a baseline.

There is one more optional, but highly recommended, step:

9. Develop a SARIMA model and compare its performance to Prophet. Did it do better?

You now have all the steps required to successfully complete this project. I highly recommend that you try it on your own first. At any point, you can refer to the following sections for a detailed walkthrough. Also, the entire solution is available on GitHub: https://github.com/marcopeix/TimeSeriesForecastingInPython/tree/master/CH20. Good luck!

20.2   *Data preprocessing and visualization*

We'll start by preprocessing the data in order to train a Prophet model. At the same time, we'll visualize our time series to deduce some of its properties.

First we'll import the required libraries.

```
import numpy as np
import pandas as pd
import matplotlib.pyplot as plt

from fbprophet import Prophet
from fbprophet.plot import plot_cross_validation_metric
from fbprophet.diagnostics import cross_validation, performance_metrics

from sklearn.metrics import mean_absolute_error

from itertools import product

import warnings
warnings.filterwarnings('ignore')
```

I also like to set some general parameters for the figures. Here we'll specify the size and remove the grid from the plots.

```
plt.rcParams['figure.figsize'] = (10, 7.5)
plt.rcParams['axes.grid'] = False
```

Next, we'll read the data. You can download it from this Statistics Canada (www150 .statcan.gc.ca/t1/tbl1/en/tv.action?pid=1810000201), although you are likely to get a more up-to-date version of the dataset since I only had data up to November 2021 when writing this book. If you wish to recreate the results shown here, I suggest you use the CSV file in the GitHub repository for this chapter (https://github.com/marcopeix/ TimeSeriesForecastingInPython/tree/master/CH20).

```
df = pd.read_csv('../data/monthly_avg_retail_price_food_canada.csv')
```

In its original form, the dataset contains the monthly average retail price of 52 products, from January 1995 to November 2021. We wish to specifically forecast the retail price of 1 kg of round steak, so we can filter the data accordingly.

```
df = df[df['Products'] == 'Round steak, 1 kilogram']
```

The next step is to remove unnecessary columns and only keep the REF_DATE column, which contains the month and year for the data point, and the VALUE column, which contains the average retail price for that month.

```
cols_to_drop = ['GEO', 'DGUID', 'Products', 'UOM', 'UOM_ID',
        'SCALAR_FACTOR', 'SCALAR_ID', 'VECTOR', 'COORDINATE', 'STATUS',
        'SYMBOL', 'TERMINATED', 'DECIMALS']

df = df.drop(cols_to_drop, axis=1)
```

We now have a dataset with 2 columns and 323 rows. This is a good time to visualize our time series. The result is shown in figure 20.1.

```
fig, ax = plt.subplots()

ax.plot(df['VALUE'])
ax.set_xlabel('Date')
ax.set_ylabel('Average retail price of 1kg of round steak (CAD')

plt.xticks(np.arange(0, 322, 12), np.arange(1995, 2022, 1))

fig.autofmt_xdate()
```

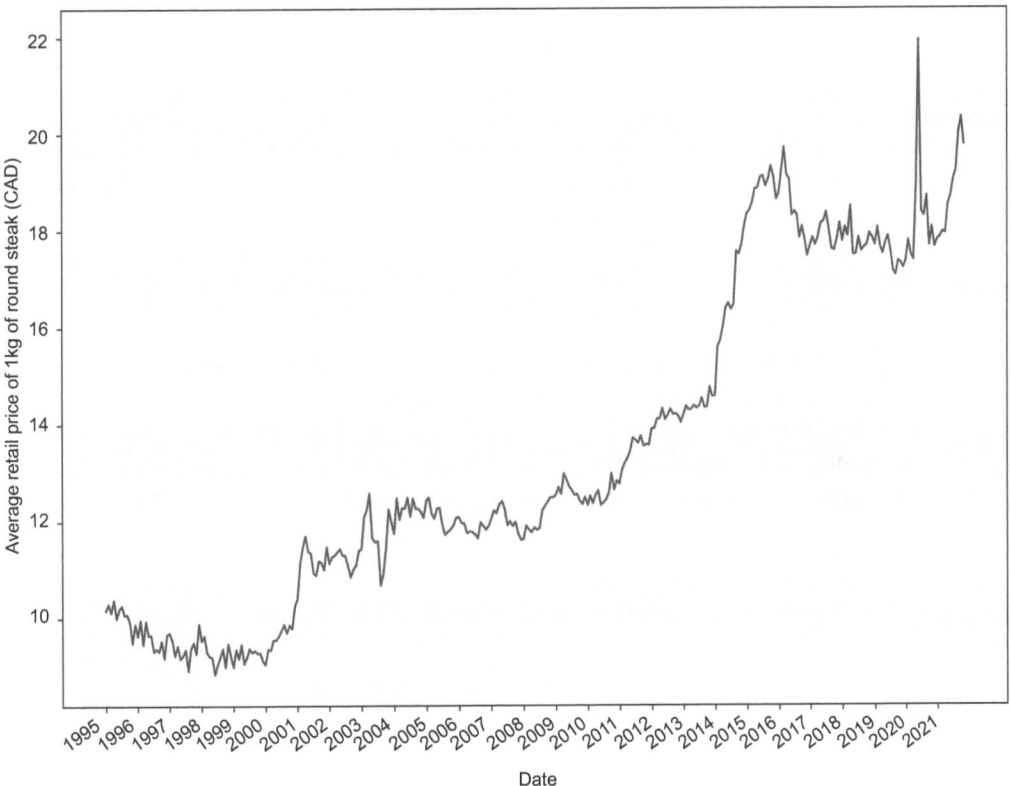

Figure 20.1   Monthly average retail price of 1 kg of round steak in Canada from January 1995 to November 2021. There is a clear trend in the data as it increases over time. However, there does not seem to be any seasonality here. This might be a sign that Prophet is not the best tool for this problem.

Figure 20.1 shows a clear trend in our data but there is no visible seasonality in this time series. Thus, Prophet might not be the best tool for this type of problem. However, this is pure intuition, so we'll test it against a baseline to see if we can successfully forecast our target.

20.3 *Modeling with Prophet*

We have preprocessed our data and visualized it. The next step is to rename the columns according to Prophet's naming convention. The time column must be named ds and the value column must be named y.

```
df.columns = ['ds', 'y']
```

Next, we must format the date correctly. Right now our datestamp only has the year and month, but Prophet also expects a day in the format YYYY-MM-DD. Since we are working with monthly averages, we must add the last day of the month to the datestamp, since we cannot report the average retail price of January until the very last day of January.

```
from pandas.tseries.offsets import MonthEnd

df['ds'] = pd.to_datetime(df['ds']) + MonthEnd(1)
```

Our data is now correctly formatted, so we'll split our dataset into train and test sets. Our objective is forecasting the future 36 months, so we'll allocate the last 36 data points to the test set. The rest is for training.

```
train = df[:-36]
test = df[-36:]
```

We can now address hyperparameter tuning. We'll start by defining a list of possible values for changepoint_prior_scale and seasonality_prior_scale. We won't include any holiday effects, as they likely will not impact the price of goods. Then we'll create a list of all unique combinations. Here we'll use the mean squared error (MSE) as a selection criterion, because it penalizes large errors, and we want the best-fitted model.

```
param_grid = {
    'changepoint_prior_scale': [0.01, 0.1, 1.0],
    'seasonality_prior_scale': [0.1, 1.0, 10.0]
}

params = [dict(zip(param_grid.keys(), v)) for v in
    product(*param_grid.values())]

mses = []
```

Now we must define a list of cutoff dates. Recall that this is a workaround for using Prophet with monthly data. The cutoff dates specify the initial training set and the length of the testing period during cross-validation.

In this case, we'll allow for the first 5 years of data to be used as an initial training set. Then each testing period must have a length of 36 months, since this is our horizon in the objective statement. Our cutoff dates thus start in 2001-01-31 and end at the end of the training set, which is 2018-11-30, and each cutoff date is separated by 36 months.

```
cutoffs = pd.date_range(start='2000-01-31', end='2018-11-30', freq='36M')
```

We can now test each parameter combination, fit a model, and use cross-validation to measure its performance. The parameter combination with the lowest MSE will be selected to generate predictions over our test set.

```
for param in params:
    m = Prophet(**param)
    m.fit(train)

    df_cv = cross_validation(model=m, horizon='365 days', cutoffs=cutoffs)
    df_p = performance_metrics(df_cv, rolling_window=1)
    mses.append(df_p['mse'].values[0])

tuning_results = pd.DataFrame(params)
tuning_results['mse'] = mses

best_params = params[np.argmin(mses)]
print(best_params)
```

This indicates that both `changepoint_prior_scale` and `seasonality_prior_scale` should be set to 1.0. We'll thus define a Prophet model using `best_params` and fit it on the training set.

```
m = Prophet(**best_params)
m.fit(train);
```

Next, we'll use `make_future_dataframe` to define the forecast horizon. In this case, it is 36 months.

```
future = m.make_future_dataframe(periods=36, freq='M')
```

We can now generate predictions.

```
forecast = m.predict(future)
```

Let's append them to our test set, so it's easier to evaluate the performance and plot the forecast against the observed values.

```
test[['yhat', 'yhat_lower', 'yhat_upper']] = forecast[['yhat',
➡ 'yhat_lower', 'yhat_upper']]
```

Of course, our model must be evaluated against a benchmark. For this example, we'll simply use the last known value of the training set as a prediction for the next 36 months. We could alternatively use the mean value method, but I would consider the mean in recent years only, since there is a clear trend in the data, which means the mean changes over time. Using the naive seasonal method here is not valid, since there is no clear seasonality in the data.

```
test['Baseline'] = train['y'].iloc[-1]
```

Everything is set for evaluation. We'll use the MAE to select the best model. This metric is chosen for its ease of interpretation.

```
baseline_mae = mean_absolute_error(test['y'], test['Baseline'])
prophet_mae = mean_absolute_error(test['y'], test['yhat'])

print(prophet_mae)
print(baseline_mae)
```

From this, we obtain an MAE of 0.681 with our baseline, while Prophet achieves an MAE of 1.163. Therefore, Prophet performs worse than the baseline, which simply uses the last known value as a forecast.

We can visualize the predictions in figure 20.2.

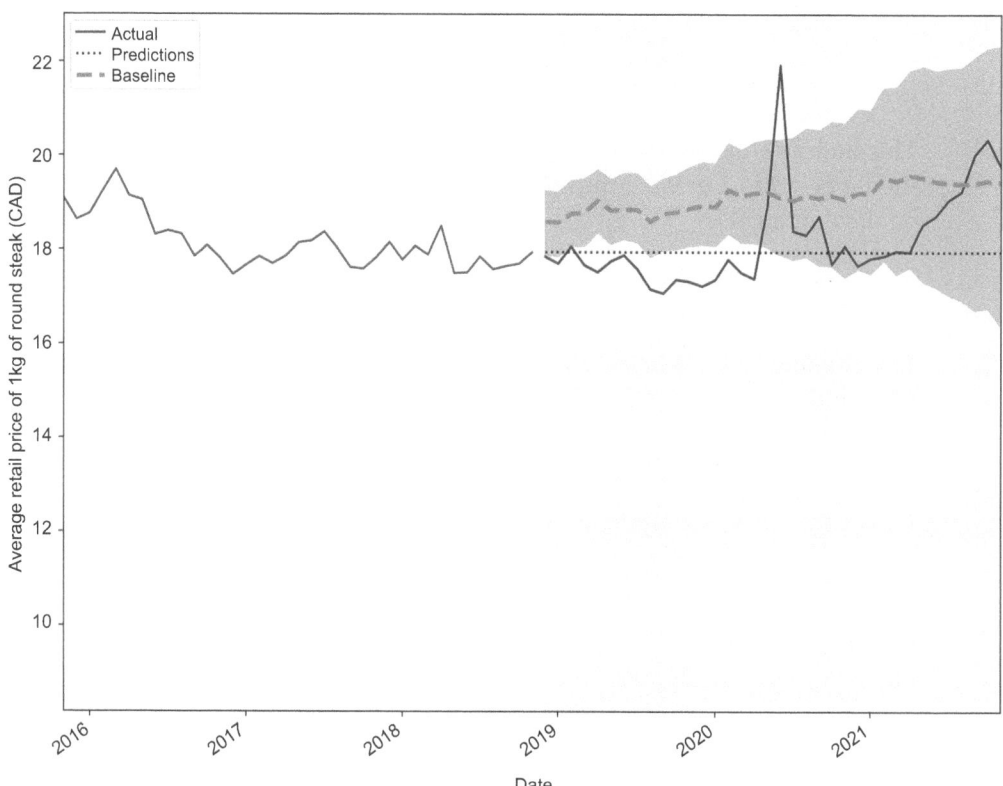

Figure 20.2   Forecasting the monthly average retail price of 1 kg of round steak in Canada. We can see that Prophet (shown as a dashed line) tends to overshoot the observed values.

```
fig, ax = plt.subplots()

ax.plot(train['y'])
ax.plot(test['y'], 'b-', label='Actual')
ax.plot(test['Baseline'], 'k:', label='Baseline')
ax.plot(test['yhat'], color='darkorange', ls='--', lw=3,
➥ label='Predictions')

ax.set_xlabel('Date')
ax.set_ylabel('Average retail price of 1kg of round steak (CAD')

ax.axvspan(287, 322, color='#808080', alpha=0.1)

ax.legend(loc='best')

plt.xticks(np.arange(0, 322, 12), np.arange(1995, 2022, 1))
plt.fill_between(x=test.index, y1=test['yhat_lower'],
➥ y2=test['yhat_upper'], color='lightblue')
plt.xlim(250, 322)

fig.autofmt_xdate()
plt.tight_layout()
```

We can also visualize the components of the model in figure 20.3.

```
prophet_components_fig = m.plot_components(forecast)
```

Figure 20.3 shows the components of the Prophet model. The top plot shows the trend component, which has many changepoints. This is because we allowed the trend to be very flexible by setting `changepoint_prior_scale` to 1.0, as it resulted in the best fit during cross-validation.

The bottom plot shows the yearly seasonal component. This component is likely helping Prophet achieve a better fit, but I doubt there is a tangible reason for price of goods to decrease toward September. This highlights the curve-fitting procedure of Prophet. It's also a great example of a case where domain knowledge could probably help us better fine-tune this parameter.

We have thus found a situation where Prophet is not the ideal solution. In fact, it performed worse than our naive forecasting method. We could have anticipated that, since we know that Prophet performs best on strongly seasonal data, but we could not be sure until we actually tested it.

The next portion of the project is optional, but I highly recommend that you complete it, as it shows a complete solution to a time series forecasting problem. We have tested Prophet and did not obtain satisfying results, but that does not mean we must give up. Instead, we must search for another solution and test it. Since we do not have a large dataset, deep learning is not a suitable tool for this problem. Therefore, let's try using a SARIMA model.

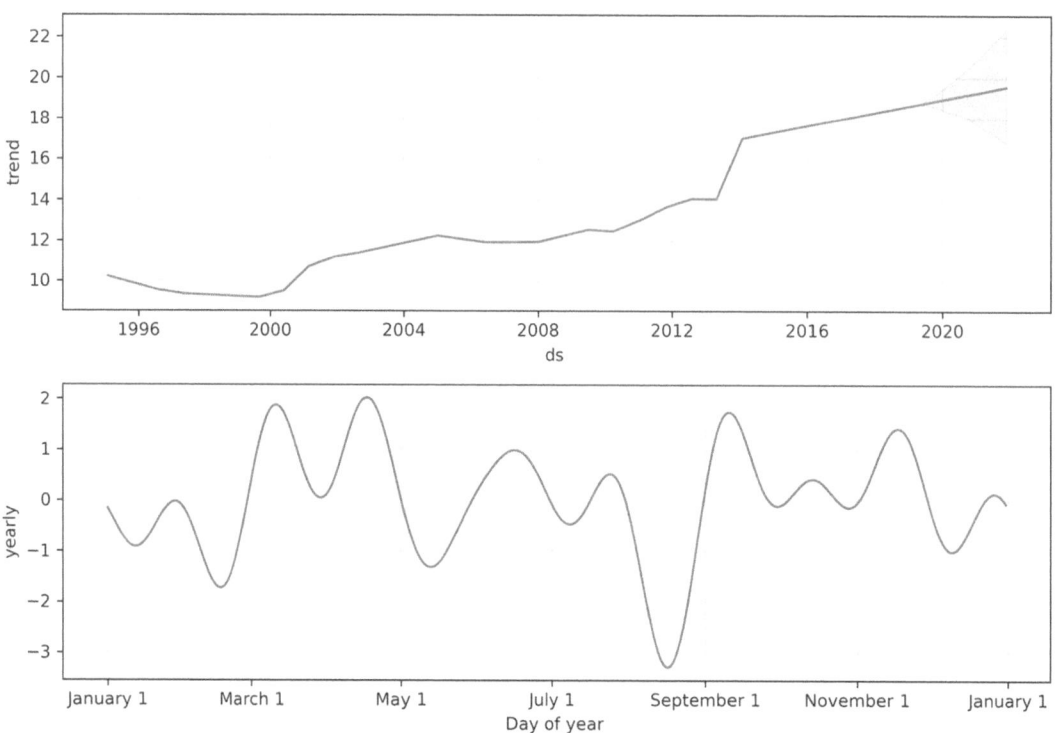

Figure 20.3   Components of the Prophet model. The top plot shows the trend component, with many changepoints, as we set `changepoint_prior_scale` to a high value, allowing the trend to be more flexible. The bottom plot shows the yearly seasonal component. Again, this component likely improves the fit of the model, but I doubt there is tangible reason to reduce the price of goods near September, for example.

20.4   *Optional: Develop a SARIMA model*

In the previous section, we used Prophet to forecast the monthly average retail price of 1 kg of round steak in Canada, but Prophet performed worse than our baseline model. We'll now develop a SARIMA model to see if it can achieve better performance than our baseline.

The first step is to import the required libraries.

```
from statsmodels.stats.diagnostic import acorr_ljungbox
from statsmodels.tsa.statespace.sarimax import SARIMAX
from statsmodels.tsa.stattools import adfuller
from tqdm import tqdm_notebook
from typing import Union
```

Next, we'll test for stationarity. This will determine the values of the integration order d and the seasonal integration order D. Recall that we are using the ADF test to test for stationarity.

```
ad_fuller_result = adfuller(df['y'])

print(f'ADF Statistic: {ad_fuller_result[0]}')
print(f'p-value: {ad_fuller_result[1]}')
```

Here we get an ADF statistic of 0.31 and a p-value of 0.98. Since the p-value is greater than 0.05, we conclude that the series is not stationary. This is expected, since we can clearly see a trend in the data.

We'll difference the series once and test again for stationarity.

```
y_diff = np.diff(df['y'], n=1)

ad_fuller_result = adfuller(y_diff)

print(f'ADF Statistic: {ad_fuller_result[0]}')
print(f'p-value: {ad_fuller_result[1]}')
```

Now we have an ADF-statistic of -16.78 and a p-value much smaller than 0.05. We thus conclude that we have a stationary time series. Therefore, $d = 1$ and $D = 0$. Recall that SARIMA also requires the frequency m to be set. Since we have monthly data, the frequency is $m = 12$.

Next, we'll use the `optimize_SARIMAX` function shown in listing 20.1 to find the parameters (p,q,P,Q) that minimize the Akaike information criterion (AIC).

Listing 20.1   Function to select the parameters that minimize the AIC

```
def optimize_SARIMAX(endog: Union[pd.Series, list], exog: Union[pd.Series,
  list], order_list: list, d: int, D: int, s: int) -> pd.DataFrame:

    results = []

    for order in tqdm_notebook(order_list):
        try:
            model = SARIMAX(
                endog,
                exog,
                order=(order[0], d, order[1]),
                seasonal_order=(order[2], D, order[3], s),
                simple_differencing=False).fit(disp=False)
        except:
            continue

        aic = model.aic
        results.append([order, model.aic])

    result_df = pd.DataFrame(results)
    result_df.columns = ['(p,q,P,Q)', 'AIC']

    #Sort in ascending order, lower AIC is better
    result_df = result_df.sort_values(by='AIC',
  ascending=True).reset_index(drop=True)

    return result_df
```

We'll define the range of possible values for p, q, P, and Q, generate a list of all unique combinations, and run the `optimize_SARIMAX` function. Note that we do not have exogenous variables.

```
ps = range(1, 4, 1)
qs = range(1, 4, 1)
Ps = range(1, 4, 1)
Qs = range(1, 4, 1)

order_list = list(product(ps, qs, Ps, Qs))

d = 1
D = 0
s = 12

SARIMA_result_df = optimize_SARIMAX(train['y'], None, order_list, d, D, s)
SARIMA_result_df
```

Once the search is complete, we'll find that $p = 2$, $q = 3$, $P = 1$, and $Q = 1$ is the combination that results in the lowest AIC. We can now fit a model using this parameter combination and study its residuals in figure 20.4, which turn out to be completely random.

```
SARIMA_model = SARIMAX(train['y'], order=(2,1,3),
➥ seasonal_order=(1,0,1,12), simple_differencing=False)
SARIMA_model_fit = SARIMA_model.fit(disp=False)

SARIMA_model_fit.plot_diagnostics(figsize=(10,8));
```

We can further support our conclusion by using the Ljung-Box test. Recall that the null hypothesis of the Ljung-Box test is that the data is uncorrelated and independent.

```
residuals = SARIMA_model_fit.resid

lbvalue, pvalue = acorr_ljungbox(residuals, np.arange(1, 11, 1))

print(pvalue)
```

The returned p-values are all greater than 0.05, so we cannot reject the null hypothesis and instead conclude that the residuals are indeed random and independent. Our SARIMA model can thus be used for forecasting.

We'll generate predictions over the horizon of our test set.

```
SARIMA_pred = SARIMA_model_fit.get_prediction(287, 322).predicted_mean

test['SARIMA_pred'] = SARIMA_pred
```

Then we'll evaluate the SARIMA model using the MAE.

```
SARIMA_mae = mean_absolute_error(test['y'], test['SARIMA_pred'])

print(SARIMA_mae)
```

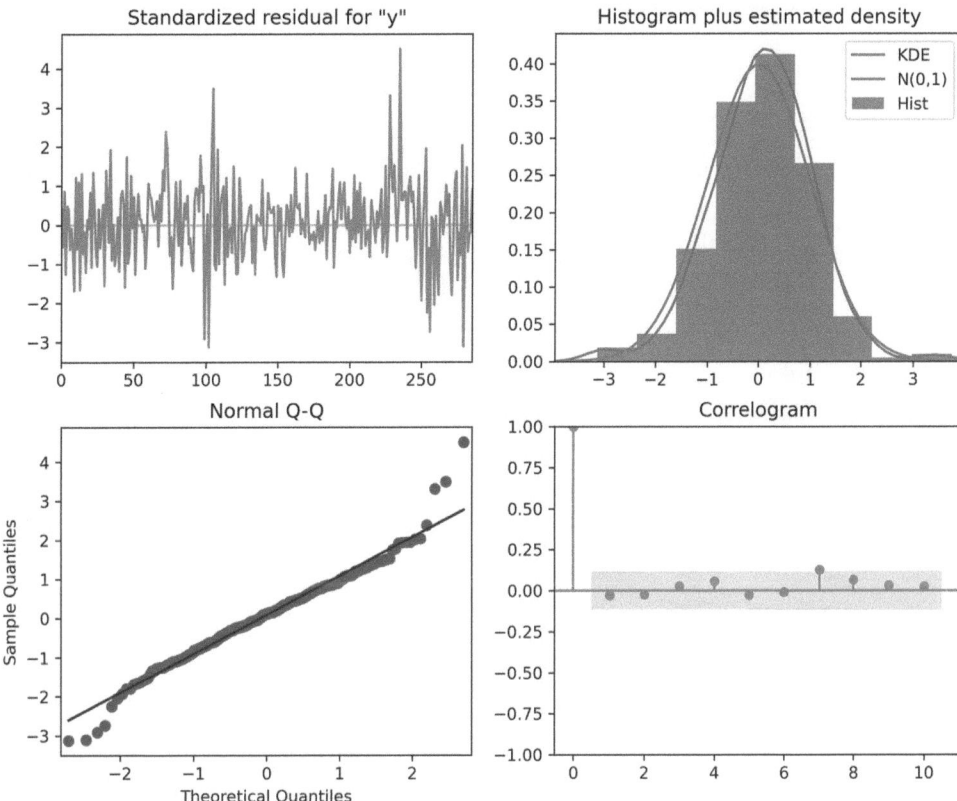

Figure 20.4   Residuals of the SARIMA(2,1,3)(1,0,1)$_{12}$ model. The top-left plot shows the residuals over time, which are completely random with no trend and a fairly constant variance, just like white noise. The top-right plot shows the distribution of the residuals, which is very close to a normal distribution. This is further supported by the Q-Q plot at the bottom left. We see a straight line that lies on $y = x$, so we can conclude that the residuals are normally distributed, like white noise. Finally, the correlogram at the bottom right shows no significant coefficients after lag 0, which is the same behavior as white noise. We can conclude that the residuals are completely random.

Here we obtain an MAE of 0.678, which is just slightly better than our baseline, which achieved an MAE of 0.681. We can visualize the forecasts of the SARIMA model in figure 20.5.

```
fig, ax = plt.subplots()

ax.plot(train['y'])
ax.plot(test['y'], 'b-', label='Actual')
ax.plot(test['Baseline'], 'k:', label='Baseline')
ax.plot(test['SARIMA_pred'], 'r-.', label='SARIMA')
ax.plot(test['yhat'], color='darkorange', ls='--', lw=3, label='Prophet')

ax.set_xlabel('Date')
ax.set_ylabel('Average retail price of 1kg of round steak (CAD)')
```

```
ax.axvspan(287, 322, color='#808080', alpha=0.1)

ax.legend(loc='best')

plt.xticks(np.arange(0, 322, 12), np.arange(1995, 2022, 1))
plt.fill_between(x=test.index, y1=test['yhat_lower'],
    y2=test['yhat_upper'], color='lightblue')
plt.xlim(250, 322)

fig.autofmt_xdate()
plt.tight_layout()
```

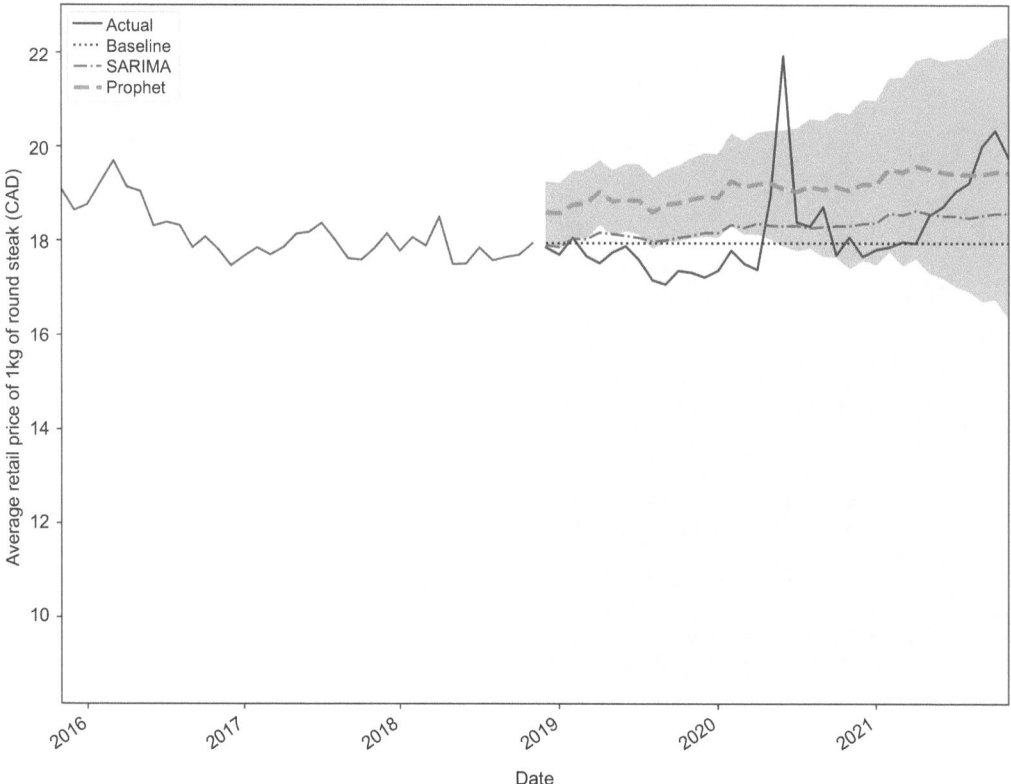

Figure 20.5   **Forecasting the monthly average retail price of 1 kg of round steak in Canada. The SARIMA model, shown as a dashed and dotted line, achieves the lowest MAE (0.678), but it is only slightly better than our baseline (0.681), which is shown as a dotted line.**

While SARIMA performed better than Prophet, the difference in performance against the benchmark is negligible. This is a situation where we must ask ourselves if it is worth using the more complex SARIMA model for such a small difference. We can also investigate further to determine if there are external variables that could help us forecast our target, as it seems that using past values only is not enough to generate accurate predictions.

20.5 *Next steps*

Congratulations on completing this capstone project! This was special and different from what we have seen, as it turned out that we were addressing a fairly complex problem, and we could not come up with a very performant solution. This situation will happen as you tackle different time series forecasting problems, and it's where domain knowledge, gathering more data, and using your creativity to find external factors that can impact your target come into play.

Take this opportunity to make this capstone project yours. We studied only one target, but there are 52 goods to choose from. Pick another target and see if you can generate predictions that perform much better than a baseline model. Feel free to also change the forecast horizon.

If you want to go above and beyond, many government websites have open data, making them a gold mine for time series datasets. Here are the links to NYC Open Data and Statistics Canada:

- NYC Open Data—https://opendata.cityofnewyork.us/data/
- Statistics Canada—www150.statcan.gc.ca/n1/en/type/data

Explore these websites and find a time series dataset you can use to practice your forecasting skills. You will likely encounter a challenging problem, forcing you to search for solutions, and ultimately making you better at time series forecasting.

Going above and beyond

This chapter covers

- Consolidating your learning
- Managing difficult forecasting problems
- Exploring beyond time series forecasting
- Sources of time series datasets

First of all, congratulations on making it to the end of this book! It has been quite a journey to get here, and it required a lot of your time, effort, and attention.

You have gained a lot of skills for time series forecasting, but there is, of course, a lot still to learn. The objective of this chapter is to summarize what you've learned and outline what else you can achieve with time series data. I'll also encourage you to keep practicing your forecasting skills by listing various sources of time series data.

The real challenge lies ahead of you, as you apply your knowledge to problems, either at work or as a side project, where the solutions are unknown to you. It is important that you gain confidence in your skills, which can only come from experience and practicing often. It is my hope that this chapter will inspire you to do so.

21.1 Summarizing what you've learned

Our very first step in time series forecasting was to define a time series as a set of data points ordered in time. You also quickly learned that the order of the data must remain untouched for our forecasting models to make sense. This means that data measured on Monday must always come after Sunday and before Tuesday. Therefore, no shuffling of the data is allowed when splitting it into training and testing sets.

In chapter 2 we built naive forecasting methods that used very simple statistics or heuristics, such as the historical mean, the last known value, or repeating the last season. This is a critical step in any forecasting project, as it sets a benchmark for more complex models, revealing whether they are actually performant models. These benchmarks can also question the use of some advanced models since, as you have seen in this book, there are situations where advanced forecasting models do not perform much better than the baselines.

Next, in chapter 3 we encountered the random walk model, a situation where we cannot apply forecasting models. This is because the value changes by a random number at each step, and no forecasting technique can reasonably predict a random number. In such a case, we can only resort to naive forecasting methods.

21.1.1 Statistical methods for forecasting

We then dived into the moving average and autoregressive processes in chapters 4 and 5. While real-life time series will rarely be approximated by a pure $MA(q)$ or $AR(p)$ model, they are the building blocks of the more complex models that we developed later on, such as the $ARMA(p,q)$ model. What links all these models is that they assume the time series is stationary, meaning that its statistical properties, such as the mean, the variance, and autocorrelation, do not change over time. We used the augmented Dickey-Fuller (ADF) test to test for stationarity. For this test, the null hypothesis states that the series is not stationary. Therefore, if we obtain a p-value less than 0.05, we can reject the null hypothesis and conclude that we have a stationary process.

While we could use the ACF and PACF plots to find the order q of a pure moving average process or the order p of a pure autoregressive process, respectively, in chapter 6 the $ARMA(p,q)$ process forced us to design a general modeling procedure, in which we select the model with the lowest Akaike information criterion (AIC). Using this model selection criterion allows us to select a model that is not too complex but that still fits the data well, hence achieving a balance between overfitting and underfitting.

Then we studied the model's residuals, which is the difference between the predicted and actual values. Ideally the residuals behave like white noise, meaning that they are totally random and uncorrelated, which in turn means that our model explains any variance that is not due to chance. One visual tool that we can use for residual analysis is the quantile-quantile (Q-Q) plot, which compares the distribution of a sample to another theoretical distribution, in this case, the normal distribution. If they are identical, we should see a straight line that lies on $y = x$. We also used the

Ljung-Box test to determine whether the residuals were independent and uncorrelated. The null hypothesis of this test states that the sample is uncorrelated and is independently distributed. Therefore, if we obtain a p-value that is larger than 0.05, we fail to reject the null hypothesis and conclude that the residuals are random. This is important, because it means that our model has captured all the information from the data, and only the random variations remain unexplained.

From this general modeling procedure, we further extended it to much more complex models, such as the ARIMA(p,d,q) model for non-stationary time series in chapter 7. Recall that we used this model to forecast the quarterly earnings per share of Johnson & Johnson.

Then we moved on to the SARIMA$(p,d,q)(P,D,Q)_m$ to account for seasonality in time series in chapter 8. Recall that seasonality is the periodic fluctuations we see in the data. For example, the weather is hotter in the summer and colder in the winter, or more people drive on the road during the day than during the night. Using a SARIMA model allowed us to accurately forecast the monthly number of passengers for an airline.

Next, we discovered the SARIMAX$(p,d,q)(P,D,Q)_m$ model, which added external variables to our model in chapter 9. Using that model, we were able to forecast the real GDP in the United States.

Finally, we concluded the statistical forecasting methods in chapter 11 with vector autoregression, VAR(p), which allows us to forecast multiple time series in a single shot, but only if they Granger-cause one another. Otherwise, the model is invalid.

21.1.2 *Deep learning methods for forecasting*

Complex statistical models for forecasting reach a limit when the dataset becomes too large, usually at around 10,000 data points. At that point, statistical methods become very slow to fit and start losing performance. Furthermore, they fail to model nonlinear relationships in data.

We thus turned our attention to deep learning, which thrives on large datasets with many features. We developed various deep learning models to forecast the hourly traffic on I-94 between Minneapolis and St. Paul in Minnesota. Our dataset had more than 17,000 rows of data and six features, making it a great opportunity to apply deep learning.

We started in chapter 14 with a simple linear model that has only an input and an output layer, with no hidden layer. Then we built a deep neural network, which adds hidden layers and can model nonlinear relationships.

We moved on to a more complex architecture in chapter 15, with the long short-term memory (LSTM) network. This architecture has the added advantage that it keeps information from the past in memory, in order to make a prediction for the future.

We also used a convolutional neural network (CNN) in chapter 16, as they effectively perform feature selection using the convolution operation. We used a CNN in conjunction with an LSTM to filter our time series before feeding it to the LSTM network.

We added one final model to our toolset in chapter 17—the autoregressive deep neural network, which uses its own predictions to make more predictions. This architecture is very powerful and is behind some of the state-of-the-art models in time series forecasting, such as DeepAR.

Throughout the entire deep learning section, the models were easily built because we first performed data windowing. This crucial step involves formatting the data in such a way that we have windows with training examples and test examples. This gave us the flexibility to quickly develop models for a wide variety of use cases, such as single-step forecasting, multi-step forecasting, and multivariate forecasting.

21.1.3 Automating the forecasting process

We put a lot of manual work into developing our models, and we developed our own functions to automate the process. However, there are many libraries available that make time series forecasting easy and fast.

It's important to note that while these libraries speed up the forecasting process, they also add a level of abstraction that removes some of the flexibility and fine-tuning capabilities that we had available when we developed our own models. Nevertheless, they are great tools for rapid prototyping, because the time it takes to create a model is very short.

One such library is Prophet, which is an open source project from Meta and probably one of the most widely used forecasting libraries in the industry. However, it is not a one-size-fits-all solution. It works best on strongly seasonal data with many historical seasons for training. In such cases, it can quickly produce accurate predictions. Since it implements a general additive model, it can take into account multiple seasonal periods as well as holiday effects and changing trends. Furthermore, Prophet comes with a suite of utilities to visualize the predictions and the components of your data, and it includes cross-validation and hyperparameter tuning functions, all within a single library.

This summarizes everything that we have discussed and applied so far. While you have all the tools you need to be successful with time series forecasting, you'll also need to know how to manage situations where your attempts at predicting the future do not work.

21.2 What if forecasting does not work?

In this book, you learned how to be successful at forecasting time series. We worked through a wide variety of situations, from forecasting quarterly earnings per share to predicting the retail price of steak in Canada. For every scenario, we managed to create a performant forecasting model that was better than a baseline and generated accurate predictions. However, we might encounter situations where nothing seems to work. Thus, it is important to learn how to manage failure.

There are many reasons why time series forecasting can fail. First, perhaps your data should not be analyzed as a time series at all. For example, you might be tasked to forecast the number of sales for the next quarter. While you have access to historical data for the number of sales over time, perhaps sales are simply not a function of time. Instead, maybe the number of sales is a function of ad spending. In that case, instead of considering this problem as a time series, we should consider it as a regression problem, using ad spend as a feature to predict the number of sales. While this example is simplistic, it shows how reframing the problem differently may help you find a solution.

Another case where time series forecasting will fail is when your data is a random walk. Recall from chapter 3 that a random walk is a time series where each step has an equal chance of going up or down by a random number. Therefore, we are really trying to predict a value that is changing randomly over time. This is not a reasonable thing to do, since no model can predict a random number. In that case, we must resort to using naive forecasting methods, as shown in chapter 2.

One other possible avenue for solving a difficult forecasting problem is to resample your data. For example, suppose you are forecasting the temperature outside. To collect your data, you place a thermometer outside and record the temperature every minute. We can consider whether working with temperature data recorded every minute makes sense. Chances are that the temperature will not vary much minute by minute. It may also introduce unnecessary noise if you have a very sensitive thermometer that records changes of 0.1 degrees or less. This is a situation where resampling the data will make sense and allow you to build performant forecasting models. Here you could resample the data so you have a temperature reading every hour. That way you'll smooth out the time series and be able to uncover a daily seasonality. Alternatively, you could resample the data daily and uncover a yearly seasonality.

Thus, you should explore different resampling possibilities with your time series data. This idea can also come from your objective. In the temperature forecasting example, it probably does not make sense to forecast the temperature for the next minute. No one is likely to be interested in that. However, forecasting the temperature for the next hour or the next day has value. Therefore, resampling the data is the way to go.

Finally, if your forecasting efforts fail, you might want to reach out to someone with domain knowledge or look for alternative data. Domain knowledge comes with experience, and people with expertise in a certain field can better guide data scientists to uncover new solutions. For example, an economist knows that gross domestic product and unemployment are linked, but this connection may be unknown to the data scientist. Thus, a domain expert can help the data scientist uncover a new relationship and look for unemployment data in order to forecast gross domestic product.

As you can see, there are different ways of managing difficult forecasting problems. In some cases, you might get absolutely stuck, which can mean that you are working on a very advanced problem that has not been tackled before. At this point, having an academic partner who can lead a research team in trying to solve the problem may be the best option.

There is always value in failure, and you should not feel defeated if a forecast fails. In fact, a failed forecast can help you become a better data scientist, because you'll learn to recognize which problems have a good chance of being solved and which don't.

21.3   *Other applications of time series data*

This book focused entirely on forecasting techniques where the objective is to predict a continuous numerical value. However, we can do more than forecasting with time series data. We can also perform classification.

In time series classification, the goal is to identify whether a time series is coming from one particular category. An example application of time series classification is analyzing data from an electrocardiogram (ECG), which evaluates the heart's condition. A healthy heart will generate a different ECG than a heart with issues. Since the data is gathered over time, this is a perfect situation for applying time series classification in a real-life situation.

> **Time series classification**
>
> Time series classification is a task where the objective is to identify whether a time series comes from a particular category.
>
> For example, we could use time series classification to analyze heart-monitoring data and determine if it comes from a healthy heart or not.

We can also use time series data to perform anomaly detection. An anomaly is basically an outlier—a data point that is significantly different from the rest of the data. We can see applications of anomaly detection in data monitoring, which in turn is used for application maintenance, intrusion detection, credit card fraud, etc. Taking application maintenance as an example, imagine that a global e-commerce company is tracking page visits over time. If the page visit count suddenly falls to zero, it's likely there is a problem with the website. An anomaly detection algorithm would notice the event and signal the maintenance team about a problem.

> **Anomaly detection**
>
> Anomaly detection is a task where the objective is to identify the presence of outliers or abnormal data.
>
> For example, we could track the expenses on someone's credit card. If there is suddenly a very large expenditure, this may potentially be an outlier, and maybe the person is a victim of fraud.

Anomaly detection is a particularly interesting challenge, because outliers are often rare, and there is a risk of generating many false positives. It also adds another layer of complexity, since the scarcity of the event means that we have few training labels.

NOTE   If you are curious about this type of problem, I recommend reading two papers from Microsoft and Yahoo where they expose how they built their own frameworks for time series anomaly detection: Hansheng Ren, Bixiong Xu, Yujing Wang, et al., "Time-Series Anomaly Detection Service at Microsoft," arXiv:1906.03821v1 (2019), https://arxiv.org/pdf/1906.03821.pdf; and Nikolay Laptev, Saeed Amizadeh, and Ian Flint, "Generic and Scalable Framework for Automated Time-series Anomaly Detection," *KDD '15: Proceedings of the 21th ACM SIGKDD International Conference on Knowledge Discovery and Data Mining* (ACM, 2015), http://mng.bz/pOwE.

There are, of course, many more tasks that we can perform with time series data, such as clustering, changepoint detection, simulation, or signal processing. I hope that this encourages you to further explore what is possible and what is being done.

21.4   *Keep practicing*

While this book has provided you with many opportunities to apply your knowledge in the form of exercises, real-life scenarios in each chapter, and capstone projects, it is important that you keep practicing to truly master time series forecasting. You will gain confidence in your skills and encounter new problems that will inevitably make you better at handling time series data.

To do so, you'll need to access time series data. The following list identifies some websites where you freely access such data:

- *"Datasets," on Papers with Code*—https://paperswithcode.com/datasets?mod=time-series.

  A list of close to a hundred datasets (at the time of writing) for time series analysis. You can filter them by task, such as anomaly detection, forecasting, classification, etc. You will likely encounter datasets used for research papers, which are used to test novel techniques and establish state-of-the-art approaches.

- *UCI machine learning repository*—https://archive.ics.uci.edu/ml/datasets.php.

  This a very popular source of data for many machine learning practitioners. Click the link for the Time-Series data type, and you'll find 126 time series datasets. You can also filter by task, such as classification, regression (forecasting), and clustering.

- *NYC Open Data*—https://opendata.cityofnewyork.us/data/.

  This website catalogs numerous datasets from the city of New York. You can filter by domain, such as education, environment, health, transportation, and more. While not all of the datasets are time series, you can still find many of them. You could also check whether your local city provides openly accessible data and work with that as well.

- *Statistics Canada*—www150.statcan.gc.ca/n1/en/type/data.

  This is a Canadian governmental agency that gives free access to a great amount of data, including time series data. You can filter by domain, but also by frequency of sampling (daily, weekly, monthly, etc.). Search your own government's websites to see if you can find a similar resource.

- *Google Trends*—https://trends.google.com/trends/.
  Google Trends gathers data about searches from all around the world. You can search for a particular theme and segment by country. You can also set the length of the time series, which changes the sampling frequency. For example, you can download the last 24 hours of data, which is sampled every 8 minutes. If you download the last 5 years, the data is sampled every week.
- *Kaggle*—www.kaggle.com/datasets?tags=13209-Time+Series+Analysis.
  Kaggle is a popular website among data scientists where companies can host competitions and reward top-performing teams. You can also download time series data—there are over a thousand datasets at the time of writing. You can also find notebooks that use these datasets to inspire you or give you a starting point. However, be careful—anyone can publish a notebook on Kaggle, and their workflow is not always correct. Note that you'll need to create a free account to download the dataset on your local machine.

You now have a wide variety of tools and resources for practicing and honing your skills. I wish you good luck in your future endeavors, and I hope that you enjoyed reading this book as much as I enjoyed writing it.

appendix
Installation instructions

Installing Anaconda

The code in this book was run on a Windows 10 computer using Jupyter Notebooks with Anaconda. I highly recommend using Anaconda, especially if you are on a Windows machine, as it automatically installs Python and many libraries that we'll use throughout the book, such as `pandas`, `numpy`, `matplotlib`, `statsmodels`, and others. You can install Anaconda's individual edition, which is free, from their website (www.anaconda.com/products/individual). It comes with a graphical installer, making for an easy installation. Note that at the time of writing, Anaconda installs Python 3.9.

Python

If you follow the recommendation of using Anaconda, you will not need to install Python separately. If you do need to install Python separately, you can download it from the official website (www.python.org/downloads/). The code in this book used Python 3.7, but any later version of Python will also work.

Jupyter Notebooks

The code in this book was run on Jupyter Notebooks. This allows you to immediately see the output of your code, and it's a great tool for learning and exploration. It also allows you to write text and display equations.

Assuming you installed Anaconda, Jupyter Notebook will also install on your machine. On Windows, you can press the Windows key and start typing `Jupyter Notebook`. You can then launch the application, which will open your browser. It will display a folder structure, and you can navigate to where you want to save your notebooks or where you cloned the GitHub repository containing the source code.

GitHub Repository

The entire source code for this book is available on GitHub: https://github.com/marcopeix/TimeSeriesForecastingInPython. At the root of the repository, there is a data folder that contains all the data files used throughout the entire book.

The repository is organized by chapter. Each folder contains a notebook that will run all the code and generate the figures for that specific chapter. You can also find the solutions to the exercises there. Provided that Git is installed, you can clone the repository and access it on your local machine:

```
git clone https://github.com/marcopeix/TimeSeriesForecastingInPython.git
```

If Git is not installed, you can download and install it from the Git website (https://git-scm.com/downloads). I then recommend those on Windows use Git Bash to run the preceding command.

Installing Prophet

In this book, we use the Prophet library, a popular forecasting library that automates most of the process. Windows users might have some trouble installing the library, even when using Anaconda.

To install the library, you can run the following commands at your Anaconda prompt:

```
conda install libpython m2w64-toolchain -c msys2
conda install numpy cython matplotlib scipy pandas -c conda-forge
conda install -c conda-forge pystan
conda install -c conda-forge fbprophet
```

Installing libraries in Anaconda

If at any time you need to install a particular library while using Anaconda, you can do a Google search: conda <package name>. The first result should lead you to the https://anaconda.org/conda-forge/<package name> website, where you will see a list of commands that will install the package. Usually, the first command will work, and it will have the format conda install -c conda-forge <package name>.

For example, to install TensorFlow 2.6 with Anaconda, you can run conda install -c conda-forge tensorflow at your Anaconda prompt.

index